UP AHEAD
IN THE DISTANCE

EAGLES

UP AHEAD
IN THE DISTANCE

RIK FORGO &
STEVE CAFARELLI

TiME PASSAGES

Published by Time Passages, LLC
4157 Mountain Road, #231
Lake Shore, MD 21122
www.timepassages.net

First paperback edition: November 2022.

ISBN, Paperback (978-1-7343653-3-7)
ISBN, Ebook (978-1-7343653-4-4)

Library of Congress Control Number:
2022937478

Cover design by Todd Bates.
Cover illustration by Daniel Belchí Lorente.

A portion of the proceeds from this book will be donated to ...

Overcoming Multiple Sclerosis, whose tireless efforts to inform, educate, and empower people who suffer from this terrible disease are inspiring.

For details visit: overcomingms.org

Judy's Run for Stroke Awareness, an organization dedicated to promoting public awareness for stroke detection, prevention, and recovery, and where families and loved ones can find help.

For details visit: judysrun.com

ACKNOWLEDGMENTS

For Maureen, Emily, and Glenn

A project like this can't be completed without a lot of help and support, and I had plenty. First thanks go to my wife, Maureen, who endured so many "book widow" days and weekends. I thank her for love, support, and boundless patience. None of this happens without her. Thanks also to my daughter, Emily, who has been such a supportive cheerleader for me throughout this project. I am grateful for her constant encouragement and optimism in both me and the world around us.

I owe a special debt of gratitude to Steve Cafarelli, my co-author and friend, who did not flinch at the enormity of this project. He brought his love for music, the Eagles, and country-rock with him. Most importantly, he brought the understanding, wit, and reasoned insight of a true musician. If drummers are the foundation of a band, I'm glad Steve is behind our kit.

Sometimes in the throes of a long editorial project you get lost, fumble your words, and, especially on those sleep-deprived days, forget the basic rules of English. I am grateful to our managing editor, Melissa Clarke, for her upbeat attitude, professionalism, and keen editing skills. Melissa, who by day is the founder and editorial director of the Americana Highways blog, kept us on schedule, focused, and out of rabbit holes. Likewise, our copyeditors and proofreaders—Danielle Anderson, Rachel Rube, Melissa Clarke, and especially Stephen K. Peeples and Rory Aronsky— made it their mission to help keep us literate. Our intrepid editorial staff and researchers—Nick Deriso, Andrew Vaughan, and Steve Wosahla—did their best to leave no stone unturned in the Eagles' historical timeline. We didn't get every story, but we tried. They covered a lot of ground, and their contributions were considerable and appreciated.

Accuracy was key as we compiled these stories. We reached out to Eagles' management for fact checking, but they did not respond. We then went to the next-best source: L&M's Eagles Fastlane (www.eaglesfans.com), the largest and perhaps most-respected Eagles fan site on the internet and Facebook. Lisa Mielke and Melissa Prepster, a.k.a. L&M, spent months painstakingly reading each story to fact-check our work. They weren't shy about pointing out inaccuracies, and we respected their guidance. Did we get everything right? Only the band members know for sure. But we tried our best and are grateful to L&M for keeping us on the straight and narrow.

Forensic rock and roll research is the best way to describe our process. We combed through countless books, magazines, newspaper stories, and websites to ferret out the smallest details. But nothing is a substitute for being there, so we reached out to people involved in the Eagles' story—both at the individual and industry levels—to learn about their experiences. Special thanks to Richard Fernandez, Eagles' road manager from 1972 to 1977, who helped us understand what life on the road was like for the band.

Special thanks as well to Rip Pelley, former director of artist development at Elektra/Asylum during the band's first run, who gave us insight into how radio affected the band's marketability and stature. Rip also gave us first-hand play-by-play of the Eagles' studio albums from the label's point of view—very few people could offer that discerning perspective. A special thanks also goes out to Eagles album designer Kosh, and rock photographers Henry Diltz, Norman Seeff, David Alexander, and Aaron Rapport.

Thanks to former WKMI/Kalamazoo Program Director Jim Higgs who helped us understand his role in the band's "The Best of My Love" story, and to Tom Leadon who explained his backstory for "Hollywood Waltz" in such vivid detail. Special thanks also to Robb Strandlund, co-writer of "Already Gone," who explained the little-known origin story for his song, and to Danny O'Keefe, whose experience with the Eagles while recording his album *So Long Harry Truman* provided a helpful glimpse into how the band helped other artists. And a special thanks goes to Cindy Johnson and Jeri Jenkins, founders of Home at Last in Miami, for sharing their experiences and photos of the Eagles with us.

Producing a book takes a village. Eternal thanks to our *Time Passages* villagers: Steven Fox for his sage legal advice and incredible patience; Jack Spatafora for his help with our informational graphics; Charles Atcherson for allowing us to tap his vast musical knowledge; Daniel Belchí Lorente and Todd Bates for creating such a wonderfully rich and detailed book cover; Yvette Gilbert for her intricately detailed illustrations that were both touching and funny; Teri Greenberg for her excellent book indexing skills; Canadian publishing queen Sandy Graham, exec extraordinaire of *Cashbox* magazine and *Record World International*, for opening her news libraries to us and extending her friendship; Henry Diltz Photography for opening its photo archives for us and to its archive director, Gary Strobl, for his photo selection help; and MJ at Gryphon Publishing Consulting, LLC for her expertise in managing the photo rights labyrinth.

And, finally, a heartfelt thanks to Glenn Frey, the inspirational force that helped create and drive the Eagles. I believe the talent of the other members of the Eagles would have lifted them to success without him, but not in the way we remember and cherish. Rest in peace, Glenn.

—*Rik Forgo*

ACKNOWLEDGMENTS

For Susanna

It all starts with family. Thanks to my wife, Susanna, who has been my partner for almost 30 years. I am grateful for her friendship and support for this project and all my endeavors. I also want to thank our kids, Tyler and Jason, who sometimes put up with me being grumpy when I'm overwhelmed by deadlines. Many thanks for your patience and support.

I thank Rik Forgo for the opportunity to work on this book and for co-authoring it with me. I appreciate his support and guidance and confidence in me, and for helping to corral the long and complex history of this significant American band into an organized timeline without missing any of the details along the way.

Though two people are listed on the cover, the number of folks involved behind the scenes was significantly more. For that reason, I'd like to thank the entire roster of *Time Passages* team members for all their efforts and contributions. From designers to fact checkers to IT technicians, everyone should be commended for a job well done. I owe a debt of gratitude to our wonderful editors and proofreaders, Danielle Anderson, Rachel Dube, Melissa Clarke, Stephen K. Peeples, and Rory Aronsky. I also must thank Andrew Vaughan, Nick DeRiso, and Steve Wosahla for their research and assistance in the development of this book.

I want to thank my friend, Rich Handley—a guy who knows a thing or two about both non-fiction writing and timeline-based works—for his guidance and encouragement during the project.

And, finally, when I am not writing about musicians, I enjoy being one, so I would like to thank all my musical friends, partners, and bandmates for playing music with me and for helping keep me both sane and inspired along the way. "Song Power" indeed!

— *Steven Cafarelli*

HOW TO USE THIS BOOK

Time Passages books track a band's history one season at a time. The important moments in a band's origin story appear as an event. Dates are estimated using the best data available, and are nested within a specific season. These events are categorized to give readers a view of milestones for different band members that illustrate how their individual stories overlap and sometimes co-mingle. Informational graphics help illustrate important milestones in each band member's story, keeping pace with everything from singles releases to collaborations, touring partners, and televised appearances. Those informational graphics cover:

PATHWAY ALBUMS

Albums recorded by band members prior to joining the band. Timothy B. Schmit, for example, recorded with Poco before joining the Eagles. Those recordings are given the spotlight to help describe the "pathway" to the band.

PATHWAY SINGLES

Singles released nationally by labels for bands or band members prior to joining the Eagles.

ALBUMS

Albums released by the band, including album charting information cross-referenced against singles including chart data.

SINGLES

Singles released by the band, including chart data from the three major radio/sales monitoring trade publications, *Cashbox*, *Billboard*, and *Record World*, including regional breakdowns of where the singles were being added to radio station playlists and how long they stayed on the charts.

AWARDS & HONORS

Recognition of awards and honors bestowed on the band and its individual members, including Grammy, Hall of Fame, and other music industry awards, as well as pop culture awards.

END NOTES

Citations for the source material for stories, briefs, and other information at the end of each article. Full listings of all citations can be found at the end of the book.

COLLABORATIONS

Identifies when members of the band participated with other artists in duets/group sessions, or provided studio support for other musicians. These listings are exhaustive, but incomplete as there is no absolute way to capture every collaborative instance (many collaborations are uncredited). The intent is to show how band members contributed their talents to—and were sought out by—other artists.

NUGGETS

Small anecdotes, news bites and other tidbits that inform about what's happening with the band and its members. Gathered data come from newspaper and magazine articles, trade papers, and interviews.

ON SCREEN

Appearances on television and in movies are cited, along with the date of the appearance for the band or individual band members. Citations are based on verifiable sources and are exhaustive, but may not be complete because records for every appearance may not be published.

ON THE ROAD WITH...

Tracks who the band toured with or appeared onstage with for a given season. Tours and tour partners are highlighted, as are appearances with other artists for one-off shows for rock festivals and televised concerts. The listing is exhaustive, but not complete.

RELEASES

Tracks the release of albums and singles from the band, its individual members, and bands they participated in prior to joining.

CONTENTS

CHAPTER 3: ON THE BORDER

CHAPTER 4: ONE OF THESE NIGHTS

CHAPTER 5: HOTEL CALIFORNIA

PREFACE

When Eagles' "Take It Easy" was released by Asylum Records at the beginning of May 1972, the single went on to dominate the Top 40 and album-oriented airwaves that summer. The hip-swinging track offered infectious, free-spirited lyrics that made listeners snap their fingers and dance. It earned critical acclaim from the rock press as singles flew off record store shelves. It was a promising start.

That summer, the rock charts were dotted with one-hit wonders. **Commander Cody**'s "Hot Rod Lincoln" was rising with a bullet, **Looking Glass** had a huge hit with "Brandy," and **Raspberries**' "Go All the Way" was making noise too. But the Eagles' formula was different; there was more depth to this band than just one song, one hit. While some bands rode a lone wave up the charts, Eagles were destined for a longer run. Or at least that's what Asylum president **David Geffen** envisioned. His instincts proved correct.

Officially named Eagles but known colloquially as the Eagles, the band has a colorful, cinematic story that's been told by many over the years. But our storytelling offers a slightly different approach. We do our best to document their history. We gathered information from a vast array of sources for the most complete story possible. We scoured years' worth of newspapers and magazine articles, dozens of related books, and a trove of online resources, ultimately cataloging more than 2,100 citations. We gathered data from the record industry's trade magazines to learn what radio stations were putting Eagles records on the air. And we spoke to artists, managers, and executives who worked with the Eagles to better understand how their efforts behind the scenes affected the band's evolution, breakthrough, and success.

The first book in this series, *Eagles: Before the Band*, dived into the histories of each of the band's members and the people who managed them. In this book, we pick up the story with a quick recap, then charge ahead into the band's first public performance for their peers as Eagles and the tour that followed. Though Joe Walsh and Timothy B. Schmit didn't join the band until the mid-to-late 1970s, we track their histories to provide a view of how their careers evolved.

We designed the book's format to place the reader in the moment. Stories are listed chronologically by season, so the reader can see all the events that happened in the band's timeline. Each season includes informational graphics that document milestones, releases, collaborations, tour partners, and awards. The season-by-season approach offers a glimpse of what other events were unfolding at that same time and provides added context to things that occur later.

Our goal is to paint as detailed a picture as possible about the Eagles' career. Consider it a one-stop shop for all the favorite stories about the band's first iteration. What was the inspiration for "The Best of My Love"? How was the outro for "Hotel California" conceived? How did Eagles end up with both of Poco's bass players? We tried to answer these questions and hundreds more along the way. We hope you enjoy the portrait we've painted.

—*Rik Forgo & Steve Cafarelli*

SOARING START

David Geffen had a feeling about Eagles.
He signed them, sent them off to Colorado to become
a band, and then to London to record their debut
album. Their first single went Top 10. Geffen wasn't
surprised—it was part of the plan.

The "sound from heaven" that came from Eagles' four-part harmonies convinced a reluctant **Glyn Johns** to produce the band. Asylum Records president **David Geffen** had begged him to, but Johns initially decided against it after the band's miserable "audition" in Boulder, Colorado, in mid-December 1971. Undaunted, Geffen asked him to reconsider. He agreed, and the quartet nearly flopped again in their second attempt in L.A. But the harmonies they sang for him on "Most of Us Are Sad," with only acoustic guitar accompaniment, changed his mind. The next day, he was flying back to England to set up in Olympic Studios— the same lauded studio where Johns had recorded the **Rolling Stones**, **Humble Pie**, and **The Who**.

"[When] we were ready to record...Glyn was our favorite producer in reputation," Bernie Leadon said, "because he can work in both capacities as engineer and producer, so he was a really good choice." Leadon, perhaps the producer's strongest advocate when the band was trying to choose someone to provide the musical direction, was enamored with Johns' approach. "Each one of us has a lot of respect for various engineers, but Glyn controls the sound like one of us would play our instrument," he said. "We were also looking for a guy who was super experienced and could help direct all of us. A really important factor was that Glyn was an engineer and producer, too. There's only a few people like that. He's one of the hardest-working people I've ever met in my life. When we record, he's like a fifth member of the group."

Frey, Leadon, and bandmates Don Henley and Randy Meisner settled into a small apartment in London in January 1972 and took practically no time for anything else but recording. "[They] picked us up, took us to the studio, and then we'd go back to this little place and drink ourselves to sleep," Henley said. "Next day, we'd get up and do it all again." Johns commanded the studio and pushed the band into areas they might not have gone otherwise. His first move was to focus the group on a more acoustic approach and concentrated on the vocal blends that had piqued his interest in Los Angeles. "On 'Take It Easy,' I got Bernie to play double-time banjo; they all thought it was a bonkers idea, but it worked. It was already a great song, but that one little thing made it different," Johns said.

"We learned tons and tons from Glyn," Henley said, including "how to cut through a lot of bullshit in arranging songs and how to shape them up real fast in the studio. He helped us take professional attitudes and mold them into professional recording artistry. He also taught me a lot about myself."

Yet Johns had a tough time discerning enthusiasm from the band. He had a clear idea of the sound he wanted to get with them, but thought they didn't like it much at the time. "They didn't seem to be over-enamored of what was going on," he said. "I couldn't even get them excited on playback—we finished the record and played it back, and they still weren't jumping up and down, which I put down to them being insecure, which they were then."

Insecure or not, Eagles returned to L.A. from London after their two-week session, but Geffen still wasn't completely happy. The distribution of songs and writing credits was generally even, except for Henley who co-wrote one song and was the lead singer on just one cut—"Witchy Woman." Geffen's partner, **Elliot Roberts**, had called Henley's voice "golden," and they wanted the drummer to have more vocal presence.

Neither Geffen nor the band was happy with the studio cut of **Jackson Browne**'s "Nightingale," so Johns returned to Los Angeles and the band re-recorded it. Once that track was laid down, Geffen and Roberts set to work to promote the upcoming single and album. They planned to unleash the Eagles on the music world in May 1972, and took out full-page ads in *Billboard*, *Cashbox*, and *Record World* to generate buzz.

The band now had just one task remaining before the LP could be released—get the album cover designed. **Crosby, Stills & Nash** had tapped the creative fountain of **Gary Burden** and his photographer partner **Henry Diltz** for the trio's first album and they suggested Eagles use them too. The covers Burden and Diltz created had become epochal in the late 1960s and early 1970s, among them albums by **Cass Elliot**, all of **Neil Young**'s solo work, and **The Doors**. **The Mamas and the Papas**' *If You Can Believe Your Eyes and Ears* album cover with the photo of Elliot, **Denny Doherty**, **John Phillips**, and **Michelle Phillips** in a bathtub became iconic. So too did CSN's eponymous debut, picturing the three musicians sitting on a battered red couch in front of an abandoned house. The pair also created The Doors' iconic *Morrison Hotel* album cover, after the band had illicitly snuck into the flophouse's lobby to pose for Diltz's photo inside the front window.

Having Burden and Diltz handling a band's cover design was an impressive sign of stature in the rock music community, and Geffen and the Eagles wanted them. Beyond that, after meeting, there was genuine camaraderie between Burden, Diltz, and the band. Leadon considered them the "cool guys" to have work on your album.

When the time came to get started, there wasn't much of a plan. Leadon described the concept as "go to the Troubadour and stay there until closing, and then we would drive to Joshua Tree." For the trip to the national park in March, the band packed a bag of peyote buttons, trail mix, bottles of tequila, water, and blankets. They would head east into the California desert and shoot photos of whatever happened there. Leadon brought his banjo, and once the Troubadour bar closed, they hit the highway.

Joshua Tree was a symbolic choice that aligned with the band's Southwestern visage, but it also matched up spiritually. The desert was right in line with the works of **Carlos Castaneda** and his ephemeral medicine man, Don Juan, which they were reading at the time. When they rolled into Joshua Tree at 4:30 in the morning, Frey openly wondered how they found the campsite in the dark. Each of them ceremoniously ate peyote buttons, then they lit a fire, and started brewing some peyote tea. As the sun rose, the band spotted a hawk flying above, which proved inspirational to Frey.

Burden said his process for developing the covers always involved a collaboration with the artist. "I listen to them, I listen to the music and [it] generally informs me what it wants to look like and say, visually," he told *Figment News* in 2013. "As I often say, I have never made *my* album cover. I lend my expertise to a project in service to the artists and the music. It's always about the music." He said he liked to take bands out of their comfort zone as well by taking trips that would get them away from their girlfriends, telephones, or anything that would interfere with his artistic direction.

On the trip to Joshua Tree with the Eagles, Burden employed peyote and its psychedelic effects as another creative tool, he admitted. "I hasten to add, no one was hog-tied and force-fed anything," he said, almost defensively. "It is my belief that if you are in the desert you should be in the desert. It was a mutual agreement and what came of that commitment has certainly served the band well, no? The images of the first album cover I think really set the tone for visually what Eagles are."

Artistically, the Joshua Tree adventure was a success for Burden and Diltz. All the Eagles sales and marketing materials for the debut album emerged from the shots taken on that trip. Images of the band in the desert sitting atop boulders, unsmiling with brooding, smoldering visages, would soon make their way onto full-page ads in the music trade magazines and then the consumer press.

The *Eagles* album package would become a bone of contention between David Geffen and Burden and Diltz, who had taken wonderfully gritty photos of the band around their pre-dawn campfire. They were also inspired when they spotted the hawk—thinking it was an eagle—flying high above with its wings spread wide against a peerless blue sky.

When Burden returned to his studio, he merged the photos into an album cover that folded out into a poster, with the campfire photo at the bottom visually ascending to the image of an eagle at the top. No one captured a photo of an eagle in Joshua Tree (or the hawk), so Burden found a stock photo of an eagle and superimposed it on the cover, Diltz said. It was a unique approach at cover design at the time.

That creativity was crushed, however, by Geffen, who chose economy over art. Diltz said that Geffen, without consulting him, Burden, or the band, ordered the cover glued shut, which eliminated the poster. "The inside spread was upside down when you opened the cover," Burden said. Diltz said it "didn't make sense to anyone" that way. But even so, the *Eagles* cover art still hit its mark and conveyed the mystical, mythical image the band wanted.

Geffen understood the value of building anticipation and that spring began teasing the album's release on June 1. He began dropping hints in the trade press that his new band had completed its work with Glyn Johns, and their debut single was ready to fly.

continued on Page 23

BOYD ELDER

Along with graphic designer **Gary Burden** and photographer **Henry Diltz**, artist **Boyd Elder** is closely associated with Eagles' 1970s album covers. Elder created the painted-and-adorned animal skull sculptures pictured on the covers of *One of These Nights* and *Their Greatest Hits (1971–1975)*.

Hailing from West Texas, Elder grew up splitting his time between El Paso, his birthplace, and Valentine, a tiny desert town about 150 miles south of El Paso that was largely platted out by his great-grandfather for the railroad decades earlier. As a creative and imaginative child with a wild streak, Boyd was drawn to art and took an early interest in drawing and painting. He was also interested in cars and motorcycles, so as a teen he combined his love of art, cars, and bikes by detailing and pinstriping his friends' hot rods and bikes.

Elder won numerous awards as an art student, and, following the suggestion of a high school teacher, headed to Los Angeles to study painting and sculpture at the Chouinard Art Institute. He attended on a series of Disney scholarships and graduated in 1968.

Meanwhile, outside of school, Elder hung around L.A. and Hollywood haunts like the Troubadour and the Whisky a Go Go and became friends with prominent musicians like **Cass Elliot**, **David Crosby**, and **Joni Mitchell,** as well as unknowns like Glenn Frey, who all liked his art as much as he liked their music. Intentionally or not, Elder became part of the L.A. music scene.

Still, after graduating, he didn't opt to stick around Los Angeles, but instead headed back home to Texas, returning to familiar, less-manic territory to raise his family (he and partner Luann had the first of their two daughters that year) and create more new experimental art.

"When I moved back to Texas [from Los Angeles], everybody thought I was crazy," Elder recalled. "You had to live in New York or Los Angeles or nobody would know you're alive."

In April 1972, Elder took some of his early

resin and plastic sculptures back to L.A. to put on an art show he called "El Chingadero," after the nickname given to him by Chouinard friend **Rick Griffin** (a Spanish term that colloquially translates to "The Fucker"). Burden and Diltz helped stage the opening reception at the gallery of **John Van Hamersveld**, another friend from Chouinard. With many of his L.A. artist and musician friends attending on Easter Sunday, Elder, like Diltz, also recalled Frey, Henley, Leadon, and Meisner were light on material for their first gig in front of their peers as Eagles: "They had six or seven songs," he said. "They played them all the way through, and when they got to the end, they played them again."

Back home in Valentine, Elder suffered a tragedy when his studio in the family's auto repair garage caught fire in May 1973. Losing all his art supplies and many of his creations, his career was in dire straits. Around this time, he recovered by painting and decorating the skulls of horses, bulls, deer, and other animals in a new series he called "American Fetish—RIP."

Some of Elder's early skull art pieces caught the eye of the Eagles camp. Burden, who had brought Elder in among the characters depicted on the back cover of *Desperado* in early 1973, would later commission Elder to provide the skull and lettering for *One of These Nights*. That and *Their Greatest Hits (1971-1975)* would become Elder's best-known works, which he viewed as both a blessing and a curse.

"Most fine artists have their work in museums or collections," Boyd said a couple years prior to his passing in 2018. "My work is in millions of households all over the world. The skull image became an icon. [*One of These Nights*] really vaulted [Eagles'] career into multiplatinum sales. That's when all the fun ended, for everybody. It got so serious." [247, 256, 262, 1786, 1787, 1788, 1789, 1790, 1791]

Geffen was out to convince radio station programmers and disc jockeys they should embrace all of Asylum's emerging artists, so he expended capital—monetary and otherwise—to elevate his entire stable. In *Billboard*'s April 1, 1972, edition, he boasted expectations his label would ring up more than $3 million in sales that year, and gushed over the recently released albums by **Jo Jo Gunne**, Jackson Browne, and **Judee Sill**. And he emphasized the debut Eagles album would be released soon, and the band would be touring with Neil Young to start the summer.

Geffen stepped up his assault on the trade press in May after Asylum released "Take It Easy" as the album's advance single on May 1. He secured a front-page story in *Cashbox* that week about all his new acts. Photos of Browne, Sill, Jo Jo Gunne, **David Blue**, **Linda Ronstadt**, **Joni Mitchell**, **Jay Ferguson**, **Ned Doheny**, **J.D. Souther**, and, of course, Eagles all adorned the May 27, 1972 *Cashbox* cover.

As "Take It Easy" gradually began getting airplay across the United States, *Record World* reported that Atlantic Records CEO **Ahmet Ertegun**, who had backed Geffen's Asylum label play, predicted the Eagles' debut 45 would be #1 in six weeks. While "Take It Easy" didn't quite reach Ertegun's lofty projection, its presence on the radio was distinctive and enduring. By the album's June 1 street date, the single was already in the Top 40, and by July, *Eagles* was a runaway hit.

For four frustrated, struggling musicians who couldn't buy a break just one year earlier, a hit single and album out of the box represented a huge turnaround. Now the Eagles focused figuratively and literally on the road ahead.

SPRING 1972

 RELEASES
▶ **Eagles**, "Take It Easy" (single)

 NUGGETS
▶ Everyone is awaiting the album by **David Geffen**'s new group Eagles on Asylum. The fantastic single is "Take It Easy."
—*Record World*
▶ The Eagles' debut album is nearly ready. It took **Glyn Johns** three weeks to record and produce it at Olympic Studios in England. It will be on the airwaves across America soon.—*Record World*

Eagles Play First Gig for Friends at Elder's 'El Chingadero' Opening

When the Eagles returned from London after recording their debut album with producer **Glyn Johns**, **David Geffen** and Asylum Records got busy preparing for the album's launch on June 1, 1972, and the debut tour that would follow.

The four band members already had some experience on the road together. Glenn Frey and Don Henley had roomed togeth-

er while touring with **Linda Ronstadt** in 1971, and, along with Bernie Leadon and Randy Meisner, played as a band in Colorado under a name given them by Ronstadt's manager **John Boylan**: **Teen King and the Emergencies**. Before they left for London, they had worked out harmonies and arrangements on new songs they were writing, stage-testing them at small clubs in Aspen and Boulder, and even back in L.A. at the Westlake School for Girls near UCLA.

But the first show Frey, Henley, Leadon, and Meisner played together for an audience of their hometown rock and roll peers was at Texas artist **Boyd Elder**'s "El Chingadero" exhibit at a gallery in Venice, the bohemian-hip L.A. beach community just south of Santa Monica, on April 2, 1972. They played using "Eagles" as their stage name.

Elder was a talented contemporary multimedia artist from El Paso who had moved to California in the mid-1960s to study at the Chouinard Art Institute in Downtown Los Angeles. He also lived a rock and roll lifestyle and hung out at clubs like the Whisky a Go Go and the Troubadour and developed friendships with the singer-songwriters, many of them residents of nearby Laurel Canyon, who helped turn those spots into cultural meccas.

Elder also became friends with graphic designer **Gary Burden** and his photographer partner **Henry Diltz**, who both lived in the canyon and worked with some of the most influential artists of the country-rock movement of the late 1960s and early 1970s.

Burden and Diltz organized the month-long "Chingadero Show" to provide exposure for their friend's art. It also presented an opportunity to introduce the new band they were working with on an album cover.

Elder's opening reception on Easter Sunday was a well-attended affair that brought out some of the biggest stars of the era, among them **Joni Mitchell**, **Cass Elliot** of **The Mamas and the Papas**, and **Mark Volman** of **The Turtles**, as well as still-unknown singer-songwriters **Jackson Browne** and **Ned Doheny**, musician and photographer **Joel Bernstein**, Geffen, Burden, Diltz, and artist friends of Elder's including **John Van Hamersveld**, whose gallery hosted the exhibit. Another mutual Chouinard friend, **Rick Griffin**, created a poster for the show, which was far from an uptight, too-hip gallery exhibit. It was ultra-casual, with mattresses laid out on some spots on the floor as artists and singers with guitars sat cross-legged, breaking into spontaneous singing and harmonizing.

The event's highlight was a short set by Frey, Henley, Leadon, and Meisner, about seven or eight songs. The brevity was in part because that was about as many originals as they'd written by then.

"They only had a few songs," Diltz said in the 2020 documentary *Laurel Canyon*, "so they kept singing 'Witchy Woman' over and over, and everybody was dancing."

Eagles may have been playing in front of L.A.'s musical elite, but the band members knew they weren't quite ready for prime time, and appreciated the encouragement they heard from people after the set.

"We weren't really fit for public presentation at that point," Henley said. "But we were just happy to be hanging out with that crowd. It was the greatest thing because all the people trying to write songs and trying to make records were very supportive."

Just four weeks later, on May 1, Asylum would release "Take It Easy" to radio stations and record stores nationwide, and launch four more Troubadour bar habitués toward worldwide fame. Elder's relationship with Burden, Diltz, and the Eagles would soon result in more collaborations that further established the band's visual image. [256, 1791, 2077]

SUMMER 1972

 RELEASES
- ▶ **Eagles**, *Eagles* (album)
- ▶ **Eagles**, "Witchy Woman" (single)

 NUGGETS
- ▶ *Eagles* LP is a "home run" and compares favorably to **Creedence Clearwater Revival** at their height. "**David Geffen**, like **Wes Farrell**, has become a legend in the business." —*Record World*
- ▶ Eagles will join **Neil Young** in the early summer, which will coincide with Young's soon-to-be-released album *Journey Through the Past.* —*Billboard*
- ▶ Eagles: Last month we said this would be a smash because **David Geffen** makes virtually no mistakes. It broke in Boston. It jumped on WCFL, KOL and WBBQ. It looks like a biggie. —*Kal Rudman, Record World*
- ▶ **Paul Ahern**, formerly promo man for Warner-Elektra-Atlantic and sales rep at Capitol Records will now head promos at Asylum Records. —*Cashbox*

continued on Page 31

TAKE IT EASY

By: Jackson Browne, Glenn Frey
Side B: Get You in the Mood (Frey)

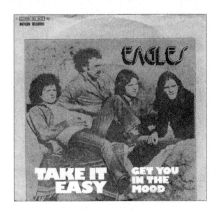

Asylum's **David Geffen**, **Jerry Sharell**, and **Paul Ahern** pushed the Eagles' first single in an all-out marketing assault—along with the full force of Atlantic Records' prodigious promotional team—on radio stations. Program directors and DJs took the hint and turned the infectious "Take It Easy" into the nation's theme song for the summer of 1972.

AIRPLAY

The first wave of radio stations to put "Take It Easy" on the air were clustered in the Northeast, Midwest, and South. Ahern had run promotions for Atlantic Records in Boston, so his radio station contacts up north may have proven helpful. In mid-May, the song was a sleeper AM hit, and landed on 98% of playlists nationwide by early June. Though billed as a Los Angeles band, West Coast stations weren't as quick to pick up the Eagles.

58 PLAYLIST ADDS Summer 1972

Region	May	June	July	Regional Airplay
Northeast	7	7	1	25.8 %
Southeast	5	9	1	25.8 %
Midwest	4	10	0	25.8 %
Southwest	3	3	1	12.1 %
West	3	4	0	12.1 %

FIRST-WAVE STATIONS Stations that added the song in the first 30 days

KGB-San Diego / KPRI-FM-San Diego / KJR-Seattle
WCOL-Columbus / WSAI-Cincinnati / WIXY-Cleveland / KIOA-Des Moines
WMEX-Boston / WBRU, WPRO-Providence / WGLI-Long Island / WDRC-Hartford / WVBF-FM-Framingham
KLIF-Dallas / KILT-Houston / KAKC-Tulsa
WROV-Roanoke / WRNO-New Orleans / WBBQ-Augusta / WVVS-Valdosta, GA

CHARTS

Billboard		
#12 August 5, 1972		
Cashbox		
#9 July 29, 1972		
Record World		
#6 August 5, 1972		

HIGHEST CHARTING WEEK: RECORD WORLD - August 5, 1972

SINGLE	ARTIST	# PREV WK
1. Daddy, Don't You Walk So Fast	Wayne Newton	1
2. Alone Again (Naturally)	Gilbert O'Sullivan	5
3. Brandy	Looking Glass	4
4. If Loving You Is Wrong	Luther Ingram	3
5. Where Is the Love	Flack & Hathaway	8
6. TAKE IT EASY	EAGLES	6
7. Too Late to Turn Back Now	Cornelius Brothers	2
8. School's Out	Alice Cooper	11
9. How Do You Do	Mouth & MacNeal	9
10. Long Cool Woman	Hollies	15

Sources: Billboard, Cashbox, Record World

BROWNE, FREY DELIVER ANTHEM OF SUMMER '72

Glenn Frey had a feeling a song **Jackson Browne** was composing might be something special. Frey lived in the same low-rent apartment complex as Browne in Echo Park, between Downtown Los Angeles and Hollywood, and was scouting songs for the Eagles' debut album.

Browne had started and shelved what would become "Take It Easy" while working on his debut album in 1971. And he had no plan to revisit it anytime soon.

Browne's inspiration to start the song was an argument with his manager, Asylum Records founder **David Geffen**, over what other musicians should support him in the studio. Geffen wanted **Carole King**, hot with her breakthrough *Tapestry* album, to play on Browne's LP. But Jackson objected. It wasn't that he doubted her—he had never even met her. He thought Geffen's request didn't feel organic and didn't want to develop his first album that way.

Bristling, Browne took a two-week break from sessions at Crystal Sound Recorders studio to collect himself and went on a road trip through small towns in Arizona and Utah in search of inspiration.

While driving through Arizona, he found it curious how many women were driving around in pickup trucks, which he had never seen in Los Angeles. One day in Flagstaff, as he was loitering on a street corner near the center of town, he saw a beautiful woman in a Toyota pickup drive by slowly and give him the once-over; he knew right then she would be in the second verse of a song he was writing.

When he returned to Los Angeles, Browne focused on finishing his album at Crystal Sound. He knew the song wouldn't be on his current album, and was getting frustrated over what to do about the second verse, so he packed it away and turned his attention back to recording.

Enter Glenn Frey.

Weeks earlier, Browne had first played him part of the song, sung him the first verse, and told him about the trip to Arizona and the woman in the truck. Frey said, "That's cool. Is it done?" Browne said no, but Frey made it clear that the Eagles wanted to record it and offered to help him finish. Browne was flattered but declined.

Meanwhile, an excited Frey took the unfinished song back to his Eagles bandmates, and they instantly liked it. Short on tracks for their album, the group encouraged Frey to approach Browne again. Frey got on the phone, nagged him about it, and asked if he could finish it. Browne, occupied with his own album, finally relented.

"After a couple of times when I declined to have him finish my song, I said, 'all right,'" Browne said. "I finally thought, 'This is ridiculous. Go ahead and finish it. Do it.'"

Frey took it home and came up with the

TAKE IT EASY *

Produced by GLYN JOHNS

*A single from **EAGLES** forthcoming album on ASYLUM RECORDS | AS-11005

David Geffen promoted the Eagles, backed by the full strength of Atlantic Records' marketing division. Full page ads ran in *Cashbox*, *Record World*, and *Billboard* magazines weeks before the band's debut album was released in June 1972.

verse about the woman Browne described. The lines *"It's a girl my Lord in a flatbed Ford/slowin' down to take a look at me"* were Frey's lyrical contribution to the song, but more importantly, he also revised the chorus and the arrangement. He swapped out the Toyota for a flatbed Ford, which blended wonderfully with the verse about the small town of Winslow (which sounded better than Flagstaff), where Browne had, indeed, broken down.

When Frey played his friend the completed song, Browne was delighted, especially with how Frey had modified the arrangement to accentuate the chorus. It was a watershed moment for Browne, who decades later still looked back at it with reverence.

"Girl, Lord, Ford, I mean all the redemption—girls and cars and redemption all in this one line," Browne said during the *History of the Eagles* documentary. Later, in an interview with KNX-FM in Los Angeles, Browne told the DJ, "The way I was singing the verse and the chorus, there was almost no chorus. It took Glenn to go, 'Take it eeeeeeasyyyy.' I probably sang something like 'Take it ea-sy.' It took an arrangement." It was a lesson in collaboration for Browne, who said that as the Eagles' version dominated the Top 40 and album-oriented airwaves, he was convinced Frey's approach was correct. "I learned it [the Eagles] way."

The single quickly found its way onto the charts, climbing into the Top 10 two months after its release. It surged to #6 on

Record World's singles chart on August 5.

On its release, *Rolling Stone*'s **Bud Scoppa** called it "simply the best sounding rock single to come out so far this year." He said the single had everything: danceable rhythm, a catchy, winding melody, and intelligent, affirmative lyrics, all tied together with a progressively powerful arrangement that mixed electric guitar and banjo, crisp vocals, and four-part harmony at just the right moments for maximum dramatic effect. Scoppa said Frey's vocals fell somewhere between Browne's and **Rick Nelson**'s.

The band loved the song from the start. Randy Meisner first heard it on the radio in his apartment in Studio City just north of Hollywood. "It was great to hear and be able to send it to your parents," he told *San Francisco Weekly* in 1998. "I love the way **Glyn Johns** mixes. It's so clean and nice. It sounded so good."

The primary appeal of "Take It Easy," Don Henley told *Rolling Stone* in 2016, "is that it evokes a sense of motion, both musically and lyrically. The romance of the open road. The lure of adventure and possibility—Route 66, the Blue Ridge Parkway, Pacific Coast Highway. Great American writers from Thomas Wolfe to Jack Kerouac to Wallace Stegner have addressed this theme of restlessness of the American spirit, of our need to keep moving, especially from East to West, in search of freedom, identity, fortune, and of this elusive thing we call 'home.'" [1, 209, 1109, 1152, 1395]

"The Eagles 'Take It Easy' is simply the best sounding rock single to come out so far this year."

Bud Scoppa, *Rolling Stone*

Bernie Leadon, Randy Meisner, Don Henley and Glenn Frey are Eagles. Four veterans of the L.A. country-rock scene who play the cleanest, tightest, most life-affirming music around today.

Their debut album has prompted *Rolling Stone* reviewer Bud Scoppa to comment, "they'll stand proudly right next to the best recordings of the Byrds, the Buffalo Springfield, Burrito Bros. and the other premiere Los Angeles groups."

Their debut single, "Take It Easy," has received chart comments like these: 46 • Billboard, 23 • Cashbox and 37 • Record World.

Eagles. A breath of fresh air on Asylum Records and Tapes.

Use the Power **18** VOTE

ASYLUM RECORDS

Asylum Records gave the Eagles' "Take It Easy" a strong marketing push in June 1972. Atlantic Records' Chairman **Ahmet Ertegun** handled distribution and lent Atlantic's promotional heft to Asylum. This full-page ad ran in the late June editions of *Billboard* and *Record World* magazines and helped fuel the single's run to *Record World*'s #6.

COLLABORATIONS
▶ **Timothy B. Schmit** played bass guitar on **Redwing**'s album *What This Country Needs*.

ON THE ROAD WITH …
▶ **Eagles**: Asule, Black Oak Arkansas, Humble Pie, Jethro Tull, Jo Jo Gunne, Mahavishnu Orchestra, Neil Young, Procol Harum, The Edgar Winter Group, Uriah Heep, Yes
▶ **Poco**, with Timothy B. Schmit: Blood, Sweat & Tears, Cornelius Brothers & Sister Rose, J.J. Cale, Leon Russell

Promo Surge: 'Take It Easy' Breaks in Boston, Nationwide

David Geffen knew something good was happening in spring 1972. He had launched his fledgling Asylum label with albums and singles from **Judee Sill**, **Jo Jo Gunne**, **David Blue**, and **Jackson Browne**, and his artists were getting good-to-strong reviews from the trade and national press. But Geffen had not played his Eagles card yet.

He knew how to get his artists onto the airwaves and leveraged the trade press masterfully for Eagles. "Take It Easy" was delivered to radio stations well in advance of its May 1 release, and by mid-May, the band had already been featured in trades including *Record World*, the trendier trade magazine of the era. Most program directors across the country were subscribers.

Geffen also hired the relentless **Paul Ahern**, who previously ran promotions for Atlantic Records in Boston, to oversee the album side of the business at Asylum. He also hired industry vet **Jerry Sharell** to

handle the pop music promotion. Together, their roles were to do whatever was necessary to get the band on the radio. The capper was when Atlantic Records chief **Ahmet Ertegun** ensured that the full might of Atlantic's promotional army was fully behind the band. Ahern, who would later become Glenn Frey's roommate at the fabled "Kirkwood Casino and Health Club" (Frey's home on the corner of Kirkwood and Ridpath Drive in Laurel Canyon), would offer program directors **Rolling Stones** tickets, tchotchkes, assorted freebies, and an array of other things to get deejays to spin the song.

A Boston native, Ahern had played bass in a high school garage band, but turned his interest in the business side of music into a career. To promote Eagles' debut album and single, he started in his hometown and visited every radio station there. Almost instantly, the band started showing up on playlists all over Beantown. Ahern spread that in a major push, making his way south, then west, back north, and eventually across the country. *Cashbox*, the top competitor to *Billboard* in the record charts, reported that "Take It Easy" was added to playlists in Roanoke, Virginia, and then New Orleans. *Cashbox* added the single to its "Radio Active" list, which used weekly phone-in surveys from markets across the nation to keep track of new playlist additions. The single was off to a great start.

Geffen continued the promotional onslaught by taking out full-page ads in *Cashbox* and *Record World* the follow-

31

continued on Page 36

Eagles' Debut Album Makes An Indelible Opening Mark

Eagles' debut album landed at the beginning of June 1972 with much fanfare—**David Geffen** had made sure of that. The self-titled album combined the talents of four experienced musicians who had been immersed in country-rock for several years—Glenn Frey, Don Henley, Bernie Leadon, and Randy Meisner.

Geffen pitched the band as a unique group that sported four lead singers who were also accomplished songwriters. They still had room to grow as songwriters, but no one could argue about their singing abilities. Their harmonies were otherworldly from the start. Frey and Henley would later be inducted into the Songwriters Hall of Fame, so they grew into that role too.

The band took a balanced approach with the album, with all four members taking turns on lead vocals and sharing songwriting credits. Three singles were released over the course of 1972, with each charting in the Top 20—a stellar start by any measure. Two of those three were written by friends of the band: "Take It Easy," penned by **Jackson Browne** (with a nota-

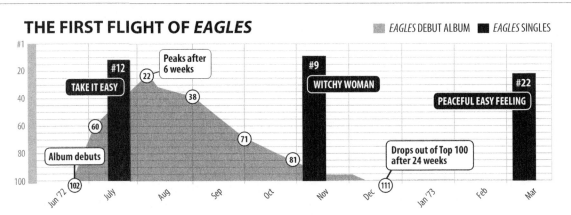

THE FIRST FLIGHT OF *EAGLES*   *EAGLES* DEBUT ALBUM ■ *EAGLES* SINGLES

Eagles got more airplay than most bands' debut albums. The LP sold well through the summer and into the fall, but slid out of the *Billboard* Top 100 albums chart in December, even as "Witchy Woman" was climbing into the Top 10. Later, when the band's third single, "Peaceful Easy Feeling," climbed into the Top 20, album sales did not benefit from that single's success. At this stage the group was still a singles band. The music industry operated on singles in the days before FM and album-oriented radio music became powerful. The album would be certified gold by the RIAA a year and a half later in January 1974; it would not achieve platinum status until March 2001.

Sources: Billboard, Recording Industry Association of America

ble assist from Frey), and "Peaceful Easy Feeling," an original by **Jack Tempchin**. "Witchy Woman" was a collaboration between Leadon and Henley that reached #9 and was the only charting single written solely by Eagles.

"Witchy Woman" was also the highest-charting single from the album. When he was with the **Flying Burrito Brothers**, Leadon had started working on a minor-key riff with Eastern Asian influences. He took the music to Henley, who added the tom-tom beat and gave the finished product a little more of an R&B flavor. Henley's lyrics were inspired by American novelist and painter **Zelda Fitzgerald**, along with an amalgam of girls he had met in Los Angeles clubs. The haunting song rose slowly on the charts, reaching the *Billboard* Top 10 by mid-November.

While "Witchy Woman" was Eagles' best chart performer, the tone of the album was clearly set by the first iconic guitar strums of "Take It Easy." The album's advance single, it remains an optimistic, upbeat song that might not have been recorded by the Eagles if not for Frey's resourcefulness and persistence in pushing Browne to let him complete it. Frey took the lead vocals and it became part of country-rock lore.

Frey also sang lead on "Peaceful Easy Feeling," the song he picked up from Tempchin, a friend he had met when they played the coffeehouse circuit in San Diego in the early 1970s. Tempchin was inspired to write "Peaceful" after meeting a waitress in El Centro, halfway between San Diego and Yuma. They were sup-

ELEKTRA/ASYLUM INSIDER

EAGLES' FIRST EFFORT WAS PRIMARILY A TOP 40 ALBUM. Not much sales early on from the LP, but radio loved the first single and the band. It was the perfect summertime song. After **Jackson Browne**'s "Doctor My Eyes" and "Run, Run, Run" by former **Spirit** leader **Jay Ferguson**'s **Jo Jo Gunne**, it gave **David Geffen** his third Top 100 hit with the new imprint. He and Asylum were becoming a force to be reckoned with in the music industry. Atlantic Records pushed every Asylum single hard, and radio gave their releases a genuine look, which was not always the case for an upstart label.

The leadoff single, "Take It Easy," got radio play across the board—Top 40, country, AOR (album-oriented rock, mostly on FM), and easy listening stations were all playing the tune. It's not easy to get a four-genre crossover record on your first release. "Witchy Woman" also circled the Top 10, but "Peaceful Easy Feeling" was just too much of a ballad for the up-tempo Eagles and didn't fare as well. Nonetheless, the Eagles were now on the map in four radio formats. Atlantic was firmly behind this upstart label and Round 2, *Desperado*, was well set up. And I think that Atlantic and **Ahmet Ertegun**'s support was critical.

—Rip Pelley, former National Director of Artist Development and Promotion, Elektra/Asylum Records

posed to leave together after his show, but she disappeared, a moment that got him started on "Peaceful."

Later in Los Angeles, he met up with Frey, Browne, and **J.D. Souther**, and played the song for them. Frey liked it and asked Tempchin if the Eagles could record it. He agreed, and the next day, he was blown away when Frey gave him a demo the band had recorded. Years later, Frey still spoke fondly of the song and of wanting it to have a **Poco** vibe. It has "a happy, country-rock quality, but a bittersweet irony about it that I thought was really great," Frey said in the liner notes of *The Very Best of the Eagles*. "I still love that song. Love singing it."

Frey also wrote two songs for the Eagles' debut LP. The first, a sincere, low-tempo ballad called "Most of Us Are Sad," was the song that changed producer **Glyn Johns**' mind about producing them during the group's second-chance audition. The band worked in excellent harmonies, but the song lacked the polished feel of other ballads Frey would later write, like "Tequila Sunrise" and "Lyin' Eyes." Frey's other writing credit, "Chug All Night," was a raucous cut with a thumping Meisner-driven bass buildup.

The most experienced musicians in the band, Leadon and Meisner, earned three writing credits each on the album. After "Witchy Woman," Leadon sang lead on "Train Leaves Here This Morning," a song he co-wrote with his former **Dillard & Clark** bandmate **Gene Clark**. Its wandering lyrics and a slow folksy shuffle gave it a

Tallahassee Democrat
July 2, 1972

Eagles has made its debut in a manner at least as impressive as **America**–the much-talked about group of a few months back. And they are making their mark with an irresistible single called "Take It Easy." The precisely placed harmonies of this four-man group of veteran rockers spice the whole album with a distinctive flavor. The group leader is Bernie Leadon, a former Burrito Brother. If you liked America's approach to music, you may like Eagles even better.

– Bud Newman

Tampa Tribune
July 29, 1972

Eagles is a fine album because grade-A sauce was used as the basic food. The ingredients: Bernie Leadon and Randy Meisner. Leadon being a seasoned studio veteran and ex-**Flying Burrito Brother** and Meisner having done a stint with **Poco**, plus an excellent guitarist-singer named Glenn Frey and a drummer named Don Henley; add English super-producer Glyn Johns; a pile of pleasant material–some of it (especially "Chug All Night") is outstanding. Eat heartily.

– Rory O'Connor

The Hackensack Record
July 30, 1972

Debut albums by new groups face a mortality hazard to that of newborn infants in the Amazon jungle, and it's only by the freakiest of chances I gave Asylum's *Eagles* the hearing it deserves. "Take It Easy," is climbing the charts. Country-rock? Yes. Easy-going? Yes. And the vocal harmonies are among the best you'll hear these days. Bernie Leadon is on guitar and banjo, and Glenn Frey is on slide guitar. Hope this group manages to stay together.

– Allen Macaulay

latter-day **Byrds** feel, but Eagles' distinctive harmonies set their version apart from Dillard & Clark's. Leadon and Meisner's "Earlybird" opens with bird tweet special effects that Henley found "corny." But the song was an otherwise punchy track, driven by Leadon's banjo and Frey's well-placed guitar distortion.

Meisner's "Tryin'" is an upbeat cut with a rhythmic swagger that ventures from country-rock into the pop-rock formula so popular in that era. The lyrics are optimistic, work-focused, and seemingly autobiographical. *"I'm just arriving in the city and there's music on my mind/Lookin' for my destination and my home is far behind"* aligns with his getting to work with Eagles. His other contribution, "Take the Devil," is a deliberately paced rocker that gives Leadon the opportunity to exercise some Gainesville licks. They were solid, often overlooked contributions to the debut album.

When the Eagles finished recording with Johns in London, they had nine songs completed. But Henley sang lead on just one of them, so Geffen asked them to cut one more in Los Angeles—Jackson Browne's uplifting "Nightingale." Henley's lead vocal gives the song a richness that blended well with the musical hooks Browne had already baked into the cut, and it especially shines as Hen-

The cover of the Eagles' debut album was conceptualized by **Gary Burden** and **Henry Diltz**. They designed it to open out into a poster, but prior to production, Asylum chief **David Geffen** chose economy over artistry and had the cover glued shut.

ley belts out *"Here comes my baby/Singing like a nightingale."*

The album performed well into the fall of 1972, but fell off the charts in November, even as "Peaceful Easy Feeling" was climbing into the Top 20. Yet the success of three charting singles gave the label hope. Another album would be queued up for 1973, though the Eagles' label was no longer just Asylum. After a corporate merger, Elektra was in the mix now too, and the incoming execs would not be excited about the "fucking cowboy album" the band would soon deliver. [15, 209, 1226, 2033]

ing week, and the song was picked up in San Diego, Hartford, Harrisburg, and San Jose. *Record World*'s survey of college radio stations showed pickups at the University of Houston and Swarthmore College in Pennsylvania. The song was attracting a strong and varied audience.

By the first week in June, just one month after its release, "Take It Easy" was on 98 percent of radio playlists nationwide, according to *Cashbox*'s Radio Active Report. A full-page promotional ad appeared in *Billboard* in mid-June, and by the end of the month, the song had finally appeared on playlists at CKLW-Detroit in Frey's hometown. Sharell, Ahern, and the entire Atlantic Records promotional team kept pushing programmers hard, and by mid-July, the song had achieved a sustained upward momentum. It had reached #37 on the *Record World* singles chart on July 22, the same week *Cashbox* logged it as #12, two spots above **Elton John**'s "Rocket Man." It rose as high as #12 on the *Billboard* Hot 100 chart.

As August rolled around, the quintessential California summer song began to fade on the airwaves and charts. By mid-month, its rank had fallen to the mid-20s to upper-30s on all three trade magazines' charts, and by September, the epic inaugural ride was over. But Geffen released the band's next single just as the first was beginning to wane on the charts. "Witchy Woman" began making chart noise just as Indian Summer arrived. [24, 587, 1592, 1683, 1684]

Geffen Thanks Fast-Moving Program Directors, Deejays

David Geffen ran Asylum Records in a more personal way than many record label chiefs in the early 1970s, interacting directly with many of the artists he signed. While his relationship with the Eagles soured after a few years, he took great care in making sure the fledgling band got airborne. In a letter to *Record World*'s **Kal Rudman**, published in Rudman's column "The Quarterback" in the magazine's June 10, 1972 issue, Geffen thanked program directors for giving the Eagles a chance:

"Dear Kal: I sure would appreciate it if you could give me a few lines in the Quarterback to thank you and the many program directors and major top 40 stations who didn't 'wait and see' on the Eagles, but went on it right away and really established an important group and important record from the very beginning. Since Asylum Records and I are new to the radio business, it is very encouraging to know that so many people give new things a chance. I am sincerely grateful." –David Geffen, President, Asylum Records

Rudman's weekly column evolved into an important source for industry news and gossip. Getting an endorsement from Rudman could help bring life to a group, and his backing certainly didn't hurt the Eagles' chances. Geffen was savvy in his approach to working other programming execs and deejays, too. The Communicator Network was a loosely affiliated group of radio stations across the country, and for a short time in the early 1970s, the consortium had an outsized impact on AM radio programming trends. Stations like KJRB-Spokane, Washington; WTBC-Tuscaloosa, Alabama; WAEB-Allentown, Pennsylvania; WCHB-Mount Pleasant, Michigan; KLEO-Wichita, Kansas; KRSP-Salt Lake City, Utah; WRNC-Raleigh, North Carolina, and dozens of others worked to coordinate playlists.

Record World acknowledged that impact when the Eagles' debut single was released. "'Take It Easy'-Eagles (Asylum), ho hum... smash record...another one brought about by the Communicator Network...tons of major markets on it...just putting it here to let you know who really made it happen," the magazine wrote. It recognized Geffen's work and acknowledged the Asylum president's gratitude. "The Communicator Network has proved to be a very good and important way of breaking new acts and new singles and I sure am glad that you and all these stations got it together," Geffen wrote to the network's board of directors. "If other record companies don't know where [the network] is at yet, tell them to call me."

Geffen and Atlantic Records CEO **Ahmet Ertegun** were high on the entire album and pushed out a then-aggressive 200,000 copies to record stores nationwide. He would continue working the phones as the Eagles hit the road in support of their debut album. Geffen had the band flying early, but the fast-growing stable of artists at Asylum would soon bring distractions that would take his eye off the Eagles' ascent. [4, 576, 1522]

Linda Ronstadt Joins Team Geffen, Signs with Asylum

Within nine months after he founded Asylum Records, **David Geffen** had assembled a roster of 13 artists, including the newly formed Eagles, **Joni Mitchell**, **Jo Jo Gunne**, **Jackson Browne**, **Judee Sill**, and **David Blue**, among others. His latest signing was **Linda Ronstadt**, who became labelmates with Don Henley and Glenn Frey, members of her one-time backing band before they were Eagles.

Ronstadt was the emerging vocalist Geffen lured away from Capitol Records after her five years on the label with the **Stone Poneys** and as a solo artist. He was beaming when he made the announcement in May 1972.

"We've never not been hot," Geffen said, confirming the signing to *Cashbox*. "Half of our first releases have been hits, not only here but overseas as well, particularly in England, France, and Germany." And he was looking ahead to promising new solo albums from Mitchell and **J.D. Souther**.

Ronstadt's third album for Capitol, titled *Linda Ronstadt* and released in January 1972, featured Frey and Henley in the band backing her on six of the album's 10 tracks, three of them recorded live at the Troubadour. Randy Meisner and Bernie Leadon also contributed to the studio tracks as session musicians and backing vocalists. Ronstadt's mostly live album served as a kind of Eagles' nest.

By the following year, Ronstadt would unveil her Asylum debut *Don't Cry Now*, with

continued on Page 41

THE LOGISTICS KID

Richard Fernandez (center) with Larry Penny (left) and longtime Eagles roadie Tommy Nixon at the *Desperado* photo shoot at Paramount Ranch in December 1972.

FERNANDEZ TAPPED AS EAGLES' ROAD MANAGER

While producer **Glyn Johns** was working with Eagles on their debut album in London in early 1972, he had taken a shine to **Richard Fernandez**, an enterprising young man with a knack for hauling gear. They met and became friends when Fernandez was road-managing **Faces**, the **Rod Stewart**-fronted band in London, and Johns was recording the band at Olympic Studios. When the Eagles were preparing to embark on their first tour coinciding with the album's June 1 release, Asylum Records president **David Geffen** was looking for someone to handle tour logistics, and Johns nudged Fernandez toward the band. He and the group hit it off well and thus began his nearly six-year run supporting them.

Fernandez had already come a long way in a short time. He was raised in East Los Angeles in a family that appreciated jazz. The first concert he attended was a **Duke Ellington** performance, and his father shared stories about how he spent three weeks in New York after returning from Europe during World War II going to see **Art Tatum**, **Dizzy Gillespie**, and **Eddie Condon**.

Fernandez loved music, especially jazz, and wanted to be around it, but wasn't musically inclined. So he found another way that was less about musical notes and more about the harmony of logistics. He became popular with high school bands because he owned a station wagon big enough to haul musical gear, and he soon found himself roadie-ing regularly.

Drafted into the U.S. Army and stationed in

Greece in 1967, Fernandez further burnished his logistics cred—and learned a few tricks of the airport trade—by scheduling and hustling top-secret military briefcases through foreign airports. When he got out of the service, he returned to Los Angeles, and his friend, **Larry Vallon**, recruited him to work with L.A. concert promoters **Jim Rissmiller** and **Steve Wolf**, who had formed a company called Concert Associates. Vallon and Fernandez then developed expertise in hauling equipment to and from venues up and down the California coast, as well as making regular setups at the Whisky a Go Go on the Sunset Strip.

"One day Larry called me up and informed me that he was doing a show with the Faces and they need an extra hand to finish up the last three weeks of their tour," Fernandez told *Time Passages*. "He asked me to come down and meet **Billy Gaff**, their manager, and **Pete Buckland**, their head production person. I spoke with Billy, and he gave me airline tickets and told me he would get the band to the airport and for me to get them on the plane and to the gig in San Francisco once we landed.

"After the three weeks," Fernandez said, "we ended up in New York City. After the last show, Billy asked me to meet him and the band in his room. When I got there, they asked if I wanted to move to London and work with the band. So, I moved to London to learn about touring in Europe."

Fernandez was shuttling Stewart and the Faces to shows in Europe and then hustling them back to Olympic Studios where they were recording with Johns in 1971. "I was the first one there before the band arrived and the last one to leave after the band took off," Fernandez said, adding that Johns kept an identical early/late schedule, so they became close and forged a lifelong friendship. That

> "
>
> I REMEMBER ONE NIGHT I SAID [TO GLYN JOHNS], 'HOW ABOUT THAT BAND OVER THERE [IN ASPEN]?' HE SAID, 'THEY PLAY AND SING IN TUNE.' AND I SAID, 'WELL, THAT'S A GOOD START.'
>
> — RICHARD FERNANDEZ

friendship eventually brought him to the Eagles.

"I remember we took about two weeks off to do gigs on the continent and Glyn took off for Aspen," Fernandez said. Johns' trip was to see Geffen's new band, the as-yet-unnamed Eagles, who auditioned for him in Boulder that December. "When he came back, he didn't really say much. And I remember one night I said, 'Hey, how about that band over there?' And he never even said their name or anything. He said, 'You know what, they play and they sing in tune.' And I said, 'Well, that's a good start.'"

When Fernandez moved back to America, he was still working Faces tours and asked Johns to let him know about any touring jobs that might become available. "He called me in California and said, 'Hey, David and **Elliot** [**Roberts**] just called up and they are looking for a tour manager for that band I worked with. They're called the Eagles.'"

Fernandez said Johns talked to Geffen and Roberts, and they told him to "come on down." Shortly after, they had worked out the details of his new gig road managing the band.

There was an issue at the start, however. Fernandez was starting a short Faces road trip that overlapped the first few Eagles gigs.

Fernandez was concerned at first because he was already committed to the Faces tour. "I told them I wasn't sure if I was going to be able to cover [their first few gigs], and Elliot said, 'That's all right, we will get them through their first three shows.'" Those first few gigs were handled by a small crew led by **John Barrick**, a former Troubadour bartender and the first tour manager for **The Byrds** who also became a close friend of the four Eagles. "The Sad Cafe," the song Henley and Frey wrote years later for *The Long Run*, was dedicated to Barrick.

Fernandez got a sneak peek at Frey, Henley, Leadon, and Meisner performing live just as he was starting his Faces tour, before the Eagles' first official tour began.

"I went to one of their rehearsals and actually met them before I started working with them," he said. "I went down to S.I.R. [Studio Instrument Rentals, on Sunset in Hollywood] and it was kind of funny because I walked in [wearing] a suit."

The band, of course, was decked out in blue jeans and t-shirts, but they all still hit it off well, he said. When his Faces tour ended in September 1972, he finally caught up with the Eagles in Florida, where they were opening for **Yes** and **Eggs Over Easy** at the Hollywood Sportatorium in Pembroke Pines just north of Miami.

Touring with the Eagles started out as a small-time affair, he said. The band would fly commercial, usually in coach, and when it wasn't far enough to fly, they would travel between shows in two cars. "It was a rental from one of those companies like Hertz, and it was probably a '72 Ford or Chevy station wagon and a sedan," he said. "I would drive the station wagon with the luggage and either Glenn or Bernie would ride with me, and Randy and Don would ride in the sedan. Sometimes Bernie or Glenn would drive."

Fernandez served an important behind-the-scenes role for the Eagles. While the band worked on their setlists, songwriting, and performing, Fernandez was fine-tuning the tour itinerary. He kept track of equipment, coordinated arrivals and setups with the venues, and directed roadies and other support staff. He also was responsible for making travel arrangements and confirming lodging, food, and other special requests for the group, which could sometimes get complicated.

Fernandez said his crew back then was small, just three people: **Larry Penny**, **Tom Nixon**, and himself. "My job [was] to get [the band] to the gig and off the

gig," he said, "and [provide] whatever space they feel they need to be in to perform their art."

Eagles quickly earned their reputation as one of the hardest-touring bands in rock history, and for the bulk of their heyday, Fernandez' tour logistics management consumed between six and eight months per year. He also became an important personality in the Eagles' operation.

Even though he came much later in the band's evolution, Don Felder described the road manager as a devoted and well-liked member of the crew.

"He would sit in the lead car with a map navigating his convoy of Eagles cars, vans, and trucks across the country," Felder said.

Fernandez observed the "genius" of Bernie Leadon on the road, no doubt finely tuned during Leadon's tenure with the **Flying Burrito Brothers** and **Dillard & Clark**. Fernandez said that if the road crew or hotel or restaurant people didn't get things just the way he liked, Leadon would take command of the situation in his own unique way. For example, Fernandez said, if Leadon didn't appreciate the way the restaurant cook was making his eggs, "he would just go back there and make them himself."

Later, when **Irving Azoff** began traveling with the band, Eliot wrote, Azoff would hand Fernandez a stack of $100 bills to make whatever problems that might emerge go away. Fernandez told *Time Passages* he couldn't specifically remember that happening, but also smiled and noted it was nearly 50 years ago.

Fernandez's role as road manager for the Eagles helped launch his wildly successful career. He built a reputation on that role, but by February 1977, that relationship would come to a bittersweet end in Montreal. [6, 1619, 1620, 1635, 1685, 1694]

> MY JOB [WAS] TO GET THESE GUYS TO THE GIG AND OFF THE GIG AND [PROVIDE] WHATEVER SPACE THEY FEEL THEY NEED TO BE IN TO PERFORM THEIR ART.
>
> — RICHARD FERNANDEZ

her cover of Eagles' "Desperado" the first single. The album was the first of Ronstadt's many collaborations with producer **Peter Asher**, half of the British 1960s duo **Peter & Gordon**, and earned her first gold LP. Although Ronstadt's once-unknown backing band had taken off as Eagles by then, Frey made a guest appearance on two tracks, singing harmony on Souther's "The Fast One" and playing steel guitar on "Everybody Loves a Winner," co-written by **William Bell**, **Booker T. Jones**, and **Bill Williams**.

It turned out Ronstadt owed one more album to Capitol, and when *Heart Like a Wheel* was released in 1974, it became her biggest album to date and her first #1. Frey was once again by her side on guitar with Henley manning the drums on the album's closing track, James Taylor's "You Can Close Your Eyes." [587, 1821, 1822, 1823]

Down and Out, Walsh Hires Azoff as New Agent, Manager

Long before Joe Walsh became an Eagle, he was influencing the trajectory of the band's career. Inspired by Walsh's choices, the Eagles would eventually find themselves working with his producer, **Bill Szymczyk**. Even before that, they chose to work with Walsh's manager, **Irving Azoff**, who would help take the Eagles to lofty heights few bands could imagine.

Azoff officially partnered with Walsh in 1972, helping the guitarist remove himself from a management situation that had deteriorated and left him desperate and burned out. After leaving the **James Gang**, Walsh was certain that Belkin Productions and co-founder **Mike Belkin**, who managed the band and Walsh himself, were being untruthful about why he was leaving the organization. "[Belkin] told people that I was addicted to heroin and that I was drying out," Walsh said. "He knew it was a lie, but he was anxious to play me down. He was afraid the James Gang wouldn't make money without me."

Taking time off to figure out his next move, Walsh spent half a year attempting to strategize. Mostly, he said, "I just got drunk a lot. I was totally down and out, living in Colorado," Walsh reflected. "Lost. Couldn't get any gigs...the IRS was auditing me three years running. My manager didn't even care."

Walsh, who had met Azoff during his James Gang days, recounted how the then-booking agent re-entered his life: "Out of nowhere, Irving came up, saying he believed in me. He was a booking agent and wanted to at least keep me working until I could straighten my career out." Walsh first hired Azoff as an agent, while still retaining management services with Belkin.

Walsh started playing with the **Barnstorm** trio and they recorded their first record, but he still thought he was dealing with what he called "bad management." Feeling he wasn't getting a fair chance, he fired Belkin and briefly hooked up with **Humble Pie** manager **Dee Anthony** before pleading with his agent, Azoff, to become his new manager. According to Walsh, "He said, 'Shit, I'm flattered. That means I don't

continued on Page 45

ODD PAIRINGS: TOUR STARTS WITH JETHRO TULL, YES

Eagles began touring at the beginning of June 1972 supporting their debut album with dates in Canada and the Pacific Northwest, opening for a succession of progressive rock bands that weren't even close to matching their own musical style or appearance. Dressed in jeans, work shirts, and sneakers, the group ambled onstage looking like a laid-back garage band, a stark contrast to most of the headliners they opened for.

That was especially true of progressive rock band **Jethro Tull**, fronted by lead singer and flute player **Ian Anderson**, whose stage presence was more akin to theater than rock and roll.

It wasn't the first time on the road for the Eagles as a band. They had played tune-ups at The Gallery in Aspen, Colorado before jetting off to record their first album in London in early 1972.

Shortly after joining them April 2 for their gig at **Boyd Elder**'s art exhibit, Geffen packed the band off to support **Joe Cocker** on a six-show tour that started in Spokane, Washington. Two months later, on June 1, release day for the *Eagles* album, they were back in Los Angeles to open one night for **Neil Young**.

But Eagles' first real tour started in Calgary, Canada, as the band kicked off a string of shows opening for Jethro Tull. The band went from Calgary to Spokane to Kansas City, Missouri, bookended by shows in Las Vegas, Dallas, Houston, and San Antonio before earning a 10-day break near the end of June.

Reviewers gave some notice to the new kids in town. The *Kansas City Star* said the "warmup band" was solid rock and included a passing reference to the Eagles' new hit single. And while the review was congratulatory about a new band nabbing such a choice spot on Tull's tour, it said, "The only problem [is] that Jethro Tull's part of the concert was so exciting, it's hard to remember the warmup [band] later." A month later, another reviewer for *The (Montreal) Gazette* said the band outshone their headliner, which that night was **Procol Harum**. "Their three- and four-part harmonies were a delight to hear throughout the show."

Touring with prog-rock greats presented a different experience for the band. "We opened up with Jethro Tull and they didn't say anything to us the whole time," said Glenn Frey, who eventually took to calling the group's leader Ian Anderson "The Leaping Leotard."

While Tull kept its distance, the other bands the Eagles supported were warmer, including Procol Harum and its leader, **Gary Brooker**, who the Eagles were booked to open for midway through June 1972. Both bands had singles quickly rising on the *Billboard* Hot 100 chart, with Procol's recut "Conquistador" at #34 and Eagles' "Take It Easy" right behind at #35.

"What a great bunch of guys," Frey said on **Dan Patrick**'s radio show in April 2015. "We used to hang out with them after work and we hit some Holiday Inn bars. And there'd be a piano and Gary Brooker would go over there and they'd sing pub songs all night. We had a really nice time hanging with them."

The feeling was mutual for Brooker. "Well, we had never heard of them, but nobody else had either," he told **Redbeard** on his *Raised on Radio* show in April 2017. "They were nice guys. They were youngsters on the way up, well—they were two years younger than me—but at that time they had their first record out that was...climbing up the charts. It was a nice, successful billing because they were just happening, and we had already had a few albums out that had

Jethro Tull frontman **Ian Anderson** performs in Denver in 1973.

done well. They were very impressive with great vocals and all good players. Still are."

Eagles opened for **Humble Pie**, **Black Oak Arkansas**, and **Uriah Heep** between multiple dates supporting Procol Harum and the **J. Geils Band**, and completed their inaugural summer with a long run of shows supporting another prog-rock heavyweight, **Yes**. Lead singer **Jon Anderson** said that by the end of that leg, his bandmates and the Eagles had become good friends.

"We finished our show, 15,000 people," Anderson said. "We get...backstage, there's no lights. It's all dark, and it's like, 'What the hell is going on?' And there were the guys with flashlights like, 'C'mon this way, the lights are going to open up.' It was so dark we couldn't see anybody and then all of sudden the lights came on, and there was a table set up with the Eagles standing behind [it] with two dozen pies. They threw these cream pies at us, and I joined in, and it was the best time ever."

So, why would Eagles open their careers supporting bands so different from their own musical style? The one constant was their labels. Most of the bands the Eagles supported that summer were on Warner Bros. labels or their affiliates, including Atlantic Records, ATCO, and Island Records. It was **Ahmet Ertegun**, Atlantic's co-founder and president, who had provided the nudge Geffen needed to launch Asylum and Atlantic became the new label's distributor. Ertegun's backing extended to promotion and marketing, including tour support.

Even if the fan bases were a bit mismatched, Yes, Jethro Tull, and Procol Harum were all performing before large crowds every night, and those large-venue shows were key to getting the Eagles off the ground. Putting them in front of that many rock and roll fans was important for exposure, experience, and cash—though not necessarily in that order—until the band built a following of its own. [1597, 1598, 1599, 1600, 1601]

SPOTLIGHT ALBUM | J.D. SOUTHER

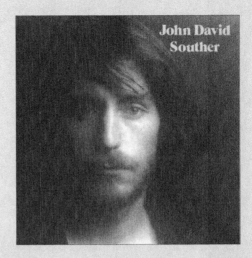

John David
Souther

J.D. SOUTHER
John David Souther
Asylum Records, August 1972

Never officially a member of the Eagles, **J.D. Souther** was firmly entrenched in the band's inner circle and arguably something of an "unofficial" member. The Songwriters Hall of Fame inductee was not only a labelmate and friend of the band, but also co-wrote some of their best-known songs. Hits like "The Best of My Love," "New Kid in Town," and "Heartache Tonight," as well as one-time concert staples "Doolin-Dalton" and "James Dean," are among the list of titles partially credited to Glenn Frey's former partner in the duo **Longbranch/Pennywhistle**.

In fact, **David Geffen** had suggested that Souther be part of the initial Eagles lineup, but ultimately, Souther felt like he'd be an unnecessary "fifth wheel" in a group already loaded with talent. Additionally, Souther had enough self-awareness to recognize that he was less of a "band guy," going as far as mentioning how he had historically been labeled as an individual who "does not work well with others." He preferred to stay home with his girlfriend, **Linda Ronstadt**, and write songs.

"I told Geffen I'd rather remain friends with those guys," Souther explained in a 1979 interview. "You know, I'm not really a team player."

So in 1972, Eagles released their debut album, and Souther, the solo artist, put out an eponymous disc of all original songs for the label.

The opening jangly strains of "The Fast One"—later covered by Ronstadt—sounded like a mid-tempo country-rock track that could have fit in well on the Eagles' debut. It set the tone for the record. Other notable tracks include "Run Like a Thief" (later recorded by **Bonnie Raitt**), a re-interpretation of "Kite Woman" from the *Longbranch/Pennywhistle* LP, and a cut that would become familiar to Eagles faithful years later—"How Long."

While the latter tune was never properly recorded and released by Eagles in their heyday, it was nevertheless a song they played in their live set during the early four-piece days, with Frey, Henley, and Meisner each taking a verse as lead vocalist.

What's old apparently does become new again, because when the Eagles released *Long Road Out of Eden* in 2007, their first full-length studio record since *The Long Run* 28 years earlier, they included a newly recorded version of "How Long" (this time with Frey also covering the verse originally sung by Meisner) and released it as the album's first single.

Souther's lone wolf ways may have been personally endearing to friends, but his solo album had a disappointing run. It wouldn't be long before Geffen asked him to reconsider joining a group. And in 1974, Souther would take the offer. [225, 363, 1579, 1580, 1590, 1808]

have to be an agent anymore,'" and accepted the offer.

Azoff didn't have the means to open his own office, so he was advised by his lawyer—who also represented **David Geffen**—to work under Geffen's company and to bring Walsh with him. It wouldn't be long before he'd cross paths with the Eagles and both camps would realize they could help each other in their quests for world domination. [1, 363, 481]

FALL 1972

 RELEASES
▶ **Poco**, with Timothy B. Schmit, "Good Feelin' to Know" (single)
▶ **Barnstorm**, with Joe Walsh, "I'll Tell the World" (single)
▶ **Barnstorm**, with Joe Walsh, *Barnstorm* (album)
▶ **Barnstorm**, with Joe Walsh, "Turn to Stone" (single)

 NUGGETS
▶ Radio station enthusiasm for **J.D. Souther**'s new song, "How Long," is strong. —*Cashbox*
▶ Eagles and **Jackson Browne** are returning to the studio in December and January, respectively. —*Record World*

 COLLABORATIONS
▶ **Don Henley** (drums, vocals), **Bernie Leadon** (banjo, guitar, vocals), and **Randy Meisner** (bass guitar, vocals) provided musical support on **Rick Roberts**' album *Windmills*.
▶ **Bernie Leadon** played guitar on **Rita Coolidge**'s album *The Lady's Not for Sale*.

 ON THE ROAD WITH ...
▶ **Eagles:** Black Oak Arkansas, Eggs Over Easy, Gentle Giant, Humble Pie, J. Geils Band, J.D. Souther, Jackson Browne, Mahavishnu Orchestra, Yes
▶ **Poco**, with Timothy B. Schmit: Ballin' Jack, Chet Nichols, It's a Beautiful Day, John Mayall, Pure Prairie League, Rare Earth, T. Rex, Ten Years After, The Beach Boys, the Doobie Brothers
▶ **Barnstorm**, with Joe Walsh: Curtis Mayfield, Grin, Mahavishnu Orchestra, Mark-Almond, Pure Food and Drug Act, Pure Gold, the Edgar Winter Group

Eagles Guest on Rick Roberts' Debut Solo LP, *Windmills*

Singer-songwriter **Rick Roberts** is most famous for his tenure in the band **Firefall**, where he wrote and sang their big hits "You Are the Woman" (1976) and "Just Remember I Love You" (1977), the latter featuring Timothy B. Schmit.

But it was in the fall of 1972 that Bernie Leadon's fellow **Flying Burrito Brother** alumnus released his first solo album, *Windmills*, for A&M records. The liner notes read like something of a "who's who" list of musicians, including **Jackson Browne**, **Al Perkins**, **Chris Hillman**, **Byron Berline**, **David Crosby**, and **Joe Lala**, not to mention three-fourths of the then-current Eagles lineup.

"The Eagles were all friends of mine," Roberts explained. "Bernie had been in the Burritos with me and Don Henley and I used to play poker twice a week together for about two years. Jackson was an acquaintance, as well. They were all close friends

continued on Page 49

ASYLUM COLLECTIVE: GEFFEN CHANGES APPROACH

Show business mogul **David Geffen** didn't earn a reputation for being ambitious by playing it safe or by staying in one place for too long. Following his career steps—even in his earliest days in the music business—almost requires a scorecard to keep track.

Geffen began his music career as an agent working for the William Morris Agency, where he brought on **Laura Nyro** as a client. He believed so strongly in the talented and engaging singer-songwriter that he soon quit his job at WMA and opened his own management company with Nyro as his sole client.

Shortly after, Geffen saw the potential in joining forces with artist manager **Elliot Roberts**—whose Lookout Management was already handling heavyweights like **Crosby, Stills & Nash**, **Joni Mitchell**, and **Neil Young**—and thus the Geffen-Roberts management company was born in 1969.

In an industry where contracts had been historically bad and unprofitable for rock musicians, the partners sought to make Geffen-Roberts an artist-oriented management operation unlike any the record industry had ever seen—on a handshake.

"We were beyond artist-friendly," Roberts asserted. "The people we worked with were our friends...that was what was unique about what Geffen-Roberts was."

With Geffen in particular, the artists had an ally who was not only savvy with business dealings, but also had a true love and appreciation for good music and artistry, as well as the creative process. The two sides to Geffen's persona seemed to be just what was coveted by the musicians: a late-1960s hippie idealism toward art that could co-exist peacefully alongside an ambitious 1970s mercenary method of operation.

Jackson Browne soon was added to the Geffen-Roberts roster, which led directly to the creation of the Asylum label in 1971. Geffen aggressively shopped Browne to get him a record deal, but no one was biting. Geffen told Atlantic Records' **Ahmet Ertegun** that Browne was sure to make him a lot of money, to which, according to Geffen, Ertegun glibly responded, "I have a lot of money. Why don't you record Jackson Browne and you, too, can have a lot of money?" A deal was made with Ertegun for Geffen to have his own label with distribution and marketing support from Atlantic, and Asylum was born.

"[Geffen] was going to keep it really small," Browne confirmed. "It was going to be a real family label—six or eight people, that's all."

Don Henley agreed: "The name was Asylum Records because it was going to be a sanctuary for artists where they would not be mistreated, and they would be nurtured and taken care of so they could develop their art and their craft."

Eagles, additions to the Asylum stable later in 1971, were, indeed, fully on board with the concept. The confidence they had in the "Asylum Approach" was cemented one night while sitting in a sauna.

As the legend goes, Glenn Frey, along with initial Asylum artists Browne, **J.D. Souther**, and **Ned Doheny**, were all disrobed with Geffen in the warm humidity of his steam bath when he made a promise that seemed apropos given the intimate setting: "I want to keep Asylum Records very small," he vowed. "I'll never have more artists than I can fit in this sauna."

Geffen's approach wasn't just small and inclusive, it was, at least at the outset, nurturing too. "If an artist on Asylum is good but doesn't sell big, we would never drop him from the label," Geffen told

Billboard in 1972. "For example, **David Blue** can stay on Asylum as long as he wants. But all our contracts are just handshakes, and acts can leave us any time they want to."

Roberts added that the company's focus was on growing artists. "One of our frustrations in dealing with record companies was that they were trying to sell product and we were trying to build artists," he said. "Our philosophy is to build our artists. Each record doesn't have to be a million-seller."

This was a concept the Eagles and their labelmates could get behind. The question was, would it ring true in practice, and, if so, for how long? [1, 204, 205, 693, 694, 1287]

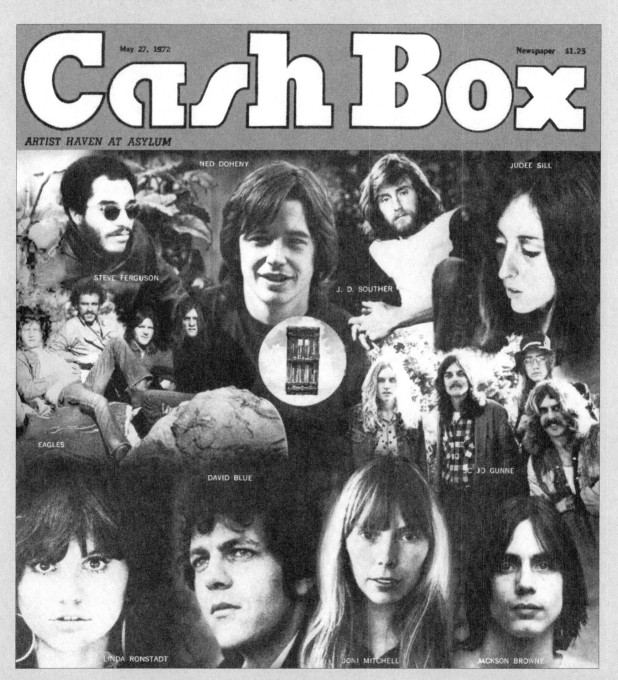

May 27, 1972

Newspaper $1.25

Cash Box

ARTIST HAVEN AT ASYLUM

NED DOHENY

JUDEE SILL

STEVE FERGUSON

J. D. SOUTHER

EAGLES

JO JO GUNNE

DAVID BLUE

LINDA RONSTADT

JONI MITCHELL

JACKSON BROWNE

BARNSTORM
Turn to Stone
ABC-Dunhill Records, August 1972

By spring 1972, Joe Walsh had left the **James Gang** and moved to Colorado, but the money and fame he had grown accustomed to as part of Ohio's most famous power trio did not follow him to the Rocky Mountains.

With **Barnstorm**, a new trio comprised of himself, drummer **Joe Vitale**, and bassist **Kenny Passarelli**, along with friend and producer **Bill Szymczyk**, Walsh began charting a new musical path at producer **James William Guercio**'s new Caribou Ranch studio in Nederland, Colorado. Although the ten tracks the group recorded for their debut album were creative and musically respectable, the album flopped. But one song, "Turn to Stone," would emerge as the true keeper from the session—just not right away.

"Turn to Stone" is a nominal rock anthem that became—and remains—a fan favorite. Years later, the Eagles occasionally added it to their setlist. Co-written by Walsh and Detroit rocker **Terry Trebandt**, it became Walsh's second post-James Gang single. Walsh told *Rolling Stone*'s **Richard Bienstock** the song was his commentary about the Nixon Administration and the Vietnam War.

"It's a song about frustration," he said. "Also, I attended Kent State. I was at the [May 4, 1970] shootings. That fueled it, too. In those days it felt like the government's priority was not the population. They had an agenda that was about something other than doing what was necessarily good for the country."

Musically, the song differed in approach from the rest of the cuts on *Barnstorm*, which largely embraced the emerging country-rock trend coming out of California in the late 1960s and early 1970s. The LP's first single, "I'll Tell the World About You" was hailed by *Melody Maker*'s **Richard Williams** as the best rock and roll song he had ever heard. Radio interest and sales fell flat, though, so ABC-Dunhill Records turned to the more James Gang-esque "Stone" as the album's second single. But giving fans a little taste of James Gang wasn't enough and that version never charted.

"Turn to Stone" was a creative itch Walsh simply couldn't scratch. He, along with producer **John Stronach** (who produced **REO Speedwagon**, **Keith Moon**, and **Rufus**), re-cut the song two years later for his first solo album, *So What*, out in late 1974. While the *Barnstorm* version exuded more raw power and abandon, the recut version was more than a full minute shorter, cleaner, and more radio-friendly, and included Glenn Frey, Randy Meisner, and Don Henley providing backing vocals.

"Stone" was the best cut on the album, so radio stations gave it a spin. Although it stalled at #85 on the *Record World* chart, it was a rebirth of sorts for Walsh. He may not have yet fully recaptured his James Gang mojo, but he was on the comeback trail. [225, 363, 1579, 1580, 1590, 1808]

and very good musicians, and they came up with a lot of ideas that added a great deal to the album."

Randy Meisner, the third Eagle on the record, would later reconnect with Roberts when they formed the **Meisner-Roberts Band** in 1987.

Despite a resume that included a tenure as **Gram Parsons**' replacement in the Burritos, Roberts considered himself a player with more pop sensibilities than a country music aficionado, and those influences are heard on *Windmills*.

He suggests that the folkier sides of **The Byrds** and **Buffalo Springfield** were a big inspiration, although the album is not devoid of the country stylings that undoubtedly rubbed off on him. This is most notably heard on the LP's lone cover, a remake of **Harlan Howard**'s "Pick Me Up on Your Way Down." Album opener "Deliver Me" and the acoustic "In My Own Small Way," which features impressive banjo work by Leadon, are other highlights.

"I called in a lot of markers," Roberts said. "Don Henley drummed on nine cuts and sang backup. Randy Meisner was on five." [231, 1502]

Geffen Sells Asylum Records To Warner Communications

David Geffen's Asylum Records quickly established itself as a successful label, in large part due to the achievements of Eagles' debut album in the latter half of 1972. But beyond that, there were no guarantees the band would continue their ascent toward global superstardom. In fact, the group was known for internal friction, so there was always a question whether they would survive as a band or split up before reaching the pinnacle.

Along with **Jackson Browne**, Eagles were Asylum's most reliable asset. But Asylum's other assets weren't as strong and that, coupled with Geffen's strong affection for cinema and theater, was why, roughly a year after Asylum's launch, he entertained an offer from Warner Communications Inc. to buy 50 percent of the company.

Geffen named a price of $7 million, which he thought would be too exorbitant even for this major corporation to accept, given that Asylum was not nearly that profitable. The label's earnings of around $150,000 its first year were solid, but not awe-inspiring. To Geffen's surprise, Warner agreed, but with a couple caveats: he was to not only step down from his role in artist management, but also agree to sign a seven-year employment contract with WCI.

Geffen made the decision to sell without consulting **Elliot Roberts**, his partner at Asylum, who didn't particularly endorse the move. Still, Roberts' protestations were minimal since he was the minority owner of the label, and the sale was going to put a significant sum of money in his pocket. Roberts, who had already sensed Geffen would become bored with Asylum and seek to network his way into the movie business, would take over more artist management responsibilities while Geffen would run the label.

The deal went down in 1972 around

continued on Page 51

PATHWAY ALBUM | JOE WALSH

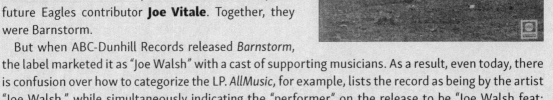

BARNSTORM

Barnstorm
ABC-Dunhill Records, October 1972

Barnstorm was not a Joe Walsh solo project, though the record-buying public likely didn't know it. Fronted by the guitarist, the band also featured bassist **Kenny Passarelli** and drummer, multi-instrumentalist, and future Eagles contributor **Joe Vitale**. Together, they were Barnstorm.

But when ABC-Dunhill Records released *Barnstorm*, the label marketed it as "Joe Walsh" with a cast of supporting musicians. As a result, even today, there is confusion over how to categorize the LP. *AllMusic*, for example, lists the record as being by the artist "Joe Walsh," while simultaneously indicating the "performer" on the release to be "Joe Walsh feat: Barnstorm."

True, Walsh's name appears under the composer credits on nine of the 10 Barnstorm tracks (including six times as the sole songwriter). But by his own assessment, Barnstorm should have gotten more credit as a band.

"I wanted to be a band, not a solo artist," Walsh reflected on Barnstorm. "Vitale, especially, should've gotten more credit 'cause it wasn't all me. When Vitale and I work together, that's how we got those songs. It was in every aspect a collaborative effort. I wanted it to be a band like **Traffic**," he explained further in a 2018 interview on *In the Studio*. "Traffic songs aren't **Steve Winwood** songs, they're Traffic songs."

While Walsh's previous power trio, the **James Gang**, was known for harder-rocking sounds, the first Barnstorm album reflected the artist's desire to grow beyond that. Engineered by future Eagles producer **Bill Szymczyk** and the first album recorded at **James Guercio**'s soon-to-be famous Caribou Ranch studios near Nederland, Colorado, the album opened with "Here We Go," setting the mood with a spacey, ethereal tone, serving as a statement of intent for a band unwilling to be limited by "power trio" expectations.

Other standouts like "One on One" and "Bird Call" served as signposts in the listener's journey through a textured and highly produced musical landscape. Walsh even brought in Don Henley's former Shiloh bandmate **Al Perkins** to play pedal steel guitar on "Midnight Visitor."

While the LP is largely devoid of the crunch associated with the James Gang (particularly prior to their *Thirds* album), the fan-favorite anthem "Turn to Stone" gives a nod to the past with its stomping electric guitar riff and a vocal delivered with conviction and purpose. The tune would make an encore appearance in 1974 when Walsh re-recorded it for his first (or third, depending on how you classify the Barnstorm records) solo album, *So What*. [1310, 1310, 1527, 1528]

Thanksgiving, but many of the artists on the Asylum roster didn't find much to be thankful for when they learned about it. Not insignificantly, Warner now owned half the artists' publishing rights, and the bands and creatives who had signed on to work with a small, artist-minded label were now part of a large corporate enterprise.

In the Eagles camp, Don Henley felt a sense of betrayal; he had heard about the promises Geffen made in his sauna to Glenn Frey and Jackson Browne that Asylum would remain small and familial, and be true to its name as a haven for artists.

"We woke up one morning and read about it in the paper," Henley lamented.

Geffen attempted damage control among his agitated clients by assuring them he and **Elliot Roberts** would remain involved, and little would change. But like Henley, his labelmates also had difficulty viewing the sale to Warner as anything but a betrayal. It wasn't the first or last time they would taste the unpleasantries of the music business, but among the Eagles, this especially unsavory development would have a direct influence on the songs they were writing for their second LP, *Desperado*.

"David had his eye on the horizon," Frey later reflected. "He might have been standing there holding hands with all the young country-rockers, but he had a vision that ultimately would take him far away from us."

Indeed, further changes and broken promises were not far off, as WCI's merger of Asylum with Elektra Records in mid-1973 was on the horizon. [1, 574, 695, 1287]

Elektra and Asylum Merged; Geffen Becomes New Chairman

When **David Geffen** sold Asylum to Warner Communications Inc. for $7 million in 1972, he thought he'd set a price so high, the corporation wouldn't buy. WCI surprised him by accepting his terms, and a year later Geffen was convinced he'd pegged the price too low. Combined with plummeting Warner stocks, the music industry wunderkind was not happy.

To placate Geffen as well as attempt to reverse WCI's fortunes, its new CEO, **Steve Ross**, favorably renegotiated Geffen's stock options and elevated his salary to $1 million annually (nearly $6.5 million in 2022 dollars). The deal hinged on a proposed merger of two of the corporation's record labels: Elektra and Asylum.

Ross wanted badly to revitalize Elektra. As a college student, **Jac Holzman** created the label in 1950. He focused on folk with artists such as **Theodore Bikel**, **Judy Collins**, and **Phil Ochs** through the mid-1960s, then ventured into rock and pop with signings including the **Paul Butterfield Blues Band**, **Love**, **The Doors**, **The Stooges**, **MC5**, **Harry Chapin**, **Carly Simon**, and **Bread**.

But by 1973 Elektra was still the least successful of Warner's three primary labels, behind Warner Bros. and Atlantic. Ross believed Elektra had gambled and lost on too many artists, and its roster had become bloated. Holzman now had other plans and wanted out. Ross needed someone to get the ship back on course. He saw

continued on Page 55

RELEASE
Mid-August 1972

WITCHY WOMAN
By: Bernie Leadon, Don Henley
Side B: Early Bird (Leadon, Meisner)

After the Eagles first single, "Take It Easy," peaked on the charts in early August 1972, the marketing brains at Asylum Records wasted no time in pressing a new single, "Witchy Woman." It was a potent cut that climbed higher in all three trade magazines—*Cashbox*, *Record World* and *Billboard*—and stayed on the airwaves far longer than its debut album predecessor. It was the band's second-straight Top 10 single.

AIRPLAY

Radio stations in the South were among the first to add "Witchy Woman" to their playlists with Richmond's WLEE leading the way. Southern stations like WBBQ in Augusta, Georgia, and KRHM in Austin, Texas also quickly added it. The song was an August mid-month release and Midwest stations added it in September; the band's appeal there was strong and growing. Notably, stations in the West were again slower to adopt the song.

31 PLAYLIST ADDS Summer-Fall 1972

Region	Aug	Sep	Oct	Regional Airplay
Northeast	1	6	3	32.2%
Southeast	3	3	2	21.6%
Midwest	0	7	2	29%
Southwest	2	1	0	9.7%
West	0	1	0	3.2%

FIRST-WAVE STATIONS Stations that added the song in the first 30 days

WJET-Erie

KILT-Houston
KRMH-Red Mesa, AZ

WLEE-Richmond
WBBQ-Augusta
WBAM-Montgomery

CHARTS

Billboard

9
November 18, 1972

Cashbox

11
November 25 1972

Record World

8
November 25 1972

HIGHEST CHARTING WEEK: RECORD WORLD - November 25, 1972

SINGLE	ARTIST	# PREV WK
1. I'll Be Around	Spinners	2
2. I'd Love You to Want Me	Lobo	3
3. I Am Woman	Helen Reddy	6
4. I Can See Clearly Now	Johnny Nash	1
5. If You Don't Know Me By Now	Harold Melvin & The Blue Notes	7
6. Papa Was a Rolling Stone	Temptations	11
7. Nights in White Satin	Moody Blues	4
8. WITCHY WOMAN	**EAGLES**	**9**
9. If I Could Reach You	Fifth Dimension	10

Sources: Billboard, Cashbox, Record World

LEADON, HENLEY CONJURE MYSTICAL 'ZELDA' CUT

"Take It Easy" was peaking as summer 1972 faded, so the band's management and label promotion team—**David Geffen**, **Jerry Sharell**, **Paul Ahern**, and **John Hartmann**—queued up "Witchy Woman" as the second single from the critically well-received *Eagles* album.

Geffen worked the same network of programming directors nationwide that had made "Take It Easy" a hit, and trade magazines *Record World* and *Cashbox* quickly told their record and radio industry subscribers about the band's forthcoming follow-up.

Co-authored by Bernie Leadon and Don Henley, the song grew out of a piece of guitar music that Leadon spun up, with Henley adding the lyrics and the rhythm track's signature tom-tom beat.

"The female character is a composite," Henley told St. Louis's KSHE-95 listeners during a 2016 interview. "I had been reading a book about the life of **F. Scott Fitzgerald**'s troubled wife, **Zelda**, who, in her 30s and 40s, drifted in and out of psychiatric hospitals suffering from schizophrenia—or more likely, bipolar disorder—while her husband's health and career spiraled downward, due to his abuse of alcohol." In other interviews, Henley said the visage of the woman in the song was also an amalgam of the girls he had met at Whisky a Go Go and the Troubadour.

After *Record World* and *Cashbox* spotlighted the new single in mid-August, "Witchy Woman" made its debut on their charts at #74 and #99, respectively; it didn't appear on the *Billboard* Hot 100 chart until September, when it debuted at #78.

The single also began showing up on playlists regionally in mid-August, breaking first in Richmond, Virginia. The following week it broke across the South and Southwest in Augusta, Georgia; Montgomery, Alabama; and Houston, Texas.

The single peaked on the *Cashbox* Top 100 singles chart at #13 in November but rose to #8 in *Billboard* and #9 on the *Record World* singles chart.

It was a milestone for both the song's writers. Leadon had written songs recorded by **Dillard & Clark** and the **Flying Burrito Brothers**, but none ever charted. The songs Henley had written for **Shiloh** never got airplay or made the charts either.

But now, just six months after Eagles' debut album took flight, Leadon and Henley landed their first-ever Top 10 single as songwriters, and the band's second consecutive Top 10 hit.

By the 1972 year-end holidays, "Witchy Woman" was on the fade. But Asylum had a third card to play from the Eagles' debut album, one that would leave all the players, radio listeners, and record buyers with a peaceful easy feeling. [208, 209]

FELDER, EAGLES INTRODUCED AT BOSTON CONCERT

Although Don Felder wouldn't join the Eagles until after he had been called into the studio to contribute guitar to a couple of tracks for their third album, *On the Border*, out in spring 1974, he and Bernie Leadon had known each other since their high school years in Gainesville, Florida.

By 1972, Felder had relocated to Boston, where he attended Berklee College of Music and was working with his band **Flow**.

"The Eagles happened and we were coming through town," Leadon recalled in a 2019 conversation with music journalist **John Beaudin**. "I called him, or he called me; he came down to the show. ... I remember he was kind of playing and showing off for the other guys in my band. And they're like, 'Oh, yeah, like, you're really a rock guitar player, man.'"

Felder himself recalled in his memoir that the Eagles were in town on their first tour, at a Boston gig opening for **Yes**. He met the other three for the first time in Eagles' dressing room. His initial impressions were that Frey was perhaps the most confident, Henley the most high-strung, and Meisner the most timid. When Felder and his fellow former Floridian started to jam, Felder agreed the guys were impressed with what they heard.

Felder recalled Frey telling him to "come to L.A.," echoing advice he had heard from Leadon, who had been encouraging Felder to do the same for years. "You gotta come back west with me. That's where it's all happening," he would tell Felder over a few beers backstage wherever he was playing. "I've made some great contacts and I'm sure I can get you some work."

Up until then, Felder and his wife Susan had preferred living in the Northeast and hadn't seriously entertained making a move west. His first fateful meeting with the Eagles might not have changed anything that day, but it arguably sparked a new

Glenn Frey (right) and Don Felder talk backstage at the Santa Monica Civic Auditorium in 1975.

conversation. Two months later, they made the move, heeding Leadon's advice that he'd never regret it.

The encouragement Felder received from his future bandmates to set up camp in California did not, however, include an offer of gainful employment with them or anyone else at the time. Arriving with about $300 and a guitar, Felder told writer **John Tobler** in 1977 that he soon found himself financially at "a point of sheer, total desperation." Just at that point, fortunately, Felder was offered a gig to play guitar for **David Blue**, an Asylum labelmate and author of "Outlaw Man," a song Eagles would later cover for their *Desperado* album.

"The Eagles," Felder said, "sort of helped recommend me for [the job with Blue], which really helped a lot. I got to know them, and **Graham Nash**, and some other people that were in that same management office while I was working for David." [218, 1390, 1501, 1518]

Geffen as the right leader to take the helm.

The deal was announced in August 1973 and included a new job title for Geffen. As chairman of the freshly merged Elektra/Asylum Records, he immediately put his mark on the company by dropping 25 of the combined roster's 35 artists. He fired the art director and the entire publicity, promotion, and production staffs. And he began investigating moving the New York-based Elektra to Los Angeles. As **Marc Eliot** wrote in his 1998 book *To the Limit: The Untold Story of the Eagles*, "Geffen was, for all his generational devotion to artists, first and always a businessman."

However, for the artists who remembered "the old sauna story," as Don Henley once referred to it, the Elektra/Asylum deal represented yet another turn for the worse. Plus, there were increasingly disturbing conflicts of interest.

"David was the Eagles' manager," Glenn Frey explained. "David was the Eagles' publisher. David was the Eagles' record company. So, there was, like, nobody negotiating with anybody."

Asylum co-founder **Elliot Roberts** seemed to chalk it up to a series of circumstances that unfolded over time. "[Geffen and I] were arguing amongst ourselves and negotiating with ourselves, and both

DAVID WAS THE EAGLES' MANAGER. DAVID WAS THE EAGLES' PUBLISHER. DAVID WAS THE EAGLES' RECORD COMPANY. SO, THERE WAS, LIKE, NOBODY NEGOTIATING WITH ANYBODY.

— GLENN FREY

saw that was very unhealthy... The dream that we had of Asylum being this familial company we saw didn't have the merit two years down the line once it became successful that it seemed to have when David conceived it."

Some Asylum artists were growing upset with the label and its management even before the company's merger with Elektra. Other artists felt a sense of resigned acceptance.

"When we came to the States to be managed by them, it came at a period when David and Elliot could have really done a lot for us," said **Gerry Beckley** of **America**, who were signed to Warner Bros. and living in the U.K. when Geffen worked hard to sign them to Geffen-Roberts. "After six months of working for them, the situation changed greatly. They tried to maintain a stable of far too many acts."

"There were too many people there," an annoyed **Jackson Browne** told a *Crawdaddy* magazine journalist in 1974. "How many male singer-songwriters can you represent? I don't think David Geffen wants to be a manager anymore and I don't think he's qualified to be one now because he's a corporation president and things are different."

With Geffen now heading the new Elektra/Asylum company, the disenchanted Eagles

continued on Page 57

PATHWAY ALBUM | TIMOTHY B. SCHMIT

POCO
A Good Feelin' to Know
Epic Records, September 1972

Eagles' debut album sent three singles up the charts and established the band as a successful act right out of the gate. But **Poco**—which in many ways provided the blueprint for the Eagles' country-rock crossover approach, not to mention both of their bass players, Randy Meisner and years later Timothy B. Schmit— had no such luck.

Poco was considered "too rock for country and too country for rock" when the band released their first album, *Pickin' Up the Pieces*, in 1969. Three years later, despite having a high-energy stage show, three studio LPs, and a Top 30 live album on their resume, the band was still looking for that elusive big break. When they released *A Good Feelin' to Know* in September 1972, expectations were high among the five band members and their label, Epic, that this album would be the one to finally break through to substantial success.

Poco co-founder and leader **Richie Furay** had recently moved out of Los Angeles to mountainous Colorado, and his new surroundings inspired him to write the title song. The band's track was upbeat, positive, and rife with the characteristics radio professionals deemed appropriate for a sure-fire hit.

"A Good Feelin' to Know" was the centerpiece of a collection of well-crafted and well-produced songs that truly represented a group effort. **Paul Cotton** wrote three, and Schmit contributed two: the breathy ballad "I Can See Everything," sung in his trademark high-tenor, and the moody "Restrain," which would also later appear on the *Poco Live* album in 1976.

Furay contributed two other solo compositions including the lush ballad "Sweet Lovin'" written about the birth of his daughter "Timmie" Suzanne. The child had been named in homage to Schmit, her dad's friend and bandmate.

Epic released the title track as the album's first single. But its energy didn't generate any excitement on the radio or among record buyers. Inexplicably, it didn't even chart. Furay was devastated. Scanning the radio dial in hopes of hearing the song, he repeatedly heard "Take It Easy" instead.

As he explained in his 2006 memoir, "The song's lead singer was Glenn Frey, who not long before had sat on the floor of my living room watching Poco and wishing he could be in our shoes. Now the tables had turned. Frey and erstwhile Poco member Randy Meisner had the AM radio hit that continued to elude us."

"'[A] Good Feelin' to Know' was designed to be a hit," confirmed album producer **Jack Richardson**. "I have had any number of people over the years say, 'Gee, we can't understand why it didn't make it.'"

Unbuoyed by a hit single, *A Good Feelin' to Know* struggled to its peak at #69 on the *Billboard* album chart, lower than any of Poco's previous four albums.

The lack of success directly brought about a significant turning point for Poco. Furay, feeling lost and frustrated, reached out to **David Geffen** for advice. Geffen enticed him with a proposed supergroup concept that would be "as big as **Crosby, Stills & Nash**." Furay's departure for this new band would not only change the dynamics for Schmit and the rest of Poco's members, but also lure in "unofficial" Eagle **J.D. Souther**. [1503, 1504, 1508, 1509, 1511]

began considering life after Geffen. They wanted a manager who would represent their interests, and their interests alone.

The first person they contacted was Geffen's old William Morris Agency compatriot **John Hartmann**, who he had recruited into Asylum to help launch the Eagles with promises of an ownership stake that allegedly never materialized. That conversation with Hartmann—and Geffen's reaction to it—would forever change the relationship between Geffen and the band. [1, 6, 38, 39, 570, 589, 1190, 1288, 1482]

WINTER 1972-73

 RELEASES
▶ **Eagles**, "Peaceful Easy Feeling" (single)
▶ **Poco**, with Timothy B. Schmit, "And Settlin' Down" (single)
▶ **Various Artists**, with Bernie Leadon, *Music from Free Creek* (album)
▶ **James Gang**, with Joe Walsh, *The Best of the James Gang featuring Joe Walsh*

 COLLABORATIONS
▶ **Joe Walsh** played electric guitar on "Hummingbird" on **B.B. King**'s album *The Best of B.B. King*.

 NUGGETS
▶ Eagles are rehearsing at Long Joe's Fat Chance Recording Studios in Tarzana. —*Record World*
▶ **David Geffen** picks up management of **America**. —*Record World*
▶ Eagles booked to tour with **Jethro Tull**. —*Record World*
▶ Warner buys Asylum Records; Geffen gets seven-year deal. —*Cashbox*

 ON THE ROAD WITH ...
▶ **Poco**, with Timothy B. Schmit: Trapeze
▶ **Barnstorm**, with Joe Walsh: Mott the Hoople

Azoff Joins Overwhelmed Geffen-Roberts Management

When Illinois native **Irving Azoff** headed for Los Angeles in 1971, he was part of the migration of music industry hopefuls (including Boston-based Florida native Don Felder who arrived a year later) who collectively heeded the adage popularized by newspaper magnate **Horace Greeley** who in 1865 famously said, "Go West, young man."

Ambitious, brash, and hungry, Azoff brought with him **Dan Fogelberg**, his roomate at the University of Illinois, with

continued on Page 60

CROWE MEETS EAGLES BACKSTAGE IN SAN DIEGO

Long before **Cameron Crowe** became an internationally renowned author and filmmaker, he was a plucky teenager who just wanted to write about rock music. And in the summer of 1972, just weeks after the Eagles released "Take It Easy," Crowe got one of his first interviews by slipping backstage at the San Diego Civic Theatre to interview the band for the *San Diego Door*, the city's underground newspaper. It would be his first of many connections with members of the Eagles over the years.

Crowe was born in Palm Springs, California, the youngest of three children in a middle-class family. His father was a real estate agent and his mother taught sociology and English literature at a local college. The family eventually settled in San Diego, and Crowe sped through his early school years. He skipped kindergarten and two grades in elementary school and graduated from the University of San Diego High School at just 15 years old. Being so much younger than the rest of his classmates made fitting in difficult for him, and being afflicted with nephritis, a disease that inflames the kidneys, made him sickly in a way that didn't help him gather friends.

Many of those experiences would later inform Crowe's books and films. But at that moment in 1972, he was just a nowhere-near-famous high school music journalist who wanted to write a feature about a new country-rock band.

He was a big fan of "Take It Easy," and wanted to know more, Crowe wrote in a *Rolling Stone* article in 2015. Eagles were due in town soon, opening for the R&B outfit **Cold Blood** and the prog rock pioneers **Procol Harum** at the San Diego Civic Theatre. So Crowe and photographer friend **Gary Elam** bought tickets to the show and hatched a plot to simply slip backstage. Even with these two veteran bands on the bill, Crowe's interest was firmly set on an interview with the Eagles.

Crowe grabbed his portable tape recorder, Elam brought along a camera, and at the Civic the pair found Eagles' road manager, **Richard Fernandez**, and the concert's promoter, **Larry Vallon**, and asked for an interview with the band. Fernandez and Vallon said OK and gave the pair backstage passes for after the show. The Eagles opened that night with an a cappella version of **Steve Young**'s "Seven Bridges Road," Crowe recalled, then strapped on their instruments as Frey strummed that iconic opening to "Take It Easy."

"On stage, Eagles play a clean, uncluttered set with a euphoric touch of joy," Crowe wrote in his 1972 review. "The aura surrounding them is one of impending super-stardom, much like the presence of **Yes**, **Jethro Tull**, **Carole King**, and **Procul Harum** [sic] in their earlier days." Recalling that night again in 2016, Crowe added that the Eagles "were fierce and joyful, playing with the piss and vinegar of a young band hitting its early stride."

After Eagles' set, Crowe and Elam went backstage to a tiny dressing room, where the band was eager to talk. They patiently answered Crowe's questions, and their answers provided a snapshot-in-time view of where they had been and were heading, creatively and financially.

They spent hours discussing their separate musical journeys. Don Henley talked about his earlier band, **Shiloh**, and Bernie Leadon discussed his time with **Hearts & Flowers** and **Dillard & Clark**. Randy Meisner was less effusive, but Crowe's story gave his readers a little of his backstory, which focused on how he helped start **Pogo** (later **Poco**) with **Richie Furay** and **Jim Messina**.

"If you like us, you should check out **John David Souther**," Frey told Crowe, giving a shout-out to his old bandmate, Asylum labelmate, and Eagles collaborator.

Since Eagles were emerging as country-rock's first commercially successful band, Crowe wanted to know why they had no steel guitar. "Bernie's the steel guitar," Frey said. Henley agreed, adding that Leadon "has one of those things that bend the strings to make it sound like a steel guitar."

Talk of the absence of a steel guitar led to a wider discussion of why there were only four Eagles. "**Sneaky Pete** [**Kleinow**] from the [**Flying Burrito Brothers**] isn't working," Leadon said. "We could have gotten him. But the reason we didn't was because the two of us [Frey and Leadon], when we started this band, could barely hold it together [on guitars]. We wanted to get really strong by forcing ourselves to do it."

Frey agreed. "When you've got five guys in a band, someone can always be lazy in a song," he said. "There will always be four other guys working. We have to play harder, and it's a lot leaner. But there's a little more air...a lot more open spaces."

Would there be any solo albums? "Not me," Frey said. "I don't think so, though I must say that any of the four of us could have easily done a solo album," Leadon added.

Would they invite their famous "friends" into the studio? "We want to record ourselves," Leadon said.

What did they attribute to the success of their first album? "We have a very good manager, a very good record company, and a very good producer," Henley said.

Do you plan on becoming a singles band? "We will probably always do albums," Frey said. "I don't think we will ever cut a forty-five."

At the end of the interview, Crowe had the group huddle together for a photo that became his favorite piece of Eagles memorabilia. The fuzzy image showed the band in front of their amplifier with their arms draped around each other in camaraderie. They exchanged phone numbers and kept in touch.

Their relationship with each other grew over time. A year later, Crowe would be hired by *Rolling Stone*, and became one of the few journalists at the magazine the Eagles trusted. They invited Crowe to the studio when they were recording their second album, *Desperado*. Frey became something of a big brother to the young writer, occasionally offering him essential life advice on relationships and even how to hold his alcohol.

The two met up again in 1975 when Crowe wrote a feature that put the Eagles on the cover of *Rolling Stone*. They'd both grown up considerably by then, and the band was flying high on record charts and headlining major tours.

After his tenure with the magazine, Crowe parlayed his rock and roll beginnings into a successful career as a writer and filmmaker. He authored the screenplays for the iconic 1980s teen movies *Fast Times at Ridgemont High* and *Say Anything* (and directed the latter), and won an Oscar for the screenplay of *Almost Famous*, the semi-autobiographical 2000 film he also directed that vividly and very accurately captured the life of a rock band on the road in the early 1970s.

As a homage to his past mentor, Crowe based the charismatic lead character in *Almost Famous*, aspiring rock star Russell Hammond (played by **Billy Crudup**), largely on Glenn Frey. [479, 1596, 1616, 1618, 1619, 1685]

whom he was now sharing an apartment. Azoff had booked gigs and tours for Fogelberg and the band **REO Speedwagon** from Champaign, where UI was located. At 16, Azoff was promoting local bands in clubs throughout the Midwest. Among his more memorable bookings included his first gig for REO, whose members played for beer, pizza, and $10 a man.

"People were moving here on both the business and musician side from all over the country to taste the American dream," Azoff recalled when asked what brought him to the West Coast. "It became the melting pot for music."

Azoff, who read *Rolling Stone* and idolized the likes of promoter **Bill Graham** and music executive **David Geffen**, quickly took a liking to the burgeoning West Hollywood club scene centered around the Troubadour (with Dan Tana's restaurant a stone's throw away), the Whisky, and after September 1973, The Roxy.

In the Troubadour bar, Azoff would see luminaries like Geffen and **Bob Dylan**'s manager **Albert Grossman** and observe lots of yelling that all seemed normal. The aspiring industry mogul initially got a job as a booker for **Jerry Heller**'s Heller-Fischel Agency, which included shows at The Roxy, the new club launched by Geffen and his industry compatriots **Lou Adler**, **Elmer Valentine**, and **Peter Asher**.

Drawing upon the trial-by-fire approach he developed working the Midwest, Azoff went to Geffen in search of a job. He quickly landed a position at Geffen-Roberts, the artist management partnership between Asylum Records co-founders Geffen and **Elliot Roberts**.

By then, Geffen-Roberts' client roster included **Crosby, Stills & Nash**, **Neil Young**, **CSNY**, **J.D. Souther**, **Joni Mitchell**, **Poco**, and **America**. Along with Fogelberg, who released his solo debut *Home Free* in 1972, Azoff brought Joe Walsh, who had been down on his fortunes after leaving the **James Gang**.

While at Geffen-Roberts, Azoff began booking shows at The Roxy. He also knew the Eagles were at a critical juncture in their career and were having second thoughts about their producer, **Glyn Johns**. Azoff, who was readying Walsh's breakthrough solo album *The Smoker You Drink, The Player You Get*, played the band the masters produced by **Bill Szymczyk** and recommended they work with him. The band was looking for growth and Szymczyk would eventually provide that, but they would first return to London with Johns. With Geffen focused on his expanding Asylum roster, America and Poco also exited Geffen-Roberts, along with their managers **John Hartmann** and **Harlan Goodman**.

Also transformative was Roberts' decision in 1974 to part company with Geffen, and carry on as head of Lookout Management, taking Young, Mitchell, and Souther with him.

Eagles would soon align with Azoff when he formed Front Line Management. With his commitment to his artists at all costs, Azoff's moxie would soon be transformed into the character known as "Big Shorty," a nickname first referenced by **Cameron Crowe** in a 1978 *Rolling Stone* article. Azoff would help make the California dream come true, not only for himself, but also for his new band. [699, 2071, 2072, 2073, 2074]

The Odd Couple: Frey, Henley Become a Songwriting Team

It's easy to think of "Frey-Henley" as a familiar, collaborative entity. Today the two names seem to naturally go together, much like "Jagger-Richards" or "Lennon-McCartney." And, indeed, throughout the Eagles' catalog from 1973 forward, rarely will one name be attached to a song without the other. This partnership began in earnest while writing songs for *Desperado*.

"They were not a team yet [on the debut record]," according to Bernie Leadon. "Henley only wrote half a song on the first album, with me: 'Witchy Woman.'"

Glenn Frey had tallied three credits on *Eagles*, along with a fourth for "Get You in the Mood," the non-album B-side of "Take It Easy." Prior to the Eagles, like Henley, Frey's name was attached to a few songs from records by former bands. Still, when they co-founded Eagles, Frey considered himself far from established in the songwriting world.

"Don and I as individuals had not written a lot of songs, period, prior to the days of the Eagles," Frey explained in a segment for VH1 in 1994. "Our team was born a little bit out of desperation, a little bit out of fear, a little bit out of insecurity."

In the same program, Henley agreed: "Songwriting was new to me."

Whether the two were being modest or simply dismissive of earlier efforts they considered below their standards ("The stuff I wrote for **Shiloh** was mostly crap," Henley has said), they welcomed the opportunity to work with and learn from their more accomplished friends.

"**J.D.** [**Souther**] and **Jackson** [**Browne**] co-wrote a lot of the Eagles songs with us," Henley said. "They had already been signed, of course, by a label and were considered a viable entity by record company big shots. So, we looked up to them."

The respect for the nascent songwriting duo from their seasoned peers was mutual.

According to Browne, "[Glenn had] boundless energy and Don was really very analytical and methodical and had the patience and desire to hammer these songs into exactly what he wanted. They made a really good combination."

Browne said the serious and reserved Henley and the rambunctious and enthusiastic Frey were "like the Odd Couple" and it worked for them.

Randy Meisner agreed: "Glenn was more of a street-tough guy. He and Henley were a real good combination in the beginning because both guys were real intelligent and knew what they wanted, and yet were so completely different. They somehow filled in each other's personalities."

From Frey's point of view, the decision to join forces may have been influenced by a pragmatic need to step up their game to a

continued on Page 66

DESPERADO EVOLVES INTO 'OLD WEST' CONCEPT LP

The Eagles thoroughly embraced the "western" side of country-rock with their second album, *Desperado*.

Inspiration for the album's concept came, at least partly, from an obscure coffee table book on Old West outlaws titled *The Album of Gunfighters*, authored and published by **J. Marvin Hunter** and **Noah H. Rose** in 1951. The book was a gift to the band from their friend **Ned Doheny**, a singer-songwriter also on **David Geffen**'s roster.

The large-format book was replete with photographs—including many images of dead outlaws—and extended captions describing the bandits, sheriffs, marshals, and badmen of the American West in vivid detail. Hunter and Rose threw in some well-known gangsters from the 1920s and 1930s as well.

In the winter of 1972-73, Henley and Frey were developing songs for the follow-up to *Eagles* when the notion of a concept album began to emerge.

Concept albums were popular in the late 1960s and early 1970s. **The Beatles**' *Sgt. Pepper's Lonely Hearts Club Band* was probably the best-known of the bunch, and **The Who**'s *Tommy* and **Marvin Gaye**'s *What's Going On* were doing well, critically and commercially.

But no one had ever done a successful country-rock concept album. Eagles decided to gamble and fill that void.

"We had a gunfighter's photo album in the house and one night we started writing a song about the Doolin-Dalton gang," Glenn Frey told the *Los Angeles Times* in 1974. "We were going to do an all-encompassing album about rebels or outlaws that didn't have a time reference. The Daltons would have sufficed for that entire period. We also started writing a song about **James Dean** the same night, the one that ends up on the new album [*On the Border*]. We also might have had songs about [**John**] **Dillinger** or [**Marlon**] **Brando**."

The night they had started working on what would become the opening *Desperado* track, "Doolin-Dalton," the Eagles and friends **Jackson Browne** and **J.D. Souther** had been in the audience at the Troubadour seeing folk legend **Tim Hardin** perform. After the show, they met at Souther's house in Laurel Canyon, where Frey said they came up with the idea of doing an album about "all the angst-meisters."

"It was going to be all of the anti-heroes," Frey told **Cameron Crowe** in 2003. "James Dean was going to be one song, and the Doolin-Dalton gang was going to be another."

Souther recalled that night of inspiration to *Billboard* in 2016, mentioning Doheny's gift. "The first thing [Browne, Frey, and I] ever tried writing together was the stuff that was on [the] *Desperado* album," he said. "[The book] had a chapter in it about the Doolin-Dalton gang. We started talking about it, ranting and raving through the night about the role of the outlaw and using that as a metaphor."

The saga begins to unfold on Page 34 of *The Album of Gunfighters* in a chapter entitled "The Doolin-Dalton Outlaw Gang," which opens with a photo of the bullet-riddled corpse of Bill Doolin, and the tale of how his gang met up with the gang led by Bill Dalton.

The next five pages recount the story of exploits in Kansas and Oklahoma, by gang members including Arkansas Tom, Tulsa Jack Blake, Crescent Sam, Bill Raidler, and George Newcombe (alias "Bitter Creek," the title of an unreleased song from *Desperado*, though not about the bandit).

"We sort of saw ourselves living outside the law," Frey said, suggesting parallels between themselves and these outlaws.

The outlaw images emanating from the book's

J. Marvin Hunter and **Noah H. Rose** wrote the coffee table book *The Album of Gunfighters* in 1951. Eagles contemporary **Ned Doheny** gave the book to the band and it served as an inspiration for many of the songs that were recorded for *Desperado*. The book was replete with photos of dead outlaws lying in state, including members of the notorious Doolin-Dalton Gang, whose crimes across Kansas and Oklahoma in the 1890s were legendary.

photos and the mental images created by the text were inspiring. **David Blue**'s "Outlaw Man" and Randy Meisner's "Certain Kind of Fool" all filled the western theme. Bernie Leadon's "Twenty-One" and "Bitter Creek" fit the mold as well, and the latter was suggested by Frey, Leadon said. Henley and Frey teamed up for "Tequila Sunrise," and Browne and Souther joined them in writing "Doolin-Dalton."

"I'm sure some of this Indian and Mexican influence was with us when we were doing *Desperado*," Frey told *Melody Maker* in 1975. "We had a great time doing the little links between songs, the banjo and traditional thing."

The comparison between gunslingers and guitar-slingers aside, the band was making a larger statement with *Desperado*. The sophomore album was, according to Henley, designed to be "our big artistic commentary on the evils of fame and success, with a cowboy metaphor." The band—or at least Henley and Frey—were already cynical about the industry in which they were relative newcomers.

"I think we knew early on that fame was a fleeting thing," Henley said in retrospect. "That you get up just to get torn down eventually, and that [music] is a fickle business. That's what [*Desperado*] was all about: that we would all be hung sooner or later. Or hang ourselves."

Several years after *Desperado*, the Eagles would deliver their second concept album. *Hotel California* was also set in the American West but would explore a far more contemporary theme. [6, 81, 209, 263, 1646, 1647, 1648]

RELEASE
Mid-August
1972

PEACEFUL EASY FEELING
By: Jack Tempchin
Side B: Tryin' (Meisner)

The third song released from the Eagles' debut album didn't ascend quite as high up the charts as the album's first two singles, but **Jack Tempchin**'s easy-going, sleeping-in-the-desert-with-a-million-stars-all-around ballad offered up a popular, calming tune that radio listeners embraced in winter 1972-73. And it gave the band its third consecutive Top 20 single.

AIRPLAY

The Eagles' first two singles were initally picked up by radio stations in regions that seemed to belie their Southern California origins. "Take It Easy" got airplay first in the Northeast and "Witchy Woman" in the South. "Peaceful Easy Feeling" was picked up in the Midwest first. But the all-over-the-map trend likely had more to do with Asylum Records' promotions directors **Paul Ahern** and **Jerry Sharell**'s travel schedules than any particular region favoring the band.

35 PLAYLIST ADDS Winter 1972-73

Region	Dec	Jan	Feb	Mar	Regional Airplay
Northeast	2	3	2	0	20 %
Southeast	0	3	5	1	25.7 %
Midwest	2	5	7	0	40 %
Southwest	1	0	1	0	5.7 %
West	0	0	2	1	8.6 %

FIRST-WAVE STATIONS Stations that added the song in the first 30 days

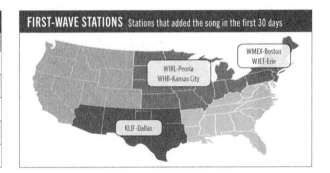

WMEX-Boston
WJET-Erie
WIRL-Peoria
WHB-Kansas City
KLIF-Dallas

CHARTS

Billboard

#22
March 10, 1973

Cashbox

#20
March 10, 1973

Record World

#18
March 10, 1973

HIGHEST CHARTING WEEK: RECORD WORLD - March 10, 1973

SINGLE	ARTIST	# PREV WK
1. Killing Me Softly With His Song	Roberta Flack	2
2. Could It Be I'm Falling in Love	Spinners	1
3. Last Song	Edward Bear	7
4. Love Train	O'Jays	5
5. Dueling Banjos	*Deliverance* soundtrack	3
6. Also Sprach Zarathustra	Eumir Deodato	13
7. Daddy's Home	Jermaine Jackson	9
8. Rocky Mountain High	John Denver	10
18. PEACEFUL EASY FEELING	**EAGLES**	12

Sources: Billboard, Cashbox, Record World

TEMPCHIN'S LOST DATE INSPIRES TOP 20 SINGLE

In the early, grueling days when Glenn Frey and **J.D. Souther** were performing as the duo **Longbranch/Pennywhistle**, they carried their own instruments from their cars to coffeehouses, auditoriums, and local halls.

In those coffeehouse days, there was a circle of singer-songwriters who played those venues that the duo befriended. Among them was **Jack Tempchin**, an Ohio-born, San Diego-raised singer-songwriter and self-professed hippie, who they had met during a shared a gig at a local club in San Diego. Frey and Tempchin would become good friends and collaborate on many songs over the years, including Frey's "You Belong to the City," "Smuggler's Blues," and "The One You Love." Tempchin, along with **Robb Strandlund**, also penned "Already Gone," one of the Eagles' staple rockers.

But one spring day in 1971, eight days removed from **David Geffen** signing the as-yet-unnamed Eagles to their first contract, Tempchin was strumming his guitar at **Jackson Browne**'s house in L.A.

"Glenn came in, and he heard me playing my new song, and he recorded it on a cassette tape," Tempchin recalled. "He said, 'Jack, I've just put a new band together, and we're going to play for all the record companies. Do you mind if we work up the song?'" Tempchin gave Frey the go-ahead to work on the arrangement.

Tempchin said he wrote "Peaceful Easy Feeling" for a waitress he met while playing a coffeehouse gig in a mini-mall in El Centro, California, east of San Diego.

"The waitress said I could go home with her later," he told *Rolling Stone* in 1978. "Then she just disappeared," he said laughing. He said he had already told his friends to leave—he was going home with her—but he ended up sleeping on the linoleum floor of the coffeehouse. That's where the idea for a song hit him.

"I started writing the lyrics on the back of a poster [advertising my show]," Tempchin said. "The poster is in the Rock and Roll Hall of Fame now. I wrote some really stupid lyrics and then I kept writing and all of a sudden I noticed I had written the phrase 'peaceful easy feeling.'"

Tempchin introduced more women he had met into the song to flesh it out, but said the real magic happened when Frey took the song and rearranged it in just one day.

"Glenn...took the song and put just the right musical arrangement, just the right attitude," he said. "He recorded it in an amazing way so you feel like you are out in the desert. So, he came back the next day and played me a cassette of the [the band] playing 'Peaceful Easy Feeling.' Then a week later, Glenn got three giant record execs to come into this tiny rehearsal studio [to hear the Eagles' songs], and they got signed and that was it." [336, 582, 1295, 1390, 1391]

level more consistent with their label's other proven songwriters.

"We're hanging in the same world with **Neil Young**, **Joni Mitchell**, Jackson Browne," he stated. "There must have been some unspoken look that Don and I gave each other that said we'd better write some good songs or they're not going to keep us around."

Henley found a common ally in Frey, at the time remarking, "The only two people to think alike in this group are Glenn and me and we've always wanted every song to be the best it can be. We didn't want any filler."

Writing "Desperado" for their second album bonded the newly formed songwriting team. "Tequila Sunrise," "Out of Control," and "Doolin-Dalton," the latter co-credited also to Browne and Souther, were penned around the same time. The Frey-Henley team—absent entirely from the debut album—had clearly established a blueprint they would build upon in their future collaborations.

Henley believed he and Frey were not on the same level as Meisner and Leadon as instrumentalists, who Henley commented were "incredible on their instruments." However, Henley thought he and Frey could best contribute to the band as the primary songwriters, or certainly the most prolific ones. "We've just taken it upon ourselves that [writing] is our department," he said.

Frey and Henley joining forces to take things to a new level as songwriters also pushed them into greater leadership roles. In hindsight, it's hard to argue with success. Still, for a band conceived as a democratic

unit with four equal participants, this twist would inevitably contribute to tensions and power struggles that would eventually fracture the founding four's lineup. [1293, 1494, 1495, 1523]

Leadon, Ronstadt Lend Talents To *Music from Free Creek*

Two years after the Summer of Love ended, rock artists were still spreading their musical affections around, and spontaneous jam session albums were popular. But jams featuring the caliber of artists that *Music from Free Creek* offered were rare.

Although the album's title and cover art imply a hippie-themed jam session at some far-off meadow near a sparkling river in Northern California, it was actually a series of sessions recorded at the brand new Record Plant in New York between June and August 1969.

Organized by **Todd Rundgren** sideman **Moogy Klingman**, the super sessions included an all-star lineup of 1960s and 1970s rock stars like Rundgren, **Jeff Beck**, **Keith Emerson** (Emerson, Lake & Palmer), **Mitch Mitchell** (Jimi Hendrix Experience), **Chris Wood** (Traffic), and an undercover **Eric Clapton**, who participated as "King Cool" for contractual reasons.

The sessions also included a pre-Eagles Bernie Leadon along with a blossoming **Linda Rondstadt** in a nod to the burgeoning West Coast country-rock scene.

When Charisma Records released *Music from Free Creek* as a double album four years later in 1973, presumably delayed because of all the legal red tape, the album was divided into different groupings. There were isolated sessions led by Clapton, Beck, Emerson, **Harvey Mandel**, and Klingman, and another where the spotlight was on Ronstadt, accompanied by Leadon and members of **Three Dog Night**.

The Ronstadt date was, by Klingman's own admission, a bit misplaced among the other acts. The sessions had been winding down as Ronstadt and her backup band, **The Corvettes**, led by Leadon, were in New York playing shows at the Bitter End. *Free Creek* co-producer **Earle Doud** invited her and the band to the Record Plant to take part in the sessions.

Ronstadt didn't want to get involved in a long musical jam where she would be an accessory, so she agreed to sing two songs in a country music session. They included "Living Like a Fool" and "He Darked the Sun," a gender-altered version of the song co-written by Leadon and **Gene Clark** ("She Darked the Sun") for the **Dillard & Clark** album *The Fantastic Expedition of Dillard & Clark*.

The production values on this Leadon-Ronstadt remake were much improved from the twangy bluegrass version released by Dillard & Clark a year earlier. Ronstadt's silky voice polished all the original's rough edges. Indeed, it was so good, she re-recorded it for her upcoming *Silk Purse* album, released in 1970.

By the time *Free Creek* was released, Leadon and Ronstadt already had a strong rapport. He had backed the singer on her studio version of "Different Drum." And they had common friends from the Troubadour and their still-widening country-rock circles that included Dillard, Clark, and **Gram Parsons**. As Leadon and The Corvettes were backing her on her East Coast tour in 1969, the *Free Creek* sessions were likely a welcome change of pace.

Leadon would continue working with Ronstadt on and off for many years, and she, of course, was instrumental in connecting him with the Eagles. [1588, 1589]

SPRING 1973

 RELEASES
- ▶ **Poco**, with Timothy B. Schmit, "Go and Say Goodbye" (single)
- ▶ **Eagles**, *Desperado* (album)
- ▶ **Eagles**, "Tequila Sunrise" (single)

 NUGGETS
- ▶ **Glyn Johns** is about to cross over the Atlantic to remaster Eagles' new album, *Desperado*. —*Record World*
- ▶ Eagles' *Desperado* is finding airplay at colleges like Carnegie-Mellon (WRCT, Pittsburgh) and Univ. of Illinois (WPGU-Champaign, Ill.) which have picked it up. —*Record World*
- ▶ **J.D. Souther** is no longer afraid to talk to his audience and has improved a lot based on his performance at the Felt Forum in New York, where he opened for new Asylum artist **America**. Souther's set included "New Gospel Song," "Duelin' Daltons" [sic] and a McDonald's comedy quickie that would have been best left to **Biff Rose**. —*Cashbox*

NUGGETS (cont.)
- ▶ Eagles tour is taking them to New York in support of their new album, *Desperado*. —*Record World*

 COLLABORATIONS
- ▶ Joe Walsh (arranging, electric guitar, 12-string guitar, synthesizer, backing vocals) contributed to **Michael Stanley**'s album *Michael Stanley*.
- ▶ Joe Walsh played slide guitar on **Manassas**' (Stephen Stills) album *Down the Road*.
- ▶ Glenn Frey sang backing vocals on **David Blue**'s album *Nice Baby and the Angel*.

 ON SCREEN
- ▶ Eagles appeared on the ABC-TV show *In Concert*. This marked their first of five total appearances on the program over the years. They appeared with **Linda Ronstadt** and **Jackson Browne**.

 AWARDS
- ▶ Eagles, **15th Annual Grammy Awards:** Best New Artist, nominated. Lost to **America**. Also nominated in the same category: **Harry Chapin**, **John Prine**, and **Loggins & Messina**.

 ON THE ROAD WITH ...
- ▶ **Eagles**: Billy Preston, Chi Coltrane, Gram Parsons & Emmylou Harris, J. Geils Band, J.J. Cale, Lester Flatt & The Nashville Grass, Little Feat, Livingston Taylor, Nils Lofgren, Ringo Starr, Rory Gallagher, Roxy Music, Ry Cooder, Spooky Tooth, Stevie Wonder, Faces
- ▶ **Poco**, with Timothy B. Schmit: Gentle Giant, Humble Pie, J.D. Souther, Nitty Gritty Dirt Band, Peter Frampton, Strawbs, the Edgar Winter Group, Yes
- ▶ **Barnstorm**, with Joe Walsh: Blue Öyster Cult, Vinegar Joe, Wishbone Ash

Tom Waits Releases 'Ol' '55,' Knocks Eagles' Cover Version

More than a few music fans have been introduced to **Tom Waits** because the Eagles recorded a cover of "Ol' '55," a song from his March 1973 album *Closing Time*, for *On the Border*. The band's rendition was a stunner, with its gorgeous melody, rich harmonies, and Frey and Henley trading lead vocals.

"[Waits] was being signed to Asylum Records at the time and **David Geffen** played a couple of tracks from *Closing Time* for Don [Henley] and I when they were still, I guess, in demo form," Frey explained. "That's how we heard the song."

As an artist, Waits is, perhaps not unlike **Bob Dylan**, often credited with being a talented songwriter, but some find his less conventional, gravelly voice an acquired taste. Not surprisingly, the *Closing Time* track lacks the pop sensibilities of the Eagles' vocal delivery, and the vocal harmonies are not quite as lushly layered, but it embodies a lot of originality, character, and soul that some prefer.

Waits, a 2011 Rock and Roll Hall of Fame inductee, described the piece as "kind of an old song about my car, a 'car' song" in a 1973 interview with *Folkscene*. On the surface, it certainly is a song about a car, but the author may have been downplaying the real magic in the composition. It's the mood Waits conveys about the protagonist's journey in that vehicle that is more significant. It's six in the morning, the sun is rising, and other autos on the road are hastily flying by him, but nothing takes him from the state of bliss he's in after leaving a presumably passionate night with his love interest.

Singer **Bob LaBeau**, who, like Waits, had spent extensive time at the San Diego Heritage Coffeehouse folk music club, believed that "Ol' '55" was inspired by Waits' relationship with an attractive waitress named **Pam Bowles**. The pair apparently had an intense, but short-lived romance that made a big impression on the songwriter.

Around then, LaBeau recalled, Waits "started writing a bunch of really pretty, sensitive songs. I think 'I Hope That I Don't Fall in Love with You' [also from the *Closing Time* album] might have been written about her. And I think he wrote 'Ol' '55' at the same time."

Coupling the wistful romantic lyric with the backdrop of a beloved 1955 vehicle creates a sense of nostalgia, but in a 1976 interview, Waits dismissed the notion, claiming that the inspiration was largely contemporary. "I drive a '55 Cadillac," he said. "That's the car I've always driven. It has nothing to do with nostalgia."

Known to be opinionated and outspoken, Waits wasn't thrilled with the Eagles' interpretation of his song. Much like country rock pioneer **Gram Parsons**, who once referred to the Eagles' stylings as being akin to "a plastic dry fuck," Waits may have considered the *On the Border* version too clean and polished.

"I frankly was not that particularly crazy about their rendition of it," Waits told WAMU Radio in Washington D.C.

"The song is about five years old—it's one of the first songs I wrote so I felt like it was kind of flattering that somebody wanted to do your song but at the same time I thought their version was a little antiseptic."

Regardless of how he felt about the song's artistic merits, undeniably, the Eagles' rendition was a big boost financially.

"It put Tom on an entirely different level economically," Waits' friend and Troubadour bartender **Louie Lista** opined. "That kind of prosperity makes certain things possible. [Eagles' recording of "Ol' '55"] gave Tom a certain prosperity and power that I think he used wisely."

Members of the group were understandably defensive when they got wind that Waits was trash-talking their version of the song. **Jack Tempchin**, who knew a thing or two about having material covered by the band, recalled, "They read that and went, 'Well, okay, we ain't gonna record any more of his songs!'" [99, 1478, 1501, 1529, 1530, 1532]

Johns Tightens Studio Rules For *Desperado* Sessions

Eagles' relationship with **Glyn Johns** produced some great works, but from the start, the band and the producer often didn't see eye to eye, especially when it came to rock and roll. And it would get personal.

"Glyn thought we were a nice, country-rock, semi-acoustic band, and every time we wanted to rock and roll, he could name a thousand British bands that could do it better," Don Henley explained.

Johns classified Glenn Frey as an "aver-

continued on Page 71

JIM ED NORMAN

Jim Ed Norman has earned a reputation as one of Nashville's most respected record producers and label executives, with a résumé including a stint as president at Warner Bros. Records Nashville. But Norman's entry into the music business all started with Don Henley and the Eagles.

Born in Fort Meyers, Florida, Norman headed west to attend college at North Texas State University, where he met Henley.

"I was walking down the sidewalk one day, and a fellow was sitting in his apartment playing his guitar with the door open," Norman recalled. "I just walked in and said, 'Hi, I'm Jim Ed Norman.' He said, 'Hi, I'm Don Henley,' and we got together and started playing music."

Norman played piano and guitar, and before long, he and Henley were working together in **Felicity**, which would eventually become

Shiloh. After moving to Los Angeles, the band recorded their first and only LP in 1970, released by Amos Records. Norman would earn writing credits on two tracks: the earthy "Swamp River Country" and the instrumental "Du Raison."

When Shiloh fizzled, Henley took up Glenn Frey's offer to tour with **Linda Ronstadt**, which led to the Eagles. The new band's success also provided opportunities for Henley's former bandmate, who got the call to arrange and conduct the strings on the *Desperado* album.

Standing in the studio with album producer **Glyn Johns** and the London Philharmonic Orchestra was a nerve-wracking debut as a conductor: "My knees were shaking," Norman recounted. "I don't mind saying that...I mean, it was my first time!"

From there, Norman gained further experience as an arranger for other notable acts including Ronstadt and **America**. He would also work with the Eagles again as both arranger and performer, playing piano on songs like "Take It to the Limit" and "Lyin' Eyes."

Later in the decade, he started producing and achieved his first major success in this capacity when he produced two songs for **Jennifer Warnes**, including her 1977 hit "Right Time of the Night."

From there, Norman's sessionography as producer grew rapidly as he continued to work with a steady stream of artists. His varied list of credits includes names like country-pop crossover singer **Anne Murray**, Bay Area country-rockers **New Riders of the Purple Sage**, and Glenn Frey as a solo artist, as well as a significant number of country artists including **Charlie Rich**, **Hank Williams Jr.**, and **Michael Martin Murphey**, and **Mickey Gilley**, whose mega-honky tonk near Houston was later the setting for the movie *Urban Cowboy*.

Norman was named vice president of A&R for Warner Bros. Records Nashville in 1983, and the division's president the following year. The multi-talented musician-executive remained active in many different capacities until he retired in 2004 and headed to Hawaii.

Old habits die hard, and his retirement was short-lived. In Honolulu, Norman got involved in music business education and supported talent on the local music scene. He returned to work in Nashville in 2010 as an independent producer and an executive for Curb Records.

In 2016, Norman was invited onstage at the Grand Ole Opry, where he was honored with the Bob Kingsley Living Legend Award, presented yearly to an individual who has contributed significantly to the history of country music. [19, 29, 29, 1546, 1547]

age" rock guitar player. "Glenn Frey and I never got on. He thought they were a rock and roll band and they weren't. They were a harmony band. The sound they made vocally was extraordinary. They were a country-rock band. But Frey, because he came from fucking Detroit, thought they were a rock and roll band. But they wouldn't know rock and roll if they fell over it."

Still, the success of *Eagles* spoke louder, so it was back to London to record the follow-up, *Desperado*, with Johns once again behind the sound board.

"He was the key to our success in a lot of ways," Frey conceded a few years later.

"He'd been working with all these classic English rock and roll bands...**The Who**, the [**Rolling**] **Stones**...he didn't want to hear us squashing out **Chuck Berry** licks. I didn't mind him pointing us in a certain direction."

That said, disparate points of view between producer and artist didn't become less of an issue the second time around. In addition to the fundamental difference of opinion on the Eagles' desire for "a tougher sound," as Frey called it, Johns pushed hard for a more democratic approach at a time when Henley and Frey were taking it upon themselves to become the band's chief songwriters and de facto leaders.

Bernie Leadon, speaking to rock historian **John Beaudin**, said Johns "was very adamant that Meisner and myself should be pushed forward as well and it not just turn into 'the Glenn and Don Show' immediately, which is I think what they wanted. They were pretty pushy, honestly. But Glyn Johns kind of created the balance that exists on the first two albums."

In his 2014 memoir, Johns confirmed Leadon's take on the situation. He said while recording *Desperado*, "I openly encouraged Bernie's and Randy's involvement in the process, as I could see signs of small cracks appearing while Don and Glenn forged ahead in their desire to control the destiny of the band, gently treading on the other two as they went."

From the start, Leadon had a strong supporter in Johns, who respected the string player's talents and country-rock pedigree. "Apart from Bernie Leadon, who was quite experienced, the others were naive and looked to me for arrangements and sound," Johns observed.

Another cause of friction may have been differing opinions on Johns' "no drugs" policy in the studio, with Frey being the primary objector.

"The others I got on great with, [but] Glenn wanted to get high in the studio and I wouldn't let him," Johns said. "I spent years, very long days, with people stoned out of their tree and the minute I had control over them I decided I wouldn't put up with it because I'd wasted so much of my life waiting for people to get their shit together."

Refreshingly, most of the stories about the Eagles' time working with Johns don't degenerate into conflicting "he said/she said" tales. Often, both parties agreed as to what happened.

"It really irritated him that Randy and I would sneak off and smoke weed," Frey said. "He'd tell me, 'You smoke grass and then you don't say what's on your mind when it comes to mind. Now it's a week later and you're talking about something that you should have ironed out seven days ago. And that's juvenile…'"

Frey was able to see the situation somewhat diplomatically, adding, "What can you say? It's true. He pointed out a lot of bad habits in everybody."

Personal tensions aside, when it came time to record their third album, *On the Border*, the band again signed up with their incumbent producer. That undertaking would commence overseas with Johns. However, it would not be seen through to completion. [66, 88, 1534, 1535]

Grammys: America Tops Eagles, Prine, Chapin for Best New Artist

Eagles had reason for high optimism as winter gave way to spring in 1973. The band had just capped a successful first year and scored three Top 20 hits with "Take It Easy," "Witchy Woman," and "Peaceful Easy Feeling." They were putting the finishing touches on their second album, *Desperado*, shooting for release in March. Against that backdrop the red carpet rolled out on March 3 for the 15th Annual Grammy Awards, which that year moved away from its usual environs of New York or Los Angeles and instead took the stage at the Tennessee Theatre in Nashville.

The Eagles were nominated for Best New Artist. Their competitors were a strong collection of singer-songwriters who would go on to enjoy successful careers: **Loggins & Messina**, **John Prine**, **Harry Chapin**, and the group that was, at least outwardly, most similar to the Eagles, **America**, which had also been nominated for Best Pop Performance by a Duo or Group. The Best New Artist Grammy ultimately went to America, which had racked up three Top 10 hits in 1972 with "A Horse with No Name," "I Need You," and "Ventura Highway."

The Grammy Awards have, through the years, been variously viewed as outdated, uninformed, and just fickle when it comes to selecting its honorees, an opinion that was not lost on the show's critics that year.

"Ever since the Grammy balloting was initiated in 1959 as a sort of recording equivalent of the motion picture Oscar, there has been a strong emphasis on albums and singles that reflect conservative, 'easy listening' tastes," wrote *Los Angeles Times* pop music critic **Robert Hilburn** the day of the ceremony. "**Bob Dylan**, for instance, doesn't have any Grammys; **Henry Mancini** has twenty."

This criticism has played out for many years on, and several head-scratchers have resulted, including Best Hard Rock/Metal Performance going to a rightfully surprised **Jethro Tull** in 1989 and a Best Hard Rock

Performance award for **Pearl Jam** in 1996 that had lead singer **Eddie Vedder** proclaim in his acceptance speech, "I don't know what this means."

It's tough to know what was on the minds of the Recording Academy when they made their selections in 1973. As usual, art and commerce seemed in conflict. Both America and the Eagles were perceived similarly at that time, but America had three charting original singles.

By contrast, Glenn Frey co-wrote "Take It Easy" with **Jackson Browne**, and **Jack Tempchin** wrote "Peaceful Easy Feeling"; only "Witchy Woman," a collaboration between Don Henley and Bernie Leadon, was solely written by the Eagles. Further, America's self-titled debut LP had reached #1 on the *Billboard* album chart, while *Eagles* had peaked at #22. On paper, it seemed like America may have been a reasonable choice.

If those high-charting records were on the minds of Academy voters, they were also on the mind of **David Geffen**, who was quietly working hard to bring America to Geffen-Roberts and Asylum Records.

The Eagles were not yet aware of Geffen's plans for America and members **Gerry Beckley**, **Dewey Bunnell**, and **Dan Peek**. Years later Glenn Frey admitted a hint of jealousy because of the attention Asylum lavished on the group. Geffen signed America without the Eagles' knowledge—they found out about it from the British music industry newspaper *Melody Maker*.

"That grated," Frey told **Fred Goodman**

in his book, *The Mansion on the Hill*, "because we felt they didn't have our substance, but were having monster hits and riding in limos. We started to think about these things."

Frey's anger wasn't directed at America as much as it was toward Geffen, along with his partner **Elliot Roberts**, and their promotion and marketing staff at Asylum Records.

It also spilled over into life when when they weren't touring. **Richard Fernandez**, then the band's road manager, would be sent on the road to support America by Geffen-Roberts. "That would bug [the Eagles]," Fernandez said. "They'd be like, 'What are you doing that for?'"

And then the Grammy loss to America was seen as a slap. "Mmmm, that wasn't fun," Fernandez said, adding that the band, and especially Frey, was perturbed. "[The Eagles] were a better band in all areas, and that was behind it," he said. "He didn't understand the recognition they were getting. And I kind of agree with him. You hate to say it. I mean, I love Gerry [Beckley] and Dewey [Bunnell]. They're nice people. I worked with them. I took them on the road, and they have written some great tunes. But it's different. Among artists, I think that everybody felt that the Eagles were a step above at every level."

The band members were disappointed on Grammy night, but ultimately took the loss in stride, Fernandez said. Disappointment would turn into determination as Eagles headed to the Netherlands to play in the Pop Gala '73 festival on March 10. The *Desperado* tour was now in full swing in Europe. [1685, 1816, 1817, 1818, 1819]

Eagles Adopt Folk Standard 'Silver Dagger' as Set Opener

The crowd settled in at a BBC soundstage in London, and there was an eerie quiet as Glenn Frey, flanked by Bernie Leadon and Randy Meisner, crowded in around the microphone, leaned in and began harmonizing:

"My daddy waaaaaas a handsome devil
He had a chain five miles long
From every link a heart did dangle
For every maid he'd loved and wronged."

Frey's voice resonated, but Leadon, Meisner, and Don Henley, from behind his drum kit, made the harmonies energetic. The subject matter wasn't uplifting, but the a cappella treatment was near-perfect.

The song was a folk standard adapted from a **Joan Baez** arrangement from 1959. They only sang one verse from the traditional folk song, then broke into "Take It Easy." The Eagles first played "Silver Dagger" at the College of the Holy Cross in Worchester, Massachusetts in June 1973, according to Setlist.fm, and for the rest of 1973 and into 1974 the band usually opened with "Silver Dagger," then segued into "Take It Easy."

Written from a female perspective, the folk song tells the story of a woman who has forsaken a potential suitor after heed-

Randy Meisner, Glenn Frey, and Bernie Leadon crowd around the microphone to harmonize on "Silver Dagger" on a BBC soundstage in May 1973.

ing the warnings of her mother to avoid the advances of men.

One variation, "Katy Dear," written from the male perspective, references the silver dagger the spurned suitor turns on himself.

Although Baez's version makes an early reference to the knife, there is no Shakespearean tragedy in her version. Rather, in the fourth verse—the one the Eagles chose not to sing—she paints a contemplative resignation to live a celibate life:

"Go court another tender maiden
And hope that she will be your wife
For I've been warned and I've decided
To sleep alone all of my life."

"Silver Dagger" was melodically similar to many songs in American folk music, and specifically to many that originated in Britain in the late 1880s and evolved in the southern Appalachians. Distant variants can be heard in "Man of Constant Sorrow," "Drowsy Sleeper," and, most notably, "Come All Ye Fair and Tender Ladies," sometimes misidentified as "Silver Dagger" by some Eagles setlist curators.

Variations on the song have been recorded over the years, including **Wilmer Watts and the Lonely Eagles**, who recorded "Sleepy Desert" in 1929. Baez brought her version to popularity in the early 1960s.

Eagles had retired "Silver Dagger" from their setlists by late 1974. But in the summer of 1975 the bandmembers chose another song with an a cappella intro. **Steve Young**'s "Seven Bridges Road" gave the Eagles a new showcase for their soaring vocal harmonies that became even more popular in concert. [2078, 2079]

PARAMOUNT UPRISING

BAND RIDES HIGH FOR *DESPERADO* SHOOT-'EM-UP

When the Eagles shot their first album cover in early 1972, they traveled into the California desert with art director **Gary Burden** and photographer **Henry Diltz**, and the result was a collection of photos that captured the essence of the boots-and-denim, long-haired, L.A. country-rock fraternity.

For the second album's cover shoot later in December, they again called upon Burden and Diltz, but they upped the ante significantly this time.

On a theatrical movie set with a ghost town vibe—the renowned Paramount Ranch in Agoura Hills, California, where countless westerns had been filmed—the group decked themselves out in period pieces to match the 19th-century cowboy motif that was to serve as the theme for the new album, titled *Desperado*.

Randy Meisner has fond memories of the shoot: "We had a great time. It was…at an old movie ranch. Everyone was trying to shoot everyone else and play cowboy, like in the old movies."

"This was 1972, and it could easily have been 1872. It just looks so real," Diltz said, referring to the crusty, dusty "movie outfits" they rented for the day. "You can just see those guys would have been outlaws if they'd been born in another century. As soon as they put the clothes on, they were there."

It's fitting that the threads were authentic Hollywood western film costumes because Diltz did shoot movie film in addition to stills. Burden had set a loose script for the photoshoot. It wasn't highly structured, but it had some goals they wanted to achieve.

"We wanted to make an image that would fit this

conceptual music they had put together that was that story of the parallel of the guitar player of the '70s and the gunslinger of the 1870s," Burden explained in the documentary *Under the Covers*. The premise of the shoot would be, "these four guys come to town, and they've decided to stop working and to take the easy way and become outlaws. So, they go in and rob the bank, and they come out...and in the process, they get killed."

"They played cowboys all day, shooting each other [with blanks], falling down," Diltz remembered. "[Burden and I] had a rough plan: 'Well, let's get the Eagles to back out of a bank with a money bag like they robbed the bank. And we'd film that whole tableau or photograph it. Actually, I had a Nikon motor drive and a Bauer Super 8mm movie camera, in the other hand that I wasn't even looking in; I was just holding it there. So, I got movies and stills at the same time." Some of this footage would be aired on TV in 1974 during the Eagles' appearance on *Don Kirshner's Rock Concert*.

Diltz said they spent about an hour doing a dry run of the scene before the key gunfight shots. "So

they would...come out and stand there in a tableau...moving around," Diltz recalled in *Under the Covers*, adding that the sepia-toned imagery looked so authentic to the era they were portraying.

"When the actual gunfight happened the first time, they all came backing out of the bank, emptying their rifles and six guns," Diltz said. "The roadies were running down the street all firing [guns] and yelling, rolling in the dirt—it was just amazing. These guys totally transformed into outlaws."

Diltz followed up to get every moment on film. Glenn Frey recalled Diltz meticulously capturing images of the "dead."

"After all the smoke cleared and most everyone was lying dead in the street," Frey said, "Henry just took the Super 8 and [pans] over one guy's body, then passes another guy's boot and up his body." The photo shoot was a success.

Burden and Diltz's original plan for the *Desperado* cover was to picture the band as a gang of outlaws on the front and show them shot dead by lawmen and lying in the gutter on the back, along with photos in a gatefold depicting the bank robbery. The

As part of Asylum Records' marketing campaign for Eagles' *Desperado*, the label blew up one of **Henry Diltz'** many unused stills from the December 1972 Paramount Ranch photo shoot for a double-wide billboard overlooking the Sunset Strip in West Hollywood.

EAGLES
DESPERADO

SD 5068

ASYLUM RECORDS

Asylum Records, 9120 Sunset Blvd., Los Angeles, Calif., 90069

front and back cover concepts were kept; however, echoing the fate of the first album's fold-out poster cover, the centerfold idea was kiboshed to save money on packaging.

While the quartet of Eagles is shown posing on the front, the gang shown on the back had grown to a sextet of slain outlaws. Bookending the band's prone bodies are shootout extras **Jackson Browne** and **J.D. Souther**.

Standing over them triumphantly are the lawmen, played by Eagles roadies **Larry Penny**, **Richard Fernandez**, and **Tommy Nixon**; road manager **John Hartmann**; producer **Glyn Johns**; Burden; and, rolling a joint, **Boyd Elder**, the Texas artist and Burden-Diltz-Eagles associate who would soon create the original artwork depicted on the covers of future Eagles albums *One of These Nights* and *Their Greatest Hits (1971-1975)*.

Fernandez, who was the Eagles road manager from 1972 to 1976, remembered the outing fondly.

"That was an interesting day," he told *Time Passages*. "That was a lot of fun. We smoked a lot of weed; weed, peyote, and tequila shots. Glenn played cowboy with Gary Burden and [Henry] Diltz directing things. And everybody was in costume. I remember coming in like a week before we all went to Western Costume and just got cowboyed up. And I love the photo on the back cover with the musicians like Jackson and J.D. that are dead. There's all of us in the back, you know, the management."

Fernandez said it lasted all day. Everyone arrived at 10 a.m., and the photoshoot went on until about 6 p.m. Everyone on the set was exhausted, "but we were loaded too," he said, grinning.

The band themselves had frequently offered a similar musician-outlaw comparison when explaining the idea behind *Desperado*, although, in retrospect, Don Henley has been more critical of the claim.

"The metaphor was probably a little bullshit," Henley conceded when talking to writer **Marc Eliot** in the late 1990s. "We weren't outlaws; we were living outside the laws of normality. We were in L.A., staying up all night, smoking dope, living the California life, and I suppose we thought it was as radical as cowboys in the Old West." [6, 1111, 1491, 1492, 1493, 1505, 1525, 1525, 1685, 2124]

Among the hundreds of images **Henry Diltz** captured during the *Desperado* photo shoot is this little-known pastoral portrait of Don Henley, Glenn Frey, Bernie Leadon, and Randy Meisner in formal western wear.

DESPERADO

After a whirlwind year that saw them go from
unknowns to Top 10 country-rock stars, the Eagles
focused on duplicating that success. As band
members gathered material for their second album,
they wanted the world to know they weren't just
musicians—they were songwriters, too.

'Desperado' Becomes Henley, Frey's First Collaboration

"Desperado," the title track of the second Eagles LP, released in April 1973, is as much a classic as almost any other song in the band's catalog, even though their version was never released as a single.

Linda Ronstadt's version, which appeared on her **J.D. Souther**-co-produced *Don't Cry Now* album released the same year, did more to popularize the song at the time.

"['Desperado'] didn't get much love or attention when it was released on our second album," Henley said in 2016. "And then Linda Ronstadt recorded the song…and everything was different after that."

Along with "Doolin-Dalton," "Desperado" was one of two original compositions that served as centerpieces to the album's western concept. Perhaps even more importantly, as noted earlier, "Desperado" also is the song identified as the one that birthed the collaborative Henley-Frey team.

"[It's] the first song Don Henley and I wrote together," Frey told **Bob Costas** in a 1992 interview. "This song would stand the test of time."

"Desperado" began with a concept that had been burning a hole in Don Henley's back pocket for a while.

"I showed [Glenn] a partially formed chord progression and a melody that I'd been carrying around with me since the late 1960s," Henley said. "Its style was largely based on the old songs of **Stephen Foster**, sometimes known as the 'Father of American Music,' who wrote over 200 songs."

Henley's reference point was the 19th-century composer of standards like "Oh! Susanna" and "My Old Kentucky Home," a tad removed from early-1970s rock and roll. But Frey knew where Henley was headed with his idea.

"What blew my mind was that Glenn knew who Stephen Foster was," Henley said. "He immediately got it, understood intuitively what I was going for, and proceeded to add structure, including some additional chords and lyrics, to a song fragment that had been lying dormant for years. Glenn had an encyclopedic knowledge of the canon of American popular music."

Frey told **Cameron Crowe** in 2003 that Henley's original working lyric opening the song referenced a friend named "Leo," but "Leo, my God, won't you come to your senses" became the more familiar "Desperado, why don't you come to your senses" as the song was molded into the Old West concept that would run through the album.

As a finished piece, the ballad, which closed Side 1 of the vinyl versions of both *Desperado* and *Their Greatest Hits*, might be one of the best examples of Henley's soulful, gravelly delivery on record. But he's personally not too keen on the performance.

"I don't hate it, [but] I could've done better because I didn't get a chance to sing it more than three or four times," Henley said in a 2015 interview with radio personality **Howard Stern**. Financial concerns influenced this decision as producer **Glyn**

81

continued on Page 84

RELEASE
Early June
1973

TEQUILA SUNRISE
By: Don Henley, Glenn Frey
Side B: Twenty-One (Leadon)

"Tequila Sunrise" was the most commercially viable track of the eleven songs on Eagles' second LP, *Desperado*. Musically similar to "Peaceful Easy Feeling"—which was the last single the band released just three months prior—the song could not find solid footing on the radio. It was a sign of things to come as the band ran headlong into the sophomore jinx.

AIRPLAY

When "Tequila Sunrise" was released, there was far less enthusiasm from radio stations nationwide. Playlist additions were an important barometer of success for the industry, and a month into its release, it was on just 10% of radio stations nationwide, according to *Cashbox*'s survey of primary and secondary markets. The song has since developed adoring fan loyalty, it became the band's first single to miss the Top 20.

17 PLAYLIST ADDS Summer 1973			
Region	Jun	Jul	Regional Airplay
Northeast	3	1	23.5 %
Southeast	3	1	23.5 %
Midwest	5	2	41.2 %
Southwest	0	1	5.9 %
West	1	0	5.9 %

FIRST-WAVE STATIONS Stations that added the song in the first 30 days

KJR-Seattle

WHB-Kansas City
WEBN-FM-Cincinnati
WIFE-Indianapolis
WDGY-Minneapolis
KIOA-Des Moines

WPOP-Hartford
WEDO-Pittsburgh
WJET-Erie, PA

WCAO-Baltimore
WKWK-Wheeling
WFOM-Marietta

CHARTS

Billboard	HIGHEST CHARTING WEEK: CASHBOX - July 28, 1973		
#64 July 21, 1973	SINGLE	ARTIST	# PREV WK
	1. Bad, Bad Leroy Brown	Jim Croce	7
Cashbox	2. Yesterday Once More	Carpenters	8
	3. Smoke on the Water	Deep Purple	9
#40 July 28, 1973	4. Shambala	Three Dog Night	3
	5. Natural High	Bloodstone	6
	6. Boogie Woogie Bugle Boy	Bette Midler	12
Record World	7. Get Down	Gilbert O'Sullivan	13
	8. Touch Me in the Morning	Diana Ross	24
#40 July 28, 1973	**40. TEQUILA SUNRISE**	**EAGLES**	**44**

Sources: Billboard, Cashbox, Record World

FREY, HENLEY RAISE GLASS TO 'SHOT OF COURAGE'

While "Desperado" has the significant distinction of being the first song written by the team of Glenn Frey and Don Henley, "Tequila Sunrise" was composed in the same week.

The title came from Frey and was also the moniker for a then-popular cocktail made with tequila, orange juice, and grenadine that visually resembled a scenic Southern California sunrise.

According to Henley, "[Frey] was ambivalent about it because he thought that it was a bit too obvious or too much of a cliché because of the drink that was so popular then." Henley encouraged him not to be dismissive of the title, because it could work as a double entendre, representing the dejected lover witnessing daybreak after spending the whole night drowning his sorrows.

It isn't a stretch to say the songwriters mirrored their own experiences in the lyrics. As Henley recalled, the bridge lyric of "'take another shot of courage' refers to tequila—because we used to call it 'instant courage.' We very much wanted to talk to the ladies, but we often didn't have the nerve, so we'd drink a couple of shots and suddenly it was, 'Howdy, ma'am.'"

At the same time, the song also fit nicely into the *Desperado* album's outlaw theme. The strumming acoustic guitar pattern, which Frey described as being "kind of **Roy Orbison**, kind of Mexican," produced a lonely desert vibe punctuated by Bernie Leadon's weeping B-Bender tones. (The B-Bender, invented by **Byrds** alumni **Gene Parsons** and **Clarence White**, was a relatively new guitar accessory that could significantly "bend" a guitar's b-string to create a sound similar to a pedal steel guitar. Leadon had also used a B-Bender for his "Peaceful Easy Feeling" solo on the first album.) The lyrics—which vary from first- to third-person throughout the song—could perhaps reflect tales of a drifting cowboy traveling into town as a "hired hand" and soon moving on.

At the time, like the *Desperado* album, "Tequila Sunrise" charted poorly, never moving higher than #40. In 1976, the song would rise again, on Side 2 of *Eagles: Their Greatest Hits (1971–1975)*.

Notably, live performances of "Tequila Sunrise" filmed in 1973 in places like London and Holland indicate an additional bridge and verse were at one time considered for the song. The extra bridge featured Frey on lead vocals prior to the song's coda:

"Think/Guess I'll go to Mexico,
  Down to where the pace is nice and slow,
  And there's no one there I know

  ~

  It's another Tequila Sunrise,
  Wondering if I'm growing wise or telling lies"

[6, 209, 1152, 1404]

Johns was under orders to not spend too much money, and an excessive number of takes for any given track were apparently not in the budget.

As the clock was running on Henley's vocal session at Island Studio, the London Philharmonic Orchestra's meter also kept ticking. The large ensemble was set up behind him, which he found rather disconcerting, partially because he found it intimidating to sing in front of an orchestra, but also because the musicians didn't seem to hide their disinterest in the project. Apparently, they even brought chessboards and played chess with each other in between takes. It was just another session to them.

"They were bored shitless, and I was scared stiff. I had never sung in front of a large orchestra before, and I was only given about four or five takes to get it right," Henley told *Rolling Stone* in 2016.

It may have made sense to record the lead vocal separate from the orchestra, but that was not the protocol laid out at the session. "[Glyn Johns] was into doing it live," Henley said, conceding that this may have helped in some ways and hurt in others: "It gives it a certain humanity. [The vocal] is flawed, like humans are. I could have sung it a lot better."

His **Shiloh** bandmate, **Jim Ed Norman**, had written the string arrangements and was conducting the orchestra. It was Norman's first studio experience with a big ensemble. Henley commended his mate by saying, "He was nervous, too, I think, but he didn't let it show. He somehow conjured up an air of authority, and the players responded to him. They were, after all, getting paid."

Later in the decade, by the time the Eagles were working on *Hotel California* and *The Long Run*, they had—fairly or unfairly—developed a reputation as perfectionists and perhaps had earned the privilege of dictating more of their own terms. But money, deadlines, and non-musical influences were always a factor, and especially so during the early years of the band.

Henley summed up the process, saying, "We weren't always ready to let a song go, but after a while, you have to just let go, especially if you're working within the constraints of a budget and a time frame."

Whatever misgivings he might have about the Eagles' original 1973 recording of "Desperado," Henley, Frey, and the band doubtlessly created one of their enduring staples. In addition to Ronstadt, **Kenny Rogers**, **Johnny Cash**, and **The Carpenters** are among the pop and country luminaries who have recorded versions of the song. [1190, 1496, 1506]

SUMMER 1973

 RELEASES
▶ **Barnstorm**, with Joe Walsh, *The Smoker You Drink, the Player You Get* (album)
▶ **Barnstorm**, with Joe Walsh, "Rocky Mountain Way" (single)
▶ **Poco**, with Timothy B. Schmit, "Here We Go Again" (single)
▶ **Eagles**, "Outlaw Man" (single)

NUGGETS

▶ Glenn Frey, **David Blue**, and Randy Meisner are making the rounds at Los Angeles radio stations in full cowboy gear and in front of a Southwestern Stage Lines wagon, doing promos for the Eagles' new LP, *Desperado*. —*Cashbox*

▶ Don Henley visits Record World to discuss Eagles' upcoming East Coast tour to support *Desperado*. —*Record World*

 ON SCREEN

▶ Eagles appeared on the NBC-TV show *The Helen Reddy Show* (Episode 1.3). **Cheech and Chong**, **Mac Davis**, and **Gladys Knight** also appeared.

▶ Eagles appeared on the ABC-TV show *In Concert* (Episode 1.14). **Mike Bloomfield**, **Jim Croce**, and **Dr. John** also appeared.

▶ **Barnstorm**, with **Joe Walsh**, appeared on the NBC-TV show *The Midnight Special* performing "Rocky Mountain Way." **Richard Pryor** hosted.

▶ Eagles appeared on the ABC-TV special *Good Vibrations from Central Park '73*. Sponsored by Dr. Pepper and performed at Wollman Rink in a pouring rain, the Eagles were third on the bill behind **Sly and the Family Stone** and **The Temptations**. **John Sebastian** and **Melissa Manchester** also appeared.

 ON THE ROAD WITH ...

▶ **Eagles**: David Blue, Joni Mitchell, King Crimson, Neil Young, REO Speedwagon, Santa Monica Flyers (Neil Young's band)

▶ **Poco**, with Timothy B. Schmit: Foghat, Mark-Almond, Robin Trower, Spooky Tooth, the Edgar Winter Group

▶ **Barnstorm**, with Joe Walsh: Bachman-Turner Overdrive, Cactus, Dr. Hook & the Medicine Show, Electric Light Orchestra, Focus, Hot Tuna, J. Geils Band, Manassas, Mott the Hoople, Poco, REO Speedwagon, Ted Nugent and the Amboy Dukes, The Flock, Wishbone Ash

TV Cameras Zoom In for Eagles' *In Concert* Close-Ups

Eagles' early success was a cocktail blending equal parts good music, great talent, and strong promotion.

David Geffen and Atlantic Records were wheels in constant motion keeping the band on the airwaves. **Jerry Sharell**, who orchestrated Asylum's singles promotions, and **Paul Ahern**, who handled album promotions, along with **John Hartmann**, were key staff. Along with the marketing might of Atlantic, Sharell and Ahern made sure that deejays and program directors nationwide were spinning the Eagles on the air.

Two months after Asylum released the second Eagles album, *Desperado*, the label began pushing the band into a new medium: television.

The Eagles' TV debut was on ABC's late-night series *In Concert* on August 3, 1973, the first of five appearances on the show. The series was produced by former **Monkees** manager and eventual Rock and Roll Hall of Famer **Don Kirshner**. *In Concert* competed with NBC's similar series *Midnight Special* and aired from 1972 to 1975, though a spin-off called *Don Kirshner's Rock Concert* was branded in 1973.

Kirshner would book some of the biggest rock bands of the day and pitched the show to a late-night audience. But even with an after-prime-time audience, the show had its controversies. The first episode was filmed at Hofstra University with **Alice Cooper**, **Bo Diddley**, **Curtis Mayfield**, and **Seals & Crofts**. Everything was fine until

continued on Page 94

'SATURDAY NIGHT'

MEISNER'S MEMORIES HATCH ODE TO LOVE, REGRET

Glenn Frey and Don Henley took increasingly central roles, both as bandleaders and songwriters, as the Eagles continued their musical flight. Frey would later memorably compare bands to a football team, where some people played quarterback, while others simply served as linemen.

Early on, however, there were far more collaborative moments—perhaps most notably "Saturday Night," the only song from their first four albums credited to all four founding members. This lovely waltz brought the rootless wanderings of *Desperado* back home for a frank discussion on the price of matrimony for those who prize their freedom and individuality.

In keeping with his usual way of contributing, Randy Meisner provided the song's initial spark. "That's what usually happened," he said in *The*

History of the Eagles documentary. "I'd get a verse or two, and I'm done, and they would help fill in the blanks."

This time, Meisner hit upon the promise of the weekend as a youth, and how those evenings of fun and freedom inevitably slip away as responsibilities take a more central role in adulthood.

"I was sitting there one night, and I came up with the line 'What ever happened to Saturday night?'" Meisner later told *Rolling Stone*. "When I was younger, I would be out partying, and with girls and having fun. And that's what it was about: Whatever happened to it? And the answer was, 'You're older now.'"

Henley and Frey took over, deepening the contextual emotions and fleshing out the main character.

"Saturday Night" presents itself in the breeziest

of manners, thanks to delicate work from co-writer Bernie Leadon on the mandolin and **Jim Ed Norman** at the piano. But there were eventually much darker themes at play, as Henley sings with a brokenhearted melancholy that makes clear he knows just what's at stake for these former lovers.

The lyrics paint a portrait of an innocent courtship just beginning, with Henley's voice hearkening back to a past that now seems dreamlike. The moon shines brightly, time moves slowly, and "the bluebird is high on the wing."

If the relationship is a dance, these are the first steps. There is hope, optimism, and marriage. But doubt enters the union in the next stanza, as the wife innocently asks, "Was I alright?" The question is vague and there is no answer, but the song's tone, like the relationship, becomes darker after the first chorus.

> "The years brought the railroad
> It ran by my door
> Now there's boards on the windows
> And dust on the floor
> And she passes the time at another
> man's side
> And I pass the time with my pride"

The protagonist seems to grow despondent over his loss of identity as their marriage unfolds. Despite his best intentions, a deep-set desire to roam had never left him. Perhaps sensing this reticence toward commitment, his lover drifts, embarks on an affair, and soon he's alone, left to *"pass the time with my pride."*

Henley was developing a particular flair for this kind of storytelling, and it was something Don Felder—who would begin a lengthy collaboration with the Eagles a few years later—said he quickly recognized. Complications in Henley's love life would make their way into their songs, Felder said, and, in turn, they would make those songs far better.

Over time, the band developed a kind of gallows humor about it. "We were all waiting for the day that [Henley and his girlfriend] would break up," Felder told *Fox News* in 2014. "We would be thinking, 'Come on, Don; break up, break up, break up! We need a ballad for this record!'"

Desperado, as a meditation on Old West themes, had plenty of them, but none that cut so deeply into issues of the heart.

"Saturday Night" also touches on how modernity can change a place, as the railroad's arrival seems to become a broader metaphor for lost innocence. The home they shared together is eventually boarded up, and, like the small town where they first fell in love, it's simply abandoned. He yearns for those early, simple days that were Saturday nights.

All that's left is the question of whether to try once more—or, more particularly, how to avoid making the same mistakes again.

"Someone show me," Henley sings with exquisite world-weariness, "how to tell the dancer from the dance."

It was a theme that clearly sparked something within Henley, since he would return to the notion of love as a dance on "Waiting in the Weeds" from the Eagles' 2007 reunion album, *Long Road Out of Eden*.

"*If finding love is just a dance, proximity and chance,*" Henley sang decades later, "*you will excuse me if I skip the masquerade.*"

In both cases, the dancers spin in distracting circles, and the narrator seems no closer to sorting things out. [1971, 1972]

> "
>
> I WAS SITTING THERE ONE NIGHT, AND I CAME UP WITH THE LINE 'WHATEVER HAPPENED TO SATURDAY NIGHT?' WHEN I WAS YOUNGER, I WOULD BE OUT... WITH GIRLS HAVING FUN. AND THAT'S WHAT IT'S ABOUT: WHATEVER HAPPENED TO IT? AND THE ANSWER WAS, 'YOU'RE OLDER NOW.'
>
> — RANDY MEISNER

Sophomore Jinx Hits as 'Cowboy Album' Arrives

When the Eagles began working on their second album, they built it around the theme of Old West gunfighters and badmen, drawing inspiration from the book, *The Album of Gunfighters*. The resulting album, *Desperado*, rustled up ten tracks (eleven counting Bernie Leadon's 48-second banjo instrumental) of original work, save for **David Blue**'s "Outlaw Man," which still fit perfectly within the album's theme.

"Doolin-Dalton," an under-appreciated gem, leads off the album, weaving a tale of how politician-turned-outlaw Bill Dalton seeks vengeance for the death of his two brothers in a failed Coffeyville, Kansas, bank heist in the 1890s. He meets cowboy Bill Doolin "working cheap, just biding time," and together they head down their own road to eternity.

Co-written by **Jackson Browne**, Glenn Frey, Don Henley, and **J.D. Souther**, "Doolin-Dalton" evoked the spirit of the Old West perhaps better than any other track on the album.

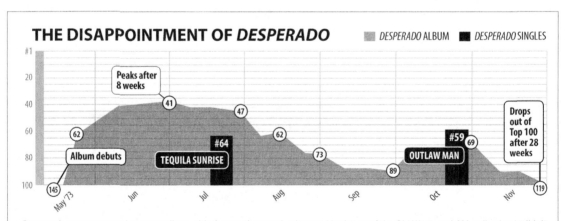

THE DISAPPOINTMENT OF *DESPERADO* ▨ *DESPERADO* ALBUM ▪ *DESPERADO* SINGLES

Peaks after 8 weeks — 41

47

62

62

73

89

#64 — TEQUILA SUNRISE

#59 — OUTLAW MAN — 69

Drops out of Top 100 after 28 weeks

Album debuts — 62

145 — May '73   Jun   Jul   Aug   Sep   Oct   Nov — 119

Desperado was a nuanced concept album with themes that revolved around bad men of the Old West, and AM radio simply didn't know what to do with it. It started out relatively strong for a band's sophomore effort, likely because fans were expecting more "Take It Easy"-style songs. They didn't get that, and sales and airplay took a quick nosedive. The oft-forgotten "Outlaw Man" buoyed the band for a short time in the fall, but the album slid out of the charts quickly after that. The album did develop a cult following on album-oriented FM stations and got some airplay; it was certified gold by the RIAA in September 1974. Nearly 30 years later, in March 2001, it achieved 2x platinum status.
Sources: Billboard, Recording Industry Association of America

Henley's weary vocals paint a picture of gritty men with nothing to lose on the dusty plains of Kansas and Oklahoma. Frey's isolated rhythm guitar sets the background as Henley renders their state of mind... *"Easy money and faithless women/Red eye whiskey for the pain."* Frey takes the lead vocals in the second stanza and the contrast between Henley's raspiness and Frey's smooth delivery offer a duality that seems to mirror the Bill Doolin–Bill Dalton pairing, almost as if Frey and Henley were acting out those roles in the studio.

The Doolin–Dalton portrait returns twice in the LP, once with Leadon's double-time banjo stylings in a short instrumental, and again with a nearly five-minute reprise that brings the story to a conclusion and expertly intertwines itself with "Desperado."

The rest of the songs mostly fit within the Old West motif, or at least approached it. Frey and Henley collaborated on "Tequila Sunrise," easily the most commercial song on the album. Leadon's "Twenty-One" is a bluegrass-tinged romper that certainly could have been a **Dillard & Clark** cut; his "Bitter Creek" is a slower-tempo number with a Muscle Shoals feel. Neither were commercial enough for a single, but they both were essential in stitching together the necessary fabric of this collection.

"A Certain Kind of Fool," co-written by Randy Meisner, Frey, and Henley, gives Meisner an opportunity to stretch his high-

ELEKTRA/ASYLUM INSIDER

THERE REALLY WASN'T A TOP 40 HIT ON THE ALBUM. With crossover play among several radio formats, "Tequila Sunrise" got out there and people knew it, even though the chart numbers were less than stellar. "Outlaw Man" was a total bomb. But wait. "Desperado" was getting airplay. Not as a single, not a Top 40 hit, but AOR and Top 40 stations were playing it. And with the Eagles touring, it took the band to a new level through non-traditional means.

Months later, **Linda Ronstadt** covered it for her album and did TV appearances with the Eagles together singing the tune. And then the album began to sell. By happenstance, "Desperado," the song, had set them up once again. Now the Eagles had growing album sales and a couple signature Top 40 hits. What's more, their live performances were top-notch and well-attended. I drove two hundred miles in college to see them— long before I knew my future. I actually ran into Glenn Frey and chatted for a few minutes at our no-tell motel in the modest college town of Athens, Ohio. Little did I know that I would be enjoying Thanksgiving dinner at his Detroit Royal Oak home with his family a few years later and breaking his new band's records on the radio.

—*Rip Pelley, former National Director of Artist Development and Promotion, Elektra/Asylum Records*

range vocals and has a dramatic hook that draws the listener. The one song where all four Eagles collaborated was "Saturday Night," a folksy homage to the lost art of courtship, which is yet another highly underrated song in the Eagles' catalog. The only cut that seems out of place is "Out of Control," co-written by Frey and Henley. With a thumping baseline and a garage-rock attitude, it doesn't fit the mold of the other tracks.

As much as the band and their producer **Glyn Johns** thought *Desperado* was a creative success, airplay and sales of the album were underwhelming. Johns suspected why. "I actually thought [*Desperado*] was going to be a monster hit album, and it really should have been. It's disgraceful that it wasn't, although it's gone platinum now and all the rest of it, but it should have just taken the world by storm. It has become a milestone, and one of those records...which are definitely considered as going down in the annals, so people tell me, and I'm very proud of it. But it's very strange that it wasn't a hit at the time, although there is a very good reason for that, and that was that the record company were not on the case. [**David**] **Geffen** had just taken over Elektra, and he was more involved with signing **Bob Dylan**."

Despite its slow start, the album still reached gold status in September 1974. Now certified double platinum, it has outsold the debut album. Not bad for a cowboy "concept" album. [15, 133, 231, 590, 591, 1484, 1501]

Rolling Stone
May 10, 1973

Although [*Desperado*] is a unified set of songs, it's not a rock opera, a concept album or anything pretending to be much more than a set of good tunes that just happen to fit together. Don Henley's rough voice is the one of experience, and it helps make "Desperado" and "Saturday Night" memorable. It won't cure your hangover or revalue the dollar, but it will give you many good times. With their second consecutive job well done, the Eagles are on a winning streak.

– Paul Gambaccini

Phonograph Record
June 1973

The amazing thing about [*Desperado*] is that it was not planned thematically. The album does not lack for single material ... the tunes stand well on their own merits. The only sore spot is the production. It falls short of [Glyn] Johns' earlier work. The undermixed vocals, especially on the more raucous songs, give it that old **Rolling Stones** quality. It didn't seem an effective way of presenting the Eagles' vocal, melodic lines which are so important to the overall presence.

– David Rensin

New Musical Express
May 26, 1973

I love the Eagles' first album dearly, and its successor no less. The Eagles are, for what it's worth, currently producing the finest music to ever emerge from the country-rock school. Around the album are dotted songs like "Outlaw Man" and "Tequila Sunrise," which has to be one of the nicest song ever written after a drink. Listen to the Eagles and glory in them. In their own un-derstated way, they're becoming one of the most rewarding and worthwhile groups in the world.

– Charles Shaar Murray

BARNSTORM

The Smoker You Drink, The Player You Get
ABC-Dunhill Records, June 1973

Barnstorm's second album, *The Smoker You Drink, the Player You Get*, was meant to establish once and for all that the trio was a band, not just a Joe Walsh solo project.

"My first solo album was called Barnstorm," Walsh explained around the time of the sophomore release. "I meant for the album [as well as] the group to be called Barnstorm, but I didn't really specify. There was some confusion after my first solo album came out as to what, in fact, was 'Barnstorm'—was it the group or the album?"

The confusion hadn't cleared up when *The Smoker You Drink...* was ready for release: ABC-Dunhill's album cover design again billed it as a Joe Walsh record. Walsh called the tussle over how to brand the album a "minor disagreement," but the label insisted it be released as "Joe Walsh," and promised him that the third LP would be billed as "Barnstorm featuring Joe Walsh."

The album's opening track—an irresistible mid-tempo shuffle titled "Rocky Mountain Way"—is easily the album's most famous song. While the lyrics offer a nod to the Colorado residence Walsh took up prior to his Barnstorm days, the song is probably best known for his use of the "talk box"—a piece of hardware that modifies a guitar amplifier's output to include "voice sounds" by routing a tube into the performer's mouth. Sound engineer **Bob Heil** built the first one for Walsh. Along with **Peter Frampton**'s "Show Me the Way" and "Do You Feel Like I Do," "Rocky Mountain Way" is arguably among rock music's most iconic examples of the talk box in action. It was likely the first in rock and roll.

Debut album producer **Bill Szymczyk** was again at the controls. Expanding the "Barnstorm is a band" concept, bassist **Ken Passarelli** wrote and sang lead vocals on the pleasant "Happy Ways," while drummer and multi-instrumentalist **Joe Vitale** wrote and took lead vocals on "Bookends" and "Days Gone By." Rounding out the unit, they added keyboard player **Rocke Grace**, who contributed the instrumental "Midnight Moodies" and shared credit with the other three on "Rocky Mountain Way."

With Walsh supplying the remaining tunes, the group created a well-rounded collection that included rock and pop stylings, dreamy sequences, Latin, funk, and more.

"We are really young still and haven't reached any peak at all," Walsh said in 1973. "There are musicians getting to know each other in the band, getting off on each other's ideas and goofing around like we'd found a new toy to play with. This is still going on and we hope it continues for as long as possible."

Despite Walsh's optimism for Barnstorm's longevity, changes were ahead, and he'd be singing a different tune just a year later when his next album was released. [361, 1543, 1544]

WALSH FINDS 'ROCKY MOUNTAIN WAY' IS BETTER

Joe Walsh has a special place in his heart for "Rocky Mountain Way," the favorite of all the songs he recorded, he told SiriusXM radio host **Howard Stern** in 2012.

The song was developed at a critical juncture in Walsh's career, after ABC-Dunhill had released Walsh's first post-**James Gang** album with his new band, **Barnstorm**, and it had not done well. The decision to leave the James Gang had been difficult, and now the mental and financial stress from it weighed more heavily on him. He was conflicted about leaving the band, had a disinterested manager who didn't seem to care about his troubles, and was enduring his third straight year of IRS audits.

To cap it off, he had his first falling out with the producer, **Bill Szymczyk**, who discovered him in Ohio. That spat prompted Walsh to produce himself, so he and Barnstorm took off for Florida at the end of 1972 to start laying down tracks at North Miami's Criteria Studios for what would become the band's second album, *The Smoker You Drink, The Player You Get*.

Walsh, **Joe Vitale**, **Kenny Passarelli**, and

PATHWAY SINGLE | JOE WALSH

BARNSTORM
Rocky Mountain Way
ABC-Dunhill Records, June 1973

Rocke Grace teamed in the studio with engineer whiz kids **Ronnie** and **Howie Albert**, who had worked with producer **Tom Dowd** recording the *Layla and Other Assorted Love Songs* album with **Eric Clapton**'s alter ego band, **Derek and the Dominoes**, in summer 1970. A year and half later, the Alberts had worked at Criteria with **Stephen Stills** and **Chris Hillman** on the celebrated **Manassas** double LP, out in April 1972.

"Rocky Mountain Way" was a complete band effort, and writing credits went to all four Barnstorm members. It was one of the first tracks they started and, months later, one of the last finished.

In Vitale's 2008 memoir *Backstage Pass*, written by his wife **Susie Vitale**, he said the band was developing tracks for *The Smoker You Drink* in

January 1973 when Walsh was tinkering with a slow blues shuffle. "This really needs slide," Vitale recalled Walsh saying.

Walsh was taught to play slide guitar by one of his good friends, **Duane Allman** of the **Allman Brothers Band**. Allman was a session ace who also recorded frequently at Criteria before his death in a tragic motorcycle crash in Georgia in October 1971.

By the *Smoker* sessions, Walsh felt comfortable enough with his developing slide guitar skills to finally use them on a recording.

"Joe picked up his guitar and we started messing around with that shuffle," Vitale said, adding that they wrote the framework for the song in about half an hour.

Szymczyk and Walsh eventually reconciled, and the tapes from Miami were shipped back to Colorado to be finished at Caribou Ranch. With the music already completed, the only thing left to consider were the lyrics. Vitale said the track simmered for three or four weeks, and while they developed the other tracks, Walsh worked on the lyrics. They didn't immediately come to him, but the precariousness of his current situation was heavy on his mind.

"I was in Colorado, I had left the James Gang, and I was worried that I might have made a mistake," Walsh said. "I have an album done, which was the first Barnstorm album, and I'm mowing the lawn. I didn't have any words for 'Rocky Mountain Way,' but we had the track done. And I was dead in the water about this song. What is it about? So, I look up and there's the front range of the Rocky Mountains, and there's snow on them in the summer, and it knocked me back because it was just beautiful. And I think, 'Well, I have committed, it's too late to regret the James Gang, the Rocky Mountain Way is better than the way I had, because the music was better."

Walsh said the lyrics just fell in place after that.

"'*He's telling us this/He's telling us that/It changes every day*,' that's the James Gang manager." Walsh said.

"'*And we don't need the ladies/Crying 'cause the story's sad*,' that's giving up the regret of leaving the James Gang," he added.

"I got all the words at once and I ran into the house to write [them] down, and the lawn mower kept going over into the neighbor's yard and it ate the garden. It was an expensive song to write," he said, laughing.

Vitale said that when they got back to the studio, Walsh wandered around putting the finishing touches on the lyrics. He settled in the control room, spent time upstairs in the pool room where the windows afforded a view of the mountains, and any other quiet place he could find, and then finished the words.

When he came back downstairs to record it, their friend Stephen Stills had joined the band in the control room, offering suggestions and support.

Szymczyk said the only thing they kept from the original session in Miami were Vitale's drums and piano parts. "We wind up overdubbing everything else, and doing it all over again," he said. "All the guitars and synthesizers and talk box and everything, up at the ranch. The track and the overdubs were done maybe a year apart—it was one of the first tracks he started and the last ones we finished for that album."

Walsh overdubbed that incredible slide part by layering six or seven guitar parts on the basic rhythm track, resulting in a rich guitar sound that comes from Walsh, not studio trickery.

"Joe was really excited because it was almost like being able to play a new instrument," Vitale said. "After Joe's performance everyone in the control room stood up and applauded. We were all impressed with his new talent."

The studio session was satisfying for Walsh too. "One of the things that makes it great is that it's a bunch of guys playing in a room. That groove you can't do with Pro Tools," Walsh told Stern, referring to the computer software that many artists and studios use today to cut tracks.

"Rocky Mountain Way" was better than the way Walsh had on the charts. The single found radio welcoming, reaching #23 on the *Billboard* Hot 100 chart and #13 on *Cashbox*'s chart. [132, 1500, 1809]

Cooper went on stage and wheeled out his hyperbolic rock and horror extravaganza. That proved too much in Cincinnati, Ohio, where the program director at ABC's affiliate WKRC-TV pulled the show from the air in disgust.

But the Eagles were quite wholesome by comparison. The band's three-song set in August featured "Tequila Sunrise," "Earlybird," and "Witchy Woman," and was recorded at UCLA as the second act on the show's card following **Ike & Tina Turner**.

They were likely tired for the appearance. Two days prior, they had been in New York's Central Park filming with **The Beach Boys** for their *Good Vibrations from Central Park* special, which also aired on ABC later that month. The band shared the stage with **Sly and the Family Stone**, **Melissa Manchester**, **The Temptations**, and **John Sebastian**, as well as The Beach Boys.

For the Eagles, handling a television show was quite different than a normal concert gig, according to former Eagles road manager **Richard Fernandez**, who remembered the *In Concert* appearances.

"TV is different from doing a live [concert]," he told *Time Passages*. "I always felt like TV people were too, 'You're going to do it this way...this is the way we do it,'" he said, pointing in various directions as if directing. "I mean, it's better now, to be honest with you."

Fernandez said that as road manager, it was his job to keep the band isolated and fend off producers' demands for unnecessary practice runs. "I would want them concentrating on what they need to do out there."

The Eagles would appear twice more on ABC's show in 1973, and three times total in 1974. The band also made appearances in summer 1973 on the NBC primetime variety program *The Helen Reddy Show.*

They didn't travel far for the *In Concert* or *Helen Reddy* appearances, which were usually shot on a soundstage in Los Angeles, "most likely at KTLA or one of those further down in Hollywood," Fernandez said.

A year later, the band would be back onstage in front of the cameras with **Linda Ronstadt** and **Jackson Browne**, and new Eagle Don Felder. [700, 1685]

FALL 1973

 RELEASES
▶ **Poco**, with Timothy B. Schmit, *Crazy Eyes* (album)
▶ **Poco**, with Timothy B. Schmit, "Magnolia" (single)

 ON THE ROAD WITH ...
▶ **Eagles**: Neil Young, Dan Fogelberg
▶ **Poco**, with Timothy B. Schmit: Leon Russell, Little Feat, Mary McCreary, the Doobie Brothers, the Marshall Tucker Band
▶ **Barnstorm**, with Joe Walsh: Argent, Blue Öyster Cult, Focus, Leon Russell, Montrose, Mott the Hoople, Orphan, Paul Butterfield, REO Speedwagon, Robin Trower, Slade, Terry Reid

 ON SCREEN
▶ **Randy Meisner** appeared in *Easy to Be Free*, a 20th Century Fox documentary about **Rick Nelson** on tour with his **Stone Canyon Band** in 1972.

NUGGETS
▶ **J.D. Souther** is mulling over plans to join up with **Chris Hillman** and **Richie Furay**. —*Record World*
▶ **David Geffen** will direct operations for the combined Elektra-Asylum. —*Cashbox*

COLLABORATIONS
▶ **Glenn Frey** sang lead and harmony vocals on the single "The Fast One" on **Linda Ronstadt**'s album *Don't Cry Now*.
▶ **Joe Walsh** played slide guitar on the song "Sweet Maria" on **Rick Roberts**' album *She Is a Song*.
▶ **Don Henley** (backing vocals) and **Glenn Frey** (harmony vocals) contributed to **Jackson Browne**'s album *For Everyman*.
▶ **Joe Walsh** played guitar on **America**'s album *Hat Trick*.
▶ **Joe Walsh** played synthesizer on **The Fabulous Rhinestones**' album *Freewheelin.'*
▶ **Joe Walsh** played electric guitar on the singles "Teenage Queen" and "Uncomplicated" on **Rick Derringer**'s album *All American Boy*.

Geffen Dabbles in Hollywood Club Scene, Opens The Roxy

On his way to becoming one of the world's biggest showbiz magnates, nothing was off the table for **David Geffen**, including starting his own nightclub. In 1973, he decided to do just that, but for a practical reason: the need to promote his stable of artists.

At the time, the Troubadour in West Hollywood, owned by legendary music promoter **Doug Weston**, was the most powerful club in town. Weston was, as described by *Los Angeles Times* pop music critic **Robert Hilburn**, "arguably the godfather of the Southern California sing-er-songwriter movement in the late 1960s and early 1970s, someone whose unshakable belief in the inspirational power of music made [the Troubadour] both a showcase and meeting hall for much of the best young talent of a generation."

The problem, as far as Geffen was concerned, was that Weston had an unreasonable amount of power since the Troubadour was the only place in town with enough muscle to successfully break a band. As such, Weston was able to dictate terms that managers, agents, and artists might not otherwise find acceptable.

It was common for Geffen and his artist management partner **Elliot Roberts** to spar with Weston over bookings. After a failed attempt to negotiate an appearance by Asylum artist **David Blue**, Geffen threatened to create his own club that would not only be a venue for him to promote his artists, but also would create competition for Weston's Troubadour.

With most anyone else, this might have been an idle threat—and it was likely received as such—but Geffen was not someone to be easily dismissed. Thus, it was not surprising when The Roxy Theatre—Geffen's new club—opened its doors at 9009 Sunset Boulevard on September 20, 1973.

Geffen partnered in his venture with other heavyweights in the music business, including Roberts; Dunhill Records founder **Lou Adler**, who famously guided **The Mamas and the Papas** through a series of mega-hits in the mid-to-late 1960s; Hollywood club entrepreneur **Elmer**

continued on Page 99

RELEASE

Early September
1973

OUTLAW MAN

By: David Blue
Side B: A Certain Kind of Fool
(Meisner, Henley, Frey)

Thematically, *Desperado* met the Eagles' goal of showing off their musical range. They wrote cohesive songs that met the LP's Old West theme well, but overlooked one thing: the album needed a commercially viable rocker. The last two songs they released were similar ballads ("Peaceful Easy Feeling" and "Tequila Sunrise"), so they needed to unleash an upbeat cut as the album's second single. The problem was that there wasn't a solid candidate. There were only two real options: "Out of Control" and "Outlaw Man," but neither was commercial enough to be radio-ready. Ultimately, "Outlaw Man" was chosen and it flopped. The band learned a valuable lesson, and they wouldn't release another LP without a strong, edgier song.

AIRPLAY

Radio stations had grown quite fond of the Eagles by the summer of 1973. Program directors had quickly added all their singles to their playlists. But the cover of **David Blue**'s "Outlaw Man" was different. It just didn't catch on. Never mind that Blue himself released the single two months earlier and it only reached #73. Radio stations gave the song a cursory listen, but it had the fewest station "adds" of any of the Eagles' releases to date. It became their first brush with disappointment.

11 PLAYLIST ADDS Fall 1973

Region	Sep	Oct	Regional Airplay
Northeast	3	0	27.2 %
Southeast	1	1	18.2 %
Midwest	3	1	36.4 %
Southwest	0	0	0.0 %
West	2	0	18.2 %

FIRST-WAVE STATIONS Stations that added the song in the first 30 days

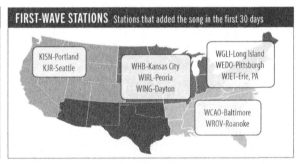

KISN-Portland
KJR-Seattle

WHB-Kansas City
WIRL-Peoria
WING-Dayton

WGLI-Long Island
WEDO-Pittsburgh
WJET-Erie, PA

WCAO-Baltimore
WROV-Roanoke

CHARTS

Billboard

#59
October 27, 1973

Cashbox

#49
October 13, 1973

Record World

#68
October 20, 1973

HIGHEST CHARTING WEEK: CASHBOX - October 13, 1973		
SINGLE	**ARTIST**	**# PREV WK**
1. Higher Ground	Stevie Wonder	2
2. Half-Breed	Cher	1
3. Ramblin' Man	Allman Brothers	3
4. Angie	Rolling Stones	9
5. Keep On Truckin'	Eddie Kendricks	11
6. That Lady	Isley Brothers	7
7. My Maria	B.W. Stevenson	8
8. China Grove	Doobie Brothers	10
49. OUTLAW MAN	**EAGLES**	**49**

Sources: Billboard, Cashbox, Record World

LACKING A ROCKER, 'OUTLAW MAN' GETS THE NOD

In the canon of Eagles singles, most are widely recognized. "Outlaw Man" is an exception. It profiles more like an album track from *Desperado* than a world-renowned hit. This makes sense because it was one of the few singles released by the band that did not chart well.

While Eagles had already shown a willingness to serve up singles from other writers by releasing **Jack Tempchin**'s "Peaceful Easy Feeling" from their first LP, with "Outlaw Man" they were releasing a version of a song also released by its composer the same year. Written by **David Blue**, "Outlaw Man" was the opening track on his *Nice Baby and the Angel* LP.

The band's version fit perfectly with their outlaw concept for *Desperado*, and since Blue was a fellow Asylum artist, it made even more sense to include it on the album.

"We all heard Blue's version before it was released and I think Glenn suggested the song fit the theme of the album and that we should work it up," Bernie Leadon said.

While Eagles' rendition is fairly faithful to Blue's arrangement, they took some liberties with the song's final verse by cutting the first half and inserting a double-time groove for the second half. This created a more dramatic, galloping sense of urgency.

Additionally, there were some lyrical tweaks. Blue, for example, originally sang of "heading to San Francisco in a '56 Chevrolet," but the Eagles instead "headed for Oklahoma" and killed the line about the Chevy to keep things consistent with the album's 1800s timeframe. Interestingly, concert bootlegs reveal that Glenn Frey, who sang lead on the track, would sometimes use the "'56 Chevrolet" line when performing the song live.

Production-wise, the Eagles' version is highlighted by their trademark harmonies, and near the end of the song as the double-time section fades, Randy Meisner plays some tasty-but-aggressive bass lines, which help add more stomp to the delivery.

"Outlaw Man" may have worked well on the album thematically and musically, but as a single, the song was only thrust into the limelight because *Desperado* was devoid of up-tempo, radio-friendly tracks, and the album was considered, at least then, a stiff.

"We needed some rockers," Leadon said matter-of-factly. "We weren't writing very many at the time." And just as the band knew that was the biggest problem with *Desperado*, the suits at Elektra/Asylum also knew that was the album's fatal flaw.

In the press, **David Geffen** was supportive of the band's decision to record *Desperado* as a concept album and likened the effort to an Americanized version of **The Beatles**' *Sgt. Pepper's Lonely Hearts Club Band.*

But privately he was fuming and exasperated, calling the approach crazy, especially on the heels of such a successful debut album.

Atlantic Records then-President **Jerry Greenberg** wasn't nearly as kind. Looking back in 2016, Don Henley remembered Greenberg's reaction was: "Jeez, they've made a fucking cowboy album."

Geffen's concerns, at least about album and singles sales, seemed initially correct. *Desperado* was very slow out of the gate and its first single, "Tequila Sunrise," though eventually a fan favorite, had stalled at #64 on the *Billboard* Hot 100 in the summer of 1973. "Tequila" and "Peaceful Easy Feeling," the third and final single released from the band's debut album just three months earlier, were both laid-back ballads with similar musical vibes.

After "Tequila," the *Desperado* question became what to release as the follow-up single. The album's title track might have been a strong choice at another time, but the idea of releasing three straight ballads for a band that increasingly wanted to show off its rock and roll cred was a non-starter. "Doolin-Dalton" was a well-crafted song that was perfect for the album, but wasn't commercially viable. Likewise, "Bitter Creek" and "Twenty-One" were solid Bernie Leadon cuts, but neither was suited for Top 40 radio.

That left "Out of Control" or Blue's "Outlaw Man" as the up-tempo choices, and the latter got pressed as a single. It died hard, and barely improved upon the "Tequila" performance: *Cashbox* charted it as high as #49 on its Top 100 singles chart, but it never rose above #59 on *Billboard*'s Hot 100.

Rather than cueing up a third single, the band packed it in. "Desperado" may have charted if it had been released as a single, as the Eagles certainly had a strong track record with ballads at that point. But the album's middling performance was so disappointing for the band that they instead chose to focus on gathering material for their next album.

The absence of a true rocker single may have hurt their marketability, and that played a part in the group wanting to change their approach to making music. They wanted to be more rock and roll.

But when the Eagles went back into Olympic Studios in London to get started on their third album with producer **Glyn Johns**, they found that his attitude about the kind of music they should record had not changed.

Discontent with Johns had already been fomenting for some time, and the band already had a vowel-challenged producer in mind to bring more rock and roll edginess into the studio: **Bill Szymczyk**.

The producer already had a formidable track record helping **B.B. King**, the **James Gang** and, most notably, Joe Walsh. With Szymczyk in the studio, the Eagles would never again release another album without a rocker that was at least as strong as their ballads. [15, 1404, 1545]

Valentine, who had already had experience running Sunset Strip institutions such as the Whisky a Go Go and the Rainbow Bar & Grill; and **Peter & Gordon** alumnus **Peter Asher**, the fast-rising artist manager and record producer who would share production credits on **Linda Ronstadt**'s 1973 record *Don't Cry Now* and go on to serve as her producer for the remainder of the 1970s and into the 1980s. Asher's office was out the back door and just across the alley from the Troubadour.

The Roxy, as it came to be known by musicians and fans, was, like the initial promise of Asylum Records, designed to be artist-friendly. "It's going to have the best lighting, best sound, dressing rooms," Adler said shortly before the opening. "Everything to make the performer comfortable."

Geffen added, "We want [The Roxy] to be a great place, somewhere artists are eager to play. We want to create some excitement on the Strip."

Neil Young headlined on the club's debut night with **Graham Nash** opening, the latter being a late replacement for **Nils Lofgren**, who would have performed if not for an unfortunate bout of laryngitis.

The performers on the stage weren't the only well-known artists in the venue: the audience included such musical luminaries as **Elton John**, **Carole King**, and most notably as it relates to the story of Geffen, **Cher**.

That night, Geffen became smitten with the singer who rose to fame in 1965 as half of the **Sonny & Cher** duo, and in short time

they began seeing each other romantically. It was an unusual relationship for Geffen—who would come out as a gay man many years later—as it was his first significant heterosexual love affair.

While The Roxy was launched as an artist-friendly venue, there is a counter argument to be made that not everything about Geffen opening a new club was good for the performers, or at least not for the artists already in his stable, including the Eagles.

As Geffen achieved greater success, entrepreneurial endeavors such as a nightclub would be seen as distractions to his other duties as head of the Asylum label.

Though the undertaking was ostensibly designed to benefit groups like the Eagles, the band's second album, *Desperado*, was, at best, floundering. They might have been better served had Geffen focused on his management responsibilities without spreading himself thinner with ambitious new conquests like The Roxy and, as **Glyn Johns** observed, attempting to sign **Bob Dylan** to his label. [1115, 1541, 1542, 1581]

Felder Joins Asylum Stable; Hits Road Backing David Blue

When Don Felder, along with his wife Susan and dog Kilo, relocated to Los Angeles in 1973, they were rolling the dice he'd make it big in the City of Angels.

It involved leaving behind a stable existence in Boston, where his music career was lagging, but at least his wife's gainful employment as a secretary at the Harvard

History Research Center kept money coming in to support their young family.

Pulling up stakes was a tough decision for the couple; after all, the thought of chasing down the dream of stardom on the West Coast had been in the back of Felder's mind for years but he had never acted upon it. In summer 1972, the Felders—with Susan's reluctant support—opted to take the chance.

The Gainesville, Florida native knew at least one person in Los Angeles: his Floridian pal Bernie Leadon, who had been encouraging him for the better part of a decade to grab his guitar and make the jump westward.

After driving across the country, Felder and Susan arrived at Bernie's place in Topanga Canyon only to find that his lone contact was about to leave town for a few weeks to tour with the Eagles. With Leadon's house vacated, he suggested they crash on his floor, but advised they start looking for an apartment—and presumably work to pay for it—right away.

Felder's first steady musical job was backing Asylum artist **David Blue**, a gig he described in a 1977 interview with writer **John Tobler** by saying the employment "was offered to me and it was either handling that job or maybe taking a straight job, which was the absolute last resort."

Felder's comments at the time perhaps oversimplified the events leading up to the Blue gig. He clarified in his 2008 memoir that he'd already, in fact, been working "straight" jobs to support himself since setting up camp on the West Coast.

After donning a jacket and tie, shearing off some hair, and slicking back the rest to "look respectable," Felder showed up at a staffing agency and eventually landed a job with a decidedly un-rock-and-roll employer: IBM. This helped pay the rent while he was taking whatever music gigs he could get and looking for that elusive break.

Attempts to sign on with several bands, including a slot in **J.D. Souther**'s touring group, offered potential but didn't pan out. Still, it was through Asylum—home to Souther and the Eagles—that he met **David Geffen**, **Elliot Roberts**, and **Irving Azoff** and eventually networked his way into regular work with Blue. Leadon, naturally, made the introductions to the Asylum leadership and endorsed his fellow six-stringer as a more-than-capable musician.

Felder said after the Eagles had recorded Blue's "Outlaw Man" for their *Desperado* album, Geffen decided to put Blue—a folk-rock singer, songwriter, and musician—on some live bills and promote him as a West Coast version of **Bob Dylan**. Roberts discussed the position with Felder, who solidified his candidacy by claiming that he was a proficient lap slide and mandolin player—even though that claim was an outright lie.

Within days, Blue called and asked him to audition. In a gutsy move, Felder pleaded with his potential employer to delay the tryout for a few days, explaining he had to work his day job. Fortunately, Blue was amenable, but Leadon suggested it wasn't such a wise move. This opportunity was too good to be anything but a top priority, and it certainly was worth taking a day off from work.

"I'm going to have to take a lot more time off than that," Felder told him. "I've only got four days to learn how to play lap slide and mandolin."

On short order, Felder boned up on the required skills and familiarized himself with Blue's material from a tape provided to him by Asylum. Felder said he auditioned at **Joni Mitchell**'s home in Laurel Canyon—where Blue was staying while Mitchell was out on tour—and he was welcomed aboard.

Felder's tenure backing Blue began in September 1973 and marked a major turning point in both musicians' careers. Blue's initial dates with Felder on guitars proved successful enough to earn continued management support, and soon Blue was opening for local shows the Eagles were performing prior to the *Desperado* tour.

Touring work followed where Blue opened for **David Crosby** and **Graham Nash**, and ultimately another opportunity for Felder emerged when he spent a few months filling in for flu-stricken Crosby-Nash guitarist **David Lindley**. Lindley, in fact, had been a member of Blue's band prior to Felder's joining, but with the guitarist ailing, Felder did double-duty on the tour and collected double the pay.

Still, nothing could compare to the life-changing event that would happen in 1974 when Glenn Frey decided the Eagles needed some aggressive slide guitar playing on tracks for their upcoming *On the Border* LP; Felder would get the first call. [218, 1501]

Souther Flies In to Help Finish 'The Best of My Love'

When the Eagles landed at Olympic Studios in London in late September 1973 to begin recording their third album, to be titled *On the Border*, they were less than inspired. The months of work the band put in on *Desperado* had not borne any hit singles and, although the album did develop a cult following among fans on FM radio, the effort did not translate into commercial success.

Back in the U.K. to work again with producer **Glyn Johns**, the excitement wasn't there. Four weeks of sessions produced just two viable songs for the upcoming album, and Glenn Frey and Don Henley were struggling to complete yet another mellow love ballad, "The Best of My Love."

Frey had started developing the melody months earlier in Los Angeles; **J.D. Souther** credited a **Fred Neil** record for the inspiration. The song's sound came from a tuning exploration, Frey said: "I was playing acoustic guitar one afternoon in Laurel Canyon, and I was trying to figure out a tuning that **Joni Mitchell** had shown me a couple of days earlier. I got lost and ended up with the guitar tuning for what would later turn out to be 'The Best of My Love.'"

Frey worked up the core music, and Henley then collaborated with him on the lyrics. Like many other songs they co-wrote, the words and music came together at their favorite booth in the back behind the bar of Dan Tana's restaurant in West Hollywood. They even gave a thank-you for "Best" in the album's liner notes to the restaurant's

continued on Page 103

PATHWAY ALBUM | TIMOTHY B. SCHMIT

POCO
Crazy Eyes
Epic Records, September 1973

Poco's 1973 album, *Crazy Eyes*, represented the end of a major chapter in the band's history: It was the last with their co-founder, leader, and primary focal point, **Richie Furay**.

After putting all their best efforts into their previous LP, *A Good Feelin' to Know*, only to see it fail commercially, Furay had decided that his days in Poco were numbered. He reached out to **David Geffen**, who offered an alternative.

Hatching plans to form a new supergroup with **J.D. Souther** and ex-**Byrds**, **Flying Burrito Brothers,** and **Manassas** member **Chris Hillman**, Furay was reasonably sure that *Crazy Eyes* was to be his final Poco record. But not wanting to leave his band members in a bind, he decided to participate in the new album, which had already been in the planning stages.

Furay's bandmates knew nothing of this while recording; they wouldn't find out about his plans until the end of the sessions. Contributions from all band members were significant—so much so that a double album was considered before a decision was made to pare the song list down to a single LP.

There was something of a **Gram Parsons** theme running through the album, with two songs related to the doomed country-rock-pioneering ex-Byrd and ex-Burrito who would die coincidentally just days after the album's release. Additionally, the title track was a Furay original written about Parsons that had appeared in Poco sets as early as 1968, albeit as an acoustic number. In contrast, the band, along with producer **Jack Richardson**, transformed it into an epic, heavily orchestrated, highly produced track that would clock in at almost 10 minutes. (In an interesting parallel, the Eagles' forthcoming *On the Border* album would also include two tracks with Parsons connections.)

Other notable pieces include **Rusty Young**'s bluegrass-y instrumental "Fool's Gold," **Paul Cotton**'s environmentally savvy "Blue Water," and Timothy B. Schmit's mid-tempo number, "Here We Go Again." Rounding out the album was Furay's Poco swan song, a piece of pure pop perfection titled "Let's Dance Tonight." All told, *Crazy Eyes* was a relatively unified group effort, which should have helped convince doubters that the other band members would be able to continue without Furay.

Reaching #38 on the charts, the album outperformed *A Good Feelin' to Know* and was relatively successful by Poco's standards, but it was a case of "a day late and a dollar short" for Furay, whose next stop was the **Souther-Hillman-Furay Band**.

Poco's remaining members would decide to carry on without him, with each taking on more responsibility. This was especially true for Schmit, whose writing style and voice were arguably the most similar to their departing principal member. [1186, 1269, 1504, 1510]

maître d', Guido. Only Henley knows for sure who inspired his lyrics, but he was dating actress **Suzannah Martin** at the time.

The song, which would become the band's first #1 single, touched on the frailty of love and the anguish of slow-motion breakups. When *Rolling Stone* asked Henley about his inspiration for the song, he said, "That was the period when there were all these great-looking girls who didn't really want to have anything to do with us. We were just scruffy new kids who had no calling card. We could be cocky at times—which was really just a front—but we weren't very sophisticated or confident. We were typical, frustrated, young men. We wanted the girls to like us, but we had all the immature emotions that young men have—jealousy, envy, frustration, lust, insecurity, and the lot.

"At the same time, however, we were also becoming quite adept at brushing off girls who showed any interest in us. 'If you want to be with me, I can't possibly give you the time of day. I want that girl over there who couldn't care less if I live or die.' Hence the line in 'Desperado': 'You only want the ones that you can't get.' We knew ourselves even then. Even in our immaturity we had some insight into our flawed little characters."

"Best" wasn't finished when the band arrived in London to start recording. Johns lamented they arrived with "very little material and a pretty disparate bunch." Low on inspiration and facing their deadline, the band reached out to Souther, their friend and frequent collaborator.

"We actually worked on it over the phone until he came to England to see us," Frey told *Melody Maker*. "'[You Never] Cry Like a Lover' came about the same way, working on the phone over all that distance." On Souther's arrival, they worked out the missing bits. His contribution was the bridge: *"I'm going back in time and it's a sweet dream/It was a quiet night and I would be alright/If I could go on sleeping."* Henley declared it was "perfect."

The London sessions only produced "Best" and "Cry Like a Lover." The band told Johns they needed to go back to Los Angeles and work on more songs, but they actually had other plans. The frequent arguments over Johns' insistence that they stay true to their country-rock origins, his unwillingness to give the band more say in their sound—his decision to keep just two or three microphone on Henley's drums was contentious—and more trivial arguments over things like Johns' policy of no drugs in the studio were fueling an insurrection. The band had heard the work that producer **Bill Szymczyk** had done on Joe Walsh's *The Smoker You Drink, the Player You Get*, and liked it. The Eagles would soon make a pivotal decision that would adjust their attitude—and their music—forever. [15, 81, 209, 584, 1726, 1727, 1728, 1811]

Eagles Draw Ire by Insulting New York Dolls...in New York

New York City rightfully has a place among the globe's most famous cities, alongside Paris, Rome, and London. The iconography of the "Big Apple" includes

continued on Page 107

FALL OF THE GRIEVOUS ANGEL

EAGLES INSPIRATION PARSONS DIES IN JOSHUA TREE

When **Gram Parsons** died on September 19, 1973—like others who burned out before ultimately fading away—he sealed his legacy.

In the eyes of the world, Parsons remains perpetually 26 years old, youthful, and beautiful. He is sometimes called the "Father of Country-Rock," though he was one of numerous 1960s musicians who pioneered the kind of music the Eagles and others would play.

It's especially ironic considering Parsons wasn't out to combine rock and country as much as to play traditional, pure country music, but with the hipper, image-driven visuals and mind-altering substances associated with rock bands. Parsons rejected the term "country-rock," preferring to call it "Cosmic American Music."

Parsons' ardent devotees think of him as a musical deity, while detractors consider him a terminally doomed addict and "trust-fund kid" credited too much for his innovations while his peers are overlooked.

Whether one considers Parsons underrated or overrated, the two needn't be mutually exclusive. There were many conflicting facets to Parsons' character. He was irresistibly charismatic and charming, but frustratingly self-centered. He didn't have the most technically proficient voice, but his singing stirred tremendous emotions in listeners. He was creative and driven, yet at times undisciplined and unprofessional.

Not surprisingly, his associates and friends acknowledge his human flaws but also speak with incredible reverence and compassion for this special individual who was a tragic figure.

From the start, Parsons' life was a study in duality. He was born into incredible wealth, as his maternal grandparents owned one-third of Florida's orange groves, but also into alcoholism and depravity. "We're talking about a very classic Tennessee Williams play here; Southern money and alcoholism and just a tragedy," his bandmate in the **Flying Burrito Brothers** and **The Byrds Chris Hillman** recalled.

Parsons' father (who committed suicide), mother (who died from cirrhosis), and stepfather were all alcoholics. Parsons emerged from this background as a sensitive, introspective young man, with lots of money and baggage.

Parsons headed west in 1966 with his college group, the **International Submarine Band**. In Los Angeles, they cut the early county-rock album *Safe at Home*. His big break came in February 1968, when he met Hillman at a Beverly Hills bank and was invited to jam with The Byrds. Hillman's pre-Byrds background was playing mandolin in bluegrass bands, and Parsons convinced the band to try their hand at country.

As they recorded in Nashville and Los Angeles, a legal dispute erupted with producer **Lee Hazlewood** and his record label, who claimed Parsons was still under contract.

That dispute—and **Roger McGuinn**, Hillman, and Byrds producer **Gary Usher**'s sense that Parsons' profile on the album was getting too high—resulted in the removal of his lead vocals from three songs before *Sweetheart of the Rodeo* was released in summer 1968. Byrds and rock fans scratched their heads about the album, and country radio avoided it.

Parsons bailed on a scheduled Byrds tour of South Africa, ostensibly due to his opposing apartheid, but also to stay put and hang around with **Keith Richards** and the **Rolling Stones**. This prompted McGuinn and Hillman to fire him. It wouldn't be the last time he was kicked out of a group.

Parsons reconciled with Hillman the following year, and the two formed the Flying Burrito Brothers and recorded *The Gilded Palace of Sin*, widely considered their best work. *Burrito Deluxe* followed in May 1970, with future Eagle Bernie Leadon as a full member and contributor. If the first Burritos LP was marked by Parsons' complete dedication and discipline, the sophomore effort was a rag-tag affair, with Parsons disinterested or, at best, behaving unprofessionally.

> ## GRAM, IN FACT, ASKED ME TO GO TO FRANCE WITH HIM TO HANG OUT WITH THE ROLLING STONES, BUT GRAM HAD A TRUST FUND AND I DIDN'T. I'M VERY GLAD I DIDN'T GO...HAD I GONE I CERTAINLY WOULD NOT HAVE ENDED UP WITH THE EAGLES.
>
> ## — BERNIE LEADON

While preparing for a show, Hillman realized Parsons was missing. He found him at a Stones recording session, sitting in the corner, stoned and reluctant to leave. Hillman recalled the scene: "**Mick Jagger**, the other professional in this business, comes over to him and says, 'Gram, you have a responsibility, you have a show to do tonight. Chris is here, go with Chris. We're working.'"

Parsons' drug-induced decline continued. After numerous spotty performances, Hillman was forced to fire him from the band he'd co-founded.

"Gram, in fact, asked me to go to France with him to hang out with the Rolling Stones," Leadon said, "but Gram had a trust fund and I didn't." Leadon declined, which turned out to be a good career move. "I'm very glad I didn't go because he got into heroin. And had I gone, I certainly would not have ended up in the Eagles."

By 1973, Parsons had hooked up with future country superstar **Emmylou Harris** at the urging of Hillman, who often forgave Parsons' flakiness and served as a guiding force in his friend's career. Parsons recorded his first solo album, *GP*, with Harris playing "**Tammy Wynette**" to his "**George Jones**." Heroin, pills, and alcohol were a big part of the recording process, but the results were good and the future looked promising.

While recording his second solo LP, *Grievous Angel*, Parsons had seemingly cleaned up his act, but really hadn't. He had just learned to be sneakier, as friend and road manager **Phil Kaufman** explained: "He was hiding what he was doing, whereas before he would be more blatant about his drinking and his drugs."

While the album was being recorded, another former Byrd, **Clarence White**—one of the greatest country-rock/bluegrass guitar pickers—was killed by a drunk driver while loading gear into his vehicle. The musical fraternity was greatly affected by the senseless death, and Parsons was no exception. He showed up to the funeral completely loaded, which others felt was disrespectful. Most famously, Parsons punctuated the moment, joined by Leadon, by singing a heartfelt and impromptu a cappella version of "Farther Along," a traditional gospel song the Burritos had recorded.

Perhaps more significantly, Parsons and Kaufman made a fateful pact. "We thought Clarence wouldn't have chosen that type of funeral if he had had his choice," Kaufman said. "Gram decided that we didn't want that to happen to us. If anything should happen to us we would like to be taken out [to Joshua Tree]."

Parsons wrapped up the recording of *Grievous Angel*, but didn't live to see its release. He made a trip to his beloved Joshua Tree to celebrate the album's completion, according to Kaufman. Parsons' estranged wife, Gretchen, was told the purpose was to dry out and clean up his life.

Parsons and a few friends checked into the Joshua Tree Inn on September 18, where Gram took a lethal dose of substances. His heart stopped in the early morning hours of September 19.

It seemed everyone had seen the writing on the wall. "If Gram was here today," Kaufman quipped, "he'd still be dead. He was heading in that direction."

Leadon believed Parsons had a death wish: "He set out to become legendary by dying young. He saw that it worked well for **James Dean** and **Hank Williams**. I think he thought that was a great idea, to live a tragically excessive life, die a tragic hero, and become immortal. And he pulled it off."

Parsons' stepfather made plans to take his body back east for burial. Meanwhile, Kaufman vowed to keep the pact they had made at White's funeral. Kaufman and a friend borrowed a hearse, showed up at Los Angeles International Airport, purported to be there on official business, and effectively stole the corpse.

They drove out to the desert, dumped five gallons of gasoline on the coffin, and dropped a match. But it was anything but a proper cremation. In fact, the body didn't fully incinerate. Thirty-five pounds were left of the singer's remains, which his family eventually buried in New Orleans.

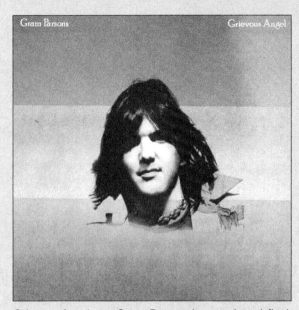

Grievous Angel was **Gram Parsons**' second, and final, studio album. Recorded in summer 1973, it included help from his close friend **Emmylou Harris**, **Linda Ronstadt**, and Eagle Bernie Leadon.

Kaufman, who still maintains he was simply honoring his friend's wishes, received a fine. It wasn't for snatching the body—there was no law on the books for that—but rather for stealing the coffin and leaving bodily remains in the desert.

In New Orleans, Parsons' gravesite was engraved with the quote "God's Own Singer," a bizarre footnote to an already bizarre tale. After all, "God's Own Singer" was a song on the second Flying Burrito Brothers album that was neither about Parsons, nor sung nor written by him. It was written and sung by Bernie Leadon.

Thus marked the undignified demise of one of the Eagles' great inspirations. "[The Flying Burrito Brothers] were the original outlaw band. And I must say, in all honesty, the Eagles really developed out of that whole syndrome," Hillman said. "And I'll never forget Glenn Frey and **J.D. Souther** opening for us as **Longbranch/Pennywhistle**. Glenn Frey was just in awe of Gram...he learned about stage presence and how to deliver a vocal, and don't think Glenn Frey wasn't in that audience studying Gram. He was." [231, 247, 306, 307, 308, 544, 739, 739, 1507, 1536, 1537, 1538]

Broadway, Times Square, the Statue of Liberty, Central Park, and the Empire State Building, to name just a few.

"The City," as it's called by folks in the region, is the central hub of the greater New York Metropolitan area, which is home to well over 20 million people. It's a financial and cultural epicenter, known for picturesque bridges, rivers, and skylines.

New York Dolls, in hindsight, might not conjure up the same thoughts of grandeur. They were never really stars. Rather, they're more remembered today as cult heroes: punky cross-dressers that pre-dated punk, but were influential to bands like **Kiss**, the **Ramones**, and the **Sex Pistols**.

In 1973, the Dolls were, in fact, the darlings of the New York glitter-rock scene. They brought a mix of **Rolling Stones** swagger and **David Bowie** androgyny, decked out in platform shoes, eyeliner, and feather boas. As *Vogue* writer **Kristin Anderson** explained, the Dolls were "at once tough and preening, [and they] bridged the androgyny of glam with what, in their wake, would become punk." At their height, they were undeniably a "New York" entity; it was built right into their name.

Not many bands making their first New York appearance would take pot shots at a popular local band, but the Eagles famously did when Glenn Frey called them "a bunch of sissies" onstage. At that point, the Eagles didn't think they were getting the attention they deserved. "Even with a Top 10 single," Frey explained, "we weren't **The Beatles**. We realized we weren't creating mass hysteria and then things started to cool out. We'd be doing 'Take It Easy' at the end of the set and no one would pay attention to the other songs."

Naturally, regional journalists were present and reported this sure-to-be provocative quip, thus beginning a long-running cold war between the Eagles and the media, especially the East Coast writers.

Ironically, despite the disdain Frey had for the whole ethos of the nascent punk movement, the rash decision to insult the locals was, in and of itself, a very "punk" move. The move gobbed in the face of local popular opinion, which created a minor public relations fiasco for a band that was still clawing its way up and had yet to achieve the fame they did later in the decade.

It wasn't particularly surprising to think that Frey and company might have held a low opinion of the Dolls when considering the disparity between what they represented and what the Eagles did.

Starting with the imagery, the L.A. quartet in denim and t-shirts downplayed visuals and stage presence, believing their music was not only far more important, but also strong enough to stand on its own without a big, flashy production. Conversely, the glitter scene was more about spectacle, with the consensus among detractors being that the bands involved could barely play their instruments.

"We don't go in for glitter or glam rock," Henley remarked in 1974. "We don't wear gorilla suits or aqualungs. Ultimately the music survives and that's what we're most interested in."

Frey poked the bear further by having the audacity to question whether the East Coast fans and critics were having the wool pulled over their eyes, incapable of recognizing quality musicianship or musical output.

Today, those who defend Frey's point of view might reference the more than 200 million Eagles records sold worldwide to support the theory that he was eminently qualified to be an arbiter of musical art and craftsmanship. For all their critical acclaim, the Dolls never scored gold, or developed a following beyond New York.

Still, when Eagles members would be seen wearing "Song Power" t-shirts as they were wont to do in the '70s, many felt (or still feel) the implied sentiments reeked of pretentiousness and arrogance, where humility may have been deemed more tasteful.

"God only knows what me, a microphone and a big PA could have done that night. You know, it's hard to.... We were..." Frey told *Rolling Stone* in 1992, struggling to find words for the Dolls incident. Henley, also in on that interview, finished his sentence. "... angry young men, using that anger to propel ourselves forward. It's not like we lost a lot of sleep about the New York Dolls."

"I think the New York critics were a real bur under our saddle," Frey added. "We became the symbol of that 'laid-back, rich and don't give a shit California lifestyle,' you know what I mean? 'These guys aren't struggling artists. Are you kidding? Even when you're just coming out, they think you jump in your convertible and go to the beach, and then, when the sun goes down,

you go to the club. We just had a problem with the New York critics. The New York Dolls were their flavor of the month, so that was probably why that came out."

Henley said he didn't understand what the Dolls hoopla was about, but admitted that the Eagles would do things that irritated the press every once in a while.

"The resentment of us was part of a larger resentment," Henley said. "There was always a cultural rivalry between New York and L.A. New York has a certain amount of chauvinism about itself, and we fed the fires by talking back. Instead of ignoring it, we always had some rebuttal, which in retrospect was probably not a good idea. And then communications [with the press] broke down completely. There was **Irving Azoff**'s famous statement: "He is an Eagle and as such does not talk to the press."

According to Frey, "That's when they started treating us nicer." [66, 1190, 1404, 1531, 1533]

Eagles Court Hartmann; Geffen Circles the Wagons

David Geffen's deal to sell off his majority stake in Asylum Records to Warner Communications Inc. in 1973 and become chairman of WCI's newly merged Elektra/Asylum label was a shock to the industry and the bands he represented. It was a bold move by WCI chief **Steve Ross**, who needed someone to improve both labels' economic woes. The fast-rising Geffen was an obvious choice. But when it came to communication with the artists and staff he had carefully cultivated, Geffen managed it clumsily, and angered more than a few of them.

One person who found himself in the deal's crossfire was agent **John Hartmann**.

Hartmann, like Geffen and his partner **Elliot Roberts**, rose from the William Morris Agency mailroom to become a booking agent and eventually the WMA liaison to **Elvis Presley**'s legendary manager, **Colonel Tom Parker**. Hartmann signed acts to WMA like **Chad & Jeremy**, a then-unknown **Sonny & Cher**, and **Buffalo Springfield**.

When Geffen and Roberts created Asylum with a relatively modest artist roster, they also kept their management team small. They hired people they were familiar with and trusted, including Hartmann and another former WMA agent, **Harlan Goodman**.

After Asylum hired both in 1970, Hartmann became one of the principal day-to-day managers for the Eagles. He, Geffen, and Roberts had all secretly watched the pre-Eagles as they rehearsed in a small hall on Ventura Boulevard in the San Fernando Valley prior to signing the band. Hartmann even took part in the famous *Desperado* photo shoot on the Paramount Ranch western movie set in December 1972, posing as one of the posse

FINDING THE RIGHT MANAGER IS KINDA LIKE FINDING THE RIGHT GIRL. WHEN YOU FINALLY GET THE PERFECT ONE, YOU WANT ONE THAT'S YOUR OWN AGE AND HAS BEEN THROUGH THE SAME TRIP AS YOU. WE WERE ALWAYS THE YOUNG GUYS DOWN THERE. NOBODY PAID MUCH ATTENTION TO US.

— DON HENLEY

standing over the "bodies" of the Eagles' outlaw gang.

Along with elevating him to the E/A chairmanship, Geffen's deal with WCI also required him to sever management ties with the artists he had developed and signed to the label. The management side of the business was left to the overburdened Roberts.

"Geffen just split the management scene entirely and became a record company president, turning the whole thing over to [Roberts and Hartmann]," Don Henley explained to *Rolling Stone* in 1975.

"It wasn't the same after that. Elliot's insights were great, but he'd been through all that stuff with Joni and Neil and Crosby and all those guys," Henley said. "Finding the right manager is kinda like finding the right girl. When you finally get the perfect one, you want one that's your own age and has been through the same trip you have. We were always the young guys down there. Nobody paid much attention to us. We found out our management company had signed **Poco** and **America** by reading *Melody Maker*."

When the group found out about Geffen's WCI deal in the press, they were angry. Over drinks at Dan Tana's restaurant, a favorite hangout a couple doors down from the Troubadour, they asked Hartmann if he would manage them. Frey liked him, even though the Eagles weren't his only responsibility at Asylum then.

Hartmann and Goodman were doing what they could to keep up with the ever-growing needs of Asylum's now-ponderous stable, but both were growing disenchanted. Then there was Geffen's long-standing promise of an ownership stake in Asylum, and Hartmann realized that with the Warner deal, those promises may never materialize.

So, according to Hartmann, in the presence of Frey and Henley, he told the band, "Yeah, OK."

But a skeptical Hartmann didn't really think there was a solid offer on the table from the Eagles. "To me, it was a product of drinking and smoking and whatever," he told an interviewer as part of the PBS feature *Inventing David Geffen*.

Unknown to Hartmann, Frey called Geffen the next morning and said Hartmann would be managing the Eagles. Geffen, livid, summoned Hartmann to his office and confronted him.

"You're leaving with the Eagles," Hartmann said, requoting Geffen's accusation from that morning. "I said, 'We were drunk out of our minds and who knows what that all meant?'"

Nonetheless, Geffen fired him before he could quit. And he wasn't done. Geffen then reached out to Henley and Frey and threatened to "bury" the Eagles if they left Asylum, reminding them that he owned their records and publishing rights. The smart move was for them to stay with Asylum, and they did. But they would not forget.

Hartmann landed on his feet. He and Goodman both walked out of Geffen-Roberts and would soon strike deals to represent Poco and America. Meanwhile, Asylum was already short-staffed and losing both made the situation far worse.

Geffen asked another recent Asylum hire, **Irving Azoff**, to take on a broader role to fill the gap, including day-to-day management of the Eagles. It was a move Geffen would later regret, even acknowledging at the time, "This guy is going to be trouble." The label chief had a clue the diminutive Azoff might be a threat but had no idea just how big. [88, 790, 1582, 1583, 1584, 1585, 1586, 1694]

Ronstadt Elevates 'Desperado'; Records It for *Don't Cry Now* LP

After the anemic chart performances of both "Tequila Sunrise" and "Outlaw Man," Asylum opted not to release any more singles from *Desperado*. Unfortunately, that initially relegated the title track to obscurity, Don Henley later told *Rolling Stone*, until **Linda Ronstadt** covered it for her 1973 *Don't Cry Now* album.

"The company was expecting us to give them more 'hits' like 'Take It Easy,' 'Witchy Woman' and 'Peaceful Easy Feeling,'" Henley said. "In fact, the *Desperado* album was not a commercial or even a critical success, but it served its purpose by establishing us as a band that was willing to roll the dice, to take chances artistically, and not just play it safe and do the expected thing."

Yet "Desperado" became one of the band's best-loved songs and a stand-alone concert staple anyway. Credit goes to two familiar collaborators: **J.D. Souther** and **Linda Ronstadt**. She recorded this update of "Desperado" under the watchful eye of Souther, who'd co-written a suite of songs around the "Doolin-Dalton" theme for *Desperado*.

And something magical happened.

Ronstadt was a native of the American West, and she brought an easy authenticity to the narrative, along with name recognition. Souther, with whom she'd recently started a romantic relationship, had an insider's intuition about how to guide her through the lyrics. The results, Henley said in the *History of the Eagles* documentary, were "poignant and beautiful."

Ronstadt's new label bosses at Asylum chose to release two other songs instead, and the highest-charting pop single was "Love Has No Pride," which stalled outside the Top 50 in early 1974. The arrival of *Don't Cry Now* co-producer **Peter Asher**, who would soon take over full time, likewise heralded her classic era.

By then, Ronstadt's recording of "Desperado" had long since become a deep-cut favorite, resonating well outside of the tight-knit group of listeners who'd initially followed the Eagles into their Old West-themed sophomore release. She'd definitively proven that the song could stand on its own. As critic **Stephen Holden** noted, not

"Desperado" was an obscure track in the Eagles catalog, albeit a deep-cut favorite among Eagles fans, but its stature changed when **Linda Ronstadt** chose to record it for her *Don't Cry Now* album in 1974.

long after *Don't Cry Now* landed on store shelves, her "straightforward yet heartfelt reading" afforded "Desperado" a "stature that does not require a conceptual context in order for it to work."

The Eagles once again had their early mentor to thank. Frey took a moment while inducting her into the Rock and Roll Hall of Fame in 2014 to note how Ronstadt's rendition of "Desperado" gave the young band "a big shot in the arm." Soon, they wouldn't have any need for such kind gestures. [1731, 1732, 1733, 1734, 1735]

continued on Page 114

TENSIONS RISE AS EAGLES, JOHNS START THIRD LP

When it comes to the Eagles' recording relationship with **Glyn Johns**, compatibility issues and disparity between philosophical outlooks had been present from the start. Still, the results had been good—commercially, with respect to the first album, and artistically, with respect to the second.

So, when it was time to record the third, *On The Border*, the band again shipped off to London to work with Johns. They planned 12 weeks of recording, but after six weeks, and only two tracks completed, everything fell apart.

"They came to England again to do the album, but they were unhappy because they didn't particularly like being in England," Johns said in an interview with **John Tobler**. "They weren't happy with each other, they weren't writing very prolifically, they were finding everything rather

difficult, they were totally insecure, and fairly miserable, and the experience wasn't very good. We had six weeks, and at the end of it, we hadn't got an awful lot done. I think they blamed me as much as anyone for that, which is the producer's lot really, and you just accept it, but obviously, I don't accept the blame."

There was some truth in what Johns claimed, but he also failed to adjust with the band's growth. He seemed more interested in fostering democracy within the band. With each passing record, the Eagles' primary leaders—Glenn Frey and Don Henley—were more willing to assert themselves. This not only led to friction with the veteran British producer, but also added to tensions in a band that featured two other musicians—Bernie Leadon and Randy Meisner—who were feeling increasingly marginalized. The stage was set for a major implosion. Less than halfway through the sessions, the band was finished with Johns.

The centerpiece of their ongoing struggles seemed to have been the disconnect that had been there since day one: the Eagles wanted to toughen up their sound, while Johns maintained they were better suited to be a country-oriented vocal band with sweet harmonies.

"The whole thing was that Glenn Frey wanted the Eagles to be a rock band and, of course, that is what they became when I stopped producing them," Johns remarked.

Henley would describe situations where Johns would be dismissive and condescending when the band told him they wanted a harder-edged sound. Henley famously told a story where he asked Johns to make his drums sound more like those of **Led Zeppelin**'s **John Bonham**, only to be brushed off with the quip, "You don't play like John Bonham."

Speaking with author **Marc Shapiro**, Randy Meisner was diplomatic but forthright: "Glenn and I were basically not getting along with Glyn as far as what we wanted to do," he said. "Glenn was probably more upset than I was but, at the time, I know I felt we needed the bass in there a little more and a harder drum sound. Glyn just didn't want to do that. No punches were thrown, but there was certainly plenty of bad feelings."

With the sessions aborted, the band departed London, and **Irving Azoff** was tasked with setting them up in a Los Angeles studio and hiring another producer.

Reflecting on the sessions later, Johns admitted the endeavor had been anything but smooth, but he deflected responsibility for it. "The six weeks in the studio were a disaster area, but I will sit here and tell you that it had nothing at all to do with

me," he insisted. "There were a lot of hang-ups, individually and with each other. But what it boils down to is they weren't ready to make another record."

Johns also held to his position that Meisner's and Leadon's roles shouldn't have been reduced. "I didn't agree with the way [Frey] and Henley were trying to take control of the band to the detriment of the other guys," he said. "So, they had me removed and they went and got **Bill Szymczyk** and spent a year making that record, which gives you a bit of a clue. I spent six weeks making the first two albums."

The two London tracks were "You Never Cry Like a Lover," which would become the second song on the LP, and, more significantly, "The Best of My Love."

While previous success—particularly with the three singles from the debut album—established the group as a moderately successful, up-and-coming band with potential, "The Best of My Love" would unexpectedly rise up the charts, hit #1, and catapult the Eagles into superstardom.

Predictably, Johns felt a sense of vindication when that single topped the charts. "I must say it put a large grin on my face when 'Best of My Love' hit a year later [after the firing]," he delighted. "That was the record that really put them on the map."

The Glyn Johns-versus-Eagles conflict is a significant sidebar in the band's history. It's hard to dismiss the producer's point of view when considering what the band accomplished under him. It's also hard to dismiss the artists' point of view when considering what they accomplished going forward without him. In the end, it seems both parties had valid perspectives on what was good for the band. [1, 6, 1404, 1494, 1539, 1540]

> "
> THEY WEREN'T HAPPY WITH EACH OTHER, THEY WEREN'T WRITING VERY PROLIFICALLY, THEY WERE FINDING EVERYTHING RATHER DIFFICULT...WE HAD SIX WEEKS AND, AT THE END OF IT, WE HADN'T GOT AN AWFUL LOT DONE. I THINK THEY BLAMED ME...I DON'T ACCEPT THE BLAME.
>
> — GLYN JOHNS

Geffen-Roberts Out, Azoff In: Eagles Tap New Manager

While working under **David Geffen** as a staff member, **Irving Azoff** got to know the members of the Eagles, and was increasingly called upon to put out their fires. The most famous anecdote occurred when Glenn Frey was incensed over a botched transportation arrangement for a gig. When the band realized they could miss their flight, Frey requested a limousine and manager **Elliot Roberts** reponded: "Glenn doesn't get a limo" and that he should "get a hippie in a cab and go to the fuckin' airport."

Azoff assured him he could take care of it, and a few calls later, a limo was on the way.

The band was already dissatisfied with their current management, which was still reeling from Asylum's sale and merger with Elektra. Don Henley described feeling betrayed when Geffen started "signing people right and left" and believed that Geffen's changing roles created a "huge conflict of interest." Azoff was interested in managing the Eagles and saw the potential for a partnership that could be mutually beneficial.

"We just wanted to find a new manager," Henley said, "and get on with our primary mission, which was music. Fortunately for us, Irving was there."

Fortunately, indeed. "The first night we met Irving," Frey said, "Henley and I and him got in a room together. There was something about it. We started telling Irving our problems with the band, our producer, how we wanted our records not to be so clean and glassy, and how we were getting the royal fuckin' screw job. ... [Azoff] was perfect from the start. Here was a guy, our own age, going through exactly the same thing, catching his rising star the same time we were. We decided that night that Irving would manage us."

"I stayed out on the road with them for ten days," Azoff told former Elektra/Asylum Chairman **Joe Smith** in his book *Off the Record*. "Immediately they came to me because **Jerry Rubenstein**, their business manager, was also a business manager for Geffen-Roberts. Jerry had taken all the money from the tour to pay back commissions to Geffen-Roberts, so there was a war from day one that I was trying to mediate. They were very unhappy with the *Desperado* LP that **Glyn Johns** produced. I thought the album was poorly produced too."

Johns was the most immediate problem, so Azoff offered a suggestion. He played them some tapes that **Bill Szymczyk** mixed for Joe Walsh and said, "You need to go back in [the studio] with someone like Szymczyk—we need to hear some more guitars."

The band agreed and that led to scrapping most of their London work. They hired Szymczyk and brought in Bernie Leadon's old bandmate, Don Felder, to sit in on a couple of tracks. Geffen was livid. "That was the turning point," Azoff remembered. "I'm not taking any credit for the turning point in their music, but it turned."

Azoff said that Geffen and Roberts reneged on his compensation about six months later,

continued on Page 119

BARNSTORM
Meadows
ABC-Dunhill Records, January 1974

Joe Walsh has always been known as the life of the party, the winking (now-reformed) hard-living rock star. So, what to make of kinder, gentler moments like "Meadows" from **Barnstorm**'s second album, *The Smoker You Drink, the Player You Get?*

In truth, a subtle introspection has always run through his music, from the dreamy uncertainties of "Take a Look Around" on the **James Gang**'s first album and "Pretty Maids in a Row" on *Hotel California*, to the quiet romanticism of "Rosewood Bitters" on *The Confessor* and "Spanish Dancer" on *Analog Man*. So, "Meadows" isn't the exception that proves any fun-loving rule. It's actually part of a continuum of moments when Walsh pulled down his fast-lane-driving jokester's mask to reveal something much deeper.

The Smoker You Drink, the Player You Get would become his breakout post-James Gang moment in 1973 with a huge assist from "Rocky Mountain Way," a more predictably rollicking song that came to Walsh while he was cutting the grass in his newly adopted hometown of Boulder. Walsh thoughtlessly dashed inside to scribble out the lyrics, and the still-running lawnmower continued through a neighbor's garden.

Typically zany stuff in those years.

But Walsh then followed that Top 25 single with the much quieter "Meadows," which also found inspiration in wide-open spaces, this time in Massachusetts. "I was driving around one morning and it was foggy," Walsh later told DJ **Redbeard** of *In the Studio*, "and I looked across this meadow, and it was beautiful. There were horses. It was a horse farm, and there was this old falling-down barn."

The moment drew Walsh in, and he began to take in the setting's finer details. "The thing I noticed for the first time was there was about a half-mile wall," he added, "and there's walls all over New England that used to be property dividers. The farmers would pile rocks up along the border of their land, to clear the land to farm. And I was kind of lonely and it was a real foggy morning, and I was in a very thoughtful mood."

A song about the barriers lovers put between themselves was born, taking Walsh a world away from the joyous party vibe of "Rocky Mountain Way." Perhaps predictably, "Meadows" stalled at #89, some 66 spots lower than the album's upbeat lead single. But, in its own deeply personal way, "Meadows" once again completed a surprisingly complex portrait of who Joe Walsh really is. [1828, 1829]

FELDER SITS IN FOR 'GOOD DAY IN HELL,' AND STAYS

Don Felder got a call to do some session work in January 1974. Recently transplanted from the East Coast, he and his pregnant wife were living in rustic Topanga Canyon just outside of Los Angeles. He had played some live shows with **David Blue**, and had been backing **David Crosby** and **Graham Nash** on some concert dates. But Felder was still looking for a steadier gig when Glenn Frey dialed him up.

According to Felder, Frey said, "We were wondering if you could come into L.A. tomorrow, to the Record Plant, and help us out with a song we're recording for this new album. We need someone who can play some real dirty slide on it, and we obviously know you can play and thought you might be interested."

Felder accepted the invitation and told Frey he'd see him the next day. Felder met **Bill Szymczyk**, and later learned it was the band's producer who had suggested that if the Eagles wanted to toughen up their sound, they might consider adding another guitar player to the lineup.

Frey was connecting the dots. "I've been a Don Felder fan for about a year and a half, ever since I heard him playing in a dressing room in Boston one night," he later told *Crawdaddy*'s **David Rensin**, who observed the Eagle was brimming with excitement.

"I saw him at a concert in L.A. and asked if he'd come down and put some slide on 'Good Day In Hell,' but with every take, he just blew us all away," Frey said. "If he isn't **Duane Allman** reincarnate, I don't know who the fuck is."

When "Good Day in Hell" went well, Szymczyk and the band threw "Already Gone" at Felder, who laid down a blazing new lead guitar intro, and suddenly the three-chord song had lots more rock and roll firepower.

Throughout it all, Felder continued to think he

was doing one-off session work, but the very next day, he received another phone call, this time asking him to join the band.

Frey credited Felder's impressive performance for winning him the job: "I think he came in and played guitar so damn good," he said, "I think we all kind of decided that we wanted him."

Don Henley agreed: "I think Glenn and I kind of flashed on it at the same time. I think Glenn called me up or something and said, 'I think we'd better get this guy in the band,' and I said, 'I think you're right.'"

"We had a discussion last night after you left and decided that we all want you to join the band," Frey told Felder the next day.

"We never thought there'd be more than four Eagles, but we've had a band meeting and we've decided we'd like you to join us. You'd really fit in. Will you, Don? Will you join the Eagles?"

When a shocked Felder could only say yes, Frey told him to come back to the Record Plant the next day.

Felder wondered how it would go over when he broke the news to Nash and Crosby. Fortunately, Nash was empathetic and encouraging; he told Felder that being in a band was better than being a sideman and gave his blessing.

"As soon as the possibility of joining the Eagles came up, I flashed on all the possibilities of players and voices," Felder reflected later, speaking with **Barbara Charone** of *Hit Parader*. "I looked at all the players and pieces and how they had been put together, plus the versatility of the group. And it was a mindblower."

Among other things, Felder's addition allowed the band to play double-lead guitar riffs and solos while a third acoustic or electric guitar could keep working with the rhythm section during solos and instrumental passages.

> BERNIE AND FELDER ARE PROUD GUITAR PLAYERS AND TO ME, AND I DON'T MEAN TO MAKE THEIR WORK COMPARATIVE, BUT RESPECTIVELY, THEY'RE CARRYING ON THE WORK OF CLARENCE WHITE AND DUANE ALLMAN.
>
> — GLENN FREY

As Frey explained, "We really felt that we wanted to have a third guitar player. As a matter of fact, the guy who's now our road manager, **Tommy Nixon**, who helped write 'Out of Control' [from *Desperado*] used to come on stage and play rhythm guitar on [that song] so that Bernie and I could play the harmony solo. Yeah, we thought five pieces would work to some advantage that way."

Frey went on to praise both his fellow Eagles guitarists. "I love to say this. Bernie and Felder are proud guitar players and to me, and I don't mean to make their work comparative, but respectively, they're carrying on the work of **Clarence White** and Duane Allman."

But from his very first Eagles session, Felder had observed the tensions within the band. When Randy Meisner heralded Felder's arrival, he might have made an understatement when he said, "We sure could use some sanity."

As Felder further reflected in his memoir *Heaven and Hell*, "A reporter from *Rolling Stone* once quoted me as saying I felt like I was joining a band that was just breaking up. 'Bernie was bouncing off the wall and Randy was threatening to quit,' I told him. 'It was like walking with a keg of dynamite on your back with the fuse lit, only you don't know how long the fuse is.'"

"What I didn't say," Felder wrote, "is that it felt like this all the time. ... Not a day passed during the recording of [*On the Border*] when someone didn't blow his top, throw something, or stalk out, slamming the door behind him. Each was fighting for control of the band and the musical direction it was taking."

On Felder's first day as an official Eagle, each member approached him to offer congratulations, but his pal Bernie Leadon reportedly whispered in his ear, "Don't say I didn't warn you." [218, 1501]

DAN FOGELBERG

Dan **Fogelberg** had already released his debut album, *Home Free*, to limited acclaim when his new friend Joe Walsh took over as producer for the follow-up, *Souvenirs*, in 1974. Prior to that, the Illinois-born Fogelberg spent years as a Nashville sessions guy, an unknown L.A. folk singer, and an opening act for **Van Morrison**.

Fogelberg took part in sessions for Walsh's *So What* the same year, but only as a faceless figure in the background. Walsh, who shared manager **Irving Azoff** with Fogelberg, aimed to right this obvious wrong. Walsh made *Souvenirs* into a passion project, playing on 10 of the album's 11 tracks. In a sign of things to come, Walsh's future Eagles bandmates Don Henley and Glenn Frey also appeared.

Something clicked. *Souvenirs* raced to #17 on the *Billboard* Top 200 in early 1975 and was eventually certified platinum. The radio-ready "Part of the Plan" led the way, becoming the first of Fogelberg's eleven Top 40 singles. Newfound interest eventually lifted *Home Free* to million-selling status, too. A star was born, along with a lasting connection.

Fogelberg and Walsh developed an easy rapport through shared experiences. Fogelberg was in the studio at the same time the Eagles were recording *On the Border*, and Fogelberg opened for the Eagles for a couple of years.

"It took all the pressure off, and it was nice being out with friends," Fogelberg told *Rock Around the World* in 1977. "We were all the same band as far as we were concerned really, and they would go out of their way to help me."

Frey returned to sing backing vocals on "Hard to Say," striking gold again as it became a Top 10 1981 smash from *The Innocent Age*. Fogelberg's sixth album proved to be a commercial and critical peak, spinning off two other Top 10 hits, including "Leader of the Band," a tribute to Fogelberg's musician father.

Fogelberg later toured with Walsh's longtime bandmate **Joe Vitale**. Timothy B. Schmit was part of Fogelberg's band up until the Eagles finally reunited in the '90s, and Fogelberg always remained close with Azoff.

"Irving and I met at the University of Illinois, moved to L.A. together in the early 1970s, knocked on doors together," Fogelberg told

Joel Hirschhorn in 2003. "Irving was seminal in helping me achieve success, and he also protected me. So, I had the total freedom to create just music. 'You do the music, I'll take care of the business.' He completely understood me."

It was Azoff who pegged "Leader of the Band" as a potential hit. "That surprised me," Fogelberg told Hirschhorn. "I'm always surprised by what does and doesn't work."

Along the way, Fogelberg became forever linked with the Eagles, though he apparently didn't mind. After all, their friendships informed the music. "Myself, the Eagles, and the **Flying Burrito Brothers** kind of pioneered that sound in California," he acknowledged in an interview with *The Oklahoman* in 1995.

The Eagles later took part in a salute to Fogelberg, who died in 2007 after a three-year battle with cancer. *A Tribute to Dan Fogelberg* featured their cover of "Part of the Plan," though it took a heroic effort on Walsh's part.

Jean Fogelberg, Dan's widow, got an early commitment from Walsh in June 2011 to participate, initially as a solo act for an update of "Part of the Plan." "He played all the instruments except the keyboards and he sang the lead vocals and harmonies," Jean said in the tribute album's liner notes, "before it was decided that the rest of the Eagles would join him on the track."

Scheduling became an issue, however, as the group launched the lengthy *History of the Eagles* tour. Walsh took tapes with him on the road, staying in contact with Jean as he tried to fit in time to add the others. By the time they finally had the chance, in December 2015, Frey was battling a stomach ailment. Henley and Schmit added their vocals, and "Part of the Plan" was as complete as it would ever be.

Walsh's track notes included an emotional message to Fogelberg: "I miss you, Danny." Jean said Walsh was "one of the few people on the planet that Dan didn't mind calling him 'Danny.'" Ultimately, she said he became "the hero of this song story" and that "Joe went above and beyond to honor Dan."

Frey died the following January. [1830, 1832, 1833, 1834]

---

and he quit. "When they figured out that several acts would be going with me, they said 'No, you have to stay.' I went back to the acts and said I was going to stay, and Henley and Frey talked me out of staying. They said they were going to leave, even if I didn't."

Azoff arranged a meeting between the band, Geffen, and Roberts to assert a fundamental conflict of interest with the duo still managing the band. When the Eagles expressed their desire to break ties entirely Geffen was furious with Azoff, feeling he had again been betrayed by one of his staff.

Nevertheless, Geffen didn't try to dissuade the group from leaving. He still ran their record label and would continue to benefit financially if the band succeeded, regardless of who was managing them. The relationship between Geffen and Azoff was adversarial, but the choices each made reflected their personalities as businessmen.

In Azoff's case, his complete willingness to go all out for his clients and protect them at all costs was precisely what appealed to the Eagles so much. They didn't call him "Big Shorty" for nothing. [1, 6, 88, 481, 2132]

WINTER 1973-74

 RELEASES
▶ **Barnstorm**, with Joe Walsh, "Meadows" (single)

 NUGGETS
▶ Glenn Frey, guitar case in hand, bumps into **Olivia Newton John**—brand new to Los Angeles—by chance at the Sunset Marquis hotel in West Hollywood and they have a friendly chat about their touring lives. The next day she receives a dozen red roses from Frey welcoming her to the states. And their paths never cross again. —*Olivia Newton John, Don't Stop Believin'*
▶ Don Felder, formerly of David Blue's backup band, has joined the Eagles as a fifth member. —*Record World*

 ON THE ROAD WITH ...
▶ **Eagles**: Dan Fogelberg, James Montgomery Blues Band, Jesse Colin Young, John Martyn, Linda Ronstadt, Maria Muldaur, McKendree Spring, Ned Doheny
▶ **Poco**, with Timothy B. Schmit: Cheryl Dilcher, Leo Kottke, The Guess Who
▶ **Barnstorm**, with Joe Walsh: REO Speedwagon

 COLLABORATIONS
▶ **Joe Walsh** played slide guitar on the singles "Whiskey Night," "Open Up," and "Start A New Life" on **REO Speedwagon**'s album *Ridin' The Storm Out*.
▶ **Bernie Leadon** played electric, acoustic and resonator guitar on the singles "Return of the Grievous Angel," "Hearts on Fire," and "In My Hour of Darkness" on **Gram Parsons**' album *Grievous Angel.*

 ON SCREEN
▶ **Joe Walsh** appeared on the ABC-TV show *In Concert.* **Cheech & Chong** and **Bonnie Bramlett** also appeared.

Johns Out, Szymczyk In: *On the Border* Sessions Move to L.A.

Tasked with finding a studio in Los Angeles and a new producer to replace **Glyn Johns** so the Eagles could finish *On the Border*, **Irving Azoff** secured time at Record Plant, on West Third Street, a few minutes' drive from the Troubadour, Dan Tana's, and the Sunset Strip.

Azoff looked no further than his own stable to fill the producer slot. His client Joe Walsh had recently recorded *The Smoker You Drink, The Player You Get* with **Bill Szymczyk**, who'd also been Walsh's **James Gang** producer.

The Eagles were impressed by Szymczyk's track record, having been a producer for not only Walsh and his more electric guitar-oriented music, but also for others like blues royalty figure **B.B. King**.

While Johns would regularly dismiss the band's desire to feed their rock and roll influences, Szymczyk didn't confine the band in a mellow, harmony-singer box. He was willing to indulge their instincts to broaden their sounds beyond "limp-wristed L.A. country-rock," as Frey once referred to it, and that excited the band.

"I saw through the Eagles as far as their acoustic L.A. cowboy [persona goes] and saw rockers dying—screaming—to get out," Szymczyk said, looking back. "I think I helped them."

While Johns had given Henley the brush-off when he asked to have the drums sound more like **John Bonham**'s, Szymczyk was more receptive.

After two albums with producer **Glyn Johns**, the Eagles decided to chart a new musical course for their next album, *On the Border*, by hiring **Bill Szymczyk** (far right), who had produced the **James Gang**, the **J. Geils Band**, Joe Walsh, and **B.B. King**.

"They asked me questions like, 'How many mics do you put on the drums?'" he recalled. "And when I said, 'Seven or eight or nine,' they went, 'Yeah, yeah, yeah! That's good!'"

Henley was certainly moved by that notion, according to Szymczyk: "Glyn used two or three (mics) at the most. Don wanted to be a rock drummer, and he heard the sounds they were getting on rock records. That's what he wanted."

With the band and producer seeming like a mutual fit, they could begin working, but not before Szymczyk reached out to his predecessor in an act of professional courtesy.

"I agreed [to produce them], but on one condition: that I check in with Glyn and that he was OK with it," he said. "He was one of the producers I had looked up to for a long time."

When Szymczyk reached Johns in London, he got the impression the feelings between the band and their former producer were mutual: "He said, 'Better you than me, mate!'"

Years later, Henley opined that Szymczyk immediately brought "freedom and fun. Bill was much less rigid than Glyn Johns in his approach to recording and producing. We in the band had much more of a say in how things were done." [15, 88, 1404, 1495, 1523]

YAZZ ART MAKES 'BEAUTIFUL' *BORDER* STATEMENT

Eagles had leaned on the artistic talents of **Gary Burden** and **Henry Diltz** for their first two album covers. As the group approached the end of production for their third album, Burden again helped them project the imagery they wanted.

Burden found the artwork that adorned the cover of *On the Border* at a rummage sale. The painting of an eagle carrying a snake against the setting sun and a Devil's Tower-like background was simple yet striking. He bought it for just a quarter without knowing it was an original or who the artist was.

"I just thought it was a beautiful thing," Burden said in his blog in 2009, almost a decade before his death. "When it came time to create the artwork for *On the Border*, I pulled out this piece of art, which I had been thinking about, and suggested it to the

band for the album cover. Everyone agreed it would be perfect."

Burden did some research to secure the image rights and learned the painting was by Navajo artist **Beatien Yazz**, which translates to **Little No Shirt**. Yazz picked up his mail at a trading post on the Navajo reservation near Wide Ruins, Arizona, so Burden had Elektra/Asylum send the royalty payment there.

"The record company sent a sizable check to the artist, and we never heard if he got it or not," Burden wrote. "If so, it must have come as a surprise—money out of the blue. I always have felt good that millions of people who bought or saw this Eagles album cover, who never would have been exposed to this wonderful Navajo art otherwise, got to see it and hold it in their hands. A

painting by a great Navajo artist immortalized by a rock and roll band's album cover is a very good cross-cultural exchange thing."

Yazz, or **Jimmy Toddy**, as he is commonly known, did receive the check, according to his late son, **Irving Toddy**. Irving replied to Burden's blog post four years later and said his father, then 86 years old, was "honored and surprised to have his art featured on the album cover." Another son, **Marvin Toddy**, said his father was 94 and living in New Mexico in 2022; he had stopped painting in the early 1990s after his eyesight deteriorated.

Although the Eagles cover gave his art a broad audience, Yazz was already one of the world's foremost contemporary Native American painters. His traditional fine line paintings, which typically featured everyday life on the Navajo reservation, had won him awards at every major showing of Native American art in the United States.

Yazz started as a youngster at Wide Ruins when the proprietors of the Navajo trading post recognized and nurtured his painting skills in the mid-1930s. A museum in Springfield, Illinois, became the first venue to exhibit his work when he was just 10 years old. His creative ambition took a brief detour as a teenager when Yazz lied about his age and joined the U.S. Marine Corps during World War II, becoming one of the famed Navajo Code Talkers.

His career as an artist took off in the 1950s when his illustrations appeared in two well-received books, *Spin a Silver Dollar* and *Paint the Wind*, both later condensed by *Reader's Digest* and featured on the

New Eagles
are soarin' your way
with an album
that's gonna take you
border to border.

asylum

popular *Cavalcade of America* television show. Yazz was nearly 50 years old when the check from Elektra/Asylum was delivered to the Wide Ruins Trading Post.

Once Burden had received approval to use the artwork, he turned his attention to the rest of the album cover. He credited his "friend and brother" **Rick Griffin** for creating the distinctive type used on the back cover. Griffin was already rock illustration royalty thanks to the memorable psychedelic art he provided for an array of **Bill Graham** shows, **Jimi Hendrix** and **John Mayall**, and, of course, the **Grateful Dead**. Diltz shot the album's inside double-sided poster photographs, with the band decked out in denim-on-denim attire. Then Griffin applied his signature style to all the text that adorned the back cover, giving the band's name, album title, and song names a bold Southwestern-yet-psychedelic flavor.

In the liner notes on the album's back cover **Bill Szymczyk** earned top-billing as the album's producer and engineer, with assistance credits also extended to **Allan Blazek** and **Gary Ladinsky**. But the band also gave credit to **Glyn Johns** for producing and engineering two singles from the abbreviated sessions in London, "You Never Cry Like a Lover" and "The Best of My Love." Szymczyk also earned credit for remixing portions of those songs.

Special thanks were given to Eagles manager "**Irv**" **Azoff**, **Jackson Browne**, Don Felder, the band's road manager **Richard Fernandez**, Asylum President **David Geffen**, publicist **Jennie Halsall**, road manager **Tom "The Good Bull" Nixon**, Don Henley's former **Shiloh** bandmate **Al Perkins**, **Elliot Roberts**, **J.D. Souther**, Geffen-Roberts artist manager **Ron Stone** and to the "fire gods Nido and Wotan," a reference that remains one of the band's enduring liner note mysteries.

The final note also offered a vague tribute to former Elektra/Asylum promotions director **Paul Ahern**, who was also Glenn Frey's roommate during the band's early years. "Extra special thanks to

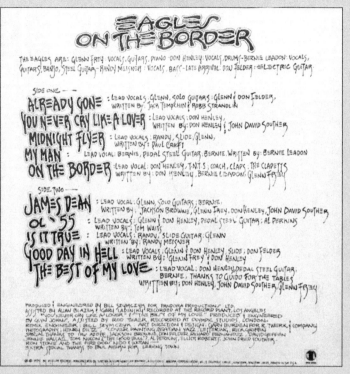

Gary Burden gathered a unique set of talents for the *On the Border* cover. **Beatien Yazz**, **Rick Griffin**, and **Henry Diltz** created a complete LP package.

Paul Ahern for leaving town," the band inscribed as the final line on the back cover. This curious note had a degrees-of-separation connection. The band hired Szymczyk to finish the album at Azoff's behest. Azoff also represented Joe Walsh and **Dan Fogelberg**. While the Eagles and Szymczyk were recording *On the Border*, Walsh was in Colorado producing Fogelberg's *Souvenirs* LP. And tucked in the liner notes of that album, also released in 1974, Fogelberg wrote: "Special thanks to...Paul Ahern, for coming back to town."

With *On the Border*, the Eagles continued projecting their country-rock image even though the album's music was breaking those bonds. And while not as elaborate or thematic as *Desperado*, the *On the Border* package remained distinctive. And Yazz's art set the tone. Burden in 2009 reveled in still having the original Yazz artwork in his collection and wrote that he still thought it was a beautiful thing.

"Now it's a famous beautiful thing." [2109, 2110, 2111, 2112]

ON THE BORDER

Eagles were bitterly disappointed by *Desperado*'s commercial failure. They were determined to explore a different path in their musical journey. A new producer would bring freedom and a new musical attitude. Turbulent times were on the horizon, but so was late-arriving success that lifted the band to heights they'd only seen in their dreams.

SPRING 1974

RELEASES
- ▶ **Eagles**, *On the Border* (album)
- ▶ **Poco**, with Timothy B. Schmit, "Faith in the Families" (single)
- ▶ **Poco**, with Timothy B. Schmit, *Seven* (album)

NUGGETS
- ▶ ABC agrees to air the huge California Jam outdoor concert, including the Eagles' set, over four spring *In Concert* specials hosted by **Don Kirshner**. The concert will exceed the size of Woodstock, but not the cultural significance. —*Record World*
- ▶ **Irving Azoff** creates Front Line Management, representing four music acts: Eagles, Joe Walsh and **Barnstorm**, **Dan Fogelberg**, and **REO Speedwagon**. Front Line also represents two producers, **Bill Szymczyk** and **Allan Blazek**, who produced Eagles' *On the Border*. —*Cashbox*
- ▶ Eagles are heading to Great Britain this summer to headline a series of one nighters. They last toured England in 1973 as the support band for **Neil Young**. —*Cashbox*

COLLABORATIONS
- ▶ **Timothy B. Schmit** was a performer on **Bob Neuwirth**'s album *Bob Neuwirth*.
- ▶ **Timothy B. Schmit** provided backing vocals on the singles "Rikki Don't Lose That Number," "Barrytown," and "Pretzel Logic" on **Steely Dan**'s album *Pretzel Logic*.

ON SCREEN
- ▶ **Michael Stanley**, with **Joe Walsh**, appeared on the NBC-TV show *Don Kirshner's Rock Concert*. **Bill Szymczyk** gathered **Dan Fogelberg**, **David Sanborn**, Joe Walsh, and **Joe Vitale** to back Stanley as "Michael Stanley's Super Session." **Ike & Tina Turner** also appeared.

ON SCREEN (cont.)
- ▶ Eagles headlined on the syndicated TV show *Don Kirshner's Rock Concert* (Episode 1.20). **Jackson Browne** and **Linda Ronstadt** also performed.
- ▶ Eagles appeared on the ABC-TV show *In Concert: California Jam - Part I*, alongside **Black Oak Arkansas**, **Black Sabbath**, **Deep Purple**, **Earth, Wind & Fire**, **Emerson, Lake & Palmer**, **Rare Earth,** and **Seals & Crofts**.

ON THE ROAD WITH ...
- ▶ **Eagles**: Dan Fogelberg, Jackson Browne, Jesse Colin Young, Leo Kottke, Linda Ronstadt, REO Speedwagon, The Edgar Winter Group, The Marshall Tucker Band
- ▶ **Poco**, with Timothy B. Schmit: Commander Cody, Henry Gross, James Cotton Blues Band, King Crimson, Pure Prairie League, Robin Trower, The Doobie Brothers, The Kinks
- ▶ **Barnstorm**, with Joe Walsh: The Marshall Tucker Band

'Eagles Limited' Math: The Division From Addition

The arrival of Don Felder changed the dynamics of the Eagles enterprise as spring 1974 approached. When the band began, the four founding members divided profits equally. But the Eagles' world had changed since Bernie Leadon gave **David Geffen** a "do you want us or not" ultimatum in his Sunset Strip office in Los Angeles.

In the almost two years since then, Geffen had sold off Asylum Records to Warner Communications, and the band had brought on a new manager, **Irving Azoff**, who was closer to their age and willing to fight for their right to do whatever.

continued on Page 131

RELEASE
Late April
1974

ALREADY GONE
By: Jack Tempchin and Robb Strandlund
Side B: Is It True? (Meisner)

A new album, a new producer and fresh material with commercial appeal got the Eagles' *On the Border* LP out of the gate quickly in spring 1974. "Already Gone" proved to be the rocker needed to get the band back to charting in the Top 20, giving radio a reason to play them again and allowing them to move on from the disappointment that lingered around the then-commercial failure of *Desperado*.

AIRPLAY

"Already Gone" hit the airwaves first on WIXY-Cleveland, and then program directors around the country began spinning the single and keeping it on the charts from mid-April through August. Midwest and Northeast stations continued their warm embrace, but the band emerged as a crossover group after the single was put into heavy rotation in Tennessee, Georgia, Virginia, Alabama, Texas, and Louisiana. Stations in the Southeast had emerged as the Eagles' most faithful region, with most singles they released becoming "automatic adds" going forward.

36 PLAYLIST ADDS Spring-Summer 1974

Region	Apr	May	Jun	Regional Airplay
Northeast	1	1	8	27.7 %
Southeast	0	7	6	36.1 %
Midwest	1	3	5	25 %
Southwest	0	2	0	5.6 %
West	1	1	0	5.6 %

FIRST-WAVE STATIONS Stations that added the song in the first 30 days

WIXY-Cleveland
WDGY-Minneapolis
WLAV-Grand Rapids
KLEO-Wichita

WBRU-Providence
WMMR-FM-Philadelphia

KGB-San Diego
KPRI-FM-San Diego

WROV-Roanoke
WSGN-Birmingham
WFOM-Marietta
WKWK-Wheeling
WMPS-Memphis
WLAC, WMAK-Nashville

KLIF-Dallas
KZEW-Dallas

CHARTS

Billboard
#**32**
June 29, 1974

Cashbox
#**17**
July 6, 1974

Record World
#**19**
July 6, 1974

HIGHEST CHARTING WEEK: CASHBOX - July 6, 1974

SINGLE	ARTIST	# PREV WK
1. Billy Don't Be a Hero	Bo Donaldson and the Heywoods	2
2. Rock the Boat	Hues Corporation	4
3. Be Thankful for What You Got	William DeVaughn	3
4. Rock Your Baby	George McCrae	9
5. Sundown	Gordon Lightfoot	1
6. If You Love Me, Let Me Know	Olivia Newton-John	6
7. Hollywood Swinging	Kool & The Gang	8
8. Annie's Song	John Denver	12
17. ALREADY GONE	**EAGLES**	**17**

Sources: Billboard, Cashbox, Record World

'ALREADY GONE' SIGNALS A HARDER EAGLES EDGE

As evidenced by **Jackson Browne's** "Nightingale," **David Blue's** "Outlaw Man," and **Gene Clark's** (co-written with Bernie Leadon) "Train Leaves Here This Morning," the Eagles were always open to recording songs by outside writers. They had already earned good airplay with **Jack Tempchin's** "Peaceful Easy Feeling," and they would again see potential in another song the San Diego native had co-written called "Already Gone."

Tempchin's collaborator was tunesmith **Robb Strandlund**, a pure country singer with a twangy delivery. The two, in fact, conceived "Already Gone" as a country song when they wrote it one night at the Back Door Coffeehouse in San Diego, where Tempchin was booking musical acts and sometimes performing.

"I booked [Strandlund]—he and I were going to do this show," Tempchin recalled. "But we looked at our refrigerator in the back room, and there was a jug and we started drinking some hard cider. We got feelin' pretty good…we wrote 'Already Gone' in about 20 minutes. Then we went onstage and played it."

The song wasn't about a breaking relationship with a girl, Strandlund told *Time Passages*. Rather, it was two songwriters conjuring an impromptu ballad that railed against the recording industry.

"We were backstage between shows drinking some wine when we started complaining about the music business slimeballs we were dealing with in Los Angeles," Strandlund said. "We both felt we were the talent and they were leeching off of it. Without us they had nothing, so we started to say we were 'already gone.' And we started to write a song. We were trading verses and after about ten each, [we] decided to write them down," he said. "After settling on three, we took to the stage, taped the lyrics to a mic stand, and opened the show with it. Jack was friends with Glenn Frey, so that's how the song got to the Eagles. Glenn changed the lyrics from 'my friend' to 'my girl' to improve its commercial appeal."

Tempchin, according to a 2017 article by journalist **Dale Kawashima**, figured Glenn must have heard it that night. "He must have been there, because he called me a couple of years later. He said, 'You know that country song you wrote? I think I can make a great rock record out of it.'"

The details may be fuzzy, because in a more recent interview with *Billboard*, Tempchin suggested the Eagles learned about the track after obtaining a tape of the song. Tempchin theorized a recording may have surfaced after he coaxed Jackson Browne into performing it with him at a show in Escondido, California. This rendition of events seems more consistent with the story told by Frey.

"I got a tape of the song from Jack Tempchin in my mailbox at 1740 La Fontaine Court, the house in Coldwater Canyon where I lived for 16 years," Frey said. He indicated the residence held many great memories. "A lot of music happened there. 'Already Gone,' though, arrived in the mail."

What is indisputable, though, is that Frey had a strong vision of where he could take the song and what it could be, much in the same way he saw huge potential in Browne's "Take It Easy." And Frey saw this one as a rocker, not a country ditty.

"They called Glenn 'The Lone Arranger,' because he would just hear the song and he would know what kind of record it should be," Tempchin complimented. "He would look into the vast vault of his knowledge of every type of American music, from Philly to bluegrass...he knew it all."

Strandlund would record the song himself and release it on his 1976 self-titled album, although his version would retain the original country feel, with a lilting bounce and quiet cross-sticks on the snare drum.

The fierce electric guitar licks executed by Don Felder that punctuated the Eagles' version, as well as Randy Meisner's thumping bass lines, were musical passages unique to the recording that would kick off the *On the Border* album. Their take almost comes off as a statement of intent for a band with not only a new record, but a new producer, a new guitar player, and a new dedication to

Robb Strandlund (above) wrote "Already Gone" with **Jack Tempchin** in a San Diego coffeehouse, but the song wasn't about a girl at the time. Rather, it painted an unflattering picture of the recording industry.

cranking up their rockier side.

As Frey explained, "I left England [and former producer **Glyn Johns**] behind and had a much more positive energy in the recording studio. The 'all right, nighty-night' at the end of ["Already Gone"] was sort of typical of the spontaneous feeling we wanted on our records. ... I was much more comfortable in the studio with **Bill [Szymczyk]**, and he was more than willing to let everyone stretch a bit. 'Already Gone'—that's me being happier; that's me being free."

Also the leadoff single from *On the Border*, "Already Gone" put the Eagles back into the Top 40 in the weeks after its release on April 19, 1974. [209, 336, 598, 1447, 1448, 1486]

The band had also freed itself from a restrictive studio relationship with famed producer **Glyn Johns**. Now, with a new studio attitude and a producer willing to let them rock, they brought in Felder to give them a harder rock edge and then invited him to join the band. These were dramatic changes.

With *On the Border* completed, it came time to discuss how to divvy the album's proceeds with a fifth band member. Does an expert guitarist who the band actively recruited and brought into the fold get an equal share of everything when he arrived more than halfway through the recording session? And further, should he get an equal share of proceeds from touring and merchandise sales?

Over the years, the Eagles have been understandably silent when it comes to discussing financial matters, and the alleged details of how Eagles Limited was set up surfaced only after the band fired Felder in February 2001. He and the band exchanged lawsuits, and Felder published a tell-all book in 2009, *Heaven and Hell: My Life with the Eagles,* that explained his side of the story.

With a change to the four-way income split necessary now that Felder was the fifth member, the group met in Azoff's office, and everyone agreed they would all be full partners in a new legal entity, Eagles Limited. All proceeds from touring, merchandising, and recording royalties would run through the company and be divided five ways, Felder said.

But the new guitarist was credited on just two songs, and that point was emphasized by Felder's longtime friend Bernie Leadon, who didn't think an equal split was fair. Felder said that Frey mediated a bit, saying that there were no "side men" with the Eagles, and that everyone there knew how that felt.

But others agreed with Leadon, so Azoff suggested that Felder get one-fifth of the profits for the cuts he played on, "Good Day in Hell" and "Already Gone." Felder happily agreed, and the band managed its finances that way through and beyond their breakup in 1980.

The Eagles Limited relationship would continue through hell freezing over in 1994. But things would change in 2001, and a disappointed Felder would find himself on the outside looking in. [1826, 1827, 1879]

Felder Debuts as Eagle With *On the Border*

When Asylum released *On the Border* in March 1974, the credits listed Don Felder as a "late arrival."

"*On the Border* was two-thirds completed when we did 'Good Day in Hell' and asked Felder to play slide," Frey remembered. "Every take we did just got better and better. My first reaction was this could be a great five-piece band. Felder kicks our rock stuff in the ass and makes the country songs better with his mandolin playing."

Felder's arrival marked a turning point for the Eagles' sound, as it evolved from a country-rock-rooted sound to an edgier rock foundation. It also coincided with the transition from producer **Glyn Johns** to **Bill Szymczyk**,

continued on Page 135

Eagles Rebound with New Studio Attitude, Sound

On the Border was released in March 1974 and certified gold within two months. The third Eagles album was the fastest-selling to date.

The record was transitional, bridging what had gone before with what was to come. The band recorded two of the songs ("You Never Cry Like a Lover" and "The Best of My Love") with their original producer, **Glyn Johns**, and the remainder under the watch of their new producer, **Bill Szymczyk**.

Despite being credited in the liner notes as a "late arrival," Don Felder was not included on the LP's promotional poster, which featured a photo from an earlier shoot of the four-piece lineup without him. But when the needle dropped to the vinyl, his contributions to "Already Gone" and "Good Day in Hell" made an immediate impression on listeners.

The latter, a Henley/Frey vocal duet, is one of two *On the Border* songs about the recently departed **Gram Parsons**.

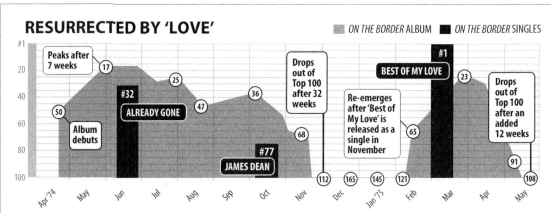

The Eagles' approach toward music—along with their producer—changed for their third album, *On the Border*. There was more rock and roll and a little less country-rock. The album got off to the the best start of any Eagles' LP to date, debuting at #50 on *Billboard*'s Top 100 Albums chart. Heavy airplay for "Already Gone" gave it a strong initial lift and helped keep it in the Top 25 for most of the summer, but the release of "James Dean" did not maintain that momentum. It fell out of the Top 100 albums in November and it wasn't until "The Best of My Love" was released as a single that the album surged back into the Top 25, where it stayed for another 12 weeks. It would be certified gold by the RIAA in June 1974, and, like the other albums in the Eagles catalog, would go 2x platinum in March 2001.

Sources: Billboard, Recording Industry Association of America

"'Good Day in Hell' was written while Gram was alive," Glenn Frey pointed out. "It just was a symptomatic scene and I saw it at the Topanga Corral [a hip honky-tonk roadhouse] where, you know, there were just a couple of girls who were just hanging out with him because he was Gram Parsons and nobody was telling him that he was killing himself. Nobody was a good enough friend… to sit him down and say, 'Hey, you're very talented and you're going to waste here.'"

The poignant "My Man" is the other song about Parsons, written by Bernie Leadon about his **Flying Burrito Brothers** colleague. According to Don Henley, though, Leadon originally was thinking about another musician friend who had recently died.

"Bernie originally started writing a song about **Duane Allman**," Henley said, "because he and Duane used to be friends and every time Duane would see him, he would say, 'Hey! My man!' And so that's where that originally came from and then Gram died and sort of got written into the thing, as well."

"Already Gone" gave the band an uncharacteristically aggressive start to the album, courtesy of Felder. They had already cut the song by the time Felder arrived in the studio. Frey had recorded the solo guitar intro but thought it could be improved on. "So, my solo, we didn't feel it was enough to carry it," Frey said, adding that three or four days after the "Good Day in Hell" session they asked Felder to recut the intro. "I said,

WARNER COMMU-NICATIONS had just bought both Asylum and Elektra Records and combined them. **David Geffen**, still CEO of Asylum, built and ran the new team, complete with L.A. marketing, sales, and promotion teams. Atlantic Records was no longer involved.

With Eagles' popularity growing, and tour dates doing well, the anticipation for *On The Border* was strong. It didn't have that "hair stand up on your arm" hit single—or so we thought. "Already Gone" seemed the best of the bunch—up-tempo tunes get radio play more easily. Top 40 and AOR stations stepped up and gave it a shot. It got decent airplay, but barely reached *Billboard*'s Top 30. Radio wanted the Eagles to happen. We wanted the Eagles to succeed, but you've got to have hits to stay on the radio. Next was "James Dean" and we knew it wasn't going too far, but there was no other choice. It did exactly what we thought—mid-charted. Now what? We got a beloved band, touring was terrific, and no big Top 40 chart hit since "Take It Easy" and "Witchy."

When the "singles release sheet" (corporate notes projecting future releases) came out, "Ol' '55" was next. "Hmmm," the field staff thought, "that's going to be another mid-charter." Everybody loved **Tom Waits**, another Asylum artist, but Top 40? Then I got a call from a station in Kalamazoo, where **Jim Higgs** had "The Best of My Love" soaring as an album cut. Based on that call, four months later, it attained #1 in the nation and their first gold single.

—Rip Pelley, former National Director of Artist Development and Promotion, Elektra/Asylum Records

'Hey, why don't you come and put something against this lead part that I did?'" And Felder obliged.

When asked if "Already Gone" gave the band its first true rock and roll single, Frey agreed it did. "Yeah, I think so. I mean 'Witchy Woman' was a rock and roll song, but ["Already Gone"] was more of a flat-out rock and roll song."

The title track, "On the Border," is a rebellious anti-establishment piece Henley described as being political and related to the Watergate Scandal. "James Dean," with its 12-bar-blues pattern and catchy middle-eight section, is perhaps the closest the Eagles ever got to old time rock and roll. A harmony-rich interpretation of Tom Waits' "Ol' '55" also brings more diversity to an album that represents a band seeking to break down the musical borders they felt had confined them. That's not to say there isn't anything familiar on the album. Randy Meisner sang a pretty ballad called "Is it True," while another Meisner song—a cover of **Paul Craft**'s "Midnight Flyer"—was banjo-heavy and would have fit well on either the Eagles' debut or sophomore album.

Perhaps the most remarkable track on the album is the stunning closer, "The Best of My Love," a gorgeous acoustic holdover from the Glyn Johns sessions.

Though *On the Border* sold quickly out of the gate, it didn't reach its stride until "The Best of My Love" hit the airwaves.

"We had more or less given up hope for the success of the *On the Border* album and we'd begun work on the next album," Henley recalled in 2016. "So, when 'The Best of My Love' took off, it was like a resurrection, a miracle." [6, 1501, 1603, 1820]

Asbury Park Press
August 25, 1974

On the Border is pure American rock 'n roll with a touch of country music for flavor. Both sides of the album begin with two excellent rockers, "Already Gone" and "James Dean." The former is easily the best on the album and sounds a lot like "Take It Easy," the song that propelled the Eagles to stardom three years ago. Other tracks that deserve attention are "Ol' '55" and "James Dean." Don Felder instills a magic-like presence and adds much needed energy and zest.

– Bob Santelli

Salem Capital Journal
April 13, 1974

Many more kilowatts were involved in making *On the Border* than previous Eagles albums, and about the only acoustic stuff you hear is a little banjo. The country flavor of *Desperado* has been abandoned; it's more sophisticated, but just as easy to listen to. For dessert there's a **Jackson Browne** tune called "James Dean," a nostalgic goodie called "Ol' '55," and a very preachy thing, "My Man." It's pure Eagles. A lot more up-tempo, but certainly no disappointment.

– David P. Bond

Rolling Stone
May 23, 1974

On the Border is a tight and likeable collection, with nine potential singles working in its favor with only one dud in the set ("Midnight Flyer") to weigh it down. [The album] is good enough to make up in high spirits what it lacks in purposefulness. And that might even be a fair trade if the Eagles would only decide they've already mastered this stuff, reign in their hit-making instincts and channel their energies into projects less easily within their grasp.

– Janet Maslin

who had overseen Joe Walsh's *The Smoker You Drink, The Player You Get.*

"I just love rock and roll," Frey said, talking with **Barbara Charone**, writing for *Hit Parader,*. "But all that stuff only makes sense when you do 'Peaceful Easy Feeling,' that puts the 'James Dean' in proper perspective. Y'see, the focal point for what we do is a multi-faceted formula. We're not a single-minded band. From 'Midnight Flyer' to 'On the Border,' who could have possibly thought that the same band would do these two songs. But all that keeps your group experience interesting."

"The acquisition of Don Felder on lead guitar has also been a major breakthrough—both in recording and performing," **David Rensin** observed in *Crawdaddy*. "He makes the Eagles a five-piece country band by playing mandolin, allows Leadon to take up instruments heretofore confined to studio overdubs and, by playing occasional rhythm guitar, lets Frey pound the keyboards."

In the months following the release of *On the Border*, the Eagles were elated to have Felder in the fold.

"I feel better than ever since he's joined," bassist Randy Meisner said. "It's much fuller onstage now."

Frey echoed the sentiment, calling himself a fan since he heard Felder playing in a dressing room in Boston. It was the night he gave Felder the nickname "Fingers," following Leadon's intro that he had the lightest fingers on the Stratocaster. [66, 67, 1719, 1720]

Walsh, Vitale Join Lennon for Secret Record Plant Sessions

In the late 1980s and early 1990s, Joe Walsh would become an official member of the first two versions of **Ringo Starr & His All-Starr Band**. While those public appearances would be widely celebrated, Walsh's much earlier jam with another former member of **The Beatles** was a far more legendary affair.

In the spring of 1974, **John Lennon** was famously in the middle of his "Lost Weekend," the roughly year and a half when he was estranged from wife **Yoko Ono** and living in Los Angeles while ingesting large quantities of drugs and alcohol.

Along with producing **Harry Nilsson**'s *Pussy Cats* LP and recording tracks for his own *Rock 'n' Roll* album with producer **Phil Spector**, Lennon's studio time in L.A. included a series of confidential jams at the Record Plant, where the Eagles had recorded most of *On the Border* and would eventually record some of *Hotel California*.

These invitation-only jams included some of the biggest names in rock and roll, like Lennon's former Beatle Ringo, members of the **Rolling Stones** including **Keith Richards** and **Bill Wyman**, and **Faces** guitarist (and soon-to-be Stone) **Ronnie Wood**.

Walsh, along with his **Barnstorm** drummer and songwriting collaborator **Joe Vitale**, were delighted when one day they got the call to join in a jam. Engineer **John Stronach**, who was overseeing the sessions, was the one who reached out on Lennon's behalf.

continued on Page 138

WALSH TURNS TO MUSIC TO COPE WITH TRAGIC LOSS

•••

While Joe Walsh was on a plane home from Los Angeles to Boulder, Colorado, tragedy was unfolding for his family. Walsh's wife, **Stefany Rhodes**, and the couple's not-quite-three-year-old daughter, **Emma Kristen**, were driving to a playgroup date on the west side of Central Boulder when a driver ran through a stop sign and crashed into their green Porsche.

The impact spun the sports car with such force that it hit a fence across the street. Emma sustained massive head injuries and was taken to the hospital; she was taken off life support later that night.

It was a devastating time for Walsh and Rhodes, and a few years later, he suggested having a drinking fountain and a memorial plaque erected at her favorite park. Rhodes agreed, and it was dedicated in North Boulder Park near the playground on May 1, 1976. Inscribed on the plaque was:

This fountain is given
in loving memory
of
Emma Walsh
April 29, 1971-April 1, 1974

Rhodes met Walsh when she was a student at Boston University, and they married after she graduated in 1971. They moved to Boulder from Cleveland, Ohio, when he left the **James Gang** and started **Barnstorm**. The family's life revolved around Joe's music, and they often slept on the floor of **James Guercio**'s Caribou Ranch studio while the band worked on songs with producer **Bill Szymczyk**.

But the tragedy ended their marriage. "Over the...next year, my wife and I, we just weren't strong enough to get through the grief and so we separated and eventually got divorced," Walsh told *Rolling Stone* in 2016.

Walsh wrote "Song for Emma" as a way of dealing with his grief. He created a touching, strings-adorned goodbye to help him find that closure. In his lyrics he cynically wondered why "He" took her, and chastised God with "He made your mama cry." With those words, Walsh told his departed daughter that her parents both grieved, that they didn't understand, and that she would be missed. The song ended with a heartfelt "Goodbye. Bye, love."

Walsh wouldn't let anyone work on the song with him but Szymczyk. "There was nobody that could do that but me," Szymczyk told **John Tobler** of the BBC. "I took a four-track recorder up to his house, and he played the piano part over and over—there was no one take. It was a really emotional time, and that night I took all the four tracks, went down to the studio, and he went to bed. He didn't hear the track again until I had done everything to it, then he came in and sang it."

Walsh had friends in Boulder and Los Angeles who helped him cope as well. "I met a girl in Los Angeles, and my song 'Help Me Thru the Night' was to her about being there for me," Walsh said. "Because I was a wreck. But she was there so that I could grieve Emma." Both songs were on Walsh's next album, *So What*.

Years later, the wounds from the loss healed somewhat, and Walsh has tried to use the experience to help others.

"The worst thing that can happen to someone is losing a child," he said. "That happened to me, so I know. That was a long time ago, and I'm at peace with it now. It was a kind of goodbye to her. That song was good because it gave me closure on it, and I could move on. I think of her often, and she was a good little kid.

"Having had that experience, sometimes I am in a position to be able to comfort people," Walsh added. "I'm in a position to put an arm around them and tell them they are not alone. I've talked to several parents whose sons were killed in Iraq or Afghanistan, and they know about my daughter. Sometimes they'll contact me to let me know their kids were killed in the war and that they were fans, or that my music really helped them deal with their grief. That's a good thing that came out of it."

In the early 1980s, Walsh struck up a relationship with **Stevie Nicks**. The pair got close and, while in Colorado, Walsh took Nicks on a two-hour ride through snow-covered Boulder, which led them to North Boulder Park where Emma's water fountain was erected. Nicks said Joe explained that his daughter's only complaint was that she couldn't reach the drinking fountain to get a drink.

"As soon as we got [to the park], I knew there was going to be a tiny little drinking fountain in that park," Nicks said in the liner notes for her *Timespace: The Best of Stevie Nicks* album. "Everybody thinks Joe was so nuts, and he is, but Joe has a sensitive side that goes far, far beyond that. I just knew the one thing that she asked for was the thing he would put in her park."

That day spawned an inspirational moment for Nicks, who co-wrote "Has Anyone Ever Written Anything for You?" with veteran soundman **Keith Olsen**. But she wouldn't record the song without Walsh's consent, noting that the subject of Emma's death was taboo.

"I had to immediately call Mr. Walsh and clear it with him, or it could never have been printed," Nicks said. "because that is a subject that is not talked about at all." Walsh agreed, and Nicks recorded the song. It was on her well-received *Rock a Little* album in 1985, and later on *Timespace*.

Though the memorial for Emma sits solemnly in Boulder, she was buried in Rhodes' hometown cemetery in Ipswich, Massachusetts. [132, 221, 223, 224, 225, 444]

> EVERYBODY THINKS JOE WAS SO NUTS, AND HE IS, BUT JOE HAS A SENSITIVE SIDE THAT GOES FAR, FAR BEYOND THAT. I JUST KNEW THE ONE THING THAT [EMMA] ASKED FOR WAS THE THING HE WOULD PUT IN HER PARK.
>
> — STEVIE NICKS

"John called one night and said, 'Do you guys want to come down to the Record Plant and jam with John Lennon?'" Vitale remembered in his hilarious memoir, *Backstage Pass*. "We went, 'Get out of here! Are you kidding?'"

Vitale recalls he was absolutely awestruck upon arrival at the studio. "There was John Lennon sitting at the piano with Ringo on drums..." he explained. "They pointed to us and then motioned to some instruments, signaling us to sit in. So, within two minutes of our arrival, we were jammin' with these guys."

Walsh and Vitale attended these weekly jams about three times, with one stipulation from the organizers: keep it quiet. "Please, no cameras," they were told. "Don't tell anybody. Keep this to yourselves." They did that, but apparently the word still got out.

"The jams were going to last another week or two, but someone must have let it leak," Vitale said. After the third week, "there were a few thousand fans waiting in the parking lot to get a glimpse of John Lennon and his friends. ... Unfortunately, that was the end of the John Lennon sessions." [1345, 1623, 1624]

Eagles, 300,000-Plus Rock Fans Survive 'California Jam'

While scouring the internet for vintage live music clips from the early 1970s, fans of bands like **Black Sabbath**, **Black Oak Arkansas**, and **Rare Earth** will doubtlessly find videos of these acts playing on a big stage with a giant rainbow backdrop, facing a sea of people in an audience seemingly stretching to the horizon.

The event was the California Jam of 1974, which on April 6 featured eight groups playing for a massive crowd of between 300,000 and 400,000 people (250,000 tickets were sold). In addition to the aforementioned bands, the diverse bill also included host **Don Imus** and headliners **Emerson, Lake & Palmer** and **Deep Purple**, funk legends **Earth, Wind & Fire**, soft rock duo **Seals & Crofts**, and, of course, Eagles.

Though it didn't draw the 400,000-plus people Woodstock did in August 1969, California Jam still boasted big numbers, and at the time was compared to other major festivals of the era.

It was a peaceful event, which differentiated it from December 1969's Altamont concert in Northern California, a gathering notorious for an incident where things got violent and a Hell's Angel gang member stabbed a concertgoer to death. Bernie Leadon had played at Altamont as a member of the **Flying Burrito Brothers**, but his appearance with the Eagles at California Jam was far less frightening.

The *Sun-Telegram* of San Bernadino County referred to the attendees as "a joyful sun-splashed crowd" half a mile long, and the paper's review of the concert quoted performers who described a largely orderly and non-hostile event.

Virtually playing in their hometown, a short drive east of Los Angeles, the Eagles

Glenn Frey and Bernie Leadon play onstage at the Ontario Motor Speedway at the California Jam rock festival. The concert attracted between 300,000 and 400,000 people in an event that set records for loudest amplification system.

had an opportunity to show off their new five-piece lineup to a huge audience, but it was not to be. Conspicuously absent was their new addition, Don Felder.

The band had arrived home on a flight the previous night, and according to Felder, he was paged at the terminal after the plane touched down at Los Angeles International Airport. An urgent message was delivered that his pregnant wife, Susan, was going into labor and he was needed home. Although a helicopter was arranged to be on-call the following day to rush him to the gig, by early afternoon, the baby had not been delivered and it became evident that Felder wasn't going to make the show.

But the Eagles did perform as a five-piece anyway. Frequent Eagles collaborator **Jackson Browne** agreed to sit in with the band, and the group was introduced as "Eagles with special guest Jackson Browne." Browne jumped from acoustic guitar to piano, complementing the band on a set of songs that included a few he had a hand in writing, such as "Take It Easy" and "James Dean."

Glenn Frey played the lead guitar part on "Already Gone" in Felder's stead, and with both Frey and Leadon frequently playing electric six-string, the band used the show as a chance to flex their new-found rock muscle.

Journalist **Barbara Charone** reviewed

continued on Page 141

PATHWAY ALBUM | TIMOTHY B. SCHMIT

POCO
Seven
Epic Records, April 1974

Six years after the group's co-founding by **Richie Furay** and **Jim Messina**, **Poco** in 1974 was still viewed by many as the next big thing that never was.

Critically praised for their high-energy live shows and tremendously influential—most notably to the Eagles—for their early blend of country and rock, Poco always seemed on the verge of a big breakthrough, but the hits hadn't happened.

Messina was gone by 1970, and then, in 1973, Furay had been courted away by **David Geffen** to form the **Souther-Hillman-Furay Band**. Geffen predicted a new supergroup with Furay, ex-**Byrd** and ex-**Flying Burrito Brother** co-founder **Chris Hillman**, and Eagles' friend and co-writer **J.D. Souther** would become the new **Crosby, Stills & Nash**.

For folks in the industry, and likely many fans, the thought of Poco without Furay was a doomed venture with little potential. The band members knew they were unfairly viewed as sidemen to Furay and set out with something to prove.

"Poco was always more than just Richie," steel guitar player **Rusty Young** clarified in an interview with author **Jerry Fuentes**, explaining that the underdog status gave them motivation to prove their critics wrong. According to future Eagle Timothy B. Schmit, Poco's bassist and co-lead vocalist, "It took us just five minutes to decide to carry on as a four-piece."

Though the band forged ahead with their pride intact, it still was a trying time for all involved. Guitarist **Paul Cotton** felt he had to make adjustments to adapt his playing to suit a band with only one guitar player; Young needed to step up his songwriting game. Stylistically, Schmit had more in common with Furay as a writer than Cotton did, and he and the others were given opportunities to carry more of the load.

Poco's first LP of 1974—indeed, they'd have two—was named *Seven* as a nod to it being their seventh album. Released in April, it was wrapped in a relatively sparse cover, with the Poco name in a horseshoe logo pictured against a solid, earthy-green background. Designed by future actor and comedian **Phil Hartman**, brother of Geffen-Roberts artist manager **John Hartmann**, the logo has been used by the band ever since.

The album's leadoff track, Cotton's "Driving Wheel," featured the three remaining vocalists—Cotton, Schmit, and drummer **George Grantham**—trading leads on the first three lines. The song asked who would become the "driving wheel" to steer the good ship Poco into this new era. The answer? They'd all take turns in the wheelhouse. But they were venturing into uncharted territory. Schmit landed three songs on the album, none of which are considered among his finest work with the group. "Just Call My Name" had none of the country-rock stylings the band was known for; its attempt to be a little edgier was unremarkable.

The same could be said for the more pop-styled "Skatin'" or the lilting track with the unusual title of "Krikkit Song (Passin' Through)." Cotton's "Angel" was a moody piece that at times bordered on brooding, though "Faith in the Families" was more poetic and is a bit of a hidden gem in the Poco catalog.

Young contributed a Colorado-inspired, harmony-rich bluegrass number, "Rocky Mountain Breakdown," with a lead vocal sung primarily by Schmit with some help from Grantham.

Overall, the record was not without its charm, but it was more indicative of a band finding its footing after taking a hit. "Poco Seven was a transitional album," Schmit would say a year later, and few would disagree. [1504, 1515]

the band, saying, "They looked great, they sang great, they played great and most importantly they sacrificed individual aims for group goals."

Backstage, Frey cryptically commented, "The magic bands are the ones who live their trip onstage. If you're in a band like the Eagles, you've got to focus on yourself and amplify that image. You have to exaggerate what you do without prostituting how you feel about yourself." [218, 596, 1404, 1602]

Asylum Night: Eagles, Ronstadt, Browne Appear on *Rock Concert*

Behind his drum kit midway through the Eagles' set on the nationally televised *Don Kirshner's Rock Concert*, Don Henley put on sunglasses. And as the camera pulled back wide, the rest of the Eagles were donning them, too. Seconds later, they were ripping thorough a rousing version of "James Dean" for the television audience.

These were clearly good times for the band, who had just welcomed new Eagle Don Felder into the group, and the appearance was filled with genuine smiles and laughter. The show aired in April 1974, and the band brought friends **Linda Ronstadt** and **Jackson Browne** with them, making the entire show a calling card for Asylum Records' top-shelf acts.

Pop and rock stars on television was a booming trend by the mid-1970s. Networks were looking for popular recording stars who had the chops to make it in front a live televised audience. There was no shortage of candidates—**Donny & Marie Osmond**, the **Captain & Tennille**, **Tony Orlando & Dawn**, **Glen Campbell**, **Johnny Cash**, and **Helen Reddy** all had variety shows.

Eagles appeared on Reddy's show in early 1973, but otherwise stayed off primetime. The late-night shows proved to be a better fit, and the band had made several appearances on ABC's *In Concert* series. Appearing on Kirshner's popular show gave them even more exposure, but to a hipper, younger, more music-hungry audience than watched the primetime variety shows.

Already a legend as a music publisher, from **Tin Pan Alley** to **The Monkees**, Kirshner had been hired by the ABC television network as executive producer and host of *In Concert by* ABC in 1972. In fall 1973, he went independent and launched the syndicated *Don Kirshner's Rock Concert*, which leveraged the same formula he had developed for ABC and was seen in more than 150 television markets.

With his extensive industry contacts and influence, Kirshner had access to great acts and even dreamed of bringing **The Beatles** back together for a one-time TV event. He never achieved that goal, but did lure the day's most popular bands onscreen, including the coup of getting the **Rolling Stones**, **Earth, Wind & Fire**, and the **Doobie Brothers** on his debut episode.

Midway through his second season, Kirshner landed an all-Asylum night with the Eagles, Ronstadt, and Browne. The show was timed to air just one month after the band had released their third LP, *On the Border*, and its leadoff single, "Already Gone," was already rising up the charts like a bullet.

The hour-long show included ten Eagles songs, including "Peaceful Easy Feeling," "Already Gone," "Midnight Flyer," "Twenty-One," "Doolin-Dalton," "Take It Easy," and "Desperado," which featured Ronstadt singing lead (her cover from *Don't Cry Now*

had just been released as a single). And as he had many times before, Bernie Leadon joined Ronstadt on two other songs that night, "Silver Threads and Golden Needles" and "It Doesn't Matter Anymore."

Two-thirds of the way through, Browne took the stage for "Your Bright Baby Blues" and "Looking Into You." In the show's final number, Ronstadt and Browne joined the band for "Take It Easy," which the band played as credits rolled.

The show was great for exposure for the band, but the novelty of rock acts on TV in the 1970s began to fade almost as fast as it emerged. Weekly shows such as *American Bandstand* and *Soul Train* that were dedicated to lip-syncing artists endured, but weekly live music shows on TV like *In Concert*, *Don Kirshner's Rock Concert*, and *The Midnight Special* faded in popularity, even when some specials were simulcast in stereo by local FM stations as an alternative to then-still-primitive TV sound technology.

"Television has been very useful in the past, although I think that in its present context its usefulness has been almost completely served by this time," Eagles manager **Irving Azoff** told *Record World* in 1975. "Rock television is becoming less and less important because their packaging has become diluted. The important acts aren't doing TV anymore and there are just too many shows. I'm very protective as a manager and we can't live with the loss of control in the selection of acts, the quality of sound, and in the post-production process.

"Rock television became what making records was in 1964. You cannot expect an artist who spends eight weeks recording his album to spend 45 minutes making his [TV] appearance. What artist who cares can compromise his performance to the extent that the producers of rock and roll TV demand?"

Azoff's mid-1970s view of the mixture of rock and television was correct. Six years later when MTV rolled out its juggernaut network, the idea of spending more than just 45 minutes on a video production took root.

After a brief feeling-out period, many of Azoff's primary clients—including Glenn Frey and Don Henley in their post-Eagles solo careers—became major players in the emergence of music videos at the dawn of the MTV era in the early-to-mid-1980s. [545, 546, 1359, 1564, 1649, 1884]

Azoff Expands His Burgeoning Empire with Front Line, Full Moon

Dan Fogelberg, with his producer Joe Walsh guesting, opened a show for the Eagles at the Shrine Auditorium near downtown Los Angeles in late 1974. In the incestuous L.A. music scene, it was hardly a coincidence these three artists shared the bill. They were, after all, clients of **Irving Azoff** and three of the debut acts signed to his new Front Line Management venture, launched in the spring.

The ambitious manager—who'd already worked his way up and through Associated Booking Corp. and Geffen-Roberts Management—was primed and ready to go solo now that he had the Eagles under his wing.

They were soon to break big with their *On the Border* album, and Azoff may well have been a catalyst in making that happen.

Joining the aforementioned artists on Front Line's roster were **REO Speedwagon**, Eagles producer **Bill Szymczyk**, and *On the Border* assistant producer **Allan Blazek**. When Front Line added five-octave soul singer-songwriter **Minnie Riperton**, Azoff remarked, "We will continue to diversify in our managerial aims and trends. Front Line will eventually represent every type of concert act."

The company's impressive client list would grow to include **Boz Scaggs**, **Steely Dan**, and **Jimmy Buffett**, among many others. Azoff's decision to form Front Line was partly the result of the Eagles' dissatisfaction with how Geffen-Roberts handled their business dealings, and the band signed with him for management because he had quickly proved he'd fight like hell on their behalf every step of the way.

"People keep saying I'm just lucky, that my artists would have been successful anyway," Azoff once mused. "I still have this driving obsession to prove to people that I have something to do with my artists' success."

Managing his acts was his primary focus, but Azoff didn't stop there. Shortly after launching Front Line, he formed Full Moon Productions, another firm aimed at delivering talent to major labels.

In his first major deal he guided Fogelberg to a contract with Epic Records, which seemed fitting since Fogelberg was one of four principals in Full Moon, along with

continued on Page 145

'ON THE BORDER': EAGLES TURN EYE TO POLITICS

The Eagles' country-rock sound and some exceptional ballads were the band's calling cards through their first two albums. The songs were uncomplicated and drew inspiration from themes of love, loneliness, and just having fun. Through two albums, there had been no hint of either political overtones or commentary on social issues.

With *On the Border*, the group sought a harder rock and roll sound, so they switched producers. It worked. But that wasn't where the experiment ended. The band would spread their collective wings with their lyrics, too.

The Eagles may have never become poster children for protest songs, as did British bands like **The Beatles**, **The Who**, and **The Kinks**, or American artists like **Buffalo Springfield**, **The Byrds**, **Jefferson Airplane**, and **Curtis Mayfield** had before them in the 1960s and early '70s.

But the Eagles did begin experimenting with political observation in their lyrics with *On the Border*, specifically the title cut, written at the height of the Watergate scandal leading up to Richard Nixon's resignation from the U.S. presidency on August 9, 1974.

It was a complex issue for a band then known for its country-rock sound and style. There was an atmosphere of political paranoia gripping the nation during the Watergate era that had basis in fact, as history has shown.

The opening lines of "On the Border" speak to jockeying political parties descending on a confused electorate, with "Big Brother" (the right-wing Nixon administration) trying to put its thumb on the scale to change the outcome.

The refrain is a metaphor for regular people who aren't paying keen attention (they are "out on the border") and are just trying to live their lives and stay out of the fray ("I'm walking the line").

The song then turns its focus to wiretaps on citizens who wonder why the government is listening in on their conversations. The final stanza

throws another log on the Nixon mistrust fire by suggesting there are consequences: *"And we wanna know whose wing are you under/You better step to the right or we can make it hard."*

"On the Border" was an uneven attempt at political commentary, but it was the band's first effort on that front. Don Henley, Glenn Frey, and Bernie Leadon all earned writing credits for the song. They weren't entirely happy with how it turned out.

"This track ['On the Border'] turned out to be completely different from what I had envisioned," Henley told *Rolling Stone* in 2016. "There was a clash of styles and influences in that song, and I'm not sure it ever became what it could have been, musically.

"As for the lyrics," Henley said, "there was a lot going on in the country at that time regarding the impeachment of Richard Nixon. The whole Watergate debacle was coming to a head. Interestingly, not unlike now, there were a lot of people concerned about the government overstepping its bounds with regard to issues of privacy. It's much like the [John] Ashcroft world we're looking at today. So that's what the verses ended up being about. It's an odd song.

"I like Glenn's cool little R&B guitar part in the tag, though, and at the very end there's something almost inaudible," Henley added. "Someone—it had to be Glenn or me—says, 'Say goodnight, Dick,' which was a phrase made famous on *The Smothers Brothers'* show when Tommy says, 'Say goodnight, Dick.' We were addressing Nixon, because at that time it was pretty clear that he was on his way out, so that was our little kiss-off to Tricky Dick." [15, 140, 209, 397, 398]

himself, former Asylum promotions man **Paul Ahern**, and Joe Walsh. All of Fogelberg's albums going forward were recorded under Full Moon and Epic.

Azoff didn't limit Full Moon's breadth to just Epic or Columbia; he branched as a sub-label under Asylum, Warner Bros., and Reprise Records where he recorded artists like **Johnny Lee**, **Grand Funk**, **Chicago**, and Chicago singer **Peter Cetera** as a solo act.

Azoff's biggest achievement with Full Moon, however, was amassing his stable of talent into the soundtrack world. Full Moon would produce the megahit multiplatinum soundtracks for *Urban Cowboy*, *Fast Times at Ridgemont High*, *Heavy Metal*, and *Blade Runner*, which all scored hits high on the *Billboard* charts. Full Moon would continue producing records into the 1990s. [488, 489, 597, 610, 1322, 1481, 1561, 1563, 1604]

Resigned to Reality: Walsh Disbands Barnstorm, Goes Solo

Future Eagle Joe Walsh spent nearly two musically satisfying years with **Barnstorm**. He began to grow in ways he felt he couldn't with his former power trio, the **James Gang**. Free from the guitar-god image he now eschewed, he began experimenting with songs with softer edges and more contemplative lyrics. He developed a songwriting partnership with his drummer and sideman, **Joe Vitale**, and even let new band members

Kenny Passarelli and **Rocke Grace** join in the collaborative process.

Barnstorm found success with cuts like "Turn to Stone" and the crowd-pleasing "Rocky Mountain Way," but nearly two years into their existence they were still opening for groups like the **Climax Blues Band** and **REO Speedwagon**.

Those concerts were consistently billed as "Joe Walsh and Barnstorm." As a practical matter, having Walsh's name above the band's was necessary since Barnstorm had little name recognition. Walsh's name on the marquee sold tickets, but that fact annoyed him. While he was finally enjoying the creative freedom he craved and was nestled in the warm cocoon of his own hand-picked band, he couldn't elevate them to headliners without invoking his own name. His persona had overshadowed what he worked so hard to create. And he knew it.

Walsh told **Chris Charlesworth** of *Melody Maker* in 1973 that he never felt his label properly marketed and promoted Barnstorm. Instead, it preferred to present the albums as Joe Walsh projects, cashing in on his James Gang caché and name recognition.

The band's self-titled debut album was called Barnstorm, but "Joe Walsh" appeared on the cover. With their second album, *The Smoker You Drink, The Player You Get,*

> THE EAGLES ARE AN IDEAL EXAMPLE OF MY IDEA OF BAND... BARNSTORM WAS ALMOST A BAND, BUT NEVER QUITE AN EAGLES; IT NEVER GOT FROM JOE WALSH AND BARNSTORM TO JUST BARNSTORM. I WISH IT HAD, BECAUSE, IT'S REALLY LONELY IN THE SPOTLIGHT.
>
> — JOE WALSH

ABC-Dunhill dispensed with Barnstorm altogether; it was a straight-up Joe Walsh LP. Indeed, the label dropped 1,000 radio spots for the album across the country that helped break it in Seattle, Boston, and Los Angeles. It was all-in with the album being by "Joe Walsh." Following ABC-Dunhill's lead, the trade press even reviewed the new album as a solo effort.

With two albums in the books and strong reviews for *Smoker* and "Rocky Mountain Way," the band began making plans for their third album. They had an aggressive tour schedule in 1973, and an equal effort was planned in 1974.

But fate intervened in tragic fashion when Walsh lost his toddler daughter Emma in a traffic crash. The touring stopped and Walsh slipped into depression. His marriage to **Stefany Rhodes** ended soon after and Walsh's dependence on alcohol and drugs grew. The band got back together in June and performed a few shows in July and September, but there was no more wind in their sails.

Walsh told the BBC's **John Tobler** that Barnstorm wasn't disbanded because of disagreements or band infighting. Rather, he said, it had just run its course by 1974. He had started work on his next album, *So What*, but it would be a solo affair with an all-star cast of supporting players, including, among others, Glenn Frey, Don Henley, and Randy Meisner.

Meanwhile, Barnstorm's drummer, Vitale, was working on his own solo album, *Roller Coaster Weekend*. Passarelli accepted a job playing bass for **Stephen Stills**' band, **Manassas**. Any lingering doubts Barnstorm might still be together were gone.

Even though Walsh's second attempt at being in a band had ended, he was still enamored with the concept. About a year after, Walsh said he was still searching for one, and he had a good idea what it might look like.

"I'm always looking for a band," Walsh told *Creem*'s **Jaan Uhelszki** in June 1975. "The Eagles are an ideal example of my idea of a band. There's five guys in the Eagles and everybody adds a fifth. When you see the Eagles, you know Glenn is there, Randy is there, Don is there, Bernie is there, and Don Henley is there. Everybody is there, but it's the Eagles. Barnstorm was almost a band, but not quite an Eagles; it never got from Joe Walsh and Barnstorm to just Barnstorm. I wish it had, because, you know, it's really lonely in the spotlight."

Ironically, it was the musical and personal connections made during Walsh's *So What* sessions that put him on a course to join the Eagles. Walsh and Henley co-wrote "Falling Down," and he and the band members grew more familiar with each other.

So when Bernie Leadon poured a bottle of beer over Glenn Frey's head later in 1975 and walked away from the band, Walsh was

an obvious candidate to replace him. [1501, 1527, 2036, 2081]

SUMMER 1974

 RELEASES
- ▶ **Poco**, with Timothy B. Schmit, "Rocky Mountain Breakdown" (single)
- ▶ Eagles, "Already Gone" (single)
- ▶ Eagles, "James Dean" (single)

 NUGGETS
- ▶ Eagles will be leaving Asylum to go with Joe Walsh and **Dan Fogelberg** to Epic Records, with Epic picking up the court costs. Eagles' asking price was a cool half million. —*Cashbox*
- ▶ Eagle Glenn Frey presents **J.D. Souther** with a scrapbook of every newspaper clipping where the names of the **Souther-Hillman-Furay Band** members were misspelled. —*Record World*
- ▶ Eagles and **Allman Brothers** play a free benefit concert for the North American Indian Fund at Boston Gardens; neither group accepted any money for the gig. —*Record World*
- ▶ *Cashbox* apologizes to the Eagles, their management, and **David Geffen**, president of Asylum Records, for erroneously stating that the group was leaving the label. The Eagles are happy with Asylum. Apologies were also extended to Joe Walsh and ABC Records for suggesting Walsh would bolt to Epic Records. —*Cashbox, (one week later)*
- ▶ **Linda Ronstadt** releases "Desperado" as the third single from her *Don't Cry Now* album, produced by **J.D. Souther**, to strong reviews. —*Record World*
- ▶ **David Geffen** announces that Asylum Records has re-signed the Eagles to an exclusive long-term recording contract. —*Cashbox (three weeks later)*
- ▶ Eagles' *On the Border* is certified gold by the Recording Industry Association of America. —*Record World*

continued on Page 149

AZOFF AVERTS EAGLES DRUG BUST IN BAHAMAS

"He may be Satan, but he's our Satan." That's how Don Henley famously acknowledged Eagles manager **Irving Azoff** at the band's induction into the Rock and Roll Hall of Fame in 1998. Azoff developed a well-earned reputation as a manager who protected his artists at all costs, even if it meant making more than a few enemies along the way.

"We're in a dog-eat-dog business," Azoff reflected. "Show me anybody that's going to be responsible for guiding or managing an artist's career that's made too many friends and I'm gonna show you somebody that sold out their artist and did a crappy job."

Glenn Frey and Don Henley picked up a pretty good vibe from Azoff from the get-go, but knew for sure their manager had their backs after he got them out of a jam they referred to as "The Bahamas Incident."

In summer 1974, about half a year into the band's relationship with Azoff, Frey and Henley decided they needed a break from work. As Frey explained in 1978, "The Eagles were in the middle of a tour. We had two days off and didn't want to stay in New York."

Because they were big gamblers and constantly playing cards, Frey continued, "We decided to go to the Bahamas and gamble for our two days off. Henley, myself, Irving, [and] a pilot [took] off for the Bahamas."

Later retellings indicate that others, including Bernie Leadon, also took the trip.

Despite being rock stars during a very drug-fueled time in rock history, all parties agreed that in order to avoid trouble when leaving domestic boundaries, no one should be "holding" anything that could get them arrested. They all agreed to "go in clean," as Henley worded it.

"Turns out everybody except [Henley]...had some kind of dope on him," Frey said. "Irving, on the plane over, took 20 Valiums and put them into a sugar package and stuffed them in his shoe. I put half an ounce of marijuana in my boot."

If the gamblers were betting they'd not be checked, they wagered incorrectly.

"[The custom officials] wanted to search us, because we looked terrible," Felder admitted. "We had really long hair and patches on our jeans...and [had] not slept."

Intent on asking the group questions and doing searches, the officials pulled all the travelers aside. Azoff volunteered to be searched first, and there was no chance for him or Frey to ditch the substances inside their footwear.

Henley and Frey were prepared for the worst, only to be surprised when Azoff emerged a few minutes later—free to continue onto the flight. The officials then approached the others. They searched Henley and decided to skip searching Frey.

Frey told *Rolling Stone* that Azoff tried to bribe the interrogators by "pulling out a fistful of twenties," which was their gambling money for the trip, about $5,000, and when that proved unsuccessful, he used all his guile and salesmanship to defuse the matter.

Azoff claimed he didn't have a Valium prescription bottle with him, because his father was a pharmacist. Then he reasoned that Frey—who he confessed was in possession of marijuana—shouldn't be arrested for it because he's a rock star who "brings such enjoyment to people." Azoff attempted to convince the officials they would end Frey's career if he couldn't play the dates on the band's upcoming schedule due to a drug bust.

Henley, who conceded he never really did know what exactly Azoff said, described it as "nothing short of miraculous, really. Because I thought for sure that we were going to be in the slammer."

"That was a real-life panic situation," Frey said. "That required more fortitude than doing a concert deal with **Bill Graham** or something. ... [Azoff] saved our ass from winding up with an international drug charge." [481, 1152, 1404]

NUGGETS (cont.)
► Joe Walsh is working on his new LP, which will be called *No One Can See You When Your Eyes Are Closed.* —*Record World*

COLLABORATIONS
► **Don Felder** played slide guitar on the single "Tattooed Man From Chelsea" on **Michael Dinner**'s album *The Great Pretender.*

ON SCREEN
► Eagles appeared on the ABC-TV show *In Concert: California Jam - Part IV.* **Earth, Wind & Fire** and **Seals & Crofts** also appeared.

ON THE ROAD WITH …
► **Eagles**: Billy Joel, José Feliciano, Lynyrd Skynyrd, Marvin Gaye, the Allman Brothers Band, The Beach Boys, the Souther-Hillman-Furay Band, The Stampeders
► **Poco**, with Timothy B. Schmit: Aztec Two-Step, Lynyrd Skynyrd, Procol Harum, Snafu, the Outlaws
► **Barnstorm**, with Joe Walsh: Lynyrd Skynyrd

Geffen Nudges Souther, Hillman, and Furay to Form 'Supergroup'

"You'll be as big as **Crosby, Stills & Nash**."

That's what **David Geffen** reportedly predicted in 1973 when he pitched the idea of a country-rock supergroup to a dejected **Richie Furay**. Furay was devastated to see the success the Eagles were having while his own band, **Poco**, who had influenced the Eagles so greatly, toiled away without scoring that elusive big radio hit.

Geffen followed the original 1969 CSN template by suggesting a new group that would feature not only Furay, but also two other seasoned singer-songwriter-musicians among the country-rock elite: **J.D. Souther** and **Byrds** and **Flying Burrito Brothers** co-founder **Chris Hillman**.

On paper, it seemed like an ideal situation. Furay was not only the undisputed leader of Poco, but also an alumnus of **Buffalo Springfield** like **Stephen Stills** and **Neil Young**.

Hillman, bassist in the classic Byrds folk-rock years, was a key figure (along with **Gram Parsons**) in crafting the band's milestone *Sweetheart of the Rodeo* album in 1968. He and Parsons would further pioneer the nascent country-rock movement when they formed the Burritos. And there was also the Geffen solo act—and the guy Geffen had wanted to be a member of the Eagles—J.D. Souther. By putting these three men together as the **Souther-Hillman-Furay Band**, a new act was formed with great potential.

The group, often referred to as "SHF" in print, would be rounded out by other musicians in much the same way bassist **Greg Reeves** and drummer **Dallas Taylor** had completed the **CSNY** lineup for the *Déjà Vu* album in 1970.

Keyboardist **Paul Harris** and steel guitar player **Al Perkins** had both played alongside Hillman as members of **Manassas**, a group led by Stills that released albums in 1972 and 1973. Perkins also had been a member of **Shiloh** with Don Henley.

Session ace **Doug Altman** was first tapped to be the drummer for the band, though **Jim Gordon** replaced him early on. Gordon is

continued on Page 153

JAMES DEAN

By: Jackson Browne, Glenn Frey
Side B: Good Day in Hell (Henley, Frey)

The Eagles wanted to prove they were more than a ballad band, so for the second single from *On the Border*, they released another rolling rocker, the infectious "James Dean." But the subject matter might have been too targeted and radio listeners may not have had the affection with the cult Hollywood legend that some members of the band had. Whatever the reason, the song didn't capture the interest of radio listeners. Released in August, it took more than a month for stations to begin spinning the single. It gained momentum in October, but never rose above #49.

"James Dean" broke first in Roanoke, Virginia, on WROV, which was a dependable secondary station for the Eagles. But the song had the weakest nationwide penetration of any single they had released to date, and it was picked up primarily among Southern stations. It was a disappointing follow-up to "Already Gone," which had performed well earlier that summer. But the "Best" was yet come.

7 PLAYLIST ADDS Summer 1974				
Region	Aug	Sep	Oct	Regional Airplay
Northeast	0	1	0	14.3 %
Southeast	0	6	0	85.7 %
Midwest	0	0	0	0 %
Southwest	0	0	0	0 %
West	0	0	0	0 %

FIRST-WAVE STATIONS Stations that added the song in the first 30 days

WMEX-Boston
WROV-Roanoke
WKLO-Louisville
WKWK-Wheeling, WV
WFOM-Marietta, GA
WMPS-Memphis
WBBQ-Augusta

Billboard	HIGHEST CHARTING WEEK: CASHBOX - October 12, 1974		
#77 October 12, 1974	SINGLE	ARTIST	# PREV WK
	1. Nothing From Nothing	Billy Preston	2
Cashbox	2. I Honestly Love You	Olivia Newton John	3
#49 October 12, 1974	3. Can't Get Enough	Bad Company	8
	4. Earache My Eye	Cheech & Chong	4
	5. Beach Baby	First Class	6
Record World	6. You Haven't Done Nothin'	Stevie Wonder	7
	7. Then Came You	Dionne Warwick & Spinners	8
#89 October 19, 1974	8. Another Saturday Night	Cat Stevens	9
	49. JAMES DEAN	**EAGLES**	**52**

Sources: Billboard, Cashbox, Record World

BROWNE, FREY PAY HOMAGE TO LEGENDARY ACTOR

The same night in late January 1972 when Glenn Frey, Don Henley, **Jackson Browne**, and **J.D. Souther** went to see **Tim Hardin** at the Troubadour, they went back to Laurel Canyon and wrote the outlaw-themed "Doolin-Dalton." They also completed a song that Browne and Souther had started many months before—but the rollicking rocker didn't quite fit the Old West motif the band was conjuring up for what would become the *Desperado* album. So "James Dean" got shelved. But it wasn't forgotten.

"When it came time to do *On the Border*, we got 'James Dean' right off the shelf and said, 'Let's finish this,'" Frey told *Rolling Stone*. "I always thought the best line in 'James Dean' was, '*I know my life would look alright if I could see it on the silver screen.*' You just don't get to do that."

Dean was a young Indiana-born actor who had done a couple commercials, studied at the Actor's Studio in New York with **Lee Strasberg**, and performed small roles in TV shows and movies before starting his short-but-illustrious Hollywood career. He rose to prominence in 1955 with his performance in *East of Eden*, and cemented his legacy in *Rebel Without a Cause*, a stirring drama about a rebellious teenager struggling to cope with the expectations of his parents and society.

With his distinctive red Harrington jacket, pompadour haircut, and anguished expressions, he became a poster child for the angst-ridden teens of the early 1950s.

Young America felt those emotions and embraced him. His final movie, *Giant*, was also critically acclaimed and his star grew brighter. But, at the height of his popularity in 1955, he died in a car crash that only magnified his cult of personality. The teen idol was just 24 years old.

Frey, Souther, and Browne were excited to pen a song that celebrated the life of the anti-hero. "James Dean was the first rock and roll casualty," Frey said. "He's the guy who trademarked blue jeans, white shirts, and a light spring jacket. Jimmy Dean, he's my first hero, that first angry young man, rebel without a cause. I had a lot of heroes, a couple of high school friends, but James Dean...." Henley admitted the legendary aura that Dean gave off never really reached his home in East Texas, but he helped write the song nonetheless. Though all four contributed to the song, only Browne and Frey received writing credits.

The song remains a favorite among fans, even though it didn't chart well when it was released in 1974. Musically, it has '50s licks that paint the backdrop of Dean's era, and the song's lyrics are fun and clever, giving a playful nod to his roles, a teen's life in the '50s, and his larger-than-life persona: "*Well talk about a low-down bad refrigerator* [a 'cool' reference], *you were just too cool for school. Sock hop, soda pop, basketball and auto shop, the only thing that got you off was breaking all the rules.*"

And, of course, the final verse refers to Dean's death, where "*along came a Spyder*," meaning the Porsche 550 Spyder that Dean died in, that "*picked up a rider*" and took him down the road to eternity. As a capper, the addictive refrain "*Too fast to live, too young to die, bye-bye*," ushered out the song and projected Dean's visage into the heavens.

The song wasn't just fun for fans. The Eagles loved it as well. "That was a really fun song to play," Randy Meisner said. "They brought that to rehearsal. Anything that was jumpin' I loved to play on bass 'cause a lot of the slower songs were just two notes on a bass. We played 'James Dean' in Detroit. Every once in a while, you get this feeling that you're **The Beatles** or something. Everything went right that night, every song clicked perfectly, and the crowd just loved us." [15, 67, 88, 132, 209, 462, 1197]

Screen legend **James Dean**, pictured on the set of his final movie, *Giant*, near Marfa, Texas, inspired **Jackson Browne**, Glenn Frey, Don Henley, and **J.D. Souther** to collaborate on a song by the Eagles that became a fan favorite.

best remembered for three things, only one of which is positive: he was a member of **Derek and the Dominos** with **Eric Clapton**; he co-wrote the group's most famous song, "Layla," taking credit for the piano coda riff his girlfriend at the time, **Rita Coolidge**, claims he copped from her; and in 1983, in a schizophrenic psychotic rage, he murdered his mother. Percussionist **Joe Lala**, whose resume included work with Joe Walsh and **Barnstorm**, would also contribute to the Souther-Hillman-Furay Band.

While the CSN comparison Geffen touted early on is a tenable one, he was quick to make a distinction between the two bands in his comments to the press. "I suppose every three guys who sing together will get compared to CSN," he said in 1974, "but this is very much its own thing. They sound nothing like CSN. They have their own sound entirely. It's good, strong, valid, original."

It was such an obvious recipe for success that the group, reportedly and likely facetiously, thought of calling themselves "Big Bucks." They were talented and established musicians in a project led by a man with an impeccable track record. But big success, in fact, did elude them.

"They didn't get together on their own," Geffen said, taking responsibility. "A lot of

[THE SOUTHER-HILLMAN-FURAY BAND] DIDN'T GET TOGETHER ON THEIR OWN. A LOT OF THE PROBLEMS CAME FROM THE FACT THAT THIS WAS A FIGMENT OF MY IMAGINATION.

— DAVID GEFFEN

the problems came from the fact that this was a figment of my imagination."

Overlooked at the start was the fact that Souther was not—even by his own admission—a "band" guy who was used to making compromises. Furay—who had a history working with a group that operated like a family—found Souther's lack of diplomacy toward songwriting choices unsettling, and problems arose from the very beginning.

"Richie and I were oil and water," Souther admitted, as reported by author **Barney Hoskyns**. "Souther-Hillman-Furay was David Geffen's attempt to make me mainstream in the wake of the Eagles' success. I think he thought I would be the **Neil [Young]** of the group. It didn't work out because there was too much pressure early on."

SHF released their self-titled debut in 1974, and while opinions vary on the worth of the compositions, chart success was not forthcoming. It's fair to say the group never really jelled as a unit or found the intangible "magic" associated with great bands. They stuck around long enough to release a second LP, *Trouble in Paradise*, which hit the shelves in 1975, but by most accounts, the group was on borrowed time long before that. Perhaps the SHF saga lends credence to the idea that great art can't always be manufactured.

Not surprisingly, all three of the Souther-Hillman-Furay principals would release solo albums in 1976. [247, 599, 1269, 1608]

Rumors Suggest Eagles-E/A Divorce, But Label Re-Signs Band

Eagles first signed with **David Geffen**'s Asylum records in 1971, and by summer 1974, they'd released three albums on the label (which had merged with Elektra in 1972). The first album had been certified gold, and the second was on the verge of reaching that distinction.

The most recent, *On the Border*, had been released in March and sales were steadily growing. In August, *Cashbox* reported Geffen's announcement that he had re-signed the band to a long-term record contract on Asylum.

But the scuttlebutt in Los Angeles wasn't as rosy just one month earlier. *Cashbox* published a report that there was "serious talk" about the Eagles leaving Asylum and following **Dan Fogelberg** and Joe Walsh to Epic Records.

"Word has it that that the Eagles' asking price was a cool half million and that Epic will pick up court costs that might ensue should Asylum take them to court over breach of contract," *Cashbox*'s **David Budge** wrote in his "Points West" column published in the July 24, 1974 issue.

Cashbox's sources were dead wrong, because Walsh—who was only producing Fogelberg's *Souvenirs* LP with Epic—did not leave ABC-Dunhill. Just one week later the

magazine published a retraction, openly apologizing to Geffen and stating that "the Eagles are completely satisfied with their Asylum affiliation." Likewise, the magazine apologized to Walsh and ABC President **Jay Lasker** for implying Walsh was departing.

Were the Eagles negotiating with Epic or other labels? Their disenchantment with Geffen and Asylum was no secret, so it's possible conversations took place over drinks at some point. But nothing ever materialized.

Asylum resigned the band the very next month, an indication that E/A may have needed to make a move to secure its new cash cow. Then again, the *Cashbox* mess might have provided leverage the band needed to bring Geffen to the table on favorable terms. The Eagles' relationship with Geffen was not always smooth, but the renewed deal would last them through the remainder of the decade, covering all the major releases prior to their initial breakup. [603, 1607, 2085, 2086]

FALL 1974

 RELEASES
▶ **Poco**, with Timothy B. Schmit, *Cantamos* (album)
▶ **Poco**, with Timothy B. Schmit, "High and Dry" (single)
▶ **Eagles**, "The Best of My Love" (single)

 ON THE ROAD WITH …
▶ **Eagles**: Barnstorm, The Beach Boys
▶ **Poco**, with Timothy B. Schmit: Chad Stuart, Dave Mason, John Sebastian, Loggins & Messina

NUGGETS

▶ Eagles were the musically stronger group than their stage partner, **The Beach Boys,** in New York's Central Park.
—*Cashbox*

▶ Joe Walsh accepts Rock Music Awards' Best Group "Rocky" for the Eagles, and surprises presenter **Raquel Welch** with a kiss before leaving the stage.
—*Record World*

▶ Eagles' *Desperado* is certified gold by the Recording Industry Association of America. —*Record World*

▶ Eagles played a benefit concert in Saratoga Springs, New York for the American Song Festival. —*Record World*

COLLABORATIONS

▶ **Don Henley** (backing vocals), **Glenn Frey** (guitar, backing vocals), and **Bernie Leadon** (backing vocals) provided musical support on **Randy Newman**'s album *Good Old Boys*.

▶ **Don Henley** provided harmony vocals on **Jackson Browne**'s album *Late for the Sky*.

▶ **Joe Walsh** played slide guitar on **Billy Preston**'s album *The Kids & Me*.

▶ **Timothy B. Schmit** played bass guitar (uncredited) on **Tom Rush**'s album *Ladies Love Outlaws*.

▶ **Don Henley** and **Randy Meisner** provided (uncredited) "participation" on the singles "One Day I Walked" and "Desperados Waiting for a Train" on **Tom Rush**'s album *Ladies Love Outlaws*.

▶ **Joe Walsh** (production, electric 12-string guitar, electric 6-string guitar, acoustic 12-string guitar, ARP bass, backing vocals), **Don Henley** (drums, backing vocals), **Glenn Frey** (backing vocals) and **Randy Meisner** (backing choir vocals) provided musical support on **Dan Fogelberg**'s album *Souvenirs*.

▶ **Glenn Frey** (acoustic guitar), **Don Henley** (drums, backing vocals), and **Timothy B. Schmit** (bass guitar) provided musical support on the song "You Can Close Your Eyes" on **Linda Ronstadt**'s album *Heart Like a Wheel*.

Under Deadline Pressure, Eagles Cancel European Tour

When *On the Border* was released in March 1974, the Eagles kicked off a tour to support it by playing a televised set on *Don Kirshner's Rock Concert*. Immediately after, the group embarked on an ambitious 40-city tour of the United States and Canada—perhaps overly ambitious.

Now headliners, they had announced dates for the European leg of the tour, to start in early May in Glasgow, Scotland, before heading to London and the rest of Europe. The band had not been overseas since opening a series of dates for **Neil Young** in England and Scotland in 1973, but their fan base in the United Kingdom and across Europe was growing despite the band's lack of overseas support from Elektra/Asylum.

Meanwhile, the clock was ticking on developing and recording new material for their next as-yet-unnamed album, and something had to give.

The truth was that the Eagles had barely started their fourth effort by September 1975, eventually titled *One of These Nights*. It would be another nine months before they completed recording. But there was plenty of pressure to make progress. Just after the band completed their last summer gig with **The Beach Boys** in Jersey City, New Jersey, in mid-September, E/A announced the tour's overseas leg had been cancelled.

It was a rare instance of an Eagles cancellation. E/A said those shows would be made up a few months later, but when the that

155

continued on Page 158

Dan Fogelberg (left) and Joe Walsh play on ABC's *In Concert* late-night show on December 5, 1974.

WALSH HELMS SHIP ON FOGELBERG'S *SOUVENIRS*

The scene in L.A. in the early 1970s was an incestuous one where musicians, managers, and promoters all seemed to be involved with each others' projects. So it was no surprise when **Dan Fogelberg** retained future Eagle Joe Walsh, whom he'd met through his manager, to produce his 1974 record, *Souvenirs*. After all, Fogelberg's manager was also **Irving Azoff**, who managed both Walsh and the Eagles.

Though he was living in Los Angeles, Danville native Azoff had seen Fogelberg perform during a trip home to Illinois and was impressed. "You're the one," he told Fogelberg. "I'm ready for the big time. And I think you're ready for the big time, too."

Fogelberg's first record, *Home Free*, had been recorded in Nashville, though it wasn't particularly successful. Azoff brought Fogelberg to Columbia Records president **Clive Davis**, who offered him a recording deal but thought the artist's debut may have been hampered by being too countrified. With that in mind, Walsh was tapped as the new producer with an eye on introducing more pop and rock sensibilities into the mix.

"I've always wanted to produce but I never thought I could," Walsh explained to *Melody Maker* in 1975. "I didn't think I was ready and I was having enough trouble getting my own things on tape without worrying about anybody else's. But at some point, I figured it was time to try, and I was interested in Dan because I really related to his music."

Walsh not only produced the record but also played guitar on almost every track, and the final results were impressive. Most famous is the album's opening track, "Part of the Plan," an irresistibly delightful composition with wonderful melodies similar to the type of material L.A. songwriters like the Eagles and **Jackson Browne** were churning out. The song would also reach #17 on the *Billboard* charts, but this was just one song on an LP that didn't suffer from a sophomore slump. Other highlights include the harmonious "Illinois," the bluegrass-based "Morning Sky," and "Better Change," where Don Henley can be heard singing harmony. In fact, three Eagles contributed to the album: Henley (who also played drums on the aforementioned "Better Change") and Glenn Frey sang backing vocals on "(Someone's Been) Telling You Stories," while Henley and Randy Meisner provided background vocals to the record's closing track, "There's a Place in the World for a Gambler."

The record, according to Fogelberg, represented "my L.A. days, running with the Eagles. They were all over that record, we were buddies, and we were touring. The thing that I'm most proud of with that record is that it opened the door to the people I wanted to work with."

Besides the Eagles, a host of other L.A. musicians guested on the album, including **Graham Nash** and **America**'s **Gerry Beckley**.

Speaking about Walsh, Fogelberg said, "It was a perfect match, working with Joe...Joe allowed me my freedom in the studio, but still supplied very capable direction."

The feeling between them was mutual. Walsh had been studying under **Bill Szymczyk** for several years by then, and said he was running out of energy in his solo career.

"I was in a position where I was pretty well drained as an artist," Walsh told **John Tobler** in 1983, "but I had a lot of energy in terms of getting someone else's brains down on tape—so I

made a commitment to work with [Fogelberg] on *Souvenirs*, although I'm not really sure, to this day, what a producer does. If I had to write it down, I would be at a loss, but basically, I think if you can get an artist's brains on tape without losing anything in the translation, you're an effective producer, and that's what I tried to do with Dan."

Souvenirs is more steeped in the singer-songwriter tradition and doesn't sound much like the **James Gang** or even **Barnstorm**, lending credence to the notion that Walsh's talents were far more diversified than some may have believed based on his harder rock credentials.

"It's hard to say what a producer does because so many producers do different things," Walsh suggested. "I just tried to be an extension of Fogelberg in whatever way he needed it."

Fogelberg, who passed away in 2007 after a battle with cancer, was honored ten years after his death with an album called *A Tribute to Dan Fogelberg*. On that disc, Eagles contributed a cover of "Part of the Plan" with Joe Walsh taking the lead vocal.

Fogelberg once suggested on his website that he was briefly considered a member of the Eagles many years ago.

"No, I was never asked to join the Eagles," he clarified, but described a conversation where it was contemplated. "I was considered among many others when they were re-organizing the group before the *On the Border* album, but Don Henley and I had a long discussion and we both realized that I wouldn't be the right choice. They were moving in one direction, and I was heading in another." [69, 70, 1572, 1573, 1574, 1575, 1576, 1577, 1945]

[*Souvenirs* represented] my L.A. days, running with the Eagles. They were all over that record, we were buddies, and we were touring. The thing I'm most proud of with that record is that it opened the door to the people I wanted to work with.

— Dan Fogelberg

didn't happen. The only trip to Europe the Eagles made was to take part in **Elton John**'s Wembley Stadium Extravaganza. The band wouldn't return to Europe until April 1977.

The group split time between Criteria Studios in Miami and the Record Plant in Los Angeles compiling tracks for the new LP with producer **Bill Szymczyk**. Six months later, they released *One of These Nights*, the album that finally established them as an A-list band in America. Their fans in Europe would soon forgive them for making them wait so long. [132, 604, 1373, 1871]

Desperado Rustles Up Eagles' Second Gold Album

Desperado, the Eagles' second album, is titled after one of their finest songs, arguably exceeded in popularity only by "Hotel California." In fact, in 2015, *Rolling Stone* readers voted "Desperado" #2 on a list of the group's best songs.

But the album's commercial reception did not match the wider success of its title track. It was actually some months after *Desperado* debuted in 1973 that attention really turned to the song's quality, courtesy of **Linda Ronstadt**'s stunning version on her *Don't Cry Now* album.

Now considered an Eagles classic, *Desperado* failed to make the Top 40. Chartwise, it was the band's biggest failure. Even the two singles released from the album, "Tequila Sunrise" and "Outlaw Man,"

couldn't make it into the *Billboard* Top 50.

It wasn't until the Eagles forged a harder-edged sound on their subsequent album, *On the Border*—thanks in no small part to the addition of guitarist Don Felder—that interest in the group's earlier albums increased.

Over time, sales for *Desperado* picked up enough for the Recording Industry Association of America to certify the album gold on September 23, 1974, almost a year and a half after its release.

In retrospect, the album always carried some risk. Typically, bands refrain from venturing into concept album territory until they're well established in the music business. The western imagery on the album's cover and the Wild West outlaw themes of the material took the group down a narrow path. Country-rock lovers and many critics admired the album's audacity and the sheer quality of its songs and musicianship. It remains one of the finest country-rock albums of all time.

Despite the critical acclaim, its relative commercial failure convinced Glenn Frey and Don Henley that the easygoing, folksy whimsy the band perfected in their Troubadour days was not going to cut it in the mainstream.

Bernie Leadon, the most attuned to country music of the five members, felt differently but lost out to his more forceful bandmates, and the Eagles would leave their bluegrass-tinged origins for a much more commercially attractive rock sound on future projects. [2087]

Lawsuits Fly as Azoff, Belkin Square Off to Manage Walsh

Joe Walsh signed a personal management deal with **Mike Belkin** in 1969. Belkin and his brother, Jules, mainly as concert promoters, had played a significant role in putting Cleveland, Ohio on the rock and roll map.

"They really got Cleveland established as an absolute must-stop in the touring world for every major band, from the **Rolling Stones** to **Bruce Springsteen**," **David Spero**, a DJ at WMMS in the 1970s and later a colleague of the Belkins, recalled to the *Cleveland Jewish News* in June 2019. "They really made this town a must-stop for every major artist—and then they extended it to a bunch of other cities."

Walsh's personal management deal with Mike Belkin saw Belkin receiving twenty-five percent of Walsh's recording earnings, twenty percent of his publishing, and fifteen percent of any other entertainment-related earnings. Undoubtedly, Belkin played a significant role in building the career of the **James Gang**, but Walsh was never comfortable with life in the limelight.

In 1970, **Pete Townshend** invited the James Gang to support **The Who** on a European tour after seeing Walsh's guitar work first hand when the Gang opened for The Who in Pittsburgh. The world was opening up for Walsh, but he was not, at that point, prepared to embrace fame. Walsh declined an invitation to join **Humble Pie** in England and instead opted to recharge his batteries by moving to Boulder, Colorado. That was when Walsh's problems with his manager came to a head.

Belkin, according to Walsh, wholly misrepresented the reason behind his move to Colorado. Those smears alleged that he retreated to the Rocky Mountains to recover from a heroin addition that stifled his career. Walsh was no stranger to drugs an alcohol, but he went to Colorado to rebuild his career. Belkins' claims, he said, were more about hiding the fact that the James Gang wouldn't be successful without Walsh.

Everything came to a head in October 1974 when Belkin Productions, headed by Mike Belkin, filed a lawsuit in the Superior Court of Los Angeles against **Irving Azoff** and ABC Records President **Jay Lasker**, as well as ABC Records Executive Vice President **Howard Stark**. The lawsuit alleged the three individuals interfered in Belkin's management relationship with Joe Walsh.

Previous suits filed by Belkin alleged ABC Records and Azoff had interfered in Belkin's attempts to secure Walsh a record deal with another label. Belkin claimed that ABC Records refused to deal with him as Walsh's manager and that Azoff ruined his relationship with Walsh, forcing him to end his contact with the singer/guitarist in 1974.

Azoff and his lawyers denied all charges and fought back with a countersuit of $500,000 in compensatory damages and $1.5 million in exemplary compensation. The following year, Azoff finessed Walsh into the Eagles, ensuring the fame-reluctant guitarist would get his wish to be in a band already experiencing life in the fast lane. [613, 1562]

WINTER 1974-75

 RELEASES
▶ **Joe Walsh**, "Time Out" (single)
▶ **Joe Walsh**, *So What* (album)

 NUGGETS
▶ Eagles add a fifth member to the band, Don Felder, formerly of **David Blue**'s backup band. —*Record World*
▶ The Hollywood holiday season started with an Eagles-**Dan Fogelberg** show in Santa Monica. Fogelberg's encore included Eagles, his producer, Joe Walsh, **J. D. Souther**, **Jackson Browne**, and **Linda Ronstadt**. Fogelberg's "Auld Lang Syne," along with "The Best of My Love," and "Take It Easy" were a perfect start to 1975, even if the 3,000 balloons that were to fall from the rafters at the stroke of midnight waited until Souther was finished with his set—a bit after midnight. —*Record World*
▶ The new Eagles album is said to be very R&B influenced. Hmmm. —*Record World*

 ON THE ROAD WITH ...
▶ **Eagles**: Dan Fogelberg
▶ **Poco**, with Timothy B. Schmit: Dave Mason, Peremiata Forneria Marconi
▶ **Joe Walsh**: REO Speedwagon, the Charlie Daniels Band

 COLLABORATIONS
▶ **Glenn Frey** (guitar) and **Don Felder** (rhythm guitar) played on **J.D. Souther**'s album *You're Only Lonely*.
▶ **Glenn Frey**, **Don Henley**, and **Randy Meisner** provided backing vocals on **Joe Walsh**'s album *So What*.

 COLLABORATIONS (cont.)
▶ **Timothy B. Schmit** (harmony vocals), **Bernie Leadon** (harmony vocals), **Randy Meisner** (bass guitar), **Glenn Frey** (guitar), and **Don Henley** (drums, harmony vocals) provided musical support on **Danny O'Keefe**'s album *So Long Harry Truman*.
▶ **Randy Meisner**, **Don Henley,** and **Timothy B. Schmit** provided uncredited participation on **Tom Rush**'s album *The Circle Game*.
▶ **Joe Walsh** played guitar on **Ray Manzarek**'s album *The Whole Thing Started With Rock & Roll Now It's Out Of Control*.

Solemn Walsh, Eagles Record 'Help Me Thru the Night'

While Joe Walsh wouldn't join the Eagles until December 1975, both artists were part of **Irving Azoff**'s stable, and their paths had crossed plenty of times prior to that. In some ways, Walsh was always headed towards becoming an Eagle.

After exiting the **James Gang** and recording another two albums with **Barnstorm**—intended as band albums but officially released as solo albums—Walsh grew into a full-fledged solo artist with his *So What* album, recorded in the winter and spring of 1974 and released that December.

Among the *So What* tracks was "Turn to Stone," a re-record of the Barnstorm favorite penned by Walsh and **Terry Trebandt** in 1972. The new version featured Don Henley, Glenn Frey, and Randy Meisner singing harmonies, as they also did on an especially melancholic acoustic ballad, "Help Me Thru the Night," a highly personal piece

continued on Page 163

PATHWAY ALBUM | TIMOTHY B. SCHMIT

POCO
Cantamos
Epic Records, November 1974

It was common in the 1970s for an artist or band to release more than one album a year, and this was true for **Poco** in 1974. In November, they released *Cantamos*, the follow-up to their first post-**Richie Furay** album.

While *Seven* rocked hard at times and reflected a band trying to find their footing after losing their most important member, *Cantamos* was a country-rock gem that found the group cultivating more familiar territory.

The title translates to "we sing" in Spanish and the album cover featured a cut-out window that revealed an inner-sleeve illustration of the group harmonizing with each other in what appears to be the backroom of an otherwise empty saloon. Instruments including an acoustic guitar, lap steel, and banjo surround the group and set the mood for an album of heartland Americana songs with titles like "Sagebrush Serenade," "Western Waterloo," and "One Horse Blue."

True to Poco's origins, *Cantamos* combined both rock and country elements, but there was more emphasis on traditional country instrumentation this time around. Dobro, mandolin, steel guitar, and banjo are featured throughout, and some of the darker elements of *Seven* were replaced with high-energy songs that proved the group learned a thing or two from co-founder Furay.

Pedal steel guitar player **Rusty Young** emerged as a writer on *Cantamos*, contributing a trio of songs including, most significantly, the opening track ("Sagebrush Serenade") and the snappy "High and Dry." This was a direct reaction to an ominous lecture he received from **David Geffen** when Furay departed.

"Tim (Schmit), **Paul** (**Cotton**), **George** (**Grantham**), and I were sitting in a room," Young recounted in **Jerry Fuentes**' 2008 Poco biography, *Legend*. "David Geffen came in and he went down the line. He pointed at Paul and said, 'Now, you write and sing, don't you? You're going to be alright.' He went to Tim. 'You write and sing songs too. You're going to be alright.' Then he went to George and me and said, 'You don't write and you don't sing, do you? You guys are in trouble!'"

The message motivated Young to step up his game. He would later begin singing many of his compositions for Poco, but in 1974, new material from him usually meant more vocals for Timothy B. Schmit, who sang all three of Young's songs on *Cantamos*. Of course, Schmit also sang his own songs, which included the moody-but-melodic "Bitter Blue" and a wonderfully forlorn country piece called "Whatever Happened to Your Smile." Cotton again brought the goods with a collection of songs that included the western-flavored "Susannah" and "Another Time Around."

"*Cantamos* is definitely our best [album]," Schmit proclaimed at the time. "We still haven't got hit records, singles, but those will come." Schmit's optimism notwithstanding, Poco had still not delivered a commercially viable single in eight albums. Epic's patience was wearing thin. [1504]

PATHWAY ALBUM | JOE WALSH

JOE WALSH
So What
ABC-Dunhill Records, November 1974

So What was Joe Walsh's first post-**Barnstorm** solo album, though former bandmates **Joe Vitale** and **Kenny Passarelli** contributed to four tracks and one track, respectively. The liner notes also credit an assortment of studio and guest musicians including future **Fools Gold** drummer **Ron Grinel**, popular L.A. session drummer **Russ Kunkel**, Eagles friend **J.D. Souther**, who contributed guitar and vocals, and three Eagles.

The *So What* cover, picturing Walsh wearing aviator goggles and a scarf (what he might have worn if he'd been piloting the biplane pictured on the cover of *The Smoker You Drink, The Player You Get*), further reflects a Joe Walsh solo record.

Possibly because some of Walsh's most famous early works, including "Funk #49," "Walk Away," and "Rocky Mountain Way," have an edge, he's often classified as a gutsy rocker with an overdriven electric guitar. But Walsh's material was always more eclectic than his reputation, and the songs on *So What* are no different.

"Welcome to the Club," a stomping boogie number, and "Time Out" (co-written with **Terry Trebandt**) were not unlike some of his well-known classics, and Walsh even takes another stab at "Turn to Stone," a rocker first recorded for the 1972 *Barnstorm* LP, this time just a little "more polished," as *AllMusic* describes it.

Meanwhile, "Falling Down" softens the grit and replaces it with strummed acoustic guitars. It's the type of song that serves as evidence Walsh was not such an oddball fit to eventually join the Eagles, despite some opinions in the rock press at the time. The track's co-writer, Don Henley, can be heard singing background vocals on the tune. In fact, Henley, Glenn Frey, and Randy Meisner all appear on *So What*, with the trio singing harmonies on "Turn to Stone" and the poignant "Help Me Thru the Night."

The latter song emerged from the pain Walsh was suffering at the time after losing his young daughter in a car crash. The other notable song on the album that reflected Walsh's grief was the even more touching and painful "Song for Emma."

"Both of those songs were on my next album, *So What*. I called it that because I had this 'so what' attitude. I was angry," Walsh reflected when looking back in 2016. "I was really mad at God. And I felt that was a great reason to drink."

So What was certified gold by the RIAA just a month after its release, selling a cool 500,000 albums in four weeks. [799, 1609, 1610, 1611]

about Walsh's desperate state of mind following the death of his daughter and the dissolution of his marriage.

Henley also sang backup on "Falling Down," which he and Walsh co-wrote, as well as "Time Out," another Walsh/Trebandt tune.

In late 1975, the Eagles would again guest on a performance of "Help Me Thru the Night" when they joined Walsh for his television appearance on *Don Kirshner's Rock Concert*. For this appearance, Meisner was replaced by Don Felder, who, along with Frey and Henley, would play acoustic guitars and contribute harmonies backing Walsh's lead vocal.

With the quartet of musicians sitting on stools center stage, they delivered a remarkable acoustic performance that should have dispelled any notions Walsh might not be a good fit with the Eagles. [225, 1500]

SPRING 1975

 RELEASES
▶ **Poco**, with Timothy B. Schmit, *The Very Best of Poco* (album)
▶ **Eagles**, "One of These Nights" (single)

 ON THE ROAD WITH ...
▶ **Eagles**: Dan Fogelberg, Linda Ronstadt, Minnie Riperton, Seals & Crofts, The Charlie Daniels Band
▶ **Joe Walsh**: Bachman-Turner Overdrive, Climax Blues Band, Humble Pie, James Cotton Blues Band, John Entwistle, Johnny Winter, Kansas, Kingfish, Leo Sayer, Link Wray, Ray Manzarek, Strawbs, The Elvin Bishop Group, Thin Lizzy

 NUGGETS
▶ Eagles' *One of These Nights* tour is a virtual sellout before the first show. Speaking of the boys from L.A., the Eagles and Joe Walsh have been added to the **Elton John/Beach Boys** Wembley show. In related news, **Irving Azoff** has appointed Joe Walsh to A&R position at Full Moon Records. —*Record World*
▶ At **Joe Walsh**'s Shrine Auditorium concert, [Elton John] "Captain Fantastic" himself was leaping onstage to accompany Joe in an encore of **The Beatles**' "Get Back." Joe appeared onstage for his encore suspended in a bird cage, playing and singing to his heart's content. —*Cashbox*
▶ Eagles will open three, and possibly more, shows for the **Rolling Stones** this summer. Meanwhile, **Jim Ed Norman** recently finished up arrangements for the Eagles' new album. —*Record World*
▶ Promoter **Howard Stein** says the Eagles/Fogelberg show is the hottest American package on the road. Ticket grosses are among the highest of any tours so far this year. The package has sold out three shows in Chicago, two SRO shows in New York, and two in Passaic, New Jersey. —*Record World*

 COLLABORATIONS
▶ **Glenn Frey** provided backing vocals on **John Prine**'s album *Common Sense*.
▶ **Bernie Leadon** provided banjo, acoustic guitar, resonator guitar, bass guitar, and backing vocals on the singles "Bluebird Wine," "The Bottle Let Me Down," and "Sleepless Nights" on **Emmylou Harris**' album *Pieces of the Sky*.
▶ **Joe Walsh** played guitar on **Joe Vitale**'s album *Roller Coaster Weekend*.
▶ **Joe Walsh** played guitar and synthesizer on the singles "Solid Gold," "One Night Stand," "Move Over Ms. L" (with a guitar solo), and "Back Door Sally" on **Keith Moon**'s album *Two Sides of the Moon*.
▶ **Bernie Leadon** played rhythm guitar and was co-producer on **David Bromberg Band**'s album *Midnight on the Water*.

continued on Page 171

JOE VITALE

Joe Vitale (second from left), a musical collaborator with Joe Walsh in the early 1970s, later became a key support player with the Eagles on their *Hotel California* and *The Long Run* tours.

Drummer, keyboardist, and flute player **Joe Vitale** has toured and/or recorded with an impressive roster of rockers, from **Crosby, Stills & Nash** and **Neil Young** to **Peter Frampton**, **John Lennon** to **Bill Wyman**, and **Ted Nugent** to **Eric Carmen**.

But Vitale's personal and musical association with longtime buddy Joe Walsh will always be the defining element of his career.

They met in Kent, Ohio, before Walsh started his rocket ride to stardom with the **James Gang.** Vitale had just begun pursuing his childhood musical dream. As a kid, "I was always pounding on my mom's pots and pans," Vitale told *Rolling Stone* in 2020. "My dad said, 'Guess what? You're going to be a drummer.'"

But with disparate musical interests and lifestyles, Walsh and Vitale weren't instant friends.

"We were in rival bands in college. He was in the greaser band, doing like **Four Tops** songs, and I was in the hippie bands doing the **Byrds** and **Beatles** songs," Walsh said, talking with *BAM* in 1981. "We didn't like each other. I didn't like any drummers particularly, and he didn't like guitar players. We decided to get together because he hated me less than any other guitar players, and I hated him less than any other drummers."

Vitale's early touring gig with **Ted Nugent**'s **Amboy Dukes** set the stage for his foundational relationship with Walsh. The Amboy Dukes opened for the James Gang in October 1971 in Florida, and Walsh invited Vitale to hang out.

"He said that he was going to do something different and he was going to put a new band together, and he wanted me to play drums in it," Vitale told *Rolling Stone*. Walsh's post-James Gang group **Barnstorm** was born, but first someone had to break the news to Nugent:

"Ted was really sweet about it; he was so nice. He gave us his blessing and said, 'Listen, you guys should be in a band together.'"

The next January, Vitale joined Walsh in Colorado. Something clicked creatively between them, and their talents complemented each other. Vitale followed up his key role in Barnstorm by collaborating with Walsh on a pair of signature songs—"Rocky Mountain Way," Walsh's first Top 25 single, and "Pretty Maids All in a Row," which would appear on *Hotel California*. Five decades later, Walsh and Vitale were still collaborating.

"We both have the same kind of humor, a very dry humor and way to look at the world," Walsh told the *Tribune-Chronicle* in 2015, "and I just feel really comfortable around [Vitale]. I've never shown him a musical idea [and asked] 'What do you think of this?' where he didn't turn around and make it better."

More importantly, however, Vitale and Walsh got to the point where they could communicate almost telepathically.

"First, we're friends," Vitale said to the *Tribune-Chronicle*. "We've always been friends, whether we work together or not. We respect each other and each other's space. We've worked together so many times, just jamming on stage. We don't have really, really charted out music. He knows where I'm going and I know where he's going."

That closeness helped when Walsh left Vitale behind to join the Eagles, a group which already boasted singing drummer Don Henley. Vitale never begrudged Walsh's decision and kept busy playing other gigs with the likes of Frampton and Crosby, Stills & Nash until Walsh eventually resumed solo work. Their time together smoothed the way when Vitale was subsequently added as a sideman on the Eagles' lengthy tour supporting *The Long Run*.

"We were working all the time, just bouncing back and forth. He'd go back and forth from the Eagles and I'd go to Crosby, Stills & Nash or whatever. Then we'd get together and make more records," Vitale told *Rolling Stone*. "Then he brought me into the Eagles band. They were doing a lot of Joe Walsh music on tour. He wanted me to play drums because I played drums on the records. Also, I was able to give Don Henley a break when he'd go out and sing out front."

Besides being a vital presence on the road and in the studio with Walsh, Vitale co-wrote a trio of songs on three different Walsh LPs: *Songs for a Dying Planet* from 1992; *Ordinary Average Guy* in 1991 (including the album-closing "School Days," which featured Vitale on lead vocals); and *You Bought It - You Name It* from 1983.

Vitale also collaborated on two tunes apiece on three other albums: *Got Any Gum?* from 1987, *But Seriously, Folks...* from 1978 (among them, the touching "Indian Summer"), and Barnstorm's 1972 debut album. The drummer earned sole composing credit on a pair of tracks from *The Smoker You Drink, the Player You Get* in 1973, as well.

If those days with Walsh had always been loose and fun, Vitale said joining the Eagles tour was like becoming part of a well-oiled machine.

"We would go on the stage and Glenn Frey would say [to the audience], 'You're paying; we're playing.' That's the way they treated it," Vitale told the *Canton Repository* in 2020. "Every night was a special show. They were very intense about us playing the parts just as they were recorded. There was no flash and no jamming. People pay a lot of money to see the Eagles, and they give them their money's worth." [1887, 1888, 1889, 1890]

RELEASE
Mid-November
1974

THE BEST OF MY LOVE

By: Don Henley, Glenn Frey, J.D. Souther
Flip Side: Ol' '55 (Tom Waits)

No one at Asylum Records—or within the Eagles—thought "The Best of My Love" would be a hit. The band wanted move past their work with producer **Glyn Johns**, and the song wasn't even considered as a possible single until **Jim Higgs**, a program director at Kalamazoo's WKMI-AM, took a shine to it. Months later, high demand forced Asylum to release it and it to everyone's amazement it became the band's first-ever #1 record. It also served as the springboard for their meteoric rise a year later.

AIRPLAY

"The Best of My Love" was a classic slow roller. WKMI put it on the map by playing the album version of the song in August 1974. Secondary stations like WROV-Roanoke, WBBQ-Augusta, and KIMN-Denver added the song three months later. "Best" then broke in Cincinnati, Memphis, and Detroit, and by January 1975 the single version was appearing on playlists nationwide, including the huge markets of New York and San Francisco.

108 PLAYLIST ADDS Summer 1972					
Region	Aug	Nov	Dec	Jan	Feb	Regional Airplay
Northeast	0	1	5	5	3	13 %
Southeast	0	3	18	9	6	33.3 %
Midwest	*1	1	14	4	1	18.5 %
Southwest	0	0	8	6	1	13.9 %
West	0	1	5	10	7	21.3 %

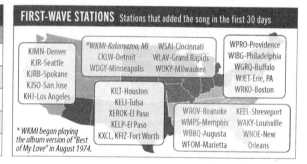

FIRST-WAVE STATIONS Stations that added the song in the first 30 days

KIMN-Denver
KJR-Seattle
KJRB-Spokane
KJSO-San Jose
KHJ-Los Angeles

*WKMI-Kalamazoo, MI   WSAI-Cincinnati
CKLW-Detroit   WLAV-Grand Rapids
WDGY-Minneapolis   WOKY-Milwaukee

WPRO-Providence
WIBG-Philadelphia
WGRQ-Buffalo
WJET-Erie, PA
WRKO-Boston

KILT-Houston
KELI-Tulsa
XEROK-El Paso
KELP-El Paso
KXCL, KFJZ-Fort Worth

WROV-Roanoke   KEEL-Shreveport
WMPS-Memphis   WAKY-Louisville
WBBQ-Augusta   WNOE-New
WFOM-Marietta   Orleans

* WKMI began playing the album version of "Best of My Love" in August 1974.

CHARTS

Billboard	HIGHEST CHARTING WEEK: BILLBOARD - March 1, 1975		
#1 March 1, 1975	SINGLE	ARTIST	# PREV WK
	1. THE BEST OF MY LOVE	EAGLES	2
	2. Have You Never Been Mellow	Olivia Newton-John	5
Cashbox	3. Black Water	Doobie Brothers	4
	4. My Eyes Adored You	Frankie Valli	7
#4 February 22, 1975	5. Some Kind of Wonderful	Grand Funk Railroad	3
	6. Lonely People	America	6
	7. Pick Up the Pieces	Average White Band	1
Record World	8. Lady Marmalade	LaBelle	17
	9. Nightingale	Carole King	10
#3 March 1, 1975	10. Lady	Styx	14

Sources: Billboard, Cashbox, Record World

MICHIGAN DOUBLE-TEAM PROPELS 'BEST' TO #1

Kalamazoo, Michigan, disc jockey **Jim Higgs** had a keen ear for hit music. Spinning records on Michigan AM radio, Higgs had a track record for finding hit songs that weren't on labels' radar. He helped break **Nazareth**'s "Love Hurts" long before anyone else added it, and played a central role in getting the Eagles their first #1 hit as well.

Higgs was music and program director for the influential western Michigan radio station WKMI-AM (1360) in Kalamazoo in summer 1974. His station had already been playing "Already Gone" from *On the Border*, and thought listeners might like several other cuts on the LP. But he was especially drawn to the last track on Side 2, the slow love ballad "The Best of My Love."

"I was kind of an Eagles fan from [their] first album, and when I got the *On the Border* album, I thought, 'Well, Eagles, they do some pretty good stuff. I'll check it out and see if it has some potential as a feature album cut,'" Higgs told *Time Passages*, describing the once-per-hour spotlight feature the station ran for selected singles on newer albums. "We didn't play much off [*Desperado*], but with *On the Border*, I thought there were several [songs] we could use. ["The Best of My Love"] was a nice catchy tune."

The song began to catch the ears of listeners around August 1974, seven months before it topped the *Billboard* chart. "My overnight [deejay] **Gary Outlaw** had been playing 'The Best of My Love' on his all-night show and

his request sheets every week showed more and more people requesting it," Higgs said.

The song had not been released as a single at the time, but he put the LP track into WKMI's regular rotation, and it became a smash in Kalamazoo. Local record stores sold out of the album and Higgs said stores were telling him it was because of "Best."

Higgs let **Rip Pelley**, Elektra/Asylum's promotion director in Michigan, know that the song was a fast-mover. Back in Los Angeles, the Eagles' label, Asylum, stubbornly kept pushing that summer's single, "James Dean," hoping it would catch fire.

"We were headed for the third single," Pelley told *Time Passages*. "It was going to be 'Ol' '55.' That was it. Then, probably a month before we knew they were going to release the third, Jim calls me up and says there's an album cut that's getting huge phones on the weekend. And at the time, I was like, 'Let me know what happens, because there's nothing I can do at the moment. Because 'Ol '55' is is slated as the third single and that's that.'"

A week or two later, Pelley said, Higgs called him back and said, "You know what? This is getting so many phones that I'm going to chart the record," meaning he was going to track it on their published playlist.

It was a bold move by Higgs, and Pelley knew that it might force the label into a different direction. As the Detroit and Michigan rep for Elektra/Asylum, it was his job to let the suits in Los Angeles know when something was happening. Once WKMI began charting the single, other stations would likely follow.

"I said, 'Okay, I have to run this up the flagpole,'" Pelley explained. "So, I called my main boss in Los Angeles, **Kenny Buttice**, who was vice president of promotion, and I said to him, 'Look, we got some action out here.' He said, 'Ripper, don't even think about it. The Eagles want 'Ol '55,' and we're going with 'Ol '55' and that's it.'"

As a "lowly" Detroit rep, Pelley didn't press the issue. But then Higgs came back to him a week later and said the record had surged from #30 to #15.

"I called Kenny back and said, 'Kenny, this thing is freaking exploding. You can't ignore it any longer,'" Pelley said. Buttice said he would make some phone calls, but by the time he got back to Pelley, "The Best of My Love" album cut had already reached #1 in Kalamazoo.

The situation created a marketing conundrum for Asylum. "Ol' '55" was a Glenn Frey favorite and **Tom Waits**, who wrote it, was also an Asylum artist. "But the field team thought ["Ol' '55"] was not a Top 40 hit," Pelley said. "We needed to come with something hard-hitting or a nice love ballad, and 'The Best of My Love' made sense as we needed a hit and Jim had proven its potential consumer popularity. I don't know if the Eagles finally agreed or if they even knew about it, but they did not want 'The

Best of My Love,'" he said, noting the falling out with their former producer, **Glyn Johns**; "Best" was one of the Johns songs on the album. "They wanted a [**Bill**] **Szymczyk** song to move forward."

With the band firm on releasing "Ol' '55" and the label reading the tea leaves for "The Best of My Love," Pelley and Buttice played some marketing sleight of hand with the single. The original plan was to release "Ol' '55" on both single sides, what's called a "double A-side" (one mono, one stereo for radio). Buttice decided to release the commercial or "retail copy" with two sides, one "Ol' '55," the other "The Best of My Love." The 7" single was simply marked "promo" and went out to the radio stations and "Best" immediately garnered the airplay.

When WKMI finally got the pressed single in November, Higgs had already been programming it for nearly four months. Even though that was typically the lifespan of a hit single, Pelley asked Higgs to keep spinning it. That decision wasn't a difficult choice. "I decided we were going to treat 'The Best of My Love' as the A-side and the requests went crazy," he said, even after four months of play. Meanwhile, Pelley and Buttice were sweating their decision not to push "Ol' '55" harder.

"Kenny told me, 'You're going to live or die by this one,'" Pelley said. "'You better make sure it works.'" He was anxious, but ultimately, he didn't sweat long. Even though Higgs had been playing the album cut for

Elektra/Asylum Promotion Director **Rip Pelley** (left), WKMI-AM Program Director **Jim Higgs** (center), and E/A Regional Promotion Director **Bert Stein** pose with an Eagles-signed *On the Border* LP cover in 1975.

months, he took the single version to #1 in Kalamazoo as Pelley successfully pushed it into all the secondary Michigan markets.

Then, **Rosalie Trombley**, the nationally respected music director at Detroit's biggest station, CKLW, picked it up based on the secondary Michigan airplay and sales, which launched it into the stratosphere. It became the band's first #1 on March 1, 1975, when it bumped **Average White Band**'s "Pick Up the Pieces" from the top. It stayed there for just one week, but the mark was made.

More drama unfolded when it was discovered that while pressing the single, Asylum opted to unilaterally cut the 4:34 track

down to just three and a half minutes. Don Henley was reportedly so upset by this move that he demanded the abbreviated single be pulled from record stores.

The label's executive promotion staff in Los Angeles defended the decision by claiming that radio stations wouldn't play it in its original long form, which was a poorly reasoned argument since Higgs had been successfully playing that LP version from the start, although major market radio was a bit more stringent in their short-form policy.

Bad feelings about that decision lingered, and when the single passed the one-million-sold mark, Eagles manager **Irving**

Azoff, along with Don Henley and Glenn Frey, exacted some revenge. Azoff had the gold record framed with a pie-slice piece cut out and captioned it the "The Golden Hacksaw Award." The trio then went down to Elektra/Asylum headquarters late one night and, according to Elektra's then-head of production, **Keith Holzman**, they bolted the award to a wall in the lobby on La Cienega to show their displeasure. Holzman told *Time Passages* in 2022 it remains a mystery who approved the track being shortened, but offered he thought it was expertly done.

Despite the initial lack of enthusiasm about "Best" from both the label and the band, both Higgs and Pelley played big roles in the song's success. The band thanked Higgs later that year by sending him a framed copy of the LP, complete with autographs. Though the signatures have faded over the years, it still hangs proudly in his home office.

Pelley's moves with "Best" helped earn him a promotion to director of regional artist development, and would eventually become national artist development director and, later, national field promotions director in Los Angeles for Elektra/Asylum, positions he held from 1977 to 1981.

Higgs was semi-retired and operating WAKV-AM, a small radio station out of his home, in 2014 when the Eagles' *History of the Eagles* tour made its way to Michigan. Higgs' daughter, **Dianna Stampfler**, connected with the band's management team and received concert passes. The Eagles met them backstage before the show and the band members, especially Detroit native Frey, were so captivated by Higgs' story that they were almost late taking the stage. Frey capped the affair by regaling the audience with the story of how Higgs helped "Best" became the Eagles' first and best. [15, 220, 221, 1723, 1729, 1730]

Former WKMI-AM Program Director **Jim Higgs** (center) poses backstage with the Eagles during the *History of the Eagles* tour in 2014.

Eagles Join O'Keefe in Studio For *So Long Harry Truman*

Eagles were busy finishing their fourth LP in January 1975, but between the sessions for *One of These Nights*, the band members found time to support other artists they knew and admired.

That winter, Bernie Leadon lent his guitar talents to **Gram Parsons**' posthumous *Grievous Angel* album, and Glenn Frey and Don Felder joined **J.D. Souther** in the studio as well. Randy Meisner, Don Henley, and Frey also helped out Joe Walsh and **Tom Rush** on their upcoming releases later that winter.

Singer-songwriter **Danny O'Keefe** was another artist who had become part of the Eagles' growing circle of friends, and they joined him in the studio to help him record his fourth album, *So Long Harry Truman*.

O'Keefe was a recent arrival in Los Angeles when the sessions began. After releasing three country albums, he was looking for a change of pace. Born in Wenatchee, Washington, he found his musical footing in the early 1960s singing and playing guitar in coffeehouses in Minneapolis. He was inspired by blues and folk artists like **Rev. Gary Davis**, **John Hurt**, and **Lightnin' Hopkins**, as well as local Minnesota players like **Dave Ray** and **John Koerner**.

But O'Keefe said it was listening to **Miles Davis**' epic 1959 album *Kind of Blue* that launched him into his career as a musician. He briefly joined a psychedelic rock band called **Calliope**, but returned to his

Eagles tried to help their artist friends in the studio when they could. The band joined **Danny O'Keefe** as he recorded his new album in 1975.

country and folk roots when he recorded *Introducing Danny O'Keefe* for Seattle-based Jerden Records in 1966.

Then he hit the New York folk music circuit and was signed by Atlantic Records' legendary chairman **Ahmet Ertegun**. With Ertegun producing, he released his second album, *O'Keefe*, in 1970, an uneven collection of songs that needed some polish, but also revealed a promising young artist. The Top 10 hit "Good Time Charlie's Got the Blues" was the album's highlight.

O'Keefe released his second Atlantic album, *Breezy Stories*, produced by **Arif Mardin**, in 1973, but it didn't reach the heights of his previous album. So O'Keefe decided to head west.

"I had been recording in New York with

Arif Mardin, who I loved working with, but I wanted a change," to a sound that felt more like the West Coast, O'Keefe told *Time Passages*.

He moved to Los Angeles and was hanging out socially with a lot of the local players. He began looking for a producer, and **John Boylan** was among those recommended to him, so they met and discussed O'Keefe's new project.

"[John] and I hit it off and I think he understood the direction I wanted to go," O'Keefe said. Boylan was already well acquainted with the friends O'Keefe had cultivated. The new kid in town had met all the members of the Eagles while they were recording their first album, and knew **Linda Ronstadt** and her band too.

"I can't remember if [Boylan] asked them, or if they volunteered," O'Keefe said of the Eagles guesting on his *Truman* sessions. "We were all in the same circle then and they were friends. I liked their songs, and they liked mine. John probably asked them if they were interested, but I honestly don't remember how it came to pass. Linda was also a friend and liked the [*Truman*] song 'Quits' and had actually considered recording it for herself."

Boylan assembled a formidable group of country-rock musicians of the era for the sessions. Ronstadt, whom Boylan had previously managed, and her bandmate, eventual Top 40 artist **Andrew Gold**, joined O'Keefe and the Eagles in the studio. **Jackson Browne**'s talented sideman **David Lindley**, along with

Sneaky Pete Kleinow and former Wrecking Crew member and first-call session multi-instrumentalist **Larry Knechtel** also joined in.

Pianist **Roger Kellaway**, an Oscar-nominated composer who backed **Joni Mitchell** for a time in the early 1970s, played piano on four of the album's tracks, and the always-in-demand jazz saxophonist **Tom Scott** lent his talents to a track.

The Eagles played and sang harmonies on three cuts: "So Long Harry Truman," "Covered Wagon," and "Steel Guitar." Henley also played drums on the title cut, and joined in backup harmonies by Leadon and Ronstadt.

O'Keefe's vocals were inspired and Dylan-esque. Henley and **Joyce Everson** provided backing vocals for "Covered Wagon," an upbeat song that opens with a 1970s funk groove, then breaks off into a Southern rock blues guitar centerpiece for O'Keefe. But the closest thing to full Eagles support was laid down in "Steel Guitar," with Glenn Frey playing a straight-fire rhythm and Lindley magnificent as the steel guitar centerpiece. Randy Meisner joined on bass and Henley added backing vocals. Always known for his ability to arrange a song, Frey favorably tinkered with this one, O'Keefe said. But the session didn't involve many other ad hoc arrangements or changes.

"My instinct is to always let players find their way through a song after I've played it for them," he said, "making sure they know all the chords and the inspiration and feel. 'Steel Guitar' is a song [that drew] on the older history of country music, which we were all schooled in."

"Delta Queen" was pure Louisiana jazz and O'Keefe's vocals were deep and penetrating. "It's Been a Good Day" was the session's most commercial piece, with a polished sound reminiscent of **Boz Scaggs'** late 1970s compositions. "Hard Times" was an intense, guitar reverb-laden cut that offered a cathedral-like effect with tight harmonies. "Quits," the song Ronstadt liked, might have been the best song on the entire album.

Despite O'Keefe's strong songwriting and excellent support, the album didn't fare well on the radio or on the charts. Country-rock musicians were still struggling with zero airplay from either country or rock stations and confused record labels that still didn't know where to focus their marketing. *So Long Harry Truman* may have been O'Keefe's most accomplished effort to date, but the album never rose higher than #189 on *Record World*'s album chart. And that was unfortunate because O'Keefe's new-direction LP was a worthwhile listen. It remains so today. [1621, 1627, 1628, 1629, 1630, 1631]

Eagles Head Back to High School For Sweaty WCFL Promotion

The last time the Eagles played before a high school crowd, in early 1972, they were barely a band. Then relatively unknown outside of their friends at the Troubadour, the group played before tweens and teenagers at the Westlake School for Girls in Bel-Air near UCLA as one of their warmup shows before embarking on their first tour.

Three years later, the Eagles were on the verge of releasing their fourth album, *One of These Nights*, and a radio station promotion would put them before another crowd of teens.

The band collaborated with Chicago Top 40 disc jockey **Larry Lujack** on a promotion where they would be "raffled off" to a Chicago-area high school that best represented a sense of camaraderie and team spirit. When the Eagles came to Chicago that summer, they would play a free concert at the chosen high school; Lujack would attend to hand out free albums and other tchotchkes. In return the Eagles would get a Lujack-led prime time interview on WCFL to promote *Nights*.

The "WCFL School Spirit" contest was held in April 1975, and a month later, McHenry High School in McHenry, Illinois delivered a whopping 54,000 signed petitions to win the Eagles concert. A month after that, the band showed up in Johnsburg, a suburb just north of Chicago. **Dan Fogelberg** and his band, **Fools Gold**, were the night's opening act.

The conditions were almost unbearable. The stage was set up in a sweltering auditorium one floor above the school's indoor swimming pool, so the humidity was oppressive. Undaunted, hundreds of students lined up for the show, and school journalists were given access to Randy Meisner and Fools Gold.

"We're not nervous, and we wanted to come," Meisner told the young writers. "We were in high school once and wanted to come back to see if it has changed."

During the show, Glenn Frey paused a few moments to talk about the band, explaining to the students that each of the five band members shared the songwriting duties, before he introduced Don Henley as the band's drummer and one of the writers of "The Best of My Love," which had given the group their first #1 record just four months before.

Days later, they headed east to perform with **Linda Ronstadt** and **Seals & Crofts** in Virginia and then joined the **Rolling Stones** in Kansas City as part of their 1975 American tour. In June, the Eagles would head to London to perform with **Elton John** and **The Beach Boys**. Eagles would perform before hundreds of thousands of fans through 1975, but none worked harder for a show than the students at McHenry High School. [2022, 2023]

The Crusade: Szymczyk Closes Out Manic *Nights* Sessions

Bill Szymczyk got more than he bargained for when he agreed to go into the studio with the Eagles. *On the Border* took six weeks to record, not counting the time the band put in with **Glyn Johns** in London. But it took six months to wrap up work on *One of These Nights*.

They did most of the work at Criteria Studios in Miami, where concierge service Home At Last arranged for the band to stay at 461 Ocean Boulevard, the same house that **Eric Clapton** made famous the year before. Other crew members stayed at nearby houses, in the same general area. The seasoned producer likened it to a "crusade."

"We'd always get more of a swamp sound in Florida," Szymczyk told the *Palm Beach Post*. "The

WCFL developed a promotional flyer that was distributed to high schools in the Chicago area to win a free concert with the Eagles. McHenry High School won.

best thing about working and living in Florida is it got them out of their hometown, and by doing so made them a hell of a lot more comfortable. They were in a much more creative, non-hassle environment than in L.A. They wrote more because they were interrupted less."

Szymczyk's experience was more lengthy and challenging than anything he had done before. **Rich Wiseman** of *Crawdaddy* interviewed him the night he finished production on the LP. Wiseman's article was part of a more extensive feature on rock producers.

"I'm finishing the new Eagles album tonight," an exhausted Szymczyk explained. "It's like winning a crusade. It's taken a long time. There are a million and one reasons, the most honest of which is that the material wasn't ready when the studio time was booked."

Szymczyk said that Eagles' pal Joe Walsh, whom he recorded many times, habitually wrote songs in the studio; the band had picked up that tendency, which led to them all playing six months of catch-up with *Nights*.

"With them, producing is really weird because they're five completely different individuals," he continued. "You got a laid-back Texas serious person, you have a De-

YOU GOT A LAID BACK TEXAS SERIOUS PERSON... A DETROIT MANIAC RAVING GREASER, AND A FLORIDA LEAD GUITAR PLAYER WHOSE ATTITUDE IF THINGS DON'T GO RIGHT IS 'I DON'T CARE'... MR. NATURAL IN BERNIE AND MEISNER, WHO'S PARANOID ABOUT EVERYTHING.

— BILL SZYMCZYK

troit maniac raving greaser, and a Florida lead guitar player whose attitude if things don't go right is, 'I don't care,' he cruises with it. You have Mr. Natural in Bernie, whose attitude is 'Fuck it, I'll go to the beach.' And you have Meisner, who's paranoid about everything.

"I've often said when I'm dealing with the Eagles, I'm the Henry Kissinger of rock and roll," Szymczyk said. "I was living with two of them in their house, Glenn and Don's, in the beginning of this album and had to leave and go to the hotel because Kissinger wouldn't stay in Sadat's house if Golda was on the telephone all the time."

Regardless of his locale, the band usually trusted their producer and respected his judgment and fairness. He acknowledged that as they developed the album, he left some of it to their "I've-always-done-it-this-way" tendencies, but they were open to refinement and everyone ended up chipping in.

"I'm going to New York next to do **J. Geils**," Szymczyk told Wiseman. "They're great. Six crazy people, but not anywhere as bad as their media image. They're six pussycats. It's funny, the Eagles have this laid-back, L.A. pickers image, and they're maniacs." [132, 2094, 2122]

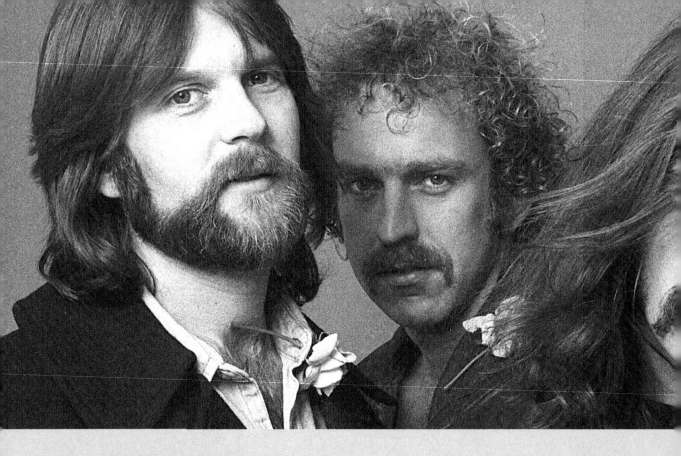

'EL CHINGADERO' TAGGED FOR *NIGHTS* COVER ART

Boyd Elder's association with the Eagles didn't begin with the skull art depicted on the album cover for *One of These Nights*. The Texas-born artist and troublemaker had known the Eagles for a number of years and even made an appearance in the western photo shoot for the *Desperado* album. But his career took a big swing upward when one of his creations landed on the cover of the Eagles' follow-up to *On the Border*.

While attending the Chouinard Art Institute in Downtown Los Angeles in the mid-1960s, Elder did more than network with musicians; he was fortunate to cross paths with creatives of all types. One such individual was a California-born artist he met in 1965 named **Rick Griffin**. The two became close friends and a Christmas gift Griffin sent in 1972 proved to be a historical piece of inspiration.

"Rick Griffin sent me a present packed in an apple crate and lettered 'To Boyd' in Olde English," Elder explained. "Inside was the breastbone of a Thanksgiving turkey he'd scalloped and pinstriped."

Several months later in 1973, with his art supplies decimated after a fire ravaged his studio on the family ranch in tiny Valentine, Texas, Elder was presented with another "gift" of sorts, this time from a neighbor who was working as a ranch hand who gave him "two wild steer skulls—a bull and a cow skull."

The artist remembered Griffin's painted turkey breast and, drawing further inspiration from Native American and Chicano culture, painted and decorated the steer craniums, tricking them out not unlike how he had pinstriped his friends' vehicles as a teen growing up in El Paso.

"I painted the skulls like they were the gas

tanks of motorcycles," he explained. "One of those [skulls] is the one that was used on *One of These Nights* that was turned into the Eagles album cover."

Elder said Don Henley and Glenn Frey became interested in the skull creation when he shared a slideshow of photos of his first two skulls with them in Dallas, where the Eagles were playing a show. In a 1978 interview, Elder said the original skull the album cover was based on was in Frey's possession, while the second skull had been given to **Joni Mitchell**.

The style, which Elder called "American Fetish— RIP," has been described as "mystical Southwest," and successfully captured the mood the band was looking for. It was the fourth, and last, cover made for the Eagles by designer **Gary Burden**.

"This album came at a time when the band and

the music was poised to make a seismic shift from folk/country/rock headed towards a more polished and sophisticated music and "look" that culminated with *Hotel California*," Burden wrote in his blog in September 2009.

"I decided to focus on the front cover and create a magical talisman to represent and express the powerful dark magic of the band and the music," he said. "I went to a friend, artist Boyd Elder. I wanted to use one of his pieces for the cover and have him do the lettering for me. Boyd is a guy I first met before I got involved in rock and roll when as a designer at an L.A. architectural firm it was one of my responsibilities to buy art for installation as a part of our interior spaces for a series of bank buildings we were designing. I used to go to the local art colleges to scout for good

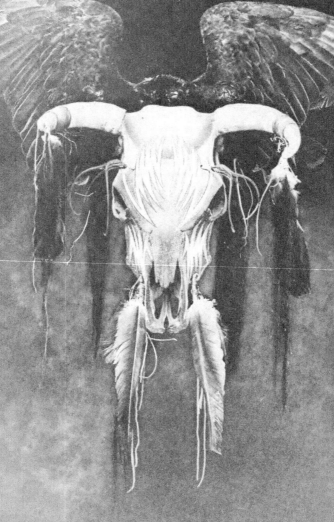

EAGLES
ONE OF THESE NIGHTS
7E-1039

**A NEW ALBUM. A NEW SINGLE.
A NEW EXPERIENCE.**

All Of These Nights, 1975: **June 19** Rotterdam, Holland **June 21 & 22** Wembley Stad., London, England **June 26 & 27** Pine Knob, Detroit, Mich. **June 29** Oakland Stadium, San Francisco, Ca **June 30** Civic Center, Sacramento, Ca

SD-5054   SD-5068   7E-1004

ON ASYLUM RECORDS & TAPES.

promising young artists. Boyd was one of those people and later on our wives and children were all a part of our extended 'family' along with dear friend Rick Griffin and his wife and daughters. Boyd and I worked together often over the years."

Burden said he chose this particular piece of art because it represented, to him, where the band was coming from and where they were going.

"The cow skull is pure cowboy, folk, the decorations are American Indian inspired and the future is represented by the more polished reflective glass beaded surfaces covering the skull. All set against the dark eagle feather wings that speak of mysterious powers.

Texas artist **Boyd Elder**, aka "El Chingadero," poses for photographer **Henry Diltz** at their friend **Gary Burden**'s house in January 1975 with the cow skull sculpture that **Tom Kelley** would soon photograph for the cover of the Eagles' *One of These Nights*.

"Technically the challenge was to make this totemic image command a presence in the room. So, I made it stand up off the page by debossing large areas and doing incredibly detailed and elaborate embossing in the wings and feathers. The photographer's drop cloth background is this cosmic blue to black of deep space," Burden added. "This always has and still does feel like some powerful object when you hold it in your hand. Something independent and 'of a piece.' Not the usual 'album cover' with a friendly, inviting portrait of a group of guys, a band. I was nominated for a Grammy for this album cover. I didn't win but as they say, 'It's being nominated that counts. You're already a winner.'"

The sexual revolution of the 1970s was well underway by the time Burden's *One of These Nights* album package was considered, and the Grammy statuette went to **Jim Ladwig**, who designed the **Ohio Players** album package for their LP, *Honey*. The album cover featured a gorgeous nude model drenched in honey, holding a honey jar and ladle, and strategically photographed to keep an R-rating. The photos were beautifully conceived by former *Playboy* photographer **Richard Fegley**, and when opened the gatefold essentially served as a pin-up poster.

Although it was the last cover Burden did for the band, he looked back at those experiences with reverence.

"I am grateful for the amazing times we shared," he wrote in 2009, "from before they were signed to a record label to the crazy, psychedelic, American Indian Shaman magic, mind bending adventures on our trip to the desert for the first album cover. Historically hilarious. They are without a doubt some of the funniest human beings I have ever met." [247, 256, 257, 262, 1786, 1787, 1788, 1789, 1790, 1791, 1856, 2137]

ONE OF THESE NIGHTS

After three years as a band that merely flirted with success, the Eagles got a full measure of it when "The Best of My Love" surprised everyone by going to #1. Then *One of These Nights* exploded, elevating them to A-list headliners. They were improving with each album, but had even more in store as they prepared for their *Hotel* check-in.

SUMMER 1975

 RELEASES
- ▶ **Eagles**, *One of These Nights* (album)
- ▶ **Poco**, with Timothy B. Schmit, *Head Over Heels* (album)
- ▶ **Poco**, with Timothy B. Schmit, "Makin' Love" (single)

 NUGGETS
- ▶ Joe Walsh joins the Eagles onstage for "Rocky Mountain Way," and in Kansas City, Walsh and the Eagles joined **Keith Richards** and **Ron Wood** in an impromptu jam in the latter's room. —*Cashbox*
- ▶ While the Eagles were onstage at Wembley, Don Henley's graduating class was holding their 10-year reunion at the American Legion Hall. —*Sounds*
- ▶ "Lyin' Eyes" has finally been released as a single on the heels of *One Of These Nights*. "Lyin' Eyes," which has been a favorite DJ go-to-the-bathroom (or whatever) album cut because it's long enough to provide time for such things, has been edited for AM; at press time, the length is unknown [ed. note: single was 4:14, album cut was 6:22]. —*Record World*

 COLLABORATIONS
- ▶ Don Henley and Glenn Frey, credited as "Sons of the Desert," provided backing and harmony vocals on the song "Somebody Must Be Wrong" on the **Souther-Hillman-Furay Band**'s album *Trouble in Paradise*.
- ▶ **Don Felder** played mandolin on **Pure Prairie League**'s album *Two Lane Highway*.

 ON THE ROAD WITH ...
- ▶ **Eagles**: Atlanta Rhythm Section, Billy Preston, Commodores, Dan Fogelberg, Dave Mason, J. Geils Band, J.D. Souther, Jimmy Buffett, Joe Walsh, Leo Kottke,

 ON THE ROAD WITH ... (cont.)
Montrose, Poco, Roger McGuinn, Rufus & Chaka Kahn, Seals & Crofts, The Gap Band, The Rolling Stones, Tom Waits, Trapeze
- ▶ **Poco**, with Timothy B. Schmit: Aerosmith, Bachman-Turner Overdrive, Dave Mason, Eagles, Eric Clapton, Frank Marino & Mahogany Rush, Kansas, Nils Lofgren, Kingfish, Seals & Crofts, Slade
- ▶ **Joe Walsh**: Blue Öyster Cult, Point Blank

Eagles, Walsh Join Elton John For Historic Wembley Concert

Elton John knows how to throw a party. He gathered some of the biggest acts of the day at Wembley Stadium in London for a stupendous one-off event called the Midsummer Music Extravaganza on June 21, 1975.

More than 72,000 people gathered in the hot summer sun to witness a ten-hour show featuring John as the headliner, along with an impressive array of supporting acts including fellow British rockers **Stackridge**, popular American bands **Rufus** (featuring **Chaka Khan**) and **The Beach Boys**, and both Joe Walsh (as a solo artist) and the Eagles.

Promotions for the show began early in the spring. The band members even filmed a commercial resembling a late-night used car ad, with all four Eagles lined up alongside a car and waving. When the acts finally made it to the stage, though Elton was riding high with his 1974 *Greatest Hits* compilation and considered the top draw on the bill, press reports indicated that other bands—particularly The Beach Boys—outshone him that day. This was largely because after playing

Don Henley plays onstage during **Elton John**'s Midsummer Music Extravaganza at Wembley Stadium in London in June 1975.

through a few favorites, John elected to play the entirety of his new album, *Captain Fantastic and the Brown Dirt Cowboy*, which had been released only about three weeks prior. Much of the audience was not yet familiar with the new material.

Conversely, The Beach Boys were in full nostalgia mode, jamming on all their plentiful hits and mostly leaving the deeper cuts off the setlist. Many of the well-known songs they performed were from their hugely successful *Endless Summer* compilation released in 1974, which featured their early classics from 1962 through 1965.

Others suggested that the Eagles, too, may have stolen the show with their impeccable harmonies and well-rehearsed performance. They played the title track from the just-released *One of These Nights* album, as well as the Randy Meisner-sung "Too Many Hands," but the rest of the original material in the set was drawn from the first three records. Joe Walsh, who had performed his own set earlier, foreshadowed things to come when he joined the Eagles for the final two songs of their set: a cover of Chuck Berry's

"Carol" and their recent chart-topping hit, "The Best of My Love."

Bernie Leadon, who sang "Train Leaves Here This Morning" at Wembley, was, of course, still officially in the Eagles for this gig, but according to Don Felder, his departure was feeling more and more imminent. The association the band had with Walsh at this show, he said, helped solidify Walsh's candidacy to join them as a replacement for Leadon.

"Everybody foresaw down the line an eventual departure by Bernie and it was in the back of everybody's mind of what to do: Would we continue as a four-piece or add a fifth piece?" Felder said. "In the meantime, Walsh had been around and... that relationship had been developing, so when it reached a point where Bernie finally made his last commitment, the obvious, most logical choice that had naturally progressed to that point, was Joe."

Walsh already practically considered himself an Eagles by the time of the Wembley show. Still, his official booking on the bill had him as a solo act, and he played with a great bunch of musicians backing him.

"That was a good band," Walsh told **John Tobler** in 1983. "At that point, I knew I was going to be in the Eagles, although it wasn't yet on paper. There was **Willie Weeks, Andy Newmark**, **David Mason** the keyboard player, and at various times **Ricky Fataar**, **Bryan Garofalo**, **Paul Harris**, **Joe Vitale**, **Jay Ferguson**...I had built up a bunch of songs through **James Gang** days, **Barnstorm** and post-Barnstorm, and I really had put together a pretty good group, although I was running out of energy to oversee it all."

Walsh said he was very proud of the band he assembled for Wembley, and was equally proud of the live LP that group would record later in the year, *You Can't Argue with a Sick Mind*. He also knew, however, that his days of being exclusively a solo artist were ending. [738, 1404, 1501, 1636, 1637, 1638, 1639]

'I Wish You Peace' Nearly Starts a Fight

Patti Davis, the daughter of **Ronald Reagan**, who in a few years would begin an eight-year run as president of the United States, received a co-writing credit for the song "I Wish You Peace" on the Eagles' *One of These Nights* album.

The credit for it came about through her relationship with Bernie Leadon, who met the actor-turned-politician's daughter after returning to Los Angeles in the wake of a tour supporting *On the Border*.

At the time, Davis' right-wing Republican father was the governor of California. Nev-

> AT THAT POINT, I KNEW I WAS GOING TO BE IN THE EAGLES, ALTHOUGH IT WASN'T YET ON PAPER ... [*SICK MIND*] WAS LIKE MY LAST STATEMENT, THE END OF A PHASE BEFORE I WENT BACK INTO A BAND SITUATION.
>
> — JOE WALSH

continued on Page 187

RELEASE
Late May
1975

ONE OF THESE NIGHTS

By: Don Henley, Glenn Frey
Side B: Visions (Felder, Henley)

"The Best of My Love" put the Eagles in the public eye just months before they released their new single, "One of These Nights." Radio loved it and the record-buying public pushed the song to the top of the charts, giving the band back-to-back #1 singles for the first time. With Bill Szymczyk producing, the song blended an R&B backbeat with great lyrics, entrancing harmonies, a scorching guitar solo, and dueling falsettos from Don Henley and Randy Meisner to create a rich sound worthy of the #1 single they achieved.

AIRPLAY

"One of These Nights" was the first Eagles single picked up immediately by every major market. KYA-San Francisco, KHJ-Los Angeles, and WPIX-New York City added the song to their playlists as soon as it was released. Secondary stations nationwide added the single too, and nearly every station kept the song in their rotations all summer long. Automatic playlist adds are a signal that a band has arrived, and with "Nights," the Eagles reached new heights.

110 PLAYLIST ADDS Summer 1975					
Region	May	Jun	Jul	Aug	Regional Airplay
Northeast	1	12	7	1	19.1 %
Southeast	5	17	8	2	29.1 %
Midwest	0	17	5	1	20.9 %
Southwest	0	6	0	4	9.1 %
West	5	16	1	2	21.8 %

FIRST-WAVE STATIONS Stations that added the song in the first 30 days

KYA-San Francisco
KNDE-San Francisco
KHJ-Los Angeles
KJRB-Spokane
KENO-Las Vegas
KJSO-San Jose

CKLW-Detroit
WABX-FM-Detroit
KSHE-FM-St. Louis
KDWB-Minneapolis

WCFL-Chicago
WZUU-Milwaukee
WIXY-Cleveland
KLEO-Wichita

WRKO-Boston
WIBG-Philadelphia
WDRC-Hartford
WNEW-New York
WPRO-Providence

KILT-Houston
KELI-Tulsa
KBBC-Phoenix

KONO-San Antonio
KZEW-Dallas
KDKB-FM-Phoenix

WSGN-Birmingham
WAPE-Jacksonville
WMAK, WLAC-Nashville
WHBQ-Memphis

Billboard	HIGHEST CHARTING WEEK: CASHBOX - July 26, 1975		
#1 August 2, 1975	**SINGLE**	**ARTIST**	**PREV WK**
	1. ONE OF THESE NIGHTS	EAGLES	2
Cashbox	2. Please Mr. Please	Olivia Newton John	4
#1 July 26, 1975	3. The Hustle	Van McCoy	1
	4. Jive Talkin'	Bee Gees	9
	5. I'm Not in Love	10cc	7
	6. Listen to What the Man Said	Wings	3
Record World	7. Swearin' to God	Frankie Valli	8
#1 August 2, 1975	8. Someone Saved My Life Tonight	Elton John	12
	9. Midnight Blue	Melissa Manchester	11
	10. Rockin' Chair	Gwen McCrae	10

Sources: Billboard, Cashbox, Record World

CHARTS

FREY, HENLEY BRING R&B GROOVE TO 'NIGHTS'

The title cut from *One of These Nights* was not what the record-buying public expected from the Eagles in the summer of 1975, but they liked it just the same. "One of These Nights" had a distinctive, loping rhythm & blues groove unlike anything they had ever produced. Further, it was being played on AM *and* FM radio, and in an unexpected crossover shift, the track was being spun in discotheques. Go figure.

Within two short months, "Nights" rushed to the top of the charts, giving the band two straight #1 singles. But this latest success was by design, not dumb luck or fate. The Eagles had detached somewhat from their country-rock moorings with *On the Border* and had now set sail into uncharted waters with this new album—especially the title song.

They'd begun work on "Nights" in Florida, with Glenn Frey at the keyboard as Henley worked out some general ideas for this session-opening song's larger narrative. The completed track would indulge the Michigan-born Frey's longtime passion for the soul music of Detroit legends like **The Spinners**. It took some work and a few cross-country studio sessions, but they got there.

The writing began like many Frey-Henley efforts—in separate rooms. "I started the music, Don started the lyrics," Frey said. "What usually happens is when we get the thing fused together, he gets involved in the music, and I get involved in the lyrics. We cut the basic track in Miami in Criteria Studios. We took it to L.A. and put in the drone guitars and [Don] Felder's solo on, and then back to Miami to put the vocals on."

Bill Szymczyk, who had a pedigree in producing blues legends, was a willing participant in their experiment with fusing rock and R&B. Frey pointed to Szymczyk's work as a '60s-era freelance engineer on **B.B. King**'s "The Thrill Is Gone" and **Aaron Neville**'s "Tell It Like It Is." So Szymczyk instantly understood what Frey was going for when they discussed the studio techniques used by producer **Thom Bell** for those classic Philly soul records—including Bell's suggestion that the drummer put a wallet on the snare drum to dampen the sound.

Henley eventually settled into a four-on-the-floor rhythm in keeping with those old songs. "Glenn and I had always been fans of the records that were produced in Memphis by **Willie Mitchell**," Henley told *Rolling Stone* in 2016. "Especially the **Al Green** records where...drummer **Al Jackson Jr.**, would hit the snare and ride the tom-tom at the same time on the backbeat."

The Eagles were so engrossed in these age-old rhythms they considered naming the entire project *Wallet on the Snare*. But sessions for *One of These Nights* eventually took them far afield of these sounds.

The band also felt emboldened enough to take chances they hadn't before, including the dueling falsettos by Henley and Randy

Meisner, which was one of the first times Henley tried a higher vocal range on tape. Don Felder added his infectious guitar solo, which he said he treated like a saxophone solo that **David Sanborn** might play.

Lesser known was Felder's role in developing the bass line for the song. As the track developed in the studio, Meisner was snowed-in at home in Nebraska, so Felder offered to play bass as the band worked out the song. And, he said, he ended up writing and playing that iconic bass introduction to the single and the entire bass line for the song.

"One of These Nights" put on full display just how far Henley and Frey had come with their songwriting; it became more mature and polished with each successive album. They made careers out of turning a melodic phrase in a way that gave listeners a meaningful, but not always pleasant, touchstone. They were now writing for adults, people their own age experiencing the same things, not concocting cute singles for kids.

In *On the Border*'s "The Best of My Love," they offered the heart-tugging lines, *"You see it your way/ And I see it mine/But we both see it slippin' away."* Those lyrics force the listener to consider a couple's mounting irreconcilable differences, but masterfully project that disil-

> WE MADE A QUANTUM LEAP WITH 'ONE OF THESE NIGHTS.' IT WAS A BREAKTHROUGH SONG. IT IS MY FAVORITE EAGLES RECORD. IF I EVER HAD TO PICK ONE, IT WOULDN'T BE 'HOTEL CALIFORNIA,' IT WOULDN'T BE 'TAKE IT EASY,' FOR ME, IT WOULD BE 'ONE OF THESE NIGHTS.'
>
> — GLENN FREY

lusionment with just an ember of hope. Such lyrical touches were missing on the debut album, but hints of them emerged on *Desperado*. *On the Border* showed continued growth, and by *One of These Nights*, the songwriting team's lyric sophistication was on full display.

"A lot of things came together on *One of These Nights*—our love of the studio, the dramatic improvement in Don's and my songwriting," Frey wrote in the liner notes of *The Very Best of the Eagles*. "We made a quantum leap with 'One of These Nights.' It was a breakthrough song. It is my favorite Eagles record. If I ever had to pick one, it wouldn't be 'Hotel California'; it wouldn't be 'Take It Easy.' For me, it would be 'One of These Nights.'"

"One of These Nights" also became the first—and remains the only—single with a Henley vocal to lead off an album's release. Frey was the lead singer on the first singles from all three previous albums: "Take It Easy" from the debut LP; "Tequila Sunrise" from *Desperado*; and "Already Gone" from *On the Border*. Singles with Frey singing lead would also be the first released from *Hotel California* ("New Kid in Town") and *The Long Run* ("Heartache Tonight"). [15, 209, 1801, 1802, 1899]

ertheless, Davis, an outspoken liberal, held political leanings in stark contrast to her father's. Even after having spent some time together, Leadon didn't know she was the governor's daughter.

"I had mentioned my father a few times, and Bernie had gotten the impression he was someone powerful, but assumed he was the head of a corporation or something like that," Davis recounted in her memoirs.

The two began a serious relationship; Davis would accompany the Eagles on a trip to Europe and soon they'd move into a house in Topanga. This was a move her parents felt would play poorly in the press, as her conservative father would soon be throwing his hat in the ring for the 1976 presidential nomination.

"She essentially wrote the song, and I wrote the second verse; [that's] the way I remember it," Leadon told *Rock History Music* journalist **John Beaudin**. "And then I came up with the arrangement to record it. But I wasn't writing too many songs at the time, and I wanted that song recorded."

Despite Davis being more politically aligned with Don Henley than her conservative family, the Eagles' drummer neither liked the song nor appreciated Davis' input or presence in the studio. In a 1977 interview, Henley matter-of-factly described Leadon's two songwriting contributions to *One of These Nights* by saying, "'Journey of the Sorcerer' and 'I Wish You Peace' were Bernie's songs, and he wanted to do those songs. So, we did those songs."

It was largely an effort to keep peace, but

years later, Henley would be far less diplomatic, claiming "I Wish You Peace" was not up to the band's standards and that Davis was "butting in." By all accounts, Leadon had insisted the track be recorded. Henley was particularly irked when he'd see press that suggested Davis "wrote songs for the Eagles."

Leadon's version of the story is consistent. "Henley and Frey didn't want that song on the album," he admitted. "And this is one of those stupid stories, but I basically let it be known that if they didn't record that song I was going to break [Henley's] arm or something like that."

The irony was not lost on Leadon: "It's absurd, right? The song is 'I Wish You Peace,' but I'm going to break your fucking arm if you don't record it," he laughed. "It shows you the insanity of life sometimes."

As for Davis, she expressed regret that her song may have contributed to hastening Leadon's departure. "I didn't really notice at first that Bernie's relationship with the group was starting to fracture, but it would soon become apparent," she reflected. "I didn't know, when I sat on my bed writing a song, that it would increase the tensions that already existed." [6, 1404, 1501, 1613, 1614, 1615, 1617]

With Nod to B.B. King, Eagles Consider 'After the Thrill is Gone'

B.B. King was already a blues legend when he recorded "The Thrill Is Gone" in New York in October 1969, but his version of the song broke him out of the Chitlin' Circuit

continued on Page 195

Eagles Flex Musical Diversity In Mixed-Genre Juggernaut

Primed by the #1 *Billboard* success of "The Best of My Love" from *On the Border*, the Eagles could have gone into making their next album with an agenda of simply "repeating the formula." Instead, they continued to feed their artistic impulses and delivered their most ambitious, well-rounded record to date.

Much like **The Beatles** would grow album by album, with *Revolver* a natural precursor to their landmark *Sgt. Pepper's Lonely Hearts Club Band* album, *One of These Nights* is also a transitional record between the early country-rock efforts the Eagles were known for and their career-pinnacle LP, *Hotel California*.

That's not to say they traded in commerciality and monetary reward for artistic integrity.

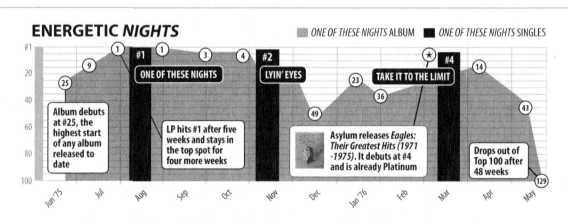

ENERGETIC *NIGHTS*

■ *ONE OF THESE NIGHTS* ALBUM   ■ *ONE OF THESE NIGHTS* SINGLES

ONE OF THESE NIGHTS — #1

LYIN' EYES — #2

TAKE IT TO THE LIMIT — #4

Album debuts at #25, the highest start of any album released to date

LP hits #1 after five weeks and stays in the top spot for four more weeks

Asylum releases *Eagles: Their Greatest Hits (1971 -1975)*. It debuts at #4 and is already Platinum

Drops out of Top 100 after 48 weeks

Jun '75 · Jul · Aug · Sep · Oct · Nov · Dec · Jan '76 · Feb · Mar · Apr · May

One of These Nights bolted off the starting line quickly in the summer of 1975. It debuted on the *Billboard* Top 100 albums at #25 and booted **Paul McCartney & Wings** out of the top position on July 26. It was the first time Eagles had ever held a #1 on the album chart, and they kept it for five weeks before being knocked out by **Elton John**'s *Captain Fantastic* LP. Buoyed by "One of These Nights" and "Lyin' Eyes," which rose to #1 and #2, respectively, on the singles chart, the LP slid in December, but rose as "Take It to the Limit" became a Top 5 single, and *Eagles: Their Greatest Hits (1971-1975)* gave the band two Top 25 albums simultaneously.

Sources: *Billboard*, Recording Industry Association of America

BILLBOARD TOP LPs & TAPE, July 26, 1975

1. **EAGLES**, *ONE OF THESE NIGHTS*
2. Paul McCartney & Wings, *Venus and Mars*
3. The Captain & Tennille, *Love Will Keep Us Together*
4. Elton John, *Captain Fantastic and the Brown Dirt Cowboy*
5. Average White Band, *Cut the Cake*
6. Rolling Stones, *Made in the Shade*
7. Isley Brothers, *The Heat Is On*
8. Earth, Wind & Fire, *That's The Way of the World*
9. James Taylor, *Gorilla*
10. Rolling Stones, *Metamorphosis*

Eagles never made a secret of the fact that they wanted both recognition for their art and to be handsomely compensated for it. With *One of These Nights*, they delivered an album that showed their creative progress as well as an ability to write and record radio-friendly smash hits.

While Don Felder was billed as a "late addition" on the credits for *On the Border* because he had only jumped on board toward the end of that album's sessions, he was a fully participating band member for *One of These Nights*. Bernie Leadon, too, was still among the ranks, even if his eventual departure seemed evident. The album serves as the best representation of the band's original four-piece lineup with the addition of Felder.

The band members still had plenty of room to grow as songwriters, though they had come a long way since their debut album.

Glenn Frey said the band's locale was instrumental in their songwriting for *Nights*. "We live in Southern California and we're a song band," he told pool reporters over a phone line. "We don't write guitar riffs or rock 'n' roll tracks for somebody to scream over. We write, etched with respect for the popular song."

"Writing songs is still a mystery to me," Don Henley told **Mary Campbell** of the Associated Press. "I don't know how we get from one concept to the end of the song. But I know it's hard work. We agonize over prepositions; we take it very seriously. The trick about writing songs is to reach as many people as possible without lowering your standards."

The songwriting did mature, and looking

ELEKTRA/ASYLUM INSIDER

WHILE "THE BEST OF MY LOVE" WAS A BIT OF A FLUKE AND BECAME #1 because it was a great radio song, the Eagles "brand" certainly helped it along. But was this really the Eagles? We have "Peaceful," "Tequila," "Desperado," and now another ballad, "Best." While radio loved the group, and the fans loved the group, most rock publications like *Rolling Stone* and *Creem* still were not sold.

We knew there was a "hidden tiger" in this group and this tune, this album—*One of These Nights*—proved us right. It absolutely exploded on radio, and sales went through the roof. What everyone was looking for finally came to pass. We finally had another Eagles up-tempo home run, with hard rock overtones that crossed heavily into the AOR format as well. And it triggered heavy sales on the band's previous LPs. We had a "supergroup" on our hands.

Some say it was the addition of Don Felder and Leadon taking a back seat on the guitar work. Leadon wanted to hang onto the country-rock roots, but Frey wanted to rock. I would agree. Felder added that missing spark and the Frey/Henley writing team jelled. Felder's guitar solo in "Nights," was a harbinger of things to come in *Hotel California*.

The band was now a household name and a radio fixture—they became what we would call radio station playlist "automatic add," and "Lyin' Eyes" was just that.

—Rip Pelley, former National Director of Artist Development, Elektra/Asylum Records

back, it was clear to Henley that this was an eclectic blend of material.

"Stylistically, the *One of These Nights* album is all over the map, but it worked as a coherent whole," Henley said when looking back in 2016. "In those days...you could mix different styles on the same album. The Beatles had made it acceptable."

The record opens with the title song, a track drenched in R&B and featuring one of Henley's most soulful vocals. With his gravelly but gorgeous voice, he delivered a lead that was both emotive and mysterious, and by the end, both he and Randy Meisner were belting out the song's coda in falsetto.

"Singing the title track was a pretty big moment for me," Henley said, "particularly the falsetto parts."

Henley also provided a drum rhythm on this one unlike others in the Eagles canon, playing the backbeat on the snare and ride tom at once, a technique he credits hearing on **Al Green** records with **Al Jackson Jr.** behind the drums. Additionally, the band was aware of the burgeoning disco scene, and Henley laid down a danceable "four-on-the-floor" rhythm in 4/4 time, thumping his kick drum on each quarter note.

"Too Many Hands" is next in line, one of two lead vocals on the album by Randy Meisner. He co-wrote the rocker with Felder, and once again, the country-rock sound that had served the Eagles so well on past recordings was replaced by heavier guitars and tabla-oriented percussion.

"Hollywood Waltz" slows things down with a pretty and harmonic tune fused with forlorn lyrics that, when taken literally, spin a melancholy tale of a world-weary woman worn down by innumerable love affairs gone wrong. But the song is actually an allegorical tale where the band's adopted home of

Phonograph Record
June 1975

One of These Nights is brimming with self-assurance, and for good reason. Group-written material has improved with each album, right along with playing and singing. [It] makes the Eagles' earlier work seem tentative and cautious. The album may well turn out to be milestone in this band's...halting search for a distinct identity. The title track is irresistible and boasts falsetto vocals by Meisner, who often does this sort of thing, and Henley, who doesn't.

– Bud Scoppa

Let It Rock
September 1975

I can't think of anything good to say about *One of These Nights*. What's so distressing is that it's not a bad album by any stretch of the imagination—it just falls short of everything the Eagles have done in the past. If they had a lousy track record this might easily be the first winner. They haven't and this isn't. The Eagles have become too set in their ideas, churning out too many soundalike songs, all lacking the character of the originals. Pass [this album] by.

– Mick Houghton

Los Angeles Times
July 20, 1975

The title track...underscores the middle ground that the Eagles' quintet has carved for itself between pop, country, and rock. Though there is a strong dose of country in its approach, the Eagles' sound mixes the three styles in a way that makes it impossible to fully describe the band's sound by merely applying two of them. [They] have established their own musical identity. The new album has some rough spots, but its most telling moments are convincing indeed.

– Robert Hilburn

Los Angeles plays the main character.

Bernie Leadon weighed in with a pair of songs, "Journey of the Sorcerer" and "I Wish You Peace." The former is a spacey instrumental that would eventually be tapped for use by the BBC television series *The Hitchhiker's Guide to the Galaxy* but stands out as something of an oddball track on an Eagles record. The latter song was co-written with **Patti Davis**—Leadon's then-girlfriend and the daughter of future U.S. President Ronald Reagan—and serves as something of his Eagles swan song. Both songs were included as a way to exercise diplomacy among the ranks.

The back-to-back, one-two punch of "Lyin' Eyes" and "Take It to the Limit" delivered the other two Top 10 singles from *One of These Nights* (along with the #1 title track).

"Lyin' Eyes," which helped to establish the Eagles as storytellers, clocks in at more than six minutes, hardly the stereotypical "two-minute pop song." Nevertheless, a 4:14 edit was a huge hit single due to Glenn Frey's immaculately smooth lead vocal, richly layered harmonies, and, moreover, the tremendous craftsmanship on the part of the Frey/Henley songwriting team.

That same team helped Meisner finish "Take It to the Limit," a song he brought in that would become the highlight of the Eagles live set and would invoke standing ovations night after night. It also would prove to be the most significant song of Meisner's career, in the Eagles or otherwise, and rightly so. It's a gem worthy of the recognition it has received.

"Visions" was contributed by Felder, and

although many may feel it pales in comparison to some of the better-known songs on the album, it holds a special significance as the only lead vocal the guitar player performs on an Eagles record.

"After the Thrill is Gone" may nick its title from **B.B. King**'s "The Thrill Is Gone," but the Eagles song is a different animal. Frey and Henley split the lead vocals as they did on tracks like "Doolin-Dalton" and "Ol' '55" on past albums—and revisit the subject of the fallout after success, which they'd been musing about as early as *Desperado*. "*What can you do when your dreams come true and it's not quite like you planned?*" Henley asks.

The band was happy with *One of These Nights* at the time.

"I think it is one of the best Eagles albums," Frey told **John Tobler** in April 1977. "That particular song, 'One of These Nights,' before we recorded 'Hotel California,' was the best single individual record we ever made as the Eagles."

Frey's affection for the LP was affirmed when awards season rolled around. The album received four Grammy nominations in 1978, including a win for Best Pop Vocal Performance By a Duo, Group or Chorus for "Lyin' Eyes." The band also scored nominations for Record of the Year ("Lyin' Eyes") and Album of the Year. Producer **Bill Szymczyk** was nominated for Best Producer of the Year.

A huge success creatively, critically, and commercially, *One of These Nights* seemed nearly impossible to top—until the band did it with their next album. [618, 1501, 1995]

THE ACACIAS ARE BLOOMING

Bernie Leadon (left) and his brother, Tom, joined Glenn Frey and Don Henley to write "Hollywood Waltz" in 1975.

LEADON BROTHERS USHER IN 'HOLLYWOOD WALTZ'

"**H**otel California" became the quintessential rock music commentary for the decadence of life in Southern California in the late 1970s, but it wasn't the Eagles' first attempt at sizing up the "City of Angels." That first try emerged from a song originally written by Bernie Leadon's brother, **Tom Leadon**, called "Hollywood Waltz."

A pleasantly haunting cut from the *One of These Nights* album, "Waltz" was unusual in that it was a straight-up country song on an Eagles album. Its inspiration was drawn from the springtime flora in nearby rural, rustic Topanga Canyon, which captivated both Leadon brothers.

"I was really struck by the brilliant spectacle of all of the many acacia trees in the mountains there, all blooming at the same time so brightly with their golden-yellow flowers," Tom told *Time Passages*. "So, the idea came up—I can't be sure which of us first voiced the idea—to write a song about it, and we were both enthusiastic."

But flowers weren't the only thing that inspired Tom. He had moved to Los Angeles at the end of 1972 to break into the music business, but his girlfriend remained in Gainesville, Florida, as he got established. As springtime arrived, so would the girl, and Leadon had a rental house ready.

The memory of the acacias and the arrival of his girl got his creative juices flowing. The day before she arrived, he wrote the entire song and played it for her and some musicians he was jamming with at the time. Everyone seemed to like it.

"I probably made a demo on a cassette or a four-track tape," he said. "It sat there on my shelf in a box when I moved a few times, along with the lyrics written in my notebook."

The song sat in the box for a few years. Tom was rehearsing with the house band in a club in West L.A. one afternoon in late 1975 when the club owner told him his brother Bernie wanted him to call. Tom left the club and found a phone booth on the street and called his older brother back.

"He was in Miami during a break from recording the *One of These Nights* album," Tom said, adding that Bernie had remembered the acacias song and wanted to offer it to Glenn Frey and Don Henley. "Of course, I was all for that!"

Bernie was having some trouble recalling details about the song, so he asked Tom to sing it. "I sang a verse and a chorus, and then he stopped me and said that was enough. He told me that Glenn and Don would probably want to rewrite the lyrics to fit with their concept for the album."

Tom said the notion of them changing the song didn't bother him. He admired Frey and Henley's work as songwriters and feared that if he required them to ask him first about making changes, it might cause delays, and they might do something else. "So, I told Bernie to tell [them] to change it however they wanted to."

Excited about the prospects of having one of his songs on an Eagles album, Tom kept Bernie's call a secret. He tried not to even think about it. "I didn't want to get my hopes up only to get crushed and have people asking me about why the song didn't make the album," he said, noting that a close friend experienced that before and remembering how dispiriting it was for him. So, he waited patiently.

Leadon didn't find out whether the song had made the final cut until the Eagles had wrapped up in Miami and returned to Los Angeles. Don Felder broke the good news to him. "Then Bernie invited me over to listen to the final mix that he had on

a reel-to-reel tape—when he played it over the studio monitors, I was pretty excited," Tom said.

The song's lyrics were rewritten by Henley and Frey, while Bernie and Tom earned writing credits as well. The recast song, arranged in 3/4 time, opens optimistically, welcoming the springtime and birds singing. But the optimism darkens as the song enters the second stanza that, when taken literally, paint a melancholy portrait of a serially used, too-eager-to-please coquette who "*looks another year older, from too many lovers who used her and ran.*"

But lyrics in Eagles songs aren't always as they appear. Frey said he and Henley were big fans of lyrics with hidden, deeper meanings. "We've been asked a million times, 'What does that song mean?'" Frey said in the *History of the Eagles* documentary. "You know, you write songs and send them out to the world. And maybe somewhere in that song is some stuff that's just yours, that they're never going to figure out."

Frey was speaking about "Hotel California" in that moment, but the Eagles' lyrics had run deep long before that epic single. And "Hollywood Waltz" was a prime example. While the vivid imagery of the lyrics seemed to cast a harsh light on the cruelty of some relationships, that's not what the song was about. For them, the meaning was more personal. It was about them and their relationship with Southern California, and specifically Los Angeles.

"There's a line in this song on our new album, 'Hollywood Waltz,'" Henley told *Phonograph Record* in 1975, referring to the lyric, "*Some nights she looks like an angel/And she's always willing to hold you again.*" "And it's true," Henley continued, "the nights after it rains, Los Angeles is the most beautiful city in the world. The sun goes down, you're up on Mulholland, all of a sudden you see

THE NIGHTS AFTER IT RAINS, LOS ANGELES IS THE MOST BEAUTIFUL CITY IN THE WORLD. THE SUN GOES DOWN, YOU'RE UP ON MULHOLLAND, ALL OF A SUDDEN YOU SEE THIS INCREDIBLE LIGHT SHOW—IT'S JUST A TURN-ON. OTHER DAYS, IT'S SMOG AN' DIRT CITY.

—DON HENLEY

this incredible light show—it's just a turn-on. Other days, it's smog an' dirt city."

Two years later, Henley's perception of the song's meaning had not changed much.

"We're right here in the middle of it. California is a microcosm," he told *Crawdaddy* in 1977. "We could all move to New Mexico and forget it, say, 'To hell with it. Let it fall into the ocean. Let them breathe the shit in the air.' We could afford to do that. I'd rather go down with the ship and stay here. That's what we were trying to say in 'Hollywood Waltz'. California is simply a metaphor for the whole country. Maybe the whole world."

The Eagles never released "Waltz" as a single, but **Buck Owens**, a key architect of country music's "Bakersfield sound" and a well-known host of the syndicated *Hee Haw* variety show, recorded it and took it to #49 on the *Cashbox* Country Singles chart in July 1976. Both Leadon brothers were big Owens fans growing up and were delighted the country legend picked up the song.

"I drove all the way from Topanga Canyon to Tower Records on Sunset Boulevard in Hollywood to get a copy of the single," Tom said.

Grateful for the opportunity the Eagles gave him, Leadon looked back fondly on the experience. Even though the lyrics were almost entirely changed, he took pride that his original melody remained. And he welcomed the musical changes.

"My solo acoustic version was understandably much more laid back," he said. "They used three minor chords in their arrangement where I had just one on each chorus. At the end of each chorus to conclude the title phrase, they added a short instrumental interlude with upbeat rhythmic accents. Then when they repeated the title at the end of the last chorus, they went into more forceful accents before building up to a crescendo instrumentally, with a synthesizer tastefully added.

"Finally, they brought the intensity back down dynamically to the very understated last chords. All in all, a very nice arrangement, I thought, and I was pleased with it."

Leadon said although the lyrics were changed, "*Springtime and the acacias are blooming*" and "*Southern California*" survived in the first verse, as

Country legend **Buck Owens** liked the Eagles' "Hollywood Waltz" so much that he cut it for his *Buck 'Em* LP in 1976. The 45 rose to #49 on the *Cashbox* Country Singles chart. After almost 20 years recording for Capitol, this was the first of two albums Owens cut for Warner Bros.

did the verse's last line, "*The birds are a-singing' as I drift away.*" Leadon said the "drift away" lyric at the end of the chorus was probably a subconscious nod to his friend **Dobie Gray**, who was near the top of the charts at the time with the single "Drift Away."

As for the Eagles' lyrical changes?

"I liked their lyrics," Tom said. "I think 'Hollywood Waltz' is a good title. My version didn't have a strong title like that. I like the environmental concerns they expressed, which speak to the way a really beautiful area has been trashed by people—many of them motivated by greed. And yet the Eagles express how sometimes the beauty of the area shines through in spite of all that, which gives us hope for the future." [83, 1656, 1852, 1930]

and into the mainstream as a worldwide blues ambassador.

The Mississippi-born King took some risks recording it, including employing the relatively untested future Eagles producer **Bill Szymczyk**, who took him down innovative production paths—strings on a blues record?—that had R&B aficionados scratching their heads. But those risks paid off handsomely when the track became King's first million-selling single, and emerged as his signature song.

Glenn Frey and blues legend **B.B. King** share a laugh during sessions for the *B.B. King & Friends—80* album, recorded for King's 80th birthday in 2005.

Szymczyk would work with a different "Thrill" six years later, recording the Eagles' sort-of answer to King's cut.

"The Thrill Is Gone" was written in 1951 by **Roy Hawkins** and **Rick Darnell** as a mournful song sung by a man coming to terms with a toxic relationship. The Eagles' "After the Thrill is Gone" wasn't a direct response to King's classic, but when asked by *Rolling Stone* if King's song was on their minds when they wrote it, Don Henley acknowledged it had been.

"We were, of course, aware of B.B. King's song, which was a straightforward statement," he said. "But we wanted to explore the aftermath. We know that the thrill is gone—so, now what?"

The lyrics of that aftermath have been open to many interpretations, but they have a much broader reach than King's. At its core, "After the Thrill is Gone" ponders life after one has achieved his or her dreams, and it weaves in lyrical turns that could apply to a relationship fading due to neglect or even musical careers that are reaching crossroads.

The song cuts right to the chase in its opening lyrics, speaking to the familiarity that often breeds complacency: "*Same dances in the same old shoes/Some habits that you just can't lose*," and then it considers what a man might lose "*after the thrill is gone*." The ensuing lyrics alternately touch on rising and fading passions, poorly defined relationships, and even writer's block, which the band was certainly beginning to struggle with more often at this juncture in their career.

Looking back, Glenn Frey was fond of the song and its inner meanings. "It's a sleeper," Frey said. "That record is a lot of

continued on Page 197

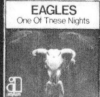

The release of *One of These Nights* was a watershed moment for the Eagles, and not just because of its three Top 10 hits in 1975-76. The album launched the band to superstardom and boosted huge interest in their back catalog. All their previous LPs re-emerged on the *Cashbox*, *Record World*, and *Billboard* album charts. Further, it helped push those albums to RIAA gold status. This promotional ad touted the achievement.

self-examination, hopefully not too much. There was a lot of double-meaning and a lot of irony. *'Any kind of love without passion/ Well, that ain't no kind of lovin' at all…'—* pure Henley."

Henley thought the song was "very good," yet was overlooked in the Eagles' catalog. "It's me and Glenn, working together," he said. "He did the verses with a little help from me. I did the bridge. As exciting as the whole Eagles thing was at times, some of the luster was beginning to wear off. We were combining our personal and professional lives in song."

There was a taste of cynicism in the lyrics as well, as the original working title, Henley told **Cameron Crowe**, was "Here's Another Hidden Commentary on the Music Business Disguised as a Love Song."

"After the Thrill is Gone" was never released as a single, but critics in 1975 loved it. When *One of These Nights* jumped to the top of the album charts—and as reviews of the day were coming in—acclaim was being lauded on the title track and "Lyin' Eyes." But "Thrill" was consistently considered one of the album's top three tracks.

Elektra/Asylum released Randy Meisner's "Take It to the Limit" as the LP's third single rather than "Thrill," but the track was placed on the flip side. Like many of the deeper Eagles cuts in their catalog, "Thrill" was embraced by other artists. **Cal Smith** added it to his *My Kind of Country* LP later in 1975, and Tanya Tucker recorded it for her *Lovin' and Learnin'* album a year later. **Lori Lieberman** also cut a version for her

Letting Go album in 1978.

Frey was the Eagle with the most affinity for R&B, so it made sense he would take inspiration from King. He got to work with King in 2005 on the legend's 41st album, *B.B. King & Friends—80*, sharing vocals with him on "Drivin' Wheel." [15, 209]

3rd Encore Excesses: Big Money, Adventures…Love 'Em, Lear 'Em

Glenn Frey once looked back on the 1970s and said, "I seem to remember that the wine was the best, the drugs were good, and the women were beautiful and, man, we seemed to have an endless amount of energy. Hangovers were conquered with Bloody Marys and aspirin…[we] were resilient."

By the time the band toured in the summer of 1975, they were bonafide stars with their fame still ascending. Though they sang like angels, their life upon the road was not entirely angelic, with all the trappings and excesses of a pre-HIV 1970s rock star paradise at their disposal.

For a band of the Eagles' stature, groupies were readily available and presented both an occupational benefit and hazard to the band and its road crew. Randy Meisner and Don Felder were married with children, which may have served as at least a minor deterrent to entertaining women on the road, but Don Henley, Frey, and Bernie Leadon were single and perhaps in a more ideal position to take advantage of these types of rock and roll perks. Leadon was often described as a bit of a loner, but it has been suggested that confirmed bachelors Henley and Frey wel-

continued on Page 199

PATHWAY ALBUM | TIMOTHY B. SCHMIT

POCO
Head Over Heels
ABC Records, July 1975

Poco had come to believe Epic Records had failed to adequately promote them for years, so when their contract ended in 1975, they signed a deal with ABC Records. Epic offered to retain the band and threatened to continue releasing competing Poco and Poco-related albums if they departed, the group took their chances and rolled with the new label.

The first release on ABC was *Head Over Heels*, which hit the shelves in July 1975. The opening track, Timothy B. Schmit's "Keep on Tryin,'" is a Poco classic and easily the most notable song on the album. It's a sparse arrangement designed to spotlight the band's sweet, harmonic vocals and features nothing more than Schmit, drummer **George Grantham**, and guitarist **Paul Cotton** singing over a lone acoustic guitar. Multi-instrumentalist and nascent vocalist **Rusty Young** doesn't even appear on the track.

Other songs on the LP feature Poco's typical full-band approach, including songs like Young's "Lovin' Arms," "Sittin' on a Fence," and "Making Love," which all feature Schmit singing lead or in tandem with Cotton and Grantham. The latter track also adds piano provided by no less a celebrity than **The Band**'s **Garth Hudson**.

Cotton contributed standouts like the moody "Let Me Turn Back to You" and a cover of **Steely Dan**'s "Dallas," while Schmit added a few more of his own, including the album's upbeat closer "I'll Be Back Again." Like most artists, Poco at the time felt that their new disc was among their best work.

"*Seven* was a transitional album and *Cantamos*, the first album where we hadn't used a producer, was only one step above that," Schmit opined while touring in support of Head Over Heels, which he said was "the strongest album we've had in a long while."

Epic quickly proved it wasn't bluffing when it said it would retaliate with competing Poco products when in September the label released *The Very Best of Poco*, a gatefold double album collecting select previously released singles and album tracks. The group, at least publicly, was unfazed by this, taking the stance that the more Poco albums on records store shelves, the better.

"It's great," Schmit remarked. "It can only be good...it was all the record company's idea."

He also foreshadowed things to come by adding that their former label was "still sitting on a live album and they've got a whole bunch of songs that were never put on albums, going right back to the time **Richie** [**Furay**] was in the band—stuff from the *Crazy Eyes* sessions for instance." Much of this material would be formally released in upcoming years, some sooner rather than later. [1504, 1515, 1622]

comed the women that greeted them in every city, or even back home in L.A. In some respects, the band itself was a mistress that kept the duo from settling into more long-term relationships with women.

"[Frey and I] would have girlfriends and live with them for a while," Henley reflected, "and then we'd get ready to do an album and we'd move back in together. Dudes on a rampage."

Speaking to journalist **Anthony DeCurtis** circa 1990, Henley expanded on this idea: "The music always came first. I think we wanted it that way. I mean, it would have been nice—we wanted to have relationships with girls and have the band, too. But it just didn't seem possible. We were wedded to the muse or the vision—whatever it was and however murky it might have been."

Though romantic ties to girlfriends would dissolve and road life presented relationship challenges, there is a famous piece of Eagles lore that Henley in 1975 once chartered a Learjet for his then-girlfriend, **Fleetwood Mac**'s **Stevie Nicks**, and flew her across the country to be with him and flew her back for her Mac tour date a day later, a practice called "Love 'em and Lear 'em."

"Hey, Learjets were a lot cheaper then," he joked to *Off the Record* author Joe Smith (also Elektra/Asylum chairman from 1975-1983), before clarifying by saying, "and when I speak of sending one for Stevie, that kind of thing did not happen every week. Once in a while we would do something completely over the top like that, and it was simply our way of coping with the absurdity

of making so much money and being so famous at such an early age."

About the Nicks charter, Henley said, "I got a lot of shit about that from the band," and it only happened once.

Women were, however, only one facet of the fast-living lifestyle the Eagles found themselves part of. There was also drink and drugs, gambling, and tales of colossal hotel room destruction (including demolition that sometimes involved the use of a chainsaw after Joe Walsh joined the band).

When considering the rock and roll climate of the times, it's perhaps unfair that

continued on Page 206

LYIN' EYES

By: Don Henley, Glenn Frey
Side B: Too Many Hands (Meisner, Felder)

RELEASE
Late September
1975

As America approached its bicentennial year, the nation had a new musical darling: Eagles. The band, again, ascended into the Top 10 with another single, "Lyin' Eyes," but it fell just one place short of becoming the band's third-straight #1 song, stalling at #2 in November 1975. The cut had strong crossover appeal and found airplay on AM and FM radio, and it found country music fans as well. It rose to #8 on the *Billboard* Hot Country Singles chart, and made some noise internationally too, making it to #3 in Ireland, #7 in New Zealand, and #23 in the United Kingdom.

AIRPLAY

With "One of These Nights" and now "Lyin' Eyes," Eagles singles quickly became automatic adds in all the major and secondary radio markets. The band needed just one month to saturate the airwaves and reach 90% of playlists nationwide. While they were a nationwide sensation by now, stations in the Southeast remained their biggest draw, representing more than 30 percent of all reported radio station playlist adds. The song was also picked up by country stations in the Midwest and West like WXTC-Peoria, Illinois, WITL-Lansing, Michigan, and KLAK-Denver, Colorado.

94 PLAYLIST ADDS Fall 1975

Region	Sep	Oct	Nov	Regional Airplay
Northeast	5	11	1	18.1%
Southeast	15	15	0	31.9%
Midwest	8	14	1	24.5%
Southwest	3	7	0	10.6%
West	3	10	1	14.9%

FIRST-WAVE STATIONS Stations that added the song in the first 30 days

KXFM-San Bernardino
KHJ-Los Angeles
KIMN-Denver
KCBQ-San Diego
KYA, KFRC-San Francisco
KJR-Seattle
KILV-San Jose
KGW-Portland
KYNO-Fresno
KTLK-Denver

CKLW-Detroit
WZZM-Grand Rapids
WSAI-Cincinnati
KQWB-Fargo
WING-Dayton

KSLQ-FM-St. Louis
KIOA-Des Moines
WHB-Kansas City
WLAV-Grand Rapids
WCFL-Chicago

WKBW-Buffalo
WRIE-Erie, PA
WORC-Worcester, MA
WKQT-Pittsburgh
WBLI-Long Island

XEROK-El Paso
KELI-Tulsa
KLIF-Dallas
KRIZ-Phoenix

WBBQ-Augusta
WORD-Spartanburg, SC
WNOX-Knoxville
WTMA-Charleston, SC

WLCY, WFUN-Miami
WLAC-Nashville
WAKY-Louisville
WAPE-Jacksonville

CHARTS

Billboard		
# 2 November 8, 1975		

Cashbox		
# 3 October 25, 1975		

Record World		
# 3 November 15, 1975		

HIGHEST CHARTING WEEK: BILLBOARD - November 8, 1975

SINGLE	ARTIST	PREV WK
1. Island Girl	Elton John	1
2. LYIN' EYES	**EAGLES**	**4**
3. Calypso/I'm Sorry	John Denver	2
4. Who Loves You	Four Seasons	6
5. Miracles	Jefferson Starship	3
6. Heat Wave/Love Is a Rose	Linda Ronstadt	9
7. They Just Can't Stop It	Spinners	5
8. This Will Be	Natalie Cole	10
9. Feelings	Morris Albert	9
10. The Way I Want To Touch You	Captain & Tennille	14

Sources: Billboard, Cashbox, Record World

FREY, SOUTHER SPOT 'LYIN' EYES' AT DAN TANA'S

When you walk into Dan Tana's restaurant on Santa Monica Boulevard in West Hollywood, you literally see red, whether it's the bright red leather horseshoe tables with red-and-white-striped tablecloths draped over them, or the bright red jackets worn by the barkeeps at Mike's Bar.

The iconic Italian restaurant's scarlett walls are adorned with pictures of famous guests and regulars, not to mention **Jerry West**'s signed Los Angeles Lakers jersey. Dangling from the ceiling in the dimly lit room are clusters of fiasco bottles, and above the fireplace are pieces of a train track the Southern Pacific Railroad used to ride east and west along Santa Monica Boulevard. Glenn Frey and Don Henley gave those track fragments to the restaurant in the 1970s, and they've been there ever since.

But that wasn't the only gift the Eagles gave Dan Tana's around then—they gave it a place in music history too. As they turned the corner on January 1975, the band was working up song ideas for their next album, *One of These Nights*. Two doors east of the Troubadour club, the restaurant was a fashionable spot for musicians and Hollywood's elite. It also was a popular gathering spot for rich men and beautiful women.

As legend holds, frequent Eagles collaborator **J.D. Souther** was in town one night and he, Frey, and a few other friends crowded into Table 4 of the restaurant, a favorite spot not far from the bar.

The iconic song was born that night, but the details have been embellished over the years—and amplified by the enormous success of the song. Henley wasn't even there that night. Fortunately, Frey's recollection of the night was crystalline, even if he wasn't the first to utter the phrase "lyin' eyes."

"One night we were drinking in a bar when I spotted this stunning young woman; two steps behind her was a much older, fat, rich guy," Frey said in the audio commentary of the *Hell Freezes Over* concert film. "We all started laughing and one of the other guys commented, 'Look at her, she can't even hide those lyin' eyes!' Immediately, we all began grabbing for cocktail napkins to write down lyrics to go with that great observation."

"[The song] was just about all these girls who would come down to Dan Tana's looking beautiful," he said, "and they would be there from eight o'clock 'til midnight and have dinner and drinks with all of us rockers and then would go home...because they were kept women."

Frey and his friends saw a lot of beautiful women around Hollywood who were married to wealthy, successful men, and wondered if they were unhappy. That curiosity created quite an inspiration.

Frey took the song back to the house he was sharing with Henley in Trousdale, just south of Mulholland Drive, and the lyrics started flowing.

"The house was up on Briarcrest Lane—that's where we wrote 'One of These Nights,' 'Lyin' Eyes,' 'Take It to the Limit,' 'After the Thrill is Gone,' and a couple of other tunes for the *One of These Nights* album," Frey said. "But 'Lyin' Eyes'—the story had always been there. I don't want to say it wrote itself, but once we started working on it, there were no sticking points. Lyrics just kept coming out, and that's not always the way songs get written. I think songwriting is a lot like pushing a boulder up a hill. I'd love to get the legal pad for 'Lyin' Eyes' again, because I think there were verses we didn't use."

"'Lyin' Eyes' is one of the songs written when Glenn and I were roommates in a house we rented up in Trousdale," Henley said. "It was built in 1942 by the actress Dorothy Lamour. Glenn and I lived at opposite ends of the house and we actually converted a music room to a full-on recording studio. The house was located at the highest point on the hill and we had a 360-degree panorama. In the daytime, we could see

After furiously scribbling his ideas for "Lyin' Eyes" on a cocktail napkin at Dan Tana's, Glenn Frey went back to his Los Angeles home (above, 1975) and started working with Don Henley on lyrics.

snowcapped peaks to the east and the blue Pacific to the west. At night, the twinkling lights of the city below were breathtaking. The place had a couple of nicknames—'the house with the million-dollar view' and 'The Eagles' Nest,' of course. We had some great times up there. As for 'Lyin' Eyes,' Glenn's pretty much responsible for that track and for the title, the choruses. I helped out with the verses and perhaps with the melody. It's really Glenn's baby."

Elektra/Asylum didn't provide the full version to radio stations. The album version clocked in at a robust 6 minutes, 22 seconds—making it one of the longest singles the band had ever released—but the label shortened it considerably for radio. To get the song more compatible with the commercial-oriented AM program directors, the label gutted the entire second verse, the second chorus, and four lines in the middle of the third verse to get it to a still-long, but more manageable 4:14. Those length restrictions didn't really apply to FM radio, and some stations chose to play the longer version, *Cashbox* reported.

Not everyone was enamored with the song at its release. *Rolling Stone* columnist **Dave Marsh** wrote in his review of *One of These Nights* in July 1975 that the song was "a conventional country western cheating heart song stretched to six minutes to no apparent purpose or effect."

Others weren't so critical.

"'Lyin' Eyes' is a perfect example of what is so extraordinary about the Eagles," wrote **Christine Brown** for *Knight News Service*. The song is a "poignant, sympathetic vignette about a girl who tried for and grabbed the brass ring—in this case marrying a wealthy older man—only to find the prize permanently tarnished."

Radio and the music-buying public loved the song. Relatable and catchy, it easily crossed over into other genres. "Lyin' Eyes" rose to #2 in *Billboard*'s Hot 100 singles chart. It also became the Eagles' first Top 10 single on *Billboard*'s Country Singles chart, rising to #8. The band won a Grammy for Best Pop Vocal Performance by a Duo, Group or Chorus in 1976 and was nominated for Record of the Year. The song has been covered by a range of country artists including **Lynn Anderson** and **Kenny Rankin**, but perhaps the best sign of the cut's acceptance in country music was from **Dolly Parton**, who covered the song on her own syndicated TV show in 1977. "The Eagles are one of my favorite bands," Parton told her audience. "I think, really, one of the main reasons for their success is the songs they write, and here's a song that I wish I'd written. But who wouldn't?"

Apart from the shared lead vocals on "After the Thrill is Gone," "Lyin' Eyes" was the only lead vocal for Frey on *One of These Nights*. The progression toward Henley taking lead on more Eagles songs had begun. [209, 1603, 1691, 1714, 2106, 2107, 2108]

EAGLES DRAFT JIMMY BUFFETT FOR OPENING ACT

The summer was winding down in August 1975 and the Eagles needed a show opener. They had finally finished their exhaustive support of the **Rolling Stones**' Tour of the Americas '75 that summer, and after a few shows in the Northeast, they headed south. They would need an opening act for their August 3 show in Columbia, South Carolina. **Jimmy Buffett**, then relatively unknown, got the call.

Buffett and the Eagles were rock artist contemporaries. He started his musical career at roughly the same time as the band, but his label—the **Andy Williams**-owned Barnaby Records—cast him as a country music artist. He eschewed that tag recording for ABC/Dunhill label, and developing his signature "island escapism" sound with distinctly Floridian and Caribbean themes.

Buffett was defining his style as the Eagles took off in 1972, and with his **Coral Reefer Band** had developed a small-but-loyal cult following by mid-

1975, when the Eagles became superstars. "One of These Nights"—both the single and the album— were #1 on their respective charts when the band reached out to Buffett. It was a welcome surprise for him, and he got more than he expected from the show.

"I was introduced to the band in the dressing room of the [Los Angeles] Coliseum," Buffett recalled during his speech inducting the Eagles into the Rock and Roll Hall of Fame in 1998. "I don't remember how I got on the bill, but I was just excited to be there. It didn't matter that nobody had paid to see us, or that they misspelled my name on the marquee. I was an opening act prepared to receive my fair share of opening act abuse from the promoter, the audience, and probably the headline act. But that didn't happen that night."

Buffett got an up-close, first-time look at the Eagles earlier on the day of the show when

Tommy Nixon, one of the band's road managers, invited him to watch the soundcheck.

"I sat there with all the members of the Coral Reefer Band in awe," Buffett said. "And when it was over, we strolled back through the empty arena towards our dressing room, and I said…'That is the kind of band we want to become.'"

The enormity of the opportunity wasn't lost on Buffett, who added, "We were opening for the Eagles, the best American band of my generation and many to follow. Any band worth their salt started as an opener for somebody. Opening for the right band at the right time could be your stairway to heaven."

Getting invited to the soundcheck was unexpected, but there was another surprise. Just as he was leaving to go onstage, Glenn Frey and Don Henley walked into his dressing room, introduced themselves, and complimented his music.

"They said, 'If there's anything you need, just ask for it.' It was a pleasant shock to say the least," he said of that first meeting. In their short conversation, Frey told Buffett that he enjoyed his recent single, "A Pirate Looks at 40," and then the duo wished him luck and disappeared out the back door.

Buffett took the stage and played with vigor, and he and his band drew polite applause from the crowd. It was a game-changing gig for him, and set wheels in motion that would help his career.

"I was able to watch and learn from them over the next few years," he said. They played benefits together and the Eagles introduced him to their manager, **Irving Azoff**, who eventually came to manage him as well. When the band launched its *Hotel California* tour in March 1977, Buffett returned to stage as their opening act, a role he would repeat often before their breakup in 1980, and one he would return to after their reformation in 1994.

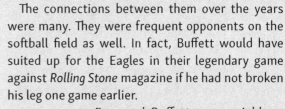

> [AT THE SOUNDCHECK] I SAT THERE WITH ALL THE MEMBERS OF THE THE CORAL REEFER BAND IN AWE. AND WHEN IT WAS OVER WE STROLLED BACK THROUGH THE EMPTY ARENA AND TOWARD OUR DRESSING ROOM, AND I SAID 'THAT IS THE KIND OF BAND WE WANT TO BECOME.'
>
> —JIMMY BUFFETT

The connections between them over the years were many. They were frequent opponents on the softball field as well. In fact, Buffett would have suited up for the Eagles in their legendary game against *Rolling Stone* magazine if he had not broken his leg one game earlier.

Frey and Buffett were neighbors in Aspen, Colorado for a time, which might have led to the time in 1977 when they both appeared on stage together at Aspen High School following a **Hunter S. Thompson** interview at the school. The taped interview concluded with Buffett and Frey singing the then-new "Margaritaville" to the crowd, with hysterical modified lyrics that included being out of cocaine.

The connections to the Eagles didn't end when the band broke up. Buffett tapped Timothy B. Schmit to play bass for his band in the breakup aftermath, and Schmit left a lasting legacy in his time supporting Buffett. Likening the devotion of Buffett's loyal fan base to that of the Deadheads who faithfully followed the **Grateful Dead**, Schmit dubbed Buffett's fans "Parrotheads" in jest. The name stuck.

The history and affection between Buffett and the Eagles was punctuated with the band's Rock Hall induction. They asked Buffett to give the speech, in which he recognized the generous camaraderie the band had shared with him over the years. He also credited their longevity.

"They are…one of the signature bands that began in the '70s and is still alive and kicking ass. They have laughed, frolicked, cried, and fought. But most of all, they have beaten the odds and are as popular today as they were during that incredible summer back in 1972.

"And here I am today," he said, grinning sheepishly, "still opening for this goddamned band." [1835, 1836, 1837, 1838, 1839]

the Eagles are often singled out as a band any more rambunctious than their peers. In most ways, the Eagles' lives were like those of other rock stars of the era, but perhaps the dichotomy between their image as a band of sweetly harmonic troubadours and their behind-the-scenes activities was a striking contrast that made for engaging press. But the group didn't seem to entirely downplay the backstage antics, either, as they christened their traveling party with a name: "The 3rd Encore" referred to the band's famed after-parties.

"Almost every night when we were on the road, we would throw this fabulous mixer," Frey said. "We'd hand out '3E' buttons, and we'd invite all the key radio people and as many beautiful girls as we'd meet from the airport to the hotel."

Though the group would eventually pen a song, "Life in the Fast Lane," intended to serve as a cautionary tale about the dangers of cocaine and fast living, excesses were simply a product of the era.

"**Led Zeppelin** might argue with us, but I think we had the greatest traveling party of the decade," Frey proudly proclaimed. [6, 1404, 1625, 1626]

Absent Eagles Win Best Group, Song at *Rock Music Awards*

The front desk at the Holiday Inn in Chicago, where the Eagles overnighted on August 9, 1975, was littered with phone messages, telegrams, and flowers from well-wishers. The band had just performed before a sell-out crowd at Chicago Stadium when they returned to learn that they had won awards

for Best Group and Best Song Composer at the first-ever nationally televised *Rock Music Awards*. Though the band wasn't there to accept the prizes, their friend and eventual bandmate Joe Walsh loped onstage to receive them and shocked presenter **Raquel Welch** with a kiss as he left the stage.

"You really kissed her?" Glenn Frey quizzed Walsh, his eyes wide and demanding, as quoted by **Cameron Crowe** a year later in a *Rolling Stone* feature. "Did you ask her about silicone?" Frey asked saracastically, before turning his attention back to Crowe. "Naw, naw, naw. Don't use that. That's a cruel remark. Besides, we can't be roguish underdogs anymore. We have to be gracious winners," he said, as Crowe described him grinning and flipping a cigarette into his mouth.

Things had changed considerably for the Eagles in the year leading up to the *Rock Music Awards*. *On the Border* had performed well commercially and "The Best of My Love" had topped the singles charts. While the awards season had come and gone without a sniff of recognition for the band, a familiar face—**Don Kirshner**—was about to put their faces on national television again.

Eagles had made frequent appearances on ABC's popular Kirshner-produced late-night network series *In Concert* and his own syndicated *Don Kirshner's Rock Concert*. The impresario now planned to cultivate that growing dissatisfaction with the pop-leaning music awards elite by producing a new music awards show aimed at becoming the anti-Grammy Awards: the *Rock Music Awards*.

Outwardly, it seemed like Kirshner was scratching the right itch. Rock music fans' complaints were that rock as a genre was repeatedly marginalized by the Recording Academy. Grammy voters were out of step with the times and too old and biased to properly judge rock's brightest stars. And the Grammys felt old. In February 1976, the then 18-year-old annual telecast completed its sixth straight year with crooner **Andy Williams** as host.

Many in the industry, like *Rolling Stone*'s **Dave Marsh**, complained that rock was systematically left out of the annual Grammy accolades, as evidenced by the lack of hardware for **The Who**, **The Beach Boys**, and **The Band**. Newer stars like **Elton John** and **Jackson Browne** were fonts of creativity, but they were also ignored by the Academy (John was recognized eventually, but Browne, to this day, remains shamefully Grammy-less). And disco was beckoning at the same time punk rock was busting out in New York and London.

Kirshner saw that old-new division and looked to exploit it. His show would have some distinct differences. While voting members of the Recording Academy choose Grammy winners, Kirshner gave selection authority to a 12-member panel of rock music journalists and deejays.

Radio stations had only just started picking up "The Best of My Love" when the Grammys aired in March 1975 and the band did not receive a nomination. But by the time the *Rock Music Awards* aired at the end of August, the Eagles' star was quickly rising and "Best" had already reached #1. That ex-

tra time seemed to help as the "Rocky" award for Best Song Composer went to Don Henley, Glenn Frey, and **J.D. Souther**. By contrast, the Grammy equivalent went five months earlier to **Alan** and **Marilyn Bergman** and **Marvin Hamlisch** for "The Way We Were." And as a capper for the evening, the Eagles also won the Rocky for Best Group.

Though Kirshner seemed to have had the selection process well thought out and secured top talent to appear, the production values could not overcome bad writing, ridiculous costumes, technical miscues, and the overall schlock of the evening. It was at best a low-budget television variety show with A-list musicians. The script was so bad that Elton John questioned aloud on camera whether he should actually read the lines. He did, reluctantly. **Keith Moon** and **Alice Cooper** ad-libbed their way through their bits (and Moon seemed to frighten his squeaky-clean co-presenter, **Olivia Newton-John**).

Speaking to *Circus Raves* almost six months after receiving the award, Don Henley was apathetic. "Yeah, we won, I don't know how or why!" he told **Steven Rosen**. "It doesn't mean a whole lot, it really honestly doesn't. I mean, it's a flash, a little adrenaline pump to be watching the television and not knowing what was going to happen and then win. That's another crazy thing, like all of your life, from 13, 14, you think, 'Boy, what would it be like to have a really big hit record and be really well-known and go on tour?' And when you get there and look in the Holiday Inn mirror when you hear that your

continued on Page 209

SCHMIT'S 'TRYIN'' BECOMES POCO'S BIGGEST HIT

The leadoff track from **Poco**'s *Head Over Heels* album, Timothy B. Schmit's acoustic composition "Keep on Tryin,'" was released by ABC Records as the album's first single in September 1975. It's a curious bit of trivia that Randy Meisner and Schmit, who would both play bass for Poco and the Eagles, also wrote and sang songs that suggested one should "keep on tryin.'"

The Schmit contribution to *Head Over Heels* is an acoustic ballad that remains one of Poco's more memorable tracks. Despite peaking at a modest #50 on the charts, it still became the band's biggest single to date. "Keep on Tryin,'" however, would be added to the Eagles' setlist during the early shows of Schmit's tenure with the group.

Initial reviews of Poco's effort were strong. **Bruce Westbrook** of the *Waco Tribune-Herald* complimented the LP, calling it "a virtually flawless piece of work," and added that "was particularly true of the laid back ["Keep on Tryin'"] in which the vocals are so strong and so well done that they require almost no instrument accompaniment." **Terry Jordan** of the *St. Joseph News-Press* in St. Joseph, Missouri, said Poco not only survived the loss of lead

PATHWAY SINGLE | TIMOTHY B. SCHMIT

POCO
Keep on Tryin'
ABC Records, June 1975

singer **Richie Furay**, it delivered an album no one was expecting, and called Schmit's vocals "familiar and mesmerizing."

Poco guested on *The Midnight Special* in January 1976 and performed the track with **Rusty Young** strumming one acoustic guitar as band members stood around microphones vocalizing—not unlike the Eagles' renditions of "Seven Bridges Road."

Poco's performance sounded great, but during the song the camera suddenly, inexplicably, cut to B-roll footage of chickens! Chickens? Frankly, it made no sense. And at that point, the single had long since fallen off the charts anyway. Schmit would have to wait a few more years when, as a member of the Eagles, he'd finally score that massive hit with a different breathy ballad he'd sing in his distinctive tenor. [343, 1504, 2089, 2090]

album is number one for the fifth week in a row, you don't feel any different. You're just the same person, the same cat, the same guy. A lot of people have all sorts of drastic reactions, ego trips, but that's bull. You can't get too blown out about it or too high on the hog because it's like a pro ballplayer, you only run three or four years, five years maybe, and then you either get too old or too tired or too rich and you quit."

Henley wasn't alone in his apathy for this particular award. The *Rock Music Awards* telecast would only last two more years before television and viewers grew tired of the format. Even the beneficiaries of the awards turned against them. **Linda Ronstadt**, who won the award for Best Female Artist all three years the trophies were handed out, didn't show up to receive it, flippantly calling it the "Who Cares Award." [76, 88, 622, 1966]

FALL 1975

RELEASES
▶ **Joe Walsh**, "Song for Emma" (single)
▶ **Poco**, with Timothy B. Schmit, "Keep on Tryin'" (single)
▶ **Eagles**, "Lyin' Eyes" (single)
▶ **Joe Walsh**, "County Fair" (single)
▶ **Eagles**, "Take It to the Limit" (single)

NUGGETS
▶ Irving Azoff was confined to the back of his limo during an Eagles concert in Anaheim with a bout of mono, but he was not suffering from the half-million concert gross. —*Cashbox*

COLLABORATIONS
▶ **Don Felder** played guitar on **David Blue**'s album *Com'n Back for More*.
▶ **Bernie Leadon** played banjo and acoustic guitar on the singles "8 Ton Crazy" and "Wide Eyed and Legless" on **Andy Fairweather-Low**'s album *La Booga Rooga*.

ON SCREEN
▶ Eagles appeared on the NBC-TV show *The Midnight Special*. The band performed "One of These Nights."
▶ Eagles appeared on the syndicated TV show *Don Kirshner's Rock Concert* (Episode 3.15), recorded at the Santa Monica Civic Auditorium with 4,500 people attempting to fit into the 3,000-seat hall.

ON THE ROAD WITH …
▶ **Eagles**: Bee Gees, Dan Fogelberg, Fleetwood Mac, Jackson Browne, Kenny Rankin, Linda Ronstadt, New Riders of the Purple Sage, REO Speedwagon, the Charlie Daniels Band, the Marshall Tucker Band, Toots and the Maytals
▶ **Poco**, with Timothy B. Schmit: America, Little Feat, McKendree Spring, the Doobie Brothers, the Outlaws, Tom Waits
▶ **Joe Walsh**: 10cc, Elton John, Emmylou Harris

Bob Dylan Signs with Asylum: Geffen Lands His 'White Whale'

David Geffen wanted to bring **Bob Dylan** into the Asylum stable for a long time. Geffen's wandering eye for talent was one of the reasons the Eagles became so eager to find a manager with fewer conflicts of interest and hired **Irving Azoff**.

But the animosity felt by some artists in Asylum's cavalcade of stars didn't prevent Geffen from chasing artists he idolized. So

continued on Page 212

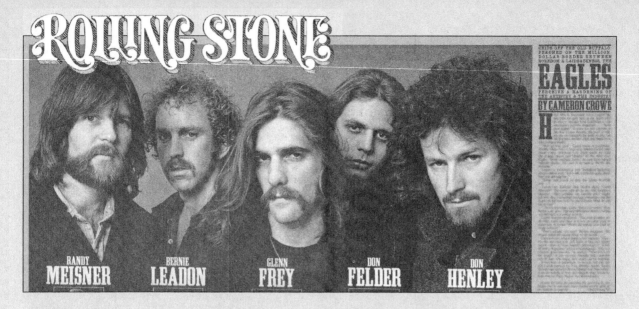

ROLLING STONE

RANDY **MEISNER** — BERNIE **LEADON** — GLENN **FREY** — DON **FELDER** — DON **HENLEY**

CHIPS OFF THE OLD BUFFALO PERCHED ON THE MILLION DOLLAR BORDER BETWEEN BOREDOM & LAISSACKNESS, THE **EAGLES** PERCEIVE A HARDENING OF THE ARTISTRY & THE INDUSTRY **BY CAMERON CROWE**

SOARING EAGLES LAND ON *ROLLING STONE* COVER

All due respect to **Shel Silverstein**'s satirical "Cover of the Rolling Stone," made famous by **Dr. Hook & the Medicine Show** in 1972, scoring a *Rolling Stone* cover was an achievement most bands coveted in the 1970s. On September 25, 1975, the Eagles accomplished this feat for the first time.

"The Eagles: Chips off the Old Buffalo" captioned the magazine's full-page cover image of the *One of These Nights*-era quintet drinking beer on the bow of a boat. Glenn Frey and Bernie Leadon appear shirtless, and Don Henley, Randy Meisner, and Don Felder are decked out in unbuttoned denim shirts. **Cameron Crowe**'s cover story remains one of the most significant pieces of journalism about the notoriously rock press-averse band.

Crowe, who had met the band after their first record while they were still a quartet, spent months with the group this time around, getting a firsthand look into the Eagles' world. "It was a different time for journalism," he said in 2015, "a long way from our current world of quick sit-downs or rote, 45-minute junket interviews."

In the journalist's estimation, the group was tired of being pigeonholed as a generic, laid-back

CHIPS OFF THE OLD BUFFALO

SEPTEMBER 1975

Southern California band. "Frey and Henley," Crowe said, "wanted the article to be completely representative of how seriously they took the mantle of being a premier American band."

Crowe began his extended feature with the band behind the mics at Super WCFL Studios in Chicago with "Superjock" **Larry Lujack**.

"I remember reading somewhere that the Eagles do the best 'ooo's [harmonies] in the business, what do you say to that?" Frey flashed a sly grin, and said: "Ooo's for bucks, Larry. That's our motto. The only difference between boring and laid back is a million dollars." Lujack chortled.

"Hey, is it true you guys want to sound like **Al Green**?" he asked. Don Henley responded deadpan: "That's actually very true, we almost called this record *Black in the Saddle*."

The morning show banter continued, and then Lujack spun "One of These Nights" for the first time on WCFL, and his segment ended. Free from the deejay's ramblings, Crowe then went in search of what made the Eagles tick.

Crowe was given unheard-of access to the band for the article, he remembered in a 2016 *Rolling*

Stone article recounting the experience.

"I spent many months with the band: sitting in on their exacting studio sessions, joining them on the road, tagging along with them at bars and clubs around Los Angeles, watching them take social nuances and inhabit all haunts that would later...turn up as iconography in their songs," Crowe observed.

Still just 18 years old, Crowe stayed with Frey and Henley for a couple weeks in their "million dollar view" hideaway overlooking Los Angeles. While he was there the songwriting team would write parts of the songs that would fill *One of These Nights*.

"I was there, with the tape recorder on, as they wrote 'Lyin' Eyes' and 'After the Thrill is Gone,' the title song and many others," Crowe recalled, "including an unrecorded gem called 'When a Bad Boy Meets a Bad Girl in the Night.'"

Crowe's access gave him insight into a central theme that both Frey and Henley had visited upon before and would return to often over the next three years: the aura of Southern California, and realizing that essence in their music.

"Though Henley was from Texas, and Frey from Detroit, their goal was to capture the California zeitgeist. As they looked out on that glittery horizon, the songwriters kept topping each other with ideas and phrases that could have layers of meaning," Crowe said, remembering that Henley had once said to Frey that "nothing can just skim the surface."

"The partnership was electric," Crowe said, "a guided missile of creativity. I had a front-row seat for their process, and wanted the [*Rolling Stone*] piece to show their chemistry from the inside out. For a notoriously press-shy group, this was off the grid. They left no doors closed and no avenues off-limits. It was journalistic nirvana, and the Budweiser flowed as we talked for many hours over many nights."

THE [FREY-HENLEY] PARTNERSHIP WAS ELECTRIC, A GUIDED MISSILE OF CREATIVITY. I HAD A FRONT-ROW SEAT FOR THEIR PROCESS, AND WANTED THE *RS* PIECE TO SHOW THEIR CHEMISTRY FROM THE INSIDE OUT.

—*CAMERON CROWE*

When he was finished Crowe had completed an exhaustive feature story with photos by **Neal Preston** that sprawled out across five full pages of the then-tabloid 11x14 newsprint magazine.

All the then-current Eagles were quoted in the story, but it read predominantly as a series of interviews with Frey and Henley. This is unsurprising to those who knew of the inner dynamics of the band, and the subject of the duo's single-minded dedication even came up in the piece, where Henley described his Eagles commitment as "a 24-hour-a-day trip," and Frey said, "Sure, Don and I are more into it than the others."

Crowe described the remaining Eagles as having more of what today we would call a "work-life balance." But Frey and Henley didn't seem to make much of a distinction between their personal lives and their lives as Eagles. It's not entirely clear from the article whether their all-encompassing approach to the band is fueled by desire or by a sense of responsibility, though it was probably a combination of both.

Other topics covered include many common motifs long associated with the Eagles: the constant quest for artistic integrity and the production of quality material, the desire to make money without compromising one's craft, a cynical view about the music business, and the differing band personalities that led Frey to comment, "We never expected to get this far, anyway. I thought we'd break up after our first album."

As Crowe reflected, "Looking back, I think the article caught the excitement, dedication, and humor of the end of the Eagles' first career act... Just around the bend was *Hotel California*—more angst, more peaks, more fireworks, and many more hits—but in 1975, they were still newcomers to the West Coast, still young men aiming to stake their claim and make good on all the promise of the future, shimmering ahead of them." [88, 480]

he went after Dylan. He worked toward this first by courting Dylan's friend, **Robbie Robertson**, the talented guitar player and primary songwriter for **The Band**, Dylan's former road band. Of course, The Band (independent of Dylan) had signed with Capitol Records in 1968 and become a successful act with big hits like "The Weight" and "Up On Cripple Creek."

After Robertson introduced Dylan to Geffen, the ambitious mogul soon established a friendship with the reclusive, notoriously private singer/songwriter.

Befriending Dylan was a remarkable accomplishment by itself. But Geffen wanted more. He and Robertson met in 1973, when the Woodstock, New York-based guitarist was on a trip to Los Angeles. He continued to nurture the relationship via phone after Robertson returned home.

On one of Geffen's subsequent business trips east, he met with Robertson and pitched an offer to have The Band sign with Asylum. Robertson—along with his bandmates **Levon Helm**, **Richard Manuel**, **Rick Danko**, and **Garth Hudson**—did not accept the offer at that point.

As Geffen biographer Tom King explained in his book *The Operator*, "Robertson's compatriots...were essentially country boys, and Geffen's presentation was a tad too flashy for their tastes." Still, Geffen commanded enough of a presence that the group agreed not to dismiss the offer outright and would leave the matter open to future consideration.

Meanwhile, Dylan had moved to a house in Malibu. Geffen reasoned he stood a better chance of luring in both Robertson and Dylan if the two lived near each other— and him. Geffen encouraged Robertson to move west and offered to set up a place for him and his family. Robertson accepted the offer.

Upon Robertson's arrival in California, Geffen made a bolder pitch than before: reuniting Dylan and The Band.

Geffen, of course, was hardly the first person to hatch this plot. Next to reuniting **The Beatles**, nearly everyone in the music industry believed that reuniting Dylan and The Band would be the most epic, most lucrative rock and roll event ever. But thus far, the two parties had declined any offers.

Robertson was still leery this time around, but Geffen was, if nothing else, a convincing salesman. Despite his skepticism that his bandmates and Dylan himself would be interested, Robertson eventually warmed up to the idea, and agreed to reach out to Dylan and arrange a meeting.

When they met, Geffen suggested a co-headlining tour featuring both The Band and Dylan, promising to handle all the arrangements. When Geffen also offered to waive his fee, that sealed the deal. He was willing to work under this arrangement since his eye was on the bigger prize of eventually signing Dylan to Asylum as a solo artist.

After booking the tour, Geffen pitched the idea that any road show like this should naturally be accompanied by new product to promote. When Geffen boldly predicted an Asylum release would outperform Dylan's usual sales on Columbia, his label since 1961, the artist agreed to a two-album deal with Asylum.

Dylan recorded the first LP, *Planet Waves*, with The Band in about five days in November 1973. There wasn't a lot of time to waste, as the tour was beginning on January 3. The record would be a hit by most standards, reaching #1 on the album charts, but it still grossly underperformed compared to the numbers Geffen had suggested he could generate. Whether this was due to the quick recording schedule, a lack of memorable material, spotty distribution, or Geffen simply overpromising what he could deliver is a matter of debate.

Certainly, Dylan's most famous musical period was almost a decade behind him, yet his legacy preceded him in 1974 and he was unquestionably considered a legendary artist. On the road, it seemed fans wanted to hear more of his classic material and fewer of his new offerings, and perhaps that affected album sales.

The disappointing sales led Dylan (and The Band, except for Robertson, who initially remained loyal to Geffen) to decide Asylum shouldn't be granted the rights to release the planned second album—a live record from the tour called *Before the Flood*. Geffen insisted there was a contract in place, but it turned out there was only a signed deal for the first album and the second was based more on an informal handshake agreement.

After much back and forth, Asylum released the live album, but the proviso outlined was that other labels would be allowed to bid on the record and Geffen would have to match or beat other offers. Columbia jumped back in and drove up the price in what became a bidding war. Geffen paid substantially more than he had wanted to for the rights, perhaps not wanting to suffer the disgrace of losing the "white whale" he had coveted for so long.

Geffen's "victory" was short-lived at best. Before the end of the year, Dylan had moved to a farm in his native Minnesota, written new songs, and signed a new long-term deal with Columbia. The label released his next album, *Blood on the Tracks*, in January 1975. Like *Planet Waves*, it topped the album charts. [1, 3, 1668, 1669]

Walsh Joins Eagles' Lineup, Takes Flight Onstage

Joe Walsh discovered he had much to learn when he officially joined the Eagles in December 1975. He'd worked with the group on several occasions, but never this closely or as long. He also began playing shows with them before this updated lineup had released any new music together.

Walsh's first dates in early 1976 found the band sticking closely to the set list from the previous leg of the tour supporting *One of These Nights*. There were nods to his pre-Eagles successes, as the group added "Turn to Stone," "Rocky Mountain Way," and "Funk #49." But Walsh had to quickly find his role on live renditions of prior Eagles songs like "Lyin' Eyes" and "Desperado" long before recreating his signature riff for the forthcoming "Life in the Fast Lane."

Walsh, who had earned praise from rock luminaries including **Pete Townsend** and **Eric Clapton**, quickly learned Bernie Leadon was no slouch, either. Once he was in the Eagles lineup, Walsh had to quickly learn Leadon's guitar parts because in January, the band would head to Australia, New Zealand, and Japan for a series of shows.

"I had no idea what a great guitar player [Leadon] was at coming up with off-the-wall original parts—until I had to learn them. Holy shit, this guy's good," Walsh recalled.

Fellow guitarist Don Felder frankly admitted he, too, had trouble picturing how it would go at first. "My only concern with Joe was our transition from a pedal steel and banjo band to one that played stoned-out, blacked-out, chain-saw rock 'n' roll," Felder wrote in *Heaven and Hell: My Life in the Eagles.* "I really had a difficult time seeing Joe playing what the Eagles did. It was a little like asking **Jimi Hendrix** to sit in with the **Boston Pops**."

But Walsh proved himself to be impressively adaptable as a musician, deftly moving from the harder edges of his music with the James Gang and Barnstorm to even the softest of early Eagles country-rock.

All Walsh had to do then was figure out how to fit in with the personalities of a tight-knit, battle-tested group of musical

> I HAD NO IDEA WHAT A GREAT GUITAR PLAYER [LEADON] WAS AT COMING UP WITH OFF-THE-WALL ORIGINAL PARTS— UNTIL I HAD TO LEARN THEM. HOLY SHIT, THIS GUY'S GOOD.
>
> —JOE WALSH

perfectionists who had already released four studio albums and toured the world—most particularly Don Henley.

"Joe Walsh came to me just after he joined the Eagles and said, 'You've known him the longest. Tell him to relax,'" **Richard Bowden**, an early Henley bandmate in **Shiloh**, told the *Washington Post* in 2016. "I told him to just let Don be tense. He's always been that way. When he solves one problem, he just moves on to something else to worry about."

Once Walsh had lived up to the Eagles' lofty expectations on stage, he in turn could mentor other members of the touring entourage—including former **Barnstorm** drummer **Joe Vitale**, who subsequently participated in a string of late-'70s Eagles concerts as an auxiliary member.

"Their live show is just incredible; it's impeccable," Vitale told *Rolling Stone* in 2020. "Joe warned me about that. He said, 'Listen, no jamming. Play the parts and play them every night. Play it like it's your first time you've ever played it.' I said, 'No problem. I get it.'"

The Eagles took some time off in August 1976, even canceling a few dates, to focus on finishing their follow-up to *One of These Nights*, to be titled *Hotel California*. They returned to the road that October and debuted a few of the soon-to-be-released LP's key songs, including the title track with its memorable guitar duel between Walsh and Felder.

By then, Walsh was certainly convincing Eagles concert goers he was the right guy to replace Leadon onstage.

Still, more than a few Eagles record-buyers wondered how the band could pull off replacing Leadon's country pedigree on tape with the lead guitarist responsible for ripping rockers like "Funk #49" and "Walk Away." How would that work?

The answer would soon present itself. The Eagles' next album, and first with Walsh on board, would be the band's biggest studio LP, the legacy-cementing *Hotel California*. From the tail-end of 1975 forward, onstage and off, Walsh would contribute mightily to the Eagles' music and mayhem, with wild tales of chainsaws, U.S. presidential campaigns, and "Life in the Fast Lane" on the horizon. [342, 1999, 2000]

Geffen Re-Signs Joni Mitchell, Jackson Browne to Asylum

David Geffen wasted no time in re-signing two of Asylum Records' most important acts as their original deals neared an end, securing the talents of **Joni Mitchell** and **Jackson Browne** as they hit creative and commercial peaks in the mid-'70s.

Cashbox in November 1975 reported both extensions were for five years, calling Mitchell "one of the most prolific and important composers/performers of the 1970s." Browne, the trade magazine added, "has gained measurable national prominence" after composing the Eagles' hit "Take It Easy" while releasing a trio of platinum-selling studio projects.

Mitchell had already achieved platinum-selling success before she left Reprise and kept that momentum going with her 1972 debut for Asylum. The multi-million-selling 1974 smash *Court and Spark* then became her first #1 album. The same month she renewed her deal with Asylum, Mitchell released her follow-up, *The Hissing of Summer Lawns*, which become her fourth consecutive Top 10 LP.

Not all of Mitchell's fans stuck with her, though, as she continued down a more experimental creative pathway, following her muse into still-jazzier sounds on records like *Don Juan's Reckless Daughter*, *Hejira*, and *Mingus* through the late '70s. Many of the newer fans Mitchell made with her most mainstream earlier records began to drift away.

"People seem to have a problem after *Court and Spark*," Mitchell said in **Mark Bego**'s 2005 biography, *Joni Mitchell*. "Everything was measured unfavorably against it."

Mitchell also admitted she considered simply finishing out her new extension and then retiring after a particularly negative review of *The Hissing of Summer Lawns* from *Rolling Stone*. That didn't happen, of course, as Mitchell later shifted to Geffen's eponymous label in the 1980s—and to then-modern synth-pop sounds.

Meanwhile, Browne was headed in the opposite direction on the charts. He

continued on Page 218

RELEASE
Mid-December 1975

TAKE IT TO THE LIMIT

By: Randy Meisner, Don Henley, Glenn Frey
Side B: After the Thrill is Gone (Henley, Frey)

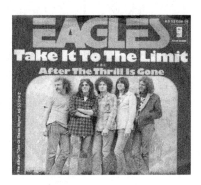

"Take It to the Limit" was the Eagles' fourth-straight Top 5 single, but it didn't follow the same path as the band's previous singles. It took more time to climb the charts, though had more staying power than any song they released since "The Best of My Love." "Limit" was virtually glued to the *Billboard* Hot 100 and stayed there for a whopping 21 weeks. When the Eagles toured, it became Randy Meisner's signature song, with fans screaming for it and then providing rapturous ovations when he finished.

AIRPLAY

Compared to the two previous singles released in 1975, "One of These Nights" and "Lyin' Eyes" respectively, "Limit" got off to a snail-like start. It was released mid-December, but radio stations didn't push hard at the outset. Telephone requests gave it momentum, and listeners were asking for it. Two months later, it had been added to 91% of all *Cashbox*'s reporting stations and remained in regular rotation for six solid months. The single's success was even more significant because it attracted very little attention from FM/AOR radio.

98 PLAYLIST ADDS Winter 1975-76

Region	Dec	Jan	Feb	Regional Airplay
Northeast	2	11	4	17.3 %
Southeast	10	18	1	29.6 %
Midwest	4	10	9	23.5 %
Southwest	3	6	5	14.3 %
West	2	11	2	15.3 %

FIRST-WAVE STATIONS Stations that added the song in the first 30 days

KAFY-Bakersfield
KISN, KGW-Portland
KIIS, KHJ-Los Angeles
KJOY-Stockton
KKAM-Pueblo, CO
KJR, KING-Seattle
KRSP-Salt Lake City
KYNO-Fresno
KXFM-San Bernardino
KYA-San Francisco

WZUU-Milwaukee
WIRL-Peoria
WCUE-Akron
WCOL-Columbus
KQWB-Fargo

KILT-Houston
KFJZ-Fort Worth
KLIF-Dallas
KXOL-Fort Worth

WCFL-Chicago
WIXY-Cleveland
KOIL-Omaha
KKLS-Rapid City, SD
KEWI-Topeka

KEEL-Shreveport
WPGC-Washington
WYRE-Annapolis
WFOM-Marietta

WPTR, WTRY-Albany
WIBG-Philadelphia
WVBF, WBZ-Boston
WPIX-New York City
WPRO-Providence

WKIX-Raleigh
WSGA-Savannah
WSGN-Birmingham
WLEE-Richmond

CHARTS

Billboard

 # 4
March 13, 1976

Cashbox

 # 5
February 28, 1976

Record World

 # 6
February 28, 1976

HIGHEST CHARTING WEEK: BILLBOARD - March 13, 1976

SINGLE	ARTIST	PREV WK
1. December, 1963 (Oh, What a Night)	Four Seasons	3
2. All By Myself	Eric Carmen	2
3. Love Machine Pt. 1	Miracles	1
4. TAKE IT TO THE LIMIT	**EAGLES**	**5**
5. Dream Weaver	Gary Wright	6
6. Lonely Night (Angel Face)	Captain & Tennille	7
7. Theme from S.W.A.T.	Rhythm Heritage	4
8. Love Hurts	Nazareth	9
9. Sweet Thing	Rufus featuring Chaka Khan	11
10. Junk Food Junkie	Larry Groce	13

Sources: Billboard, Cashbox, Record World

WITH 'LIMIT,' MEISNER FINDS HIS SIGNATURE SONG

The Randy Meisner-sung "Take It to the Limit" became the Eagles' third consecutive Top 5 hit from *One of These Nights*—and their fourth consecutive overall. It also was their first gold single, which signaled their growing stature in pop music. Midway through his career with the Eagles, it gave him his signature crowd-pleasing song.

Meisner had provided the original idea for the song, handing over a few lines he'd dashed off after a show at the Troubadour so Glenn Frey and Don Henley could complete things. "I was feeling kind of lonely and started singing '*All alone at the end of the evening, and the bright lights have faded to blue*,'" Meisner told *Rolling Stone*. "And it went from there."

That wistful moment in the Troubadour might have gotten Meisner started, but producer **Bill Szymczyk** had a feeling about the song and assigned the band's songwriters some homework.

"Around that time, I was really influencing the Eagles insofar as my great love has been black rhythm & blues," Szymczyk explained to the *BBC*'s **John Tobler**, "and I had been turning those guys on to all these various records, especially the Philadelphia International label records. The tune of 'Take It to the Limit' is based on 'If You Don't Know Me By Now' by **Harold Melvin and the Blue Notes**—I told them to listen to that record, because it was re-

ally good. So Randy started to write a real laid-back three-chorded thing, and we put strings on it. I like that record too, even though it took a little time for Randy to do it. He's got a great voice."

Szymczyk said recording Meisner's voice in the studio was challenging. But, he added, his vocal range was perfectly suited to the song. The result—a soaring promise not to give up in the face of life's hardships—was the first Eagles single not to feature either Frey or Henley on lead vocals.

The rock press loved the single. Veteran rock journalist **Bud Scoppa** praised it as an "unusual" track in the album, but called it the best lead vocal Meisner ever recorded. The true measure of Meisner's performance came from Frey. "Randy (Meisner) gets a standing ovation whenever he hits the high notes," Frey told **Chris Charlesworth** of **Melody Maker**, "and sometimes the applause goes on for two or three minutes."

"I just remember being very happy for Randy," Frey told *Rolling Stone*. "We had tried, unsuccessfully, to get a piece of material for him—or from him—that might be a hit single, or turn into one. I don't think we ever consciously tried to make a hit single. We finally succeeded with 'Take It to the Limit.' That's the first Eagles single to sell a million copies. It was our first gold single, maybe our only gold single. And when Randy would sing it in Japan—

returned with *The Pretender* in 1976, notching his best-selling album to date, then topped it with *Running on Empty* in 1978. Two years later, Browne scored his first and only #1 album with *Hold Out*. But by then, Geffen was long gone from Elektra/Asylum. [627, 2030, 2031]

Three Eagles Guest on Walsh's *Rock Concert* TV Appearance

In the pre-MTV era, a live concert television performance was one of the best ways to get an act in front of people at home, and Joe Walsh delivered a blistering set at the Santa Monica Civic Auditorium on November 26, 1975 that was filmed for broadcast on *Don Kirshner's Rock Concert*.

The bandleader/guitarist brought along three Eagles to sit in with him during the show, billed as *Joe Walsh & Friends*. With Walsh on the verge of becoming an official member of the band the following month, the performance was akin to a dress rehearsal for the lineup.

Felder was onstage for almost the entire set, though he largely filled a secondary guitarist's role, playing rhythm parts while Walsh handled the leads.

Walsh began with the introspective "Meadows" from the second **Barnstorm** record before ripping into the **James Gang** classic "Walk Away." The juxtaposition of the softer songs with the rockers offered a good indication of how Walsh's talents would fit in well with what the Eagles were already doing. Walsh's guitar acumen

would add a new dimension to the band.

Some of the songs Walsh and his band performed also flirted with "jam band" leanings, where the group would open things up a bit and incorporate Latin percussion, extended guitar solos, and occasionally even two sets of drums on stage (a common practice for popular live groups like the **Allman Brothers Band** and the **Grateful Dead**).

Accompanying Walsh on stage, in addition to Felder, were longtime partner **Joe Vitale** and session ace **Andy Newmark** on drums, bassist extraordinaire **Willie Weeks**, **Spirit** alum **Jay Ferguson** on piano, one-time Todd Rundgren collaborator **David Mason** on organ, and Ghanaian percussionist **Kwasi "Rocky" Dzidzornu**.

If that cast of characters seems a lot like the list of credits on Walsh's *You Can't Argue with a Sick Mind* record, it's not a coincidence: the show was also the source for the live album ABC Records would release early in 1976.

Henley, Frey, and Felder eventually joined Walsh front and center, each sitting on stools strumming acoustic guitars while singing a gorgeous rendition of the sadly emotive "Help Me Thru the Night." If there was one moment in the set that felt more like an Eagles show than a Walsh performance, that was it.

On the Walsh favorite "Turn to Stone," future Eagles collaborator Vitale jumped from keyboards to drums to flute, all within the same song, and the guitarist's signature tune "Rocky Mountain Way" followed this, replete with a talk-box solo. Two cover songs rounded out the show: "Get Back" by **The Beatles** (with Frey stepping onstage again to play guitar) and "Gimme Some Lovin'" by the **Spencer Davis Group**, both played in Walsh's inimitable style rather than just being rote reproductions.

While Walsh was clearly the star of the evening, by featuring what would be the entire *Hotel California* lineup minus Randy Meisner, this show feels, at least in hindsight, like a transitional moment. For all of Walsh's remarkable achievements in the James Gang, in Barnstorm, and as a solo artist, it's tough to downplay the fact that he was about to join a band whose next album would sell more than 30 million copies. [1498, 1687, 1688]

WINTER 1975-76

 RELEASES
▶ **Eagles,** *Their Greatest Hits (1971–1975)* (album)

 ON THE ROAD WITH …
▶ **Poco**, with Timothy B. Schmit: Automatic Man, B.W. Stevenson, Dave Mason, Santana, Stephen Stills

 AWARDS
▶ **Eagles, 3rd Annual American Music Awards:**
● Favorite Pop/Rock Band/Duo/Group, nominated. Lost to **Tony Orlando & Dawn**. Also nominated: **Earth, Wind & Fire**.
● Best Pop/Rock Album, *One of These Nights*, nominated. Lost to **Olivia Newton John**, *Have You Never Been Mellow*.

 AWARDS (cont.)
▶ **Eagles, 18th Annual Grammy Awards:**
● Best Pop Performance by a Duo or Group with Vocals, "Lyin' Eyes," winner. Also nominated were **Singers Unlimited,** "A Capella 2," **Captain & Tennille,** "Love Will Keep Us Together," **Simon & Garfunkel,** "My Little Town," and **Gladys Knight and the Pips,** "The Way We Were / Try to Remember."
● Album of the Year, *One of These Nights,* nominated. Lost to **Paul Simon**, *Still Crazy After All These Years*. Also nominated: **Janis Ian**, *Between the Lines*; **Elton John**, *Captain Fantastic and the Brown Dirt Cowboy*; **Linda Ronstadt**, *Heart Like a Wheel*.
● Best Album Package, *One of These Nights*, nominated. Lost to **Ohio Players**, *Honey*. Also nominated: **Rod Stewart**, *Atlantic Crossing*; **Nitty Gritty Dirt Band**, *Dream*; **Led Zeppelin**, *Physical Graffiti*; and **Carly Simon**, *Playing Possum*.
● Record of the Year, "Lyin' Eyes," nominated. Lost to **Captain & Tennille**, "Love Will Keep Us Together." Also nominated: **Barry Manilow**, "Mandy," **Glen Campbell**, "Rhinestone Cowboy," and **Janis Ian**, "At Seventeen."

 NUGGETS
▶ Eagles host party to welcome **Joe Smith** to Elektra/Asylum, with Don Henley, Joe Walsh, **J.D. Souther**, Irving Azoff, Don Felder, and Warner Bros.' **Mo Ostin**, **Carly Simon**, **Andrew Gold**, **James Taylor** and **Minnie Riperton**. —*Record World*
▶ A concert crowd impatient to hear the Eagles begins booing opening act **Tom Waits** halfway through his set at Red Rocks Amphitheater in Morrison, Colorado. When the Eagles finally take the stage the disappointed band reminds their audience that Waits was the writer of fan favorite "Ol' '55". — *Tom Waits on Tom Waits (2011)*
▶ **Byron Berline** and his band **Sundance** welcomed **Mark Cohen** and **Vince Gill** as new members. —*Cashbox*

continued on Page 222

BURNED-OUT LEADON LEAVES; WALSH JOINS BAND

Glenn Frey once remarked he never expected the original Eagles to survive past the first album. For a band comprised of such diverse personalities and talents, it's remarkable the original quartet—with the later addition of Don Felder making it a quintet—remained intact through four studio albums and almost half a decade. But that's as long as it would last.

Bernie Leadon, the founding member who brought the greatest country pedigree to the Eagles, was the first original member to leave.

Leadon's tenure in the group ended in December 1975, though by all accounts, his departure was a long time coming and surprised no one.

"We actually knew about a year and a half earlier that Bernie would be leaving the band at some point," Frey said in the year following Leadon's departure. "We knew he wasn't happy touring; we knew he was gonna leave."

In the group's second *Rolling Stone* cover feature in 1979, the departed guitar player offered his most oft-quoted explanation: "I kept asking, 'Are we going to rest next month?' and we never did.

I wanted to get in shape before the age of 30 so I could have a chance at the rest of my life. I was afraid something inside of me was dying. Leaving was an act of survival."

"Mainly, I was burnt out," Leadon told the *Minneapolis Star-Tribune* in 2002. "I wanted to go to the beach and get healthy."

The band was well aware Bernie was fed up with touring after years of working. "Bernie wasn't happy with the road," Don Henley said, "but then he'd started his road map [with his previous bands] about six years before we started traveling."

But there was more to it. Musically, Leadon was walking on a different path than the others, particularly Henley and Frey, who had emerged as the band's leaders.

"Late in [*On the Border*] we brought in Don Felder to play some lead electric guitar in a couple of songs," Leadon told **Anthony Fawcett** in the writer's 1978 book *California Rock California Sound*. "We decided to get him in the band to beef things up. I was already thinking of leaving. He's an old friend of mine and he's good. I know he can hold up. I didn't want to destroy the band by leaving, so I got a good strong friend to come in and I could bail any time I wanted.

"So I stayed and stayed and stayed, but that was the beginning of me leaving; it took two years," Leadon continued. "I was enjoying it, it was fun. But the reason I had to leave was the touring kept going on and on. Tensions between me and Henley and Frey were unnecessary—everybody was getting some money and there was no reason to compromise. And in the beginning there were no drugs. The pressure of the whole thing was really starting to wear on me, so I was really seriously thinking of leaving. I was really depressed about my music—that was just personal—and my non-acceptance in the band. I felt we could expand in some other areas 'cause we were so successful. The other guys were being very strong-willed about the way we wanted to do things. So I decided to do it."

"Bernie's expertise was country," Felder remarked. "Musically, he wanted the band to go back into country. But everyone else wanted to move towards rock."

Indeed, Bernie had brought a great deal of his sound and influence to the debut Eagles album and to *Desperado*, where acoustic guitars, banjos, mandolins, and other country and bluegrass instruments were prevalent. *On the Border* made a deliberate effort to turn down the country, **Paul Craft**'s bluegrassy "Midnight Flyer" notwithstanding. But by *One of These Nights*, it was difficult to consider the Eagles a "country-rock" band anymore.

In fact, Leadon's two contributions—the spacey instrumental "Journey of the Sorcerer" and his collaboration with girlfriend **Patti Davis**, "I Wish You Peace"—seemed out of sync with the rest of the album. His bandmates, Henley, in particular, didn't feel the songs were up to the band's standards, and has indicated they were included only to foster peace among the ranks.

Leadon also was less comfortable with riding in limousines and living the grander rock star life than his colleagues. As success came, he was increasingly concerned the band might become "sellouts" lacking musical integrity. He quipped that using the limousines and playing up the rock star lifestyle felt "like you're thumbing your nose at the audience."

"I just wasn't enthralled with the whole rock star persona and world," Leadon remarked. "I consider myself a working musician; I just like to perform for people. That pretension part doesn't really appeal."

Leadon also yearned for the simplicity of a band whose members were not as controlling as he thought Henley and Frey were becoming. In his autobiography, Felder recounted how Bernie would tell him, "You weren't there in the beginning when the Eagles were a band and everybody got two songs. That's all been forgotten, and it stinks."

At one point during the *One of These Nights* sessions, Leadon grew tired of the in-fighting and tensions, announced he was "going surfing," and took off, going AWOL for a number of days during the album's creation.

With Leadon's contributions and role diminishing, his desire for a simpler and healthier lifestyle, and his romance with Davis, all the elements of a split were lining up.

Leadon's departure wasn't a matter of if, but when. The final act came when, during a heated band meeting, he decided to "cool down" Frey by pouring a beer over his head. Not long after, he would be officially gone. It seems appropriate that Leadon's "I Wish You Peace" was the final song on Side Two of *One of These Nights*. It felt like a parting sentiment from the founding guitar player.

Over the years, the "beer incident" has been one of the most notorious pieces of Eagles lore: the mercurial Frey, the equally strong-willed Leadon, and a supporting cast of characters living in a drug-fueled world of 1970s rock star excesses and egos that combined to create chaos in the ranks.

Decades later, in the *History of the Eagles* documentary, Leadon spoke with not only hindsight, but also wisdom and maturity on his side.

"It was a spontaneous thing. I take that incident now quite seriously," he said. "It was a very disrespectful thing to do. Obviously, it was intended to be humiliating to him. ... [It's] something I'm really not proud of. It did illustrate a breaking point."

As soon as Leadon was out, the band turned to Joe Walsh, a kindred spirit who for years had seemed to be heading toward life as an Eagle. [6, 294, 626, 630, 1363, 1404, 1495, 1548, 1559, 1670, 1671, 1810, 2149]

COLLABORATIONS
▶ **Joe Walsh** and **Don Felder** played guitar on **Jeffrey Comanor**'s album *A Rumor in His Own Time*.
▶ **Randy Meisner** provided vocals on **Mac Gayden**'s album *Hymn to the Seeker*.
▶ **Bernie Leadon** played acoustic guitar and provided backing vocals on the single "Feelin' Single - Seein' Double" on **Emmylou Harris**' album *Elite Hotel*.

ON SCREEN
▶ **Joe Walsh** appeared on the NBC-TV show *Don Kirshner's Rock Concert*. Walsh played "Meadows," "Walk Away," "Mother Says," "Turn to Stone," and "Rocky Mountain Way." Walsh and the Eagles then played "Help Me Thru the Night."
▶ **Eagles** appeared on the *18th Annual Grammy Awards*, broadcast on CBS. The band won Best Pop Performance by a Duo or Group with Vocals for "Lyin' Eyes."

Eagles Protest as Geffen Orders Up an Unwanted *Hits* Album

After three months promoting *One of These Nights* around the world, the Eagles returned to Los Angeles to start work on their next album, *Hotel California*. *One of These Nights* had been a momentous success following its June 1975 release, and bean counters at Elektra/Asylum was already looking forward to its successor.

But the band members were taking a more measured approach to their next release and planned to begin recording in March with only a vague idea about when those sessions would wrap.

E/A faced a conundrum: the label had the world's hottest band, but was approaching a full year without any new product, and nothing new on the horizon. Geffen made a move that was enormously successful and further alienated the band: Elektra/Asylum released a greatest hits album in February 1976.

"None of us had a say in the decision," guitarist Don Felder said of the *Eagles: Their Greatest Hits (1971-1975)* compilation. In the end, the label did let the band have some say in things like song selection, sequencing, and graphics, but the Eagles could not refuse the release. The album featured ten cuts cherry-picked from their first four albums, and was the second to depict artwork created by Texas-born artist **Boyd Elder**.

"Let us say that we aren't really advocates of 'Greatest Hits' albums," Henley told *Melody Maker*. "They are more or less a ploy by the record company to get free sales. They don't have to spend any money to make them, and they get a lot of money back."

Henley said the band got hate letters after the Greatest Hits LP accusing the group of "selling out" and that artists like Eagles and **Steve Miller** were among the last of the "hits" holdouts (Miller would release his *Steve Miller Band: Greatest Hits 1974-78* on Capitol in November 1978). "But we didn't have anything to do with it. The record company put it out and we couldn't stop them."

Like it or not, the album's stratospheric success astounded the band.

"I never expected it to do five million," Frey told *Melody Maker* in late 1976 with genuine disbelief. "The numbers this year are staggering, and I try not to look at them anymore. It's a different kind of person that buys 'Greatest Hits' albums...people who buy them for gifts for children and not the kind who buy regular albums. I think you reach more people with them...you reach the over 25s and the under 15s a lot."

Upon its release, journalist **Barbara Charone**, writing in *Sounds*, noted the "can't fail" nature that guaranteed the album's success and observed, "It is a fine collection well put together but you're selling the Eagles short if you assume them to be merely a singles group."

Charone was puzzled why the album was missing "James Dean" and noted, "Sad that some of the band's raunchier rock 'n' roll tunes like 'Out of Control' or 'Outlaw Man' could not be included just to let the punters know there's more substance to the Eagles than back-seat-of-your-car sing-alongs."

Though he had left Elektra/Asylum well before the album's release, and Warner Bros. veteran **Joe Smith** had assumed E/A leadership, Geffen later reflected on his role in setting its enormous success in to motion.

"I remember when I decided to put out their greatest hits after four albums," Geffen said in the 2012 PBS biography, *Inventing David Geffen*. "Everybody was shocked. They said you don't put out a greatest hits album until they're on their way down. And I thought, 'No, put it out now.' And it's the biggest-selling album of all time."

But with the compilation's release, speculation abounded that uncertain times lay ahead for the band.

"More than other greatest hits collec-

tions, this album signifies the end of an era for the Eagles," Charone wrote in *Sounds*. "With the departure of Bernie Leadon and the arrival of Joe Walsh, the Eagles' future seems uncertain. As breakup rumours persistently abound, this greatest-hits package could serve as an early epitaph to one of L.A.'s finest."

By the end of 1976, events would make that speculation seem eerily prescient. [41, 94, 256, 257, 262, 442, 475, 637, 641, 1807, 1824, 1825, 2034]

Elder Returns for Eagles' Greatest Hits Album Cover

Ringing up huge catalog sales worldwide over the years, *Eagles: Their Greatest Hits (1971-1975)* has long been the best-selling album of all time in the United States. It officially took that position in August 2018, when the Recording Industry Association of America certified it "38x platinum," accounting for "sales and streams of more than 38 million copies since its release in February of 1976."

Obviously, the ten songs on the disc—all radio staples—are well known to many millions of fans. So is the image of the painted eagle skull dramatically depicted on the album cover, even if the artist who created it, Texas-born **Boyd Elder**, is lesser known. But everyone who owns a copy of *Their Greatest Hits* also owns an iconic piece of Boyd Elder art from his celebrated "American Fetish–RIP" series of painted and adorned animal skulls.

That fact led journalist **Sterry Butcher** to declare Elder "the most famous artist you

continued on Page 225

EAGLES
THEIR GREATEST HITS
1971-1975

7E-1052

TAKE IT EASY
WITCHY WOMAN
LYIN' EYES
ALREADY GONE
DESPERADO
ONE OF THESE NIGHTS
TEQUILA SUNRISE
TAKE IT TO THE LIMIT
PEACEFUL EASY FEELING
BEST OF MY LOVE

asylum

Eagles did not want a greatest hits album in their catalog, but Asylum Records didn't give them a choice. The label did give them control over the artwork, so they went back to **Boyd Elder** to create their album cover (as seen in this promotional ad that ran in trade magazines).

have never heard of" in a feature article she wrote for *Texas Monthly* in February 2018, several months before his death at 74.

Elder, of course, had in early 1975 provided the artwork for *One of These Nights*, working with independent art director **Gary Burden**. Both the cover and the album inside were well received critically and commercially, so the band and their label reconnected with Elder for the upcoming hits package.

They stuck with the painted animal skulls, this time choosing an eagle skull Elder had painted and pinstriped.

"First, the eagle skull was modeled out of clay, because it's illegal and wrong to own a real one," Elder told writer/producer and longtime friend **Stephen K. Peeples** in 2018. Elder said he had created it not for the Eagles, but for **Neil Young**. Young had declined, possibly due to a miscommunication during price negotiations.

Not too much later, Elder recalled, "the Eagles contacted me saying they had to put this greatest hits album out, and it had to be done right a-fucking-way." When he offered the eagle skull, the band agreed to pay $5,000 to use it.

Keeping with the mystical Southwestern desert motif, Elder hand-lettered "Eagles" and "Their Greatest Hits" with pointy serifs and an all-caps treatment.

Elder, working with Asylum's staff art director, **Glen Christensen**, laid the skull over a background matte. They spent a good deal of time experimenting with ways to highlight the skull before deciding on a backdrop of tiny glass beads. But in the cover photo, the beads scattered on the backdrop also resembled cocaine. Even Glenn Frey noticed the resemblance upon seeing the creation, reportedly remarking to Elder that it looked like "a field of blow."

An urban legend developed as fans assumed it was true. But the artist himself, who was as familiar with the drug as anyone in the band, flat-out denied it.

"There were rumors that when we had the photo shoot, it was pharmaceutical cocaine, and then after we did the album cover, we did all the lines," Elder said. "That was a big myth."

Though the record sold astronomically and made the Eagles a lot of money, Elder didn't get rich from it. The $5,000 paid was a flat-rate agreement, which Elder expressed regret about in 2016, talking with Texas writer **Michael Corcoran**. "If the band had cut me in just one percent of one percent," he lamented, "I wouldn't be having the money problems I have now."

But the terms of the deal he made with the Eagles in 1975 didn't stop him from working with them again years later. In 2003, a Boyd Elder sculpture graced the cover of the group's *The Very Best Of* collection.

It was a new millennium by then, but Elder's signature hand-lettering and another decorated animal skull—a sculpture he called "Black Horse Running"—flashed back to his creations for *One of These Nights* and *Their Greatest Hits* more than a quarter-century earlier. [475, 1786, 1790, 1791, 1795, 1796, 2095, 2096]

E/A-Mandated LP Soars to U.S. All-Time Best-Seller

At the dawn of 1976, the Eagles were coming off their first #1 album, *One of These Nights*, and faced a challenge to top that success the next time they went into the studio.

Eagles: Their Greatest Hits (1971-1975), released in late February, was meant to keep Elektra/Asylum's cash flowing while buying the band more time to prepare a proper follow-up. If *One of These Nights* had rocketed the band to stardom, the hits collection helped them go supernova. It featured ten songs from the band's first four albums. Eight had been hit singles—with five Top 10s including the chart-topping "The Best of My Love" and "One of These Nights"—plus the fan-favorite title track from *Desperado*, their second album. "Tequila Sunrise" was the only other single that had missed the Top 40.

There were no bonus tracks or modern-era extras like demos, live versions, or alternate mixes.

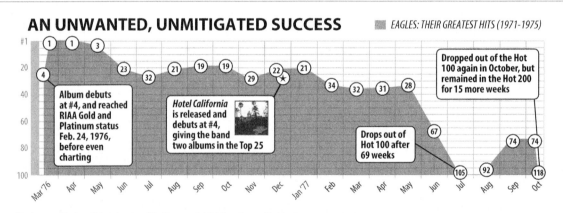

AN UNWANTED, UNMITIGATED SUCCESS   ▨ *EAGLES: THEIR GREATEST HITS (1971-1975)*

Album debuts at #4, and reached RIAA Gold and Platinum status Feb. 24, 1976, before even charting

Hotel California **is released and debuts at #4, giving the band two albums in the Top 25**

Drops out of Hot 100 after 69 weeks

Dropped out of the Hot 100 again in October, but remained in the Hot 200 for 15 more weeks

Eagles wanted nothing to do with the greatest hits album Elektra/Asylum released in February 1976; they considered it a creative sell-out. But the label released it anyway, and the compilation took off like a shot, reaching #1 on the *Billboard* Top LPs & Tapes chart in just one week. It became the first LP the Recording Industry Association of America ever certified platinum and has since shown the greatest staying power of *any* album in U.S. music history. At 38x platinum as of August 2018 (the RIAA's most recent tally), it still topped **Michael Jackson**'s *Thriller* by four million as of August 2021. Along with *One of These Nights*, it gave the Eagles two Top 20 albums at once.
Sources: Billboard, Recording Industry Association of America

BILLBOARD TOP LPs & TAPE, March 13, 1976

1. **EAGLES,** *EAGLES: THEIR GREATEST HITS (1971-1975)*
2. Peter Frampton, *Frampton Comes Alive!*
3. Bob Dylan, *Desire*
4. Fleetwood Mac, *Fleetwood Mac*
5. David Bowie, *Station to Station*
6. Carole King, *Thoroughbred*
7. Paul Simon, *Still Crazy After All These Years*
8. Rufus featuring Chaka Khan, *Rufus*
9. Bad Company, *Run with the Pack*
10. America, *History: America's Greatest Hits*

This kind of package also necessarily lacked the context that made "Desperado" such a critical element in its original song cycle, something Don Henley openly complained about. In a larger sense, as Don Felder later admitted, *Their Greatest Hits (1971-1975)* was nothing more than a "stalling tactic."

But if the point was to set the table for the career-making moment that came next, that's just what this compilation achieved. No one could have guessed how hungry the record-buying public was for a handy overview of an already-impressive recording career.

Released late in February, the LP debuted at #4 on the *Billboard* 200 and was #1 a week later. It perched there for five weeks, and was the first LP to be certified platinum—a new million-selling award established by the Recording Industry Association of America in 1976. Even after slipping from that peak, fans kept buying the album for decades.

"After the band broke up in 1980, it just kept selling and selling and selling," Eagles manager **Irving Azoff** later told *Rolling Stone*. "There became this kind of classic-rock, album-oriented-rock format, and we got so much radio airplay. And the Henley and [Glenn] Frey solo careers kept it going."

Their Greatest Hits (1971-1975) eventually emerged as the best-selling album of all time in the United States, passing *Thriller*, **Michael Jackson**'s biggest album, in 1999 and then again in 2018, when the RIAA certified U.S. sales of the compilation at 38 million, with Jackson trailing by four million. "I think when Michael Jackson sees this on television," Frey quipped to CBS the first time the Eagles surged ahead, "he's going to go out and buy a million and a half copies of *Thriller*.")

Hotel California followed *Their Greatest Hits (1971-1975)* to the top of the charts, producing two more #1 singles in "New Kid in Town" and the title song. It later settled in just behind *Thriller* as the RIAA's third best-selling album ever. The Eagles' legacy was set. [1866, 1867]

ELEKTRA/ASYLUM INSIDER

WE DIDN'T KNOW WE WERE RELEASING THE BIGGEST SELLING LP IN U.S. HISTORY. According to the RIAA's most recent U.S. sales numbers, Eagles: *Their Greatest Hits (1971-1975)* is the #1 best-selling album of all time. But it was a stopgap while we waited for *Hotel California*. In the 1970s, it seemed like forever between various groups' records, but in hindsight it was usually only between six months to a year at most. E/A Chairman Joe Smith complained about how long it took the Eagles to record what would become *Hotel*. And the money numbers being floated for that LP were reportedly around $1 million. That's what Joe reportedly put on the table, which was an outrageous cost in those days—well, in these days too.

We were on the hook to make sure this one happened. And due to the wait for this new endeavor, we opted to release *Their Greatest Hits (1971-1975)* in early '76 to make up for the delayed billing and E/A's bottomline sales projections.

—Rip Pelley, former National Director of Artist Development and Promotion, Elektra/Asylum Records

CHAINSAWS AND CREDIT CARDS

WALSH REFINES THE ART OF HOTEL ROOM MAYHEM

Joe Walsh was never embarrassed about the trail of destruction he left in his wake. "Yes, on occasion I do saw up hotel rooms with chainsaws and throw the pieces out the window. Why not?" he rhetorically asked the *Daily Kent Stater* in 1986.

Along the way, Walsh's use of a chainsaw to create a doorway to the next hotel room became legendary. There was also the $28,000 repair bill at one of Chicago's glitziest inns. But that's hardly the sum total of his wildly destructive past.

In fact, one of Walsh's more hilarious pranks was sawing off all the furniture legs in the Eagles' diminutive manager **Irving Azoff**'s room so they would be a "more manageable" height, according to *Rolling Stone*. And Walsh was particularly fond of fast-acting adhesives.

"I used to throw stuff out of the window, and trash hotel rooms," Walsh told *GQ* magazine in 2019, "and

superglue all the drawers shut, and superglue the toilet seat down, and superglue the phone to the nightstand, and all kinds of stuff."

Anyone hoping Azoff would provide some form of adult supervision, maybe cautioning Walsh on the expense and public-relations issues associated with such outbursts, ended up sorely disappointed. The band's manager was just as prone to pranks, tantrums, and spontaneous vandalism.

Azoff retaliated after his hotel furnishings were cut down to size, for instance, by having all of Walsh's stuff nailed to the ceiling. He was rumored to have set a menu on fire when the service was too slow at an upscale Beverly Hills restaurant. Azoff started at least one food fight—on a plane. He was also said to have torn a television off a wall and thrown it out a hotel window because of construction noise below.

"A lot of people think he is destructive," Azoff friend

Roger Ames of Warner Music Group told the *New York Times* in 2002, "but I don't see that. He's mischievous."

Like Walsh, Azoff expressed no regrets: "We probably threw [the hotel TV] out the window," he told the *Times*, "but we didn't tear it off the wall."

In fact, Azoff was the one who bought Walsh the chainsaw. "Then he bought me a case, so I could bring the chainsaw on the road," Walsh told the *New York Times* in a separate 2010 talk.

Walsh confessed his chainsaw usually remained in that case. "I didn't really use it but once or twice," Walsh told *GQ*. "If you have a chainsaw in a hotel, you don't really need to use it. Just having it, usually you get your point across."

Sometimes, however, using a chainsaw just once was more than enough to become part of rock and roll lore. Ask **Larry Solters**, the longtime Walsh and Eagles PR man.

Solters was awakened by a terrifying sound one night while out on the road: "I'm in my bed and all of a sudden, *grrrrrr*, and the plaster is falling off the ceiling," he told *Rolling Stone* in 2006. "Not 18 inches from the bed, I see a chainsaw blade come through the drywall."

Once the new door had been made, Walsh triumphantly exclaimed: "We've got adjoining rooms now, don't we?" A frazzled Solters called Azoff for advice on what to do. Solters said his boss told him to "go to the front desk. Tell them everything's OK. And give them your credit card."

It seemed to get worse as concert dates rolled by. "Whenever we got to the end of a tour, that's when he'd start wrecking things," **David Spero**, Walsh's 1990s-era manager, told the *Cleveland Plain Dealer* in 2013. "I just don't think he was a comfortable guy at home. He was most alive when he was performing in front of a crowd."

There could occasionally be quite a bill. A single night at the Astor Towers in Chicago with debauched comedian **John Belushi** racked up damages of nearly $30,000. Glenn Frey later praised Belushi and Walsh for setting the "world record for room trash" in the *History of the Eagles* documentary.

"There was really nice artwork, but we didn't like the wallpaper," Walsh told **Conan O'Brien** in 2016. "So, we took the paintings down and tore all the wallpaper off and put the paintings back on." The hotel's enraged owner later informed the duo that the penthouse suite where they were staying was actually his private apartment.

By the time a sobered-up Walsh reunited with the Eagles in the early '90s, the chainsaw had long since been put away. Only the lore remained, but Walsh reveled in that too. "Irving never dreamed I'd use it," the impish Walsh told *Rolling Stone* in 2016, "but now he knows about that."

He and Azoff had discovered their shared love of mayhem on the day they met, Walsh remembered. "So, I said: 'You can manage me, but first you have to help me trash this dressing room,'" Walsh he told the *New York Times*. "And we threw everything everywhere."

For his part, Walsh said his trail of carnage traced back to early years as a member of the **James Gang**, when they had an opening gig with **The Who** at the turn of the 1970s. Drummer **Keith Moon** tutored the young rocker in "this great tradition of bang! And crash!" Walsh told *Rolling Stone* in 2006.

"He taught me the art of hotel damage, of destroying things, of making things that blow up, of superglue madness and mayhem, of trashing rent-a-cars—just causing as much trouble as possible," Walsh added in the 2016 talk with *Rolling Stone*.

"I still know how," Walsh told the Aquarian in 2006. "I just don't do it anymore, but I know how." [1954, 1955, 1956, 1957, 1958, 1959, 1960, 1961, 1962, 1963, 1965]

> [KEITH MOON] TAUGHT ME THE ART OF HOTEL DAMAGE, OF DESTROYING THINGS, OF MAKING THINGS BLOW UP, OF SUPERGLUE MADNESS AND MAYHEM, OF TRASHING RENTAL CARS—JUST CAUSING AS MUCH TROUBLE AS POSSIBLE.
>
> — JOE WALSH

SPRING 1976

 RELEASES
- **Joe Walsh**, *You Can't Argue with a Sick Mind* (album)
- **Gram Parsons**, with Bernie Leadon, *Sleepless Nights* (album)
- **Poco**, with Timothy B. Schmit, *Live* (album)
- **Poco**, with Timothy B. Schmit, *Rose of Cimarron* (album)

 COLLABORATIONS
- **Don Felder** provided guitar and vocals on the song "Help Me Thru the Night" on **Joe Walsh**'s album *You Can't Argue with a Sick Mind*.
- **Joe Walsh** played guitar on **Rod Stewart**'s album *A Night on the Town*.
- **Joe Walsh** was a "guest performer" on **Talton, Stewart & Sandlin**'s album *Happy To Be Alive*.
- **Joe Walsh** (guitar), **Don Felder** (guitar), and **Glenn Frey** (producer) provided musical support on **Fools Gold**'s album *Fools Gold*.
- **Don Henley** (backing vocals), **Glenn Frey** (electric guitar, electric piano, backing vocals), and **Joe Walsh** (guitar, slide guitar) on **J.D. Souther**'s album *Black Rose*.
- **Joe Walsh** played lead guitar, acoustic guitar, and slide guitar on **Jay Ferguson**'s album *All Alone in the End Zone*.
- **Don Henley** (harmony vocals) and **Glenn Frey** (rhythm guitar, backing vocals) provided musical support on **Warren Zevon**'s album *Warren Zevon*.

 AWARDS
- **Eagles, 11th Annual Academy of Country Music Awards:** Top Vocal Group, nominated. Lost to **Conway Twitty & Loretta Lynn**. Also nominated: **Asleep at the Wheel**, **Bill Anderson & Mary Lou Turner**, and **The Statler Brothers**.

 NUGGETS
- One great aside from the Eagles/**Linda Ronstadt/Jackson Browne** show at the Capital Centre in Landover, Maryland supporting **Jerry Brown**: Irving Azoff wore a suit. —*Record World*
- **Led Zeppelin**'s *Presence* knocks *Eagles: Their Greatest Hits* out of the top LP spot. —*Billboard*
- From the desk of **Phil Walden** (Capricorn Records): "The Eagles don't say 'ain't' the same way **Marshall Tucker** says 'ain't.'" Perhaps Irving Azoff can explain. —*Record World*
- Azoff Replies: "**Jimmy Carter** doesn't say 'Maryland' the way Jerry Brown says 'Maryland.'" Perhaps a battle of the bands is in the offing? —*Record World*
- From the desk of Phil Walden: "Phil Walden can't understand why Irv Azoff isn't supporting Jimmy Carter for President. After all, Carter has always been for the little people." —*Record World*

 ON SCREEN
- Eagles appeared on the BBC-TV show *Top of the Pops* (Episode 13.12). **Brotherhood of Man**, **Tina Charles**, **Randy Edelman**, **David Essex**, **The Ladybirds**, and **Pan's People** also appeared.

 ON THE ROAD WITH ...
- **Eagles**: Jackson Browne, Linda Ronstadt
- **Poco**, with Timothy B. Schmit: The Flying Burrito Brothers, Willie Nelson
- **Joe Walsh**: Kiss, Rush

Grammys: Eagles Win First Statuette in '75 Showcase

Through their first three albums, the closest the Eagles came to claiming a Grammy win was their nomination for the Best New Artist award in 1973.

But that year, the statuette went to **America** instead.

The National Academy of Recording Arts and Sciences, which hosts and presents the awards each year, didn't look the Eagles' way again until another two years and two new albums had come and gone. Grammy voters had no interest in *Desperado* or *On the Border*, though "The Best of My Love" had delivered the Eagles' first #1 single.

But the massive commercial success of *One of These Nights* got the voters' attention when the 18th Annual Grammy Awards rolled around in 1976. Eagles won their only Grammy of the night in the Best Vocal Performance by a Duo, Group, or Chorus category for "Lyin' Eyes." The band earned two other nominations: Record of the Year for "Lyin' Eyes," and Album of the Year for *One of These Nights*. Art director **Gary Burden** picked up the album's fourth nomination, in the Best Album Package category.

Paul Simon's *Still Crazy After All These Years* won Best Album on Grammy night, February 28, but the Eagles finally took home some hardware when the Recording Academy awarded them a golden gramophone for their country-flavored song about city girls learning how to open doors with just a smile.

As the Grammys always do, the nominations drew criticism. Rock writer **Dave Marsh** criticized the entire Grammy process as irrelevant and ridiculous and blasted organizers, calling them biased and hopelessly anti-rock. The voting process, he argued, gave people long out of the business and people now working in the studios unfair equal footing—so long as they continued paying their dues.

Then Marsh reeled off a lengthy list of rock heavyweights who had shamefully never won a Grammy, including **Chuck Berry**, **Led Zeppelin**, **David Bowie**, the **Allman Brothers Band**, and **Eric Clapton**, among others. The Academy corrected some of those wrongs as the years passed, as Bowie and Clapton earned awards along the way. But Zeppelin and the Allmans had to settle for Lifetime Achievement Awards long after their prime.

While Marsh's view of the Academy was on the mark, his view of the nominees that year was off. The five nominees for Album of the Year in 1976 were works released in 1975 by Simon, **Janis Ian**, the Eagles, **Elton John**, and **Linda Ronstadt**. Each album was strong. But in that moment, Marsh couldn't see past Simon. "As an artist, rather than as a commercial force or pleasant entertainer, Paul Simon stands out like Kareem Abdul Jabbar in a kindergarten. But I'll bet he doesn't win."

Simon did win, but his field of competing artists wasn't childish. Every single artist nominated for Best Album that year was later inducted into the Rock and Roll Hall of Fame, including Ian, who finally was recognized in 2021.

With their first Grammy in hand and a new album to write and record, 1976 would be a busy year for the Eagles, who would have one more curious awards show to endure that fall. [406, 635, 777]

JOE WALSH
You Can't Argue With a Sick Mind
ABC Records, March 1976

When Joe Walsh released his *You Can't Argue with a Sick Mind* live album in March 1976, the guitarist already had been a member of the Eagles for a few months. *Sick Mind* is nothing short of a terrific live memento to put a bow on his work prior to signing on with the band, yet it's transitional at the same time.

The disc captured a blazing performance at the Santa Monica Civic Auditorium on November 26, 1975. The set, in fact, had also been shot on video for Walsh's TV appearance on *Don Kirshner's Rock Concert*. The album, however, featured only six songs and clocked in at less than 35 minutes. In an era of big, double-live LPs, about the only complaint fans and critics had about the album was its brevity.

Those who caught it at the Civic or on the tube would have noticed the show was billed as *Joe Walsh & Friends*. The guitarist brought along three Eagles to back him up: Glenn Frey, Don Henley, and Don Felder, who was onstage for almost the entire set.

You Can't Argue with a Sick Mind is a succinct but fulfilling sonic journey through Walsh's rock and roll life through 1975. The James Gang stomper "Walk Away" segues into Barnstorm's twisting and flowing "Meadows," nicely illustrating how Walsh could rock with the best of them, but wasn't beyond creating more subdued, introspective compositions. The irresistible boogie and blues of "Rocky Mountain Way" follows, where Walsh gamely calls out the TV promoter who would be airing the video version by singing, "Bases are loaded and Kirshner's at bat!"

"Time Out" from Walsh's 1975 solo outing *So What* follows before the band slows things down with the gorgeous and poignant "Help Me Thru the Night," which reflects the guitarist's mood in the wake of his daughter's death and his marriage falling apart. The track also serves as a transitional moment, representing Walsh's inauguration as a band member just a few weeks later, with soaring Eagles-style harmonies and three of his new bandmates joining him on the performance. Felder, Frey, and Henley had gathered with acoustic guitars around Walsh at the front of the stage as they played and harmonized. Performances such as this one proved he was a well-rounded musician more than capable of fitting in with his soon-to-be band.

When originally aired on *Rock Concert*, two cover songs rounded out the set: "Get Back" by **The Beatles** (with Frey onstage again to play guitar) and "Gimme Some Lovin'" by the **Spencer Davis Group**, both played in Walsh's charcteristic style that were nothing like the originals. However, with both covers scratched, the album was shorter than the TV show.

Joe Vitale features prominently throughout the disc as well, notably with his flute playing on the

LP's closer, "Turn to Stone." The song dated back to the first **Barnstorm** album before Walsh revisited it for the *So What* album. This jam-packed live version stretches almost nine minutes and rounds out *You Can't Argue with a Sick Mind.* It was an appropriate closer and exemplified the harder-rock edge Walsh would be able to introduce into the Eagles, who would incorporate the song into some sets in 1976.

The album didn't impress everyone. Veteran rock scribe **Barbara Charone** said there wasn't enough on the LP to justify its release. In a biting *Sounds* review in April 1976 she praised Walsh's electric live shows, but said this recording lacked the energy of those performances, suggesting the absence of those visuals was an important loss. Charone thought the Eagles-assisted "Help Me Thru the Night" was moving, but that a new Walsh solo studio LP would have been superior. [2004, 2005, 2006, 2138]

Fools Gold: Eagles Lend Hand To Fogelberg Bandmates

Lending a hand in the studio was becoming a regular practice for members of the Eagles. They found time to help with their friend **Dan Fogelberg**'s band, **Fools Gold**, even as their own time became more compromised.

Formed by **Denny Henson** and **Tom Kelly**, two members of Fogelberg's backing band, Fools Gold released two LPs in the late 1970s that went unnoticed. But those who find these forgotten gems—particularly the self-titled debut—might be delighted.

AllMusic suggests that "Fools Gold will warm the hearts of anyone who is a fan of such bands as the Eagles and **Poco**."

Granted, it was 1976, so this slice of L.A. country-rock sonically had less to do with Poco's early '70s country-hippie roots or the denim-clad cowboy approach of the first Eagles album. It was more like the highly produced but impeccably crafted approach the latter band took on records like *One of These Nights* and *Hotel California.*

It's not surprising, considering Glenn Frey, Joe Walsh, Don Felder, and producer **Glyn Johns** all made contributions to the Fools Gold album.

"Those guys are real good singers," Frey told rock journalist **John Tobler** in 1977, referring to Henson and Kelly, Fogelberg's guitarist and bassist, respectively. "I had a good time doing [the *Fools Gold* album]."

The duo combined to write all the songs on the album, except for two covers penned by their day job boss: the ballads "Old Tennessee" and "Love Me Through and Through." Rounding out the Fools Gold lineup were drummer **Ron Grinel** and steel guitarist/multi-instrumentalist **Doug Livingston.**

"I think I ended up doing two or three things on that *Fools Gold* album," Frey vaguely-but-correctly recalled. The "things" he referred to earned him credits as a producer on the richly layered "Rain, Oh, Rain," the peacefully moody "Sailing to Monterey," and the bluegrassy harmony number "I Will Run."

continued on Page 236

FELDER'S DEMO BECOMES BLUEPRINT FOR 'HOTEL'

Glenn Frey and Don Henley were instrumental in crafting the song that became the title cut of Eagles' biggest album. But it was Don Felder, working at his beach house in Malibu, who laid down the foundation on which the band built their signature single "Hotel California."

Felder credited his experience as a member of **Flow** with shaping the way he wrote songs: "We were a jazz fusion rock band. If you listen to jazz players, they never play the same solo twice. They throw themselves out there and improvise."

Looking to capitalize on that type of energy, Felder explained how his approach to songwriting comes from that mold, that when he sits down to write something, "instead of trying to conceptualize exactly what it should be...I'll just turn on a tape machine or my iPhone and just start playing, and let that improvising idea come out."

That's how Felder creates music in the 21st century, an update of the same process he used in the summer of 1976 when he demoed the musical piece that would become "Hotel California."

As Felder recalls, he was living the stereotypical California life—enjoying the warm Southern California weather while at his rented house on the beach—when he started noodling around on an acoustic 12-string guitar. Using the same approach of "just improvising," he stumbled upon the famous opening chord progression (though he was playing it in a different key).

Feeling he was onto something good, he tried building upon it, experimenting with different patterns and combinations until he had "about 32 bars" of this new composition.

Knowing he would very likely forget the progression he had just created, Felder said he "ran back into my little one-year-old daughter's bedroom, which, during the time she was awake, was my recording studio for demos. I just turned on the [four-track recording] machine and recorded just the 12-string part over and over and over."

He would later go back and flesh it out further, adding a drum machine to the demo. Originally, he was going for something of a reggae groove, but the closest pattern he could find on his primitive drum machine was more of what he called a "cha-cha" rhythm.

Felder laid down bass and still more guitar parts, even switching instruments at one point, musing, "Well, Joe [Walsh] would play something kind of like this, then I would play this," as he told The Indianapolis Star in 2016.

He decided to leave it alone for a little while and played with his kids. Then, over the next few hours, he kept tinkering with it. "The tempo was right, but it needed another section and a chorus, the payoff," he said. "I tried three or four different chord progressions and then finally went back down and put a bass track with a reggae feel on it."

As the track's music evolved, he thought about how to keep the drum parts uncomplicated enough to allow Henley to sing it, and to give Meisner a good backbeat to pace the song. Then he wrote two guitar parts in descending harmony, which he called a "hornline kind of thing," until he got to the end and alternated them. It was the basis of the famed outro that he and Walsh would eventually play.

Felder had been looking for a vehicle to showcase his guitar interplay with Walsh for a while: "Joe and I had been doing that [dueling guitars] together live during Joe Walsh shows [when] I was just out jamming with Joe—because I loved to play with him—before he joined the band. I wanted to be able to do that on an Eagles record."

Felder mixed down the demo and added it to a cassette he prepared for submission to the band. He had 10 to 15 ideas on the tape when he handed

> JOE AND I HAD BEEN DOING THAT [DUELING GUITARS] TOGETHER LIVE DURING JOE WALSH SHOWS [WHEN] I WAS JUST OUT JAMMING WITH JOE—BECAUSE I LOVED TO PLAY WITH HIM. I WANTED TO BE ABLE TO DO THAT ON AN EAGLES RECORD.
>
> — DON FELDER

it off to the chief songwriters, Frey and Henley.

"If there's anything on this tape you hear [that you like], let's finish writing it," Felder told them.

Most of his song ideas went unused, but at least two of them caught his bandmates' ears. One song they accepted contained the riffing that became "Victim of Love." The other was this 12-string demo with the Flamenco feel. Henley called up Felder and told him he really liked the song "that sounded like a Mexican reggae."

The working title given to the idea was "Mexican Reggae" (along with "Mexican Bolero," as Felder remembered). Felder took it as a good sign that Henley was moved enough by the piece to give it a name.

"I think I was driving down Benedict Canyon Drive at night, or maybe even North Crescent Drive (adjacent to the Beverly Hills Hotel) the first time I heard the piece," Henley recalled. "I remember thinking, 'This has potential; I think we can make something interesting out of this.'"

And so construction of the title cut began, and Felder's demo became the blueprint for the epic single. And Henley gave credit for the music to his guitarist bandmate.

"All that music [on 'Hotel California'] was written by Felder," Henley agreed. Speaking to author **Marc Eliot**, he said Felder "had been an engineer at one point, before he began to play full-time, so he was really good at it. He created the music track, and although we re-recorded it, basically all the parts were there."

Producer **Bill Szymczyk**, Henley, and Joe Walsh would also have significant input in fine-tuning the song's famous outro, as well, which was painstakingly and seamlessly stitched together with a multitude of edits and splices over several days in the studio. [1603, 1651, 1652, 1653, 1781]

Walsh, who had previously produced Fogelberg's *Souvenirs*, grabbed another production credit for the opening boogie, "Coming Out of Hiding," on which he also played guitar. [1501, 1632, 1633, 1634]

A&M Posthumously Releases Parsons' *Sleepless Nights*

The notion that **Gram Parsons** is the "founder of country-rock" has grown to almost epic proportions in the roughly half-century since his death in the California desert in September 1973. While he was inarguably one of the many deserving a mention in the evolution of this musical hybrid, some observers believe his legacy outshines his actual contributions.

Whether Parsons' importance is overrated is a matter of heated debate between his most ardent supporters and those who resist holding him up as a musical deity. It's an argument that likely won't be settled anytime soon. In either case, his early demise left his mission to bring what he called "Cosmic American Music" to the masses unfulfilled.

Still, it didn't take long for the music industry to start burnishing Parsons' legend. The morbidly titled *Grievous Angel* was the first posthumous release, fittingly packed with songs like "In My Hour of Darkness," which sounded eerily like he wrote it, intending it to be released from the grave.

The album started the ball rolling for a significant post-life career for Parsons. Three years later, A&M released *Sleepless Nights*, which it billed as being by Gram Parsons/**The Flying Burrito Brothers**, pushing more of Parsons' product into the market. It seemed little more than a cash grab to capitalize on the fallen musician.

A&M had released another Burrito Brothers retrospective in 1974, the year following Parsons' death, titled *Close Up the Honky Tonks*. While that one benefited from the new posthumous interest in Parsons, it seems a bit more legitimate an offering. After all, the band had "closed up" when they called it quits the year before, and the record included material from all the previous Burritos lineups, not just the Parsons era.

But *Sleepless Nights* was neither a proper Parsons release nor a Burritos release, rather a hodgepodge of leftovers from both the solo artist and his prior band. It appeared the label simply scraped up whatever it could find to release something "new."

Three tracks were leftovers from the solo *Grievous Angel* sessions, each featuring vocals with Parsons' singing partner **Emmylou Harris**: "The Angels Rejoiced Last Night," "Brand New Heartache," and the title track, "Sleepless Nights." All three of these, as well as the rest of the disc's offerings, were written by others. *Sleepless Nights*, in fact, was mostly a collection of classic country covers like **Merle Haggard**'s "Sing Me Back Home" and **Buck Owens**' "Together Again."

Most of those tracks—many featuring future Eagle Bernie Leadon—were demos and studio outtakes never intended for release. Referring to the nine Burritos tracks on the album, founding Burrito Brother **Chris Hillman** said, "This is all practice.

These are outtakes recorded at a studio as we were waiting to do [the band's second record, *Burrito Deluxe*]." When some of the songs were re-released on the 1988 compilation *Farther Along: The Best of the Flying Burrito Brothers*, Hillman again indicated the songs were just outtakes, and charitably commented that they're valid "from an historical perspective."

Jim Bickhart, an A&M publicist also involved in compiling the *Close Up the Honky Tonks* retrospective, was not thrilled, either, with the Burritos tracks on *Sleepless Nights*. Speaking about *Close Up the Honky Tonks*, which also contained some cover material, he said, "I remember being fairly assertive that the covers and classics the band had played on stage during the Gram era be included. I was happy to find that so many of them were presentably recorded. ... Interestingly, we felt the material we left off, most of which ended up on *Sleepless Nights*, deserved to be left off."

As such, the album often lacks focus and energy and is probably best suited for Parsons completists. [739, 1536, 1724, 1725]

Walsh, Vitale Offer 'Pretty Maids' for *Hotel*; Dylan Approves

With his first road trip as an Eagle behind him, Joe Walsh hit the Record Plant in Los Angeles in early 1976 to edit and mix his new solo project: the audio tracks from the Santa Monica Civic show he and friends, including Glenn Frey, Don Henley, and Don Felder, had performed the previous November.

After being broadcast as an edition of *Don Kirshner's Rock Concert*, the concert appeared as the live album *You Can't Argue with a Sick Mind* in March.

But solo work wasn't the only thing on Walsh's mind that spring—the Eagles were busy developing songs for *Hotel California*, and he still had a lot of work to do.

Joe Vitale, Walsh's longtime prank partner and favorite drummer-keyboardist-flute player, was in L.A. then. Walsh asked him to come over to his house and help finish a song, Vitale said. Walsh was working on a piece that so far had just a couple of lyrics and a little music for a verse. He had no title yet and was unsure where to go with it. But, Vitale added, "he had a beautiful start." So, he sat down at Walsh's antique green piano and they continued developing the song.

After about half an hour, Vitale said, they had come up with a set of changes and a melody "that seemed to work well with what he had written and, bingo, we had a song." The two worked on the song for two or three more hours to finish it off. "I wrote the chorus and added changes in the chorus, and then [Walsh] added the words," he said. "And it became a beautiful song. We were so proud of it."

After finishing the lyrics and titling it "Pretty Maids All in a Row," Walsh presented the song to Frey and Henley, who liked it. The band took it into the studio where they tinkered more with the arrangement, and once everyone was happy with it, **Bill Szymczyk** produced the track featured on *Hotel California*.

continued on Page 237

POCO COMPETES WITH POCO AFTER LABEL SWITCH

Much time had passed since the days when a young Glenn Frey would sit in **Richie Furay**'s house and listen and watch as **Poco** rehearsed. Frey's then-unnamed band opened for the country-rock pioneers at the Troubadour in Los Angeles in 1970, and a year later became the Eagles.

The success that followed for the Eagles eluded Poco. By the mid-1970s, a frustrated Furay was long gone. After eight albums, Poco bolted Epic Records and signed with rival ABC Records in 1975.

It was a messy divorce: the band's jilted label made good on its threat to retaliate by releasing competing Poco product when it issued a best-of compilation head-on with *Head Over Heels*, the band's debut album for ABC.

Things got even messier with their ex-label the following year, and Poco would face the same problem with their next album.

But that was still over the horizon in early 1976, when the band was at the Record Plant in Los Angeles co-producing the sessions with engineer **Mark Henry Harman** for the album that would become *Rose of Cimarron*.

Poco's ninth studio effort showcased songwriters **Rusty Young** and **Paul Cotton**; each contributed four songs, augmented by a pair from Timothy B. Schmit.

Modeled around the band's layered harmonies and melodic hooks, songs like Schmit's "Just Like Me" were instantly catchy. His pop gem "Starin' at the Sky" anticipated the band's later hit "Heart of the Night." Against a slew of handclaps and banjos, Young's down-home bluegrass medley "Company's Comin'/Slow Poke" is a front-porch stomper, and the Cotton-penned "All Alone Together" is a barroom country weeper accentuated by Young's pedal steel.

"P.N.S. (When You Come Around)" was a re-recording from Cotton's days in **Illinois Speed Press**, and his "Too Many Nights Too Long" is led by a fiddle and accentuated by Schmit singing a verse *en Español*.

The title song is a mid-tempo country-rocker

PATHWAY ALBUMS | TIMOTHY B. SCHMIT

POCO

Poco Live | Epic Records

April 1976

Rose of Cimarron | ABC Records

May 1976

with a Western flavor sung by both Cotton and Schmit. Young wrote "Rose of Cimarron," inspired by a brochure he had picked up in Oklahoma while on tour.

"It told a story of a woman who took in outlaws in the 1800s," Young remembered. "She fed them, mended their wounds, and sent them on their way. Or so they say."

As the legend goes, Rose Dunn, then just 15 years old, was romantically involved with George "Bittercreek" Newcomb, an outlaw linked with fellow badman Bill Doolin's cutthroat gang. According to *Songfacts.com*, "In 1893, the gang was caught in a gunfight with U.S. Marshals in Ingalls, Oklahoma. Newcomb survived, but was later killed by the Dunn Brothers, outlaws-turned-bounty hunters who also happened to be Rose's brothers. Rose was accused of tipping them off to the gang's movements, a claim she and her brothers denied."

Young wrote "Rose of Cimarron" as a narrative empathetic of Dunn and of a way of life long gone by. His dobro powered the instrumental segments, and Cotton and Schmit alternated vocals. The dramatic orchestral string arrangement closing the saga was almost cinematic in scope, perfectly suiting Young's elegy for the Old West and its colorful characters. With this track, Poco's most ambitious foray in the studio to date clocked in at almost seven minutes.

Also featuring guest appearances by multi-instrumentalist and future Eagles collaborator **Al Garth** (who flirted with becoming an official member of Poco around this time, though it never quite panned out), *Rose of Cimarron* remains a remarkably consistent album, reflecting maturity in Poco's songwriting and a renewed inspiration in their performances.

Despite its artistic achievement, *Rose of Cimarron* was typical of Poco's output; after ABC released it in May 1976, the album pleased the band's core following, but there were not enough record-buying fans to make more than a tiny dent on the charts.

It didn't help that the band's estranged label beat *Rose* to the shelves with *Poco Live* about two months earlier.

Epic had sourced the live album from a trio of Poco shows in November 1974, which contained spirited versions of songs made by the then-current four-piece lineup ("Rocky Mountain Breakdown," "High and Dry") as well as older material from the Furay days ("Restrain," "Bad Weather"). The concert favorite "A Good Feelin' to Know," originally sung by Furay, featured Schmit ably handling the lead vocals this time.

While not as classic as Poco's *Deliverin'* live album in 1971, *Poco Live* is a keepsake representing the strength of the band's "fantastic four" era, a time after Furay's departure and before Schmit would leave to join the Eagles after Poco's next album, 1977's *Indian Summer*.

Since the concert recording was already a couple of years old, and Epic released the album just as a nuisance, the label did not seriously promote it, so *Poco Live* lasted only four weeks on the *Billboard* 200 in April, rising only to #169.

Rose of Cimarron fared better, charting for 15 weeks through summer 1976 and peaking at #89. As a single, the title track had a brush the *Billboard* Hot 100 in mid-August, debuting at #94 and falling off the next week. While the argument could be made that more Poco albums in stores gave fans more options, it seemed more like the band was once again chasing its tail by competing with itself—precisely Epic's goal.

As the years passed, Young said he would hear from fans around the world who marveled at the panoramic western imagery in "Rose of Cimarron." He, too, thought it was one of Poco's all-time best.

"There are a couple songs on the top of my list," he recounted years later when asked to name his personal favorites. "First would be 'Rose of Cimarron.' I love everything about that song—from the very visual lyrics to the beautiful melody."

The song would gain another round of recognition after **Emmylou Harris** recorded it for her *Cimarron* album, released in 1981.

More recently, "Rose of Cimarron" found a new voice in another generation when Young added more lyrics and re-recorded it in 2018 with Americana-folk-West Coast-pop singer-songwriter **Chelsea Williams**.

While recording his solo album *Waitin' for the Sun* in 2017, he reimagined "Rose of Cimarron" after hearing Williams' *Boomerang* album, Young said. "The song is about a woman so I thought it would be interesting to revisit it including a woman's voice. That idea inspired me to write additional lyrics. Then, when I first heard Chelsea's voice, I thought she'd be perfect for the new version." [1504, 1721]

ON A DARK DESERT HIGHWAY...

Don Henley, Glenn Frey, and Bryan Garofalo (center) joke backstage at the Santa Monica Civic Auditorium.

HENLEY, FREY FOCUS ON CINEMATIC 'HOTEL' STORY

The lyrics to "Hotel California" have generated more discussion about potential deeper meanings than virtually all the other songs in the Eagles canon combined. And the song's lyricist, Don Henley, heaves heavy sighs when people ask about—or purportedly find—hidden meanings in his words that just aren't there.

Glenn Frey said he believed the title "Hotel California" was Henley's idea, and they envisioned it exploring the excesses of the music industry, the surrounding culture, and losing innocence that they experienced as their careers evolved.

"Hotel California" would be the first single completed for the album, and it followed a theme they had visited before with "Hollywood Waltz" from *One of These Nights*, which explored their adoptive home town of Los Angeles. But the new song would go deeper. Then, when they heard Don Felder's "Mexican Reggae" demo tape, they knew they finally had the music. Now they just needed the

lyrics. So, in March 1976, the pair began composing their song, which Henley described as "not only [about] the mythmaking of Southern California, but the mythmaking that is the American dream." And they wrote it from a mansion in Miami Beach.

Producer **Bill Szymczyk** had a home in Miami, and a phobia of California earthquakes, and got the band to indulge his request to produce them in the familiar confines of Criteria Studios in nearby North Miami. Frey would grow to love South Florida too. Spending March in the Sunshine State wasn't a tough call, so Frey and Henley leased out a house on Biscayne Bay and started work.

They listened to Felder's demo tape and talked about how the song would come together. They wanted the lyrics to have a cinematic feel and open like an episode of the *The Twilight Zone*, with rapid-fire sequences that charged the imagination. The opening line imagery started as Frey and Henley talked on an airplane.

"We wanted to write a song just like it was a movie," Frey said, alluding to **Robert DeNiro**'s film *The Last Tycoon*. "This guy is driving across the desert. He's tired. He's smokin'. Comes up over a hill, sees some lights, pulls in. First thing he sees is a really strange guy at the front door, welcoming him: 'Come on in.' Walks in, and then it becomes Fellini-esque—strange women, effeminate men, shadowy corridors, disembodied voices, debauchery, illusion... weirdness. So we thought, 'Let's really take some chances. Let's try to write in a way that we've never written before.'"

Frey said **Steely Dan**'s lyrical bravery and willingness inspired them "to go out there." The group inspired them so much that they felt compelled to refer to them in the song. "*And in the master's chambers/ They gathered for the feast/Stab it with their steely knives/But they just can't kill the beast.*" They swapped out "Dan" for "knives" for a lyrical volley back to Steely Dan's reference to the Eagles in "Everything You Did" on their *The Royal Scam*. **Walter Becker** wrote the line "*Turn up the Eagles, the neighbors are listening*" as a sarcastic, but not unfriendly, shot at the band since Becker's girlfriend loved the Eagles.

Some believe that the "*Mirrors on the ceiling*" lyric may have evolved from some of the avant-garde hotels the Eagles haunted, and "The Boat Room" at the Record Plant's 3rd Street studio in Los Angeles drew particular interest because of its hideaway bedroom with velvet walls and mirrors on the ceiling. Henley flatly denied any connection to *Rolling Stone* in 2016, asserting that the song had nothing to do with the Record Plant apart from the parts recorded there.

Frey said that "Hotel California" was definitely thinking and writing outside of their traditional songwriting box. As the songs for the album came together—"Life in the Fast Lane" and "The Last Resort" specifically—they realized they were "heading down a long, twisted corridor" and kept writing for that theme as they completed "Hotel California." "Songs from the dark side," he said. "The Eagles take a look at the seamy underbelly of L.A.-the flipside of fame and failure, love and money."

Henley said hotels had by then become an intrical part of their lives, both literally and symbolically, so that imagery took hold as the writing evolved.

"I've always been interested in architecture and the language of architecture, and, at that time, I was particularly keen on the mission style of early California," Henley told **Cameron Crowe**. "I thought there was a certain mystery and romance about it. Then, there are all the great movies and

> ## WE WANTED TO WRITE A SONG JUST LIKE IT WAS A MOVIE...THIS GUY IS DRIVING ACROSS THE DESERT. HE'S TIRED. HE'S SMOKIN'. COMES UP OVER A HILL, SEES SOME LIGHTS, PULLS IN. FIRST THING HE SEES IS A REALLY STRANGE GUY AT THE FRONT DOOR, WELCOMING HIM.
>
> ### — GLENN FREY

plays in which hotels figure prominently, not only as a structure but as a dramatic device. Films such as *Grand Hotel*, *The Night Porter*, and even *Psycho* — motels count too. There are plays like **Neil Simon**'s *Plaza Suite* and *California Suite*, which Glenn and I went to see while writing the song. We saw it as homework or research. We were looking for things that would stimulate us and give us ideas."

As the lyrics developed, images of the cinematic hotel in the story existed in the minds of Henley and Frey, but it would need to take on a physical form at some point. And as the album's development came close to conclusion the images coming into focus included places like the Green Hotel in Los Angeles and The Beverly Hills Hotel in Beverly Hills.

The latter won out and as the album and single rolled out in the winter of 1976. Although it resisted initially, the hotel accepted its image on the Eagles' album cover. And when the album was released, Elektra/Asylum arranged a press junket at the hotel in Bungalow 16. [209, 2133]

"Glenn Frey told me a long time ago that they were sold on the song once we finished it and got the chorus," Vitale told *Rolling Stone*. "Once that was done, they really put their vocal magic to it. It came out really good. We were really, really happy with it."

For Walsh, the song was an important introduction into being an Eagle, and he wanted to make a meaningful first contribution.

"To make the Eagles really valid as a band, it was important that we co-write things and share things," Walsh told **John Tobler** in 1982. "'Pretty Maids' is kind of a melancholy reflection on my life so far, and I think we tried to represent it as a statement that would be valid for people from our generation on life so far. 'Heroes, they come and go' ... Henley and Frey really thought that it was a good song, and meaningful, and helped me a lot in putting it together. I think the best thing to say is that it's a kind of melancholy observation on life that we hoped would be a valid statement for people from our generation."

The song was never released as a single, though it did get placed on the flip side of "Hotel California," which Walsh knew would delight Vitale.

"Well, that blew my mind," Vitale told journalist **Casey Chambers**. "You know, B-sides...they weren't that important, but you didn't just throw anything on there. Especially a group like the Eagles. They wouldn't throw just anything on a B-side. They didn't make any bad recordings. They were all great. To get that on the B-side of their biggest hit—I think their biggest hit of all time—was quite amazing. It blew me away."

Vitale said Walsh broke the news to him over the phone, but only hinted at it. "Joe said, 'I've got a surprise for you. I'm not gonna tell you—I'm just gonna mail your surprise to you.'"

Vitale's surprise eventually was delivered via the U.S. Mail. When he opened the package, it contained the 45-rpm single of "Hotel California."

He looked at it, then flipped it over and saw "Pretty Maids All in a Row," with "Joe Walsh & Joe Vitale" on the credit line. "I couldn't believe it."

"Pretty Maids" made an impression on another listener who knows a thing or two about songwriting. **Bob Dylan** called out the song in a rare interview with the *New York Times* in 2020. Discussing his rambling nearly 17-minute new song about the Kennedy assassination, "Murder Most Foul," Dylan gave props to Glenn Frey and Don Henley in the lyrics: "Play Don Henley, play Glenn Frey/Take it to the limit and let it go by."

In the interview, writer **Douglas Brinkley**

GLENN FREY TOLD ME...THAT THEY WERE SOLD ON ["PRETTY MAIDS ALL IN A ROW"] ONCE WE FINISHED IT AND GOT THE CHORUS. ONCE THAT WAS DONE THEY PUT THEIR VOCAL MAGIC TO IT.

— JOE VITALE

pointed to the references to Henley and Frey, and asked what Eagles songs Dylan enjoyed the most.

"'New Kid in Town,' 'Life in the Fast Lane,' 'Pretty Maids All in a Row.' That could be one of the best songs ever," he said.

High praise, indeed.

"Coming from Bob Dylan, it doesn't get any better than that," Vitale told *Rolling Stone*. "I called Joe immediately. And he goes, 'I know what you're calling about.' I said, 'This is so cool, Joe.' He was excited too. He thought that was really cool. I printed out that article and framed it." [135, 1657, 1658, 1659, 1660]

Asylum Crowd, Eagles Gather Behind Enigmatic Zevon

Jackson Browne met **Warren Zevon** in the mid-1970s and played a crucial role in his fledgling career. He helped Zevon get signed to Asylum, produced his major-label debut, and introduced him to his friends in the Eagles. However, the artists could not have been more different.

Zevon had become friends with the Laurel Canyon crowd, but he did not share the country-rocking approach of labelmates like Browne and **J.D. Souther**. Zevon's take on the so-called California dream was far darker than the troubled modern fables the Eagles were busy constructing on *Hotel California* when the eponymous *Warren Zevon* album arrived in 1976.

It wasn't surprising that Glenn Frey and Don Henley were invited to perform on Zevon's Asylum debut, given Browne's mentor role with Zevon and his history with the Eagles. Zevon's acerbic songwriting style wasn't lost on Frey and Henley when they showed up in the studio to provide backing vocals to "Gorilla, You're a Desperado." They just weren't sure how he wanted to them approach it, **Jim Sullivan** wrote for the *Boston Globe*. "Well, you want us to make fun of the Eagles?" Zevon remembered the pair asking. He replied: "No, I just want you to sing great like you do," and they said, "'OK, we'll do that then.'"

"Gorilla" was uniquely characteristic of a Zevon cut. His songs—"Lawyers, Guns and Money," "Roland the Headless Thompson Gunner," "I'll Sleep When I'm Dead," "Carmelita," and the immortal "Werewolves of London," just a few examples—were more caustic, more ironic, and so literary at times that he earned the nickname "F. Scott Fitzevon."

"His songs are like short stories; the best songs always are," Browne told *Rolling Stone* in September 2003, after Zevon lost a battle with cancer at age 56, not long after releasing his 15th and final album, *The Wind*. "They tell much more about life than books. They communicate so much more than a longer volume would."

Zevon had undoubtedly paid his dues when **Elliot Roberts** signed him to Asylum. Chicago-born, California-raised, and New York City-seasoned, at age 19, he scored a minor hit called "Follow Me" in 1966 with the folk duo **Lyme and Cybelle**.

He supported himself into the early '70s

243

continued on Page 243

'HOTEL' LYRICS EVOLVE UNDER THE PALMS IN MIAMI

When it came time to finish writing the lyrics to "Hotel California" in spring 1976, Don Henley and Glenn Frey opted to leave L.A. and drop anchor for an extended stay in Miami, not far from Criteria Studios.

A hotel would not do for this excursion, so they reached out once again to Home at Last, a local boutique company that helped artists visiting Miami to record at Criteria and other local studios by providing private Miami Beach mansions and complete concierge service.

Best friends since elementary school, Home at Last founders **Cindy Johnson** and **Jeri Jenkins** were cooking-challenged 19-year-olds when they launched the enterprise in late 1971. **Stephen Stills** and his band were their first clients when Stills recorded the first **Manassas** album at Criteria that fall and winter.

Both Johnson and Jenkins admitted they initially did not know how to cook, but said they got better with Stills' help. In-home chefs would come later. "We were all just kids," Jenkins told *Time Passages*.

As the business grew over the next decade-plus, the partners developed a network of domestic help to staff the homes. "They were dignified older ladies from the New Macedonia Baptist Church Choir who even the most irreverent rockers naturally respected and often called 'Mama,'" Jenkins said.

Through word of mouth mostly from one artist to another, and referrals from Criteria, dozens of other artists visiting Miami to record leased HAL properties and enjoyed the secluded environments, home-cooked meals, and perks like transportation to and from the studio.

"It was a far cry from the 'Riot House' on Sunset in L.A. that many of them had become used to along with the boredom that caused TV sets to fly out windows into the pool and other sorts of destructive behavior," Jenkins pointed out. "In the Miami mansions they could sunbathe by their private pool, go boating, biking, or skating around the neighborhood and have friends over for jams or poker games."

Clients included **Eric Clapton** (staying at 461 Ocean Boulevard), **Crosby, Stills, Nash & Young** (multiple locations), the **Bee Gees** (several mansions, eventually buying a few), as well as the **Allman Brothers Band**, **Jimmy Buffett**, **Joe Cocker**, **Roger Daltrey**, **George Harrison**, **John Mellencamp**, **John Denver**, **Meat Loaf**, **Barbra Streisand**, **Prince**, and more.

"It wasn't just the artists and groups," Jenkins said. "At our age, we were also dealing with the mega-producers and managers of that era—**Ahmet Ertegun**, **Arif Mardin**, **Robert Stigwood**, **Tommy Mottola**, **Tom Dowd**, and **Irving Azoff.** They felt the bands would be safe with us and we would help keep them out of trouble."

On prior trips to record in Miami, the Eagles had stayed in Home at Last properties including 461 Ocean Boulevard.

"With the Eagles, it was fast. It was innocent, it was wholesome, it was smoking pot, it was gorgeous guys, it was cool," Johnson told *Plum Miami* in 2011. "All living together. They were like the Boy Scouts."

In March 1976, this time just for Henley and Frey, Johnson and Jenkins lined up a beautiful Spanish-styled waterfront mansion at 5242 N. Bay Road, on the Biscayne Bay side of Miami Beach, with a terrific view of the Miami skyline across the bay to the east.

After catering to rock stars for half a decade, Johnson and Jenkins were experts at accommodating their clients' sometimes-quirky needs. Henley and Frey knew a lot was riding on the band's upcoming album. Topping *One of These Nights* would be no mean feat. So they wanted isolation and set strict rules, demanding no one be allowed in the house except Johnson, Jenkins, and their "sassy" maid **Delores Henderson**. No exceptions. And then the songwriters got to work.

The partners stayed at the house on North Bay Road for a few days, preparing meals and coffee for the two Eagles as they worked on lyrics for their new song. Deloris visited daily, spending a few hours helping to keep the house clean.

> WE RELATED TO THEM. GLENN FREY ROLLER SKATED ALL OVER THE PLACE. THEY LOVED LYING IN THE SUN. DON HENLEY WANTED A TAN—ALL THE TIME. THEY LOVED BEING OUTSIDE, ON THE BEACH.
>
> — JERI JENKINS

"We would bring them sandwiches and [trays of] coffee, knock on the door and leave," Johnson said. "Don and Glenn dubbed the pink bedroom 'the Hollywood Room' because they were writing the song 'Hotel California.' It was also called 'the Jayne Mansfield Suite' because it had a big pink satin headboard with scalloped mirrors all around it and mirrored end tables, real old-glamour-from-the-1950s-type thing. For rock stars to be staying there, it was kind of funny. They all made fun of it."

Henley and Frey spent three days working on the song and then emerged one morning, bleary-eyed but beaming.

"They came downstairs, Don in his white terry cloth robe, Glenn in his red flannel plaid robe, both wearing slippers," Johnson remembered. "They said, 'We just wrote the best song we've ever written.' They were really excited, and we all sat at the kitchen table."

Johnson said they first read the lyrics from their yellow legal pad and explained what each line meant.

"Jeri had her favorite line, which was the 'Mercedes bends' one," Johnson said. "Mine was, 'We haven't had that spirit here since 1969.' And they sang the song to us a cappella...and Jeri and I cheered them on. They took a lot of pride in their work."

Although stories of the Eagles' excesses during the mid-to-late 1970s purported significant drug use, Johnson and Jenkins said they didn't see much of that back then.

"The Eagles, when they started, really weren't doing coke," Johnson said. "They weren't getting high all the time. Maybe they smoked pot a little bit like anyone would. When they stayed with us at 461, they were so sweet. They were California guys. That was different because Stephen Stills and his whole entourage, which also included the **Memphis Horns**, **Peter Tosh**, and **Dr. John**, were more like Woodstock hippies. Then you had Eric Clapton, and he was very

English and very different, and the Bee Gees were family. And then you had the Eagles, who were our kind of guys."

"We related to them," Jenkins added. "Glenn Frey roller skated all over the place. They loved lying in the sun. Don Henley wanted a tan—all the time. They loved being outside, on the beach."

Later, the entire band would convene at the mansion as they recorded tracks at Criteria for *Hotel California*. Jenkins said that by the time of *The Long Run*, "it got dark." In the end, she said, when the bandmembers did not get along anymore, HAL had to set them up in three separate houses. Johnson added that they asked for blackout curtains, which she saw as a metaphor for what was happening to them.

"You could always tell when things weren't going well during a recording," Jenkins explained to *Plum Miami*. "They would leave notes for us. Joe Walsh was the practical joker of the group, but Don and Glenn could be tough. Apparently, Don wasn't happy that we always had strawberry preserves, so one time, we walked in the kitchen, and he [had written] in big letters on a legal pad: 'Do you ever think about buying a different flavor?'

And there was a leak in his bedroom, so he wrote: 'How would you feel if you felt a drip. Drip. Drip. All night on your head?' It was signed, 'Home My Ass, Don Henley.' We still laugh about that story whenever we see each other."

Criteria's business began drying up in the early 1980s, and HAL's business fell, too. Artists and producers began opening their own studios— Eagles producer **Bill Szymczyk** had opened his own Bayshore Recording Studios in Coconut Grove, just south of Downtown Miami. Many of the artists he recorded followed him there.

But HAL had earned quite a reputation by then, with notes of special thanks showing up in the credits of more than 40 albums recorded by artists and bands they hosted. Among them: the Eagles' *Hotel California*, where Johnson, Jenkins, and Home at Last are the first to be thanked.

Not surprisingly, best friends forever Johnson and Jenkins segued to real estate in the 1980s and have since achieved immense success and recognition selling—what else?—multi-million-dollar beach-front properties up and down the Florida East Coast. And they remain friends with the Eagles to this day. [2090, 2091, 2092, 2093, 2094]

The courtyard at 5242 N. Bay Road, Miami Beach, where the Eagles stayed in 1976 while recording at Criteria Studios in nearby North Miami. Home at Last co-founders **Jeri Jenkins** and **Cindy Johnson** (inset left and right, with Don Henley in 1998) hosted the property.

with a series of music odd jobs. Along with writing jingles for products like Boone's Farm wines, he took whatever session work came along, including a turn on guitar for the title track of **Phil Ochs**' *Pleasures of the Harbor.*

Zevon's 1969 debut album, *Wanted Dead or Alive*, was mostly ignored. He wrote songs for others, like "Outside Chance" for **The Turtles**, and worked as a sideman for the **Everly Brothers**' touring band. At one point, he spent a summer playing piano at a Spanish bar.

"The road, booze, and I became an inseparable team," Zevon would later admit. He'd continue down that road to a very bad place, but in 1975, these excesses were manageable.

"Zevon was like a kid that we could all see a little of ourselves in," **Elliot Roberts** observed in **Barney Hoskyns**' book *Waiting for the Sun: A Rock 'n' Roll History of Los Angeles.*

In the meantime, Browne continued to serve as Zevon's biggest cheerleader, and Jackson's famous friends began recording his material. "I brought Warren Zevon to some people's attention because he was doing some really amazing things with his music," Browne told *On Milwaukee* in 2015. **Linda Ronstadt** became a particularly effective interpreter.

It had been more than five years since Zevon's 1969 debut. Fueled by sharp intellect, rock hedonism, and flinty ambition, he had never stopped writing. Zevon's notebooks were filled with most of the songs that would make up *Warren Zevon*, including "Hasten Down the Wind," "Carmelita," and "Poor Poor Pitiful Me." Asylum's allstar cast loved recording his songs.

"Carmelita," first covered four years earlier by former Everly Brothers opening act **Murray McLauchlan**, featured Glenn Frey on rhythm guitar and backing vocals. Frey and Don Henley sang on "The French Inhaler," while Souther added harmony vocals on "Mama Couldn't Be Persuaded" and "Desperados Under the Eaves."

Browne was a consistent presence, singing on "Mama Couldn't Be Persuaded," adding slide guitar to "Backs Turned Looking Down the Path," and adding piano and harmony vocals to "Desperados Under the Eaves."

Other Zevon fans who guested on the sessions as players and singers included **Phil Everly**, **Carl Wilson**, **Lindsey Buckingham**, **Bonnie Raitt**, **Stevie Nicks**, **David Lindley**, **Bobby Keys**, and **Kenny Edwards**.

Yet Zevon never got lost among these much bigger stars. In fact, "Desperados Under the Eaves" gave him the chance to share one of his most memorable lyrics:

"And if California slides into the ocean like the mystics and statistics say it will, I predict this motel will be standing until I pay my bill."

"The songs on the first album we did, like 'The French Inhaler' and 'Desperados Under the Eaves,' are literary masterpieces," Browne told *Rolling Stone*. "Serious writers, serious lovers of language, will be

continued on Page 249

SPOTLIGHT ALBUM | J.D. SOUTHER

J.D. SOUTHER

Black Rose
Asylum Records, June 1976

By the time **J.D. Souther** approached making his second album, *Black Rose*, in 1975, it had been five years since Glenn Frey's onetime **Longbranch/Pennywhistle** bandmate had made his eponymous solo debut. During that time, Souther went along with **David Geffen**'s **Souther-Hillman-Furay Band** supergroup gambit, which failed to take off after two albums.

But throughout the early '70s, Souther had also proven himself a jack of all trades, as a songwriter, singer, musician, and producer. He had helped out his friends in the Eagles on several occasions, among them collaborating on "Doolin-Dalton" for *Desperado* and co-writing two songs for *On the Border*—"You Never Cry Like a Lover" and the band's first #1 single, "The Best of My Love."

Souther contributed backing vocals to **Dan Fogelberg** albums, had songs covered by **Bonnie Raitt** and **Linda Ronstadt**, and in 1973 co-produced *Don't Cry Now*, Ronstadt's first album for Asylum.

At the time, Souther and Ronstadt shared a home in Hollywood. One day while he was working on a song, she wandered down the hall, intrigued by what she heard. Souther was sitting on a piano bench playing his guitar when Ronstadt asked, "What is that thing at the bridge?" Souther replied he had no idea since he hadn't finished it. But she asked him if she could sing it if he completed it, and he agreed.

By the next morning, he had finished the song, and called it "Faithless Love." As he told songwriter **Louise Goffin** on her *Song Chronicles* podcast, "She put it aside for a while and then all of a sudden, it was a big song everyone knew."

"Faithless Love" made its debut on Ronstadt's next album, the breakthrough *Heart Like a Wheel*. It had an immediate hook, using the title in the first few words, a trick Souther learned from **Hank Williams**' "Your Cheatin' Heart." Souther realized he would be foolish not to cut it himself. But the time was not right.

An encounter he had with **Joni Mitchell** during a party at her producer **Peter Asher**'s house may have planted the seed for his next solo album. "She said something about my work not having caught up to my ego, something like that, and I remember thinking, 'OK, watch this,'" as Souther recalled in writer **Scott Schinder**'s liner notes for Omnivore's 2016 *Black Rose* reissue.

With Asher at the helm in the studio, he and Souther recruited an all-star cast that included **Andrew Gold**, **Waddy Wachtel**, **Danny "Kootch" Kortchmar**, and **Kenny Edwards**, as well as guest vocalist **David Crosby**, drummer **Jim Keltner**, and Eagles compatriots Don Henley, Glenn Frey, and Joe Walsh.

On "If You Have Crying Eyes," Ronstadt sang harmony to Souther's lead vocal, both underpinned by

Frey's soulful, bluesy guitar. The string arrangements laid out the ambitious musical landscape Souther and Asher sought. Asher and Souther also brought in jazz bassist **Stanley Clarke** for "Silver Blue" and flugelhorn player **Donald Byrd** for "Midnight Prowl." If you close your eyes and listened to "If You Have Crying Eyes" or "Faithless Love," it's easy to imagine Souther singing them seamlessly in the Eagles, had he been their original fifth member.

While recording *Black Rose*, Souther was living in Malibu on a property he and **Irving Azoff** had rented as a party house. The commute between Malibu and the now-defunct Sound Factory studios in East Hollywood may have been long and winding, but Souther thought waking up every day to the sounds of breaking waves made it worthwhile.

Getting *Black Rose* finished proved a challenge. At one point, when Souther was on tour, Asher told him he wanted to withdraw from the project. "You're just not prepared," he told Souther. "You have pieces of songs. It's like watching someone build a house without a blueprint." Souther asked for a second chance and was able to convince Asher to complete the project.

The album closed with the title track, powered by background vocals by **Ned Doheny**, Henley, and Frey. Souther likened the image of a black rose to broken love but called it a horticultural impossibility. "There's a deep purple rose," he told Schinder, "but no one's been able to breed a perfect black rose. So, to me, it was the perfect metaphor for the unattainable."

Black Rose represents the start of a fertile period for Souther. When he unveiled his idea for the chorus for "New Kid in Town" to the Eagles, it kicked off a renewed, year-long writing spree with Henley and Frey. Along with "Victim of Love," which he co-wrote with Henley, Frey, and Don Felder, Souther's new Eagles collaborations would soon become some of his most famous songs. [1664, 1982, 1983, 1985]

discovering them for a long time to come."

Unfortunately, none of this work led to a quick commercial breakthrough—Zevon would have to wait until 1978's platinum-selling *Excitable Boy*, with its monster hit single "Werewolves of London." Still, his first Asylum LP set the stage for all to follow.

"I think his stylistic writing, combined with that voice, made it just a little more difficult dish than some people were willing to taste," Souther said in *Accidentally Like a Martyr: The Tortured Art of Warren Zevon*. "But it was always rich in nutrients, which made his songs sound very determined—and somehow, for me, it made his vulnerability all the more poignant."

Browne memorably described Zevon as "the writer who said the things I wish I said, the things I wish I could say."

Only later did he learn that the jokes Zevon told during these sessions, hoping to ensure a collaborative and friendly atmosphere, had been written out beforehand in his songwriting notebooks. [1926, 1927, 1928, 1929]

Jerry for Prez: Ronstadt, Eagles Hold Benefit for Governor Brown

Linda Ronstadt was a power player in 1970s California rock and roll. An ever-present member of the Troubadour singer-songwriter scene since the late 1960s, she is especially remembered and honored by Eagles fans everywhere. Her manager **John Boylan** put the lineup together in the first place (the four original members made up her backing band for a show at Disneyland on July 12, 1971) and Ronstadt unselfishly encouraged them to go out on their own.

The singer's *Heart Like a Wheel* album elevated her to superstar status in 1974. She was also an influential figure in progressive politics in California throughout the decade, performing at benefit concerts to help raise funds and awareness for causes she supported. Along the way, she met **Jerry Brown**, a liberal politician who would win the race for California governor that November.

Ronstadt found Brown a refreshing change from the artists and musicians in her romantic past. "Jerry Brown and I had a lot of fun for a number of years," she recalled fondly in her 2013 memoir, *Simple Dreams: A Musical Memoir*, saying that he was "smart and funny, not interested in drinking or drugs, and lived his life carefully, with a great deal of discipline."

Brown was young, dynamic, and dating a hugely popular rock star. He was rarely out of the news, and when elected at just 36, made history as California's youngest-ever governor. As a progressive liberal, Brown opted to not live in the governor's mansion and refused to travel around Sacramento by limousine. Instead, he walked to work.

According to a *New York Times* article in March 1976, "How Jerry Brown became Governor Moonbeam," Brown was popular and ambitious. Ignoring his critics' derisive nickname, Brown decided to try his luck running for president that year.

First, though, he had to win the Democratic nomination. Entering the race late, he was way behind **Jimmy Carter**, then Georgia's governor. But with West Coast star power behind him, Brown thought he might be a contender—even if his opponent did have Macon's favorite sons, the **Allman Brothers Band**, in his corner.

Ronstadt, **Stone Poneys** co-founder **Kenny Edwards**, the Eagles, **Jackson Browne** with **David Lindley**, and **Dan Fogelberg** descended on the Capitol Center in Landover, Maryland, on May 14, 1976, to participate in a benefit concert for Governor Brown. Show highlights included Ronstadt singing "Desperado" and "When Will I Be Loved," accompanied by Don Henley, Glenn Frey, and Joe Walsh, and the Eagles dedicating "Lyin' Eyes" to Carter, who, of course, was the winner in November.

One man's recollection of the show sums up the interplay between rock and politics in the 1970s. **Jeremy Gaunt** recalled the event for *No Depression* magazine in 2012, remembering the moment Brown took the stage. "Before he started, he asked everyone in the Capital Center to take a deep breath and hold it in so that we could all get high from the dope fumes."

Glenn Frey welcomes California Governor **Jerry Brown** onstage following Eagles' performance at the San Diego Sports Arena in December 1979. It was the band's second benefit concert for Brown, supporting his second run for U.S. president.

Undaunted by the loss to Carter, Brown launched a second bid for the White House in 1979. Again, assorted California artists backed Brown, Eagles included, but it was not enough for him to win the Democratic nomination. Nor was it enough to stop Republican ex-California Governor Ronald Reagan from winning the presidency in November 1980. [643, 746, 2043, 2044]

Eagles Return Lyrical Volley To Steely Dan in Friendly War

In **Steely Dan**'s 1976 deep cut "Everything You Did," the main character finds himself in a shouting match with a wayward spouse, and in the heat of the argument, he realizes how much noise they're making. It's then that the wronged husband takes a shot at one of the era's biggest bands: "*Turn up the Eagles,*" he seethes, "*the neighbors are listening.*"

Rather than being insulted by the slam, the Eagles were actually flattered—and decided to return the favor.

"I know [Steely Dan] pretty well, and it was like [the character] was sort of saying, 'Everybody in L.A.'s playing this fuckin' record, and I'm sick of it!'" Don Henley later told *Uncut*. "It was a little bit of an acknowledgment, and a little bit taking the piss, because we had the same man-

251

continued on Page 253

HENLEY PONDERS REDEMPTION IN 'WASTED TIME'

Glenn Frey and Don Henley had successfully teamed up for some of the most melodic, introspective ballads the Eagles ever recorded in the four albums preceding *Hotel California*.

"Saturday Night" (also co-credited to Randy Meisner and Bernie Leadon) was *Desperado*'s nostalgic look back at the courtships of days gone by. *On the Border*'s "The Best of My Love" (with **J.D. Souther**) went to #1 and highlighted the struggles of a couple coming to terms with breaking up. And *One of These Nights* served up two, "After the Thrill is Gone" and "Lyin' Eyes," which both looked at love and relationships gone bad from vastly different perspectives.

As the Eagles gathered in Malibu in the spring and summer of 1976 to begin developing songs for their new album, Frey and Henley collaborated anew, and romantic and not-so-romantic relationships were once more on their minds.

Hotel California produced rockers, ballads, and in-betweeners. Among the latter was "Victim of Love," originated by Don Felder and written with further input from Souther, and "Try and Love Again," a Randy Meisner *tour de force*. But "Wasted Time" was the only ballad penned exclusively by Henley and Frey.

Closing Side 1, "Wasted Time" peers into the soul of a relationship, striking familiar chords for many listeners. Frey opens with a haunting, isolated piano that segues into Henley's melancholy vocals. Henley's lyrics bring the listener into a private world of disappointment, regret, and resigned acceptance. The song masterfully draws the picture of a love regrettably lost and examines the familiar, repeating patterns of previous relationships and the mistakes that caused the breakups. In the end, it acknowledges heartbreak and a future that will probably never be—but that the time they did spend together was not wasted after all.

Jim Ed Norman, Henley's former **Shiloh** bandmate who arranged the strings for *Desperado*, finished the song with a touching string arrangement. Norman opens the album's Side 2 with a reprise, which in the flipside days of LPs brought the listener back into the mood established at the end of Side 1.

Looking back at the song in 2016, Henley told *Rolling Stone*'s **David Browne** that the piece was inspired by "failed relationships. Nothing inspires or catalyzes a great ballad like a failed relationship. Still, it's a very empathetic song, I think."

When Frey and Henley started developing the song, Frey thought of soulful R&B singer **Teddy Pendergrass**.

"It's a Philly-soul torch song," Frey said in an interview with *Rolling Stone*'s **Cameron Crowe**. "I loved all the records coming out of Philadelphia at that time. I sent for some sheet music so I could learn some of those songs, and I started creating my own musical ideas with that Philly influence. Don was our Teddy Pendergrass. He could stand out there all alone and just wail. We did a big Philly-type production with strings—definitely not country-rock. You're not going to find that track on a **Crosby, Stills & Nash** record or **Beach Boys** record.

"Don's singing abilities stretched so many of our boundaries. He could sing the phone book. It didn't matter. We had 'Golden Throat.' Jim Ed Norman, Don's old college buddy and former bandmate—and now President of Warner/Reprise Records/Nashville—wrote all of our string charts. He was right there with us in terms of wanting to do something like **Thom Bell**. It was definitely us loving Thom Bell." [15, 41, 209]

agement—still do—but you know, they're very droll, [Steely Dan co-founder **Donald**] **Fagen**, in particular."

Glenn Frey said "Everything You Did," found deep on Side 2 of Steely Dan's *The Royal Scam*, was sparked by a real-life situation involving Fagen's principal collaborator in the band.

"Apparently, **Walter Becker**'s girlfriend loved the Eagles, and she played them all the time. I think it drove him nuts," Frey told **Cameron Crowe** for the liner notes on 2003's *Eagles: The Very Best Of.* "So, the story goes that they were having a fight one day, and that was the genesis of the line."

The Eagles were still wrapping up sessions for *Hotel California* when *The Royal Scam* landed in record stores, giving them a rare opportunity to quickly respond. "During the writing of [the title song for] *Hotel California*, we decided to volley," Frey told Crowe.

"We repaid them in 'Hotel California,'" Henley remembered of the "*stab it with their steely knives*" reference. "That was my rejoinder."

Of course, their reference—like so much else in the forthcoming album's epic opening song—was far more indirect and open to interpretation than Steely Dan's had been. The reasons were twofold.

The Eagles felt like they had a lot to live up to: "We were, and are, big Steely Dan fans. We were always quite amazed that Steely Dan was so brave lyrically," Frey enthused in an interview with **Bob Costas**. "You know, they had lines in their songs that we would sort of look at ourselves and say, 'Whoa. Would we have put that in one of our songs?'"

But the Eagles were also impishly leveraging the innuendo that always surrounded Steely Dan, since the band shared its name with a sex toy from **William Burroughs**' *Naked Lunch*. As Frey told Crowe, "We just wanted to allude to Steely Dan, rather than mentioning them outright, so 'Dan' got changed to 'knives'—which is still, you know, a penile metaphor." [209, 1743, 1744]

SUMMER 1976

 RELEASES
▶ **Poco**, with Timothy B. Schmit, "Starin' at the Sky" (single)

 NUGGETS
▶ Eagles are spending the next three weeks in Criteria Studios putting the finishing touches on their next LP, and Joe Walsh is fitting in fine. —*Record World*
▶ Eagles' summer tour drew more than 400,000 for 14 summer dates; somehow that tour wasn't as long as it started out to be. —*Cashbox*
▶ Don Felder and Joe Walsh are in New York making the rounds at radio stations in support of their new album, *California Hotel*. [sic] —*Cashbox*
▶ Bernie Leadon is in the studio with friends working on his first post-Eagles album. —*Crawdaddy*

 ON THE ROAD WITH ...
▶ **Eagles**: Boz Scaggs, Dave Mason, Fleetwood Mac, J.D. Souther, Joe Walsh, Linda Ronstadt, Loggins & Messina, Pure Prairie League, Renaissance
▶ **Poco**, with Timothy B. Schmit: Laura Nyro, Lynyrd Skynyrd, Stephen Stills, the Stills-Young Band

 COLLABORATIONS
▶ **Glenn Frey** played guitar on the single "Libby" on **Carly Simon**'s album *Another Passenger*.
▶ **Bernie Leadon** (acoustic guitar, baritone vocals) and **Timothy B. Schmit** (backing vocals) provided musical support on **Chris Hillman**'s album *Slippin' Away*.
▶ **Don Henley** played drums and provided harmony vocals on **Linda Ronstadt**'s album *Hasten Down the Wind*.

Geffen Wraps Tumultuous Short Stay at Warner Bros. Pictures

By the mid-1970s, **David Geffen** was firmly ensconced in the music industry as an innovator, skilled talent spotter, and powerhouse record company executive.

A contemporary of many of the artists he both adored and made successful, Geffen was cut from a different cloth than the typical middle-aged cigar-chomping music executives of the day. He related to artists and built success based on genuine relationships with them. **Jackson Browne** recalled in an interview with *Insight* magazine in 1989 that Geffen was unusual in that he was a fantastic businessman who could also be trusted. Geffen instinctively understood musicians, a gift that may have been under-appreciated until he stepped away from the music scene and entered an even more ego-fueled arena: Hollywood and the movies.

After signing **Bob Dylan** to Asylum Records in 1973, Geffen, at just 30 years of age, had achieved his musical ambition. Never one to rest on his laurels, he sought a new business challenge. As he said to writer **John Duka** in a 1982 *New York Times* story: "I told **Steve Ross** [in 1975] that I wanted to run a movie studio."

The chairman of Elektra/Asylum parent Warner Communications Inc., Ross was a mentor to Geffen throughout his music career, and gave the idea some thought. In December 1975, he appointed Geffen the Vice Chairman of Warner Bros. Pictures. Geffen brought the people skills he had developed as a music mogul to the role and enjoyed signing talent and dealing with directors, actors, producers, and studio executives.

During his brief stay at Warner Bros., Geffen oversaw three movies: *Oh God*, featuring comedy legend **George Burns** in the title role; *Greased Lightning*, the true story of NASCAR's first Black winner, **Wendell Scott**; and *The Late Show*, a detective comedy starring **Art Carney** and **Lily Tomlin**. All three films were low-budget affairs and financially successful at the box office, and proved Geffen had what it took to make money in Hollywood.

Unfortunately, he hated the tumultuous process. The Hollywood studio system was too hierarchical for his liking. There was way too much red tape, and bureaucracy was anathema to his entrepreneurial nature. He had built his career by making his own decisions and acting on them quickly.

"It was a nightmare," Geffen told *New York Times Magazine* writer **Don Shewey** in 1985. "I hated those meetings, everybody afraid to be responsible. ... If I have to sit and convince somebody why I'm enthusias-

tic about something, I'm already depressed."

Geffen chose to part ways with Hollywood. As he told Duka, "When I realized it was not workable, I had to leave."

Leave he did, chastened by the experience and ready to find a new challenge. But the next challenge was unexpected and frightening. A diagnosis of bladder cancer in 1977 led Geffen to quit the business to focus on treatment and healing. Three years later he'd receive a different, life-altering diagnosis. [508, 567, 2041, 2042, 2048, 2049]

Hotel Change: Henley Takes Over for Felder on 'Victim of Love'

Like the music for "Hotel California," "Victim of Love" emerged from the more than a dozen song ideas Don Felder brought to the sessions that produced *Hotel California*—but it came with an unexpected switch on lead vocals.

Building on Felder's instrumental he called "Iron Lung," the song initially seemed like it would come together quickly. Eagles completed the basic track in a single take, a most unusual outcome for the always-meticulous musicians.

Next, they had to complete the lyrics. Longtime collaborator **J.D. Souther** had the beginnings of an idea, which he shared during writing sessions in Malibu, and he, Glenn Frey, and Don Henley collaborated to finish the lyrics.

"J.D. said, 'There's something about the word 'victim' in a sentence,'" Felder told radio DJ **Joe Benson** in 2018. "I like that word, 'victim,'" Felder remembered Souther adding.

"I think that's a good hook for a song."

Felder says he thought he would be singing the lead vocal, just as he had on "Visions" from *One of These Nights*. But he got stuck after sessions moved to Criteria Studios in Miami.

"It was supposed to be a song that I was going to sing on the record," Felder told radio personality **Artie Lange**. "We got into Miami and we set up a mic one night for me to sing. I'd had about a half a bottle of wine, and I went out and tried to sing it, and after three or four takes I said, 'Hey, let's just do this tomorrow when I'm clean and sober and I can make a good attack at it.'"

According to Henley, Felder's attempts to record the track had extended for a week with dozens of unsuccessful cuts. Frustrated, Frey finally opened the talkback mic in the studio one last time and told Felder, "Okay, let's hold on that," according to *Goodnight, L.A.: The Rise and Fall of Classic Rock*. "We'll pick it up later."

"Don Felder, for all of his talents as a guitar player, was not a singer," Frey explained in *The History of the Eagles* documentary.

Henley disagreed with Felder's assertion the band had pledged to let him sing lead. "I have no recollection of anybody being promised anything," he said in the documentary. "We did let Mr. Felder sing it…it

> " **WHILE I WENT TO DINNER, I THINK DON WENT OUT AND SANG IT, JUST AS A DEMO FOR ME TO HEAR HOW HE HEARD IT—AND WHEN I CAME BACK AND HEARD IT, IT WAS GREAT.**
>
> — DON FELDER

simply did not come up to band standards. Felder demanding to sing that song would be the equivalent of me demanding to play lead guitar on 'Hotel California.' It just didn't make sense."

Later, after hearing a playback with Henley's vocal, the guitarist agreed the switch was the right call.

"While I went to dinner, I think Don went out and sang it, just as a demo for me to hear how he heard it—and when I came back and heard it, it was great."

Henley's vocal, Felder later admitted, was obviously definitive.

"It was immediately apparent to everyone, especially me, that he should sing it," Felder wrote in his book *Heaven and Hell: My Life in the Eagles*, "even though, deep down, I wasn't thrilled at losing my slot."

"Victim of Love" went on to become a treasured Eagles deep cut and was included on 1982's *Eagles Greatest Hits, Vol. 2*, while "Visions" remained Felder's only appearance as lead singer on an Eagles album. [1663, 1714, 1891, 1892, 1898, 2148]

Meisner Croons His Only *Hotel* Tune, 'Try and Love Again'

By the time *Hotel California* hit the shelves in December 1976, Don Henley had emerged as the primary go-to guy for Eagles lead vocals. His voice dominates the album. Don

Felder would be denied any lead vocals, while Randy Meisner, along with Joe Walsh and even Glenn Frey, only got one song each.

For Meisner, it was a good one: the lush semi-ballad "Try and Love Again."

How things had changed since the Eagles' debut album, where the bassist sang lead on three songs, had two sole writing credits, and shared a third credit. He took the lead vocal on his own "Take the Devil" and "Tryin'" and on Glenn Frey's ballad, "Most of Us Are Sad." Meisner also co-wrote "Earlybird" with Bernie Leadon.

Meanwhile, Henley had only one co-writing credit and just two lead vocals on their debut album, and it would have been only one vocal if the band had not added **Jackson Browne**'s "Nightingale" specifically to remedy the situation.

By the time the group released their second album, Henley and Frey had emerged as leaders. In **Beatles** comparisons, they became the "Lennon/McCartney" figures, while Meisner was relegated to "George Harrison" duties—a role sometimes described as "two songs per album."

The third album's credits bear out this perception. Meisner sang just one full lead ("Certain Kind of Fool"), in addition to one line in the chorus of "Saturday Night" on *Desperado*. He sang two complete lead vocals on each of the next two LPs: **Paul Craft**'s "Midnight Flyer" and his own "Is It True?" for *On the Border*, and his co-writes "Too Many Hands" and "Take It to the Limit" on *One of These Nights*.

On *Hotel California*, Meisner's sole con-tribution appears as the penultimate track, bookended by Walsh and **Joe Vitale**'s gorgeous "Pretty Maids All in a Row" and Henley's epic, environmentally minded closer, "The Last Resort."

After an eight-bar intro, Meisner enters "Try and Love Again" with his unmistakable tenor. The tone is moody and melancholic, fitting well not only with the immediately surrounding songs, but also with the darker mood of the whole album.

Meisner may be the only credited songwriter on "Try and Love Again," but he acknowledged a few of his bandmates also played a part in fleshing it out: "Joe [Walsh] helped me a little bit with that," he said. "I had that song for a long time and never really got it finished. I brought it in for those album sessions, we worked on it and worked on it and it turned out really good. Don and Glenn helped put it together."

Meisner delivers an earnest vocal, as the song's protagonist questions what might happen if he attempted another romance too soon after the last one's miserable failure.

While "Take It to the Limit" from the previous album will always be considered Meisner's most famous tune and his signature piece, "Try and Love Again" represents another high point.

And it would be his final writing contribution and lead vocal as an Eagle. Like the doomed romance he lamented in the song, Meisner's relationship with the band would soon dissolve and he'd be "out there on his own" trying to find his way with a new endeavor. [1785]

FALL 1976

 RELEASES
▶ **Poco**, with Timothy B. Schmit, "Rose of Cimarron" (single)

 NUGGETS
▶ Eagles will kick off a 24-city, 27-date tour of the western U.S. beginning Oct. 14 in San Diego. —*Record World*
▶ **Bill Szymczyk** opens Pandora Productions in Miami; Eagles are doing studio work there. —*Billboard*
▶ The Eagles' new album will actually be titled *Hotel California*, not vice-versa. —*Cashbox*
▶ Joe Walsh is reportedly close to signing with Portrait Records, a new West Coast-based label affiliated with Columbia. —*Cashbox*
▶ Eagles play a sold-out Forum in L.A. and work in three unreleased songs from *Hotel California*. —*Cashbox*

 COLLABORATIONS
▶ **Bernie Leadon** provided backing vocals on the song "Young Westley" on **David Bromberg Band**'s album *How Late'll Ya Play 'Til?*
▶ **Joe Walsh** played electric guitar and slide guitar on the singles "Every Sixty Seconds," "Feet," and "What's the Point" on **Bill Wyman**'s album *Stone Alone*.
▶ **Don Henley** and **Glenn Frey** provided (uncredited) backing vocals on **Ned Doheny**'s album *Hard Candy*.
▶ **Don Henley** provided harmony vocals on the single "The Only Child" on **Jackson Browne**'s album *The Pretender*.
▶ **Bernie Leadon** played electric guitar and acoustic guitar and provided vocals on **Andy Fairweather-Low**'s album *Be Bop 'N' Holla*.
▶ **Joe Walsh** played slide guitar on the song "Hollywood Vampire" on **Al Kooper**'s album *Act Like Nothing's Wrong*.

 ON THE ROAD WITH ...
▶ **Eagles**: Hall & Oates, J.D. Souther, Linda Ronstadt
▶ **Joe Walsh**: Ambrosia

Clive Davis Signs Tempchin, Funky Kings to Arista Records

If people did not know the name **Jack Tempchin**, they certainly knew his songs, "Peaceful Easy Feeling" and "Already Gone" (the latter a co-write with **Robb Strandlund**). They were both signature songs in the Eagles' canon when Tempchin set out from his native San Diego to Los Angeles to pursue his own career. He had also earned notoriety co-writing "Tijuana" with **Tom Waits**, and **Jackson Browne** and **Linda Ronstadt** had performed Tempchin's "One More Song" in their live sets by that time.

After less than a week in L.A., he found himself in a new band with **Richard Stekol** and **Jules Shear** called **Funky Kings**. Glenn Frey soon introduced Tempchin to former Columbia Records chief **Clive Davis**, who had launched Arista Records in 1974.

"We got together and we played one gig, and a manager came up and said, 'You shouldn't be playing in this bar,'" Tempchin recalled. "And then a couple weeks later, we had a record deal."

Working with **The Doors**' producer **Paul Rothchild**, the self-titled debut album *Funky Kings* came out in early 1976, followed by a tour with **Daryl Hall & John Oates**. One song that helped secure the deal was "Slow Dancing." Tempchin was at a club called The Iron Horse when he saw everyone heading to the dance floor as the band began playing a slow song.

"I noticed the people were waiting for the slow song because they wanted to squish the girl up against them," he remembered. "I thought there ought to be a song called 'Slow Dancing,' so I took that and ran with it. And at the same time I was writing it, I had fallen in love with this girl who's now been my wife all this time...and that's what poured into the song. It's just a simple thing, but I worked on it until I couldn't get any better."

Although it wasn't a hit for Funky Kings, **Johnny Rivers** heard it on the radio. As Tempchin remembered, "He said, 'Well, too bad I can't do that song—it's already a big hit.' And then somebody told him, 'No, it's not a big hit.' So, he recorded it."

As "Swayin' to the Music (Slow Dancin')," Rivers' cover made the Top 10 on the *Billboard* Hot 100 chart in 1977, and two years later, **Johnny Duncan**'s version was a Top 10 country hit.

Funky Kings disbanded after eight months and the one album, and Tempchin recorded his first solo album, *Jack Tempchin*, for Arista in 1978. Recorded in Muscle Shoals, Alabama, with session guitarist **Pete Carr**, the record included Tempchin's own version of "Peaceful Easy Feeling."

"I wasn't really well known," he reflected of the years he opened for **Chicago**, **Christopher Cross**, **Kenny Loggins**, and others, "but my songs were known. So, I got to play in front of thousands of people for years, and that was very satisfactory."

"As in baseball, not every song leads to a hit," Davis reflected in the 2017 documentary *Clive Davis: The Soundtrack of Our Lives*. "In the case of the Funky Kings, it was Jack Tempchin who had written some songs for the Eagles. But he was ultimately not able to write for the new group. There's gotta be misses. I didn't sign **Meat Loaf** and I thought **John Cougar Mellencamp** was too close to **Bruce Springsteen**."

More than 40 years after Funky Kings dissolved, Tempchin found himself telling stories and singing songs in the Clive Davis Theater at downtown L.A.'s Grammy Museum, a venue named after the record mogul who first signed him. By then, Tempchin had a much larger repertoire with songs like "You Belong to the City" and "Smuggler's Blues" and more than 30 credits on Glenn Frey's solo albums. [581, 582, 583, 645, 1707, 1708, 1712, 1713]

Eagles Debut *Hotel* Setlist Onstage in Arizona, Los Angeles

Bill Szymczyk was still in the studio in early September 1976 trying to finish up production on *Hotel California*. Elektra/Asylum wanted the next Eagles album for the Christmas season badly, so he was under pressure to wrap it up. The label had scheduled a December 8 release date and it was getting close to crunch time.

A notoriously meticulous producer, Szymczyk found himself shuttling back and forth between Criteria Studios in Miami and the Eagles' various tour stops to get feedback. He played tapes of the latest iterations and

continued on Page 262

FELDER, WALSH PERFECT DUELING GUITARS CODA

After Don Felder's multi-tracked "Mexican Reggae" home demo hooked Don Henley and the rest of the band, the Eagles continued developing the song's intricate arrangement in the studio.

Building the basic track for what would become "Hotel California" was a painstaking process, taking place over three sessions with producer **Bill Szymczyk**. The earlier versions were either the wrong tempo or in the wrong key. But the ideas, at least musically, were there from the start, as blueprinted by the demo. Szymczyk ended up splicing multiple takes to complete the song's structure.

Felder was especially looking forward to teaming up with new guitar partner Joe Walsh for the long instrumental ending, which they worked on next during two days of sessions at Criteria Studios in Miami. Felder played a 1959 Les Paul Sunburst while Walsh strapped on a trusty Telecaster.

"I always thought we would just set up two guitars, and Joe and I would just go toe to toe and have fun playing and pushing each other," Felder told WCBE radio in 2021.

And that's how the session started, Felder added, until Henley interceded.

"Joe and I started jamming, and Don said, 'No, no, stop! It's not right,'" Felder told *MusicRadar* in 2012. "I said, 'What do you mean it's not right?' And he said, 'No, no, you've got to play it just like the demo.' Only problem was, I did that demo a year earlier; I couldn't even remember what was on it."

Felder had to call his home and ask his housekeeper to go through his cassettes and find the demo. Once she did, he instructed her to play the recording while holding the phone up to the speaker.

"I had to sit down and learn something I had just made up off the top of my head for that demo," Felder recalled. "Don was right to make me go back and do that."

Somewhere along the way, the impish Walsh broke a few rules. Rather than replicating exactly the guitar parts Felder demoed that summer day on the beach, Walsh added a few asides of his own.

Even these small additions—described by Walsh in highly technical terms perhaps only a fellow guitarist would understand—ended up being very time consuming, because they had to be built into the existing musical foundation.

Walsh said he wanted to do something that sounded like "diddly diddly diddly," Felder recalled in the WCBE interview. "Since I [had] written the chord changes, I had to sit down and figure out what 'diddly diddly diddly' was over all the different chords that went by across that progression, work out my part, and then the harmony for it."

But a competitive atmosphere made it difficult for either guitarist to be 100% loyal to the demo. "He pushed me, and I pushed back," Walsh said on KIRO-TV in 2018. "Two guys going at it was really the magic of 'Hotel California.'" Felder glowingly described Walsh's additions as "Joe Walsh-isms" in the interview with WCBE. "He's just Joe."

Even within the confines of an already arranged piece, they dueled their way to a new creative peak. "It was like, 'Okay, watch this!'" Walsh told Gibson.com. "We did that on purpose, because it created tension, that effort to be the tougher guy. You can hear that in our performances."

He and Walsh practiced what they would play "literally almost bar-by-bar," Felder added, then recorded their parts in the same systematic fashion until they had "a perfect execution of that idea."

"I wound up with a [reference] cassette that had virtually the entire arrangement that appeared on the record, verbatim, with the exception of a few Joe Walsh licks on the end," Felder said to Guitar World in 2013. "All the harmony guitar stuff was there, as was my solo."

"[Felder and Walsh's greatest contributions evolved in a] two-day period working at Criteria Studios," Szymczyk remembered. "We ran lines out to the amplifiers in the studio, but they were both performing in the control room. I was in the middle, Joe Walsh was on one side, Don Felder was on the other side, and we just attacked this ending blend of solos. It took us two days, but it is still one of the highlights of my career. There was a lot of stop/start and, 'Let's try this,' and, 'That didn't work,' 'Well, if we did this with that, maybe that would work.' Piece by piece by piece until it was done. They were equal gunfighters, Joe and Don."

In the released recording, Felder and Walsh call and respond to each other for 24 bars, then at 5:39 begin a soaring harmonized section that powers "Hotel California" toward its emotional conclusion.

As Szymczyk worked with Felder and Walsh to complete the song's coda, the rest of the band, especially Henley and Frey, provided direction as bits and pieces of the outro were stitched together to form what became the famous final cut. The outro is widely considered one of the greatest guitar solos ever recorded, even if it was a duet.

For all that focus and effort, Felder still did not think "Hotel California" should be released as a single—and his marathon outro performance with Walsh was one of the reasons.

"It was six and a half minutes long, the introduction was a minute; you couldn't dance to it, it stops in the middle; it breaks down with no drums and it's got this two-minute guitar solo on the end of it," Felder told the Daily Herald in 2014. "It's completely wrong for AM radio."

"Hotel California" became the album's second consecutive #1 hit and scored RIAA gold for more than a million singles sold despite those unconventional elements. Felder said he'd "never been so happy to have been so wrong in my life." [1197, 1931, 1932, 1933, 1934, 1935, 1936, 1937, 1938]

IT TOOK US TWO DAYS, BUT IT IS STILL ONE OF THE HIGHLIGHTS OF MY CAREER. THERE WAS A LOT OF STOP/START, AND 'LET'S TRY THIS,' AND 'THAT DIDN'T WORK.' ... PIECE BY PIECE UNTIL IT WAS DONE. THEY WERE EQUAL GUNFIGHTERS, JOE AND DON.

— BILL SZYMCZYK

mixes of the tracks to the band, made detailed notes, and headed back to the studio to apply the updates.

While he was steaming toward the production finish line, the Eagles were preparing to add some of their new songs into the tour setlists. "Hotel California" had become the dramatic opening song in Eagles concerts by early 1977, but exactly when the band first played their most recognizable song live remains a mystery. However, there's evidence fans heard it onstage for the first time in Tempe, Arizona, on October 15, 1976, though the day before at the San Diego Sports Arena, the band had played its usual *One of These Nights* set.

At Arizona State University's Assembly Center, "Hotel California" was the fourth song the Eagles played that night, according to Setlist.fm, a crowd-managed site where fans can post setlists for concert dates.

ASU alum **Jeff Hammond** said he and his fellow concertgoers were unfamiliar with the new songs but were intrigued.

"Before they played 'Hotel California,' they said they were working on it in the recording studio," Hammond said. "Of course, no one had ever heard it before. I remember it was much longer than a typical Eagles song, and it sort of drifted along, kind of mesmerizing-like for quite a while," he added, noting that there wasn't much to be excited about at first. "But when they got to the guitar duet and finished the song, you could feel this vibe in the crowd like 'What the hell did I just hear?' There was definitely the experience of something no one had ever heard before."

J.D. Souther opened the evening with songs from his new *Black Rose* album, and he gave way to the Eagles, who kicked off their eleven-song set with "Take It Easy" and concluded with "Wasted Time," another song that would have been unknown to the audience.

The Eagles' concert in Tempe and another in Tucson were dress rehearsals for the shows booked at the famed Forum in Inglewood, a suburb just south of Los Angeles, from October 19-22, which would officially kick off the *Hotel California* tour. The band carefully conceived the four nights of shows, the performances were tight, and everything was recorded. Decades later, in 2017, those recordings appeared in the 40th Anniversary reissue of *Hotel California*.

After *Hotel California* was released, the band said playing those new songs onstage helped them prepare for the upcoming tour, but understood why fans weren't excited about the brand-new material.

"We worked up three of the songs for the October tour that we played and found them easy to do on stage," Glenn Frey told *Melody Maker* in December 1976. "We have been playing the title track, 'Wasted Time,' and 'New Kid in Town,' but it's difficult to do new tunes on stage. If the people haven't heard them on the radio, then they just don't pay that much attention. There has to be a repetition factor for some reason. When we start touring again in March the album will have been out two months or so and by that time, we'll be playing it all or most of it."

Don Henley looked back at those early

Eagles play live at The Forum in Inglewood, near Los Angeles, on October 19, 1976, as their *Hotel California* tour gets underway. The album wouldn't be released for another month and a half, but the band had begun adding the new songs in their setlist in September.

performances with pride. "I was delighted with the energy and grittiness of the live tracks," Henley told *Rolling Stone* after the reissue. "But we had the foresight to record those shows. I was surprised we were doing songs from the album before it even came out. That was pretty ballsy."

The Forum stand had originally been slated as a two-night affair, but demand for tickets was so great, the band added two more nights. Eagles played twenty-two-song sets before crowds of 18,000 each night, though reports said the show "exceeded capacity" every evening. As he did in Arizona, Souther opened the show and joined the Eagles for "New Kid in Town," which he then dedicated "to rock's hottest

new phenoms, **Daryl Hall** and **John Oates**."

"The Eagles debuted material from the forthcoming *Hotel California* LP, due for release in early November," wrote *Cashbox* on October 30. "The title track, reminiscent of the mood to the eerie 'Witchy Woman,' opened the concert as a large silhouette of the Beverly Hills Hotel on Sunset served as background. In a surprising move the Eagles played another new song, 'Wasted Time,' to the full accompaniment of a tuxedoed orchestra. The violin-heavy ensemble, seated above and behind the band on a specially crafted stage, added a lushly romantic feel to what was described by [Glenn] Frey in his introduction as 'a rainy day song.'"

The after-party for the first show was one

263

continued on Page 267

SZYMCZYK, EAGLES ASSEMBLE THE MASTERPIECE

The fourth Eagles album, *One of These Nights*, was their best to date by all accounts. It kept touch with the band's country-rock roots, but also served up some hard-edged rock and roll, plus a shot of rhythm & blues. Radio loved it. Eagles fans loved it. Remarkably, the band had become as popular as the **Rolling Stones** by then, at least in America—no small feat.

So, what would the Eagles do for an encore? Fans as well as Elektra/Asylum would spend the bulk of 1976 wondering not only what the band would deliver for their fifth studio effort, but also when.

Producer **Bill Szymczyk** used to churn out between six to eight albums a year before he met the Eagles. Indeed, he spent just five weeks in the studio with the band when he took over production of their third album, *On the Border*.

The pace slowed significantly with their next album, *Nights*, which took more than six months to

make. Now, the album to be titled *Hotel California* would keep E/A executives nervously twiddling their thumbs like expectant parents for nine months. For the studio-bound Szymczyk, the lyric line "you can check out any time you like, but you can never leave" took on personal significance during these sessions.

With Joe Walsh joining the band in December 1975 in time for a shakedown tour of the Far East in January, coming up with new material was naturally the first order of business. With *Nights*, the group had written most of the songs in the studio. Now, since they'd written little to nothing new since those sessions because they'd spent most of the time on tour, it became clear the new album would also be created in the studio—and mostly on the fly.

"They call me up and they say, 'Okay, we're ready to record, book some time," Szymczyk said. "'We're going to have a week or two of rehearsals before we go in and see what we've got.'"

Szymczyk booked studio time at the famed Record Plant in Los Angeles in April 1976. Getting ready, the band gathered at Randy Meisner's house, a charming place he bought from **Rick Nelson** that overlooked Universal Studios just north of Hollywood. The plan was to camp there and start writing and rehearsing. But it was not as productive as they had hoped.

"I show up, we get together, and I said, 'Okay, let me hear some tunes,'" Szymczyk said. But at first, the band had just one song ready to record: Meisner's "Try and Love Again."

"I said, 'Fantastic—it's a great song. Good start, what else you got?'" The band's collective response was "nothing."

Walsh, who had been recording with Szymczyk for years, tried to assuage his old friend and producer. "Oh, we got some licks and we got a couple of verses and we got a little bit of this," Walsh recalled during a 2019 Record Plant-hosted TED Talk-like session of the *Record Plant Diaries*. "I said, 'Don't worry about that, Bill.'"

Szymczyk understood, but also figured the songwriting phase was going to be protracted. Still, Walsh remained optimistic.

"We really didn't know how to start. We just knew that it was going to work," Walsh said during the Record Plant event. "We brought ideas in. Everybody had some pretty cool stuff, parts of songs, and I had a lot of great guitar licks and Don had some words and, of course, Glenn being from Detroit, he knew where he wanted to go. We took all of that and put it on a table like this and said, 'Okay, let's pretend this is a jigsaw puzzle. Well, this here, these two things go good here. This isn't part of that. This is going to have to be another song,' and we started that way.

> ## WE REALLY DIDN'T KNOW HOW TO START. WE JUST KNEW IT WAS GOING TO WORK. WE BROUGHT IDEAS IN. EVERYBODY HAD SOME PRETTY COOL STUFF, PARTS OF SONGS, AND I HAD A LOT OF GREAT GUITAR LICKS AND DON HAD SOME WORDS.
>
> ## — JOE WALSH

Then we presented that to Bill and little by little, things started to take shape."

Feeling more comfortable in Miami, Szymczyk moved production to Criteria Studios. Over the next seven months, the band logged production time on both coasts, with Szymczyk sometimes shuttling back and forth between Eagles tour dates with tapes in tow.

Speaking to *Crawdaddy* in April 1977, Frey seemed to buckle under the pressure of what the album required of the band.

"The demands that have been put on us," he sighed. "*Hotel California* missed so many deadlines it was put on the 'indefinite release' list. Plus, a tour had to be performed and Joe Walsh initiated into the band. Suddenly sleep becomes a planned activity. A lot of your time is not your own. I know that sounds silly. I didn't think it could be any less my own than a year ago, but it actually got to the point where it's a 24-hour-a-day job."

Life in the studio for *Hotel California* was different than any other album they had recorded. Bernie Leadon was gone, and the mischievous but creative Walsh had replaced him. Habits began forming that slowed things down. Frey allegedly restricted access to the control room while he was singing. Don Felder said Henley was habitually late.

Even the neighbors at the studio were intent on obstructing progress. The band had to delay and then re-record "The Last Resort" because **Black Sabbath** was too loud in the room next door.

After things got "unruly," Szymczyk said he laid down some ground rules, which was something of a risk since that's how former producer **Glyn Johns** found himself on the outs with the band. He wouldn't allow drinking in the studio until 6 p.m.

"I made a rule after it got a little unruly at first and

whenever it gets unruly, you need rules," Szymczyk told the *Diaries*. "I said, 'All right, guys, we have to get in here at 2 o'clock in the afternoon...so I don't want no ingestion of anything other than coffee. 6 o'clock you can get your beer, get your whatever.' You know what I mean?"

The rules may have helped in the studio, but the band found tensions elsewhere. Frey and Henley were sharing a house, but after an intense argument, Henley moved in with manager **Irving Azoff**. Meanwhile, Meisner and his wife were divorcing, and the bassist began feeling more isolated. The friendships the band had forged were crumbling. But amidst all the turmoil, their overall nose-to-the-grindstone work ethic remained unchanged—they did not work fast, but they always worked hard. And the formula for success, albeit different, was familiar.

"Don and Glenn would get a framework. Glenn was great at that," Walsh recalled. "They would get a framework of the song, a rough idea of how we're going to start, what the verses are, what the choruses are, and of course Don would take that and start writing words. Don Felder, Randy, and I would play Ping-Pong."

Whoever was on duty "got the control room," Walsh said. "We stayed away when Don was singing, of course. He would do that with Bill, and Glenn would pop in every once in a while. When it was time for Don Felder and I, we wanted to put a layer of things on. Kind of like a mariachi band's trumpets. That was the first thing we wanted to do and we wanted to play those together. We wanted to play with each other a whole part.

"Then he got the first verse and I got the second verse and then we figured, at the end, we would go at it and the last thing we did was really go at it," Walsh said. "Don Felder and I were always very competitive, but it was good. We really respected each other and we pushed each other. We pushed each other on stage and when we were playing together. It was really competitive and really serious but it was really good for creative energy. Controlled tension fuels creative energy."

Walsh said the group would then gather, and Szymczyk would sit in the control room to help them arrange it, and tell them what was going to work and what wasn't.

"We all had ideas and stuff, but Don and Glenn were great at crafting songs," Walsh said. "They just needed material to work with, and that was our job. That's gradually how it took shape. Once we got going, we started to see progress and then rather than be clueless, like in the beginning, we were on our way. The toughest thing is to get started."

There were plenty of disagreements in the studio, and Walsh admitted that heated arguments broke out. "Did we fight?" he asked whimsically. "Yeah, we fought. In any relationship, you fight, a marriage, yeah, you disagree. I always said that it was a democratic dictatorship. We got to vote but Don and Glenn decided."

Fortunately, the greatest hits collection E/A released over the band's objections in February gave the label the revenue it wanted, and it relieved some pressure. Mostly it gave the band more time to complete their work.

"Let me just say that it was a kind of a painful birth, '*Hotel California*,'" Szymczyk said. "Not too bad, once we got going, but the funny thing is that everybody thinks we knew what we were doing. That didn't really matter. We just knew it was going to work. We weren't famous yet. I mean we weren't like we are, like it turned into. But I think one of the greatest rewards for all of us is to have been part of something that affected that many people on the planet, beyond our wildest imaginations. And it's good to feel like we made a valid, profound statement for the generation that we represented." [132, 1810, 1852, 1875, 1987, 1988, 1989]

> **IT WAS A PAINFUL BIRTH, HOTEL CALIFORNIA. NOT TOO BAD... ONCE WE GOT GOING, BUT THE FUNNY THING IS EVERYBODY THINKS WE KNEW WHAT WE WERE DOING.**
>
> **— BILL SZYMCZYK**

for the ages. The band—accompanied by their entire string section—crowded into the Forum Club along with a bevy of rock celebrities. **Joni Mitchell** posed for photos with Henley, while **Linda Ronstadt**, **Boz Scaggs**, **John Denver**, **Olivia Newton-John**, Daryl Hall, and John Oates joined in the festivities. A similar party, with even more rock royalty, would join in when the Eagles opened the East Coast swing of the tour at Madison Square Garden later that summer. [41, 1977, 1978, 1979, 1980, 1981, 1986]

Warner Bros. Plans *Desperado* Film; 'Screaming' Eagles Protest

As a concept album, the Eagles' *Desperado* seemed ripe for a movie treatment—and the Hollywood management firm of Leber-Krebs, headed by **Steve Leber** and **David Krebs**, was very excited about the prospect. So were executives at Warner Bros. Pictures.

Eagles, however, were less so.

"I'm afraid it's going to turn out to be a bad movie," Don Henley said in a 1980 D.I.R. Broadcasting interview, *A Conversation with the Eagles*. "I'd rather just give it the axe than have it be a bad movie."

Eagles manager **Irving Azoff** went a step further, telling *Rolling Stone* in November 1976 that Leber-Krebs was moving forward despite the band's "screaming objections."

The tangled mess had developed earlier in the year when the company optioned the movie rights to the album concept from Warner Bros., who had earlier secured them from Asylum's **David Geffen**. Managers for **Aerosmith** and **Ted Nugent**, Leber and Krebs

were riding a wave of success with a recent adaptation of *Jesus Christ Superstar* and had a **Beatles**-focused musical in pre-production, *Cashbox* reported at the time.

According to *Billboard,* **Ray Stark** would be executive producer of the proposed *Desperado* film, and Leber-Krebs even floated the idea of creating a companion rock opera for the stage. The Eagles wanted to go their own way, however, and at one point apparently considered writing their own original script. The process dragged on for "two or three years," Henley later confirmed, before the band finally had enough. "It might be better as an album," he said. "We might be better off to leave it as it is."

Finally, the Eagles sued Warner Bros., hoping to block the licensing of the so-called "grand rights" for theatrical broadcast, *Cashbox* reported. The band had already gone directly to Leber and Krebs with their complaints, Azoff said, but got nowhere.

"We totally rejected it," he told *Rolling Stone*. "Aesthetically, we don't think they're the right people to do it."

Leber painted a different picture, arguing that Azoff was initially interested, but then things allegedly changed as the Eagles grew closer to a pinnacle of commercial success with *Hotel California*.

"Two years ago, when the Eagles weren't as big, we told Azoff about our concept," Leber told *Rolling Stone* in 1976. "He told the Eagles and they were ecstatic. As they got bigger, Irving became less enthusiastic."

Leber-Krebs' *Beatlemania* ended up becoming a surprise smash, and they moved

267

continued on Page 275

HOTEL COVER SPARKS DECADES OF SPECULATION

Hotel California is about "the dark underbelly of the American dream and about excess in America," according to Don Henley. So, the band is not singing about an actual hotel. But the photo on the Eagles' album cover depicts the real-life Beverly Hills Hotel, located on Sunset Boulevard in the famously posh city west of the Sunset Strip.

When putting together the artwork, the band called upon art director [**John**] **Kosh**, whose previous credits included some of the most iconic classic rock records of all time, including *Abbey Road* and *Let it Be* (**The Beatles**), *Who's Next* (**The Who**), and *Get Yer Ya-Ya's Out!* (the **Rolling Stones**). How did the Eagles and this album cover luminary come together? Kosh said his connection with the band was probably a by-product of the extensive work for **Peter Asher** and **Linda Ronstadt**—four covers since 1975, and eventually twenty-four altogether.

The road to *Hotel California* proved a little uneven for Kosh. While his work was well known, he found it difficult to break into the clique of Los Angeles art directors and designers in the mid-1970s. "I was the cocky kid from London, you know?" he told *Time Passages*, adding that when work was elusive, he reached out to Asher, who he knew from England. "That led to Linda Ronstadt and **James Taylor**," he said. And then **Irving Azoff** and Don Henley came calling after the band wrapped production on the album in October 1976.

"I just got this phone call from Irving, and I was invited up to his office at Front Line Management on Sunset Strip to hear their record," he said. "The whole band was there, with Frey and Henley, of course, taking up the front."

Azoff dropped an acetate pre-production single of "Hotel California" on the turntable in his office,

and "it blew me away," Kosh remembered. "I just knew this was going to be a monster. I had no doubts."

Shortly after, Frey and Henley gathered with Kosh to plan out the album's imagery. They agreed the cover should have a hotel on it, so he and his photographer, **David Alexander**, were commissioned to get shots of three different hotels to capture a "sinister" feel that Henley wanted to achieve. The project would end up being the most expensive job Kosh was ever connected to, reportedly around $40,000, partly because Henley wanted "full-resolution comps" (mock-ups) of several hotels.

Alexander said the first attempt was made at the Green Hotel in Pasadena, which, he said, didn't produce the imagery they wanted. Azoff then suggested the Beverly Hills Hotel, but that presented the team with another problem because

local photographers knew well that the hotel did not allow commercial photography or movies to be filmed there. And if there wasn't a way to get the photo they needed on the premises, they resolved to go to a higher power—or at the very least, a higher vantage point.

"To get the perfect picture," Kosh told *Rolling Stone*, "David and I had perched nervously atop a 60-foot cherry picker dangling over Sunset Boulevard in the rush hour, shooting blindly into the [setting] sun."

He also mentioned he isn't even sure whether he or Alexander took the photo because both alternated shots, with each ducking down and allowing his back to be used as a "tripod" by the other cameraman.

"Both of us brought our Nikons up in the basket, and we took turns shooting, ducking, and reloading," Kosh remembered.

The final shot captured a grainy look that they were going for, though after the album's release, many people didn't initially recognize the source of the photo. "Very few people who even know the Beverly Hills Hotel knew that it was the Beverly Hills Hotel," Alexander recalled. Despite growing up in Los Angeles, the dramatic on-high visage of the hotel was new to Alexander. "Before going up in the cherry picker I had never seen the mission architecture of the building with the palm trees and the lights that came on as the sun was setting," he said.

Kosh was not sheepish about who deserved credit for the shoot. "I'd like to point out David deserves his full photo credit," he told *Time Passages*. "He was in full control and orchestrated the shoots for me, with his soon-to-be-famous assistant, **Aaron Rapoport**. It was a grand collaboration and a joy for us all to work together. We knew we had nailed

the front cover when the first frames of the Beverly Hills Hotel at sunset hit the lightbox."

Once they had the photo, they focused on the entire album package—the front and back covers, the inner sleeve, the poster, the disc label, and the marketing and promotional materials for print publications and record stores. He decided, as he had with *Abbey Road*, to keep the band's name off the cover, reasoning that for a band as big as the Eagles, that step wasn't necessary. "[Elektra/Asylum]'s marketing department were aghast," Kosh said, "forecasting a marketing disaster."

Another little-known fact about the album cover was that Kosh also personally drew the blue neon-ish "Hotel California" script. Variations on the script appeared through the album package and helped create a unifying theme. These touches were important to the design, but they still needed approval before going too far. A few weeks later,

Hotel California's album cover imagery was designed to depict people from all walks of life, and the band role-played for the **Norman Seeff** photo shoot in a hotel room (above) that became the album's inner poster.

they gathered again in Azoff's office, where a 4'x4' dye-transfer print of the front cover was exhibited. "The whole band was beaming," Kosh chuckled.

Then Henley and Kosh returned their attention to the rest of the album package. The back cover presented an empty hotel lobby, but not the Beverly Hills Hotel. Instead, they set up a photo shoot at the low-budget Lido Hotel on the corner of Yucca Street and Wilcox Avenue in Hollywood to capture a darker perspective. The back cover was cast in an eerie yellow-orange glow of an empty hotel lobby, with just a solitary janitor leaning against a mop in an entranceway off in the distance.

The mysterious gatefold featured a photo of the hotel lobby filled with an assortment of characters seemingly out of central casting. The band stands in the center of the spread, surrounded by people seemingly "captured" by the hotel. In the foreground, a red-suited bellhop leans against a table as two men to his right whisper in the shadows. A perhaps-actress, martini glass in hand, with a low-cut dress and boa, stares suggestively. There's a pimp in a white, wide-lapelled suit and a wide-brimmed hat standing in the background. In the archways above, a nondescript figure—which some incorrectly insisted was Church of Satan leader **Anton LaVey**—peers hauntingly down at the scene below. The scene emits a spooky aura; the Overlook Hotel from **Stephen King**'s *The Shining* had a similarly eerie vibe.

That was the illusion they wanted. Kosh said the photo was simply the band surrounded by friends in the "cleverly redecorated flop house [the Lido]

in Hollywood" that Alexander assembled. "Our combined rock and roll friends were all invited."

Kosh left the setup to Alexander, who fondly remembered the day.

"There were roughly 120 people," Alexander told *Time Passages*. "I positioned them either in groups or one at a time, starting with the foreground people." He explained that the group of people on the left foreground were friends of the Eagles, while the people at the check-in counter were people he had cast and costumed.

"The only person I sort of knew a bit further back in the picture was the comedian **Milton Berle**'s brother," Alexander said. "Other than those, as I recall, we just put out the word among different groups of people who would represent a *Hotel California* social picture. The two guys on the left foreground in shadow in the white and black one-piece jump-suits just happened to be at the Lido and I stuck them in. The woman in the balcony bent over, extending her spirit over the room was

a famous model whose name I don't remember. She heard about this project and showed up. People just showed up, dressed the way they did—impromptu *Hotel California*. It was fantastic. My assistants and I spent the day lighting the space so we could just plug people in, not sure who or how many would be there. It was all pretty fun."

After countless delays, the album was finally released December 8, 1976; a few weeks later, Glenn Frey and Don Henley met with *Sounds* magazine's **Barbara Charone**, and Frey tied the song's lyrics to the cover's imagery.

"'Hotel California'...starts out with a kinda glamour as the song opens up," Frey said. "The song starts out where it's all beautiful. The hills, the L.A. Basin...then when ya examine it closer ya see the decadence. I mean the album packaging is like that, too. Something that at one time was elegant but now is decadent. See this lobby [pointing to the album cover]...just when you think it's beautiful you see this goddamn paneling over

The back cover of *Hotel California* album cover was designed to show the more pedestrian, after-the-party feeling that set it apart from the more recognized gatefold images arranged by album designer **Kosh** and photographer **David Alexander**.

here and the cheapest chandeliers in the world next to a couple of nice ones."

The band and the label loved the cover, but the Beverly Hills Hotel was not pleased. According to Kosh, the hotel was "irate" about it. They tried to sue, but Kosh said Azoff pointed out that the hotel's bookings had gone through the roof since the album was released. When recounting the story in a documentary highlighting his most famous works, Kosh recalled Azoff saying, "'Wait a minute, I just looked at your books, and you've had, like, a 35-percent increase in clientele since this album came out!'" Faced with that reality, the hotel allegedly dropped the lawsuit. More than 40 years later, the Beverly Hills Hotel remains the photo on the cover of the celebrated album.

Kosh said he was proud of his *Hotel* work and only regrets that the label "forgot" to submit it for a Grammy. "Weird, right?" Kosh said sarcastically. "I think there was some resentment for this cocky kid. I was the new kid in town, and the creative department at Asylum was kind of pissed off that I'm spending so much money, which, of course, mattered not when you sell 26 million copies by Wednesday."

That snub aside, Kosh still left with Grammy hardware that year. He was also the art director for Linda Ronstadt's *Simple Dreams*, which won the statuette. If *Hotel* had been submitted and won, Kosh would have shared the award with Henley, who received top billing as an art director in the album credits.

EAGLES   7E-1084

Henley said he wanted a collection of people from all walks of life for the gatefold. He wanted people on the edge, people on the fringes of society. He got what he asked for and then some. The effectiveness of the shoot was so profound, it spawned decades of speculation and rumors from fans and critics alike.

Snopes.com has a page dedicated to the album and its murky cover. Some of the ridiculous rumors spawned by the band's masterwork include:

• The song is about a Christian church abandoned in 1969 (a reference to not having that spirit here since 1969), and taken over by an occult group, "The Hotel of California"; debunked.

• Anton LaVey is pictured in the gatefold picture's top balcony with arms spread; debunked.

• Some or all of the Eagles were either heavily involved with the occult or were disciples of LaVey; debunked.

• The album photographs were taken in or around LaVey's headquarters for his Church of Satan; debunked.

• The song is about **Aleister Crowley**'s mansion near Loch Ness, and its lyrics point to weird occurrences that supposedly happened there (including reference to Crowley's nickname, "The Beast;"); debunked.

• The song is a reference to the Camarillo State Hospital, a state-run psychiatric hospital northwest of Los Angeles near Oxnard that was allegedly nicknamed "the Hotel California"; debunked.

• The janitor leaning on a mop in the lobby on the back cover was the propped-up corpse of a dead man; debunked.

"Hotel California" speaks to the culture of success, and wealth, and the self-destruction that comes with it, Henley said in an interview with *60 Minutes*. By this time, the Eagles were writing from first-hand experience. [2056, 2057, 2058, 2060, 2102, 2103, 2129]

on from the proposed *Desperado* project. So did the Eagles, who would soon be dumping untold time and financial investment into completing their next album as Leber and Krebs became the toast of Broadway.

"If we're going to pursue our musical careers, we don't have the time to sit down and write [a film]," Henley admitted. "Glenn [Frey] and I would love to...because God knows there aren't that many good screenplay writers in Hollywood. Most of them are hacks."

Henley believed the financial stakes were too high—that really hit home during sessions for *The Long Run*. "It takes a lot more money to make a movie than it does to make an album, though we're catching up with that," Henley added, with a laugh.

The notion of *Desperado* attached to a film project did not end with Leber-Krebs. In the mid-1980s, NBC President **Brandon Tartikoff** got behind a made-for-television movie based on an original screenplay by **Elmore Leonard**.

Envisioned as a backdoor pilot for a TV series, the film was originally titled *Duell McCall*. But Tartikoff suggested renaming it *Desperado* and acquiring the music rights from the Eagles for the theme. The band gave that project the green light, and the movie aired in April 1987.

The anticipated TV series never materialized; NBC commissioned four additional TV movies in 1988-1989 before sending *Desperado* out to pasture. [664, 665, 1820, 2001, 2002, 2052]

HOTEL CALIFORNIA

If *One of These Nights* turned Eagles into arena headliners, a huge-selling greatest hits album followed by the multi-platinum *Hotel California* elevated them to the stadium circuit. They had become America's biggest rock band. But constant touring and the pressure to one-up themselves would eventually exact a price on their personal, creative, and professional relationships.

WINTER 1976-77

 RELEASES
- ▶ **Eagles**, "New Kid in Town" (single)
- ▶ **Eagles**, *Hotel California* (album)
- ▶ **The Bernie Leadon-Michael Georgiades Band**, *Natural Progressions* (album)
- ▶ **Eagles**, "Hotel California" (single)

 NUGGETS
- ▶ Eagles played Purdue University on Joe Walsh's birthday and led a "Happy Birthday" to Walsh, complete with miner's hats with twirling lights on each helmet. —*Cashbox*
- ▶ Eagles' *Hotel California* went platinum in just two weeks. —*Cashbox/RIAA*
- ▶ Record and Tape shops in Missouri, Indiana, and Kentucky are holding a special promotion for *Hotel California*. One of 125 albums in each store has a hotel key attached that opens a door to the rest of the Eagles' catalog and other assorted E/A LPs. They are also giving away ashtrays. —*Cashbox*
- ▶ Eagles' leadoff single, "New Kid in Town," was leaked to RKO Radio by an E/A employee and the label was forced to rush-release the single. —*Cashbox*
- ▶ "New Kid in Town" is the most active single in the nation for four straight weeks. —*Record World*
- ▶ Eagles' *Hotel California* and **Paul McCartney**'s *Wings Over America* were released simultaneously and collectively knock **Stevie Wonder**'s *Songs in the Key of Life* off the top of the charts. —*Record World*
- ▶ **Phil Walden** said **Irving Azoff** registered Republican and ordered new lifts for his elevators after Walden's "short" slur. —*Record World*
- ▶ Led by enormous sales from Eagles' *Their Greatest Hits (1971-1975)* and *Hotel California*, Elektra/Asylum destroyed sales records in the Christmas season. —*Cashbox*

 COLLABORATIONS
- ▶ **Bernie Leadon** provided backing vocals on **Linda Ronstadt**'s album *Simple Dreams*.

 AWARDS
- ▶ **Eagles, 4th Annual American Music Awards:**
  - ● Favorite Pop/Rock Album, *Eagles: Their Greatest Hits (1971-1975)*, winner. Also nominated: **Peter Frampton**, *Frampton Comes Alive!* and **Stevie Wonder**, *Songs in the Key of Life*.
  - ● Favorite Pop/Rock Band/Duo/Group, nominated. Lost to **Chicago**. Also nominated: **Earth, Wind & Fire**.

Leaked: RKO Radio Chain Pushes 'New Kid' One Week Early

When the Eagles wrapped up production on *Hotel California* in the fall of 1976, they decided "New Kid in Town" would be the first single out of the chute, days ahead of the album in December.

The band, along with **J.D. Souther**, concluded its road schedule with a series of November dates in the Midwest. As the tour wound down, Elektra/Asylum was warming up its promotional machine for a big holiday season. *Hotel California* and **Jackson Browne**'s *The Pretender* were going to be centerpieces of the label's Christmas push. They expected sales to be strong, and for good reason.

One of These Nights was a monster album for the band, and "Lyin' Eyes," "Take It to the Limit," and the title cut were still getting strong airplay on Top 40 radio and album-oriented rock stations. The band and E/A were also excited about the forthcoming follow-up; anticipation had been steadily building over the summer and fall, and the label kept dropping hints in the press and on radio to stoke the fire for the release.

Producer **Bill Szymczyk** finally got the album out of the studio, and E/A queued up "New Kid in Town" for a December 2 release. Then "New Kid" mysteriously got played on the radio on November 27, a full week early. Press reports didn't say where, but Eagles Manager **Irving Azoff** said an Elektra employee had leaked the single to the RKO Radio chain and the song got prematurely aired.

As a result, Elektra/Asylum scrambled to rush-release the single across the country. E/A President **Mel Posner** signed off on the rush-release but denied it was an Elektra employee who leaked the song. It was not the end of the world in Posner's view, who said "there was no real problem on the situation."

Did the added drama do anything for the single? Certainly not as much as great Eagles' songwriting, but it may have helped with initial playlist adds on radio. A week later, one-fourth of all *Cashbox*-reporting radio stations had added "New Kid" to their playlists, including major markets like KLIF-Dallas, CKLW-Detroit, WMPS-Memphis, and WPIX-New York, making it the most added song in the country. "New Kid" entered the *Cashbox* chart at #57, and a week later it debuted on *Billboard*'s Hot 100 chart at #48. By the end of February, it was *Billboard*'s #1.

Was there really a pilfered single that caused the kerfuffle? Perhaps, but more likely it was a marketing ploy.

"[Leaking] releases was a common marketing tool back in the day," said **Rip Pelley**, former E/A promotion and artist development exec. "Sure, occasionally a tape got swiped from a studio and a non-planned leak occurred, but we used that tactic all the time with major artists—particularly in key breakout markets that housed a 'chain' radio station that could trigger five or six major adds."

With stations in all the major markets, RKO fit that bill. But however the "leak" happened, it further fueled the *Hotel California* launch, and few in either camp could complain about that. [653, 1775, 2007]

Ian Anderson Hears Familiar Chord Sequence in 'Hotel'

When **Ian Anderson**, the vocalist and primary composer for British progressive rockers **Jethro Tull**, first heard "Hotel California," he believed the song's now-legendary chord progression sounded similar to one of his own. If one were to dig up a copy of Tull's 1969 album *Stand Up*, the listener would find a composition in 3/4 meter called "We Used to Know" that features the same chord structure.

While every situation is different, the moral implications of creating a piece of musical art reminiscent of another often comes down to intent. Was an artist intentionally stealing a lick, progression, or melody? Was the writer looking to build upon it as an homage to a beloved song? Or do chance occurrences just happen because every songwriter is working with the same twelve notes that form the foundation of music in the Western world?

When listening to the pop and harmonic craftsmanship of **The Beatles** or the root-sy sounds of the first wave of country-rock bands like **Poco** or the **Flying Burrito Brothers**, it's indisputable that the Eagles, like all groups, was a band inspired by others that came before them.

But Jethro Tull? A band whose stylings were an eclectic mix of blues, classical, hard rock, and jazzy flute? It's difficult to make the connection between the band that gave the world "Take It Easy" and "Desperado" and the prog-rock band most famous for "Thick as a Brick" and "Aqualung," and infamous as the first band to win the newly established heavy metal Grammy in 1989, curiously beating **Metallica**.

While the Eagles may not have cut their songwriting teeth by listening to old Jethro Tull records, the composer of "We Used to Know" offered another theory as to how the Eagles may have ended up reusing the chordal hook. He suggested the tune had gotten into the band's collective head when they were upstarts supporting Jethro Tull on their *Thick as a Brick* tour in 1972.

"Maybe it's just something that they picked up on subconsciously and introduced that chord sequence into their famous song 'Hotel California' sometime later," Anderson mused. It sounds like a logical theory, but it's unlikely, as the "Hotel California" chord progression was blueprinted by Don Felder, who was not a member of the Eagles when they toured with Tull.

When asked about the similarity, Felder said he had no knowledge of Tull's "We Used to Know" when he produced his "Mexican Reggae" demo, with the chord progression that became "Hotel California." All he really knew about Jethro Tull was the band had a lead singer who played the flute.

Anderson himself recognized the disparity between the two bands' styles and even said Jethro Tull and the Eagles did not interact a whole lot when they toured. "They were countrified, laid-back polite rock and we were a bit wacky and English and doing weird stuff," he said. "I don't think they much liked us, and we didn't like them."

He insisted that, over the years, whenever he spoke of the Eagles borrowing his work, he did so with his tongue firmly in cheek: "It's not plagiarism. It's just the same chord sequence," he explained. "It's in a different time signature, different key, different context. And it's a very, very fine

> **IT'S NOT PLAGIARISM. IT'S JUST THE SAME CHORD SEQUENCE. IT'S IN A DIFFERENT TIME SIGNATURE, DIFFERENT KEY, DIFFERENT CONTEXT. AND IT'S A VERY, VERY FINE SONG THEY WROTE, SO I CAN'T FEEL ANYTHING BUT HAPPINESS FOR THEIR SAKE.**
>
> **— IAN ANDERSON**

continued on Page 279

RELEASE
Early December
1976

NEW KID IN TOWN

By: J.D. Souther, Don Henley, Glenn Frey
Side B: Victim of Love (Felder, Souther, Henley, Frey)

Don Henley pitched this song to reporters as a single with two "play sides," believing that "New Kid" and "Victim of Love" were both radio friendly. It had been more than a year since the Eagles had released a single, and radio and the music-buying public were hungry for new material. *One of These Nights* set a high bar, and "New Kid" met that challenge and then some. It took off like a rocket. The track was a polished, meaningful melodic ballad that showcased the band's maturity as songwriters, performers, and recording artists.

AIRPLAY

"New Kid" got an artificially fast start when the RKO Radio chain began playing the single nearly a week before its scheduled release date. Elektra/Asylum claimed it was forced to rush-release it, and radio stations nationwide picked it up immediately. The "rush" was likely marketing bluster, but the release provided fresh music to program directors eager to spin new Eagles material. While the band's past singles were gradual risers, this one was different. Their typical two-to-three month glide path to the major and secondary markets was reduced to about 45 days.

135 PLAYLIST ADDS Winter 1976-77			
Region	**Dec**	**Jan**	**Regional Airplay**
Northeast	18	2	14.8%
Southeast	37	4	30.4%
Midwest	28	8	26.7%
Southwest	11	3	10.4%
West	21	3	17.8%

FIRST-WAVE STATIONS Stations that added the song in the first 30 days

KEZI-Anaheim	WZUU-Milwaukee	WCFL-Chicago	WRFC-Athens
KHJ-Los Angeles	WIRL-Peoria	WIXY-Cleveland	WRKO-Boston
KROY, KNDE-Sacramento	WCUE-Akron	KOIL-Omaha	WRKS-New York
KJRB-Spokane	WCOL-Columbus	KKLS-Rapid City, SD	WPEZ-Pittsburgh
KING, KJR, KRKO-Seattle	KQWB-Fargo	KEWI-Topeka	WPIX-New York City
KLIV-San Jose			
KYA, KFRC-San Francisco	KRKE-Albuquerque	WZGC, WQXI, WBBQ,	WQPD-Lakeland, FL
KRSP-Salt Lake City	KELI, KAKC-Tulsa	WSGN-Birmingham	WMPS-Memphis
KCBQ-San Diego	KNUS, KLIF-Dallas	WTMA-Charleston, SC	WERC-Birmingham
KSLY-San Luis Obispo	KILT-Houston	WFLB-Fayetteville, NC	WAKY-Louisville

CHARTS

Billboard
 # 1
February 26, 1977

Cashbox
 # 2
February 26, 1977

Record World
 # 3
February 19, 1977

HIGHEST CHARTING WEEK: BILLBOARD - February 26, 1977

SINGLE	ARTIST	PREV WK
1. NEW KID IN TOWN	**EAGLES**	2
2. Love Theme from "A Star is Born"	Barbara Streisand	4
3. Blinded by the Light	Manfred Mann's Earth Band	1
4. Fly Like an Eagle	Steve Miller	8
5. I Like Dreamin'	Kenny Nolan	5
6. Enjoy Yourself	The Jacksons	6
7. Torn Between Two Lovers	Mary MacGregor	3
8. Night Moves	Bob Seger	10
9. Dancing Queen	ABBA	14
10. Weekend in New England	Barry Manilow	11

Sources: Billboard, Cashbox, Record World

EAGLES EYE THEIR REPLACEMENTS WITH 'NEW KID'

Eagles had just scored their first #1 album with the quadruple-platinum *One of These Nights*, along with two straight chart-topping singles: the record's title track and "The Best of My Love" from the previous LP. They finally made it to the top.

Inevitably, they began thinking about when it all might end. "New Kid in Town" crystallized around the doom-filled notion that fame never lasts.

"We were writing about our replacements," co-author and long time collaborator **J.D. Souther** told Songfacts.com in 2011.

Souther had handed the Eagles part of the idea that grew into "New Kid in Town." They immediately saw it as more than an obvious surface allegory about losing a girl.

"It's about the fleeting, fickle nature of love and romance," Henley said in the liner notes to *The Very Best of the Eagles*. "It's also about the fleeting nature of fame, especially in the music business. We were already chronicling our own demise. We were basically saying, 'Look, we know we're red hot now, but we also know that somebody's going to come along and replace us—both in music and in love.'"

Over the years, there has been speculation over whether there was a particular artist that inspired Henley, Souther, and Frey to write "New Kid"—including, among others, **Bruce Springsteen**, who had finally arrived the year before with *Born to Run*. Souther flatly denied any connection with Spring-

steen, but Joe Walsh suggested that other artists were at least on the periphery of the "New Kid" inspirations.

"**Hall & Oates** had just put out 'Sara Smile,'" Walsh said during the *Record Plant Diaries Project* session for *Hotel California* in March 2019. "Daryl Hall was the 'new kid,' because that song just went, boom—#1, and just parked there on the charts. Everybody said, 'Who are these guys?' When there's a new kid in town, everybody pays attention—until there's another one. That's how that song came around."

The track found a home on an album that looked deeply into their current situation as veteran rock stars amid the excesses of 1970s-era Los Angeles. But in some ways, Souther said, its genesis predated the band's current project, *Hotel California*, going back to the Old West themes they had explored on *Desperado*.

"'New Kid' emerged from our whole fascination with gunfighters as an analogy," Souther told Songfacts.com. "The point was, at some point some kid would come riding into town that was much faster than you and he'd say so, and then he'd prove it."

Things were no different in their careers, or in their lives. "There's a lot other guys like you and gals like you that want the same thing that are coming up," Souther added, "and they want their moment, too, and they're going to get it—and it's fine. It's as it should be." [1810, 1910, 1912]

Eagles Deliver a Masterwork In Platinum-Shipping *Hotel*

Just as **John Lennon** and **Paul McCartney** possessed an uncanny feel for changes in popular culture in England that was reflected in their music, Glenn Frey and Don Henley also instinctively knew when to adapt their sound for the times.

By the mid-1970s, country-rock had peaked. **Gram Parsons** was dead. **Poco** and the **Flying Burrito Brothers** could not get beyond their small but rabid cult followings. **Michael Nesmith** had given up on his groundbreaking **First National Band** concept and moved to producing multimedia projects. The musical driving force of the late 1960s and early 1970s was evolving.

Bernie Leadon, the Eagles' most direct musical connection to country, recognized the

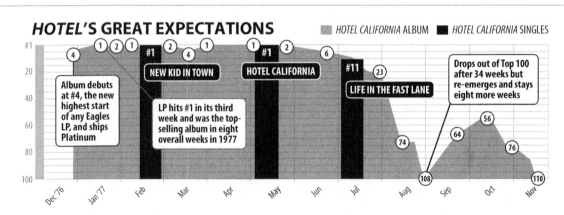

HOTEL'S GREAT EXPECTATIONS

HOTEL CALIFORNIA ALBUM   ■ HOTEL CALIFORNIA SINGLES

- **Album debuts at #4, the new highest start of any Eagles LP, and ships Platinum**
- **NEW KID IN TOWN** — LP hits #1 in its third week and was the top-selling album in eight overall weeks in 1977
- **HOTEL CALIFORNIA**
- **LIFE IN THE FAST LANE**
- **Drops out of Top 100 after 34 weeks but re-emerges and stays eight more weeks**

Each of the Eagles' preceding albums debuted on *Billboard*'s Top LPs & Tapes chart in a higher position than the one before it. *Hotel California* landed at #4 in its first week and, unsurprisingly, shipped with platinum status. *Hotel* bounced around the Top 5 for three months before putting a six-week stranglehold on #1 from late March to mid-May 1977. Along the way, it was booted from #1 by both **Paul McCartney**'s group **Wings** (*Wings Over America*) and **Barbra Streisand** (*A Star is Born* soundtrack), but the Eagles finally wrested the top spot from Streisand to launch its six-week #1 ride. **Fleetwood Mac**'s *Rumours* knocked it from its final week at #1 on May 14.
Sources: Billboard, Recording Industry Association of America

BILLBOARD TOP LPs & TAPE, January 15, 1976

1. **EAGLES, *HOTEL CALIFORNIA***
2. Stevie Wonder, *Songs in the Key of Life*
3. Paul McCartney and Wings, *Wings Over America*
4. Boston, *Boston*
5. Electric Light Orchestra, *A New World Record*
6. Doobie Brothers, *Best of the Doobies*
7. Peter Frampton, *Frampton Comes Alive!*
8. Linda Ronstadt, *Greatest Hits*
9. Steve Miller Band, *Fly Like an Eagle*
10. Rod Stewart, *A Night on the Town*

change his bandmates were looking for, particularly after adding Don Felder on guitar, which contributed to Leadon's exit a year later. With Joe Walsh's immediate recruitment, the band had more tools to take the next album in a new musical direction.

Henley also had his eye on something much more ambitious. Ahead of the album's release, Henley told *ZigZag* magazine that *Hotel California* was "a concept album, there's no way to hide it, but it's not set in the Old West, the cowboy thing, you know. It's more urban this time..."

If there was a musical purity and naïveté on an album like their debut album, *Eagles*, the band, now with Joe Walsh in tow, had found a more cynical, analytical voice.

Even the overall sound, while still very Eagles-like, had traded Leadon's folksy charm for a tougher, Walsh-infused guitar tone. Derided in later years for investing too much painstaking detail into the recording process, the Eagles, with producer **Bill Szymczyk** steering the ship, managed to strike the balance between inspiration and perspiration just right on *Hotel California*. The overall sound was polished, but never so much that the emotional essence of a song was diluted by too many takes and or excessive overdubs. Eight months in the studio was the longest time the band ever spent in the studio, though it would seem quite fast compared to their next LP. Szymczyk's efforts on *Hotel* earned him a Grammy nomination for Producer of the Year.

The album perfectly encapsulated the California sound of the mid-1970s, a dynamic fusion of folk, blues, and rock and roll, with no single genre

ELEKTRA/ASYLUM INSIDER

THE ADDITION OF JOE WALSH'S TALENT COMBINED with Bill Szymczyk's production skills took the already super-talented Eagles to another peak that was seldom seen in the music business. Not only was *Hotel California* a career-making album, it gave the entire band a place in history as one of the biggest selling groups in America—and arguably the world.

"New Kid" was pretty much a unanimous choice for the first single. It garnered incredible airplay and audience acceptance. But AOR went heavily on the "Hotel" cut, as well, which had a tremendous groundswell, and the group was demanding that it be released as the second single. It wasn't the song that held us back, it was the six-minute run time. And the group once again wouldn't permit any radio edits. Six minutes was a format anchor, but at E/A we succeeded a few years back by getting airplay for Queen's 5-minute, 55-second long "Bohemian Rhapsody"—which I also broke out of Detroit—so here we go again...and it worked this time too. "Hotel California" became a worldwide smash.

After three days on my honeymoon in the Hilton Head sun with my new bride, I got a call from **Jerry Sharell**. "Sorry buddy, the Eagles want you on the *Hotel* tour, so get your ass back here and then head to Houston." You can only imagine how that went over.

—Rip Pelley, former National Director of Artist Development and Promotion, Elektra/Asylum Records

dominating the mix. The title track, the epic cinematic Eagles tour de force, saw the band at their finest—lyrically, vocally, and musically. It also set the tone for Henley and Frey's lyrical exploration of what they saw happening around them just then. It was beautiful, haunting, and energizing, and reflected on a trek Henley would later describe as a "journey from innocence to experience."

Sometimes lost among the collection of great songs on this album is Randy Meisner's "Try and Love Again," which was the first song the band completed in the studio. Meisner, soon to leave the band, reminded older fans of the original Eagles sound with the track. Lyrically, it touched a nerve with lines like:

"Right or wrong, what's done is done
It's only moments that you borrow
but the thoughts will linger on

Meisner had the sole writing credit on the single, though he said Joe Walsh helped him complete it, and Frey and Henley helped provide polish as well.

Don Felder chipped in with "Victim of Love," based on a guitar riff he gave to Henley and Frey. And while Felder said he was promised a lead vocal on the track (Henley has suggested no such promise was made to his recollection), Henley's version was so good that Felder was left to concede that the song was better that way.

Henley and Frey also collaborated on "The Last Resort," which Frey would later dub "Henley's Opus." Written about the perils of unchecked commerce and develop-

ment, it connected the notion of "Manifest Destiny" that arose in the mid-1800s with the then-prominent suburban sprawl of the mid-1970s, which has continued unabated into the 2020s. The song's lyrics track the spread of growth across some of the nation's sacred and beautiful landscapes, following a path that Henley starts in Providence ("the one in Rhode Island") "to the great divide" and then, later, to Lahaina, Hawaii. Then he laid the responsibility at the feet of "progress" and, more precisely, developers:

"Some rich men came and raped the land
Nobody caught 'em
Put up a bunch of ugly boxes
And Jesus people bought 'em"

Frey's vocals shone impressively on "New Kid in Town," a song he co-wrote with Henley and **J.D. Souther** that contemplated who might replace them among the newcomers in rock and roll.

The most un-Eagles track at that point was the raucous "Life in the Fast Lane," with its searing guitar, courtesy of Joe Walsh. It was a track the band would likely never have created with Leadon. This was a more aggressive Eagles—a rockier Eagles—and fans and critics loved the new sound.

Has any song begun so evocatively of a time and place than "Hotel California" did with the opening line?

"On a dark, desert highway
Cool wind in my hair
Warm smell of colitas
Rising up through the air

And just where was this mystical, mythical hotel where people could check out any time they liked, but they could never leave, capturing the listener's imagination? Henley and Frey wrote the lyrics intending them to be vague and wide open to interpretation, and listeners read all kinds of crazy things into them. But the words were simply the duo's poetic reportage of the crazy world they inhabited.

As Henley told **Gayle King** of *CBS News* in 2016: "It's about the dark underbelly of the American dream. It's about excess, it's about narcissism. It's about the music business. It's about a lot of different... It can have a million interpretations."

Hotel California became a commercial and cultural phenomenon. The LP entered the *Billboard* album chart at #4 in December 1976, and after hitting the top spot in four weeks, it parked there for a couple of months. The album sold almost six million copies in its first year of release and spawned two #1 singles, "Hotel California" and "New Kid in Town."

In 2003, *Rolling Stone* magazine ranked *Hotel California* at #37 on its list of the best 500 albums of all time. According to the RIAA's most recent tally, it is also the band's second all-time biggest-selling album in the United States at 26 million copies (just behind *Their Greatest Hits (1971-1975)* at 38 million copies).

Creatively, though, the album remains the Eagles' finest musical achievement, a sentiment Henley echoed when talking to *USA Today*'s **Bob Doerschuk** in 2020. "Every band has its creative peak... We had the musicianship. We were willing to make some changes and take some risks and try to do something different from anything we'd done before." [1550, 1820, 2050, 2051]

Chicago Sun-Times
January 1, 1977

The new Eagles album, *Hotel California*, takes the band's predilection for combining beautiful music and sordid subject matter to the limit. The album is built around the theme of sorts: life in Southern California. As usual, their lyrics are impeccable. Henley and Frey turn phrases like no other songwriters practicing today, but they aren't hung up on hooks. They are telling cautionary stories, but the music keeps telling us that if we take heed, there's hope.

– Al Rudis

Circus
March 17, 1977

I'm willing to believe these guys are trying. I'm just glad I'm not buying. *Hotel California* is weary, it's loaded with sermons about Hollywood's rat race, and its gloom is not particularly attractive. The title cut is a second-rate mystery nightmare worthy of a Satan-cult episode on *Kraft Suspense Theater*. Gold stars to the guy who came up with "she was terminally pretty" and "they pay heavenly bills." How many times can you indict your lifestyle before you're finally guilty?

– Stephen Demorest

Sounds
December 1976

Track rundowns are a waste of time really—it's difficult to avoid old clichés about "trading licks" and "delicate polyrhythmic pattern." But the scam is this: there are no weak tracks. Styles vary from quiet rural to burning city sound. Joe Walsh fits ideally and the music flows majestically. *Hotel California* heralds a new lease on life for the Eagles. Forget *One of These Nights*. Remember the band for what they are–one of the finest groups to emerge from this or any other decade.

– Tim Lott

song that they wrote, so I can't feel anything other than happiness for their sake, and I feel flattered they came across that chord sequence. It's difficult to find a chord sequence that hasn't been used and hasn't been the focus of lots of pieces of music. Harmonic progression—it's almost a mathematical certainty that you're gonna crop up with the same thing sooner or later if you're strumming a few chords on a guitar." [1952, 1953, 1997, 1998]

SPRING 1977

 RELEASES
- ▶ **Poco**, with Timothy B. Schmit, "Indian Summer" (single)
- ▶ **Poco**, with Timothy B. Schmit, *Indian Summer* (album)
- ▶ **Eagles**, "Life in the Fast Lane" (single)

 NUGGETS
- ▶ Fans in Cleveland braved the freezing weather to buy tickets for the upcoming Eagles concert. **Irving Azoff** rewarded them by personally serving hot coffee while they waited. —*Cashbox*
- ▶ Eagles perform their East Coast tour opener at Madison Square Garden and the huge after-party included **Faye Dunaway**, **Linda Ronstadt**, **Mick Jagger**, **Ron Wood** (who had joined the Eagles onstage for **Chuck Berry**'s "Carol"), **Paul Simon**, **Daryl Hall** and **John Oates**, and *SNL*'s **John Belushi** and **Dan Aykroyd**. —*Cashbox*
- ▶ Eagles make the cover of *Crawdaddy* magazine with a seven-page feature on the completion of *Hotel California* and how life is different for the band. —*Crawdaddy*
- ▶ Glenn Frey, Don Henley, and Tim Schmit will provide backing vocals for **Steely Dan**'s title cut to the movie *FM*, "FM (No Static at All)." —*Record World*

 COLLABORATIONS
- ▶ **Joe Walsh** played guitar and provided "scat vocals" on the song "L.A. Nights" on **Emerson, Lake & Palmer**'s album *Works (Volume 1)*.
- ▶ **Bernie Leadon** produced the singles "The Joke's on Me" and "(What a) Wonderful World" on **David Bromberg**'s album *Out of the Blues: The Best of David Bromberg*.
- ▶ **Don Henley** (harmony vocals) and **Joe Walsh** (rhythm guitar) provided support on **Dan Fogelberg**'s album *Nether Lands*.
- ▶ **Bernie Leadon** was a "musician" on **Helen Reddy**'s album *Ear Candy*.
- ▶ **Joe Walsh** played guitar on **Andy Gibb**'s album *Flowing Rivers*.

 ON THE ROAD WITH ...
- ▶ **Eagles**: Carl Perkins, Dan Fogelberg, Elton John, Jimmy Buffett, Valerie Carter
- ▶ **Poco**, with Timothy B. Schmit: Commander Cody, ZZ Top

Classic *Hotel California* Concert Shot in Landover, Maryland

"Good evening. We're the Eagles from Los Angeles," Glenn Frey announced two songs into the band's opening night on a two-show stop near the nation's capital in March 1977. Frey's signature line made the Eagles sound like a new band, but against the backdrop of "Hotel California," the title track of their latest album, already a multi-million-seller, they needed no introduction.

When Eagles fans search YouTube for classic Eagles concert clips, the footage that most often appears is from the now-demolished Capital Centre in Landover, Maryland (known then as Largo), just outside Washington, D.C. There is the youthful Frey, his sunglasses arched back on the top of his head like he just stepped off a plane, his wavy curls dangling down over his black University of Colorado t-shirt. Don Felder is in plaid flannel and Joe Walsh is wearing his signature bandana and a t-shirt emblazoned "Telluride," a nod to the Colorado ski resort.

The spunky Walsh followed Frey's introduction by barking out his own public service announcement to the raucous crowd: "I tell you what. If you've got firecrackers, save 'em until you get home, lock yourself in a closet, and light everything you got, okay?" The impromptu remarks amused a smiling Don Felder and Frey said, "Thank you, Joe."

Director **Victoria Hochberg** filmed the twenty-one-song concert in 16mm on March 21 that year, and eight songs were included in the 2013 documentary *History of the Eagles*.

Eagles' road manager **Richard Fernandez** remembers the night vividly—and the pressure for the band to perform at its best.

"The one thing about everybody in this band, they were all pros, you know," he said in an interview with *Time Passages*. "They knew what they had to do, and they knew they had to deliver. When I saw them go in front of a large crowd in Holland for the first time at a festival, they were biting at the bit to get out there, all four of them. And they went out there and they nailed it."

The film shows the versatility of the band in its interchangeable formats. After an interlocking guitar duel between Felder and Walsh on "Hotel California," Walsh slides over to electric keys for "New Kid in Town" and then to acoustic guitar one song later on "Take It to the Limit." Frey plays piano against Felder's underlying R&B guitar licks during "One of These Nights." With three acoustic guitars (Frey, Henley, and Walsh), and four voices, Felder lays down some aching pedal steel lines that frame "The Best of My Love."

In speaking with *Time Passages*, Fernandez remembered talking to the crew to prepare for the shoot.

"The most important thing was getting the shots," he said. "We don't want to mess up anything sound-wise or with the band. Whether somebody trips over an amp now when he's onstage trying to film or something, we don't need that. Basically, it's just creating boundaries where normally, if you're not filming, you wouldn't have to create these boundaries."

Don Felder took viewers behind the scenes in Landover in his book *Heaven and Hell*.

"In the movie, there's one part on the final cut where Joe and I are standing toe-to-toe playing the two main guitar parts in 'Hotel California,'" he wrote. "Joe's wearing a bandana on his head. I say something to him, he looks at me, and we start laughing uncontrollably. Scores of people have asked me what it was I said to him that night. Well, what I actually said was, 'Hey buddy, you're showing,' pretending that he had a white powder ring around his nostrils, captured forever on film. He didn't but he thought he did, so he said, 'Oh, am I?' which set us off laughing."

After a tantalizing Felder/Walsh guitar intro during "Rocky Mountain Way," Frey

continued on Page 291

A smoggy morning view of the Griffith Park Observatory, looking south over the Los Angeles basin.

'THE LAST RESORT' PUTS PROGRESS IN CROSSHAIRS

Don Henley has made protecting the environment one of his most consistent personal goals. The biggest early hint at this lifetime passion was in the song "The Last Resort," his album-closing lament on *Hotel California*.

"'The Last Resort'... is still one of my favorite songs," Don Henley told *Rolling Stone* in 1978. "The gist of the song was that when we find something good, we destroy it by our presence—by the very fact that man is the only animal on earth that is capable of destroying his environment."

"The Last Resort" is sweeping in scope, even as Henley conveys his fears about the natural world's fate in fine detail. He begins in Providence, Rhode Island, site of the first non-Indigenous settlement established in 1636 by **Roger Williams**, then travels across the country to witness the ensuing destruction of the continent's native culture. The song finally arrives in Lahaina on the once idyllic, now overly commercialized Hawaiian Islands.

Frey called this the final piece of what he described as "the *Hotel California* puzzle. We started the song early in the record, and Don finished seven months later," he later said to **Cameron Crowe**. "I called it 'Henley's Opus.'"

A theme of movement—echoing the concept of "manifest destiny" as advanced by journalist **John L. Sullivan** in the 1830s and '40s—was key to developing the song, Frey noted. "One of the primary themes of the song was that we keep creating what we've been running away from— violence, chaos, destruction," he told Crowe. "We migrated to the East Coast, killed a bunch of Indians, and just completely screwed that place up. Then we just kept moving west."

Frey and Henley had traced those same steps, moving to California from Michigan and Texas, respectively. Along the way, they felt as if they'd discovered something sinister involving man's senseless disregard for nature.

Henley had a revelation while standing on Zuma

Beach at Malibu, looking out over the ocean. "I remember thinking this is about as far west—with the exception of Alaska—as you can go on this continent," Henley recalled, talking with Crowe. "This is where 'Manifest Destiny' ends—right here, in the middle of all these surfboards and volleyball nets and motor homes.'" Then he had a second thought: "Nah, we've gone right on over and screwed up Hawaii, too."

Frey played a small-but-important role in pushing "The Last Resort" toward completion. In many ways, however, this became a vehicle for something more personal to Henley. "I helped describe what the song was going to be about and assisted with the arrangement," Frey told Crowe, "but it was Don's lyrics and basic chord progression."

This was the first time Henley had taken it upon himself to write such an epic narrative, according to Frey.

"We were very much at that time concerned about the environment and doing anti-nuclear benefit concerts," he said during an appearance on *In the Studio with Redbeard*. He said it felt like "the perfect way to wrap up" *Hotel California*.

Henley's journey toward completing "The Last Resort" included a discussion of long-ago school lessons featuring literary themes based on nature. "There was always this juxtaposition," Henley told Crowe, between "the awesome beauty and the spirituality inherent in the natural world and the unrelenting destruction of it, wrought by this thing that we call civilization or progress."

Henley began the songwriting process with hours of research, diving into books and articles on the impact of mining, oil, timber, and cattle industries on the West. He also weaved in personal experiences, including ideas gleaned from his friendship with **Samu**—an elder with the Chumash Tribe in California—and a supposed former girlfriend from Providence ("the one in Rhode Island") who took her inheritance and moved to Aspen, Colorado, to make a new start.

Aspen, Frey argued, had become a great example—a town "where the billionaires have driven out the millionaires. Whether we're carrying the cross or carrying the gasoline can, we seem to have a penchant for wrecking beautiful places."

At that time, Samu was raising funds for an educational program aimed at preserving the tribe's culture. Eagles ended up performing benefit concerts on their behalf, while gaining a vital new perspective. "The old man feared, rightly, that the white man's culture was stripping his people of their identity," Henley said to Crowe. "They were losing the memory of their language, their ceremonies, their history."

In the end, Henley said the completed track served as a "reaffirmation of the age-old idea that everything in the universe is connected and that there are consequences, downstream, for everything we do."

A song constructed with so many vignettes, with so many details, and with so much lived experience always felt somehow unfinished for Henley. Years later, he still questioned whether the music lived up to his expansive narrative.

"It's fairly pedestrian from a musical point of view," Henley mused in the interview with Crowe, "but lyrically it's not bad." He took some measure of pride in the final verse:

> "They call it paradise
> I don't know why
> You call someplace paradise
> Kiss it goodbye"

The lyric "becomes an allegorical statement about religion—the deception and destructiveness

> **THIS IS WHERE 'MANIFEST DESTINY' ENDS—RIGHT HERE, IN THE MIDDLE OF ALL THE SURFBOARDS AND VOLLEYBALL NETS AND MOTOR HOMES. ... NAH, WE'VE GONE RIGHT ON OVER AND SCREWED UP HAWAII TOO.**
>
> **— DON HENLEY**

that is inherent in the mythology of most organized religion," Henley said.

The song's basic premise that man is always seeking new paths toward destruction proved sadly prophetic, Frey told Redbeard. "We're constantly screwing up paradise," he said. "We're putting junk into space now. ... It's unfortunate but that is sort of what happens."

Although the Eagles had dabbled in politics in their songs before ("On the Border"), the song was Henley's first attempt to bring environmental issues into the consciousness of Eagles listeners. Music critic **Dave Thompson** likened it to an update of **Joni Mitchell**'s "Big Yellow Taxi."

"The environment is the reason I got into politics," Henley told *Rolling Stone*, "to try to do something about what I saw as the complete destruction of most of the resources that we have left. We have mortgaged our future for gain and greed."

"The Last Resort" quickly became—and it remains—a fan favorite among Eagles songs, though the band is selective in where they play it live because of its subtle touches. It doesn't play well in stadiums.

And it wasn't Henley's final word on environmentalism. Beyond writing songs like "Goodbye to a River" from the 2000 solo project *Inside Job*, he also co-founded the Walden Woods Project to help protect a tract of Massachusetts land associated with the poet and writer **Henry David Thoreau**. (A portion of proceeds from the *Common Thread: The Songs of the Eagles* compilation helped underwrite the nonprofit.) Henley later helped start the Caddo Lake Institute to similarly protect Texas wetlands where he spent many of his early years.

That long journey began with the final track from *Hotel California*. "The Last Resort" is also the moment, as Frey told Redbeard, where Henley came into his own as a composer. "Don found himself as a lyricist with that song." [209, 527, 1655, 1948, 1949, 1950]

"The Last Resort" lyrics probed how unrelenting development was destroying some of nature's greatest gifts, including Hawaii, where these condos were being built in Lahaina in 2007.

pounds the keys like he's in a bar band. "D.C., give it up!" Walsh implores the audience before revving up the talk box. Later in "Take It Easy," smiles abound onstage between the three guitarists, Felder, Frey, and Walsh. The footage, with great audience glimpses that capture an era, reminds us that there was once joy in this band.

History of the Eagles also memorably catches the moment during "Take It to the Limit" when a naked woman jumps up on stage and starts dancing suggestively around an unsuspecting Randy Meisner. She kisses the smiling bassist before she is removed, and Meisner does not miss a beat. [1714, 1715, 1716, 1717]

SUMMER 1977

 RELEASES
- ▶ **Poco**, with Timothy B. Schmit, "Living in the Band" (single)

 COLLABORATIONS
- ▶ **Bernie Leadon** played banjo on the single "Cold on the Shoulder" on **Dan McCorison**'s album *Dan McCorison*.
- ▶ **Timothy B. Schmit** provided backing vocals on the song "Just Remember I Love You" on **Firefall**'s album *Luna Sea*.
- ▶ **Don Felder** played guitar on **Angelle**'s album *Angelle*.

 ON THE ROAD WITH ...
- ▶ **Eagles**: Andrew Gold, Hall & Oates, Jimmy Buffett
- ▶ **Poco**, with Timothy B. Schmit: America, Dickey Betts & Great Southern, Little River Band
- ▶ **Bernie Leadon & Michael Georgiades Band**: Linda Ronstadt

 NUGGETS
- ▶ Timothy Schmit is rumored to be one of the likely bassists to tour with **Steely Dan**, along with session keyboard player **Steve Porcaro**. —*Cashbox*
- ▶ Eagles, along with Azoff and Front Line Management, lose in softball to **Bill Graham**, FM Productions, and KSAN radio in San Francisco, but still draw 102,000 fans to their concert in Oakland Coliseum. —*Cashbox*
- ▶ Glenn Frey is in the studio with **Karla Bonoff** and she's lamenting she has to record four or five vocals for every song, then go phrase by phrase from each segment to pick the best one. "That's the way we do it," Frey tells her. "We even take syllables." To which Bonoff says, "If the Eagles can do it, I can do it." —*Crawdaddy*
- ▶ Eagles, **Chicago**, and **Cheech & Chong** team up for half-court combat in the East-West NBA All-Star game. —*Record World*
- ▶ Rumors are growing stronger that Randy Meisner may be on his way out with the Eagles. —*Record World*
- ▶ Joe Walsh's house in Santa Barbara is nearly consumed by a wildfire that left 600 people homeless. Walsh volunteered to help fight the fire but was politely turned away. —*Cashbox*
- ▶ Former Poco bassist/vocalist Tim Schmit will be replacing Randy Meisner in the Eagles. —*Cashbox*
- ▶ **Bill Szymczyk** is defending his current gig in Miami where he is helping southern rockers the **Outlaws** down a more commercial path. "If I can point something out here," he said with a smile, "history might be repeating itself, because the first Eagles album was monstrous; *Desperado* was critically well received, but commercially was a goof-up; and their third one was *On the Border*. We came back at 'em with a smasher, and that's sort of the situation now." —*Crawdaddy*
- ▶ **Kenny Rogers** joins the growing list of distinguished artists who have covered the Eagles' "Desperado," which he cut for his *Daytime Friends* album. —*Record World*

continued on Page 301

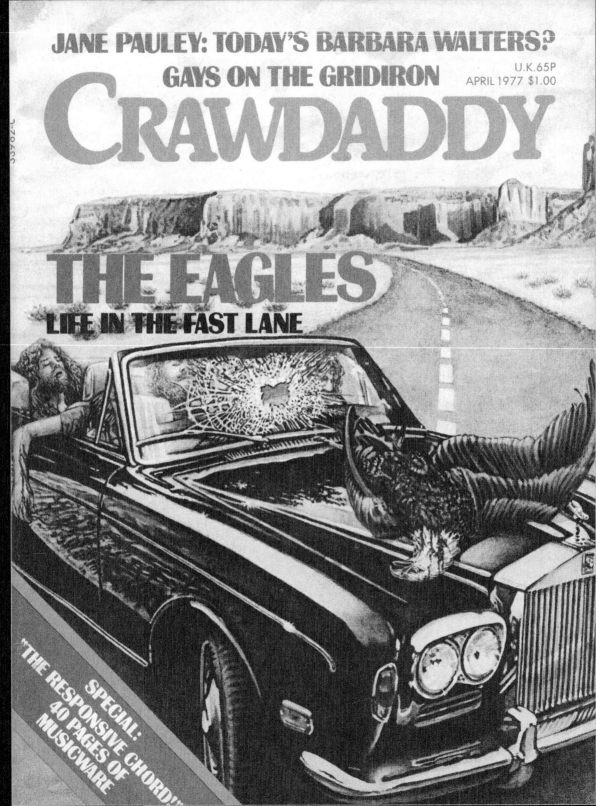

CRAWDADDY PROBES RIGORS OF FAST-LANE LIVING

Eagles suddenly had a lot in their rearview mirror by the end of 1976. The *One of These Nights* tour had ended, *Hotel California* checked in after lengthy delays, and the winter holidays were finally behind them. Rested, their plan was to launch into the publicity phase for *Hotel* in early January 1977 ahead of the concert tour in March. Management set up a press junket in Bungalow 16 of the Beverly Hills Hotel, the same auberge that adorned the cover of their new album.

Veteran rock writer **Barbara Charone** flew from London to do a feature article for *Sounds* magazine. She had a history with the band, writing three lengthy feature stories about them in 1975 and 1976. She was openly a fan of *Desperado*, less enamored with the R&B styling of *One of These Nights*, but with *Hotel*, she wrote, the band had restored her faith. Charone thought she was getting a full band interview, but only Glenn Frey and Don Henley were available that day to her chagrin. Don Felder and Randy Meisner were not even in Los Angeles, and no one knew the whereabouts of Joe Walsh.

Sounds published Charone's 6,000-word plus feature on January 8, 1977, under the headline, "Eagles: Life in the Fast Lane." The story was expansive, including the evolution of their music and a brief explanation of Bernie Leadon's departure.

Then she let Henley and Frey riff on their growth, *Hotel California*, and what was next for the band.

She opened the article with a friendly quote from **Jackson Browne**: "A friend of mine in L.A. said talkin' about music is a lot like singing about football." Charone assumed that Browne's "friend" was sports junkie Glenn Frey, who counted "Sporticus" among his many nicknames. And her affection for Frey was evident.

"Glenn Frey is the rock 'n' roll star of the Eagles," she wrote. "When he was in high school, he was undoubtedly the cool kid in class. Even today, he is the rock 'n' roll Fonz. He chose life in the fast lane as a career and football as a spectator sport. His hip Fonz posture alternates with a gentle sensitivity displayed more often in song than conversation. When Glenn Frey talks, people *listen*. Most of his opinions are delivered with a kind of cocky arrogance that makes disagreement an impossibility. His is *the* last word. Cool."

Charone turned her attention to the more reserved Henley and asked him to consider how the band's direction had changed between *One of These Nights* and *Hotel California*.

"We're a song-oriented group," Henley replied. "That's the bottom line," and explained that the band's current iteration, without Bernie Leadon

ONE OF THESE NIGHTMARES

SEPTEMBER 1977

and including Joe Walsh, was more flexible. He asserted that while the band could write country-rock stuff all day long, they could now do more. "*Hotel* proves that."

"We haven't lost touch with the everyman to use Jackson's terms," Henley said. "But you have to consciously work at it. Obviously, we're in a position where we could totally isolate ourselves. People who live in Beverly Hills who are rich and beautiful have just as many problems as people...in East L.A. Maybe they're not as desperate...oh, I don't know (throwing his hands up in frustration), there's a lot of desperation around here."

Then the conversation turned to the interview's primary focus, *Hotel California.*

"You should never lose your passion," Frey said excitedly. "Getting emotion on plastic is an art form unto itself. It defies the live act. *Hotel California* has all the passion, the story, and the life signs of *Desperado*, but with the good recording technique of *One of These Nights*. This is the first album where we've been able to put them both together."

Charone guided the pair to the rigors of the Eagles living in the fast lane, as exemplified in "Life in the Fast Lane." Henley admitted that listening to the song made him uncomfortable and hoped it would move people to consider their lifestyles—he hoped it would scare them. Frey said he enjoyed the fast life the song described but warned that it was easy to get trapped there.

"You can go on and totally waste away without having accomplished anything," he said, his tenor turning away from his cheeky Fonz alter-ego to a more serious tone. "You can't just take. I hope we can continue to keep that perspective because a lot of people have gone blind."

Henley and Frey both laughed when the pressures of leading the Eagles and writing most of the songs surfaced in the interview, alternately calling themselves "The Pressure Brothers" and "The Up Against The Wall Brothers."

"I suppose we'd eventually finish the songs and the album if we didn't have the pressure," Henley said. "But up to now, it's been that way. I remember reading an interview with Lennon and McCartney a long time ago when they said that's the only way they'd ever finish anything: having a deadline, some kind of pressure."

ONE OF THESE NIGHTMARES

Say a Prayer for the Pretenders....

BY BARBARA CHARONE

The Crawdaddy feature included images from rock photographer **David Alexander**, who caught the Eagles checking into a hotel on the *One of These Nights* tour. Some photos were included on the band's *Hotel California* Tour program.

"That kind of pressure actually works better for us," Frey added.

Charone quizzed them on the environmental issues that drove "The Last Resort," how Walsh's addition had affected the band, their perceived East Coast bias against West Coast bands, and the Eagles' own maturation process.

The story had legs, and since it was only seen in Europe, a different version of the article was re-published three months later as a cover story for the irreverent New York-based *Crawdaddy*. It was rearranged a bit, and some new quotes added, likely at the request of editors, and some 1,500 words shaved from it, but the foundation was the same. References to Charone actually "liking" the Eagles were removed, and the Jackson Browne lead-in quote was replaced with "Say a prayer for the Pretenders," from Browne's "The Pretender" to give the story an edgier feel. But the starkest difference between the two versions was in *Crawdaddy*'s cover art illustration, which became well known among Eagles fans.

The **Arthur Thompson** illustration put the Eagles either unconscious or dead inside a Rolls Royce convertible with a windshield destroyed by a now-perished eagle on the car's hood. Inside the magazine, the artwork appeared again, covering a two-page spread where the Rolls is parked in the middle of a mythical Route 1. One band member lay supine on the highway next to the car. The headline above the image was "One of These Nightmares: Say a Prayer for the Pretenders...." The tone was set.

One thread that continued through both articles was that the Eagles were eyeing their longevity and driven to succeed.

"We're survivors," Henley told Charone. "I intend to be a survivor. I intend to be around. I intend to enjoy the fruits of my labors."

And when the interview in Bungalow 16 had finally concluded, an impatient Frey sprinted to the phone and, while impersonating **Arthur Herbert Fonzarelli**, placed his bets on that night's football game. Just two hours later, Frey was holed up at Elektra/Asylum Records' office a few miles away on La Cienega, watching the game. [44, 1852]

RELEASE
Late February
1977

HOTEL CALIFORNIA

By: Don Felder, Don Henley, Glenn Frey
Side B: Pretty Maids All in a Row (Walsh, Vitale)

Fresh off a #1 single with "New Kid in Town," the Eagles didn't waste time giving radio stations another cut. "Hotel California" hit the charts fast and by March 19, the two songs were at #18 and #24 respectively. "Hotel" would climb into the Top 10 in April and claimed one week at #1 on three different charts. On the flip side the band's two new "Joes"—Walsh and Vitale—gave great balance with the tender ballad "Pretty Maids All in a Row," which, decades later, **Bob Dylan** said might be the best song ever. Not bad company, given what was on Side 1.

AIRPLAY

KSRP-Salt Lake City, KDWB-Minneapolis, and WPGC-Washington didn't wait and opted to begin playing the LP version of "Hotel" in early February; the single was released near the end of that month. Elektra/Asylum usually waited until a song began fading in the charts before releasing another, but "Hotel" was released while "New Kid in Town" was still in the Top 20. The singles passed each other in opposite directions in March. Like "New Kid," "Hotel" was an immediate add for most stations.

Region	Feb	Mar	Apr	Regional Airplay
Northeast	7	15	0	17.3 %
Southeast	7	35	2	33.3 %
Midwest	8	23	3	25.6 %
Southwest	0	11	1	7.7 %
West	6	16	3	16 %

137 PLAYLIST ADDS Winter-Spring 1977

FIRST-WAVE STATIONS Stations that added the song in the first 30 days

KTAC-Tacoma
KTNQ-Los Angeles
KXFM-San Bernardino
KCBQ-San Diego
KYNO-Fresno
KENO-Las Vegas
KFRC-San Francisco
KEZI-Anaheim
KERN-Bakersfield
KJR-Seattle

KDWB-Minneapolis
WING-Dayton
KKXL-Grand Forks
WISM-Madison
KRIB-Mason City, IA

KVOX-Fargo, ND
KKLS-Rapid City, SD
KSLQ-FM-St. Louis
WSAI-Cincinnati
WDGY-Minneapolis

WICC-Bridgeport, CT
WYSL-Buffalo
WRKO-Boston
WAVZ-New Haven
WABC-New York

KAKC-Tulsa
KTKT-Tucson
KQEO-Albuquerque
KFJZ-Fort Worth

WPGC-Washington
WISE-Asheville, NC
WFLB-Fayetteville, NC
WGSV-Guntersville, AL

WAPE-Jacksonville
WAAY-Huntsville, AL
KVOL-Lafayette, LA
WLEE-Richmond

CHARTS

Billboard

#1
May 7, 1977

Cashbox

#1
April 23, 1977

Record World

#1
April 23, 1977

HIGHEST CHARTING WEEK: RECORD WORLD - April 23, 1977

SINGLE	ARTIST	PREV WK
1. HOTEL CALIFORNIA	EAGLES	4
2. Don't Give Up On Us	David Soul	1
3. Southern Nights	Glen Campbell	5
4. Rich Girl	Daryl Hall & John Oates	2
5. I've Got Love On My Mind	Natalie Cole	6
6. When I Need You	Leo Sayer	10
7. Tryin' To Love Two	William Bell	8
8. So Into You	Atlanta Rhythm Section	9
9. The Things We Do for Love	10cc	3
10. I Wanna Get Next to You	Rose Royce	13

Sources: Billboard, Cashbox, Record World

E/A PLAYS THE SPEED GAME TO MAXIMIZE 'HOTEL'

The notion of "Hotel California" as a single puzzled Don Felder. There was no denying the song was a *tour de force*, but in an interview with the *Daily Herald* in 2014, he pondered how unconventional it was, stretching more than six minutes. Hell, the intro alone went on nearly a minute, he reasoned. You can't dance to it; there's a stop in the middle, it breaks down with no drums, and the song-ending guitar duel adds almost two minutes more. There was no way AM radio would play this as a single. And yet....

Elektra/Asylum had usually given Eagles cuts breathing room between 45s. It would issue the album's leadoff single, wait for it to peak, then send up the next release after the first had faded off the charts. It was a formula it tried for most artists with varying degrees of success—not every band could manage three charting releases per album. **Poco** struggled to get one. But in the mid-1970s, the Eagles helped E/A perfect the three-hit-singles-from-an-album formula. Three hit singles meant profitability for the label, artist, and AM radio.

There were other positives in play for "Hotel." FM radio had been playing the song since the album's release, and it was widely popular on the emerging album-oriented rock format stations. But AM radio was still where the industry's money was made via advertising, made easier by short singles.

The E/A suits asked the band for a shorter version and were flatly rebuffed. So, with the *Hotel California* LP, the label changed the three-single calculus.

E/A released the first *Hotel California* single, "New Kid in Town," in mid-December 1975, and by the end of February, it had reached #1 on *Billboard*'s Hot 100. But rather than waiting for it to fade off the charts, the label sent up the next single immediately.

With a base already built for the title track at AOR, "Hotel California" was a logical choice. Eagles fans had multiplied after *One of These Nights* and the label gambled that fans—and radio—wanted more Eagles faster, so they released the follow-up single just as the first peaked.

"New Kid" reached #1 on *Billboard*'s chart February 26, and that same week E/A released "Hotel California," which debuted at #72. Two weeks later, "New Kid" had finally fallen out of the Billboard's Top 10 to #14, and "Hotel California" leaped to #35.

The singles passed each other in opposite directions the following week, with "Hotel" jumping to #18 while "New Kid" dropped to #24; it was the first time the Eagles had two Top 25 singles simultaneously.

At the end of April, "Hotel" had reached #1 on both *Cashbox* and *Record World*'s charts, and a week later, #1 in *Billboard*, giving the band two consecutive #1 singles for the second time ("The Best of My Love" and "One of These Nights" in March and August 1975, respectively, was the first). [2115, 2116, 2117, 2118, 2119, 2120]

FAREWELL IN MONTREAL

Eagles tour manager **Richard Fernandez** (left) hustles Don Henley and **Irving Azoff** (right) into a car during the frenzied *Hotel California* tour in early 1977. By this time the band was breaking into different factions and Fernandez was managing multiple limos for different band members.

EAGLES FIRE FERNANDEZ AS *HOTEL* TOUR HEATS UP

While most bands who had reached the heights of rock fame basked happily in the glow of their success, the Eagles were a different sort. They were a complex set of personalities driven to improve on each successive album and to perfect their onstage performances. Being good wasn't always good enough. Their perfectionism proved daunting for the band and its road crew, especially as they embarked on a tour to support Hotel California. **Richard Fernandez**, who captained the band's road crew, became a casualty of those new pressures in spring 1977.

Like most other well-known bands of the era, the Eagles toured aggressively. The *One of These Nights* tour started in early 1975 and ground through to August 1976, with short breaks in between

to record *Hotel California*. Album sales were important, but since many bands then did not fully own the publishing rights to their own songs, they were especially reliant on touring to supplement their income. Eagles, at least at that stage of their careers, were no different. The band was tight-knit at the beginning, but as the group evolved into a pop culture phenomenon, pressure from their record company for new material intensified and the demands of near-constant touring began to take their toll.

Through it all, Fernandez, who became the Eagles' full-time road manager just three months into their first tour in 1972, dutifully handled the logistics that got them from city to city, hotel to venue, and car to stage and back again. It could be grueling at times, but he enjoyed his work. He had guided the band from the days of traveling coach to the upper echelons of the rock and roll jet set.

But the differences had become stark. The bosom-buddy days of the crew and the band traveling together in station wagons and sedans were long over. As the band transitioned on the road from *One of These Nights* to *Hotel California*, chartered jets, limousines, and special hotel requirements were becoming the standard. The mood had grown darker in the Eagles camp, and prickly pro-Henley and pro-Frey factions had formed within the band and the crew.

"When things became bigger and more popular, the differences between the band became more tense at times," Fernandez told *Time Passages*. "And when you're in a gig, I don't think you need that. It just became...not fun. Everything was getting bigger, and they felt like they were under a lot of pressure. It was tense. The feeling wasn't the same as when we were in smaller venues. With other bands that I worked with, when we did get into larger venues, things didn't seem to change that much. Things seemed more intense with the Eagles."

Just three short months into the *Hotel California* tour, the band flew into Canada to play at the Forum de Montréal on March 29.

What happened that day remains fuzzy, though by all accounts, the hotel reservations were fouled up and some members of the crew were forced to stay in other hotels. Fernandez's initial fear was that Don Henley's room did not meet his expectations. In fairness, the constant touring and years behind the drum kit playing and singing had been wreaking havoc on Henley's back. One of his shoulders was an inch higher than the other, and by then he needed a massage therapist to help keep him upright. He and other band members even had a crew truck that lugged mattresses from city to city to use in place of the hotel's stock mattresses.

Knowing this, Fernandez said he thought there was a problem with Henley's bed. At check-in, he said Henley tried to get his attention, but Fernandez was busy trying to complete arrangements with the hotel clerk and asked Henley to wait. "He didn't like that," said Fernandez, who added that after finishing, he returned to Henley and said, 'Okay, what do we got?' And I'm not sure if [he was upset with] the bed or the room, but we got it sorted out."

Or so he thought. Later that night he got a call from the band's manager, **Irving Azoff**, who said the band had a meeting and decided to let him go. Henley confirmed this in **Marc Eliot**'s book, *To the Limit: The Untold Story of the Eagles*. "Richard's a good guy, but I did have him fired," Henley said, adding that he felt like Fernandez had, in his view, become too unreliable.

Fernandez disagreed with Henley's assessment and told *Time Passages* that throughout his road managing career, he had kept his father's advice close to heart—"treat people fairly, work hard, and take care of family"—which he tried to apply at home and with his family on the road.

For Fernandez, the aftermath was upsetting, but not tragic. But the people around him were confused and angry. "Immediately after, my crew came by and asked, 'What's going on, what's going on?'" he said. He just replied, "Hey, I'm outta here, man."

One crew member had a stronger emotional response. "This one kid I hired, **Tony Taibi**, he grew up in the same neighborhood as me," Fernandez said. "He came up to me and says, 'I'm quitting.' I said, 'No, don't quit, dude. You got a good gig here. Don't worry about me. I'll be okay.'" Taibi did stay, and he remains a member of the Eagles crew even today; Fernandez said he was happy to play a small role in that.

The message he wanted his team to have after his dismissal, he said, was that he would be okay. And as it turns out, Fernandez was okay. He flew back to his home in Capistrano Beach the next morning. "I cooled it," he said. "I smoked a lot of pot, and [said] 'What the fuck?'"

Fortunately, in his nearly 10 years in the music business, he had developed a strong corps of friends, including heavyweights in the Los Angeles rock-tour business, and industry people like **Glyn Johns** internationally. Within the first 10 days, he got a call from Caribou Ranch Management & Studio in Colorado. The studio's owner, **James Guercio**, was looking for someone to manage road

Richard Fernandez checks his watch as **Keith Richards** prepares to go onstage at a **New Barbarians** concert. After leaving the Eagles, Fernandez started a 40-year tenure as road manager for **Tom Petty and the Heartbreakers**.

acts out of Los Angeles for Caribou Management and hired Fernandez immediately.

After almost a year booking **Chicago** tours, he saw a **Tom Petty and the Heartbreakers** concert via satellite. Petty was an emerging star in 1976, and Fernandez was impressed. He soon found his way to Petty's management team and within a year had convinced them to let him manage the Heartbreakers on the road.

The gig paid little to start, but he earned the trust of Petty and his band, became a valued crew member, and eventually earned a salary commensurate with that trust.

Looking back, Fernandez said he admires the Eagles and where they are today, and he holds no animosity toward the band. In fact, he and the band members continued to interact and get along even after they cut him loose. Fernandez was the Eagles' starting shortstop when they beat *Rolling Stone* magazine in their famed softball game in 1978, and he and Glenn Frey remained close friends until Frey's death in 2016, sometimes spending holidays together at their nearby properties on Kauai, Hawaii.

And Fernandez and Henley even patched things up. They had run into each other from time to time throughout the years, but when Henley was performing at the *MusiCares Concert for Tom Petty* in 2017, the two had a moment, Fernandez said.

"Henley and a collection of Eagles and other people performed there, and I remember he was leaving, and I was close to the door," he said. "He stopped, looked over at me, and he said, 'Richard, you're doing okay?' And I said, 'Yeah,' and he walked over and gave me a hug. He gave me a big hug, and I said, 'Hey, have a good one.' I can't have any animosity, and he helped my friend Tony Taibi. I've known Tony since the fourth grade. We remain friends to this day. I'm glad Tony listened to me when I said, 'I'm fine. Stay here. I'm going to be fine.' And you know what? [Don] took care of Tony. I'm happy for that." [1690, 1692, 1693]

Eagles Sue Geffen, Warner To Claim Publishing Rights

Six years after signing their original deal with **David Geffen** and his then-fledgling Asylum Records label, the Eagles filed a lawsuit against its new owner (Warner Bros. Music), Geffen, and three publishing companies, charging antitrust law violations and breach of fiduciary duties. The damages sought were, at least then, perceived to be in the millions.

A lot had changed since Bernie Leadon gave Geffen his "do you want us or not" ultimatum in 1971. The Eagles had become one of the world's best-selling rock bands, basking in the glow of two straight #1 albums. But the songwriting royalties deal they signed as hungry unknowns had become a festering wound by May 1977, when the Eagles filed suit to recover their copyrights, opening a high-profile, high-stakes fight with Warner and Geffen.

Caught between the legal machinations and bad blood was **Joe Smith**, Elektra/Asylum's pragmatic chairman, who wanted to protect the cash flow generated by his label's highest-earning band. Smith didn't share Geffen's emotional investment. He was more focused on the bottom line and needed the Eagles to keep Warner Communications Inc. shareholders content. Smith and Eagles manager **Irving Azoff** wrestled a bit but ultimately respected each other, and Azoff made clear the Eagles wanted the issue resolved.

"We have no problem with Elektra/Asylum," he told *Rolling Stone*. "We have just re-signed and are happy to be there. Our goal is to get back our copyrights and receive compensation for damages."

Geffen fretted over how the lawsuit affected his image, and it certainly took a beating. But after a few months, Smith convinced Geffen and the leaders at Warner Bros. to settle. The Eagles got what they asked for later that summer, and Smith thought that show of goodwill would help him quickly secure a new album from the band. But that wouldn't happen anywhere near as fast as he hoped. [1914, 1990, 1991, 1992, 1993, 1994]

Randy Newman Gets Eagles' Help on *Little Criminals*

Randy Newman's amiable *Little Criminals* took a notable step back from the biting satire found on his previous studio project, the 1974 album *Good Old Boys*. But the singer-songwriter-composer's 1977 album also included an encore appearance by a bunch of studio ringers whose day job was performing as the Eagles.

Glenn Frey, Don Henley, and Bernie Leadon had contributed vocals to a trio of songs from *Good Old Boys*, including the sharply drawn opening track, "Rednecks." Frey was a huge fan and had personally asked album co-producer **Russ Titelman** to allow the Eagles to join the sessions.

"Glenn pulled me aside at the Troubadour and said, 'Hey, man. If you ever need any background singing on Randy's record, let us know,'" Titelman later told journalist **Jim Bessman**.

continued on Page 301

Bryan Garofalo (far left), Michael Georgiades, David Kemper, Bernie Leadon, and Steven Goldstein as they appeared in this Gary Burden photograph on the back cover of the Bernie Leadon-Michael Georgiades Band's *Natural Progressions* album in 1977.

LEADON RETURNS WITH FOLKSY CO-CONSPIRATOR

In July 1977, roughly a year after officially departing the group, Bernie Leadon released his first post-Eagles album in the form of a partnership with Los Angeles-based songwriter and musician **Michael Georgiades**.

Asylum released *Natural Progressions*, billing the artists as the **Bernie Leadon-Michael Georgiades Band**, but the music sounds more like it's by a couple of folkies than a "band." The songs are all solo compositions by the two songwriters, without any additional credits from outside writers or the supporting musicians on the album. In fact, Georgiades and Leadon don't even share credits with each other; rather, there are six songs individually credited to the former and four to the latter.

The chemistry between the two—from the comfortable informality of the cover photo to the sounds in the grooves—sounds genuine, as though they had known each other for years.

Georgiades was an aspiring songwriter who had bounced from California to Hawaii and back when he first met Leadon in the early 1970s. Georgiades was living in Topanga Canyon and relaxing at home

one day when, as he described it, "I hear this really insane banjo playing in the distance and I look out there and see my girlfriend and this guy walking towards the house." The girlfriend introduced the banjoist, who happened to live next door, and it was Leadon, who at the time was playing with the **Flying Burrito Brothers**. The two musicians instantly became friends and musical co-conspirators.

Georgiades had already networked his way into a relationship with **Johnny Rivers**, who had a string of hits in the 1960s, and played on the singer's 1972 album *L.A. Reggae*.

"Bernie came down with me [to work on the record]," Georgiades remembered, and the two both scored writing credits as well. (The duo would also sing backup on Rivers' 1973 follow-up, *Blue Suede Shoes*.)

For their own endeavor, Georgiades and Leadon teamed up with former Eagles producer **Glyn Johns** to helm the sessions in 1976. It was hardly a surprising move, considering how Johns always championed Leadon's contributions to the Eagles while producing their first two albums. Because of Johns' involvement, Georgiades and Leadon would record parts of the album at Olympic Studios in London, and the rest at home in Los Angeles.

While Leadon does contribute the country instrumentation he is best known for—acoustic guitar, banjo, and mandolin— *Natural Progressions* comes across as more soft rock than country. Some songs are coated in string arrangements designed to make them more friendly to AM radio than to album-oriented rock stations on FM. At times, like on Leadon's "How Can You Live Without Love," the layered acoustics and harmonies sound like they could have been on an early Eagles record, though the songs lack the same commercial appeal. At the time, Leadon himself also acknowledged that comparisons to his former band, especially the lyrical content of the songs, might reveal significant differences.

"This music is really personal to me," he said in 1977. "It's basically music for acoustic instruments and it's pretty simple philosophically. It's maybe not as complicated as what the Eagles say. That main difference is in the ideas expressed. At this point, there is a severe diversion between the Eagles' point of view and Michael's and mine."

The Eagles, he explained, had a far more cynical outlook than he did. Considering the Eagles were wrapped up in their *Hotel California* era at the time, it would be fair to say that lyrically and musically there was a significant disparity between Leadon's new and old projects.

"The music I play with Michael is the kind that I've always played at home," he offered. "Michael and I played together for years...we'd get together, just pickin' in the house."

After Bernie Leadon (left) teamed with **Michael Georgiades**, their summer 1977 album *Natural Progressions* became Leadon's first post-Eagles LP.

Sylistically, Georgiades' songs don't sound too different from Leadon's, with Johns' production creating a uniform feel. "You're the Singer" is the closest thing to the Eagles' early country-rock sound, with more than a hint of **Jackson Browne**, although the strings and the buried mix of the drums help achieve a more soft-rock/adult-contemporary sound.

One surprise on the album involved Leadon's former manager with the Eagles, **Irving Azoff**, who was credited with background vocals on "Callin' for Your Love." He would get behind the mic once again for Glenn Frey's solo album *Partytown*, where he sang background under the pseudonym "Urban Azoff" as a member of the **Monstertones**.

Overall, the the Leadon-Georgiades songs are pleasant, but most reviews at the time insisted there was something lacking. The album had all the right ingredients, but the flavor was sometimes too bland. Whether for this reason or because laid-back Southern California music was beginning to fall out of favor by 1977, *Natural Progressions* had no traction on the radio or among fans, so there was no follow-up from the duo, nor from the pair as individuals. In fact, decades would pass before Leadon released an album of his own material, titled *Mirror*, in 2004. [1671, 1704, 1705, 1706]

PATHWAY ALBUM | TIMOTHY B. SCHMIT

POCO
Indian Summer
ABC Records, May 1977

Indian Summer was Poco's tenth studio album (twelfth overall, counting live albums), out in May 1977. By this point, most music industry types viewed **Poco** as a band whose best chances for success were long gone. Even fans thought their best years were behind them. Perhaps that's why *AllMusic* described *Indian Summer* as reflective of a band that was "treading water."

All that said, consummate professionals tend to produce professional work, and *Indian Summer* is a solid effort. **Paul Cotton**'s title track is a rich, evocative musical piece, and his "Living in the Band" lyrically recounts and celebrates the story of the fabulous buzz that Poco created back in 1969 when Cotton watched their first show from the audience.

Timothy B. Schmit has a gorgeous ballad in the melancholic "Find Out in Time" and a delightfully bouncy pop tune called "Stay (Night Until Noon)." **Rusty Young** offers an ambitious musical suite of three sewn-together songs that he calls "The Dance," which is mostly a solid offering despite the questionable misstep of having a short disco interlude in the middle; it's not entirely clear if the intent was ironic commentary on dance culture or a genuine stab at the music form that was surging in popularity.

The problem with *Indian Summer* is not that it's bad, but rather that it lacks the originality and spunk the band once had as fresh-faced newcomers. It would be the latest in a successive line of albums that failed to turn Poco into a superstar act. Something had to change and, indeed, it did four months after *Indian Summer* was released, when Schmit accepted an invitation to join the Eagles as bassist—once again replacing Randy Meisner in a band.

At a crossroads, Poco disbanded after that, with Cotton and Young forming a partnership, auditioning new members to join them in the formation of the **Cotton-Young Band**...or so they thought. They cut demos for the new project, but when it was time to do a proper record, ABC Records balked, unwilling to take a risk on an unknown entity. Instead, the label agreed to release a record if the name on the sleeve said "Poco." Poco had a degree of name recognition and was, therefore, easier to promote.

The new group led by Cotton and Young recorded *Legend*, a polished piece of vinyl more akin to adult-contemporary than country-rock, and ABC released it under the Poco name. Ironically, with this album, Poco finally gained Top 40 success with "Heart of the Night" and, more significantly, the song the group is best remembered for, "Crazy Love."

Meanwhile, Schmit joined one of the biggest groups on the planet and would be a part of the Eagles for *The Long Run*. In the end, things appeared to work out well for both bands. [1504, 1512, 1765]

When Newman got around to recording a follow-up to *Good Old Boys* three years later, Frey and Henley brought along bandmate Joe Walsh and not-quite-an-Eagle-yet Timothy B. Schmit. This time, Newman's guest stars had an even bigger presence: Frey played guitar on two songs and sang background vocals with **J.D. Souther** on three tracks. Walsh added guitar to a trio of tunes, while Henley and Schmit both appeared on one song apiece.

Along the way, Newman learned a lot about the famous attention to detail that marked a typical Eagles session.

"They were the best background singers I could get, so I got them," Newman told *Rolling Stone*. "They would go way past the point where I wanted. I'd say, 'That's good, isn't it?' They say, 'No, no, no.' They'd hear out of tune, where I didn't necessarily. They were very, very fastidious about what they did and never satisfied. They could go back over their stuff or my stuff and find a million things they didn't like about it."

The notion of having the Eagles backing him up was a little intimidating for Newman. "D'ya ever see on vacation a fat kid that's all sunburn trying to swim around?" Newman asked *New Musical Express* in 1979, puffing up his cheek like a bloated fish while he starts splashing around in imaginary water. "That's how I felt trying to sing with the Eagles." Still, he soldiered on.

Frey, Souther, and Schmit's most famous contribution was the background vocals on Newman's novelty hit "Short People." The *Washington Post* reported the satirical song was rumored to be a whimsical dig at **Irving Azoff**, the Eagles' vertically challenged yet powerful manager who was later the subject of a *Rolling Stone* profile by **Cameron Crowe** headlined "They Call Him Big Shorty."

"Short People" would become Newman's highest-ever chart single, peaking at #2. It went on to sell more than a million copies and score gold from the RIAA.

Walsh joined Frey on "Little Criminals" while Frey and Souther appeared on "Baltimore."

Walsh also took a turn on guitar for the winking "Kathleen (Catholicism Made Easier)." But they reached a new level of collaborative genius on "Rider in the Rain," a note-perfect western-themed satire featuring background vocals from the trio of Henley, Frey, and Souther. It turned into the best early-era Eagles soundalike ever recorded.

"The most notable and most fun thing they did was...Randy's funny fake cowboy

> I'D SAY, 'THAT'S GOOD, ISN'T IT?' THEY SAY, 'NO, NO, NO.' THEY'D HEAR OUT OF TUNE, WHERE I DIDN'T NECESSARILY. THEY WERE VERY, VERY FASTIDIOUS ABOUT WHAT THEY DID AND WERE NEVER SATISFIED.
>
> — RANDY NEWMAN

continued on Page 308

RELEASE
Mid-May
1977

LIFE IN THE FAST LANE

By: Joe Walsh, Don Henley, Glenn Frey
Side B: The Last Resort (Henley, Frey)

"Fast Lane" was the third single released from the chart-busting *Hotel California* LP, and its sales and airplay matched the tenor of the song. The single was fast out of the blocks—it debuted on *Record World*'s Top 100 singles at #54—but it never quite got into the Top 10, stalling out at *Billboard*'s #11. Once again, Elektra/Asylum employed the push-it-out-while-they're-hot strategy: "Hotel California" was still at #3 on the *Billboard* Hot 100 chart when "Fast Lane" debuted on the chart at #72 on May 14. But it would be a year and a half before fans could hear another new Eagles song, and it would be wrapped in a Christmas bow.

AIRPLAY

Following two straight #1 singles the Eagles remained automatic adds for most radio stations in every region of the country. The Southeast and Midwest remained fiercely loyal, and the West Coast now fully embraced them, too. "Fast Lane" surged across the airwaves early in the summer, and by the time July arrived, it was on more than 90% of *Cashbox*-polled playlists nationwide.

146 PLAYLIST ADDS Summer 1977

Region	May	Jun	Jul	Regional Airplay
Northeast	20	6	0	17.8 %
Southeast	30	15	1	32.2 %
Midwest	25	8	1	23.3 %
Southwest	8	6	0	9.6 %
West	15	9	1	17.1 %

FIRST-WAVE STATIONS Stations that added the song in the first 30 days

KING-Seattle
KLOS-Los Angeles
KYNO-Fresno
KFRC-San Francisco
KENO-Las Vegas
KJOY-Stockton
KJRB-Spokane
KROY-Sacramento
KERN, KAFY-Bakersfield
KPAM-Portland

WCOL-Columbus
WSAI, WKRQ-Cincinnati
CKLW, WDRQ-Detroit
KXOK-St. Louis
WLS-Chicago

KDWB-Minneapolis
WHNN-Bay City, MI
WLAV-Grand Rapids, MI
KQWB-Fargo, ND
WEBC-Duluth, MN

WTRY-Albany
WIFI-Philadelphia
WYSL-Buffalo
WBBF-Rochester
WAVZ-New Haven

KINT-El Paso
KRBE-FM-Houston
KELI-Tulsa
KAKC-Tulsa

WSGA-Savannah
WRBQ-Q105-Tampa
WAYS-Charlotte
WKIX-Raleigh

WMAK-Nashville
WFOM-Marietta, GA
WCAO-Baltimore
WQPD-Lakeland, FL

CHARTS

Billboard	HIGHEST CHARTING WEEK: BILLBOARD - July 2, 1977		
# 11 July 2, 1977	SINGLE	ARTIST	PREV WK
	1. Gonna Fly Now (Theme from "Rocky")	Bill Conti	2
Cashbox	2. Undercover Angel	Alan O'Day	3
# 12 June 25, 1977	3. Got to Give It Up, Part 1	Marvin Gaye	1
	4. Da Doo Ron Ron	Shaun Cassidy	8
	5. Looks Like We Made It	Barry Manilow	13
Record World	6. Dreams	Fleetwood Mac	6
# 16 July 2, 1977	7. I Just Want to Be Your Everything	Andy Gibb	15
	8. Angel in Your Arms	Hot	9
	11. LIFE IN THE FAST LANE	**EAGLES**	**11**

Sources: Billboard, Cashbox, Record World

WALSH'S TRICKY LICK INSPIRES EDGY 'FAST LANE'

A driving rocker, "Life in the Fast Lane" was yet another instant Eagles classic from the *Hotel California* album. Like the album's title track, it's a profound insight into the California culture of the day. As Joe Walsh told the BBC's **John Tobler** in Tobler and Stuart Grundy's 1983 book *The Guitar Greats*, the song reflected the high-paced L.A. lifestyle of "'run around in your Porsche' 24-hour boogie mode that unfortunately is too true for a lot of people."

The song is about excess, something all members of the Eagles had both witnessed and lived themselves. It's telling that the title came from a conversation Glenn Frey had with a drug dealer dubbed "The Count" while riding in a Corvette to a poker game.

Frey recalled the incident in 2013's *History of the Eagles* documentary: "The next thing I know we're doing 90. Holding! Big time! I say, 'Hey man!' He grins and goes, 'Life in the fast lane!' I thought, 'Now there's a song title.'"

Significantly, the track served as a perfect vehicle to integrate Walsh's gun-slinging rock guitar with the mellower California rock approach that had served them well. With Walsh, the Eagles had an extra gear.

Walsh had a particularly tricky lick he would play as a warm-up before a show. Henley heard the lick coming from Walsh's dressing room, grabbed Glenn Frey, and asked Walsh to play the part again.

"And they said, 'Well, there's our Joe Walsh Eagles song!'" Walsh told *Rolling Stone* in May 2016.

After incorporating Walsh's lick, Frey started arranging the music and turned it into a vibrant song. Henley followed up with his cautionary lyrics, and the three shared songwriting credits for what became the Eagles' hardest rock and roll cut to date. It would also become the song people most associate with Walsh as an Eagle.

Walsh was philosophical about the song beyond the lick.

"It wasn't really a statement about the guys in the band, or about anybody in particular," Walsh said. "Just it's kind of disturbing to see the extremes that the bourgeois jet set will involve themselves in."

Walsh added that when the band wrote it "we realized that running around and parties and fast cars are not really the answer—it's kind of a shallow way to approach why we are on this planet, and it probably came as a band consciousness."

Radio loved the single from the start, and *Cashbox* reported the Eagles were "harder and funkier ever" with the single. Radio loved it and it climbed the charts quickly.

They weren't wrong. The track perfectly embodied the new Eagles sound, seamlessly merging the band's mellow style with Walsh's rock edge. "Life in the Fast Lane" was the album's third single but stalled out before reaching the Top 10, peaking at #11 in July 1977. [135, 2063, 2064]

song," Titelman argued. "Glenn, Don, and J.D. Souther sang beautifully. It sounded like Randy singing lead on an Eagles record. Humorous and great."

While much of this may have been for laughs, Newman noted, the Eagles weren't fooling around.

"They didn't settle. They worked on their stuff—words [and] music, in particular," Newman explained to *Rolling Stone*. "If they had a guitar solo, it was going to be a good one, a memorable one. When I got to know them better, I teased them about the cowboy stuff. They were a long way from being cowboys."

Frey's passion for Newman's work never faded. He later returned to the Newman songbook for "Same Girl," which appeared on the late Eagles star's career-closing 2012 LP *After Hours*. Likewise, Henley covered the same song during his 1993 solo tour, and threw "Let's Burn Down the Cornfield" and "Political Science" onto his setlists as well.

Henley and Newman remained good friends over the years and Henley inducted him into the Rock and Roll Hall of Fame in 2013. In his remarks, Henley remembered a conversation he had with Newman about his biggest hit.

"That was really clever how you used the idea of short people combined with a catchy melody to make a statement about intolerance and discrimination and man's inhumanity to man," he said straight-faced. "That's what the song is really about, right?"

Henley said he looked on as Newman stared off into the distance over his glasses and replied: "It's about short people." [125, 1226, 1865, 1868, 1869, 1872]

Frey, Meisner Scuffle Over 'Limit' After Knoxville Concert

At the Eagles' Rock and Roll Hall of Fame induction in 1998, Glenn Frey spoke at the podium about the relationships between the band members. "A lot has been made tonight about disharmony," he said to the audience. "The Eagles were a very laid-back band who played music in a very high-stress situation. A lot has been talked about and speculated over the last 27 years about whether or not we got along. We got along fine—we just disagreed a lot."

Frey followed this with a rhetorical challenge: "Tell me one worthwhile relationship that has not had peaks and valleys..." This brought cheers and applause from the audience, and he suggested the good times far outnumbered the bad.

By all accounts, on the *Hotel California* tour, tensions were high among all the band members. Occasionally, things escalated to the point of fisticuffs, and one of the most notorious moments occurred after a show in Knoxville when the outspoken Frey mixed it up with the introverted Randy Meisner.

"Glenn and I got into a little fight there," Meisner told journalist **John Beaudin** in summer 2000. "It just happened. Something happened and we kind of got mad at each other and we took a swing at each other."

The showdown happened when Meisner

refused to go out for an encore to sing "Take It to the Limit." His song was massively popular, and it was his signature moment during the shows. But over time, it had become a huge stressor for him. It was partly shyness, partly a fear of failure.

"I was always kind of shy," Meisner said. "They wanted me to stand in the middle of the stage to sing 'Take It to the Limit,' but I liked to be out of the spotlight."

Knowing nothing of this, audiences would invariably erupt in delight when Meisner stepped forward to sing his song, especially when he hit an extended high note during the song's coda. His performance was a real showstopper every night.

"[The crowd] went crazy when Randy hit those high notes," Henley complimented.

But Meisner often worried he would not be able to nail that highest note. In the *History of the Eagles* documentary, Frey said that Meisner said he didn't want to sing "Limit" anymore and asked the road manager to take it out of the set.

"I confronted him about this," Frey said. "I called him up and said 'Randy, there's thousands of people waiting for you to sing that song. You just can't say 'Fuck 'em, I don't feel like it.'"

Arguments frequently occurred over his reluctance to step up and deliver this high point

I CONFRONTED HIM ABOUT THIS. I CALLED HIM UP AND SAID, 'RANDY, THERE'S THOUSANDS OF PEOPLE WAITING FOR YOU TO SING THAT SONG. YOU CAN'T JUST SAY, 'FUCK 'EM, I DON'T FEEL LIKE IT.'

— GLENN FREY

in the show. And then came the tilt the night in Knoxville when he refused to go out at all.

Meisner said he was sick that night, and claimed the band had already done three encores, so he believed he was justified in skipping another one.

"My ulcer was acting up and I had a bad case of the flu as well," he recalled. "I was too sick and generally fed up. I decided I wasn't going back out [for the encore]."

Others were not sympathetic, and the "sickness" excuse was not the first time they had heard it.

Irving Azoff opined that Meisner would have been happier if the Eagles had remained a bar band and not become superstars. He explained to author **Marc Eliot** that Meisner "began complaining between shows about having to do ['Take It to the Limit']. Increasingly, he'd piss and moan about one thing or another, mostly having a sore throat, and suggested a couple of times that maybe they ought to drop the song or have someone else sing it."

Henley offered his read on the situation with the following explanation: "He didn't want to do ['Take It to the Limit'] because he'd been up all night doing drugs with two chicks in a hotel room."

Fans may have differing opinions over who was or was not being reasonable, but the result was the same. Frey reportedly called Meisner a "pussy" and they took swings at each other before they were restrained. Frey said when security started to move in to break things up Henley told them, "Stay out of it. This is personal, and private. Real fucking private." Though Meisner would complete the tour, his decision to leave the nest had been cemented that night, and he was merely finishing out his duties.

In Don Felder's memoir, he recalled that a huge argument indeed ensued in Knoxville over Meisner's refusal to return to the stage, but that the confrontation happened two days later. Felder indicated it occurred during that show's intermission, and that the argument was about where Meisner should be standing on stage.

The facts may have been confused over time but there is also the possibility the Knoxville story is a combination of stories that have become lore, aided by fading memories and repeated retellings.

Either way, the Knoxville beef illustrates how tensions were flying high and the group was operating in, as Frey described it, a "high-stress situation."

"Glenn had somehow pushed Randy to the point that this gentle, easy going guy, who wouldn't hurt a fly, flipped," Felder said.

"Randy never knew how great he was," Joe Walsh said. "He wasn't alpha. Confrontations were really hard for him."

Looking back decades later, Meisner dismissed the altercation as water under the bridge. "We're just people," he said. "There was a time when there was a little resentment and all that stuff but, you know, when you get older, why even think about it anymore?"

In 2015, web paparazzi site *TMZ* caught some footage of an aged and frail-looking Meisner coming out of a diner with his wife, Lana, and he was asked who "got the last punch in." He diplomatically said, "Both of us," laughing it off with the implication that it was a draw.

In Young's article reporting the Frey/Meisner confrontation, the writer also dropped rumors that Meisner's time in the band might be ending and that the "favorite" to fill his role would be **Poco**'s Timothy B. Schmit. In the months that followed, Young would be proven right on both scoops. [6, 467, 1190, 1513, 1514, 1644, 1686]

Elvis Presley Dies: Frey, Meisner, Felder Early Inspiration was 42

On August 16, 1977, at just 42 years old, **Elvis Aaron Presley**, from Tupelo, Mississippi, died at Graceland, his home in Memphis, Tennessee. It devastated countless fans, including three Eagles, who looked up to Presley as a hero.

The body of the singer long known as the King of Rock 'n' Roll was found at 2:30 p.m. by **Jerry Esposito**, Presley's road manager and longtime friend. Elvis was slumped over on the floor of his bathroom upstairs in Graceland. He was rushed to the hospital, but was later pronounced dead by the infamous Dr. Nick (Dr. **George C. Nichopoulos**). Dr. Nick had been Elvis' personal physician since 1967, gradually prescribing more medications to Presley until the King became addicted to a cocktail of Demerol, Codeine, Percodan, Dilaudid, and Quaaludes.

Presley's death was a shock to the world, but not so much a surprise to those in his inner circle. It was just exhaustion, his spokesperson said. But it was more than that. Elvis's weight had ballooned. He weighed 260 pounds when he died, almost 100 pounds over his fighting weight in the mid-1960s. His prescription drug use had gotten out of control.

The news outlets were unprepared to report the event—not to mention the impact Elvis Presley's death would have on America and beyond. *CBS News*' reporting that night led with a story about the Panama Canal. Meanwhile, grieving fans were calling TV, radio, and newspaper newsrooms around the country trying to get details and make sense of the tragic loss.

Even *The New York Times* was unprepared for the news and "some mild panic occurred when editors surprisingly discovered no one had prepared an advance obituary of Presley," according to **Neal** and **Janice Gregory**'s best-selling 1980 book, *When Elvis Died.*

As shockwaves reverberated around the world, thousands of fans from all over began to descend on Memphis, Tennessee. The global community was just as shattered as Presley's loyal, adoring following. For almost everyone making popular music in 1977, Elvis was an early inspiration, and the Eagles were no different.

Glenn Frey was an Elvis fan growing up, and even carried the nickname "Teen King"—a name bestowed on him by **Linda Ronstadt**'s manager **John Boylan**—early in the Eagles' history as a tribute to Presley; the band played as **Teen King and the Emergencies** in Colorado back in 1971 before officially becoming the Eagles.

As a kid, Don Felder learned guitar playing Elvis songs. The first single Don Henley's mother bought for him was "Hound Dog," Presley's cleaned-up 1956 remake of **Big Mama Thornton**'s salacious hit single for Peacock three years earlier (penned by **Jerry Leiber**, **Mike Stoller**, and produced by **Johnny Otis**).

Randy Meisner also started playing in local bands after seeing Elvis's first (and uncensored) performance on *The Ed Sullivan Show* on September 9 that same year, when Presley gyrated through "Ready Teddy," "Don't Be Cruel," "Hound Dog," and "Love Me Tender."

Across the Atlantic, **The Beatles** chose a rock and roll journey thanks to Elvis and others. "The King is dead," said **John Lennon**, on the day Elvis died. "But rock 'n' roll will never die. Long live the King." [218, 550]

FALL 1977

 NUGGETS
▶ Eagles and **J.D. Souther** start impromptu jam session of "Rocky Mountain Way" at **Jimmy Buffett**'s wedding. —*Cashbox*
▶ Glenn Frey drops the first puck at an NHL game between the Cleveland Barons and the Washington Capitals in Cleveland–the first time a rock and roller has ever been asked. —*Record World*

continued on Page 315

REACHING HIS LIMIT

Randy Meisner sings between Joe Walsh and Don Henley during a concert in the Netherlands in May 1977.

MEISNER EXITS, IRONICALLY REPLACED BY SCHMIT

Eagles were at their apex in late 1977, an odd time to decide to quit the band, artistically and financially, but that's what Randy Meisner did when the *Hotel California* tour wrapped up.

"When the tour ended, I left the band," Meisner said. "Those last days on the road were the worst. Nobody was talking to me, or would hang after the shows, or do anything." He also claimed, "I was made an outcast of the band I helped start."

Meisner's timing suggests that **Irving Azoff** might have been right when he quipped that Meisner would have preferred the Eagles remain a "bar band" playing to modest crowds in small rooms. Certainly, Meisner had grown tired of the tension and stress of it all, and perhaps that was reason enough for him to quit.

Artist **Boyd Elder**, who created the skull pieces that adorned the covers of *One of These Nights* and *Their Greatest Hits (1971–1975)*, described to author

Marc Eliot how there had been a time when the Eagles were a tight-knit bunch of broke friends who hung out at the Troubadour. Naturally, a lot had changed in the two years since Bernie Leadon flew the nest. Now Meisner was to take off as well.

"It was a lot of fun in the beginning," Meisner reflected in 1994. "Because we were all such tight friends at the time, everybody got along with each other well." He told a similar story about his time in **Poco** and suggested that bands, in general, tended to be more fun before growing success and business interests would inevitably complicate things. The reserved Meisner possibly best summed up his relationship with music when he said, "Small crowd or big crowd, I love to play. As long as a band's friends with each other and you're having a good time, there is nothing better."

Contrasting this outlook with the personalities of the group's *de facto* leaders, it's easy to see why the relationship was eventually doomed. Though Don Henley was sometimes criticized as overly serious and Glenn Frey was extroverted with boundless enthusiasm, both shared an unapologetic desire to succeed in the rock business.

Meisner's ongoing battles with Frey and the others about his reluctance to step up to deliver his spotlight moment and sing "Take It to the Limit" certainly contributed to his split, though with tensions at a boiling point within the volatile band, it's likely an oversimplification to chalk it up to any single issue.

As with most conflicts, there are multiple sides to the story, and Henley, Frey, and Azoff would quickly point out that Meisner was not "made" into the outcast victim but that he contributed to it himself.

Like the rest of the band, Randy partook in typical rock star vices of cocaine and alcohol, and Henley remarked that Meisner was "hypersensitive" and that he "was always sick, his marriage was always breaking up...there was always something wrong for him." Azoff quite bluntly said, "In truth, Randy had become a major pain in the ass, and I think he knew it. He was probably looking for a way to leave."

In his autobiography, Don Felder recalled that he and Joe Walsh pleaded with Meisner to remain with the band, to stick it out if for no other reason than to reap the benefits financially. But Meisner decided to depart anyway. For him, it was not about the money.

The pressures of being an Eagle and the constant touring were undoubtedly factors in Meisner's eventual departure.

"I'd been singing mostly background my whole life," Meisner explained to BAM's **Dave Zimmer** in 1980. "And I figured I was missing something by not singing out more. Listening to Don [Henley] and Glenn [Frey], I knew I could do just as well or better. That's the point when I started thinking about quitting the Eagles. I was 31—a time in your life when you want to make a decision if you want to really go for something. I wasn't going to wait until I was 40." Bravado for the press? Perhaps, but it was also an indicator that he didn't want to be typecast as a former Eagle.

In the press, the Eagles cited fatigue and a desire to return to his family in Nebraska as motives for Meisner's resignation, two reasons which may not have told the whole story but were contributing factors, nonetheless. Meisner had married his high school girlfriend when they were still teenagers, and the couple welcomed a child in 1963; twins followed in 1970. Meisner returned to music with one poorly conceived album attempt in 1978, then tried again in 1980 with better results.

With the bassist slot vacated, it was important for the band to find someone who could play the low notes and sing the high notes. Meisner's tenor was a big part of the Eagles' vocal harmonies, and the consensus was that Timothy B. Schmit from Poco was the ideal candidate.

He had already once replaced Meisner, the original bass player in Poco, which was as much proof as one could get that it could work.

Schmit, a Sacramento native (and soon to be the band's first California-born member), was from the same L.A. country-rock scene that birthed the Eagles and could nail the high notes like Meisner. Schmit also wrote songs. As Poco faltered, he was starting to feel desperate for a new gig, so the timing was perfect.

Schmit said he "had been kind of disenchanted with what was going on with my career and Poco... we had 'leveled off,' we weren't thriving." He was willing to continue to collaborate with them, but, he said, "I had my eyes open to different things."

Schmit gave an interview to Crawdaddy's **Michael Barackman** earlier that summer and talked about Poco's fortunes, or lack thereof.

"Lots of people who come to see us tell us how frustrating it must be," Schmit explained, dressed in jeans and a faded One of These Nights t-shirt. "They ask, 'How do you feel about seeing the Eagles in the Top Five with a style you had before them?' I can't be brought down by something so trivial. That we were before them doesn't mean nothin.'"

What rankled Schmit Barackmen wrote, was Poco had done everything a rock band is supposed to do—toured extensively, released two albums a year—yet didn't have much to show for it. Alternately standing and pacing, Schmit went further.

"When you exist so long at the same level of popularity, it gets to be kind of fatiguing," Schmit conceded. "There's no logic in this business! **Steely Dan** doesn't go out and tour—they're not really even a band—and they fucking sell records...gold ones. Art and business don't have anything to do with each other. We're not really hurting, but we're

New Eagle Timothy B. Schmit (left) takes the stage with bandmate Glenn Frey in November 1979.

not the richest band in the world. We have to go out and work to keep our payments up."

Those frustrations were forcing him to consider a change. But a neighbor had some news that would prove welcomed. Eagles insider **J.D. Souther**, who lived across the street from Schmit in the Hollywood hills, tipped him off.

"I could see [Souther's] house from mine, and we used to hang out a lot," Schmit said. "One time I was over there, and he said, 'I'm not supposed to tell you this, you've got to keep it quiet. But I think you're going to get a call that Randy is quitting, and I'm pretty sure you're going to get [an offer to join

the Eagles].'" It was a big break. "That night, I was mentally jumping up and down for joy," Schmit said.

Souther's prediction proved correct: "I can't remember how much time passed," Schmit continued. "It wasn't that long—maybe a few days, maybe a week or two. And I did get the call. I got the call from Glenn."

Schmit said he took great care in letting his Poco bandmates know. "I went to all of their houses individually and told them I had to do something else," Schmit said. "It was important for me to do it that way. I felt kind of nervous each time, but they all understood and gave me their blessings."

Even as he was doing that, Frey asked Schmit not to share the news. "I had to keep a lid on it," he explained about the conversation he had with Frey. Eventually, though, news started leaking out in trade publications, possibly after Schmit informed his bandmates in Poco that he would be leaving.

"When you lose a bass player you've been playing with for years, it's hard to immediately establish a tight connection with someone new," Meisner told *BAM* after the release of his solo album in 1980.

"It's a matter of learning when Don is going to kick down on the bass drum and when to fill in," he added. "But Tim's a great bass player and has a really strong voice. I'm looking forward to hearing their next album."

With the Eagles' help, Schmit would cut the track that would become his signature song. Switching bass players, however, would not eliminate the pressures within the band, and a "long run" (despite the name of the next album) was not in the cards for anyone. [48, 670, 674, 1268, 1665, 1666, 1745, 1746, 1747, 1748, 1751, 1820, 2134]

NUGGETS (cont.)

▶ Eagles arranger **Jim Ed Norman** got a nice surprise when he left his production chores with **Anne Murray** to wed **Tricia Johns**. Though he had to fly back the following day, some thoughtful folks hired a plane pulling a banner to circle his house with the message "Jim Ed and Tricia with a bullet." It was rumored the Eagles had something to do with it. —*Cashbox*

▶ Former Eagle Randy Meisner signed a solo contract with E/A and is now in the studio. —*Cashbox*

▶ On a twin-bill Eagles-**Fleetwood Mac** show, the Mac's **John McVie** and **Mick Fleetwood** leave a practical joke bouquet of red roses for **Stevie Nicks** in the band's dressing room signed "The best of my love...Tonight? -Don [Henley]" Nicks was absolutely fuming at Henley's presumptiveness. Then bandmate **Christine McVie** told her the flowers were actually sent by the mischevious duo of Mick and John, who were, she said, "in hysterics." —*Crawdaddy*

▶ Leber-Krebs plans to convert the music and story of the Eagles' *Desperado* into a feature-length movie. —*Cashbox*

▶ Don Henley has corraled a bunch of his contemporaries, **J.D. Souther** and Don Felder among them, to back up **Glenda Griffith** on her debut album. —*Cashbox*

COLLABORATIONS

▶ **Don Henley** provided backing vocals on the single "Blue Bayou" on **Linda Ronstadt**'s album *Simple Dreams*.

▶ **Glenn Frey** provided backing vocals on the single "If He's Ever Near" on **Karla Bonoff**'s album *Karla Bonoff*.

▶ **Joe Walsh** played lead guitar and slide guitar on **Jay Ferguson**'s album *Thunder Island*.

▶ **Don Henley** (backing vocals), **Timothy B. Schmit** (backing vocals), **Glenn Frey** (guitar, backing vocals), and **Joe Walsh** (guitar, slide guitar) provided musical support on **Randy Newman**'s album *Little Criminals*.

COLLABORATIONS (cont.)

▶ **Don Henley** (co-producer, drums, percussion, backing and harmony vocals), **Don Felder** (electric guitar, acoustic guitar), **Joe Walsh** (guitar), and **Timothy B. Schmit** (bass guitar, harmony vocals) provided musical support on **Glenda Griffith**'s album *Glenda Griffith*.

ON THE ROAD WITH ...

▶ **Bernie Leadon & Michael Georgiades Band**: Linda Ronstadt

Souther, Henley Join Ronstadt In Studio for *Simple Dreams*

As the Eagles rose through the pop ranks in the early 1970s, so did their early, ardent supporter, **Linda Ronstadt**. Her cover version of the Eagles' "Desperado" drew renewed attention to the band when the album of the same name was slipping into obscurity.

Fast-forwarding to autumn 1977, Ronstadt's *Simple Dreams* was a terrific album featuring a gung-ho version of **Warren Zevon**'s "Poor Poor Pitiful Me" and a barnstorming rendition of **Buddy Holly**'s "It's So Easy." She delivered a moving interpretation of **J.D. Souther**'s mellow "Simple Man, Simple Dream" and the songwriter also contributed guitar and vocals on the album.

However, the stand-out track, "Blue Bayou," renewed Ronstadt's Eagles connection as Don Henley contributed inspired vocals to her dreamy version of the **Roy Orbison** classic during the sessions that summer with producer **Peter Asher**.

Henley's voice may have added richness to the track, but it might not have ever been recorded without some unsolicited advice from another Eagle and his unofficial Eagle pal.

"J.D. and Glenn [Frey] simultaneously suggested 'Blue Bayou' to me sorta like Twiddle Dee and Twiddle Dum [sic]," Ronstadt told writer **Barbara Charone** while imitating both. "We sat up all night talking like mice at incredible speeds, playing and singing half the songs we knew, all of us singing in different keys. I've got a tape of it and it's the fastest tape I've ever heard. It sounds like R2D2."

Thanks in part to Frey and Souther's suggestion, and Henley's backing vocals, Ronstadt's version of "Blue Bayou" went on to score a Grammy nomination for Record of the Year after *Simple Dreams* had topped the *Billboard* album chart for five weeks straight late in 1977. [2045, 2046, 2121]

WINTER 1977-78

 AWARDS

▶ **Eagles, 5th Annual American Music Awards:**

● Favorite Pop/Rock Band/Duo/Group, nominated. Lost to **Fleetwood Mac**. Also nominated: **KC and the Sunshine Band**.

● Favorite Pop/Rock Album, *Hotel California*, nominated. Lost to **Fleetwood Mac**, *Rumours*. Also nominated: **John Williams**, *Star Wars*.

▶ **Eagles, 20th Annual Grammy Awards:**

● Record of the Year—"*Hotel California*," winner (accepted in 2016). Also nominated: **Barbra Streisand**, "Love Theme from 'A Star is Born,'" **Crystal Gayle**, "Don't It Make My Brown Eyes Blue," **Debby Boone**, "You Light Up My Life," and **Linda Ronstadt**, "Blue Bayou."

● Best Vocal Arrangement for Two or More Voices—"New Kid in Town," winner.

 AWARDS (cont.)

Also nominated: **Heatwave**, "All You Do Is Dial," **Seals & Crofts**, "Baby I'll Give It to You," **Fleetwood Mac**, "Go Your Own Way," and **Quincy Jones**, "Oh Lord, Come By Here."

● Album of the Year—*Hotel California*, nominated. Lost to **Fleetwood Mac**, *Rumours*. Also nominated: **James Taylor**, *JT*, **John Williams** (conducting the **London Symphony Orchestra**), *Star Wars*, and **Steely Dan**, *Aja*.

● Best Pop Performance by a Duo or Group with Vocals—"Hotel California," nominee. Lost to the **Bee Gees**, "How Deep Is Your Love." Also nominated: **Steely Dan**, *Aja*, and **Fleetwood Mac**, *Rumours*.

 NUGGETS

▶ Glenn Frey, Joe Walsh, and Don Felder joined Elektra/Asylum Chairman **Joe Smith** on a trip to Super Bowl. —*Record World*

▶ Glenn Frey and **Jimmy Buffett** flew to the Caicos Islands and jumped on Jimmy's ketch *Euphoria*. They dropped anchor in a peaceful cove on the northeast coast of the Domincan Republic to ride out some bad weather. There were only three other sailboats anchored there, and Buffett and Frey were happily anonymous. They were invited aboard one of those neighboring boats—what music did they have below deck? Just cassettes of the Eagles and Buffett. —*Crawdaddy*

▶ **Jimmy Buffett** threw a standing-room only benefit concert at the Aspen School of Music where he was joined by Eagles Glenn Frey and Don Henley. The concert ended up overbooked, so police were called in to help cull the crowd. —*Cashbox*

▶ Tim Schmit has left **Poco** and will join the Eagles. His first song with the group will be a Christmas single. —*Record World*

NUGGETS (cont.)

▶ Joe Walsh weighed his pockets down in the deep end of the swimming pool of his Coconut Grove, Florida, hotel for a photo shoot for his new album. He would swim down, then come up gasping for air between shots. Every time he went down his ears would pop—he had to cancel his recording sessions that night. An elaborate camera was rented from a movie studio, but it was missing a key part that ruined the shoot. Everything had to be re-shot a week later, but this time it all worked beautifully.—*Jimmy Wachtel*

▶ **David Geffen** has resigned his post as assistant to the chairman and board member at Warner Communications. —*Record World*

COLLABORATIONS

▶ **Glenn Frey** provided additional lyrics on the single "Cocaine" on **Jackson Browne**'s album *Running On Empty*.

▶ **Glenn Frey** provided backing vocals on the single "Off Night Backstreet" on **Joni Mitchell**'s album *Don Juan's Reckless Daughter*.

Soul Pole: Szymczyk Compiles Tongue-in-Cheek Outtakes LPs

Amid the pops and clicks of a worn vinyl record there's an echo of the sound of chuckles and occasional laughs. Studio chatter rises up and trails off, and then Glenn Frey's distinctive, distant voice calls out, "I know you got that goddamned tape recorder going, Szymczyk." And more chuckling ensues.

It was 1976, and the Eagles and **Bill Szymczyk** were in Miami recording tracks at Criteria Studios for *Hotel California*. Szymczyk built a sterling reputation as a sound engineer and producer for the Eagles,

but he was also an audiophile pack rat. He liked to document everything. Although Frey audibly took notice of the producer's recorder, its presence was an open secret. Szymczyk would often leave a tape rolling between session takes and let his microphones capture the banter between the band, the producer, and others in the studio. The results were sometimes funny, profane, and filled with inside jokes. But they were mostly just good, stress-relieving fun.

Szymczyk had started leaving the tapes rolling a few years earlier, and his first victim was fellow prankster Joe Walsh. Later, the producer captured the studio antics of the **J. Geils Band**, and he left the mics on for the Eagles, too.

Later in the decade, Szymczyk began compiling these outtakes along with other bits like fake commercials poking fun at weight loss pills and the frequent punching bag of the era, New York Telephone. He compiled these recordings into limited-run LPs that he would give as Christmas gifts to band members, studio engineers, and crew. He only pressed 50 per year.

He dubbed the albums *Soul Pole* after his nickname, which blended his love for rhythm & blues with his Polish heritage. Only four of the albums were ever pressed: *Soul Pole #1* captured outtakes from Walsh, *Soul Pole #2* covered J. Geils, and *Soul Poles #3* and #4 were outtakes from the Eagles' *One of These Nights* and *Hotel California* sessions, respectively.

The Eagles recordings included cutting up between Frey, Walsh, Don Henley, and others. One included a radio interview with Frey and Henley about *One of These Nights*, which segued into a prank recording of the song with a purposely out-of-tune Don Felder hitting painfully off-key notes live on the air. The pair was confused, and then got the joke and laughed out loud. Other pieces of the Eagles outtakes included short tongue-in-cheek versions of "Hotel California" and "Pretty Maids All in a Row."

Some of the recordings made it onto the Eagles' *1972-1999 Selected Works* box set as "Random Victims," which Frey addressed in the album's liner notes.

"The evil Bill Szymczyk always ran a separate two-track machine during our recording sessions," Frey wrote sarcastically. "Besides blackmail, his other motivation was to preserve for all time some of the most idiotic things we ever did in a recording studio. Here are some gems from Bill's 'Soul Pole' collection."

The *Soul Pole* series remains a rare, but not impossible, find. At press time in August 2022, less-than-mint versions were going for around $500. [2061, 2067, 2068, 2076]

Grammy No-Shows: Eagles Absent for 'Hotel,' 'New Kid' Wins

The Eagles' history with the Grammy Awards from the early to mid-1970s was a mixed bag of success and disappointment. They lost the award for Best New Artist to **America** in 1973 and were not heard from again until they won Best Pop Vocal Performance by a Duo, Group or Chorus for "Lyin' Eyes" in 1975.

The massive success of *One of These Nights* changed things. The band had improved dramatically since their debut album, and now, after *Hotel California* became the #1 album on the charts in three short weeks and spent the first six months of 1977 in the Top 10, the accolades were not in short supply.

When the National Academy of Recording Arts and Sciences unveiled the 20th Annual Grammy Awards nominations in early 1978, spotlighting works released in 1977, the Eagles received five nods: Album of the Year for *Hotel California*; Record of the Year for the title track single; Song of the Year for "Hotel California"; Best Arrangement for Two or More Voices for "New Kid in Town"; Best Pop Vocal Group; and Producer of the Year for *Hotel California* producer **Bill Szymczyk**.

Eagles had not warmed up to music industry awards or shows celebrating them. The group was touring when it won its first Grammy in 1976. But as popular as they had been then, *Hotel California* made them America's hottest rock band and the Recording Academy wanted their star power to beef up ratings for their February 23 telecast.

Grammy show producer **Pierre Cossette** reached out to Eagles' manager **Irving Azoff** hoping to get the band to attend and perform or, at the very least, be there to collect any Grammys they might win.

Azoff was sensitive to the band's awards-show reticence, and audaciously told Cossette the band would attend only if he could confirm they had won. Of course, industry types and fans alike knew that only the accounting firm tallying the votes knew the winners in advance. Cossette declined; he did not want to compromise the show's integrity.

A series of day-long "what-ifs" then rattled back and forth between Azoff and Cossette. Azoff allegedly first offered a video clip of the Eagles performing "Hotel California," which Cossette declined. Then he then suggested the Eagles could be sequestered backstage and appear if they won. If they lost, no one would know they were there. Hopeful, Cossette took that offer back to the Recording Academy's board of directors, who eventually nixed the idea. Finally, near the end of the day, Azoff finally told Cossette's staff the Eagles would not be there at all, and to have the show's host **John Denver** accept the award for them.

But at showtime, with an audience of 6,000 music industry pros and a handful of civilians packed into the Shrine Auditorium near Downtown Los Angeles, and a televised worldwide audience of millions about to tune in, Cossette still clung to the hope the Eagles would appear. After the broadcast went live, the seven-year Grammy show producer spent much of his evening nervously pacing backstage.

When "New Kid in Town" won the Grammy for Best Arrangement for Two or More Voices, there was no Eagle in sight.

As the evening went on, the odds and Eagle would show up to accept any award slipped from slim toward none. That forced Cossette to reshuffle the order of the awards. All the members of **Fleetwood Mac**,

whose *Rumours* had also dominated the charts in 1977, showed up to collect their Album of the Year Grammy.

Cossette's last hope for the Eagles to show was Record of the Year, the prestigious final award of the night. Four of the five nominees were in the house to potentially receive it—**Linda Ronstadt**, **Barbra Streisand**, **Debby Boone**, and **Crystal Gayle**. But, *Billboard* reported, the Eagles were an hour away in Malibu when they were announced the winner (the next day Azoff issued a press release that said the band was in Miami working on their next album).

Backstage, Cossette was infuriated. He and Azoff, who did attend that night, passed each other backstage and had a heated exchange. "If you'd told me they'd won, I would have had them here," Azoff said, as recounted by *Billboard*'s **Paul Grein**, who had been shadowing Cossette all day for a magazine feature. Cossette reminded Azoff that he could not since no one knew the results until the envelope was opened. After that, Grein wrote, the tension lifted.

In the end it was **Andy Williams**, the former Grammys host and presenter for the Record of the Year, who said "I guess they couldn't be here," as he sheepishly accepted the Eagles' award. Backstage, **Stephen Stills** and **David Crosby**, decked out in formal attire, found Azoff and congratulated the band. The praise was likely welcomed, but the outfits were not.

"Rock and roll does not belong in a tuxedo," Frey told *Rolling Stone* weeks later. "When we saw [Crosby and Stills] walk out there, my fuckin' heart sank. It was like the end of an era."

Eagles weren't alone in giving the Grammys bad news that year. **James Taylor**, nominated for Best Pop Vocal Performance for "Handy Man" was also a no-show. And Ronstadt declined Cossette's request to perform. Still, the show set viewership records for the Academy, and the share of television sets tuned into the program rose from 39 percent at 9 p.m. that night to 48 percent by 11 p.m.

As is its custom, the Recording Academy told *Time Passages* it mailed the band their Grammys shortly after the telecast. Although the Academy was not able to give the band their awards in 1978, it would get another chance in 2016.

On the evening of the 58th Annual Grammy Awards the Eagles, **Jackson Browne**, and the Academy paid tribute to Glenn Frey, who had died two months earlier. After the band performed "Take It Easy," the Academy asked them to remain on the stage and NARAS' then-President **Neil Portnow** and **Ken Ehrlich**, Cosette's successor as Grammy telecast producer, made the presentation nearly 40 years after the February 1978 telecast. [408, 1951, 1952, 2003]

SPRING 1978

 RELEASES
▶ **Randy Meisner**, "I Really Want You Here Tonight" (single)
▶ **Joe Walsh**, *But Seriously, Folks...* (album)

 COLLABORATIONS
▶ Glenn Frey (guitar solo on "Till It Shines") and Don Felder (guitar on "Ain't Got No Money") on **Bob Seger**'s album *Stranger in Town*.
▶ Don Felder (pedal steel guitar), Don Henley (backing vocals), Glenn Frey (backing vocals) and Timothy B. Schmit (backing vocals) provided musical support on Joe Walsh's album *But Seriously, Folks....*

 NUGGETS
▶ **Jimmy Buffett** and his gang beat the Eagles in an extra-inning softball game in Coconut Grove, Florida. Eagles have also challenged *Rolling Stone* to a softball game in Los Angeles with the loser donating $5,000 to UNICEF.
—*Record World*
▶ Eagles perform in benefit opposing California's Proposition 15 (Nuclear Safeguards).—*Record World*
▶ Jimmy Buffett broke two bones in his leg in a prep game for the Eagles match against *Rolling Stone*, so he won't be able to play for them. Undaunted, he went on *Saturday Night Live* as the guest musician anyway, full leg cast and all. —*Cashbox*
▶ Eagles beat *Rolling Stone* in their softball game, but someone stole Glenn Frey's Eagles jacket, keys, and wallet. Dodgers manager **Tommy Lasorda** congratulated **Irving Azoff** via telegram, and told him, "I won't teach my guys to sing or play guitar if you keep your guys off the field." —*Cashbox*
▶ It keeps getting worse for Jimmy Buffett. Doctors say the leg he broke practicing for the Eagles-*Rolling Stone* game isn't healing properly, so they had to re-break it. —*Cashbox*
▶ Irving Azoff is racking up starpower for the soundtrack of the **John Travolta** movie he is producing, *Urban Cowboy*. The Eagles, Joe Walsh, and **Mickey Gilley** are in. —*Cashbox*

'The Long One': Eagles Begin Follow-Up to *Hotel California*

Eagles were Elektra/Asylum's most profitable act, and *Hotel California* delivered the goods. Naturally, the label wanted more from the band since whatever they recorded would certainly sell. So in March 1978, **Irving Azoff** coaxed the band to gather in Miami to begin work on the album that would become *The Long Run*.

The idea was to give them several months to write and record the new disc so it could be delivered in time for E/A to capitalize on the year-end holiday buying season. But that timetable did not work for the band.

The rock and roll whirlwind they'd been in for years included a grueling work schedule, massive success, and all the stereotypical 1970s rock star vices. The core band members were physically and mentally fried. Additionally, the group—and particularly Don Henley, who was now handling most of the lead vocals, felt enormous pressure to attempt to follow up one of the biggest albums in the history of rock music.

In no short order, Elektra/Asylum learned that while it could hope for a new album by year's end, that was just not going to happen. There was no backlog of unused songs ready to be recorded, nor usable outtakes from previous sessions in the can.

The label's chairman, **Joe Smith**, tried to sweeten the deal by offering a million-dollar bonus if the group could deliver in time for the holidays. Meeting that deadline was not possible because they still had not finished writing songs for the album, they said. Smith jokingly sent the band a rhyming dictionary.

The sessions for the album with producer **Bill Szymczyk** occurred in fits and starts. The group reacted with a shrug while acknowledging the mounting pressure. "Dylan says, 'They deceived me into thinking I had something to protect,'" Glenn Frey explained, "and I think that would probably be a good way to describe the first couple of months in the studio when we were working on *The Long Run*."

"We were staring down the barrel of what *Hotel California* had left for us," Don Felder said. "That's tough to beat."

"We were real uptight," Frey said of the first day in the studio. "[We were] trying to be relaxed and keep everybody loose. But the fact of the matter was that going into the studio the first time after *Hotel California* wasn't exactly what I would call a day at the races. It's just a lot of pressure was laid [on] everybody's shoulders as far as performance...the sound of the record... production [values]...material...the writing. It was an uncomfortable situation to be in. Even though everybody tried to relax, to be cool—we know we're good—we just had trouble getting it going."

The Eagles, it seemed, were going to work following their own schedule, not one dictated by their record label. When the recording began, one of the first songs the band would tackle was newcomer Timothy B. Schmit's "I Can't Tell You Why," which Frey and Henley helped turn into a soulful R&B song.

Frey said there was a reason why they chose this different direction for Schmit. "Timothy joined the band, and the real challenge, as Don and I saw it, was to get a piece of material for him that wasn't country...[and] the three of us got down to work. I said, 'You could sing like **Smokey Robinson**. Let's not do a **Richie Furay, Poco**-sounding song. Let's do an R&B song.'"

The Schmit-Frey-Henley work would eventually produce the Top 10 hit "I Can't Tell You Why" and thaT represented a solid start for the overdue album, but burnout affected the rest of the early writing and recording sessions. And there would be plenty more starts and stops over the next couple of years while attempting to finish *The Long Run*.

"We were physically, emotionally, spiritually and creatively exhausted," Henley conceded in 2016. "Our collective tank was empty. We'd been touring relentlessly, even in-between recording sessions. We should have taken a one-year hiatus, but the Big Machine demanded to be fed. Momentum had to be maintained. There were big bucks at stake, the corporate stockholders had expectations, jobs were on the line."

With expectations high, the band slogged through the arduous and laborious sessions. When *The Long Run* was finally done, it would yield some new Eagles classics and a handful of remarkable songs, including their last #1 single, "Heartache Tonight.".

Still, the album would also contain some of the more critically questionable Eagles tracks in the band's canon. The latter assessment could, and historically would, be attributed to the fatigue factor within the ranks. [6, 209, 1494, 1603, 1820]

Hitchhiker's Guide to the Galaxy Picks Up Leadon's 'Journey'

After Bernie Leadon left the Eagles at the end of 1975, he became a sought-after session musician and producer, supporting artists ranging from pop to folk to straight-up bluegrass over the next two years. Then, in 1977, an unexpected caller offered to breathe new life into one of the songs he wrote with the Eagles, an otherwise obscure track on *One of These Nights*.

Leadon's early post-Eagles credits included sessions and/or gigs with **David Bromberg, Dan McCorison, Emmylou Harris, Chris Hillman, Helen Reddy, Craig Nuttycombe, Linda Ronstadt**, the **Woodstock Mountains Revue**, and **Andy Fairweather Low**. Leadon and **Michael Georgiades**, his next-door neighbor and friend, also released an album in 1977.

But when the British Broadcasting Company reached out from London and asked for the right to use his "Journey of the Sorcerer," the inquiry seemed to come out of nowhere, or maybe from a galaxy far, far away.

Author **Douglas Adams**, who was developing the BBC comedic sci-fi radio series *The Hitchhiker's Guide to Galaxy*, was looking for a spacey but not-too-serious theme song, and recalled the dramatic "Journey" from *One of These Nights*. An Eagles fan, Adams had bought the album in 1975, and it had an immediate impact on him. He had just put it on his turntable the day he called, according to Leadon in a conversation with **John Beaudin** for RockMusicHistory.com. Adams thought the cut's cinematic feel would fit nicely with what the BBC wanted as intro music for the show. And the fact that it was, at its core, an operatic banjo instrumental checked the "not-too-serious" box. It was perfect for the production.

Led by *Hitchhiker's Guide* producer **Geoffrey Perkins**, the BBC agreed, and Adams made the call to get permission to use it. Leadon said the BBC had to go through the English branch of Warner Bros. to secure the licensing. They got the rights to use the music for a paltry £500 fee, which was about $1,000 USD at the time. In later iterations of the radio show and the 1980s television show, the BBC avoided costly renegotiations with the Eagles by using cover versions of the song pulled from different segments of Leadon's opus. The band **Illegal Eagles** recorded the cover versions to keep down production costs. The first episode with Leadon's song as the lead-in aired on March 8, 1978.

Disney started work on a big-screen adaptation of the series in 2003, and this time the producers could not circumvent Leadon without violating the synchronization portion of copyright law.

"So [Disney] had to negotiate with me," Leadon said, "and we got $175,000 for the rights for the film." Not bad for an inspiring

> **NOBODY ELSE IN THE BAND WAS IN FAVOR OF IT, BUT I THOUGHT IT WAS NICE...IT WAS A BANJO THEME, AND WE PUT SOME STRINGS ON IT, SOME BACKWARDS GUITAR, AND SOME SPACE SOUNDS... I LIKED OUR ORIGINAL TITLE BETTER: 'FELLINI IN FLORIDA.'**
>
> — BILL SZYMCZYK

but commercially forgettable track.

When they were putting together *One of These Nights* in the studio, neither Glenn Frey nor Don Henley thought the song was a good fit for the album. It clocked in at a long six-and-a-half minutes, and, while inspiring, it had no commercial appeal for AM radio. Leadon stubbornly insisted they record it, and they begrudgingly relented.

"I'm glad somebody picked up on it," Eagles producer **Bill Szymczyk** said of the BBC's choice. "It was a fairly spacey record, and I had quite a bit to do with that because by now, everybody knows there was this big rift going on [with the members of the band], and Bernie...wanted to do this instrumental.

"Nobody else in the band was in favor of [it], but I thought it was really nice, so we did it. It was a banjo theme, and we put strings on it, some backwards guitar, and some space sounds and stuff like that. I really enjoyed that cut, and I still listen to it now, but I liked our original title for it better—'Journey of the Sorcerer' seems a little wimpy for me because our working title was 'Fellini in Florida.'"

For all the rancor the song's inclusion on *Nights* caused, it has become a favorite among *Hitchhiker's Guide* fans in the United Kingdom. **Nicholas Lezard**, a columnist for London's *The Independent*, explained a mild dilemma the song had caused for fans of the show in a 2004 column.

These fans, he wrote, "to put it politely... find themselves aligned with a segment of the population with whom they would rather not be. I think it may be telling that many of the initial fans asked the BBC what the title music was and where they could get it, and were told it was 'Journey of the Sorcerer' from the Eagles album *One of These Nights*, and realized they already had it in their collections. It was not one of those songs Eagles fans listen to, then, which I think doesn't cover the song with glory."

But, Lezard reasoned, as the theme music for the *Hitchhiker's Guide*, "it works a treat," and noted that the show itself draws every Trekkie, dweeb, and "girlfriendless young male in the land."

Indeed, British novelist **Lloyd Shepherd** wrote in a 2012 blog post that he was "genuinely amazed" by the song and its origins. "What an extraordinary mixture of heritages: a gawky middle-class boy from England writes a sardonic, witty, inventive spoof of science-fiction, which is turned into a radio and TV series by similarly gawky and middle-class boys from the BBC, and to introduce it, they find a piece of music by a band who by then were the byword for West Coast rock pomposity and excess. And somehow they find the one piece of music the band recorded that sounds like British prog."

It's doubtful Leadon thought he was creating a banjo-driven **Pink Floyd**-esque piece when he composed "Journey," but

still felt he had something special even before Szymcyzk added the orchestral strings that enveloped it with its rich, dramatic feel. Those strings were highly unusual for such a folksy work.

"That was an economic decision," Leadon said about the orchestral treatment. "It was later in the production of that album, and **Jim Ed Norman** handled the string arrangements for the Eagles."

They had also brought **David Bromberg** to play fiddle alongside the **Royal Martian Orchestra** for "Take It to the Limit." But after the band finished recording, there was still time remaining on the orchestra's clock.

"The way orchestral sessions work is, first of all, you hire an arranger, and then you hire the string session players, which is usually between twelve and eighteen string players, and it's a union session, and it lasts three hours on the dot," Leadon said in his interview with Beaudin. "You get as much recording done as you can get done in the three hours, and then you're done. But I think we only had one, maybe two, to get done in that three-hour session. So, we said, 'Well, we got enough time to do another song. So why don't we do an orchestral arrangement on 'Journey of the Sorcerer?' So, we did because the other songs were essentially paying for the string sessions."

A banjo instrumental with an orchestral treatment is not something one would expect to hear every day.

"So, it's one of the extremely few kinds of funky banjo flailing songs that have a full string session on it, because who could afford to do that, right?" Leadon remarked. "The banjo is a working-class instrument anyway, but it works really great." [132, 2097, 2098, 2099, 2100, 2101]

Azoff Eyes Real Radio Life in *FM*, But Hollywood Hijacks Movie

The premise of *FM* was reflected in the reality of the day, as a ragtag group of DJs tried to hold back the corporatization of late 1970s rock radio. But the resulting movie relied on so many clichés that it ended up bombing at the box office.

Before its premiere, Executive Producer **Irving Azoff** had asked that his name be removed from the credits, telling the *Los Angeles Times* that "the film is not an authentic representation of the music business."

FM is actually a beautifully shot time capsule of a movie. Director **John Alonzo**, a cinematographer known for his work on *Chinatown*, had a knack for capturing sets, hair, and costumes as resonant of the era as this movie's star-packed soundtrack. Talented actors including **Martin Mull**, **Eileen Brennan**, and **Cleavon Little** gamely played along.

Unfortunately, **Ezra Sacks**' script didn't do them any favors, as the DJs ultimately staged a station takeover—only to be somehow validated by a previously stodgy owner at the film's conclusion. It's the sort of gift-wrapped, out-of-nowhere ending that moviegoers might have expected from a back-to-school special, but not a big-budget Hollywood production.

Azoff was roiled by Hollywood's need for

Eagles manager **Irving Azoff**'s first attempt at producing movies was the feature film *FM*, which turned into a fiasco, but with songs by Eagles, **Linda Ronstadt**, **Steely Dan**, and a host of A-list performers, the soundtrack still became a million-seller.

a happy ending at the expense of realism. The actual issue with *FM*, however, seemed to be more personal.

He claimed Universal Pictures "reneged" on a promise of creative control, which led to a few high-profile skirmishes on a variety of casting and production issues. Azoff believed he could have secured **Richard Dreyfuss** and **Dustin Hoffman** for the film, but the studio passed. And then they bickered over the film's opening date. He began publicly questioning things not long after finally getting the May premiere he'd wanted all along: "I don't know about that movie," Azoff told *Rolling Stone* in 1978. "Something's wrong. I tell the studio it's not authentic [and] they say, 'Hey, this is movieland; nothing's authentic.' I'm handcuffed."

continued on Page 325

The inside sleeve of of Joe Walsh's solo album *But Seriously, Folks...* showed just how far he would go for a laugh. The table, food, chairs, and umbrella from the underwater photo shoot were weighed down, and he almost drowned.

SERIOUSLY, WALSH SERVES UP BEST SOLO EFFORT

Comparisons with the Eagles inevitably followed Joe Walsh's fourth album, partly because *But Seriously, Folks...* was his first solo project since joining the group, and partly because all four of his new bandmates guested on various tracks.

But the Eagles were bit players in Walsh's definitive statement of purpose, as he constructed an LP deftly pairing rockers with ballads and joy and wit with a touch of nostalgia.

Walsh proved his dedication to his new band by offering every song he wrote to the Eagles, not stashing away his best for a solo project. But not everything in Walsh's deep stockpile of material could find a home on *Hotel California*—his new group simply had too many talented contributors.

"The songs he brought to [*But Seriously, Folks...*] were songs that he brought to the Eagles," Walsh's former **Barnstorm** bandmate **Joe Vitale** said later to **Rich Redmond**. "They had enough songs

because they're all great writers in that band."

Evidence of Walsh's new musical partnership abounds on *But Seriously, Folks...* as Glenn Frey, Don Henley, and Timothy B. Schmit contribute background vocals to "Tomorrow," and Felder adds a crying pedal steel to "Second Hand Store." Felder and Walsh even recall the twin-guitar interplay of "Hotel California" on "At the Station."

Still, this 1978 project was more reflective of the fun-seeking Walsh as an individual artist than the serious-minded musical perfectionists he had taken up with as an Eagle.

For starters, he wanted to avoid the tension

associated with the Eagles' sessions. "For this album, I had my studio in Miami—Bayshore Recording," producer **Bill Szymczyk** told *Music Radar* in 2015. "Rather than go right to the studio, though, Joe said, 'Let's rent a boat and rehearse this stuff.'"

A lesser-known song on the LP had the best backstory. Szymczyk, Walsh, and his crew had planned to rehearse at Szymczyk's "hideaway" cabin in North Carolina in January 1975. But a foot of snow days before scuttled that possibility.

"So we really had to hustle and try to figure out something else," Szymczyk told *TapeOp*, "and we finally got this seventy-two-foot yacht called 'The Endless Seas' up in Fort Lauderdale, and we loaded a four-track on it, a set of drums, electric piano, some guitars and amps and so on, and we went down to the Keys, and anchored down there, and made demos for a week."

One of those boat demos, Szymczyk added, was so good it became the final track because they couldn't top the recording even with superior equipment. They titled the instrumental track "Theme From Boat Weirdos."

"If you're looking for spontaneity, that was done on a four-track on a boat in the middle of the ocean, and we couldn't beat it re-recording in the studio [at Bayshore], so we used it."

The experience of collaborating aboard a swanky yacht on a sojourn through the Florida Keys led to moments like "Life's Been Good," Walsh's comic meditation on his famous rock-star lifestyle. The Top 20 hit became his highest-charting solo single.

And just as there has always been more to Walsh than his court-jester persona, *But Seriously, Folks...* had depth and breadth. The album also made room for the adult sadness of "Indian Summer," the funky reggae groove found on "Over and Over," and the stand-out "Theme From Boat Weirdos."

Still, Walsh would usually go the extra distance in the service of a prank or gag. On the album's cover, Walsh worked with prolific album designer **Jimmy Wachtel** to create an underwater dining experience with Walsh decked out in a suit eating a meal. Walsh wanted the cover lighthearted and funny, sure, but the photo shoot nearly killed him.

Wachtel told *Time Passages* he arranged the shoot

Walsh offered all of his latest songs to the Eagles for *Hotel California* first, then recorded the songs they didn't need for his *But Seriously, Folks...* solo album.

at Walsh's Coconut Grove hotel next to Bayshore Recording. He rented an expensive camera from a movie studio, and Walsh took a plunge for the shots. But a key camera part was missing, and they were forced to re-do the entire shoot a week later at a friend's pool in the San Fernando Valley.

"I had to do that a couple of times, but I did go down to the bottom of the pool and almost drowned...it was fun," Walsh said. "Not at the time, but it was fun to do. We weighted everything down, but it was very involved, and it took a long time, and I was real proud of it. It was hard to do, but when I look at it, I can't believe it either, I can't believe I was stupid enough to do that, but I was proud of it. I won't be repeating it, I can assure you!"

But Seriously, Folks... was one of Walsh's most fully realized albums, and it would have been even without all those famous friends. But it would not have been as much fun to record.

"That album is a masterpiece; Joe was on top of the world writing," Vitale told Redmond. "He had some killer songs, and that was my favorite all-time album because it was musical, and it ended up selling the most copies. It was a brilliant record."

"That album was a prize, a great one," Szymczyk agreed. [385, 1873, 1874, 1875]

In the end, Azoff only got input on the musical side of things, and that was the breaking point. Feeling like the studio had exploited him for his industry connections, an annoyed Azoff promised to approach promoting the *FM* soundtrack "as if the movie [did not] exist."

And he did. Filming started in October 1977 in Los Angeles and then moved to Houston for a week to capture an actual **Linda Ronstadt** concert. Songs from this show were to be broadcast in the film on the fictional Q-SKY Radio, said to have been based on Los Angeles AOR station KMET-FM, where Sacks was previously employed. **Jimmy Buffett** also performed live in *FM*, while sharing screen time with **Tom Petty** and **REO Speedwagon**.

The producers initially wrapped their eight-week shoot after filming Buffett's performance at the New Coconut Grove in December 1977, but then they decided *FM* "needed a more exciting ending," according to the *Los Angeles Times*. Those reshoots didn't help. Instead, the corny final act fell flat, dooming the project. *FM* finished outside of the Top 50 films of 1978, despite its budget of more than $4 million.

The same can't be said for its soundtrack, which featured songs from the Eagles ("Life In the Fast Lane"), Randy Meisner ("Bad Man"), and Joe Walsh ("Life's Been Good"), along with contributions from **Bob Seger**, **Foreigner**, **Boston**, **Boz Scaggs**, **Billy Joel**, Petty, Buffett, and Ronstadt, among others.

Reviews of the film in spring 1978 were brutal with comments like "uninspiring"

and "amatuerish." Opinions on the movie didn't age well either. *Chicago Reader* critic **Dave Kehr** called it "an embarrassing youth cult film, founded on the shaky premise that the staff of a 'progressive' L.A. rock station have to fight their management for the right to play **Olivia Newton-John**." *AV Club* critic **Keith Phipps** went further. "[*FM*] gets the standard rock-movie formula backwards by trying to base a revolution around some of the safest, least revolutionary music in the history of rock." The film's *Rotten Tomatoes* score clocked in at a lowly 20% on the website's Tomatometer, but received a more forgiving 62% Audience Score. It was probably the soundtrack.

In sharp contrast with *FM*'s box-office receipts, the soundtrack album streaked to more than a million in sales. **Steely Dan**'s new title song, "FM (No Static At All)," became a Top 30 hit. Ironically, most everything ended up working in Azoff's favor—and not just because his management clients included the Eagles, Walsh, Buffett, Scaggs, and Steely Dan. Azoff's original contract with Universal gave him a percentage of the record sales. [681, 683, 684, 685, 2069, 2070]

Hollywood Flirts with Reluctant Eagles for *Hotel California* Film

When Don Henley and Glenn Frey were holed up in a Miami Beach estate filling legal pads with the lyrics that would become "Hotel California," they both had a specific goal: the song should have a cinematic feel.

"We wanted to write a song just like it

was a movie," Frey told **Cameron Crowe**. It's an understatement to say they succeeded, and Hollywood took note. Or at least one well-placed Hollywood producer took a keen interest.

Julia Phillips had Hollywood gravitas. She and her husband, **Michael Phillips**, and co-producer **Tony Bill**, turned a $3,500 script for *The Sting* into a **Paul Newman**-**Robert Redford** vehicle that grossed $160 million and won seven Academy Awards including Best Picture in 1973. It also made her the first woman to win an Oscar as a producer. Three years later, the now-divorced pair produced **Martin Scorsese**'s *Taxi Driver*, earning high praise and a Best Picture nod. A year later they were closing production on *Close Encounters of the Third Kind* with hotshot new director **Steven Spielberg**. So, when Phillips wanted to develop a movie, people listened.

Phillips had been working up a movie concept for two years that she called *The Third Man Out the Door*. In her tell-all autobiography, *You'll Never Eat Lunch in This Town Again*, she said she always wanted to produce a film "where the music was integral to the movie" and would "incorporate the musical talent and the writing talent at the very beginning." When she heard *Hotel California* in early 1977, she drew a correlation between parts of her *Third Man* project and the album.

As Phillips developed her idea of connecting her movie plot with the nation's biggest rock band, she discovered a fatal flaw. A tiny disclaimer on the back of the album said: "(Copyright in dispute)." Film-

ing a movie where the music is integral to the plot is a non-starter when the music's copyright owner is ambiguous.

Eagles had filed a lawsuit against Warner Bros. that spring to reclaim their publishing rights for past and future works, including *Hotel California*. Most record companies would halt production in the face of these legal challenges—**Bruce Springsteen** paused his career in 1976 when his former manager enjoined him. But the Eagles meant too much to Elektra/Asylum's bottom line, so the label pressed the album with the disclaimer and sent it to the adoring masses. Cashdrawer bells rang continually, and E/A and Eagles sorted the legal issues out that autumn, much to **David Geffen**'s chagrin.

But the copyright issue was a severe roadblock to Phillips. Warner Bros. Pictures was bankrolling her *Third Man* project, so she thought if she could entice the Eagles into the game, they could negotiate an end to the bitter legal stalemate and she could continue her project.

Enter Eagles' manager **Irving Azoff**, who was dabbling in films around this time. He had co-produced *FM*, a dramedy about marginalized deejays at a fictitious L.A. radio station. The movie wandered far from his original ideas and flopped, but he learned a lot about contracts and control over film projects; he would take a more measured approach in the months and years ahead. And he was curious when Phillips arranged a lunch meeting with him that spring.

Phillips, who admittedly had developed a

continued on Page 329

Timothy B. Schmit (left) gets a hug from champagne-swigging Glenn Frey after Eagles and crew beat *Rolling Stone*.

EAGLES CRUSH *ROLLING STONE* IN REVENGE GAME

"The Eagles, on their first vacation in three years, seem more interested in finding a softball team they can beat—having lost in recent weeks to teams fielded by **Andrew Gold**, **Jimmy Buffett**, employees of several San Francisco radio stations, and their own road crew."

So said writer **Charles M. Young** in a quip in *Rolling Stone* magazine's "Random Notes" gossip section in 1977. It was the latest barb thrown at the Eagles during a press war of sorts between the band and the most prominent rock publication, which had shifted its main offices from San Francisco to New York that year. At one point, *Rolling Stone* had called out the Eagles for "loitering" onstage.

Young's observation was accurate. Glenn Frey and his Eagles band mates and road crew had taken to playing charity softball games against other bands, radio stations, and the like. But this latest jab the magazine threw at the Eagles did not tell the whole story, and Frey was going to let them know.

"What you have failed to mention," Frey wrote back, "is that the Eagles won two out of three games against Jimmy Buffett. Anytime you pencil-pushing desk jockeys want to put on your spikes, we'll kick your ass, too."

With that, the gauntlet had been thrown down. "I hadn't been looking to start a feud with the Eagles," Young explained, "I was just looking to write a funny Random Note." He should have known that the Eagles would not take the insult lying down.

"Henley for his whole life has been an inveterate writer of letters," Young said. "If someone displeases him, he can send these little masterpieces of venom. Glenn Frey is equally smart, which is to say very smart."

After some more back and forth between Young and the band, they agreed that on May 7, 1978, the Eagles would square off against the magazine. Pride was on the line, along with the promise of a $5,000 donation to UNICEF courtesy of the losing team.

For the Eagles, all five members took the field

along with an assortment of roadies and crew members. Pitcher Don Henley (donning a shirt that read "BULLSHIT" across the chest) paired up with catcher Joe Walsh. Timothy B. Schmit handled the hot corner at third base, while Glenn Frey played opposite him at first base. Don Felder played in the outfield, along with ringer **Peter Cetera** of **Chicago**.

Rolling Stone fielded a lineup of Gonzos (a nod to "gonzo journalist" **Hunter S. Thompson**) including Young and notable scribes like **Cameron Crowe** (who wrote the Eagles' first *Rolling Stone* cover story in 1975), **Ben Fong-Torres** (who would write an Eagles biography, *Taking It to the Limit*, in 2011), and rock critic and **Bruce Springsteen** biographer **Dave Marsh**. **Jann Wenner**, the magazine's co-founder and publisher, attended but did not play.

Five thousand people showed up at Dedeaux Field at the University of Southern California to watch the game, most of them fans rooting for the Eagles. The crowd included notable celebrities like **Daryl Hall**, **Chevy Chase**, **Joni Mitchell**, and even then-governor of California, **Jerry Brown**.

"I expected [Brown] to be like a politician, being kind of fifty percent for the Eagles and fifty percent for *Rolling Stone*," Young remembered. "But the Eagles had done benefits for him, so of course, he was one hundred percent for the Eagles."

Being on the Eagles turf in Southern California certainly helped them. "That gives us a big advantage," Frey boasted during the pre-game coverage. "We're used to being in front of 20,000 people in concert, so the noise won't bother us. But those *Rolling Stone* guys are accustomed to sitting alone in a room with a typewriter. They'll be nervous as hell when all those people start yelling."

Prior to commencement, the crowd rose for the national anthem, though what followed through the PA speakers was not "The Star-Spangled Banner," but rather "Life in the Fast Lane."

In the end, the Eagles were demonstrably victorious, with a commanding victory of 15-8. "They had actually played together quite a bit and were a much better team," Young conceded years later. The error-prone journalists performed poorly.

"I didn't feel entirely personally humiliated because I played OK," he said, "but the team didn't do so well. It was an amazing and completely humiliating experience."

Though the *Los Angeles Times* referred to it as a "grudge" match, the adversarial battle between the band and the magazine was based on friendly ribbing and good public relations and press as much as anything. But much like there is truth in jest, there was real animosity simmering beneath the surface. As Frey commented, "With the exception of Cameron Crowe's cover story on us, I don't think the magazine has been particularly insightful as far as it comes to the Eagles."

After the game, the two teams put aside their differences and had dinner at Dan Tana's restaurant back in West Hollywood. For the Eagles, the savory taste of victory may have even surpassed that of the fine Italian cuisine served.

Beyond the secondary business of cleats and curveballs, the Eagles did provide one bit to the press that day related to the question everyone was asking about the follow-up to *Hotel California*: The new album was about a third done and expected to hit the shelves by late summer 1978. That prediction would be off by more than a year. [343, 477, 478, 573, 666, 667, 758, 1190, 1565, 1764, 1766, 1767, 1768]

EAGLES-*ROLLING STONE* BOX SCORE

Eagles 15, Gonzos 8

EAGLES	AB	R	H	GONZOS	AB	R	H
Schmit, 3b	5	3	4	Young, c	5	1	2
Frey, scf, 1b	5	4	2	Dunning, ss	5	1	2
Cetera, cf	3	3	2	Baron, 3b, cf	5	1	3
Sargeant, lf	3	0	2	Bahrenburg, 1b	5	1	3
Hollingsworth, lf	2	0	0	Warhaftig, cf	3	0	1
Fernandez, ss	4	1	2	Bornstein, 2b	2	0	1
Bassett, 2b	3	0	1	Reitz, p	4	0	2
Vacharino, 2b	1	0	0	Gilburg, p	0	0	0
Buttice, 1b	2	0	0	Marsh, ph	0	1	0
Lanham, scf	2	0	0	Klein, lf	4	0	1
Felder, rf	2	0	1	Sabbag, 2b	1	0	0
Szymczyk, rf	2	1	1	Ford, 2b, 3b	3	1	1
Walsh	2	1	1	Crowe, rf	3	0	1
Nixon, c	1	1	1	Herbst, scf	2	1	0
Henley, p	4	1	1	Kohn, scf	2	0	0
Halem, 1b	0	0	0	Cavanaugh, rf	2	1	2
				Fong-Torres, ph	1	0	0
Total	41	15	18	**Total**	47	8	19

Gonzos	003	000	023	-8	19	5
Eagles	030	306	004	-15	18	2

GONZOS	IP	H	R	BB	SO
Reitz, L, 0-1	7	18	15	3	0
Gilburg	1	0	0	0	0

EAGLES	IP	H	R	BB	SO
Henley, W, 1-0	9	19	8	4	0

Source: *Rolling Stone*

RANDY MEISNER

Randy Meisner
Asylum Records, June 1978

When perusing the jacket of Randy Meisner's 1978 self-titled album for Asylum (not to be confused with his also-eponymous 1982 LP), one thing jumps out immediately to the discerning fan: there is no new original material. True, the record does contain an acoustic guitar and piano remake of the song he's most identified with, "Take It to the Limit," but that is the only time Meisner's name appears as a songwriter on his debut disc.

"The Eagles convinced me to try to write," Meisner said, as quoted by writer **John Einarson** in 2001. "But still to this day, writing is real hard for me. I needed co-writers, and I wasn't fast enough like Henley and Frey became."

He would team up with co-writers on his future solo albums and join in the song creation process, but on *Randy Meisner* he left the composition to others.

Still, the record is not without its high points. Covers of classic '60s songs like "It Hurts to Be in Love" and "If You Wanna Be Happy" (popularized by **Gene Pitney** and **Jimmy Soul**, respectively) are, if nothing else, an enjoyable listen. Meisner's former Eagle-mate Glenn Frey contributed a stylistically contemporary song (co-written with **J.D. Souther**) called "Bad Man," which not only opens the album but also made it onto the *FM* soundtrack in 1978.

Eagles' country influence is most notable on a song by the album's producer, **Alan Brackett**, titled "Lonesome Cowgirl." The track is a straight-ahead saloon stomper; it references Stetson hats and foreshadows the fascination with Texas honky-tonk culture that emerged a couple years later in the wake of the 1980 film *Urban Cowboy.*

The record's most significant writing contributions are the trio of songs by guitarist **Billy Lamb**, who would release an album with his band **Lazy Racer** in 1979. "Every Other Day," Lamb's best song, emerges delightfully effervescent in Meisner's and Brackett's capable hands, with irresistibly feel-good backing vocals that belie the tune's darker message of ditching a trash-talking woman. "Too Many Lovers" is an emotive ballad, while "Daughter of the Sky" is mystical and epic, with richly layered harmonies.

However, *Randy Meisner* was a better listen than a commercial success. "Randy Meisner's debut solo album is unimpressive," **Bill King** of the *Atlanta Journal-Constitution* wrote, stating that his choice of material was poor. "This one album leaves you with the feeling it should have never been made."

By November 1978, the *Fort Worth Star-Telegram* reported that "former Eagle Randy Meisner has quit the music business to work a farm in the Midwest." [6, 1749, 1750, 2123]

cocaine habit so indulgent that she moved in with her dealer for economy, pitched her "develop movie, develop music" idea to an analytical Azoff.

"You think they're **The Beatles**?" Azoff asked, hinting at the band's landmark film *A Hard Day's Night*. "No, I think they're The Beagles. Nobody's The Beatles, even The Beatles anymore," she replied.

Phillips would provide the story, she said as her pitch continued, and the Eagles would give the music. Puzzled, Azoff stopped her and said, "I don't have the vaguest idea what you have in mind, but you seem like a crazy creative person. Let me put this together."

She should have known it was not going well when it took weeks to arrange a meeting. When they finally got together at her swanky Hollywood home, she had two associates present, and Azoff brought his dog, Don Henley, and Glenn Frey. According to her autobiography, there was an ounce of cocaine on the table, and everyone but Azoff and the dog partook.

"I don't know how to tell Irving," she wrote, "but I don't think they're The Beatles. No star power. They seem sparked by the idea, but by then, everybody except Irving is pretty lit from the blow. They agree to think about it."

Henley told writer **Marc Eliot** that Phillips was a liar.

"We sat there, polite but not terribly friendly," Henley said. "We were too wary to be friendly. In an effort to loosen us up and to create some sort of camaraderie, she dragged out this huge ashtray filled with a mound of coke. One of her writers was there. She offered us some, and we said no; we didn't know her that well, and it was a business meeting. It was a little early in the day for us. I don't remember if she went ahead and did some or not, but I know for certain that we didn't. She wants to remember it that way for her own reasons. She's bitter about everything that's happened to her, but I don't know why she feels it necessary to say we did drugs with her. We were doing lots of coke in those days, every day, but not with her."

The Eagles remained dispassionate on her advances. They had terrible experiences already with "movie people," including producer **Ray Stark**, when he tried in vain to make a movie out of *Desperado*.

"They always thought we should be excited or flattered because they want to make movies out of our songs," Henley remarked in his conversation with Eliot.

"In fact, we didn't really want anything to do with it. We were pretty sure they would take our songs and ruin them," he said. "We knew enough about the film business to know you'd have to relinquish all control and that it's somebody else's vision, just like rock videos are today."

Shortly after the meeting, Azoff called Phillips to tell her to indefinitely put the project on hold, which was shorthand for "we pass." By then, it likely didn't matter because Phillips' cocaine habit was already decimating her once-promising career. [209, 2130, 2131]

SUMMER 1978

 RELEASES
- **Joe Walsh**, "Life's Been Good" (single)
- **Randy Meisner**, *Randy Meisner* (album)
- **Joe Walsh**, "Over and Over" (single)
- **James Gang**, with Joe Walsh, *So Far So Good* (album)

 COLLABORATIONS
- **Don Felder** played guitar on the single "I Go for You" on **Andy Gibb**'s album *Shadow Dancing*.
- Glenn Frey played 12-string acoustic guitar and provided backing vocals on the single "Peaceful Easy Feeling" and provided backing vocals on "Fifteen Days Under the Hood" on **Jack Tempchin**'s album *Jack Tempchin*.
- **Bernie Leadon** played acoustic guitar on the singles "My Singing Mudlark" and "Sunny Carmel Valley Day" on **Craig Nuttycombe**'s album *It's Just a Lifetime*.
- **Don Henley** provided harmony vocals on **Dan Fogelberg**'s album *Twin Sons of Different Mothers*.
- **Joe Walsh** played lead guitar on **Jay Ferguson**'s album *Real Life Ain't This Way*.

 NUGGETS
- Eagles headlined the first-ever concert at Cincinnati's Riverfront Stadium, appearing with **Steve Miller** and newcomer **Eddie Money**. The band drew 55,000, and they were scheduled to play a softball benefit with WLS-AM (with Don Henley at 3-0 as pitcher). —*Cashbox*
- Randy Meisner starts touring in support of his new self-titled album in July in Aspen, Colorado, where he will be opening for **Jimmy Buffett**.—*Cashbox*
- Eagles pulled some interesting people to their shows in Edmonton and Winnipeg this August, most notably **Dolly Parton** and **Neil Young**.—*Cashbox*

 NUGGETS (cont.)
- Eagles received a standing ovation after their show in Chicago, which may have taken the edge off the 10-7 defeat laid on them by E/A staffers in the Windy City; the band claims the loss to the E/A staff in Chicago was 10-9, and they would have won except for **Mike Veeck**, who is the son of Chicago White Sox owner **Bill Veeck**, who was a ringer. He was responsible for four E/A runs. —*Record World*
- In the upcoming book *California Rock, California Sound*, Don Henley says he's tired of "computer clone rock" and "androgynous heartless, gutless crap." The Eagles' new album, thus untitled, responds with cuts like "Teenage Jail" and "You're Really High, Aren't You?" —*Cashbox*

 ON THE ROAD WITH …
- **Eagles**: Chilliwack, Dan Fogelberg, Eddie Money, Jesse Winchester, Judy Collins, Little River Band, Pablo Cruise, Seals & Crofts, Steve Miller Band
- **Randy Meisner Group**: Jimmy Buffett, Little River Band

Meisner Starts Solo Tour; Absence of New Material Hurts

With his debut solo album, *Randy Meisner*, in the can, Meisner set out on the road. His band, the **Randy Meisner Group**, included guitarist **Jerry Swallow**, bassist **Kerry Morris**, drummer **Kelly Shanahan**, and keyboardist **John Hobbs**.

In a mostly self-financed tour, Meisner kept the group on the road from late July through mid-September, but his album sales were poor, and the touring didn't seem to help. Reviews of both the album and live performances were often uncomplimentary. *Los Angeles Times* critic **Terry Atkinson**, covering a shared bill between Meisner and **Fleetwood Mac** alum **Bob Welch**, called the former Eagle's performance "nondescript" and suggested his rendition of "Take It to the Limit" was the only memorable part of the evening. Atkinson further commented that "Meisner demonstrated a typical, ordinary country-rock voice and stance, with little else to indicate that his loss to his former group was a serious one."

Meisner kept **Irving Azoff** as his manager after he left the Eagles, and the bassist felt as though the album didn't even make the charts in part because the Eagles did not appreciate Azoff still being involved with him as a solo artist. Moreover, he believed the band asked Azoff to make an "us or him" decision.

Meisner went to Azoff and demanded answers to why the record was not receiving proper airplay. According to Meisner, Azoff angrily threw him out of his office.

He had found Meisner difficult during his final days with the Eagles but vehemently denied any neglect or blackballing. "I may not have been the most diplomatic guy in the world, but I did try to help Randy at first until his self-destructiveness became too much," he said.

Meisner had a different view.

"Irving was too busy for me, and [Asylum] didn't have any faith in me. That really hurt," he said to author **Marc Shapiro**. "When the first album didn't work out, I was shattered. I went back to Nebraska. I was all set to retire."

It would be two years before there was another Meisner sighting in Los Angeles, but he would return with a better plan, original material, and some heavyweight friends to help him along. [1539, 1539, 2083, 2084]

FALL 1978

RELEASES
▶ **Joe Walsh**, "At the Station" (single)
▶ **Joe Walsh**, *The Best of Joe Walsh* (album)
▶ **Eagles**, "Please Come Home for Christmas" (single)

NUGGETS
▶ **Eagles** will release a new Christmas single on November 27, "Please Be Home for Christmas" [sic]; it will be the first single released with Timothy Schmit as an Eagle. —*Cashbox*
▶ Joe Walsh joins **Dan Fogelberg** onstage for the Rocky Flats Truth Force anti-nukes benefit. —*Record World*
▶ **Jack Tempchin** rolled out his self-titled debut album and gets help from Glenn Frey, **Jackson Browne**, and **Jennifer Warnes**. —*Cashbox*
▶ Don Henley and Tim Schmit are in the studio helping **Dane Donohue** finish his debut album for Columbia. **Stevie Nicks** and **J.D. Souther** are also providing backing vocals. —*Record World*
▶ **Stephen Bishop** has recorded an instrumental track on his new album called "Avocodo," which is his "tribute" to the Eagles' "Desperado."—*Circus*
▶ The Eagles played to about 650,000 people this summer on only 14 dates, making them one of the biggest concert draws in the country and competing with the **Rolling Stones**, **Fleetwood Mac**, **Led Zeppelin**, and **Bruce Springsteen**. —*Circus*

335

continued on Page 338

OF MANSIONS AND MASERATIS

WALSH COMPOSES HIS AUTOBIOGRAPHY IN VERSE

As the 1970s progressed and the often-serious Don Henley emerged as the most prominent voice of the Eagles, the rock press sometimes tagged the band as humorless or too self-righteous. But without a doubt, Joe Walsh brought irreverent humor that added needed balance. He would make faces while playing on stage, run for U.S. President on a "Free Gas for Everyone" campaign, and write songs for his solo albums like the hilarious and self-referential, self-deprecating "Life's Been Good."

Walsh assembled "Life's Been Good"—which appeared on his own *But Seriously, Folks...* album as well as the *FM* movie soundtrack in 1978—from three disparate musical concepts. He had been kicking around a catchy guitar lick (which would become the song's opening), a delicate transitionary pattern strummed further up the fretboard, and a series of chords with a reggae feel (inspired by "listening to **Bob Marley** too much," he said) that would become the backing for the

verses. When he put the concepts together, they somehow worked.

Remarkably, the song almost didn't get recorded. Walsh's producer, **Bill Szymczyk**, told *Mix* magazine that Walsh was growing more hesitant about releasing the song because he thought the public would take it the wrong way. "I was just on him constantly," Szymczyk said. "No, no,n o, no, you've got to finish this, because at this point he wasn't even going to finish it. And I told him 'You MUST finish this, this is a killer record.' So he finally agreed, and the rest is history."

But the most notable thing about "Life's Been Good" is the lyrics. In Walsh's inimitable warble, he glibly reflects on all the excesses and peculiarities of the life of fame he was living. He sang about owning mansions he had never been to, wrecking hotel rooms and having accountants pay for it, and owning a Maserati even though he no longer drove because he lost his license. With unmistakable sardonic wit, he claimed that *"everybody's so different"* now that he's famous—but he hasn't changed. At the end of each chorus, he concludes, *"Life's been good to me so far."*

While the song's lyrics read as a satirical commentary on the lifestyles of rich and famous rock stars, Walsh insists the lyrics accurately described his life at the time.

"Between *Hotel California* and *The Long Run*...we were either recording or touring and sometimes both," he explained, adding that he had a lovely home in Santa Barbara, but was never there.

"I wanted to make a statement involving satire and humor, kind of poking fun at the incredibly silly lifestyle that someone in my position is faced with," Walsh said, speaking with **John Tobler** in 1983.

"In other words, I do have a nice house, but I'm on the road so much that when I come home from a tour, it's really hard to feel that I even live here," Walsh added. "It's not necessarily me, I think it paraphrases anyone in my position, and I think that's why a lot of people related to it, but basically, that's the story of any rock star—I say that humbly—anyone in my position. I thought that was a valid statement, because it is a strange lifestyle. I've been around the world in concerts, and people say, 'What was Japan like?' but I don't know. It's got a nice airport, you know...so it was kind of an overall statement."

He described a life living on the road and credited **The Who** drummer **Keith Moon** for teaching him (during Walsh's **James Gang** days) the art of hotel destruction. Walsh would prove to be a good apprentice, which later led to his days of toting a chainsaw on tour. "Yeah, I tore out some walls with it," he admitted. "Sometimes, I wanted adjoining rooms, and they weren't available."

While most fans assumed Walsh "lost his license" for speeding in a Maserati, it was not about his driving privileges being revoked. Instead, he joked, he had lost his wallet, which

Walsh released "Life's Been Good" in May 1978 and watched it climb to #12, as it became his highest-charting single as a solo performer.

contained his license. However, he said he knew many people in his "peer group" who crashed up expensive cars, and felt like the line in the song "was poetic license; it didn't really happen to me, but it happened to 'us.'"

Walsh didn't even own the lightning-fast hyper-expensive race car memorably referenced in the lyrics. "I never had a Maserati. I finally got one because everyone was making me feel guilty," Walsh told *Rolling Stone* in 2020. "The look of sadness on their face...so I went and got a Maserati. I don't know if it does 185; I chickened out at 140."

The most accurate part of the song may have been staying out late at parties and being too loaded to find the door, as Walsh struggled for years with addiction issues. He finally cleaned up in 1994, with encouragement from Henley and Glenn Frey, in time to rejoin the reunited band, as hell was freezing over.

"Life's Been Good" became Joe Walsh's anthem, played for decades at his solo and Eagles concerts.

A decade later, in 1991, Walsh released a single that was the philosophical flipside of "Life's Been Good." "Ordinary Average Guy" eschewed stories of riding in limos and wrecking hotels, replacing them with everyday tales of going bowling with pals and picking up dog poop in the yard. [1945, 2013, 2014, 2147]

COLLABORATIONS
▶ **Bernie Leadon** played guitar and high-string guitar, and provided vocals on the singles "Ride, Ride, Ride" and "Pretty Lucky" on **Woodstock Mountains Revue**'s album *Pretty Lucky*.
▶ **Don Henley** and **Timothy B. Schmit** provided backing vocals on "Casablanca" and "What Am I Supposed to Do" on **Dane Donohue's** self-titled album.

Infighting, High Expectations Taint *The Long Run* Sessions

Eagles stopped touring at the end of summer 1978 so they could focus on songwriting, but that was only happening sporadically, so the next album was continuously delayed. The band offered up a hit single version of "Please Come Home for Christmas" for the year-end holidays, but Elektra/Asylum would have preferred an LP.

The group had failed to deliver a new album in 1977—understandable, considering *Hotel California* debuted in December 1976. They spent most of '77 and half of '78 bouncing between legs of grueling tours and laborious recording sessions spread across five different studios.

By August, the members were emotionally and physically depleted, highly irritated with each other, and all but dysfunctional. They weren't functioning as a unit any longer.

When the next Eagles album would land in stores became one of the biggest questions of 1978 and 1979. The band had company on the overdue-album bench. **Fleetwood Mac**, who had made such an incredible leap in popularity after *Rumours*, was struggling to finish their sprawling double album *Tusk*. But the Eagles got more flak about the delays from the music press. Adding to E/A's woes, the recording industry was in the middle of a remarkably bearish season in 1979 and counting on the Eagles and Fleetwood Mac to help buoy their depressed bottom lines.

The trade press kept getting conflicting information about the Eagles' progress. *Cashbox* reported in January the album would hit stores shelves in the first quarter. Two months later the date changed to May or June. *Record World* reported the band had generated enough new material to fill a double album, but that was not remotely true. As summer began the press stopped reporting on delivery dates altogether.

E/A Chairman **Joe Smith**'s $1 million bonus offer for an LP by Christmas did not fly. After recording a stopgap holiday single in the summer, the band said it aimed to wrap up sessions by fall and be back on the road by March or April of 1979. But that mark was missed too. *The Long Run* wouldn't finally roll out until September 1979.

Joe Walsh said the band was stigmatized by the weight of expectations from *Hotel California*, a feeling that was mutually shared by his band mates.

"It's hard to explain. I think we felt a burden in that *Hotel California* had really gained public acceptance beyond our wildest dreams," Walsh told **John Tobler** in 1983, "and we felt a burden in terms of how we could top it. That was a non-musical thing that kind of interfered for the first couple of months of working on *The Long Run* and I think we got a little hung up in that, and that slowed the process down a bit."

"When you try to match yourself, it gets harder and harder the more successful you are," Don Felder reflected to *Songfacts* about the challenging experience. "So, we got to a point where we realized we've got to just wrap this up and end it here and get out of the studio and get on the road. There were a lot of arguments and dissension and contentious arguments about songs and schedules. It was really not heading in the right direction."

The growing tensions within the band, the fraying of Don Henley and Glenn Frey's longtime relationship, and the creative challenge to match *Hotel California* all contributed to the lengthy debacle that became referred to by Elektra/Asylum executives as "The Long One."

Speaking to **Dave Herman** of DIR Broadcasting after the album's release, Frey said the task of recording an album after *Hotel California* was enormous.

"I mean, if you asked **Peter Frampton** what it was like going into the studio after *Frampton Comes Alive*, he'd probably give you the same answer," Frey said. "You know, like Dylan says, 'They deceived me into thinking I had something to protect.' That would be a great way to describe the couple months in the studio when we were working on *The Long Run*."

The pressures, Frey said, came from all over, and the band did their best to ride them out. And it was clear that self-doubt had crept into their mindsets, brought on by those lofty expectations.

"Performers are basically insecure peo-ple," he mused. "And I think we fortify ourselves by having other people tell us we're okay. I know myself, as a record-buying person that once I get the idea that somebody's good and if they give me one album and I think it's a right-turn away from where I think they should be going, I'm very fickle. I say 'Well, I don't like that anymore.' And I don't buy any more of their records. So, there was that [added] pressure of 'whatever we do, let's not make a mistake.'"

Along with Fleetwood Mac, the Eagles were vying to be the top American band of the late 1970s. In addition to their well-known drug usage, the excesses of both groups were running on parallel paths as each spent more than $1 million to record their new albums.

The Eagles once envisioned *The Long Run* as a double album, something Fleetwood Mac took a chance with when the experimental and sparse *Tusk* came out a month later. It confused fans who were expecting another *Rumours* (and asked to pay twice as much with a list price of $15.98, double the cost of a single disc record). That was one mistake the Eagles did not make.

Yet the irony in recording an album named after a song about perseverance and endurance was not lost on any of them, as Henley explained in a 2003 conversation with **Cameron Crowe**: "The group was breaking apart, imploding under the pressure of trying to deliver a worthy follow-up to *Hotel California*, and yet we were writing about longevity, posterity."

It was "a long and difficult album," Hen-

339

continued on Page 344

RELEASE
Early December 1978

PLEASE COME HOME FOR CHRISTMAS

By: Charles Brown, Gene Redd
Side B: Funky New Year (Henley, Frey)

Eagles had not released a single since mid-May 1977 and fans—and execs at Elektra/Asylum—were clamoring for anything from the band. Nowhere near completing their next album, *The Long Run*, the band released this Christmas 45 to satiate the label and the fan base. It jumped right into the Top 40, and stayed there beyond the holidays. Maybe that was due to its cross-holiday appeal or perhaps fans just wanted to hear a new Eagles song a bit longer. Whatever the reason, the single peaked at #18 in mid-January 1979.

AIRPLAY

Few holiday singles have moved to the airwaves as quickly as Eagles' version of "Please Come Home for Christmas." Asylum began heavily promoting the A-side in early December and in just two weeks, it became the most-added single nationwide. Once again, the Eagles' fan base in the Southeast lent its strong support on the airwaves, but across the nation the cut ruled over all other holiday songs in 1978-79. It remains an evergreen on stations and streaming services during the year-end holidays.

105 PLAYLIST ADDS Winter 1978-79

Region	Dec	Jan	Regional Airplay
Northeast	21	1	21%
Southeast	32	0	30%
Midwest	18	0	17.1%
Southwest	11	0	10.5%
West	22	0	21%

FIRST-WAVE STATIONS Stations that added the song in the first 30 days

KHJ-Los Angeles	KTOQ-Rapid City, SD	WPLR-New Haven, CT	WBBF-Rochester
KGW-Portland	WMET-Chicago	WKBW-Buffalo	WTLB-Utica, NY
KING-Seattle	WOWT-Omaha	WPEZ-Pittsburgh	WVRT-V97-Mill Hall, PA
KJR-Seattle	KEBQ-Kansas City	WGUY-Bangor, ME	WPTR-Albany
KFI-Los Angeles	WNCY-Y100-Green Bay	WIFI-Philadelphia	WDRC-Hartford
KERN-Bakersfield			
KENO-Las Vegas	KULF-Houston	WKLS-FM-Atlanta	WQXI-Atlanta
KCBQ-San Diego	KLIF-Dallas	WNOE-New Orleans	WRVQ-Q94-Richmond
KEZI-Anaheim	KILT-Houston	WCAO-Baltimore	WSGA-Savannah
KJRB-Spokane	KOPA-Dallas-Ft. Worth	WPGC-Washington	WRJZ-Knoxville

CHARTS

Billboard

#18
January 13, 1979

Cashbox

#32
January 13, 1979

Record World

#42
January 20, 1979

HIGHEST CHARTING WEEK: BILLBOARD - January 13, 1979

SINGLE	ARTIST	# PREV WK
1. Too Much Heaven	Bee Gees	1
2. Le Freak	Chic	2
3. My Life	Billy Joel	3
4. You Don't Bring Me Flowers	Barbra Streisand & Neil Diamond	4
5. Hold the Line	Toto	8
6. Sharing the Night Together	Dr. Hook	6
7. Y.M.C.A.	Village People	7
8. Ooh Baby Baby	Linda Ronstadt	10
18. PLEASE COME HOME FOR CHRISTMAS	**EAGLES**	**18**

Sources: Billboard, Cashbox, Record World

LONG RUN DELAYS SPAWN A CHRISTMAS FAVORITE

Eagles were in Miami in the fall of 1978, behind schedule and short on ideas, and outside the studio, it was sweltering hot and humid. But they had Christmas on their minds—more specifically, **Charles Brown**'s 1960 classic "Please Come Home for Christmas."

The dust from the grueling *Hotel California Tour* was settling and the Eagles were convening at the Bayshore Recording Studios in Coconut Grove, just south of Downtown Miami, to work on their increasingly overdue next album, *The Long Run*.

It was not a pleasant time for the exhausted band members, and their record company was not happy, either. *One of These Nights* and *Hotel California* made the Eagles a money-making machine and Asylum wanted to cash in on it. But the label needed the next album ASAP and was checking in with the band regularly to get status reports. But as Glenn Frey put it, "We weren't going to finish anytime soon."

"The record label was bugging us because *The Long Run* was, at this point, 6.8 months behind schedule," said producer **Bill Szymczyk**, adding that the band thought, "Well, maybe if we give them a Christmas single, they'll get off our back."

"We've always wanted to do a Christmas record," Frey told the *Los Angeles Times* in November 1978. "Whenever we talked about it, Don would mention the Charles Brown song. The last time he went to his mother's house in Texas he dug it out of his old record collection in the attic. He played it for us last September and I went crazy. I loved the song. We knew it was perfect for Don to sing. There hasn't been a decent Christmas record in a long time. So, we went ahead and recorded it."

Henley said he always had fond memories of Brown's original. "When I was growing up in East Texas, there were basically two radio stations that were interesting," he said in a 2003 conversation with **Cameron Crowe**. "There was KEEL in Shreveport, Louisiana, which I listened to in the daytime. Then there was the legendary WNOE in New Orleans, which I could pick up at night when the station boosted its signal. It broadcast this wonderful, eclectic mix of music, which was like nothing I had ever heard on pop stations in Texas. WNOE is where I first heard Charles Brown's original version of 'Please Come Home for Christmas.' It always stuck with me. Our version is very much like the original."

The track would be new Eagle Timothy B. Schmit's first-ever studio recording with the band. "We knocked it out in a matter of two or three days," Szymczyk said, "gave it to the label and they indeed did get off our back until we were finished." The band stayed true to Brown's original, save for the lyrical change to the song's incipit, which the group altered from "glad, glad news," to "sad, sad news."

For the single's B-side, they recorded "Funky New Year," an original by Henley

EAGLES

PLEASE COME HOME FOR CHRISTMAS
B/W FUNKY NEW YEAR

PRODUCED AND ENGINEERED BY BILL SZYMCZYK FOR PANDORA PRODUCTIONS LTD.

asylum

and Frey, as an ode to the New Year's Day hangover. The song opens with a slow fade-in of sounds from a New Year's Eve party and then rolls into a bass-driven funk groove that Henley peppers with tongue-in-cheek lyrics about waking up the day after partying all night long, gems like: *"Can't remember when I ever felt worse/Nothing matters and everything hurts," "I gotta perk up a little/My hair hurts,"* and *"Whose shoes are these?/Party hardy baby."*

With a single sleeve picturing all the Eagles, including new Eagle Schmit, sitting poolside with an artificial white Christmas tree, Asylum rush-released the song and it became the highest-charting holiday single in twenty years. Warner-Elektra-Asylum affiliates in Germany reported getting the shipment the day after it was pressed, which was "some sort of new record." Though the label was excited to get something—anything—from the Eagles. Still, the label would have much preferred a full-fledged album.

Label profits aside, Frey was right about the then-Christmas music market stagnation. Apart from a few new holiday offerings each year, Christmas radio in 1978 was still dominated by the likes of **Bing Crosby**, **Andy Williams**, and **Brenda Lee**. And while artists would occasionally record new holiday fare, few of their efforts ever made it to the Top 20. In fact, there had not been a Christmas single in the Top 20 since **Roy Orbison** released "Pretty Paper" in 1963.

That changed with the Eagles single, which set a new benchmark for holiday music. Eagles fans were already starved for new material by then—the band had not released anything new in more than a year and a half. "Please Come Home" shot to #18 on *Billboard*'s Hot 100 chart in just one month and, remarkably, stayed there into February long after all other holiday songs had been stashed away for the season.

The Eagles' 45 was the third time "Please Come Home for Christmas" had hit the *Billboard* Hot 100 singles chart. Brown, an American blues singer and pianist from Texas City, Texas, co-wrote the song with **Gene Redd**. Brown's single on the King label rose to #76 over the 1961-62 holiday season, after peaking at #21 on the R&B singles chart in late 1960-early 1961.

It had season-over-season staying power, hitting #1 on *Billboard*'s Christmas Singles chart more than a decade later in 1972; it had sold more than a million copies by 1968 and became a staple. Brown died in 1999 at 76 years old, but his legacy lives on in the song. The Eagles' version remains the most popular, and **Bon Jovi**, **Willie Nelson**, **Martina McBride**, and **Kelly Clarkson** are among the many artists who have recorded covers.

By mid-December 1978, Eagles' "Please Come Home for Christmas" had become one of the most-added singles on radio stations nationwide.

On December 16, WNOE in New Orleans reported to *Cashbox* it had added the single to its playlist, bringing the song, performers, and airwaves full circle. [6, 209, 1792, 1793, 1794, 1799, 1800]

ley conceded. "Everything was catching up to us. Too much pressure, too much worry, too much traveling, too many controlled substances, too much paranoia, and infighting. I missed having a normal life. Everything was pulling apart, and we were writing about longevity. Yeah, well, even if we weren't living it, we were always able to idealize it in a song about the way we'd like to be—the way we'd like to be perceived."

Henley would rank *The Long Run* sessions as being the most unpleasant of any to date: "The recording of every one of our albums had moments of ecstasy and agony. That's just the way the process works. But if I had to choose an overall favorite studio experience, it would be the *Hotel California* album. My least favorite time was the recording of *The Long Run*."

The band soldiered on, often bickering and fighting, and often not communicating at all. When they landed in Miami for *The Long Run* recording sessions, they stayed in separate houses. The band was in a dark place, but they would find the light at the end of the tunnel in September. [135, 209, 1918]

WINTER 1978-79

 RELEASES
▶ **Joe Walsh**, "In the City" (single)

 ON SCREEN
▶ **Eagles** appeared on the BBC-TV show *The Old Grey Whistle Test*, highlighted as one of the year's top acts.

 NUGGETS
▶ Eagles' "Please Come Home for Christmas" is turning into the biggest yuletide hit in years, having leaped into the Top 30 in only four weeks. There hasn't been a mover like this since **John Lennon**'s "Happy Christmas" [sic] *(War is Over)* in 1971. Elektra/Asylum reports it is selling well overseas, too. —*Cashbox*
▶ Christmas is over, but the Eagles' run on the charts is not. It's February and "Please Come Home for Christmas" is still in the Top 20. —*Record World*
▶ The long-awaited follow-up to the Eagles' smash *Hotel California* is expected in the first quarter of 1979. —*Cashbox*
▶ **Bob Dylan** on extended studio work: "I haven't done it that way, but I feel you can. You see, my records take a week or two to make. The Eagles go in and make a record, they'll take a year. Every time they go off the road, they'll go in the studio and work on it, and that's what they'll be doin' and it's important to them. And me, I don't do that, 'cause I don't have a producer." —*Circus*
▶ And in obscure instrument news, **Roger McGuinn** has traded his five-string banjo with a Vega rim and an Ode neck to Bernie Leadon for a flat-top resonator that was in his Fender Concert Tone banjo. —*Circus*
▶ Hollywood's **Bob Evans** and **Irving Azoff** will team to produce a new movie called *The Urban Cowboy* [sic] to be filmed at Gilley's in Pasadena, Texas. —*Circus*

'The Eagles': *Record World* Nipped By Henley, Frey's Sarcastic Wit

While researching British bands in 1979, Radar Records' executive **Andrew Lauder** found a single from a by-then obscure British guitar band called **The Eagles**. There's lot of duplication and near-misses in the rock band name game, but this proved an interesting tidbit since this outfit released a single ironically titled "The Desperadoes."

Lauder passed that information to an un-named source who, in turn, gave it to *Record World* that April. **Samuel Graham** and **Sam Sutherland**, editors of the music industry trade magazine's "The Coast" column, found it an interesting nugget, so they added a suspicion-sprinkled 70-word paragraph to the magazine's April 21 column. It read:

> *"We're told Radar Records' Andrew Lauder has unearthed a British single, cut in 1962, with more than a familiar ring to it. The track's featured artists were a long-forgotten Bristol ensemble named the Eagles, a fact we might have written off to coincidence until Deep Ear, source of this and other press-stopping COAST revelations, clued us in to the title: 'Desperado.' Rod Serling, where are you when we need you?"*

Gossip columns in *Record World*, *Cashbox*, *Rolling Stone*, *Sounds*, *Circus*, *Crawdaddy*, and other music trade and consumer magazines of the era were notorious for dropping innuendo, and those columns preferred to keep things light, airy, and—when they could—funny.

But this morsel had shades of implied impropriety that came close enough to the line, and Graham and Sutherland considered printing a clarification in *Record World*'s next issue. And just as they started writing it, the mail arrived.

Don Henley was a notorious letter writer

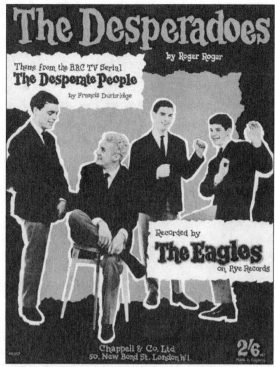

Bristol, England's **The Eagles** predated the Eagles from Los Angeles by more than a decade, as did their first single, "The Desperadoes."

in the days before email. And in this instance Glenn Frey joined him as they co-signed a letter that sarcastically corrected the record:

> *"When I was boy of 15 (1962), growing up in a remote farming community in northeast Texas, there wasn't much to do except drink beer and listen to AM radio. We could only get KOMA and, of course, BBC 1. (Sometimes on a clear night we could even get Radio Bristol. I think that was because of all the iron ore in the area.) Anyway, late one steamy summer night I was cruising down Highway 59 in my dad's car,*

listening to BBC 1, and suddenly there it was, 'Desperado,' by the Eagles. I thought to myself, 'Boy Howdy!' Eight years from now, when I move to Los Angeles and meet Glenn Frey, we can start a group and call it 'Eagles,' and then we'll wait until our second album and call it 'Desperado,' I planned it right then and there. I thought no one would ever figure it out but, gee, you guys sure nailed us."

There was more to the letter. Frey said that he, too, could pick up BBC 1 in his hometown of Royal Oak, Michigan; "Life in the Fast Lane" was copped from "a little promotional ditty released by the Hollywood Highway Department after they finished the Hollywood Freeway in 1953"; "Hotel California" is actually in Paris; and he and Henley are actually **Napoleon III** and E/A Chairman **Joe Smith**. They signed the missive, "Humbly yours, Don Henley and Glenn Frey."

Some *Record World* readers were, indeed, confused by the original note; Graham and Sutherland made clear in their follow-up column that group name and record title aside, there were no similarities between the two Eagles. And to Henley and Frey sarcastically dubbing themselves Napoleon and Smith, Graham and Sutherland retorted that they were **Santo & Johnny**.

The Eagles (the English incarnation) were a four-member band that launched in the late 1950s. The group—**Johnny Payne, Terry Clarke, Michael Brice,** and **Rod Meacham**—were students at the Con-

naught Road School, and took their name from the Eagles House Youth Club, to which they all belonged. They played local gigs and landed a deal with Pye Records, and eventually became the backup band for **Del Shannon**. They released a series of well-received singles in 1962 and 1963, including "The Desperadoes," the theme from BBC-TV serialization of author **Francis Durbridge**'s *The Desperate People.* Their first LP, *Smash Hits of the Eagles,* in 1963, was also their swan song. A variety of health issues struck the band and their producer at the end of 1964, and they packed it in. [2125, 2126, 2127, 2128]

Walsh Takes 'In the City' to Hollywood, Then to Eagles

Joe Walsh made a soundtrack contribution for a movie that bombed. It ended up being one of the best things that happened as the Eagles struggled to complete *The Long Run.*

"In the City" started as a favor for a friend, but this friend was not a member of the band. Walsh had met **Barry De Vorzon** when they were living in Santa Barbara, and the veteran songwriter and TV-film composer reached out when he was called on to work on *The Warriors,* director **Walter Hill**'s 1979 street-gang-themed film for Paramount Pictures.

"Joe and I were friends, and I just saw an opportunity to work with him—and plus, I thought it'd be great to have Joe Walsh sing the end title," De Vorzon told the *Village Voice* in 2015. Walsh agreed, and they ended up co-writing "In the City" together. When De Vorzon handed the finished song over to the studio, "of course, they were very happy about that."

Walsh was peaking creatively and commercially, having returned to solo work after *Hotel California* to produce his most complete, best-selling album ever in *But Seriously, Folks....* De Vorzon also knew that Walsh was familiar with the film's gritty urban setting, spending part of his youth in New York City.

"He explained to me that it was about gangs in New York," Walsh told *Rolling Stone* in 2016. "He and I came up with the words after reading the screenplay."

The resulting track was darker than many would have expected from Walsh, who typically played up his comedic side: "*I know there must be something better,*" he sings, "*but there's nowhere else in sight.*" But this theme of escape, even if it was against all odds, hit home for Walsh.

Walsh told the BBC in 1981 he related to the film's "gang-type city situations," based on his years in the Big Apple. But, at the same time, he wanted to make "a positive statement to go against the desperation of miles and miles of concrete and growing up in a city. That really can affect you."

His long-time producer **Bill Szymczyk** was less surprised by the maturity of Walsh's songwriting. He knew better than anyone just how complex Joe Walsh really was.

"People erect walls between themselves and the world," Szymczyk told *Rolling Stone* in 1979. "Then, depending on how the chemistry works between them and their friends, the walls come down." Walsh, Szymczyk added, employed humor to keep those walls standing. He said Walsh had a "lot of chaos in his life" that he did not want to share with the wider world.

The Warriors had respectable ticket sales over its opening weekend in early February that year, but the movie became linked to a series of violent incidents resulting in the deaths of three people. Paramount pulled the plug on promotion, and radio programmers suddenly became skittish about playing the album's songs. *The Warriors* soundtrack never got any higher than #125 on the *Billboard* 200.

"Nobody wanted to encourage the violence," De Vorzon told the *Village Voice*. "It certainly hurt the music because radio was saying, 'Uh-oh. This is too hot to handle.'"

Instead of becoming his next huge hit, Walsh's big-riffed meditation on inner-city ennui sank along with the movie.

"In the City" might have remained a lost artifact if not for the Eagles' initial difficulties while working on *The Long Run*.

"I think we felt a burden in that *Hotel California* had really gained public acceptance beyond our wildest dreams," Walsh told the BBC, "and we felt a burden in terms of how we could top it." He said they were hung up on this "non-musical thing" for a couple of months, "and that slowed the process down a bit."

Walsh was suffering from a persistent case of writer's block, according to Szymczyk. In the end, his most recent solo song wound up Walsh's next featured Eagles track.

"That's the only song he had," Szymczyk later told *Rolling Stone*. And in a larger sense, the idea of updating "In the City" suited Glenn Frey just fine: "I always liked the song and thought it could have been an Eagles record," he added, "and so we decided to make it one."

They recut "In the City," adding a more profound musical complexity to Walsh's original track, and in the end, its searching theme fit in perfectly on *The Long Run*. Over time, *The Warriors* found its own dedicated following when released on videotape, and then Rockstar Games brought the project to a new generation with a video game adaptation in 2005 that featured music from the original soundtrack. [1942, 1943, 1944, 1945, 1946, 1947]

SPRING 1979

NUGGETS

▶ Rastar Films will budget $10 million for a western being produced by **Irving Azoff** based on the Eagles album *Desperado*. The film will reportedly have music from the Eagles. —*Cashbox*

▶ Randy Meisner is back from Nebraska and working on his second solo LP. —*Cashbox*

▶ The Eagles' follow-up to *Hotel California* is now expected in May or June. —*Cashbox*

▶ The Eagles have reportedly compiled enough material for a double-album set.—*Cashbox*

▶ Producer **Irving Azoff** gave **John Travolta** a bucking bronco machine for a little *Urban Cowboy* inspiration. —*Record World*

Future Unofficial Eagle Gill Joins Pure Prairie League

Long before joining the Eagles as a regular onstage non-member in 2016, **Vince Gill** was just getting started in 1963, earning a local following with his bluegrass band **Mountain Smoke** around his native Norman, Oklahoma. When his band opened for country-rockers **Pure Prairie League** in Oklahoma City a few years later, he did not know that night would play a big part in his future.

Gill grew up playing music with his family, led by his father, a judge who played banjo. Gill had once considered a career as a pro golfer but got more enjoyment from learning to play stringed instruments and country and bluegrass music. After high school, he moved to Louisville, Kentucky, in the heart of bluegrass country, where he joined the **Bluegrass Alliance**.

Gill also spent some time with **Ricky Skaggs**' bluegrass band, **Boone Creek**, in 1976, and at age 19, left home and headed west at the invitation of master fiddler **Byron Berline**, who asked him to play guitar in his Los Angeles-based band, **Sundance**. Two years later, while in L.A., Gill accompanied a friend who happened to be auditioning for Pure Prairie League. One of the band members recognized Gill from Oklahoma City.

"They were telling me about the trouble they were having finding a guitar player to replace the one who left," Gill remembered. "They had auditioned 50 people, and no one was right. They thought they might have to put the band on the shelf; then they asked me if I wanted to audition for the job."

Pure Prairie League by 1978 had achieved modest success as a regular on the touring circuit with the **Marshall Tucker Band**, **Poco**, **Lynyrd Skynyrd**, the **Charlie Daniels Band**, the **Outlaws**, and other Southern rockers, and released seven albums. The album covers were recognizable for a cowboy character named Luke, who initially appeared on a *Saturday Evening Post* cover by **Norman Rockwell**. When the song "Amie," first released in 1972, became popular again, RCA re-released the band's *Bustin' Out* album in 1975. The year also saw their new album *Two Lane Highway*, with appearances from **Chet Atkins**, **Johnny Gimble** of the **Texas Playboys**, and **Emmylou Harris**.

Gill passed the audition and reinvigorated Pure Prairie League with his versatility on vocals, guitars, mandolin, banjo, and fiddle. His first album with the group in 1979 was *Can't Hold Back*. He would record two more albums with the band, including *Firin' Up* in 1980 and *Something in the Night* a year later, featuring "Still Right Here in My Heart." Gill left the band in 1982 for a successful solo career based in Nashville.

"I think people want to hear music that takes their minds off of all the troubles," he reflected during his tenure in Pure Prairie League. "I think they're interested in hearing music that makes them feel good; that they can maybe tap their toes to."

It's a role Gill would reprise in the next century when he joined the Eagles as an unofficial member following Glenn Frey's death in January 2016. [1752, 1753, 1754, 1755, 1756]

SUMMER 1979

COLLABORATIONS
▶ **Don Henley** provided backing vocals on the single "Singing Out Alone" on **Louise Goffin**'s album *Kid Blue*.

NUGGETS
▶ While fans and the record industry await the new **Eagles** album like manna from on high, stray Eagle Joe Walsh is working on another solo project. The flaming guitarist has announced his candidacy for the 1980 U.S. presidential election. —*Cashbox*
▶ Eagles have scheduled their first Japanese tour since 1975. Appearances in 10 cities have been scheduled, including Tokyo's Budokan Hall—appearing on the same bill is MCA recording artist **Jimmy Buffett**. —*Cashbox*
▶ Contrary to published reports, **Jimmy Buffett** will not be making his Far East debut with the Eagles on their Japan-Hawaii dates. It seems that MCA has declined to put up tour support money for the sold-out concert swing, and manager **Irving Azoff** is reportedly quite upset with MCA's decision. —*Record World*
▶ Retailers hope new releases from Eagles, **Fleetwood Mac**, and **Led Zeppelin** will lift lagging record sales. —*Cashbox*
▶ Columbia Records plans to release **J.D. Souther**'s next self-produced LP, *You're Only Lonely*, in July. He will have a lot of friends with him, including **Jackson Browne**, Glenn Frey, Don Henley, Don Felder, **David Sanborn**, **Phil Everly**, and **Tom Scott**. —*Cashbox*
▶ The marketing campaign for the upcoming Eagles album will be Elektra/Asylum's biggest promotion ever. —*Cashbox*
▶ Tim Schmit, Randy Meisner, and **Jackson Browne** will provide backing vocals on **Richie Furay**'s new LP, *I Still Have Dreams* —*Cashbox*

KOSH'S *LONG RUN* COVER REFLECTS EAGLES' SPIRIT

When considering the fabled history of monochromatic rock album covers, **The Beatles** sit atop the mountain with *The Beatles*, aka *The White Album*. Not far away is the Eagles' matte black *The Long Run*. The Fab Four weren't quite at the end of their run when they released their two-record set in 1968, but the Eagles were running on fumes by the time *The Long Run* crawled across the finish line in September 1979.

As they closed out the LP's production the band welcomed back art director [**John**] **Kosh**, who had turned the cover for *Hotel California* into a compelling piece of pop culture and one of the most recognizable covers of all time. Kosh hadn't seen much of the Eagles in the three years since the band released *Hotel*, but had kept busy designing albums for **Linda Ronstadt**, **Electric Light Orchestra**, **Dan Fogelberg**, **ZZ Top**, **James**

Taylor, **Ringo Starr**, Randy Meisner, **Andrew Gold**, the **Moody Blues**, **Karla Bonoff**, and **Aerosmith**, among many others.

Like he had with *Hotel*, Kosh took his cues mostly from Don Henley for the album's art direction. But where Henley's creative notions led to big expenses on *Hotel*, *The Long Run* would be more somber with a much lower investment, which Kosh estimated at roughly a third of what *Hotel* cost, if not less.

"Don wanted something very, very simple, with just type on the front, which was fine," Kosh told *Time Passages*. "And I mocked up about four or five different fonts, all on a black background. Some had a thin gray border, some didn't, and the typefaces [I selected] were all there for him to pick. And he just chose that particular face and I grayed it down a little bit."

The final typeface was Albertus, an old Monotype face, and the lettering used on the cover was hand-

EAGLES
THE LONG RUN

adapted for the occasion.

The cover design proved a bit different as well. A stark black, glossy cover would mean visible fingerprint marks, so he had the outer cover printed with an ultraviolet matte coating to reduce smudging. It used a standard four-color process to intensify the blacks, he said, and the inner gatefold was coated with a UV-cured high-gloss varnish.

The final front cover was solemn. Every word was in the large uppercase white serif typeface set against a black background; it was only broken up by a thin gray border set just inside the album's edges. The back cover continued the black background with a simple, centered gray box with the songs from each side listed inside it. The only name to appear on the outside was producer **Bill Szymczyk**. The album package included a poster of the band, which followed a practice started with *On the Border* that continued on all subsequent albums, with the exception of *One of These Nights*. Those pos-

ters were in color with the mostly smiling faces of the band members. The group shot for *The Long Run* was different. The stone-faced Eagles were captured in crisp black and white by veteran rock photographer **Jim Shea**, who cast side lights illuminating the black void behind them.

While Henley directed things, Kosh also had input from Glenn Frey, who, he said, would sometimes play the foil against the moody Henley, often winking and giving thumbs-up encouragement during the discussions for *Hotel* and *The Long Run*. Elektra/Asylum was in the midst of a corporate-wide cost-cutting rampage on album production, but those rules did not apply to supergroups like Eagles or **Fleetwood Mac**. Kosh would sometimes have trouble getting cooperation with E/A's creative department. When those troubles arose, help was just a phone call away.

"I would say, 'I want to do this...I want to do that,'" and [Elektra/Asylum] would say, 'I don't

EAGLES
THE LONG RUN
(5E-508)

THE NEW ALBUM ON
ASYLUM RECORDS AND TAPES.
PRODUCED BY BILL SZYMCZYK
FOR PANDORA PRODUCTIONS·LTD.
CONTAINING THE SINGLE,
"HEARTACHE TONIGHT."
(E-46545)

asylum

FALL TOUR 1979

Date	City	Venue		Date	City	Venue
10/8	Providence, RI	Civic Center		11/1	Charlotte, NC	Coliseum
10/9-10	Boston, MA	Boston Gardens		11/2	Raleigh, NC	North Carolina State University
10/12	Bloomington, IND	University of Indiana		11/4-5	Largo, MD	Capitol Center
10/13-14	Ann Arbor, MI	University of Michigan		11/8	Murfreesboro, TN	Middle State Tennessee University
10/15	Buffalo, NY	War Memorial Auditorium		11/9	Knoxville, TN	University of Tennessee
10/17	Lexington, KY	Rupp Arena		11/11-12	Atlanta, GA	Omni
10/18	Roanoke, VA	Convention Center		11/13	Birmingham, ALA	Jefferson Civic Center Arena
10/20-21	Richfield, OH	Richfield Coliseum		11/15-16	Cincinnati, OH	Riverfront Coliseum
10/22	Chicago, ILL	Chicago Stadium		11/18-19	Philadelphia, PA	Spectrum

Management: Irv Azoff and Front Line Management

SIDE ONE

THE LONG RUN
I CAN'T TELL YOU WHY
IN THE CITY
THE DISCO STRANGLER
KING OF HOLLYWOOD

SIDE TWO

HEARTACHE TONIGHT
THOSE SHOES
TEENAGE JAIL
THE GREEKS DON'T WANT NO FREAKS
THE SAD CAFÉ

Produced by BILL SZYMCZYK

Kosh's back cover for *The Long Run* was only marginally more complex than the album's front design, with a simply gray box that listed the songs. The covers were developed into an integral part of the band's marketing. Kosh (above right) set up his "cardboard tombstone" display at Tower Records' store on Sunset Boulevard the week the album was released in September 1979.

think we can do that,'" Kosh recalled. "Then **Irving [Azoff]** would get on the phone and all of a sudden they can do it."

Things ran smoothly until the album was ready to go to print. Kosh did not hear much more from Henley during the run-up for *The Long Run* art, but in his last conversation before it shipped, a misunderstanding changed their relationship.

"I had decided that to make this work I would like this really nice, soft matte finish on the cover," Kosh said. "Matte wouldn't show finger marks, and it does feel soft and nice, and then when you open it up inside was this crisp, black and white photograph in totally high [lamination], a UV gloss matte, which was exactly the opposite of what we normally do."

It was unorthodox, but he believed in the design. Henley expected something different.

"By the time Don found out, he was really pissed with me," Kosh said. "He wanted it the other way around. He wanted it glossy outside and matte inside, and I had to explain that it was too late. It's *on press.* And I mistakenly believed that we had fallen out at that point."

The Long Run went straight to the top of the charts on release. *Hotel*'s experience was similar, but where its cover had created a stir with its *Sgt. Pepper*-like gatefold, *The Long Run* was met with polite praise for its conservative, yet bold look.

Not everyone was sold.

Melody Maker's **Mark Williams**, whose 1979 review of *The Long Run* was biting, compared the cover to a "cardboard tombstone." Kosh thought that description a bit harsh, but laughed as he recalled setting up origami-like cardboard promotional boxes for the album that someone might think had a passing similarity.

Developing the cover was somewhat costlier than standard E/A art, but it was still far cheaper than the *Hotel* project. "The extra hits of the matte and gloss coatings meant two extra [print] stations [in production], which made the printing process more expensive," Kosh said, laughing. "But worth it for my 'cardboard tombstone,' don't you think?"

The project was a success, and Azoff invited Kosh back a year later to manage the art for the post-breakup LP, *Eagles Live*. And he would employ an inside joke on that cover that made English fans grin. American audiences? They didn't even know it was there. [122, 2129]

THE LONG RUN

Hotel California was the creative and commercial masterwork that cemented the group's status as America's biggest rock band. Legions of fans adored them and they sold out shows everywhere. But all was not well. It took three grueling years to complete *The Long Run*, and, after tensions reached a crescendo, the band's long fade-out began.

FALL 1979

 RELEASES
- ▶ **Eagles**, "Heartache Tonight" (single)
- ▶ **Eagles**, *The Long Run* (album)
- ▶ **Eagles**, "The Long Run" (single)

 NUGGETS

▶ Eagles are rush-releasing their first non-holiday single in three years; radio stations are putting "Heartache Tonight" into heavy rotation. The album, called *The Long Run*, ships Sept. 24. —*Cashbox*

▶ During the current Eagles tour, guitarist Joe Walsh is the last member to hit the stage at most shows; his entrance is accompanied by the rest of the group playing "Hail to the Chief"—in anticipation, of course, of Joe's successful bid for the presidency next year. Watch out, **Ted Kennedy**. Walsh gave a few campaign speeches to a largely uncomprehending Japanese audience. —*Record World*

▶ Eagles are kicking off the first leg of their U.S. tour in Providence, Rhode Island, after playing to 28,000 people in Hawaii's Aloha Stadium — the largest crowd ever assembled in the venue. —*Record World*

▶ **Irving Azoff**'s entire Front Line Management stable has new releases out; he also signs **Warren Zevon** and the **Doobie Brothers**. —*Record World*

▶ Don Henley and Joe Walsh join **Jackson Browne** for a benefit at Arlington Theater in Santa Barbara in support of the Western Gate Indian Reservation, which was having a liquified natural gas plant built on their reservation. Henley and **Stephen Stills** wore their "Walsh for President" campaign buttons. —*Record World*

▶ Joe Walsh, with the **Eagles** supporting him, held a "campaign" event in Tennessee that outdrew real presidential hopeful Ted Kennedy in attendance, 13,000 to 9,000. **Bob Seger** and Eagles PR man **Larry Solters** are his potential running mates. —*Cashbox*

 COLLABORATIONS
- ▶ **Don Henley** provided backing vocals on **Karla Bonoff**'s album *Restless Nights*.
- ▶ **Randy Meisner** and **Timothy B. Schmit** provided backing vocals on **Richie Furay**'s album *I Still Have Dreams*.

Free Gas for Everyone: Eagle Joe Walsh Runs for President

At their concerts, Glenn Frey used a standard stage line introducing the Eagles as a band from Los Angeles. But on the second night of *The Long Run* tour stop in Boston, on October 10, 1979, he had another job to do.

As a large banner unfurled from the balcony reading *Joe Walsh For President–1980*, Frey was suddenly on the stump in the unlikely role of endorsing a new political candidate.

"We need a good guitar player in the White House," Frey declared, eliciting raucous applause from the crowd.

Backstage, Walsh was acting coy about his intentions as an unlikely candidate.

"Just because I've announced doesn't mean I'm going to run," he said. But everything indicated he was serious.

With the Eagles back in the USA from a month-long tour of the Far East, Walsh had announced a populist platform ("Free Gas for Everyone") that tapped into the nation's angst after a summer of gas shortages and rationing at long pump lines.

With "Life's Been Good," Walsh had a song that could work for the campaign song and even become a national anthem.

Walsh's "run" would often tap anyone who might be in the area as a potential "Veep," including **Larry Solters**, the Eagles' publicity rep, who the trade press also identified as one of Walsh's running mates. Walsh hinted to **Steve Morse** of the *Boston Globe* that **Bob Seger** might be his running mate.

The day after the Boston show, United Press International reported that Walsh was floating a proposal to "anyone who would listen" to change the name of the nation's capital to "Walshington." The write-in candidate reportedly asked the Secret Service for protection. The wire service noted the Eagles' East Coast swing was "presumably gearing up for the presidential primaries in the spring."

"I was just watching TV and watching all the campaigning and all the baloney," Walsh said in a radio interview, talking about what spurred him to enter the race. "I do pay attention to what's going on and read the paper. And I was just so frustrated with it, you know, the political rhetoric. So, I said heck, I should just run for president. And I did it to be funny, to be humorous—somebody needs to. Remember Ford? Bumping into things? I enjoyed him. I thought I could get some press coverage. I could talk about things. And maybe get some kids who respect me because of my music to maybe get them thinking, get them mad enough where they might want to vote. And so that's really the motive I have in running for president."

But there was one problem. The Constitution requires candidates to be at least 35 years old. With Walsh still 31, he could not legally run. Given the roadblock, Walsh considered an alternative path, suggesting he might write an open letter to the American public about the issues he cared about most.

"The most important thing is to check out senators and congressmen," he observed. "There are environmentally concerned senators who are going to be bumped out this election because corporations are backing other people. So, it's not just voting for the president. I don't think the vote for president matters that much, whether they are Republican or Democrat. People have to get concerned about the environment, about the economy, and check on senators and congressmen and find people that will actually listen to people and not listen to corporations. And there are those kinds of people."

After **Ronald Reagan** defeated **Jimmy Carter** in November 1980, Walsh tabled his political ambitions for another decade. He made another "run" for office in his post-Eagles life, launching a mock vice-presidential campaign themed to the song "Vote for Me."

"There's a lot of stuff wrong and a lot of stuff broken," Walsh reflected in 2012 with *Loudersound*'s **Peter Makowski**. "I was watching the debates, and I was pretty sure that I could get elected if I just didn't say anything. These guys are putting their foot in their mouths with every third thing they say. It's hilarious, but it's also scary. I don't know why anybody in the world would want to be president, but if the whole country begged me, I'd probably consider it."

Half a decade later, even if Walsh was not

considering another run, he was still touting the skills he could bring to the office.

"I think I know how it works," he told *Rolling Stone* in 2017. "I know how to live in a complex decision-making organization. For example, the band. We got stuff done!" [1299, 1820, 1881, 1882, 1883, 1922, 1923, 1924]

Greeks and Freaks: Eagles Look Back at Frats, Debutantes

Looking back on a nonstop decade, the Eagles were pontificating about their longevity and future as the '80s loomed and its members approached middle age. In one song on *The Long Run*, "The Greeks Don't Want No Freaks," the band flashed back even further, cutting the rave-up as a nod to the 1960s fraternity rock co-authors Don Henley and Glenn Frey played in their college days.

Cutting their teeth on the Austin concert circuit, Henley's band **Felicity** played frat rock covers every weekend, including staples like "Louie Louie" by the **Kingsmen** and "96 Tears" by **? and the Mysterians**.

"Playing those frat parties was another dues-paying experience," Henley said in a conversation with *Rolling Stone*'s **David Browne** in 2016. "We witnessed a little bit of everything."

Around the same time the Eagles began recording *The Long Run* in the summer of 1978, **Bruce Springsteen and the E Street Band** toured America, and their sets included a mini-history of fraternity rock. Before introducing the song "Sherry Darling," Springsteen extolled the virtues of the raucous early-1960s rock and roll subgenre. He cited such defining records as "Louie Louie," "Farmer John" by the **Premiers**, and "Double Shot (Of My Baby's Love)" by the **Swingin' Medallions**.

"What these records had in common was that the audience was twice as loud as the band," he exulted as a vociferous Cleveland Agora audience cheered him on.

"The Greeks Don't Want No Freaks" was a cacophony of sounds, including rhythmic stomps, cheesy organ, and handclaps. With its enthusiastic background shouts, "Greeks" tried to emulate the loud and uproarious wild abandon Henley and Frey heard on the radio as teenagers and played at frat parties in their early bands.

While "Sherry Darling" (released on Springsteen's double album *The River* a year after *The Long Run*) was a lighthearted comic romp, there was a sneering and disdainful undertone to "The Greeks Don't Want No Freaks." The song portrayed its pristine heroine, a southern belle, as "a perfect little sister" but was unceremoniously fated to be found "in the bushes with the boys in the band."

The song was the B-side of the album's third and final single, "I Can't Tell You Why," released in early 1980, and climbed with the A-side up the *Billboard* Hot 100 chart to #8.

Unlike **The Beatles**, **Rolling Stones**, or Springsteen, the Eagles were not in the habit of releasing singles with unreleased treasures on the B-sides. (An early 45

continued on Page 363

WELCOME, JOE BOB—DON'T DO THAT FILL

Don Felder (far left), Joe Walsh, new band multi-instrumentalist **Joe Vitale**, and Glenn Frey joke around during warmups backstage on the *Hotel California* tour in 1978.

VITALE JOINS EAGLES FOR *HOTEL, LONG RUN* TOURS

In concert, from the start, the Eagles have performed their songs just as they sound on record. The band members meticulously crafted writing and recording their material and believed that fans shelling out hard-earned money to attend a show should hear everything the way they are accustomed to hearing it.

Critics claim that approach creates sterility in a live show and removes spontaneity from a performance, while others subscribe to the Eagles' notion that a band should not reinvent beloved songs. Judging by the history of sold-out Eagles concerts, many of their fans share the band's point of view.

As Eagles' later albums became more difficult to reproduce with only the five members pictured on the record packaging, they opened up to the idea of bringing on extra hands to help on stage.

One player who'd pitch in on later tours was **Joe Vitale**, drummer and multi-instrumentalist

from Joe Walsh's **Barnstorm** band and a veteran touring drummer for many other 1970s groups. As Don Henley emerged as the most prominent lead singer in the Eagles, there were times, like on "The Best of My Love," when it made more sense for the drummer to grab an acoustic guitar and make his way to the front of the stage to sing.

Henley also had issues with back pain, in part from singing while drumming, and it seemed reasonable that a second drummer could either relieve or redistribute his onstage strain. Vitale fit the bill: a talented, versatile musician who also played percussion, keyboards, and more on songs that did not need a second drummer.

Walsh lobbied his Eagles bandmates to hire his longtime musical partner and friend, and they agreed. But when he called Vitale at three in the morning to tell him the Eagles wanted to bring him aboard, the drummer was certain his former boss and serial prankster was trying to pull one on him.

"Listen, you've gotta get on a plane tomorrow and come out [for rehearsal]," Walsh told him. "You're gonna be in the Eagles, 'cause we need an extra guy to play percussion, drums, and keyboards. But you've gotta get on a plane tomorrow and come out to rehearsal 'cause we're gonna go to Japan."

Vitale told Walsh he wouldn't believe it unless Henley called and invited him. He assumed that would be the end of the "prank," but not too long after that, the phone rang again.

"I thought it was Joe running the joke into the ground," Vitale recalled. "I picked up the phone and said, 'WHAT?' This time, it was Henley." A really deep voice, quite different than Walsh's, said, "It's Henley. You feel like coming out and practicing with us?"

Vitale knew it was really the Eagles drummer and the offer was legitimate because Henley was anything but a prankster. Vitale flew out in the morning and, before long, was boarding another flight to Japan with the Eagles.

Since he called with a personal invitation, Henley presumably welcomed Vitale on board. Still, Don Felder, when telling the story in his 2008 biography, suggested otherwise. He claimed Henley, in fact, felt threatened by the other drummer's presence and suggested that Walsh had lobbied to make his buddy a permanent Eagle. Felder claimed Henley saw Vitale's inclusion as "a direct criticism of his competence as a drummer," and sniped that "Joe Vitale could play better drums than Don Henley with an arm and a leg cut off."

Notwithstanding Felder's claims, Vitale stayed on well past the Japan shows.

Despite being a more technically proficient drummer, Vitale respected Henley a great deal and considered him an excellent player as well. He spoke glowingly about Henley's voice, too, and said he was among the best in the business at managing the difficult job of singing while playing.

Vitale would do the drumming during certain spots in the set when Henley would perform from the front of the stage. Other times, both played the drums—each on his own kit—and Vitale would help by handling the fills while Henley just kept the backbeat. This allowed Henley to focus on his singing and gave him a break from contorting and twisting his back more than necessary.

Vitale, who the band affectionally called "Joe Bob" (which worked better when Walsh was within earshot), usually stuck to the parts as Henley had played them on the record. He made it a point to do so, respecting the band's philosophy on that matter, until one fateful night when, as Vitale explained it, "I got a little fancy on a drum fill in the song called 'Those Shoes.' It's an extremely funky song and coming out of the talk box solo where Joe and Felder were doing dueling talk boxes, I did this really funky syncopated fill."

Members of the band turned around and grinned at him. Vitale figured his fellow musicians really dug what he did. Bands like Barnstorm would occasionally stick their toe in the "jam band" waters, and when someone pulled off a chops-y fill, the other players would often nod in delight. As it turns out, that was not the case here. Vitale's bandmates were grinning at him because they knew he was going to hear from Henley.

As Vitale recalled in his 2008 memoir, "Later on at the hotel, Henley called and asked me to come over to his room for a second...Henley, wearing a hotel robe, came to the door and opened it about six inches. He said something like, 'Yeah, hey, you know that drum fill you played coming out of the solo in 'Those Shoes'?'

"So, there I was expecting to bask in this big compliment from Henley about my cool drum fill," he wrote. "I expectantly said, 'Yeah...?' And he shook his head and said evenly, 'Don't do that.' Then he said, 'Good night, Joe Bob,' and closed the door."

The boss had spoken. Vitale took it in stride and agreed to follow orders. But the next night before the show, Frey came up to him and ribbed him further. When Henley was not around, Vitale recounts, "Glenn said, with a completely straight face, 'So, Joe Bob, remember to play that fill.' They all laughed."

When telling the story in a 2016 interview, Vitale added that Frey also peeled off some large bills from a wad of cash, offering them as an incentive to play the fill again. "[There] ain't enough zeroes on those bills to play that," Vitale laughed. [218, 1309, 1345]

RELEASE
Mid-September 1979

AIRPLAY

CHARTS

HEARTACHE TONIGHT

By: Don Henley, Glenn Frey, Bob Seger, J.D. Souther
Side B: Teenage Jail (Henley, Frey, Souther)

Eagles last released a non-holiday single in May 1977. Now, after more than two years, Elektra/Asylum got its promotional engine revved, but still admitted having to "rush-release" the 45 to get it in stores by September 18. Whatever troubles the label had, it was worth it. The record-buying public couldn't get enough of the hand-clapping rocker and on October 6 the song leaped into both the *Cashbox* and *Record World* singles charts at #23 and on *Billboard*'s Hot 100 at #52. Just one month later the band would have the #1 song in America again.

Over the years, the Eagles' following among radio stations varied from region to region depending on the song, but the Southeast was, perhaps, the band's most faithful territory. Their collective decision to carry "Heartache" came as no surprise. WBGN-Bowling Green, Kentucky, was the first reported playlist add for "Heartache," according to *Billboard*. And the stations in the West, which were such slow adopters in the earlier years, showed no hesitation in adding Eagles songs.

185 PLAYLIST ADDS Fall 1979

Region	Sep	Oct	Nov	Regional Airplay
Northeast	7	21	1	15.7 %
Southeast	17	38	1	30.3 %
Midwest	6	26	3	18.9 %
Southwest	0	19	1	10.8 %
West	12	32	1	24.3 %

FIRST-WAVE STATIONS Stations that added the song in the first 30 days

KRTH, KFI-Los Angeles
KFRC-San Francisco
KROY-Sacramento
KFBG-San Diego
KJRB-Spokane
KTAC-Tacoma
KRSP-Salt Lake City
KTLK, KIMN-Denver
KJR, KYYX, KING-Seattle
KERN-Bakersfield

WNCI-Columbus
WZUU-FM-Milwaukee
KSLQ-FM-St. Louis
KBEQ-Kansas City
KDWB-Minneapolis

KKLS-Rapid City, SD
KLEO-Wichita
KIOA-Des Moines
WHB-Kansas City
WDRQ-Detroit

WPEZ-Pittsburgh
WTRY-Albany
WBBF-Rochester
WRKO-Boston
WICC-Bridgeport

KINT-El Paso
KRBE-FM-Houston
KAKC-Tulsa
KRKE-Albuquerque

WBGN-Bowling Green
WTIX-New Orleans
WNOE-New Orleans
WXLO-Miami

WPGC-Washington
WCAO-Baltimore
WYRE-Annapolis
WRVQ-Q94-Richmond

Billboard	HIGHEST CHARTING WEEK: BILLBOARD - November 10, 1979		
# 1 November 10, 1979	SINGLE	ARTIST	PREV WK
	1. HEARTACHE TONIGHT	**EAGLES**	**2**
	2. Dim All the Lights	Donna Summer	3
Cashbox	3. Still	Commodores	5
# 1 November 10, 1979	4. Rise	Herb Alpert	4
	5. Pop Muzik	M.	1
	6. Babe	Styx	7
Record World	7. No More Tears	Barbra Streisand & Donna Summer	10
# 1 November 10, 1979	8. Tusk	Fleetwood Mac	8
	9. You Decorated My Life	Kenny Rogers	9
	10. Please Don't Go	KC and the Sunshine Band	11

Sources: Billboard, Cashbox, Record World

THUMPING 'HEARTACHE' IS EAGLES' LAST #1 SINGLE

The Eagles' first album single in two and a half years, "Heartache Tonight," shot to the top of the charts quickly after being released on September 18, 1979. But it had a tough road to get there.

Glenn Frey found initial inspiration from some vintage R&B records, but then he got stuck. It took a village to finish this song, as four collaborators—Frey, Don Henley, **J.D. Souther**, and **Bob Seger**—earned songwriting credits for the stomping rock and soul shuffle.

Frey and Souther got things started after a period spent "listening to **Sam Cooke** records at my house," Souther told Songfacts.com in 2011. "So, we were just walking around, clapping our hands and snapping fingers and singing the verses to those songs. The melody sounds very much like those Sam Cooke shuffles."

But Frey felt the song needed a chorus—and more than that, it required attitude. He got both courtesy of a song-changing suggestion from Seger, his old Detroit mentor. Souther remembered the conversation as a phone call, while Frey and Seger said it happened at Frey's home on LaFontaine in Beverly Hills.

"We didn't get to a chorus that we liked within the first few days, and I think Glenn was on the phone with Seger," Souther added, "and he said, 'I wanna run something by you,' and sang it to him, and Seger just came right in with the chorus—just sang it and it was so good." And that was Seger's contribution—the chorus. But it was the heartbeat of 'Heartache.'"

It was not the first time Seger had provided Frey with a timely career assist. As a teenager, the future Eagles star had signed his first recording contract with Seger's management team. Seger produced one of Frey's early singles and brought Frey in as a guitarist and background vocalist on "Ramblin' Gamblin' Man," the title track of the 1969 debut album by the **Bob Seger System**, and Seger's first Top 20 hit single.

"The most important thing that happened to me in Detroit was meeting Bob and getting to know him," Frey told the *Detroit Free Press* in 2003. "He took me under his wing."

Their friendship, both musical and personal, would endure for decades, even after Frey's move to California led to new creative intersections with the likes of Henley and Souther. "I knew him for 50 years," Seger said in a 2016 interview with *Billboard*. "He was a great kid. I always kind of thought of him as my baby brother, a little bit. He was fucking brilliant. He was a joy to be around. I always looked forward to seeing him. It was always memorable. He had an amazing sense of humor and was just smart, whip-smart."

Whenever Seger visited the Eagles' California home base, "he always used to come over and visit me, and he'd visit Don, too, and play us stuff he was working on—and we would do the same," Frey recalled. "I seem to remember that I had the verse thing going on for 'Heartache Tonight,' and I was showing it to Seger, and we were jammin'—I think we were jammin' on electric guitars at LaFontaine—and then he blurted out the chorus. That's how 'Heartache' started. Then Bob disappeared, and J.D., Don, and I finished that song up. No heavy lyrics. The song is more of a romp, and that's what it was intended to be."

Frey's lengthy history with Seger provided an unspoken chemistry that helped "Heartache" finally get underway. Souther would ultimately downplay the lyrics, telling Songfacts.com that "there's not much to it. I mean, it's really just two long verses, but it felt really good." Henley, however, thought they had something special on their hands: "Don said, 'That's it—we're done,'" Seger later told *Rolling Stone*.

Frey was left with only one small reservation: "Glenn called me and said, 'Is four writers okay on this?'" Souther told Songfacts.com. "And I said, 'Sure, if it's good.' And he said, 'Yeah, it's great. Seger just sang this to me,' and he sang it to me and I said, 'That's fantastic.'"

Don Felder would add a sensuous turn on the slide guitar, but there was still something missing—a big drum sound. Henley was in search of a very specific feel, one that could hold its own with the song's huge narrative. Henley finally captured the sound he wanted by placing a marching-band drum on a luggage stand and then playing it with a mallet. "He did that forever," Timothy B. Schmit told *Rolling Stone*. "It took a long time."

Joe Walsh then described to *Rolling Stone* what happened next: "Glenn went out and sung his ass off on that track."

Henley's rhythm experiments weren't the only things that dragged out, as sessions for *The Long Run* stretched beyond a year. But a meticulous attention to detail had always been the hallmark of Frey's studio approach, Seger added. "He used to tell me that 'every single track's gotta be good—every single track,'" Seger remembered in the *Billboard* interview. "'We don't release an album 'til it's good.'"

The Eagles ended up splitting after *The Long Run*, but not before taking a jigsaw puzzle-like song to the top of the charts and then claiming a Grammy Award for Best Rock Vocal Performance by a Duo or Group. Ironically, "Heartache Tonight"—despite its dark, decidedly unromantic theme and a lengthy gestation period—emerged as perhaps this album's most approachable moment.

"*The Long Run* became, indeed, the long run," Frey conceded in a conversation with **Cameron Crowe**. "It was a difficult record to make overall, but I loved 'Heartache Tonight.'" [209, 1857, 1858, 1859, 1860, 1861] release of "Take It Easy" backed with the non-album cut "Get You in the Mood" was a rare exception.) In the end, "The Greeks Don't Want No Freaks" created more confusion than mystery, as an Eagles B-side was historically more of a throwaway song than something talked about in the band's canon. But given the gloom so pervasive on *The Long Run*, "Greeks" certainly helped lighten the mood. [1995, 1996]

WINTER 1979-80

 RELEASES
▶ **Eagles,** "I Can't Tell You Why" (single)

 COLLABORATIONS
▶ **Don Henley** provided backing vocals on the single "The Light is On" on **Christopher Cross**'s self-titled debut album.
▶ **Don Henley** (harmony vocals), **Glenn Frey** (harmony vocals), **Joe Walsh** (lead guitar), and **Don Felder** (guitar) provided musical support on **Warren Zevon**'s album *Bad Luck Streak in Dancing School*.

 AWARDS
▶ **Eagles, 22nd Annual Grammy Awards:** Best Pop Performance by a Duo or Group with Vocals, "Heartache Tonight," winner. Also nominated: **The Blues Brothers**, *Briefcase Full of Blues*; **The Cars**, *Candy-O*; **Styx**, *Cornerstone*; **The Knack**, *My Sharona*; and **Dire Straits**, "Sultans of Swing."

 ON THE ROAD WITH …
▶ **Eagles**: Chicago, Jimmy Buffett, Linda Ronstadt, Roy Orbison, the Amazing Rhythm Aces

 NUGGETS
▶ Special benefit concert in San Diego for **Jerry Brown** supported by Eagles, **Linda Ronstadt**, **Chicago**, and **J.D. Souther,** and with a train from Los Angeles to San Diego where riders can mingle with guest conductors **Helen Reddy** and **Jane Fonda**. —*Cashbox*
▶ **The Who**'s disastrous Cincinnati concert draws attention to concert security for big draws, and the focus turns to the next BIG show: Eagles at The Forum. Eagles management was there again serving coffee and donuts to those fans in L.A. waiting in line to get tickets. —*Cashbox*
▶ The Eagles' *The Long Run* streak at the top of the *Cashbox* Top 100 albums chart comes to an end, and is displaced by **Pink Floyd**'s *The Wall*. —*Cashbox*
▶ Eagles performed at the Las Vegas Aladdin Theater in a $20-per-seat show that helped raise $400,000 for Gov. Jerry Brown, a presidential candidate. —*Record World*
▶ Eagles make an appearance at San Francisco's Golden Gate Park on March 8 in KRFC's 8-mile "Long Run." Proceeds go to restore the park. Winners get a place in the Boston Marathon and the other prizes include radios, 50 pairs of Nike running shoes and 100 copies of *The Long Run* LP. —*Record World*
▶ **Bob Seger** has three Eagles in the studio with him—Glenn Frey, Don Henley, and Tim Schmit—helping him record songs for his new album, *Against the Wind*. —*Record World*
▶ **Bill Szymczyk** is flying across the pond to London to produce **The Who**'s upcoming album, *Face Dances*. Apparently **Pete Townshend** is a big *Hotel California* fan and, according to Szymczyk, the arm-whirling guitarist told him: "You hear how that sounds? Do that to me." Unlike the Eagles, almost all of The Who's album material is ready to record before the producer even arrives in the studio. —*Record World, BBC*

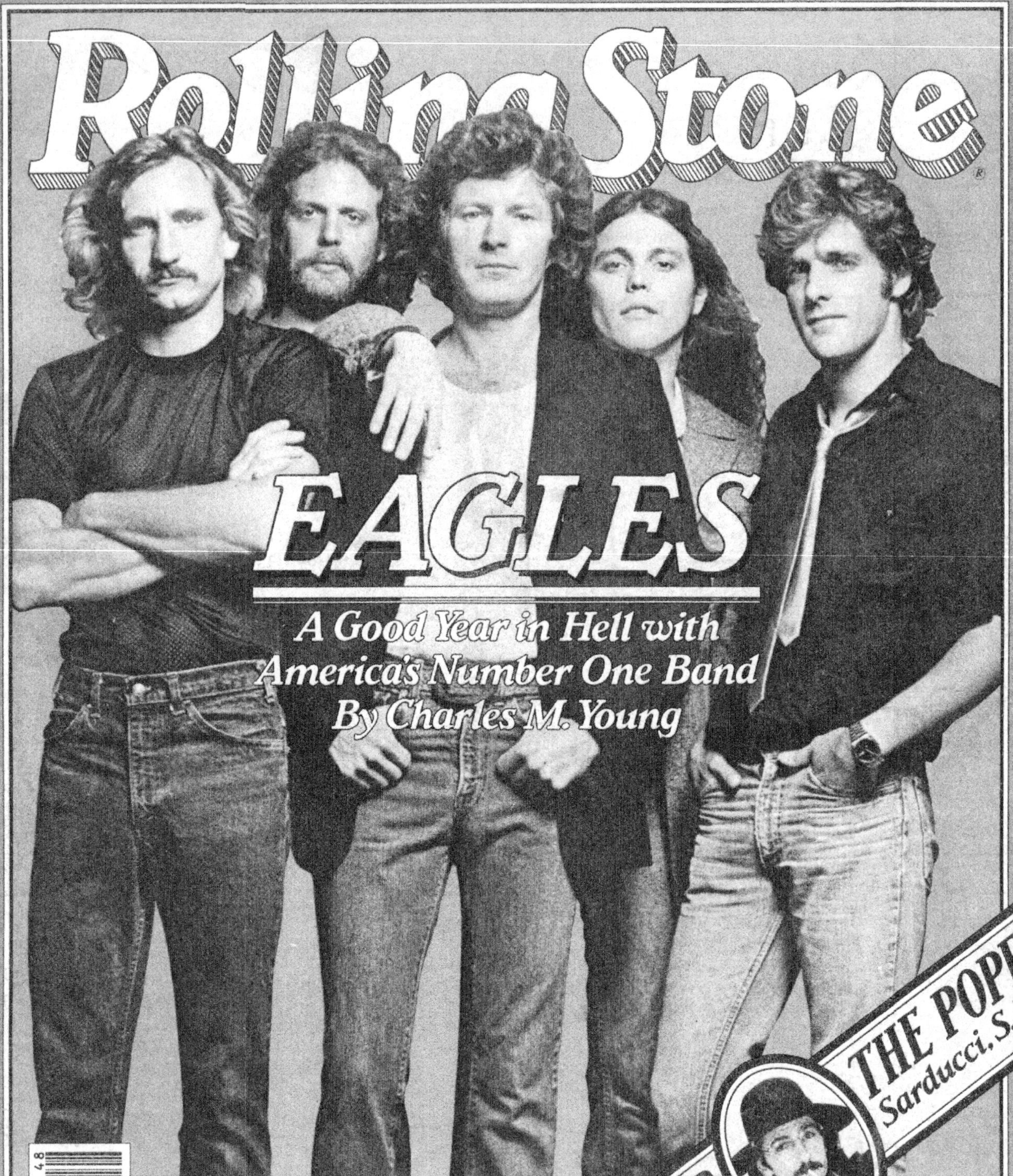

Rolling Stone

EAGLES

A Good Year in Hell with
America's Number One Band
By Charles M. Young

THE POPE
Sarducci, S.J.

I COVER
By Guido

0 748214

ROLLING STONE SPOTLIGHTS RE-EMERGING EAGLES

Four years after appearing on the cover of *Rolling Stone* magazine for the first time, the Eagles duplicated the feat in the issue dated November 29, 1979. While the first cover story described a band still on the ascent, the second cover story caught them when they were both on top of the world and nearing the end.

Two of the original members were gone, and the Eagles had reached the zenith of their career with *Hotel California*. They were attempting—and struggling—to follow up that record with *The Long Run*. The headline strewn across *Rolling Stone* was "Hell is for Heroes" (a nod to the gritty 1962 World War II drama starring heroes **Steve McQueen** and **Bobby Darin**) when the magazine hit newsstands two months after they released the album. It certainly captured the band's sentiment, and its author found himself in an unusual position.

Staff writer **Charles M. Young** spent a good deal of time with the band for the story and witnessed firsthand the making of what would become the swan song of their classic period in the 1970s.

Young's most ominous previous connection with the band was a snarky remark in his "Random Notes" column that sparked a feud culminating in the infamous Eagles vs. *Rolling Stone* softball game the previous year. One byproduct of that Eagles win was the promise of another story in the magazine, and Young got the task. He crafted an informative and humorous article subtitled "The Eagles' Slow Burn in the Rock & Roll Inferno." Young captured them at an exciting time in their history, when the Eagles were essentially the most popular band in the world. And as they were about to implode.

Young ponders the relative anonymity of the Eagles, despite their status as what he described as "*The* American band of the Seventies." The group's unquestioned leaders, Glenn Frey and Don

HELL IS FOR HEROES

NOVEMBER 1979

Henley, show up in most of the publishing credits, make the final decisions in the studio, and simply "run the show," he wrote, yet they "can walk down any street in the world and not be recognized...an anonymous monolith."

Young intermingles the backstage goings-on as the band prepares for a concert at Milwaukee County Stadium in front of 50,000 drunken teenagers, weaving off-the-cuff comments from Joe Walsh and **Irving Azoff**, and sprinkles in the back stories for Henley and Frey as the eight-page feature spread unfolds. It's a massive article, filling *Rolling Stone*'s then-robust 11x14 tabloid dimensions.

Young paints Henley as a stressed artist who is suffering from a bad back, an ulcer, and enormous pressure to follow the considerable success of *Hotel California*. He described the angst caused by the religious fear tactics imposed on him during his conservative Texas upbringing, by his "macho" high school football coach, by the political problems in the country, and by his frustration that fans don't always understand the meaning of his lyrics. He summed up his relationship with his job when he said, "Music is a lot of hard work, as far as I'm concerned...I've been criticized and maligned and misunderstood, and this is a 24-hour-a-day job, you know. This is not something you leave at the office.

"This is something I take around with me all the time. Every minute I'm awake, even when I'm asleep, I'm worried about the next album and what's going to be written on it and how it's going to do and how it's going to be accepted, and how my peers are going to react and how we're going to make it better than the last one and how the record company is on our case."

The record company was "on their case" because the September 1979 album was more than a year late. The article quotes Elektra/Asylum Chairman

Joe Smith expressing frustration over sales numbers and grumbling that their top act was slow to deliver an album. He and manager Irving Azoff, on opposing sides between the label and the band, traded barbs about each other, though both claimed they had a good relationship.

Henley and Frey also described some of the misogyny they were witnessing in the culture that surrounded them. Frey reflected that women were being viewed as "objects" for men, while Henley offered the observation that sometimes sexual relationships ended up as a commodity exchange—trading status for beauty.

Both Frey and Henley spent a fair amount of time deriding punk rock, not surprising considering their distaste for the music and that journalist Young championed the punk movement in his work for *Rolling Stone*.

The magazine had moved from San Francisco to New York in 1977, and reflecting on the article in 2012, Young said, "It's never been hip to like the Eagles in New York. When [the Eagles] were popular in the '70s, there was this thing going on here called punk rock. You know, this little subculture that came out of [seminal New York club] CBGBs [sic]. And the values of punk were very different from the values of the Eagles... [the band members] were doing something that really nobody else could do with their harmonies. There weren't any punk bands that would do harmonies at all. So, the Eagles were viewed as unhip. At the time when I wrote that [1979 Eagles cover] article, people thought I was crazy for writing about the Eagles because I came up writing about the **Ramones** and the **Dead Boys**." He added that the Eagles "weren't punk, but they were certainly pugnacious."

Most curious in hindsight was the description of the band offered by Timothy B. Schmit, still in his "honeymoon" period with the group and feeling blissful to just be a part of it. Or he was simply putting on a good face for the press.

"It's an incredibly smooth operating band now," Schmit said, "the closest to a band I've ever worked with. We have a good time without any major arguments."

Heartfelt or not, his comment runs counter to just about everything ever heard about the Eagles throughout the '70s and especially during this period. Insurmountable tensions would cause the group to disband less than a year after the story's publication. [343, 1764]

Rolling Stone illustrator **Greg Scott** attempted to capture all the varied gossip surrounding the Eagles in a single illustration for the magazine's November 29, 1979 issue.

Geffen Forms New Label, Signs John & Yoko, Elton, Donna

From mailroom boy to one of the most powerful and innovative executives the music business had ever known, **David Geffen**'s meteoric rise came to a standstill in the late 1970s. He had suffered through **Bob Dylan** leaving Asylum after his *Planet Waves* album had underperformed. He'd seen a short-lived stint as the vice-chairman of Warner Bros.' film division end abruptly in 1976 when Warner Communications topper **Steve Ross** fired him.

A bladder cancer diagnosis followed these setbacks in 1977, prompting Geffen to quit the business to focus on his health and take inventory of his life. Although he used some of his downtime to teach a non-credited music industry and arts management seminar at Yale, he remained retired throughout 1978 and 1979, despite being a young man in his early thirties.

It turned out that early retirement did not agree with Geffen. And when his doctors told him they erroneously diagnosed his cancer and gave him a clean bill of health, it primed him for a comeback.

In 1980, he returned to the fray with a new label, Geffen Records. The music industry was in a slump then and it hardly seemed the most auspicious time to pump millions of dollars into a new company when established giants of the industry were struggling. As Geffen told **Christian Williams** of the *Washington Post* in 1982, "When I wanted to start up again with Geffen Records, everybody said, 'Oh, no,

David, you can't, it's the worst possible time.' But I thought, what better time if you really want to do it?"

Geffen's punctuated his return to the music business with a startling announcement that he had signed major talent—**John Lennon** and **Yoko Ono**, **Elton John**, and **Donna Summer**—to his new company.

Geffen brimmed with enthusiasm at the announcement. "He's made a real commitment to do what he's done in the past," Geffen stated about Elton John. "He's recording, he's touring with **Nigel Olsson** and **Dee Murray**, and he's writing songs again with **Bernie Taupin**."

While successfully luring John away from MCA and providing a new home for successful disco artist Summer, the new label's most significant prize was releasing the first new music from Lennon in more than five years.

Record executive **Ed Rosenblatt**, who rejoined Geffen as the new company's president, recalled how the label made its biggest signing at the end of summer 1980.

"I get a call from **Phil Spector**, who I knew from A&M," he recounted to writer **Mike Sigman**. "He says, '[John] Lennon's in the studio—he doesn't have a deal.' 'Oh, thank you, Phil!' I go up to see David, and I say, 'Do you know Yoko?' He says, 'Of course.' I say, 'Call her, and make the deal.' Which, of course, he did."

When rumors began swirling that Lennon was back in the studio, label heads began courting the former Beatle. But Geffen took a different approach by reaching out directly to Ono. The major labels had all made

continued on Page 375

Exhausted Eagles Complete An Uneven LP, *The Long Run*

The waiting, as **Tom Petty** once sang, is the hardest part. Eighteen long months of fits and starts culminated in the release of *The Long Run* on September 24, 1979. The approach to the album's recording tested the limits of all involved. It was downright torturous. In Don Felder's book *Heaven and Hell*, he described a process whereby the band would fill up ten to twelve reels over three to five days and deconstruct them on a 24-track recorder to decipher the best takes. Producer **Bill Szymczyk**, who the band dubbed "Coach," would attempt to put the best together, often requesting new pieces and trying to splice them.

"When our master tape went by, it looked like a zebra, there were so many edits," Felder

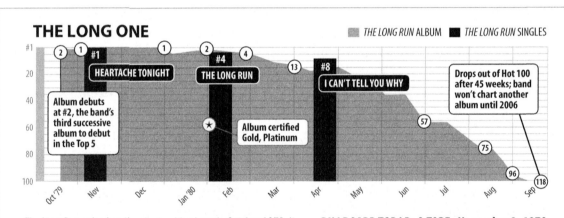

THE LONG ONE

■ *THE LONG RUN* ALBUM   ■ *THE LONG RUN* SINGLES

#1 HEARTACHE TONIGHT

#4 THE LONG RUN

#8 I CAN'T TELL YOU WHY

Album debuts at #2, the band's third successive album to debut in the Top 5

Album certified Gold, Platinum

Drops out of Hot 100 after 45 weeks; band won't chart another album until 2006

The Long Run arrived on the charts with a bang in October 1979. It jumped directly into the #2 position on *Billboard*'s Top LPs and Tape chart. Two weeks later it had dislodged **Led Zeppelin**'s *In Through the Out Door* as the country's new #1 album, holding onto that position for the next eight weeks. It remained a Top 10 album through March 1980, but began slipping down the album chart even as "I Can't Tell You Why" was climbing the singles chart. The band's tour wound down in June, along with the album's presence on the charts. By July, it had fallen out of the Top 50, and dropped out of the Top 100 by September, but not before spawning three Top 10 singles along the way.

Sources: Billboard, Recording Industry Association of America

BILLBOARD TOP LPs & TAPE, November 3, 1979

1. EAGLES, *THE LONG RUN*
2. Led Zeppelin, *In Through the Out Door*
3. Commodores, *Midnight Magic*
4. Styx, *Cornerstone*
5. Foreigner, *Head Games*
6. Cheap Trick, *Dream Police*
7. Fleetwood Mac, *Tusk*
8. Herb Alpert, *Rise*
9. Michael Jackson, *Off the Wall*
10. The Knack, *Get The Knack*

wrote, lamenting that in the pursuit of perfectionism, the band may have left some of its most spontaneous moments on the control room floor.

Frey was attracted by the concept of "who would last" and told **Cameron Crowe** that "The Long Run" was as much about longevity as his love for **Tyrone Davis**' single called "Turning Point." As a metaphor and a song concept, the band's title track was an idea they were mulling for six or seven years. Frey thought of it as a tribute to Memphis with the slide guitars of Felder and Walsh playing the parts of horns.

Frey's Detroit roots took hold on the album's strongest tracks. He leaned on his old Detroit friend **Bob Seger** for help with what would become the album's first single, "Heartache Tonight." Bassist Timothy B. Schmit had presented an idea he had been working on that became "I Can't Tell You Why." Henley and Frey joined him as co-writers, contributing harmony vocals and a sleek R&B groove guided by Frey's striking solo. It was the first song completed for the album. With Frey taking lead guitar and Walsh playing keys, it showcased the interchangeable roles the band members played throughout the sessions.

The Eagles were also releasing their new music in an ever-changing world. The raw sounds of mid-decade punk rock by **The Clash**, the **Ramones**, and **The Jam** were morphing into the more radio-friendly "new wave," with new rising stars like **Blondie**, **The Cars**, **Devo**, **Pretenders** and **The B-52's**, and who also challenged the status quo and re-energized a staid scene. At the same time, dance music was reach-

ELEKTRA/ASYLUM INSIDER

AFTER *HOTEL CALIFORNIA*, TWO AND A HALF, ALMOST THREE YEARS WENT BY before we saw *The Long Run*. The pressure of touring and top-tier success weighed heavily on the band. They weren't getting along. And once you've recorded one of the best albums of all time, how do you follow up? Well, first, bring in Timothy B. Schmit from **Poco** to fill Randy Meisner's shoes. We knew there were also writing issues, and they brought in two other songwriters, **J.D. Souther** and **Bob Seger**, to help them over the creative hump. They put Glenn back on the mic and it worked—radio jumped right back in. "Heartache Tonight" was a home run. The Eagles could do no wrong.

But the next singles were not as obvious and not as easy to promote as their predecessors. At the time, disco was at its peak, and to the ever-fickle press, the Eagles' sound began to wane. As a retort, Henley's tongue-in-cheek "The Long Run" wasn't a true Top 40 single, but we pushed it up the charts and achieved Top 10 success.

As with "The Best of My Love," ballads are hard to identify upfront as potential hits. But we all decided Schmit's tune, "I Can't Tell You Why," should get the shot. Although it was a struggle working the single, we continued the pressure and finally the record came home. Then hell froze over ...

–Rip Pelley, former National Director of Artist Development and Promotion, Elektra/Asylum Records

ing its apex in the heyday of *Saturday Night Fever*, and the **Village People**, **The Bee Gees**, **Donna Summer**, and **Chic** dominated the charts. It was getting crowded.

Against this sonic backdrop, the long-delayed *The Long Run* hit the bins, and the band sounded tentative and tired. A trio of hit singles including "Heartache Tonight," the title track, and "I Can't Tell You Why" offset songs that might not have made the cut on earlier Eagles albums, like "Teenage Jail," "The Greeks Don't Want No Freaks," and "The Disco Strangler."

"The one thing the Eagles agreed on was that we all hated disco music," Felder wrote in *Heaven and Hell*. "It seemed so unmusical and repetitive for us ballad boys."

As for infectious hooks, "Those Shoes," with Felder and Walsh on double talk box at the song's end, was based on a fashion trend Henley observed of women wearing Charles Jourdan shoes with little ankle straps. Henley decided he and co-writers Frey and Felder would turn it into a metaphor. In talking with Crowe, he envisioned women standing on their own and taking responsibility for their own lives and losses.

Henley elaborated further: "The lyric 'Once you've started wearing those shoes' meant once you've started being your own woman and taking responsibility for your own life; once you've decided not to be just decoration—an appendage to some guy— then this is all the crap you're going to have to put up with."

The song's nod to the singles scene that was full of sharks "including us," as Henley put it, cast the Eagles as play-ers among the characters they were describing. With its austere black cover, *The Long Run* accentuated the dark underbelly of the Los Angeles landscape and the cynicism of the album's creators as they were approaching middle age.

The album's closing track "The Sad Café," co-written by Henley, Frey, and **J.D. Souther**, seemed to reflect their nostalgia for the early days of hanging out at the Troubadour and Dan Tana's restaurant (scene of "Lyin' Eyes").

"We were getting older, and there was a sadness because we had seen, close-up, that everybody's dreams don't come true," Henley shared with Crowe in 2003. "Or, at least, not in the way they think they're gonna come true. Then, of course, there was the dark side. Friends and acquaintances of ours (from that era) had begun to meet untimely ends—classic cases of 'too much, too soon.' It was either that or 'too little, too late.' So, we were struggling to make sense of that dichotomy, that contradiction. Is fortune a good thing or a bad thing, you know?"

While their ambitions may have been for a double album, not much is known about what they left out. One outtake had the working title "You're Really High, Aren't You?" According to an interview Felder gave to *Fox News*, the band had worked up guitar arrangements and the lyrical ideas for the song. "But we never got around to finishing the lyrics, and we barely even finished that record before it finished us. Everybody was like, 'OK, we're done, let's quit. We've got enough to put a record out.'"

The Long Run entered the charts at #2 and claimed the top spot a week later. It yielded three Top 10 singles, including "Heartache Tonight," which reached #1. ("The Long Run" and "I Can't Tell You Why" hit #4 and #8, respectively.) The RIAA certified it platinum by February.

As the release date for *The Long Run* approached, the Eagles were already gone and out of the country. One week before the album landed in stores, the band kicked off a six-night stint in Japan, followed by a layover in Hawaii that included a memorable concert at Aloha Stadium in Honolulu on September 30, with **Jimmy Buffett and the Coral Reefer Band** opening the show.

When **Joe Smith**, Elektra/Asylum's charming but persistent chief executive, attended the opening night show in Providence, Joe Walsh had a little fun, interspersing a verse into "Life's Been Good"

that poked fun at the last year-plus and the saga of making *The Long Run*:

*"I'm making records
Joe Smith he can't wait
He sends me letters
Tells me I'm late"*

Looking back, like Henley, Felder lamented the decision not to take more time off for rest between projects. The pace was too rigorous. The tour continued through the end of the year and into summer 1980.

Until then, for nearly a decade, the machinery behind the Eagles had never stopped. The length of *The Long Run* tour and all the band's accumulated baggage would be the band's undoing. [711, 1820, 1840, 1841, 1905, 1906, 1907, 1908, 1913]

Washington Post
November 14, 1979

The Long Run is far from a disaster. There is experimentation throughout the disc, but there are no cuts...to achieve the brilliance of "Lyin' Eyes," "Hotel California," or even "Life in the Fast Lane." Eagles fans will be satisfied with this album, which is already #1 on the pop charts. "Heartache Tonight" is a hit and "I Can't Tell You Why" promises to be another. But whether any of these cuts will grow on us is questionable. These are all more solid than inspired.

– Al Aronowitz

Melody Maker
September 29, 1979

I can't account for the obvious paucity of imagination in *The Long Run*. I don't know why they've abandoned the notion of using a framework to hang their lyrics on when it's served them so successfully in the past. But I suspect the reason we've had to wait so long for this dross was because they were desperately scrabbling around for something stronger to put in place. All to no avail. This is easily the Eagles' worst album to date.

– Mark Williams

Rolling Stone
November 15, 1979

The Long Run is a bitter, wrathful, difficult record, full of piss and vinegar and poisoned expectations. Because it's steeped in fresh, risky material and unflinching self-examination, it's also the Eagles' best work in years. There's none of the tacky posturing that marred *Hotel California*, and the innocence of the "Take It Easy" era is too distant to retrieve. Wrapped in black cardboard, *The Long Run* is an invitation to a funeral, a thoughtful interment of the past.

– Timothy White

Doug Weston's Troubadour club and Dan Tana's restaurant (far right) provided the inspiration for "The Sad Café."

HENLEY, FREY WAX NOSTALGIC IN 'THE SAD CAFÉ'

Eagles concluded their last classic-era album on a nostalgic note, as "The Sad Café" returned to the place where their early dreams took shape.

Don Henley borrowed the song's name from author **Carson McCullers**' 1951 novella, *The Ballad of the Sad Café*, about a small-town café in the South that becomes a late-into-the-evening gathering spot for locals to carouse and gossip. The Troubadour in Los Angeles was similar and happened to be where Glenn Frey met Henley in 1970, as if by fate.

"[Glenn] walked up to me one night and handed me a beer, and he just started talking to me," Henley told CBS in 2015.

The venue provided them with inspiration, both on stage and off. A cast of characters including bartender **John Barrick**—who had earlier served as **The Byrds**' first road manager—shared a wealth of knowledge about music, about the business, and about the life they hoped to lead.

Soon, as "The Sad Café" co-writer **J.D. Souther** would tell *Rolling Stone*, a group of up-and-comers began to coalesce there who "schemed, dreamed, and laughed more than seems possible." In time, Henley said, this tiny West Hollywood nightclub on Santa Monica Boulevard became the "center of the universe."

So it was only natural they'd return to the Troubadour for inspiration as they slotted in songs for *The Long Run*—and to Barrick, for whom "The Sad Café" was dedicated. He ended up serving as the Eagles' first road manager, too, but he ultimately meant so much more to the band.

Henley would subsequently describe Barrick to *Rolling Stone* magazine as "our former road manager/spiritual/philosophical adviser." Barrick's most invaluable service was that he allowed the youngsters to "pick his brain," Frey said in *A Conversation with the Eagles*. "He was very much like a bard, a teacher," Frey added.

They would talk about things as momentous as how The Byrds split up, and as mundane as staying the course through required drudgery like promotional interviews. His advice was as simple as it was timeless: "Barrick said to me, 'Glenn,' he says, 'you have to lick the stamp to send the letter, not for the taste of the glue,'" Frey recalled. On the Eagles' self-titled debut, Barrick is credited as "fire keeper," likely a nod to his steadying presence during peyote-fueled desert trips that inspired both the name of the group and their first album's cover art.

At this point, however, the future Eagles were still sharpening their sound—and growing thicker skin during the Troubadour's so-called "Hoot Night" on Mondays, when new singer-songwriters would share their latest material before a jaded group of music industry promoters, producers, agents, music reviewers, publishers, and critics.

Frey, Henley, and new friends like Souther, **Linda Ronstadt**, and **Jackson Browne** became staples of the scene. "When the Troub came along, that was right up our alley," Ronstadt told author **Barney Hoskyns**. "It was small enough that you could really hear the music well and get close to it."

Yet, the Troubadour could still operate very much like a drinking establishment rather than a live music venue. Indeed, the bar was at the front of the house, and anyone could sidle up, but the stage was in the larger back room, and it took a ticket—or a good hustle—to get inside. On one memorable night, Henley almost got into a beef when a drunken fellow patron would not stop talking while Ronstadt performed onstage.

Henley asked him to be quiet, and the guy turned around to say, "I'm cool, man," Henley later remembered. "And I think I had had a couple of shots of tequila because I jokingly said, 'No, you're an asshole.'"

Frey, who was sitting nearby, went "white," Henley added. But by then the talkative drunk had lifted Henley into the air by his lapels. Frey eventually smoothed everything over, but only after first trying to convince the patron to let Henley go because he was a member of the Eagles.

"We hadn't even put out a record yet," Henley noted, so "that didn't really do any good. Nobody had heard of us." Once his feet were back on the Troubadour floor, Henley said he made a lasting vow: "I don't think I've had any tequila since then because it turns me into somebody I don't like."

Other memories that helped evolve the song were more pleasant. Henley explained to **Cameron Crowe** how a soon-to-be-famous comic worked the nostalgia into his bit.

"A train used to run down the center of Santa Monica Boulevard, right outside the Troubadour," Henley said. "**Steve Martin** actually had a routine where he'd get the entire audience to exit the club, hop a flatcar on that slow-moving train, and ride up to La Cienega, a few blocks east. Then, everybody would hop off and walk back down to the club together. I don't think that happened very many times—maybe not even more than once or twice, because the railroad people didn't like it. It was kind of dangerous and there was liability involved. Still—and I don't want to over-mythologize—it was something to remember. That was a wonderful time in Los Angeles. The city was alive with magic and a sense of possibility. People were warmer and more open than they are now."

On stage, it was not always a loose, fun environment. For up-and-comers like Frey, who had already seen an earlier musical collaboration with

> " **STEVE MARTIN ACTUALLY HAD A ROUTINE WHERE HE'D GET THE ENTIRE AUDIENCE TO EXIT THE CLUB, HOP A FLATCAR ON THAT SLOW-MOVING TRAIN, AND RIDE UP TO LA CIENEGA. THEN, EVERYBODY WOULD HOP OFF AND WALK BACK DOWN TO THE CLUB TOGETHER.**
>
> **— DON HENLEY**

Souther called **Longbranch/Pennywhistle** fall apart, there was a lot on the line.

"This unspoken thing was created between Henley and me, which said: 'If we want to be up here with the big boys, we'd better get our game together and write some fucking good songs,'" Frey later told *The Independent*. He added that their goals were twofold: to be successful but also to be taken seriously as songwriters.

The cutthroat nature of these showcases gave everything a competitive edge. Some nights, the setting was more like a musical boot camp. "The Troub was the only place where you could go and showcase for record companies," Browne said to Hoskyns. "If you were lucky, you might get to sing three or four songs that night."

Musicians would line up along Santa Monica Boulevard, hoping to be waved in by so-called "Hootmaster" **Roger Perry**. The experience was demoralizing for those who did not get on stage, and occasionally excruciating even if they did.

"The Troubadour, man, was and always will be full of tragic fucking characters—has-beens and hopefuls," Frey said in a 1975 interview with *Rolling Stone*.

The Eagles would soon outgrow the tiny nightclub as all those dreams became real. "I don't know what made the Troubadour feel like a giant place," Frey admitted in a 2007 talk with the *Los Angeles Times*. "Maybe it's because, for us, it was an open road."

In relatively short order, they had scored a gig backing Ronstadt, formed the Eagles with former Ronstadt bandmates Bernie Leadon and Randy Meisner, signed with **David Geffen**'s new Asylum imprint, and then saw that first album yield three hit singles. "We came up at a 45-degree angle," Henley told the *Times*.

But as "The Sad Café" confirmed, they never forgot the Troubadour and those days when a flat-broke Frey would bend Barrick's ear while nursing a single beer all night.

Of course, so much had changed since then—and the song reflects that, too. A precious few others made it out, too, but many did not. The Eagles themselves exited the 1970s having experienced dizzying highs and some depressing lows.

"The Sad Café," Souther said to *Rolling Stone*, was "more than anything else about losing your innocence—our innocence." [1820, 1915, 1917, 1918, 1919, 1920, 1921, 1925, 1975]

Like the Troubadour nightclub, Dan Tana's restaurant was a favorite Eagles haunt since their early days. After the Southern Pacific Railroad finally retired the line and pulled up the tracks, Don Henley, Glenn Frey, and two friends bought a piece of track and presented it to owner **Dan Tana**, along with an inscribed plaque. It reads: "To Dan, 'The Last Piece,' Southern Pacific Railroad, October 1978, Charisse, Linda, Don, Glenn."

the fatal mistake of dismissing the significant role Ono played in Lennon's personal and business life. Recognizing that to get Lennon he had to first get Yoko, Geffen contacted her, expressing his admiration, and asking for a meeting at the Dakota apartment building in New York, where the Lennons lived and had an office.

The strategy paid off. When Lennon saw a telegram from Geffen addressed to his wife, he told her, "I guess we'll go with him."

Geffen also had played his cards well when asked if he needed to hear the new music before making a deal. After answering "no" and agreeing to pay $1 million, he was well on his way to signing the couple and soon releasing the single "(Just Like) Starting Over."

Geffen would not get his first album from Elton John for another year as the artist completed his MCA contract. But the new label head was enthusiastically looking ahead to the November 17 release of the Lennons' *Double Fantasy*. A few weeks later, everything changed. On the evening of December 8, 1980, as the couple arrived home after a recording session and walked toward the entrance, the former **Beatle** was shot to death by an assailant. [1709, 1710, 1711, 2088]

Eagles Lend Voices to Seger for *Against the Wind*

When **Bob Seger** blurted out the chorus to "Heartache Tonight," it provided the creative breakthrough that helped turn a set of Glenn Frey's verses into a song that would become a #1 single.

Months later, Frey returned the favor by singing background a Seger tune, "Fire Lake," and brought Don Henley and Timothy B. Schmit with him. Later, he helped his longtime mentor with "Against the Wind," the title track of Seger's new album.

Frey was one of the few musicians Seger would acknowledge as a genuine friend. "I don't really even have a lot of friends in the business," Seger told **Steve Morse** of the *Boston Globe*. "Outside of the Eagles, I don't have anybody."

The roots of Seger's friendship with Frey went back to their days growing up in Royal Oak, Michigan. Three years his junior, Frey was in the background singing on "Ramblin' Gamblin' Man," and that earned Seger a regional, then national, hit in 1968 and began his ascent to heartland rock favorite.

Before the Eagles formed, Frey was an ardent proponent of Seger, promoting his songs to friends like **Linda Ronstadt**. Frey also boosted Seger to Henley and the band, saying, "We gotta rock like this." When in Los Angeles, Seger was a regular visitor to see Frey and Henley, and each would share their latest songs.

While Seger and his Silver Bullet Band did not break through to national popularity until 1975's *Beautiful Loser* and the double *Live Bullet* album in 1976, the follow-up platinum albums *Night Moves* and *Stranger in Town* made it clear he wasn't just a Midwest regional phenom.

Going into sessions for *Against the Wind*, Seger felt more fulfilled as a songwriter and and took a more prominent role

continued on Page 378

RELEASE
Late November
1979

THE LONG RUN

By: Don Henley, Glenn Frey, Timothy B. Schmit
Side B: The Disco Strangler (Felder, Henley, Frey)

Eagles' follow-up to the #1 hit "Heartache Tonight" didn't soar quite as high on the charts, but it still landed the group in the Top 10 of all three major industry trade publications. And it got there in a hurry. The single was released the last week of November 1979, and *Record World* charted it at #4 on February 2, 1980, a rapid rise that took less than 40 days to achieve.

AIRPLAY

Promoting Eagles singles was not difficult for Asylum Records, or Elektra/Asylum after the labels merged. "Outlaw Man" may have been a tough sell in 1973, but the Eagles had come a long way since then. Their singles were reliably commercial and easily found their way onto AM and FM playlists. But "The Long Run" was a slightly different track. It wasn't quite a ballad, but certainly wasn't a rocker either. Everyone in the band—and the label—still thought it should be the next single, so E/A gave it a promotional push and even took out full-page ads in the trade publications to boost it. The result? The song recorded more playlist adds than any Eagles single ever released to date. Once again, the Southeast led the charge with more than 50 total adds in just two months. The Northeast and West loved the single as well.

186 PLAYLIST ADDS Winter 1979-80			
Region	**Dec**	**Jan**	**Regional Airplay**
Northeast	30	8	20.4 %
Southeast	43	10	30.1 %
Midwest	28	5	18.3 %
Southwest	16	3	10.2 %
West	32	6	21 %

FIRST-WAVE STATIONS Stations that added the song in the first 30 days

KOPA-Phoenix
KCBQ, KFMB-San Diego
KROY-Sacramento
KHJ, KNX-Los Angeles
KYNO-Fresno
KTAC-Tacoma
KCPX-Salt Lake City
KJR-Seattle
KFRC-San Francisco
KMGN-FM-Bakersfield

WZZR-FM-Grand Rapids
WZUU-FM-Milwaukee
WCUE-Akron
CKLW-Detroit
WNCI-Columbus

KFJZ-Fort Worth
KELI-Tulsa
KTKT-Tucson
WKY-Oklahoma City

KSLQ-FM-St. Louis
WZZP-Cleveland
WROK-Rockford, IL
KXOK, KSHE-St. Louis
KBEQ-Kansas City

WZGC-FM-Z93-Atlanta
WRBQ-Q105-Tampa
WSGN-Birmingham
WLOF-Orlando

WKBQ-Harrisburg
WPRO-Providence
WAAL-Binghamton, NY
WLIR-FM - Long Island
WBLM-FM-Portland

WAYS-Charlotte
WBGN-Bowling Green
WNOE-New Orleans
WQXQ-Daytona Beach

CHARTS

Billboard	HIGHEST CHARTING WEEK: RECORD WORLD - February 2, 1980		
# 8 February 2, 1980	**SINGLE**	**ARTIST**	**PREV WK**
	1. Coward of the County	Kenny Rogers	2
	2. Do That To Me One More Time	Captain & Tennille	3
Cashbox	3. Rock With You	Michael Jackson	1
# 10 February 2, 1980	**4. THE LONG RUN**	**EAGLES**	**4**
	5. Cruisin'	Smokey Robinson	6
	6. Crazy Little Thing Called Love	Queen	13
Record World	7. Yes, I'm Ready	Teri DeSario with K.C.	11
# 4 February 2, 1980	8. Don't Do Me Like That	Tom Petty and the Hearbreakers	10
	9. Sara	Fleetwood Mac	12
	10. Escape (The Piña Colada Song)	Rupert Holmes	8

Sources: Billboard, Cashbox, Record World

EAGLES PEN IRONIC SONG OF SURVIVAL, LONGEVITY

Reaching back once more to Glenn Frey's early R&B influences, "The Long Run" echoed **Otis Clay**'s 1972 single "Trying to Live My Life Without You," but with a much different message. Clay sang a **Eugene Frank Williams** lyric about trying to let go of a past love, while the Eagles wrestled with the concept of career longevity.

The band had been around for years, and the last three had been challenging. The idea of capturing that long glide path in song had been something the band had been kicking around since *Desperado*, Frey told **Cameron Crowe**.

"We'd had the idea for about six or seven years," Frey recalled. "The title of the song was apropos, and it seemed to be a good title for the album—let's see who'll last. I think it was a lot about longevity, and it was also about me just lovin' **Tyrone Davis**' record 'Turning Point.' We had done some slicker production like the Philly sound, but 'Long Run' was more like a tribute to Memphis with the slide guitars playing the parts of the horns."

In a mid-tempo arrangement, the song's lyrics mull over exchanging life in the fast lane for a more laid-back approach. The goal appears to be survival in a relationship, but the subtext is clearly the band embracing its own longevity: "*You can go the distance/ We'll find out in the long run/We can handle some resistance/If our love is a strong one.*" That embrace was probably genuine at the time, but things change. By the time Elektra/Asylum released the single, Eagles had already crossed the finish line.

"Despite the extraordinary success of *Hotel California*," Don Henley told *Rolling Stone* in 2016, "we were collectively in a pretty dark place during the making of *The Long Run*. Disco had exploded, and punk was on the rise. We were beginning to see press articles about how we were passé. Those kinds of jabs were part of the inspiration for the song 'The Long Run': 'Who is gonna make it, we'll find out—in the long run.'"

"The Long Run" was the last of three Top 10 hits from its namesake album, but the Eagles were too exhausted to celebrate. They had pushed back against popular trends with the single and won, an irony not lost on Henley. New wave and punk came and went, but so did the Eagles—defiantly declaring they would only return when hell freezes over.

By 1994, though, when the Eagles put *The Long Run*-era lineup back together for the appropriately titled *Hell Freezes Over* TV special, tour, and album, Henley had a new perspective. "The group was breaking apart, imploding under the pressure of trying to deliver a worthy follow-up to *Hotel California*," he told *Rolling Stone*, "and yet we were writing about longevity, posterity. Turns out we were right. Irony upon irony." [209, 1776, 1782]

in his band. With his friends from the Eagles (including producer **Bill Szymczyk** at the helm), the backing of the famed Muscle Shoals Rhythm Section, and guests like **Bill Payne** of **Little Feat**, Seger was going for the big time and shooting for a #1 album.

"We had a chance to make it, and we wanted to make some history," he said, talking with **Dave DiMartino** of *Creem*. "At least some Silver Bullet history, if nothing else, so we could say we were #1 at least once in our lives. 'Cause the market may change... Who knows?"

If Seger was aiming for a commercial album, he wanted at least three hit singles. Both were feats he had never achieved. The first single, "Fire Lake," was a song Seger had begun writing almost a decade earlier and was intended for *Beautiful Loser*.

Seger's song about taking risks and risking love also broke new ground as it moved away from the traditional rock and roll that people expected from him. *Detroit Free Press* columnist **Kim McAuliffe** had glowing praise of Seger, who she placed "at the heart of the town's rock and roll."

"When 'Fire Lake' plays," she wrote, "it's magically a Friday night, and all the car radios are tuned to the same station, and each head and heart is fused into the ultimate expression of Detroit rock 'n' roll feeling."

Seger would entertain his West Coast friend Don Henley with stories about cruising Detroit's Woodward Avenue, but back in Seger's hometown, not everyone accepted his affiliation with the Eagles. **Robert Hilburn** of the *Los Angeles Times* observed that *Rolling Stone* critic and Detroit native **Dave Marsh** was upset by the singer's growing connection with the band, "a band many rock critics (particularly East Coast ones) argue is too laid back and smug." Writing in the *Detroit Free Press*, **John Smyntek** concurred, noting that "Seger's work has not been stir-fried but 'Glenn Frey-ed.'"

"Frey is generally accused of leading Seger astray into mellowism," Smyntek wrote, acknowledging that the singer's Royal Oak roots had been transplanted to mellow California. "A harder persona would be welcomed by his core Detroit audience."

But the charts told an opposite story as "Fire Lake," released in January, was moving up the Top 10 in February just as the Eagles' "I Can't Tell You Why" hit the Top 10. "Fire Lake" would eventually rise to #6 on the *Billboard* Hot 100, and "I Can't Tell You Why" reached #8.

After its release in late February, *Against the Wind* hit #2, vying for the top spot but blocked by **Pink Floyd**'s *The Wall* for five

> "
> I LIKED THE LINE, AND EVERYBODY I PLAYED IT FOR—LIKE DON AND GLENN—WERE SAYING 'THAT'S THE BEST LINE IN THE SONG,' BUT I COULDN'T SHAKE THE FEELING THAT IT WASN'T RIGHT.
>
> — BOB SEGER

weeks. Seger met his goal when the album reached #1 in May, aided by the title track, which had lyrics that Frey was drawn to.

"Oh, I gotta sing background on that," Frey told his old friend from Detroit.

"Okay, why?" Seger replied.

Frey was coy when he demurred and told Seger he would tell him later. It turned out that the protagonist's name in "Against the Wind," one Janie, bore the exact name of a woman Frey was dating.

"Some people don't know what goes on behind the scenes in rock and roll," Seger said, laughing at the memory in a radio interview on *In the Studio with Redbeard.*

Seger hardly needed to prove his songwriting abilities to anyone by then, but he still had moments of self-doubt. He had a hang-up with the lyrics in "Against the Wind," specifically with the grammar in the lyric "I wish I didn't know now what I didn't know then."

"I kept asking myself, 'Is that correct grammar?'" he said. "I liked the line, and everybody I played it for—like Glenn and Don [Henley]—were saying, 'That's the best line in the song,' but I couldn't shake the feeling that it wasn't right." Seger slowly came around to it and acknowledged that songwriters can't always punctuate everything they write. "I work in such a narrow medium," he said, "that I tend to second-guess things like that."

A key moment in Seger's life and career was when Frey visited his home, listened to his 1975 album *Beautiful Loser,* and

encouraged his old friend. Buoyed by Seger's newfound musical confidence, the breakthrough album would sell more than five million copies.

Looking back, Seger could remember a time when the Eagles were hitting it big, and he was still struggling. Seger shared with **Timothy White** of *Rolling Stone* that it meant a lot coming from someone successful in the industry. But he also recounted the time he got drunk in a hotel room and wistfully told Frey and Henley, "I'm gonna catch you fuckers."

"Henley just sort of looked at me," Seger remembered, "and Frey looked at me, too, but Frey didn't care. He knew what I was feeling. But I was always incredibly envious to the point where I almost hated him."

When Seger's *Beautiful Loser* and then *Live Bullet* put him on the national map, things started looking up. With *Against the Wind*, Seger blew open the start of the 1980s.

"I was a very hard-working person, but I probably wasn't the best person to be around, unless you were really in my inner circle," Seger said in his interview with **Redbeard**. "I think it wasn't until 1980 that I really opened up, and that's why I think I have such fond memories of *Against the Wind*. I think at that point, I had relaxed."

The friendship and influence of the Eagles endured over the years.

"Oh, I feed off Glenn and Don to this day," Seger told **Susan Whitall** of the *Detroit News* a decade after *Against the Wind* went to #1. "When they do something that knocks me out, it just makes me want to do something in my own vein that's just as good."

Producer **Don Was**, who worked with Seger, confirmed what the Detroit native said: "It's made him try to write deeper songs to this day." [1650, 1797, 1798, 1846, 1847, 1848, 1849, 1850, 1853, 1854, 1855]

Eagles Join Elton John in Studio For 'White Lady White Powder'

Elton John found himself in a slump in the latter third of the 1970s. The hit songs were not coming like before. In 1977, after more than ten years together, he and his longtime collaborator, **Bernie Taupin**, started exploring work with other artists. The magic that churned out songs like "Rocket Man," "Levon," "Goodbye Yellow Brick Road," and "Daniel" was missing from John's newer music.

But the two agreed to work together for a few songs near the end of the decade, and they recorded three cuts for John's *21 at 33* album, released in 1980. One of those songs, "White Lady White Powder," had a familiar Eagles sound.

John asked Glenn Frey, Don Henley, and Timothy B. Schmit to back him vocally on "White Lady" because he loved the Eagles' harmony. He and the band were already friendly, and it did not hurt that *The Long Run* was the #1 album in the nation.

Henley was at the Troubadour when John made his famed debut there on August 25, 1970. When John organized the celebrated Midsummer Music Extravaganza at Wembley Stadium in June 1975, he hand-picked the Eagles to join him, along with **The Beach Boys**, **Joe Walsh**, and **Rufus** featuring **Chaka Khan**. And Elton was friendly enough with them to join them again two weeks later for a surprise jam session during their encore at the **Bill Graham**-sponsored Day on the Green concert in Oakland, California. Weeks later, he recorded an album—*Rock of the Westies*—at Walsh's and **Bill Szymczyk**'s old haunt, Caribou Ranch in Colorado.

John truly admired the Eagles—even as some critics in the rock press viewed the Los Angeles band through a harsher lens. He struggled to understand the slings and arrows directed at them.

"With the Eagles, the songwriting and production and all the strengths that they had at the time were being subjected to such vitriolic criticism," rock columnist **Bob Harris** said in **David Buckley**'s book *Elton: The Biography*. "I remember Elton looking at me and saying, 'But this is wonderful. They write great songs, they play beautifully, what more do you want from a band?'"

John wrote the music for "White Lady" while developing song material in Grasse, France, in August 1979, and he said he instinctively felt that it would be perfect for some of the Eagles to sing on it. The question was, when? The band was constantly on the road, but they had three scheduled shows at the Forum in March 1980 that had been well-publicized. He corralled them then, and they agreed.

The subject was familiar. Taupin's "White Lady" lyrics were admittedly autobiographical and served as an overt warning about the dangers of the cocaine culture of the late 1970s and early 1980s. "*Dust settles on a thin cloud/Sends a fog drifting to a worn-out crowd/I've had my face in a mirror for twenty-four hours/Staring at a line of white powder.*" Those words were on the same highway the Eagles' "Life in the Fast Lane" drove down three years earlier.

The combination of talent for this recording was unquestionably potent. Every component of the song—the instrumentation, lead vocals, and harmonizing—was near-perfect. Early in the song, Frey's voice in the chorus is distinctive, and later, Henley and Schmit's familiar harmonizing gives the song an Eagles-like lift.

Even so, the final track seemed less than inspired. While the lyrics were poignant, they did not marry well with the bouncy beat that was John's trademark for his career's second go-round.

The song had another unexpected musical tilt. When the chorus arrives, "*And she's a habit I can't handle/For a reason I can't say/I'm in love with a wild white lady/She's as sweet as the stories say,*" it sounds like pure, unadulterated **Jimmy Buffett**.

"White Lady White Powder" was not a hit, but it was one of the better efforts on *21 at 33*. "Little Jeannie," which John wrote with songwriter **Gary Osborne**, went to #3 on the *Billboard* charts, making it Elton's highest-charting single in the United States in five years. [2008, 2009, 2010, 2011, 2012, 2015]

The Dark Run: Gloomy Songs Foreshadow Eagles' Breakup

A trio of deep, darker cuts on *The Long Run* underscores how dreary things were behind the scenes for the Eagles. In their own ways, "The Disco Strangler," "King of Hollywood," and "Teenage Jail" represent the gloomiest moments in a dismal period.

Don Felder described it as "such a dark time personally," in his book. "We were struggling to write, we were struggling with drug and alcohol abuse, and we were struggling with interpersonal relations and ego."

That toxic stew leaked into the songwriting, as the Eagles took potshots at the latest musical fad ("The Disco Strangler"), peeked inside the world of lecherous directors who would one day help spark the #MeToo movement ("King of Hollywood"), and told a sad tale of adolescent isolation ("Teenage Jail").

Themes aside, these tunes also could not be further away musically from the stomping backbeats of "Heartache Tonight," the smooth soul stylings of "I Can't Tell You Why," or the lonesome reveries found in "The Sad Café."

"The Disco Strangler," which was co-credited to Don Henley, Glenn Frey, and Felder, tells the sordid tale of a woman who is "dressed to kill" but meets her own terrible fate. "It's 'watch out for the guy on the date: He might have a knife,'" producer **Bill Szymczyk** later told *Rolling Stone* with a chuckle.

Henley makes an unusual choice with his approach to the lyric, trading in a typically

continued on Page 385

RELEASE
Mid-February
1980

I CAN'T TELL YOU WHY

By: Timothy B. Schmit, Don Henley, Glenn Frey
Side B: The Greeks Don't Want No Freaks (Henley, Frey)

Stations began adding "I Can't Tell You Why" to their playlists in early February 1980, and it took a leisurely two-month stroll into the Top 10 of all three music trade publications. Elektra/Asylum released the single just as their preceding single, "The Long Run," began to fade. The brooding ballad rose to #7 on *Record World*'s singles chart and #8 on *Billboard*'s Hot 100 in May 1980. They wouldn't hit the Top 10 again until 1996 when another Timothy B. Schmit ballad, "Love Will Keep Us Alive," rose to #1 on the *Billboard* U.S. Adult Contemporary chart.

AIRPLAY

When The Long Run's first single, "Heartache Tonight," was released, it took off like a shot and went to #1. The next single, "The Long Run," was a bit different and required a promotional push, but it still landed in the Top 10. Elektra/Asylum didn't push as hard for the album's third single, "I Can't Tell You Why," but the band still managed to complete its three-single trifecta. While their grip on stations in the Northeast loosened slightly with this single, the Southeast, West and Midwest remained old friends. *Billboard* reported that WSGA-Savannah was the first to add "I Can't Tell You Why" to its playlist in the first week of February.

149 PLAYLIST ADDS Spring 1980

Region	Feb	Mar	Apr	Regional Airplay
Northeast	10	13	1	16.1%
Southeast	22	21	1	29.5%
Midwest	9	24	0	22.1%
Southwest	4	11	0	10.1%
West	10	22	0	22.1%

FIRST-WAVE STATIONS Stations that added the song in the first 30 days

KOPA-Phoenix
KFMB-San Diego
KROY-Sacramento
KERN-Bakersfield
KING-Seattle
KIMN-Denver
KNX, KRTH-Los Angeles
KJRB-Spokane
KSPT-Sandpoint, ID
KPAM-Portland

WDRQ-Detroit
KKLS-Rapid City, SD
CKLW-Detroit
WZZP-Cleveland
KSTP-Minneapolis

KRBE-FM-Houston
KOFM-Oklahoma City
KINT-El Paso
KRQQ-Tucson

WCUE-Akron
KBEQ-Kansas City
WZUU-FM-Milwaukee
WGCL-Cleveland
WKRQ-Q102-Cincinnati

WSGA-Savannah
WCAO-Baltimore
WGOW-Chattanooga
WAKY-Louisville

WPTR-Albany
WKQT-Pittsburgh
WTRY-Albany
WBZ-FM-Boston
WPRO-Providence

WTIX-New Orleans
WRVQ-Q94-Richmond
WRBQ-Q105-Tampa
WAYS-Charlotte

CHARTS

Billboard	HIGHEST CHARTING WEEK: RECORD WORLD - April 19, 1980		
# 8 April 26, 1980	SINGLE	ARTIST	PREV WK
	1. Call Me	Blondie	2
Cashbox	2. Another Brick in the Wall (Part 2)	Pink Floyd	1
	3. Ride Like the Wind	Christopher Cross	3
# 8 April 26, 1980	4. Lost in Love	Air Supply	6
	5. Fire Lake	Bob Seger	5
	6. Working My Way Back to You (Medley)	The Spinners	4
Record World	**7. I CAN'T TELL YOU WHY**	**EAGLES**	**8**
	8. With You I'm Born Again	Billy Preston & Syreeta	12
# 7 April 19, 1980	9. Special Lady	Ray, Goodman & Brown	10
	10. How Do I Make You	Linda Ronstadt	7

Sources: Billboard, Cashbox, Record World

'NEW GUY' SCHMIT REGISTERS HIS FIRST HIT SINGLE

When Timothy B. Schmit received the call from Glenn Frey inviting him to join the Eagles, it seemed like the perfect time.

"I thought I was definitely the right guy to join the Eagles," the bassist told **Joe Basso** of *MusicRadar*. "I knew it was a very big thing being put in front of me, one of the biggest in all of music. But I knew I could do it. I knew I could fit. In my heart, I knew I was the right guy."

As a vocalist, Schmit also knew he could hit the high notes, his voice having graced **Steely Dan**'s *Pretzel Logic* and *The Royal Scam* and **Randy Newman**'s *Little Criminals* (and later Joe Walsh's *But Seriously, Folks...* and Steely Dan's *Aja*.)

When Schmit replaced Randy Meisner in **Poco** and then again in the Eagles, he was guided by his philosophy: He had to fit in.

"They'd already been rolling for six albums and just come off *Hotel California*," he remembered in an interview with **Paul Lester** of *Classic Rock*. "My role was to hop on board the train, simply add harmonies, and contribute to the songwriting—and hopefully the daunting task of trying to keep things harmonious. I had no thoughts about trying to dominate anything."

Before writing the song even began, Schmit needed to take a crash course in everything Eagles. While he lived across the street from **J.D. Souther** and knew the Eagles, he had not studied their work in enough detail to support a tour or go into the studio.

"Before doing new material for [*The Long Run*], which everybody is learning, I sat and listened to [all the Eagles] records for hours," Schmit said to broadcaster **Dave Herman**. "You know, learning the bass parts and what I would probably be singing. That was not really stimulating, but it had to be done."

When the Eagles began the arduous year-and-a-half-long project, Schmit would play a pivotal role. The bassist had something partially finished that he remembered as "a little piece of a song." Loosely based on personal experience, it drew the attention of Don Henley and Glenn Frey. Schmit believed they wanted to introduce the "new guy" in the band on a positive note. Soon, they would become his co-writers.

Henley and Frey wanted to highlight Schmit's debut with a piece that would be different than the type of stuff he did with Poco, and Frey suggested crafting a song with an R&B feel. According to Frey, "He said, 'Sure, love to try!'"

Frey soon headed to the piano, and he said, "Well, how 'bout something like this?'"

For Schmit, it all made sense. Growing up in Sacramento, he listened to Motown and Stax on the radio before playing folk and surf music.

"I was very pleased that the song they picked to work—and the one I was going to sing—was not country-flavored, or something that went in another direction," he shared with Best Classic Bands' **Russell Hall**. "I was really happy to go in an R&B direction; thrilled, actually."

"Glenn and I just wanted to surround it with everything we could," Henley added in a conversation with **Cameron Crowe**. "Glenn came up with that wonderful counterpart, very much a soul-record type thing, 'Try to keep your head, little girl.'"

The song is anchored by Joe Walsh's versatile instrumental mix of keyboards, including the guitarist playing the Hammond organ, a Fender Rhodes electric piano, and ARP string synthesizer.

For Frey, "I Can't Tell You Why" was one of his favorite Eagles songs, as Schmit sang with Henley counterpoint against the melody and what he called the "Ooh baby, baby" vocal. Henley marveled at hearing an audience of thousands of people are heard singing the opening words in unison, "*Look at us, baby....*"

"I think the piece of that song I brought touched upon that thing [Frey and Henley] wanted, something that resonated and had the potential to be very good," Schmit reflected in his Best Classic Bands interview. "And they were sure they could help shape it into a radio-friendly song...something that people might want to hear again and again. It had the sort of spark they were always looking for in their own material."

Although it was the first song completed for *The Long Run*, "I Can't Tell You Why" was not the album's leadoff single.

Timothy B. Schmit sits at the bow of a sailboat during an outing in his first days with the Eagles.

It followed "Heartache Tonight" and "The Long Run" when released in February 1980, and it peaked at #8 on the *Billboard* Hot 100 singles chart.

Schmit still can't get over that he shared co-writing credits with Henley and Frey.

"I remember when it was being developed in the studio. I knew it was a great song," Schmit said in his conversation with Basso. "I was like, 'Yes! This is an amazing debut for me.' When we finally mixed it, we had a little listening party at the studio. As people were hearing it, Don turned to me and said, 'There's your first hit.' That was pretty cool." [1820, 1842, 1843, 1844,

easygoing, almost laconic singing style for lightning-fast cadence. It all runs headlong into a heavy metal-style riff, ensuring that "The Disco Strangler" would never become a dance-floor favorite. And the cautionary tale aside, the song's subtext seemed to be saying that the disco fad was, in reality, "strangling" rock music.

"*The Long Run* placed an enormous weight on everyone's shoulders," Felder told *Record Collector* in 2008. "Instead of being fun, free, and exciting, the creative process now had this...heavy seriousness and intensity," based on expectations for following up *Hotel California*.

"King of Hollywood" culminates in another patented guitar workout from Felder and Walsh, but only after co-writers Henley and Frey take fans into the seamiest corners of Los Angeles' entertainment industry. The subsequent outro arrives like a raging response to a night gone unspeakably wrong and was probably meant to be cathartic, and would have been meant for the likes Hollywood producers like **Robert Evans** and, in the next millennium, **Harvey Weinstein**.

"This album," Timothy B. Schmit deadpanned in the 1979 *Rolling Stone* cover story interview, "has some quirky songs."

The quirkiest had to be the sludgy "Teenage Jail." With a near-suicidal main character, "Teenage Jail" crawls at such a slow musical pace, one might wonder if Szymczyk had somehow recorded it at the wrong speed. Henley and Frey, who co-wrote the track with **J.D. Souther**, completed it with grinding, chant-like vocals.

Felder said that he blamed some of the weaker points from *The Long Run* on the absence of significant creative input from Frey, who split lead vocal duties with Henley on "Teenage Jail" and sang a few lines on "King of Hollywood"; his only other lead vocal appeared on "Heartache Tonight." In *Heaven and Hell*, Felder said they only included "Teenage Jail" on *The Long Run* because it was one of the few ideas Frey brought to the others.

Unfortunately, the track was "by far [Frey's] worst writing effort," Felder added. But he was equally harsh in criticizing his own frankly bizarre contribution—a song-closing solo that Felder himself has described as "crazy." It was all "the result of a four-in-the-morning, whacked out, coked-out session, and to this day, I'm embarrassed to have played it," Felder says in *Heaven and Hell*. "It just keeps lingering like a bad smell."

Frey's squiggly synth solo certainly did not make things any less bizarre. But the Eagles were in no shape to produce anything better, much less anything more uplifting.

"Teenage Jail," like "The Disco Strangler" and "King of Hollywood," ended up on the finished track listing for the band's last album during their classic era.

"Finally," Felder added, "we exhausted ourselves, exhausted our patience, and took so many drugs that nobody could see any further solutions except to finish what we had and walk away from it." [1967, 1968, 1969, 1970]

continued on Page 387

J.D. SOUTHER
You're Only Lonely
Columbia Records, September 1979

It's unexpected to see **J.D. Souther**'s name popping up in articles about one-hit wonders. But it's true—the Amarillo, Texas-raised songwriter is listed alongside the likes of the **Vapors**, **Chumbawumba**, **The Knack**, **Soft Cell**, and **Big Country**.

Despite his illustrious songwriting pedigree, Souther has indeed scored just one Top 40 hit on the *Billboard* singles chart with a song released under his name. In 1979, the title track from his *You're Only Lonely* album hit the #1 spot on the *Billboard* Adult Contemporary chart and #7 on the *Billboard* Hot 100. It would be his first and last hit solo record. But, as Glenn Frey would often say, it was not surprising since Souther gave his best songs away.

While recording *You're Only Lonely*, guitarist **Waddy Wachtel** asked Souther to come up with something more up tempo for the album. Souther had a song written roughly six years earlier while rehearsing in Colorado with the **Souther-Hillman-Furay Band**. It was a simple song, maybe not even a finished article.

Souther recounted the story to **Dave Kawashima** of SongWriterUniverse.com: "So I played it for him and said, 'You see, it doesn't really have a chorus, and it doesn't have a bridge.' And Waddy just said, 'Sing the first verse again...' And it just sounded so catchy and sincere. We had a pretty good feeling while we were recording it that it was gonna do well."

The finished track was moody and haunting, yet the loneliness it evoked was countered by the brisk rockabilly beat that drove the song. It was pure **Roy Orbison**, an influence not lost on Souther, as he told **Dave Macintosh** of Songfacts.com: "The beat that I used for 'You're Only Lonely' is that rockabilly beat. That sort of break in it was taken from another Roy Orbison record called 'I'm Hurtin'' that I really love."

Souther had been a fan of Orbison since he was a kid. He loved the operatic quality of Orbison's vocals, telling Songfacts.com that Orbison was "one of half a dozen or so rockabilly musicians that I really loved. When I was in junior high school was the first time I really started listening to that."

Despite the success of the album and hit song, Souther balked at building his solo career and did not record another album until 1984.

He told **Jeremy Egner** of the *New York Times* in 2012, "I had plenty of money coming in, and there were a few things I hadn't done that I really wanted to do—I wanted to go to New Zealand and ski; I wanted to spend more time in Hawaii. I wanted to build a house—I built my dream house in the Hollywood Hills." [171, 575, 802]

Azoff Builds Up Front Line Stable With Fogelberg, Scaggs, Buffett

In the mid-1970s, **Irving Azoff**, the abrasive, loud, and intimidating band manager, was positioning himself as one of the most powerful artist managers in the music business.

Dan Fogelberg, his friend and first client, was building a healthy career. Fogelberg's second studio album, *Souvenirs*, made it to #31 on the *Billboard* album chart in 1975. The Eagles were climbing to the top. Another artist friend, Joe Walsh, had found emotional breathing space when Azoff pulled him out of an unhealthy management deal. And that was all Azoff thought he needed just then. After all, handling the Eagles was a full-time job all by itself.

But after keeping things small for a while, Azoff began to expand his management company, reasoning, as he told **Cameron Crowe** for *Rolling Stone* in June 1978, "The ultimate decision I came to was that the whole key to real power in the management business is not to pat yourself on the back and say, 'I did it.' I have tried to break a new act every year."

Building what he called a rock and roll fraternity, Azoff signed another longtime friend—**Boz Scaggs**.

Glenn Frey and **Jimmy Buffett** had stayed connected and become firm friends since they met at the Columbia Coliseum in South Carolina in 1975, and Frey had told him how much he liked him and his **Coral Reefer Band**'s music.

By 1976, Buffett's career was in the dol-drums; his breezy "Gulf & Western" songs were still in search of a wide audience, and he was stuck in bad record and management deals. Frey and Don Henley recommended Buffett to Azoff, who signed him to Front Line and secured a better record deal.

Buffett's next LP, *Changes in Latitude, Changes in Attitude*, and its breakthrough single, "Margaritaville," finally put him on the global musical map. It peaked at #8 pop, #13 country, and #1 adult contemporary on *Billboard*'s charts, defined the summer of 1977, and later branded a worldwide chain of restaurants, hotels, and resorts.

"[Glenn] and Don were instrumental in getting **Irving Azoff** to become my manager," Buffett said in an interview with **Jon Blistein** for *Rolling Stone* in January 2016, "and eventually open for the Eagles on the *Hotel California* tour of America, which was the rocket ship we rode to eventually becoming a headliner." But Buffett, talking with **Eve Zibart** of the *Washington Post* in July 1978, said his "biggest break was Irving renegotiating my contract." [668, 717, 2035]

Grammy: 'Heartache Tonight' Takes Best Rock Performance

"Heartache Tonight," easily the most commercial song on *The Long Run*, hit #1 on all three major singles charts in mid-November 1979, less than two months after its release. Eagles-starved fans who had waited two-plus years for the band to follow-up *Hotel California* loved the bluesy, ballsy shuffle, and so did Elektra/Asylum.

The musical landscape had changed significantly in that time. Even though the group had been touring aggressively, 36 months was a long time with no new songs on the radio. Meanwhile, emerging artists were quickly filling the void. Disco was still around but fading. Punk was making noise. Stalwart pop hitmakers of the 1970s—artists like the **Captain & Tennille**, **Tony Orlando & Dawn**, **Helen Reddy**, and **John Denver**—lost favor as record buyers went for edgier, more visual acts.

Still, the Eagles would place two more songs on the charts by spring 1980—the album's mid-tempo title track and the R&B-inflected ballad "I Can't Tell You Why." While both missed the window for Grammy consideration, the group earned a nomination for Best Rock Performance by a Duo or Group for "Heartache Tonight."

Not that they really cared. Eagles were never big fans of industry awards. The "Heartache" nomination came almost two years after the band's Grammy Awards no-show in February 1978, when they won Record of the Year for "Hotel California" and Best Arrangement for Two or More Voices for "New Kid in Town."

So it came as no surprise that when the red carpet rolled out at the Shrine Auditorium in Los Angeles on February 27, 1980, the Eagles were, instead, performing in Oakland, California, with first generation rock 'n' roll legend **Roy Orbison** as their special opening act. The band would return to L.A. a day later to appear in shows that included Orbison special guest **David Sanborn**, who played saxophone on "The Sad Café."

The Grammys went on without them, and the Best Rock Performance nominations included a mixed bag of singles and albums. Eagles won, but their competition was intense, including the **Blues Brothers** (**John Belushi**, **Dan Aykroyd**, and a band of legendary R&B musicians) for their album *Briefcase Full of Blues*, **The Cars** for *Candy-O*, **Styx** for *Cornerstone*, **The Knack** for "My Sharona," and **Dire Straits** for "Sultans of Swing." (Eagles, The Cars, and Dire Straits are now in the Rock and Roll Hall of Fame.)

Eagles would continue their tour supporting *The Long Run* through the end of July. The fateful phone call between Glenn Frey and Don Henley that confirmed the band's breakup would happen a couple months later. The Grammys would not come calling again for another 16 years. [2016, 2017]

Reluctant Eagles Agree to Record July Shows for Live Album

When Eagles manager **Irving Azoff** got on the telephone with Elektra/Asylum's **Joe Smith** in late July 1980, the conversation did not start well.

"I think we have a problem with the guys," Azoff began.

For more than a year, Smith had tried to convince the band to make one last album. At one point, he offered them $2 million to record two new songs. As the band planned to record shows Santa Monica Civic Auditorium at the end of the month, a double live album envisioned by the record company seemed like it was going to happen. And then Azoff called.

Smith recounted the conversation in his book *Off the Record*.

"We had four dates scheduled in Southern California," he wrote, "and the day before the first night I get a call from Irving Azoff, who tells me 'we have a problem.' The problem means I'm not getting the album. In my mind I'm trying to explain to [Warner Communications Inc. Chairman] **Steve Ross** why he's not going to get the $40 million to $50 million I promised him."

Smith said Azoff began to explain, but then said, "The guys want to tell you themselves."

"Glenn and Don get on the phone," Smith recounted, "and they say, 'Look, we really don't want to do this. We really don't want to spend that much time with each other. We could do a short tour and not record and be finished. But we promised you we'd do this, so we are going to give you a chance, if you can answer this question.' I said, 'What's the question?' They said, 'In 1971 the Baltimore Orioles had four 20-game winners. If you name them, we'll do the album.' God must have opened a recess in the back of my mind, and I named them—**Dave McNally**, **Jim Palmer**, **Mike Cuellar**, and **Pat Dobson**. Glenn and Don said, 'OK, we'll do the album and we'll see you tomorrow.'"

Perplexed, Smith then asked the pair, "'What would you have done if I didn't answer the question correctly?' They said, 'We'd go on tour, and you'd never have the live album.'" Smith conceded that they weren't kidding. His sports trivia comeback helped him dodge a bullet, and the project was back on.

When Frey stepped inside the 3,000-seat Santa Monica Civic once again, at the other end of the Eagles' long run, his perspective had changed.

"You know, it's funny," he said, speaking to *Los Angeles Times* pop music critic **Robert Hilburn**. "When we walked into the Civic the other day, the place seemed so small. But then Joe reminded us how big it looked the first time we played here. That's when we were just starting out, and the idea of playing The Forum (18,000 seats) was just a dream. I mean, if someone had told us we were going to play The Forum, I'd have figured I died and just went to heaven."

Frey expected the Eagles to release a double album with tracks from the Civic, The Forum, and a few other shows. He added that a few new songs still to be recorded might also be added, possibly from a local soundstage or a private party.

Against the backdrop of the scheduled shows designed to fill the live album, there was a widening rift between Frey and Henley. The rest of the band felt the tension, but they didn't suspect the band's end was near. Even the two leaders didn't know.

Then the notion of making one of those shows a benefit concert for Senator **Alan Cranston** was surfaced. It came to a vote and everyone but Felder agreed they should do it. Felder was apolitical and said he had a mistrust of politicians.

"Don and Glenn had been into fundraising for newsworthy political issues for some years," Felder wrote in his autobiography, "chiefly for the Chumash Indians and for high-profile anti-nuclear and environmental projects. I didn't mind about the apolitical events, but I didn't see the point of benefits for politicians like Cranston or Governor **Jerry Brown**."

Felder said he mostly kept his political opinions to himself as an Eagle. Mistrust aside, he did participate in fundraisers for Brown, who he considered "all right." Felder added he even successfully reached out to Brown to help find a new site for the Malibu Little League team after the team's ball field was turned into a bird sanctuary.

So, when the Eagles agreed to perform a benefit for the governor that spring, Felder had no qualms. But he didn't know Cranston, and certainly he didn't know that a snide comment he would make before that benefit would be the spark that lit the fuse for the band's implosion. [1190, 1718, 1736, 1737]

SPRING 1980

 RELEASES
▶ **Joe Walsh**, "All Night Long" (single) from the *Urban Cowboy* soundtrack.
▶ **Linda Ronstadt & J.D. Souther**, "Hearts Against the Wind" (single) from the *Urban Cowboy* soundtrack.

 NUGGETS
▶ Ex-Fugs member **Ed Sanders** plans to write an authorized biography of the Eagles. —*Cashbox*
▶ Eagles manager **Irving Azoff** is preparing to roll out the soundtrack to *Urban Cowboy*. —*Cashbox*
▶ While playing a concert in Murfreesboro (near Nashville), the Eagles spotted **Roy Orbison** backstage and, in amazement, stopped for a chat. The rock legend is now opening four shows for the band in Los Angeles and San Francisco; sax man **David Sanborn** will also join them for gigs at the Forum to play sax for "The Sad Café," which the band is adding to their playlist as a gift to L.A. fans. —*Record World*
▶ E/A is heavily cross-marketing "I Can't Tell You Why" to country and R&B radio and it's working. —*Record World*
▶ Rumors are breaking that the Eagles might be switching labels to EMI. —*Cashbox*
▶ KRNA/Iowa is running a promotion to send six lucky listeners to Los Angeles for the Eagles' concert at The Forum. Winners will also get the entire Eagles LP catalog. —*Cashbox*

 COLLABORATIONS
▶ **Don Henley**, **Glenn Frey**, and **Timothy B. Schmit** provided backing and harmony vocals on **Bob Seger & the Silver Bullet Band**'s album *Against the Wind*.
▶ **Don Henley** provided backing vocals on the singles "Ice and Snow" and "Did She Finally Get to You" on **Terence Boylan**'s album *Suzy*.
▶ **Don Henley**, **Glenn Frey**, and **Timothy B. Schmit** provided backing vocals on the single "White Lady White Powder" on **Elton John**'s album *21 at 33*.

 ON THE ROAD WITH …
▶ **Eagles**: David Sanborn, Roy Orbison

'Desperado' Helps Defuse Hostage Incident in New York

Eagles and **Jackson Browne** have a common thread beyond simply being friends and artists who helped make Asylum Records an industry power. Their gift for writing introspective songs that examine the ironies of the human condition has touched countless listeners. And one cold morning in late March 1980, that gift helped defuse a hostage situation in New York.

That morning, **Joseph Paul Rivera**, a distraught 28-year-old truck driver, walked into the Midtown Manhattan office of Elektra/Asylum Records with a simple request—to hear "Desperado" played.

Morty Gilbert, a sales manager for the company, greeted him when he arrived and explained that E/A was not a radio station; Rivera would have to call one of them to get his request played.

Gilbert was puzzled but unbothered, later telling the *New York Post* that the truck driver looked normal enough, dressed in blue jeans and a down jacket and carrying a briefcase. "He seemed to be OK, and I didn't really give it much thought."

Rivera, born in New York City, wandered further into E/A's office, repeating his "Desperado" request to other employees. He became increasingly agitated when they declined to help. **Ruth Manne**, the company's 58-year-old office manager, approached Rivera to calm him.

She didn't know that Rivera was having a mental breakdown brought on by an assault in January that had left him hospitalized with multiple facial fractures. While recovering from his injuries, a former friend sold his truck out from under him. Desperate, Rivera thought if he could talk to the Eagles, he might borrow $2,500 to hire a lawyer so he could prosecute his former friend. He also hoped Jackson Browne might give him a job.

Manne, a music industry veteran, suggested she and Rivera go into her office, where they could talk alone. Rivera agreed, but when they walked in, he snapped. He slammed the door shut, locked it, and then barricaded it with filing cabinets. He pulled out a .32 revolver and fired a shot into the ceiling. Outside Manne's office, the E/A staff panicked. "The office was in turmoil," Gilbert said. "People were crawling out."

Back-and-forth shouting occurred in Manne's office for 10 solid minutes, the E/A staff reported. Rivera finally relented and allowed Manne to make a phone call. She called the police, and within minutes, uniformed officers swarmed the lobby.

Frank Bolz, the NYPD Hostage Negotiation Team commander, took over and began a two-hour negotiation with Rivera. Bolz could not recall whether someone tried to contact the Eagles or Browne, but said even if they could have been reached, the police might not have used the artists to help defuse the situation. "You try to contact them," he said, "that doesn't mean you will let [the captor] talk to them right away. It's like ammunition. You don't want to use it, but you like to have it."

Manne said Rivera unloaded his problems on her, "which were very complicated. I became very philosophical with him. I knew if I kept him talking, he might not get violent." Rivera began talking about suicide, and Manne explained that doing so "would be a futile effort." But the two worked out a solution that involved calling a local radio station and making a request.

Bolz's team called **Larry Berger**, the station program manager at WPLJ, a New York rock radio station. Then, just before 2 p.m., **Jimmy Fink**, the disc jockey working the 10 a.m. to 2 p.m. shift, went on air and as instructed by police, said, "This is 'Desperado' for the desperate trucker." Bolz made it clear that there should be no mention of the hostage situation on the air; he did not want to risk the radio station taking over hostage negotiations.

The plan worked. Manne said that they turned on the radio and tuned it to WPLJ, and when Rivera heard the first lines of the song ("*Desperado, why don't you come to your senses/You been out riding fences for so long now...*") he burst into tears. He told police "I'm going to give you the gun." Then he handed the pistol to Manne, saying, "You can go now." The door opened and police apprehended him.

Suffering from nervous exhaustion, Manne was wheeled out of the building on a stretcher; St. Clare Hospital held her for observation but released her later that day. Rivera left in handcuffs and authorities charged him with felony kidnapping, possession of a weapon, and reckless endanger-ment. And so ended an emotionally charged day at Elektra/Asylum's New York office.

A year later, prosecutors and the court system took Rivera's situation and mindset into consideration. He pled guilty to kidnapping but his sentence was a light five years' probation. What happened to Rivera after that is unknown.

In 2020, Fink, the deejay who announced the dedication, told the *New York Post* he was unaware of who Rivera was until the next day, but he said he was happy to have helped. "Simply playing a song on the radio could diffuse a hostage situation?" he asked. "That doesn't happen very often." [161, 722, 1939, 1940, 1941]

The Run-Off: Eagles, Szymczyk Etch Inside Jokes in Vinyl

One of producer **Bill Szymczyk**'s more idiosyncratic habits was etching session-specific in-jokes onto the blank vinyl space at the center of the records he produced. That meant that every Eagles- and Joe Walsh-related album he worked on also ended up including mysterious messages.

Szymczyk got the idea from a single produced by **Phil Spector** in 1963. Studying one closely, Szymczyk found the words "Phil and Annette." It turns out Spector had a vinyl cutter etch "Phil and Annette" into the run-off grooves of around 10 singles released during the year when he married the former **Annette Merar**.

"I discovered that you could write messages there," Szymczyk told *The Record Plant Diaries Project*. "That was it for me."

Joe Walsh and **Bill Szymczyk** started the tongue-in-cheek run-off inscriptions with Walsh's early albums, and the joke continued on in all the Eagles albums through *Eagles Live*. "Never let your monster lay down" was etched into the run-off of T*he Long Run*'s Side 1.

Typically, this space would only include production-related information, like a pressing-plant batch number. Joe Walsh said he first noticed Szymczyk's penchant for adding something extra while still in the **James Gang**. "He started writing secret messages just outside of the label where the groove is in the middle, where it goes around and around," Walsh told *The Record Plant Diaries Project*.

Thirds, the James Gang album from 1971 with "With Love from Jessica and ?" carved into the so-called "dead wax" was just the beginning of what would become a fun new tradition. Next, there was "That's no banany, thats my noze" from Walsh's 1974 album *So What*. The following year,

"Don't worry, nothing will be OK" appeared on the Eagles' *One of These Nights*.

"Every time it would have something specifically to do with that album—maybe a phrase that had come up during the course of that album or something along those lines," Szymczyk told *The Record Plant Diaries Project*.

He inscribed "V.O.L. is five-piece live" on one side of *Hotel California*, which Walsh said referred to the fact that the "Victim of Love" basic track had no overdubs.

"Is it six o'clock yet" is on the run-off groove on the other side of the *Hotel California*—yet another inside joke: Szymczyk's studio rule that the band had to stay sober until 6 p.m. each day. "We didn't

393

continued on Page 395

SPOTLIGHT SINGLE | JOE WALSH

JOE WALSH
All Night Long
Full Moon/Asylum Records, May 1980

Joe Walsh's 1980 single "All Night Long" pays homage to graveyard-shift workers. It later found a home in the movie *Urban Cowboy* in the scene where **John Travolta** picked a fight with the movie's villain. But on a personal level, Walsh knew about staying up until morning's light all too well. As the 1980s dawned, he found himself without a band—and with plenty of time on his hands to indulge in a growing alcohol and substance abuse problem.

"My higher power became vodka and cocaine," Walsh later told the Associated Press. He was always prolific before, but he only made four albums over the decade, each charting more poorly than the last. In 1980, however, Walsh was still a functioning addict, and the Eagles' former manager was still opening doors for him.

Irving Azoff served as executive producer for *Urban Cowboy*, helping craft a soundtrack dominated by country songs but still making room for pop/rock songs like Walsh's. They would waft out of truck radios in the movie or, as with "All Night Long," get played on the jukebox at the local greasy spoon.

A contemporary *Billboard* magazine review took pains to connect "All Night Long" with the film's down-home country vibe, noting that it "features Eagle Walsh wailing through a rocker that has a subtle country-rock flavor." "All Night Long" fits in perfectly with the loping feel and fun-loving vibe of Walsh's "Life's Been Good" and "A Life of Illusion" singles that arrived on opposite sides of this #19 song.

But the songs hid a sad and scary truth: By the '80s, Walsh's addictions did not just keep him up all night. They had become part of his career. "Later on," Walsh said, "when I did an album that didn't do so good, I thought, 'Well, obviously I'm not drinking nearly as much as I need to.'"

Some 13 years later, Eagles bandmates Glenn Frey and Don Henley made rehab a condition for Walsh's employment when they reformed the group. Walsh went through with it and has been sober ever since. "I'm actually proud that I'm still alive," Walsh told the *Lancashire Telegraph*. "I really hadn't planned on living this long."

"All Night Long" remains a stalwart element of his solo shows, usually closing out the night, but it also became part of the Eagles' repertoire along the way. It was the second of two Walsh songs that found their way onto the *Eagles Live* album in 1980.

Out on the road today, the hard-partying lifestyle depicted in "All Night Long" is long, long gone: "The big difference now is that we sleep," Walsh told the *Salt Lake Tribune*, with a hearty laugh. "There's relevant silliness and food fights and stuff, but we don't party like the old days." [1758, 1760, 1761, 1762, 1763]

start work until 2 in the afternoon," Walsh said in *A Conversation With the Eagles*, "so around 2:30, we'd start asking him if it was six o'clock yet."

"Call it in the air" is on Walsh's 1978 album *But Seriously, Folks...*, while "Never let your monster lay down" is on *The Long Run*. "Monster is Eagle code word for having a good time or almost too many beers: Going crazy," Walsh said in *A Conversation With the Eagles*. "Because if you let your monster lay down, you go to bed, and then your mind stream goes away."

The tradition continued even past the Eagles' original classic-era tenure. Szymczyk inscribed "Is it illegal to yell MOVIE in a firehouse?" onto *Eagles Live* in 1980; "After 15 years I still can't spell Szymczyk—is it one L or two?" onto Walsh's 1981 studio project *There Goes the Neighborhood*; and "Are we done yet?" onto *You Bought It—You Name It*, his 1983 album, among others.

Sometimes, the references were so inside that no one outside the studio could crack the code. But that was part of the fun, too. "I would never tell anybody what I was going to put in there until I mastered it," Szymczyk told *The Record Plant Diaries Project*. "People would get the staff pressing and go, 'Oh, okay,' or 'What?'" [1810, 1820, 2032]

SUMMER 1980

 ON THE ROAD WITH ...
▶ **Eagles**: Christopher Cross, Heart, Little River Band

 ON SCREEN
▶ **Joe Walsh** appeared in the Universal Pictures film *The Blues Brothers*. Walsh played the inmate who sets off the dance riot in the final prison scene.

 NUGGETS
▶ **Crosby, Stills & Nash** are joined by "three stray Eagles" (Timothy B. Schmit, Joe Walsh, and Don Felder) at the Hollywood Bowl. —*Cashbox*
▶ Eagles make a return visit to the Santa Monica Civic Auditorium, which they haven't appeared at since 1973; held in association with KLOS. —*Cashbox*
▶ Eagles are in the Los Angeles Record Plant's Complex Studio B checking out cuts for their upcoming live album. —*Cashbox*
▶ **David Geffen** signs **Donna Summer** to his new label, Geffen Records, for a staggering amount—between $5 million and $10 million. —*Cashbox*
▶ The *Urban Cowboy* soundtrack, with songs from Eagles and Joe Walsh, surges past $1.5 million in sales. —*Cashbox*
▶ Eagles' double-live album is set for an October release. —*Cashbox*
▶ Elektra/Asylum is running a new promotion for the Eagles' *The Long Run*... designer Nike jogging suits. —*Record World*

'Oo-ee, Oo-ee Baby': Eagles Cover Smith's 'Sea Cruise'

The third-to-last song the Eagles played before they broke up was a cover of **Huey "Piano" Smith**'s classic, "Sea Cruise." Sandwiched in between the encores of Joe Walsh's "Rocky Mountain Way" and "Take It Easy," it was a fitting tribute to Smith and singer **Frankie Ford**, who made it popular twenty years earlier.

By the time the Eagles got to the Long Beach Arena to play the benefit concert for Senator **Alan Cranston**, they had performed "Sea Cruise" more than twenty times during *The Long Run* tour. **Steve Young**'s "Seven Bridges Road" and **Poco**'s "Keep on Tryin'" were also among the several covers in the band's setlist.

Smith, a New Orleans native, was one of the Crescent City's premier R&B players, best known for the song "Rockin' Pneumonia and the Boogie Woogie Flu." With his band, **The Clowns**, he recorded the playful "Sea Cruise" that featured a ship's horns. But in 1959, Ace Records wiped Smith's lead vocal and dubbed in the voice of white teenage singer Frankie Ford, and released the song under Ford's name. Ford's campy filmed promo clip featured him swaying inside a small boat wearing a sailor's suit. It became a smash hit, selling more than a million copies and reaching #14 on the *Billboard* Hot 100.

Over the decades, **Jimmy Buffett**, **The Beach Boys**, **Johnny Rivers**, and **Jerry Lee Lewis**, to name a few, have also recorded Smith's buoyant song.

"Sea Cruise" was on the setlist when the Eagles hit the Santa Monica Civic and recorded the shows for a live album. Although "Sea Cruise" did not make *Eagles Live*, Glenn Frey recorded it for his debut solo album, *No Fun Aloud*, two years later. Frey's version emulated the New Orleans classic built around a swinging horn arrangement and piano that stoked his affinity for R&B.

Frey's love for the song, released when he was just 11 years old, was apparent throughout the tour. When the Eagles played the Yale Bowl in New Haven, Connecticut, they headlined a bill that included the **Little River Band** and **Heart** in June 1980. Writer **Steve Wosahla**, covering the show, sat behind the stage on the wooden benches that encircled the storied Ivy League football stadium. As the show ended, he spotted someone running up the steps to his left, suddenly realizing it was Glenn Frey.

As Frey flew by, he was still singing to himself, smiling, and snapping his fingers in time to the famous line: "Won't you let me take you on a sea cruise."

"It seemed so surreal and unexpected as if the band were still playing," Wosahla remembered years later, writing for *Americana Highways*.

He saw Don Henley, Don Felder, and **Irving Azoff** milling about between encores in the makeshift backstage area as he looked up. Frey bounded up the steps, his enthusiasm propelling him to the center of the Yale Bowl stage.

"I've replayed it in my mind many times since," Wosahla told *Time Passages*. "In that moment, he was still the kid from Detroit whose voice I still try to pick out every time "Ramblin' Gamblin' Man" comes on. Whenever you talk about the dysfunction of the Eagles, I go back to that afternoon. If anyone wonders whether there were any moments of joy in all that turmoil, I can tell you that I saw one of them." [2018, 2019, 2020, 2021]

Feature Films, Take 2: Azoff Wins With *Urban Cowboy* Gamble

Irving Azoff's first venture into the movie business with *FM* had been so underwhelming he had his name removed from the credits. It was a good call; the movie was a flop.

However, the Azoff-masterminded *FM* soundtrack was a Top 5 platinum smash. Entertainment conglomerates in the mid-1970s that had both film and music divisions were figuring out how to make money from a movie and a soundtrack. As *FM* proved, a strong rock soundtrack would sell, despite the film's failure.

Azoff, undeterred, believed the movie and soundtrack concept was still viable. He just needed the right vehicle.

Then, in September 1978, he read an article, "The Ballad of the Urban Cowboy: America's Search for True Grit," by **Aaron Latham** for *Esquire*. Gilley's, a mega-honky-tonk in Pasadena, Texas, a Houston suburb, and the working-class cowboy beer drinkers and hell raisers who regularly packed the joint, fascinated Latham, as well as Azoff. He wasted no time contacting the club's owner and star attraction, country singer **Mickey Gilley**. Azoff soon purchased the movie rights to the article and secured the rights to use the honky-tonk as a location for a cool $200,000.

He told **Robert Palmer** of the *New York Times* in March 1981 why the blueprint he followed for the *Urban Cowboy* soundtrack, also a double album, was successful.

"I set out to make a record that would be palatable on FM radio...with Joe Walsh and **Jimmy Buffett** and **Dan Fogelberg** on it, and a record that would be palatable on country radio, which **Johnny Lee** and Mickey Gilley were." Azoff also noted the record "grossed more than $26 million in the U.S. alone."

Film critics received *Urban Cowboy*, starring **John Travolta** and **Debra Winger**, much better than *FM*. With Travolta's star power, the movie inspired a cowboy craze across the United States and significantly raised the profile of country music.

Significantly for Azoff, the soundtrack was another smash. Lee went to #1 on the *Billboard* Country Singles chart with "Lookin' for Love," while Gilley climbed to #3 on the trade magazine's Adult Contemporary chart with "Stand by Me." Also featuring the Eagles' "Lyin' Eyes" and Joe Walsh's "All Night Long," *Urban Cowboy* hit #1 on *Billboard*'s Country Albums chart and #3 on the Top 200 pop chart, eventually selling more than three million copies and earning triple platinum certification. [295, 487, 490, 690, 691]

Walsh Instigates Prison Riot in Landis' *The Blues Brothers*

Two of *Saturday Night Live*'s most creative and popular performers in the mid-to-late 1970s, **John Belushi** and **Dan Aykroyd** invented Jake and Elwood, the **Blues Brothers**, for a TV skit. The popularity of the R&B-loving characters, combined with the star power of Aykroyd and Belushi, resulted in a movie spinoff, *The Blues Brothers*.

continued on Page 407

Eagles and friends complete their final curtain call during a show at the San Diego Sports Arena in December 1979. From left: **Joe Vitale**, Timothy B. Schmit, **J.D. Souther**, Glenn Frey, Don Henley, Joe Walsh, and Don Felder.

FREY, FELDER SQUARE OFF AFTER BENEFIT CONCERT

When Glenn Frey called **Irving Azoff** the day after Eagles' July 31, 1980, concert to inform him he was leaving the band, there was every expectation it was just another day at the office for the volatile L.A. rockers. Threats of departures and breakups were regular occurrences. But this was the day the powder keg finally blew.

Frey's decision dissolved the group while they were a colossal arena/stadium-level act at the pinnacle of their success. But the whole band did not get the official word until later, and the Eagles' announcement to the public and their fans would follow later still.

The band's blowup was sparked by friction between Frey and Don Felder at the previous night's concert in nearby Long Beach, and was dubbed by the Eagles and press alike as the "Long Night in Wrong Beach."

The show was a benefit designed to raise money and awareness for the re-election campaign of U.S. Senator **Alan Cranston**, a California Democrat. Eagles had occasionally lent their services to fundraisers for various causes they agreed with, and supporting the Cranston campaign was their latest endeavor of this type.

Though it may have appeared to some observers as a good PR move for the band, Henley emphatically denied this. Speaking to author **Marc Eliot**, Henley said the decision to take part in the Cranston benefit was "the direct result of a visit the Eagles made to [Cranston's] office in Washington, D.C." while the band was in the area. Band members and Azoff talked with the senator at length. They felt his stance on Native American issues, the environment, and the proliferation of nuclear power plants and nuclear weapons aligned well with theirs.

Four of the five band members voted to play the benefit, with Felder the lone "no" vote. The guitar player was suspicious and untrusting of politicians, preferring the band steer clear of any political involvement. Outvoted, he still did his job and played the show but, in his autobiography, admitted he did not want to be there.

When asked pre-show about the night's event, he quipped to the press that it was "just another show" and downplayed any interest in political causes. Felder's attitude irritated Frey.

The more significant blow for Frey occurred when Cranston's wife, **Norma Weintraub**, was walking around and thanking each of the band members for their involvement. When she thanked Felder, he replied, "You're welcome…" and then, under his breath, muttered, "…I guess."

Frey overheard the aside and felt Felder had made a disrespectful comment. He was livid.

"I was seething," he remembered. "I wanted to kill Felder."

Frey and Felder had been butting heads for years and were regularly in conflict with each other, but, as Joe Walsh put it, "The real manifestation of [their contentious relationship] came that night" in Long Beach.

Looking back on the exchange years later, Felder understood how Frey found it to be insulting, but he claimed he was politically "uninformed" and that being insulting "was not my intent." He chalked it up to the overwhelming tension among the ranks, claiming "our nerves were just frayed down to raw tissue."

Rock bands with interpersonal problems commonly follow a philosophy to "leave it backstage" when the show starts, but Frey and Felder could not follow this credo at the Long Beach show. The two taunted each other between songs, making threats of physical violence to come after the performance.

As Frey recalled, "Felder looks back at me [during the show] and says, 'Only three more songs till I kick your ass, pal.' And I'm saying, 'Great. I can't wait.'"

Some of the banter was picked up in the vocal mics, leading the sound crew to pull back on the mic faders when possible.

"You're a real pro, Don, all the way," Frey sarcastically mocked.

"Yeah, you are, too, the way you handle people," Felder shot back. "Except for the people you pay; nobody gives a shit about it."

"Fuck you," Frey retorted, "I've been paying you for seven years, you fuckhead."

Though both parties mentioned the band was playing "The Best of My Love" while the two sparred, online setlists indicate they did not play that song that night. It made for excellent copy to embellish the story, of course, but whether "The Best of My Love" plays into the story or not, the irony remains: The band members sang in angelic harmony but were hardly a harmonious crew. Musically, they had blueprinted the laid-back 1970s Southern California sound and were known for titles like "Take It Easy" and "Peaceful Easy Feeling." But they had always operated in a pressure cooker.

After Frey and Felder exited the stage when the show ended, it was one of Felder's inexpensive acoustic guitars that received the biggest beating, as he made a big show of smashing it into a million pieces. Frey was unimpressed, calling Felder out by saying it was typical of him to break his cheapest guitar.

Felder does not deny he intentionally broke a lesser musical instrument and cops to the fact that the smashing of the inexpensive guitar was pre-planned. He had known Joe Walsh to destroy guitars at times when he needed to blow off some steam. Felder, reasoning that he could benefit from that kind of explosive release, asked his roadie to get that specific guitar queued up for him to grab and destroy at the end of the show.

With the shards of wood falling to the floor, other band members predictably jumped into the fray, and a lot of hollering ensued before roadies intervened to prevent anyone from getting injured. Felder angrily made a beeline to his limo and took off; Frey also departed rapidly, saying nothing further to his bandmates.

The next day, with Frey's call to Azoff, the Eagles crashed and burned.

Fortunately, for E/A's sake at the time, but more importantly for Eagles' and rock and roll's posterity, the band had fresh as well as vintage concert recordings in the can. All that remained in the aftermath was the fixing, mixing, and release of a live two-record set of songs documenting the band's near-decade flight. [6, 1152, 1644, 1714, 1769, 1770, 1771, 1772, 1773, 1774]

EAGLES LIVE COVER LEANS ON ANVIL CASE, GRENADES

ontracts are contracts: In early 1980, the Eagles had one album left on their deal with Asylum, so they soon recorded a series of concerts to help fill a live double LP. But when Glenn Frey wouldn't agree to record any new studio tracks for the live album, Elektra/Asylum Chairman **Joe Smith** knew the band was history. The internal animosity—between Frey and the two Dons, primarily—appeared irreconcilable. Yet fans were left to speculate about the band's fate for another two years until Frey and Henley were ready to roll out their first solo albums and the split was acknowledged.

Producer **Bill Szymczyk** pulled all the audio together and worked such magic in the studio that audiophiles worldwide questioned how much of the album was actually live.

As Szymczyk approached the end of his overdub-

bing duties in late fall 1980, [**John**] **Kosh** was called upon again to complete the album's art.

Kosh did not remember who reached out to him, but suspects it was Eagles manager **Irving Azoff**. Whoever the messenger was, they didn't give him much to work with.

When Kosh is in design mode and looking for inspiration, he starts to scan his surroundings. He keeps a warehouse of props that are occasionally useful—the turntable from **REO Speedwagon**'s *Hi Infidelity* came out of storage there. Poking around inside that building, he found a brown bird's nest with several eggs in it. And he thought to put some hand grenades in there to fill out the space and illustrate the band's volatile frame of mind.

He developed the nest idea over several album cover composites but later rejected the idea as a serious contender before the band even saw it.

But, he thought, it might make a good album sleeve or maybe a disc label, so he kept it around. And it eventually became the graphic for the disc labels.

Kosh knew the album would be a series of Eagles live performances and wanted an image analogous to the band being on the road. He never considered using a photograph of the band on the cover. But that did not resolve the quest for the final cover image.

"Obviously, I wouldn't care to use an existing shot," he said, laughingly feigning arrogance. "And it would probably be very difficult to assemble them for a new shoot, anyway."

He stumbled across the answer in his colleague **Aaron Rapoport**'s nearby office: a red Anvil equipment case.

Anvil cases are a well-respected brand name among musicians and photographers; they come in all shapes, colors, and sizes, but all are designed with distinctive metal bands to protect edges and corners. Kosh said he did not know how Rapoport had acquired the case, but thought it might work as a prop for the cover shot. Contrary to some Eagles urban legends, the band never used the case in an Eagles concert tour.

Kosh took the case back to his studio and stenciled a broken-block lettered "EAGLES" in gray with "86" (1930s soda counter term for sold out, and later became slang for halted or nixed) in black on the side of the case. He added similar touches to the other side and then roughed up the design by adding torn pieces of shipping labels with "MIA" and "LAX" scribbled on them in marker, indicating the band's movement back and forth between Miami and Los Angeles. When it came time to design a sticker with the band's name for the cover, he applied an inside joke from his childhood.

"There was a comic when we were kids [in

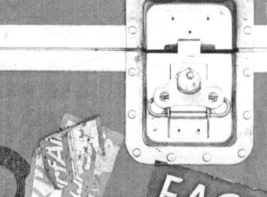

England]," he said, "They were all kind of jokey, and they were for boys. And the most serious one was called *The Eagle*. And it had **Dan Dare** the spaceman on the cover, and you'd open it up, and there'd be illustrations of planes, buses, and whatever."

The Eagle was a weekly tabloid published in England from 1950 to 1969 and revived from 1982 to 1994. It was a traditional frame-by-frame cartoon with a flying eagle emblazoned across its top-left banner, set off against a bright red background. It was the distinctive Eagle typeface Kosh wanted to employ, where the "crossbars" on the letters "E" and "L" have rounded lower edges with the sharper top edges that seem to point upward.

"I just took it and stuck it on the side of the Anvil case," he said, "and everybody my age in England got it immediately, but no one in America did."

Once all the touches had been applied, Rapoport photographed both sides of the decorated case. Kosh took those images and employed some embossing techniques he used effectively for **Linda Ronstadt**'s *Prisoner in Disguise*, **Bad Company**'s *Run with the Pack*, and **Electric Light Orchestra**'s *A New World Record*. The case's metal bands and rivets were embossed to give a raised appearance, while the sunken latch and handle at the top-center of the front of the album were recessed, just like the actual Anvil case.

The rest of the package then fell in place. There would be dual sleeves for the two discs, and Azoff suggested using helicopter aerial photographs of the capacity audience for the Eagles concert at the Yale Bowl in New Haven, Connecticut, as part of the four-part poster. The album sleeves used various concert photos from band concerts at the Santa Monica Civic, the Long Beach Arena, and The Forum, including shots of the band, likely playing "Life's Been Good" in front of a giant projection of Joe Walsh's mischievous history. Other shots included roadies with bunny ears, a blurred shot of hustling roadies, and concert stages in various stages of setup.

The record sleeves and the gatefold documented all the onstage and backstage action at an Eagles concert, including a dramatic black-and-white shot of all the Eagles' guitars lined up before a show. Kosh never met personally with the band to

One of the first designs considered for the *Eagles Live* cover art was the eagle-eggs-and-hand-grenades concept developed by **Kosh**. It was quickly eliminated as a cover option, but eventually adopted as the label art.

discuss the album's design and approval, but both Frey and Henley gave the final OK.

The cover's Anvil case eventually made its way back to Rapoport's office and stayed there until an Eagle arrived for a photo shoot one day.

Kosh said that a few years later a visiting photographer leased out Rapoport's studio for a day to photograph Frey for one of his solo albums.

"When he spotted the case," Kosh said. "And he said, 'That's mine!' And he took the case home with him. And that's a bit of history—they should have got it into the Rock and Roll Hall of Fame."

Kosh thought he had fallen out with Henley over the drummer's disappointment with the design of *The Long Run* cover. When Glenn Frey passed in 2016, Kosh attended the private memorial at The Forum in Los Angeles, where he said he and Henley connected for moment.

"I thought Don and I were harboring this sort of resentment until we bumped into each other," Kosh said. "He was clearly unaware on my mindset. We chatted briefly and then we just looked at each other and burst out laughing and said, 'What the fuck was that all about?'" [2129]

RELEASE
Early November
1980

SEVEN BRIDGES ROAD

By: Steve Young

Side B: The Long Run (live version)

Eagles had quietly disbanded by the time the double-disc live album hit the market for the year-end holiday season. The band's cover of "Seven Bridges Road" was the only single released, and they nailed it. Of course, they had been harmonizing it live onstage for years so they had plenty of practice. However, the song was only known to those fans who went to their concerts. Despite its country music leanings, radio loved the tight harmonizing. The band would not release an original single for another 14 years.

AIRPLAY

Steve Young's song was a heartfelt homage to a lonesome stretch of road near Montgomery, Alabama. Radio stations in the Southeast considered the song a natural fit. They added it to their playlists in early December and kept spinning it through March 1981. Stations in the Northeast added it, too, but the Midwest and West didn't seem as enamored. It lacked the staying power of the band's previous hits and faded with the spring. As the 1970s were left behind, the song—like many other Eagles hits—would find a home on classic rock radio.

115 PLAYLIST ADDS Winter 1980-81				
Region	**Dec**	**Jan**	**Feb**	**Regional Airplay**
Northeast	10	10	2	22.4 %
Southeast	23	15	1	36.2 %
Midwest	8	9	2	17.2 %
Southwest	3	9	0	11.2 %
West	7	3	1	12.9 %

FIRST-WAVE STATIONS Stations that added the song in the first 30 days

KFI-Los Angeles
KMJK-Portland
KERN-Bakersfield
KYYX-Seattle
KOPA-Phoenix
KCPX-Salt Lake City
KIMN-Denver
KFMB-San Diego
KIOY-Fresno
KROY-Sacramento

WGCL-Cleveland
WKRQ-Cincinnati
WNCI-Columbus
WNAP-Indianapolis
WOKY-Milwaukee

KBFM-McAllen, TX
KRUX-Phoenix
KRQQ-Tucson
KLUC-Las Vegas

WBLI-Long Island
WLBZ-Bangor, ME
WXKX-Pittsburgh
WPJB-Providence
WFBG-Altoona, PA

WHYN-Springfield, MA
WIGY-Bath, ME
WFIL-Philadelphia
WBBF-Rochester
WVBF-Framingham, MA

WKJJ-Louisville
WFBR-Baltimore
WQXI-Atlanta
WBBQ-Augusta

WRJZ-Knoxville
WSGN-Birmingham
WFMF-Baton Rouge
WSGA-Savannah

CHARTS

Billboard	HIGHEST CHARTING WEEK: BILLBOARD - February 7, 1981		
#21 February 7, 1981	**SINGLE**	**ARTIST**	**# PREV WK**
	1. Celebration	Kool & The Gang	3
	2. The Tide Is High	Blondie	1
Cashbox	3. I Love a Rainy Night	Eddie Rabbitt	4
#27 February 21, 1981	4. 9 to 5	Dolly Parton	8
	5. Passion	Rod Stewart	6
	6. (Just Like) Starting Over	John Lennon	2
Record World	7. Every Woman in the World	Air Supply	5
	8. Woman	John Lennon	17
#31 February 28, 1981	**21. SEVEN BRIDGES ROAD**	**EAGLES**	**23**

Sources: Billboard, Cashbox, Record World

ODE TO A LONESOME ROAD IS EAGLES' SWAN SONG

Eagles would gather in the showers and backrooms of sports arenas to warm up their voices back in the day. They would sing a cappella to songs like "Take It Easy" and "Seven Bridges Road." Don Felder said the natural echo and privacy in these locations offered an ideal setting.

"No matter what the mood or how bad things had been," he wrote in his autobiography, "we always had that private rehearsal together."

Felder lamented that the band had gotten away from the bonding ritual and admitted he missed the "spiritual harmony" of singing "Seven Bridges Road." But the song made a comeback of sorts when the band included it in their July 1980 sets at the Santa Monica Civic.

The track, recorded on the second of three nights at the intimate small hall, found its way onto the release of *Eagles Live* LP in early November 1980, just as the band was breaking apart but keeping it quiet from the public.

"Seven Bridges Road" became the first single from *Eagles Live*, paired with a live version of "The Long Run" as its B-side. Outlaw country artist **Steve Young** wrote the song for his *Rock Salt & Nails* album, released in 1969. The mossy trees of Woodley Road in Montgomery, Alabama, and its seven bridges—including three intersecting pairs of bridges and another stand-alone bridge—inspired the song. Woodley Road has another country music distinction in that it leads to the Oakwood Annex Cemetery, where **Hank Williams** is buried.

Young was moved to write "Seven Bridges Road" on a starry night in Montgomery, said **Jimmy Evans**, Alabama's former attorney general and a close friend of Young's back then.

"That night there was a full moon," Evans remembered. "We were in my Oldsmobile, and when I stopped, Steve got out on the right-side fender. We sat there a while, and he started writing down words."

Evans and Young had just finished a jam session with bluesman **C.P. Austin** in the nearby town of Orion, and were driving home along that long stretch of highway.

"I thought it was the most beautiful place around Montgomery that I'd ever seen," Evans added. "That road was a cavern of moss; it looked like a tunnel."

But the song almost didn't get recorded. Young's producer, **Tommy LiPuma**, thought the album should focus on folk and country music covers. Near the end of the recording session, Young told music journalist **Dave Dawson** that near the end of the recording session, they ran out of songs to record in the studio." All the studio musicians were in place and ready to record, including legendary session guitarist **James Burton**, so he started performing

"Seven Bridges Road" and everyone else joined in. After it was recorded, LiPuma admitted that the cut was good.

Young was born in Georgia and was raised in Gadsden, Alabama. He traveled all over exercising his "outlaw country" musical craft. He recorded fourteen albums over the years, and his work was in demand. **Waylon Jennings** recorded a country hit with Young's "Lonesome, On'ry and Mean," and **Hank Williams Jr.** recorded "Montgomery in the Rain," among others.

Young died at 73 due to complications from a fall in Nashville, Tennessee, in 2016. Looking back on his signature song, Young told the *Gadsden* (Ala.) *Times* earlier that year, "Consciously, when I wrote it, it was just a song about a girl and a road in south Alabama. Now I think there's almost a mystical thing about it."

While Young's gritty original presented "Seven Bridges Road" in its raw form, another artist, **Iain Matthews**, rearranged it with a more pastoral quality that caught the Eagles attention.

In the liner notes to *The Soul of Many Places: The Elektra Years, 1972-1974*, Matthews, who covered the song on his *Valley Hi* album, remembered seeing the Eagles in Los Angeles while they were both watching other bands at the Troubadour.

Matthews, one of the founders of the British folk group **Fairport Convention**, had a feeling about where the Eagles found their own inspiration.

"We were forever going back to somebody's house and playing music. Don Henley had a copy of *Valley Hi* that he liked, so I've no doubt about that being where their version of the song came from."

Glenn Frey told **Cameron Crowe** the band had, indeed, modified their arrangement after listening to Matthews' version.

"We listened to the Iain Matthews version and then modified the arrangement from that," Frey recalled. "Sometimes we start our show with it. It's something we do well—four voices, a cappella. I think the bottom line is, that's a style that comes very easily and naturally to us. It's also something that our fans really like. It's Americana."

Though the Eagles never released a non-live version of "Seven Bridges Road" on a proper studio album, the track was introduced to many when the live performance was also included on *Eagles Greatest Hits Volume 2* at the end of 1982.

Others also took a liking to Young's song. **Dolly Parton**, **Rita Coolidge**, **Joan Baez**, **Tracy Nelson & Mother Earth**, and **Alan Jackson** covered it as well.

The single would reach #21 on the *Billboard* Hot 100 chart and give *Eagles Live* the illusion of an earlier, happier era. But if one were to look in a crystal ball, one might have seen the band singing the song a cappella on future reunion tours and capturing the magic that first began in the locker rooms of sports arenas across America. [1453, 1461, 1974, 1975, 1976]

The plot was a vehicle for some anarchic comedy and a slew of classic blues and R&B musical guests. Believing they are on a mission from God to save the orphanage where they grew up, the brothers vow to get their old band back together.

The music greats in the long and rambling movie were **Steve Cropper**, **Cab Calloway**, **Aretha Franklin**, **James Brown**, **Ray Charles**, and **John Lee Hooker**. The film, directed by **John Landis**, was a hit, grossing $57 million in the United States alone. Audiences who looked closely noticed another star—an off-duty Eagle, Joe Walsh.

Walsh was good friends with Belushi, who would die of a drug overdose in 1982, and the pair had many hotel-trashing escapades in the 1970s. Walsh, talking to **Richard Bienstock** for *Rolling Stone* in 2016, recalled he had "met Belushi on the road in Chicago. He came to an Eagles concert. He showed up in my room and didn't leave for two days."

For a highly strung performer like Belushi, movie sets were painful. There was too much sitting around and waiting. Bored out of his mind one day, he asked Walsh to hang out on the set with him. Sitting in a trailer with Belushi and Aykroyd, the two *SNL* alumni had an idea: Walsh could be in the film. They needed someone to start a riot in the film's prison scene. The king of hotel room destruction was perfect for the job and accepted the role.

"I'm the prisoner that starts the riot at the end," he told **Thomas H. Green** of Artsdesk.com in June 2012, "John said, 'You gotta do this, you gotta be this guy, I need you to start a riot,' so I did.'"

As the band played "Jailhouse Rock," Walsh's character jumps on a table and starts dancing wildly, prompting the entire room of inmates to follow suit.

"The fun thing," he said, "was we had three riots to get all the camera angles, so there was me and 200 guys, and when they give the signal, we go nuts and destroy the place, then we go on break, and they set it all up just like it was, and we come in and go nuts again." [225, 2065]

FALL 1980

 RELEASES
▶ **Randy Meisner**, *One More Song* (album)

 COLLABORATIONS
▶ **Don Henley** provided backing vocals on **Melissa Manchester**'s album *For the Working Girl*.
▶ **Joe Walsh** was a "performer" on **The Beach Boys** album *Keepin' the Summer Alive*.
▶ **Don Henley** and **Glenn Frey** provided backing vocals on the single "One More Song" on **Randy Meisner**'s album *One More Song*.

 NUGGETS
▶ **Jackson Browne** puts on a set of shows at The Forum in Inglewood, and is joined by **Bruce Springsteen** and **Graham Nash** the first night, and Glenn Frey and Tim Schmit the second night with a rousing celebratory version of "Take It Easy." —*Record World*
▶ **Doug Weston** puts the Troubadour up for sale for $500,000. —*Cashbox*

Almost Live: Scattered Eagles Bid Adieu with Concert LP

With the benefit of hindsight *Eagles Live* was not the end of the story. Later chapters would extend the saga. But as 1980 drew to a close, the live album was an inglorious end to a glorious career.

Eagles, as a band, had fragmented months earlier and was over. Unfortunately, for the disgruntled, frustrated, and fatigued band members, their recording contract stipulated that they had to deliver one more album. They had very little interest in that and hit on the idea of releasing a live collection: no more songwriting, and no more toxic recording sessions. They even rejected **Joe Smith**'s desperate offer of a cool $2 million to write just two new songs. A final contractually obligated studio album appeared doomed from the start, but a live album was a viable alternative.

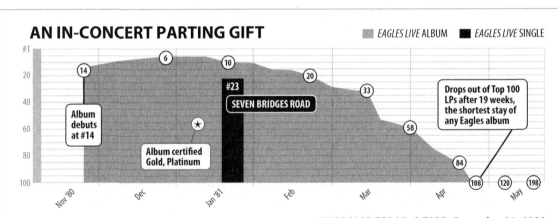

AN IN-CONCERT PARTING GIFT

■ *EAGLES LIVE* ALBUM ■ *EAGLES LIVE* SINGLE

Album debuts at #14

Album certified Gold, Platinum

#23
SEVEN BRIDGES ROAD

Drops out of Top 100 LPs after 19 weeks, the shortest stay of any Eagles album

When Elektra/Asylum released *Eagles Live*, rumors the band was on the rocks were already swirling in the music press. But while the then-expensive $15.98 double album didn't generate the buzz of the previous two LPs, it still became a Top 15 hit. There was only one single released, and the masterful harmonies in "Seven Bridges Road" helped keep it in the Top 10 through the end of January. But the absence of new original material was evident and the album began fading in the charts in February. By the end of April, it had fallen out of the Top 100 entirely after just 19 weeks.
Sources: Billboard, Recording Industry Association of America

BILLBOARD TOP LPs & TAPE, December 20, 1980

1. Kenny Rogers, *Greatest Hits*
2. Barbra Streisand, *Guilty*
3. Stevie Wonder, *Hotter Than July*
4. AC/DC, *Back in Black*
5. Pat Benatar, *Crimes of Passion*
6. **EAGLES, *EAGLES LIVE***
7. Bruce Springsteen, *The River*
8. The Police, *Zenyatta Mondatta*
9. Queen, *The Game*
10. Neil Diamond, *The Jazz Singer*

The band members had grown increasingly hostile toward each other while making *The Long Run*, the underwhelming follow-up to *Hotel California*. By the time producer **Bill Szymczyk** was patching together a live album, the members weren't even on speaking terms. Frey was frustrated and refused to fly to Miami, where Szymczyk, Henley, and the rest of the band upgraded their parts from the live tapes. New recordings would then be flown to Frey in Los Angeles for his input. Szymczyk sarcastically credited the production of the album to FedEx.

The album drew its share of detractors. **Randall Edwards**, a music critic for the *Daily Utah Chronicle*, keyed in on the slick production qualities applied to the live album, concluding that it "proves, once and for all, that [Eagles] are products of excellent splicing, dicing, and chopping by a fabulous studio La Machine." In 1983, the *Rolling Stone Record Guide* decried *Eagles Live* as "perhaps the most heavily overdubbed [live album] in history." Historically, live albums have been fixed and polished in recording studios, but it typically takes a serious audiophile to spot the overdubs.

There may be live albums that have escaped charges of having too many post-event studio fixes, but the fact that *Eagles Live* was polished to excess is hardly a surprise. The band had a reputation for being notorious studio (and live concert) perfectionists. Presented with a series of live recordings that could never match the studio perfection the band strove for, it's no wonder that the concert recordings were significantly overdubbed. And given that the band members weren't all together for the sessions, there was simply too much license to refine the work into a glossy sheen. Not that the record didn't sound exquisite, but the finished article lacked some concert authenticity.

Szymczyk defended his work in an interview with the BBC's **John Tobler**. "I beg to differ with [the notion of excessive overdubbing]," Szymczyk said. "We did patch the tracks up here and there, but everybody does that with a live album. The band does sound like their albums in concert, and I'd say that 70 percent of that record is live."

The trouble with recording a band with a singing drummer, Szymczyk said, is that "you have to make sure your vocal mic is aimed in a particular way to prevent a lot of leakage, which presents problems. So that should prove that all Henley's vocals are live because it would be almost impossible to overdub keeping a drum track and putting on a different vocal. I rest my case."

Critics assert the perfectionist Eagles over-polished the live tracks and lost some of the concert authenticity, but taken as an album,

> **SO, THAT SHOULD PROVE THAT ALL HENLEY'S VOCALS ARE LIVE BECAUSE IT WOULD BE ALMOST IMPOSSIBLE TO OVERDUB KEEPING A DRUM TRACK *AND* PUTTING ON A DIFFERENT VOCAL. I REST MY CASE.**
>
> **— BILL SZYMCZYK**

away from the troubles of the day, *Eagles Live* is a fine document of America's premier rock and roll band at its peak.

While many of the tracks were culled from the last tour (from shows performed at the Santa Monica Civic in July 1980), a handful of tunes date back to 1976. As such, fans could once again hear Randy Meisner's heartbreaking vocals on "Take It to the Limit," which was lifted from a gig at The Forum in Inglewood. Meisner appears on about one-third of *Eagles Live*, which is a bit of a curiosity considering that Timothy B. Schmit was the current bass player promoted on the album's photography.

The album begins with the band's iconic "Hotel California" from 1980, and overdubs or not, it's a scintillating version of the song that showcases a group, despite animosity and tension, playing as a highly efficient unit.

With a nod to their L.A. country-rock days, the live performance of "Desperado" is a standout piece and a reminder of happier, more hopeful times. The same is true for "Saturday Night," where Schmit sings the line in the chorus previously handled by Meisner ("She said tell me, oh, tell me...").

The biggest problem with *Eagles Live* is that the songs are such faithful, polished renditions that they don't offer much value to people who already own similar studio versions. Yet there is some value in the two songs from Joe Walsh's solo career—"Life's Been Good" and "All Night Long"—that made the cut and provided listeners with Eagles-driven versions of these tunes for the first time.

"Seven Bridges Road" was released as a single and climbed to a respectable #21 on the *Billboard* Hot 100, while the album reached #6 in *Billboard*. And that was it. Eagles were over, at least until **Irving Azoff** got the idea of an Eagles tribute album built around **Travis Tritt**'s cover of "Take It Easy" in 1993. [132, 725, 1945, 2037, 2104]

Billboard
November 22, 1980

Anxiously awaited since the Eagles played a series of small hall Los Angeles dates earlier this year for the purpose of this recording, this live set lives up to the high expectations. Though five of the 15 tracks are from 1976 performances, the bulk of this two-disk affair is from those highly acclaimed 1980 L.A. shows. The harmonies and the playing are top notch. Set selection is varied, ranging from the expected hits to lesser-known tracks. The guitar work of Joe Walsh, Don Felder, and Glenn Frey absolutely sizzles.

New York Daily News
November 17, 1980

My mailbox is clogged with "Greatest Hits" records; they're trying to cash in on Christmas with surefire product, which this double-disc certainly is, consisting of bullseye hits like "Hotel California," "Take It to the Limit," "New Kid in Town," "Life In the Fast Lane," "Desperado," and "Take It Easy." I already have all these songs on old Eagles albums so I wouldn't buy this disc, but if you have a musical friend who just came out of a ten-year coma, it's perfect.

– *Bill Carlton*

The Ottawa Citizen
November 28, 1980

Eagles Live is a heavy two-album live set focusing primarily on the band's last two albums. As expected, the Eagles' live sound is superior to a lot of bands' studio efforts. But these aren't mere repeats of past hits. There is a definitive live edge to the music and songs. Perhaps somewhere down the road we'll get a more definitive Eagles live album that focuses more on the band's truly golden age–pre-*Hotel California*, before the band got caught up in traffic in the fast lane.

– *Bill Provick*

SPOTLIGHT SINGLE | RANDY MEISNER

RANDY MEISNER
Deep Inside My Heart
Epic Records, October 1980

Duetting with **Kim Carnes** in 1980 proved to be a successful formula for country music legend **Kenny Rogers** when they sang "Don't Fall in Love with a Dreamer," a song she co-wrote.

Rogers—who figures into the Eagles' story as early as the early 1970s when he discovered Don Henley and **Shiloh**—released the song on his *Gideon* album for the United Artists label. The Carnes-Rogers duet peaked at #4 on *Billboard* in May 1980.

That fall, Epic Records also released a Carnes duet with former Eagle Randy Meisner when they picked "Deep Inside My Heart" as the first single from Meisner's *One More Song* album. Like several songs on the LP, Meisner wrote the tune with the help of **Blues Magoos** veteran **Eric Kaz**. While Meisner sings most of the lead vocals by himself, Carnes ably sings harmony and then co-lead vocals as a catchy call-and-response during chorus vocals.

Carnes appeared with Meisner and his current band, the **Silverados**, on the TV shows *Fridays* and *The Midnight Special* to reprise her role in the song. When he played songs from the new album on *Fridays*, Meisner typically traded in his familiar bass for a six-string guitar. But for "Deep Inside My Heart," he sang sans instrument with only a microphone in hand. He and Carnes stood side by side and traded lines, sometimes making eye contact and gesturing with each other. It was an atypical look for a musician known only for performing with a fretted instrument around his neck. The performance appeared to follow the exact blueprint as the Rogers-Carnes duet.

However, the song itself was far different from the more syrupy "Don't Fall in Love with a Dreamer." "Deep Inside My Heart" was an upbeat tune with percussive piano, a touch of synth, and an effervescent feel. *Billboard* magazine called the song "a devastating piece of crisp rock with a finger-snapping beat that won't quit [that is] further enhanced by Kim Carnes' background vocal."

Steve Pond, pop music columnist for the *Los Angeles Times*, said that while the record "is a typically slick L.A. studio product, it's also a state-of-the-art commercial pop disc. Far less pretentious than the Eagles' recent outings (Meisner is simply singing songs, not grappling with the Big Issues), it's tailor-made for radio airplay."

"Deep Inside My Heart" would spend 16 weeks on the charts, peaking at #22 in December 1980.

Meisner fared slightly better when the follow-up single from *One More Song*, "Hearts on Fire," reached #19. But it was not his last duet with a talented female singer; in 1982, he would also record an **Elton John**-penned song, "Strangers," with **Heart** vocalist **Ann Wilson**. [1146, 2024, 2025, 2026, 2027, 2028, 2029, 2135]

MEISNER RETURNS STRONG WITH *ONE MORE SONG*

When Randy Meisner quickly released his first post-Eagles solo album in 1978, one thing was notable just by reading the labels affixed to the vinyl: an absence of original material. Except for a remake of the Eagles' "Take It to the Limit," no songs credited the artist as a songwriter on *Randy Meisner*.

The album performed poorly, so Meisner knew the formula needed changing. A couple years later, he released *One More Song*, on which he did not rely as heavily on outside composers. He had some critical help, though, from co-writers **Eric Kaz** and **Wendy Waldman**.

"By writing these songs with Eric and Wendy," Meisner said, "I was able to put a lot of real feeling into the compositions, as opposed to just collecting songs." He referred to his first effort as "scattered" and remarked, "It's really hard, as I found out, to collect songs by other people and end up with a good album."

Kaz was a former member of the New York-based **Blues Magoos** and also worked with ex-**Pure Prairie League** leader **Craig Fuller** in the band **American Flyer**.

SPOTLIGHT ALBUM | RANDY MEISNER

RANDY MEISNER
One More Song
Epic Records, October 1980

Kaz was successful as a songwriter, having co-written **Linda Ronstadt**'s gem, "Love Has No Pride." Waldman was a Southern California artist who released a series of singer-songwriter albums throughout the 1970s for Warner Bros.

Meisner penned six of the album's nine tracks in collaboration with Kaz, or with both Kaz and Waldman. He and Kaz teamed up to write the album's first two singles, "Deep Inside My Heart" and "Hearts on Fire."

The former was a duet featuring **Kim Carnes**, who made headlines that year by teaming with **Kenny Rogers** on "Don't Fall in Love with a Dreamer." The following year she would release the hit she's most remembered for, "Bette Davis Eyes." When Meisner appeared on the TV show

Fridays in 1981 to perform many of the tunes from *One More Song*, she joined him on stage to replicate the part she sang in the studio.

"Hearts on Fire" was the album's opener and proved to be a catchy pop-rock number. Meisner described the collaboration process with Kaz: "Eric ended up working a lot on the music [on the album]...I'd hum a melody to Eric, spit out ideas, and he'd condense it down."

Adding Waldman into the mix with Kaz and Meisner, the trio produced the mid-tempo numbers "Gotta Get Away" and "Come On Back to Me," as well as the ballad "I Need You Bad" and the contemplative "Trouble Ahead."

The remaining songs on the album were from outside writers, but names familiar to Eagles' fans. **Jack Tempchin**, the songwriter behind "Peaceful Easy Feeling" and (with **Robb Strandlund**) "Already Gone," provided two songs, including the album's title track. "One More Song" was about a musician playing his last performance with a band, so it seemed quite fitting for Randy, who had departed the Eagles just a couple of years prior. Eagles friend **Jackson Browne** recommended that Meisner record it for the album.

"Jackson thought the song was right for me," Meisner remembered. "So, we sat down at the piano, made a demo of [it] and added one lyric. Instead of 'packin' away my guitar,' I sang 'packin' away my bass guitar.'"

It's easy to connect the tender and wistful message of the song with Meisner's former band, so it's apropos that two Eagles contributed to the recording. If you listen carefully, you can hear Glenn Frey and Don Henley, who joined in to provide backing vocals.

The record's closer was a cover of "Anyway Bye Bye," a **Poco** classic written by **Richie Furay** and released on the band's second album. It was a significant selection for Meisner, who, as a founding member of Poco, used to sing lead on the tune in the band's Los Angeles club days.

Overall, *One More Song* was more unified and organized than his 1978 offering. At the time of the album's release, Meisner agreed: "It feels like my career, my solo career, is starting anew. *One More*

Randy Meisner's second solo album, *One More Song*, did far better than his first effort, taking two songs into the *Billboard* Top 25. The magic for his second go-round came from the decision to record new material.

Song reminds me of the first Eagles album when there was all of this fresh spirit, and everything was just beginning."

While *One More Song* may not have made Randy Meisner a household name, it was moderately successful, with the two singles landing at #22 and #19 respectively on the charts. He would return with one final solo album in 1982, but it would not be as successful. [1504, 1539, 1893, 1894, 1895, 1896, 1897]

Don Henley and Glenn Frey sit together during the 2nd Annual MTV Video Music Awards at Radio City Music Hall in 1985, a little more than four years after the Eagles quietly broke up.

FREY DISSOLVES EAGLES WITH A FATEFUL PHONE CALL

The day after Glenn Frey and Don Felder had almost come to blows at the Long Beach Arena following the Eagles' fundraiser for **Alan Cranston**, Glenn Frey called Eagles' manager **Irving Azoff** to let him know he would not be getting involved in other projects. If Azoff dismissed it as typical end-of-tour noise, when Frey called Don Henley a few months later, its gravity became a lot more real.

A conversation that started with football quickly turned into a formal notice Frey was leaving. "He said he wanted...to do his own thing," Henley recounted to biographer **Marc Eliot** in *To The Limit*. "Not forever, he said, but for a while. He said he had some ideas for an album. I knew what he was telling me. He may have been trying to low-key it, but the message was clear."

While Henley was empathetic and knew Frey may have increasingly taken a backseat to him over the years, inside he knew things would never be the same. This might mean he, too, would have to think about his own solo album. By the time he wished Frey luck and hung up, Henley knew the Eagles' race was run.

Coming into the making of *The Long Run*, bassist Timothy B. Schmit had a sense the band might break up but admits he was in denial.

"I knew that there was some squabbling—I mean, it was obvious," he told **Joe Basso** of *MusicRadar* years later. "It couldn't be hidden—but I did not know how truly serious it was. To me, all bands fought. Another day at the office in rock 'n' roll. I didn't know how heavy the issues were."

It shocked and saddened Schmit when Frey called him and said, "It's over."

"Despite the fighting in the band, everything else was going too good," the bassist reflected. "You never think something so big is going to end."

For Don Felder, there was no call from Frey. He found out when he spoke with **Bill Szymczyk**, who was putting together the band's final album, *Eagles Live*. Azoff had already called each band member to let them know they would have to finish editing the live album without Frey.

When Felder asked the producer about the band's upcoming studio schedule, Szymczyk bluntly told him, "There is no band at this time."

"Everybody kept hoping that Glenn would reconsider, even me," Felder wrote in his autobiography, *Heaven and Hell*. "We thought he'd get the stress out of his system, do a solo album, and be back. We were at the peak of our success—the biggest band in the world. Why quit now?"

The release of *Eagles Live* in November gave the illusion the Eagles were still a unit. But there would be no public announcement and, as Felder said, "for all our fans knew, the Eagles simply vanished."

Azoff had been down this road many times before.

"The Eagles were breaking up from the day I met them," he told **Joe Smith** for *Off the Record*. "The first day I met them, in Kansas City, Missouri, we were driving to Springfield, and Bernie and I were feuding. There was talk of a breakup on that tour. At the end of every tour, they broke up. So, there is no date as to an actual breakup. One day they just kind of drifted into a divorce."

According to Henley, it took a long time for people to realize the Eagles were history. For a band whose members were miserable and not communicating, things had stopped being fun. Both management and their record company had a sense of denial, which held out hope the lucrative franchise would continue.

Or as Joe Walsh later put it so succinctly: "We just plain had to stop because it stopped making sense.

We were all in bad moods all the time. It just felt yucky." He told **Matt Wardlaw** of Ultimate Classic Rock that they were lucky they stopped before their relationships were irreparably damaged.

That did not stop Henley from taking a shot at Walsh a decade later when he told *Chicago Tribune* writer **Lynn Van Matre** that he felt the guitarist played a important role in the band's demise.

"I didn't want to talk about it before, but the hell with that," Henley confided. "I don't mind telling you, Joe Walsh was one of the reasons the Eagles broke up. He was instrumental in the disintegration of that group. He was an insidious troublemaker. He would split the band into factions. He was a very divisive presence and very covert about it. He was very hypocritical. Glenn and I used to laugh and say, 'Yeah, Joe's a very interesting bunch of guys.'"

Years later, Frey was more conciliatory about the band's demise.

In his conversation with Smith in 1988, Frey likened the Eagles to a "powder keg just waiting for someone to light the fuse." The band, he said, was serious about becoming successful, and he wanted them taken seriously as songwriters.

"The band was like a fake democracy," Frey explained. "Henley and I were making the decisions while at the same time trying to pacify, include, and cajole the others. There was always so much turbulence around our band that it made us serious all the time. There was never a day when all five guys felt good. I'd think, 'Who's gonna blow it today? Who's gonna want to fire everybody?'"

Frey told Smith his patience had worn so thin that he could never deal with those personalities again, but conceded it was necessary at the time to keep the band moving, even when everyone was in each other's faces.

> I KNEW THERE WAS SOME SQUABBLING—I MEAN, IT WAS OBVIOUS. BUT I DID NOT KNOW HOW TRULY SERIOUS IT WAS. TO ME, ALL BANDS FOUGHT. ANOTHER DAY IN THE OFFICE IN ROCK 'N' ROLL. I DIDN'T KNOW HOW HEAVY THE ISSUES WERE.
>
> — TIMOTHY B. SCHMIT

"You knew it when you were in a room with the Eagles," Frey continued. "There was a certain intensity. Perhaps a lot of it was all bluff because we were really just a bunch of skinny little guys with long hair and patched pants and turquoise. I was never tough, but I sure was mad. I think I was more for entertainment, and I think Henley was more for trying to get more out of your entertainment dollar. But underneath it all, we were best friends. We talked every day for seven or eight years. Every day, like roommates. Splitting up the Eagles, though, was not because of some rift between Henley and me. There was a rift and that didn't help, but we had come to a point where we were running out of gas artistically. We had gone from being a band that could make an album in three weeks to a band that couldn't finish an album in three years.

"In some ways, the success took a lot of the fun out of it. Putting pressure on ourselves also took a lot of the fun out of it. I think Henley took some of the fun out of it for me, and I'm sure I took some of the fun out of it for him. Looking back, I think the band lasted a couple of more years than I thought it would."

The band's fractious relationships made the group overly serious, Frey said. The tensions between Henley and Frey, Frey and Felder, Henley and Walsh, and so on, were a byproduct of finding the right blend of talent, even if the personalities did not quite mesh.

"I really felt that when it came to getting people to play with," Frey told Smith, "you didn't go around picking the nice guys, you found the guys who could play blues and rock and roll, the guys who could take the Eagles up from a country-rock band to a serious stadium filler. And it took the combined guitar talents of Joe Walsh and Don Felder to help us achieve that.

> ## UNDERNEATH IT ALL WE WERE BEST FRIENDS... SPLITTING UP THE EAGLES, THOUGH WAS NOT BECAUSE OF SOME RIFT BETWEEN HENLEY AND ME. THERE WAS A RIFT AND THAT DIDN'T HELP, BUT WE HAD COME TO A POINT WHERE WE WERE RUNNING OUT OF GAS ARTISTICALLY.
>
> — GLENN FREY

"The Eagles had its best chemistry when Don Felder and Joe Walsh were both in the band at the same time. Don and Joe were both tremendously gifted guitar players. Walsh is like an almanac. I could sit down at a piano at any given moment and play every song **The Drifters** ever recorded. But Joe can do the same thing with **Jimi Hendrix**, **Jimmy Page**, and **Eric Clapton**. I mean every single blues lick.

"But it was rare when everyone in the band got along. We used to joke around and say we're like the Oakland A's—as long as we got along on the field, it didn't matter what happened behind closed doors."

That Oakland A's analogy held true for a while, but those tensions eventually caught up with the band.

Frey told Smith that someone once asked **Bob Seger** why the Eagles broke up. "He answered them in two words," Frey said. "'Hotel California,' because it was impossible to top. For me, it ended in Long Beach, California at a benefit for **Alan Cranston**. That's when I knew I had to get out."

Years later, in an interview with the Associated Press, a more relaxed Frey conceded that the band just grew tired of each other.

"That's the way it played out," he said. "The Eagles became such a burden. I think Don and I just sort of succumbed to the weight that we felt after *Hotel California* went through the roof. You know, it could have ended there. Instead, for us, we were able to, as Don said, have a second act."

That second act would begin 13 years later, after each band member set out on solo careers with varying levels of success. Azoff was instrumental in bringing them back together in late 1993. But he had a few things of his own to accomplish first. [1437, 1644, 1645, 1876, 1877, 1880, 2136]

HELL FREEZES OVER
Isolation, Solos, and Reunification

The Eagles' nine-year evolution from happy-to-be-here rock and rollers to studio perfectionists was both rewarding and exhausting. They made great music together and challenged themselves to make each successive album better than the previous one. They almost succeeded. The legacy of music created during those nine years would make most any rock band proud, including two of the three biggest-selling albums in U.S. history: *Their Greatest Hits (1971-1975)* and *Hotel California*, which are #1 and #3, respectively.

The quality standards the Eagles adhered to produced incredibly creative work, but it was also personally destructive. Near constant touring, label pressure, and infighting created a toxic environment. They were not friends anymore. They did not want to be around each other anymore. The group finally called it quits in fall 1980. For most bands, that would be the end. The breakup ended with acrimony and hard feelings, but their creative instincts were still alive and well. Don Henley, Glenn Frey, Don Felder, Joe Walsh, and Timothy B. Schmit went their separate ways, each launching a solo career with varying degrees of success.

Glenn Frey and Don Henley enjoyed the most individual success, scoring several solo Top 10 hits in the 1980s and 1990s. Henley earned two Grammys and ten nominations by 1993, and collected two MTV Video Music Awards. Frey earned two Grammy nominations and one MTV Video Music Award. Felder, Walsh, and Randy Meisner each had strong solo moments as well. And Walsh, Bernie Leadon, and Schmit became some of the most sought-after session musicians in the business.

A new trend on radio—classic rock—kept the Eagles brand alive. These were not your typical oldies stations that spun singles by first-generation rock 'n' rollers like **Elvis**, **Little Richard**, and **Eddie Cochran**, or post-**Buddy Holly** teen idols like **Bobby Rydell** and **Fabian** deep into the night. By the 1980s, programmers and deejays had a couple decades of classic rock to choose from and an audience eager to consume it—and the Eagles were big players in it. "Hotel California," "Take It Easy," "One of These Nights," and many others were on heavy rotation at these stations years after the Eagles' breakup. And then country music helped bring the Eagles full circle.

While the band made considerable effort to shed their country-rock label throughout the years, the country music community liked it just fine. Eagles manager Irving Azoff helped organize *Common Thread: The Songs of the Eagles*, an album of Eagles covers featuring an array of country music stars. And when **Travis Tritt** reached out to the Eagles to join him in December 1993 on the video shoot for his cover of "Take It Easy," it started something. Whenever Henley was asked about when the Eagles would reunite, his patented answer was: "When hell freezes over." Tritt's request started the thaw, but Azoff lit the match. The final book in this trilogy, *Eagles: Hell Freezes Over*, will follow the band's post-breakup isolation, their solo careers, and their unexpected reunion. ■

INDEX

BIBLIOGRAPHY

[1] King, T. (2000). *The Operator*, New York, NY: Broadway Books.

[2] Holson, L.M. (Feb. 20, 2016). "The Boy from Brooklyn: David Geffen Comes Home, With Cash to Spare," *New York Times*.

[3] Singular, S. (1997). *The Rise and Rise of David Geffen*, Secaucus, NJ: Birch Lane Press.

[4] Rudman, K. (Jun. 10, 1972). "A Letter from David Geffen," *Record World*, 27(1303), p. 16.

[5] Geddy, P.A. (Oct. 28, 2015). "Don Henley: Return to Cass County," *County Line Magazine*.

[6] Eliot, M. (2005). *To the Limit: The Untold Story of the Eagles*, Cambridge, MA: Da Capo Press.

[7] Varga, J. (May 4, 1970). "Fact or Fiction? With Joe Walsh, You Never Know," *San Diego Union Tribune*.

[8] Associated Press (May 28, 1970). "Festival Will Go on Despite Ban by Court," *Alton (Ill.) Evening Telegraph*.

[9] Magnotta, A. (Aug. 17, 2018). "State Shooting," *iHeartRadio*.

[10] Recording Industry Association of America, *Eagles: Eagles*, (Jun. 1, 1972).

[11] Gibson, J. (May 5, 1972). "The Coast," *Record World*, 26(1298), p. 14.

[12] Rudman, K. (May 13, 1972). "Money Music," *Record World*, 26(1299), p. 18.

[13] Rudman, K. (May 27, 1972). "Money Music," *Record World*, 27(1301), p. 18.

[14] *Record World*. (Jun. 17, 1972). "Hits of the Week," 27(1304), p. 1.

[15] Browne, D. (Jun. 10, 2016). "Eagles Complete Discography: Don Henley Looks Back," *Rolling Stone*.

[16] Recording Industry Association of America, *Eagles: Desperado*, (Apr. 17, 1973).

[17] Recording Industry Association of America, *Eagles: On the Border*, (Jan. 22, 1974).

[18] Recording Industry Association of America, *Eagles: On the Border*, (Mar. 22, 1974).

[19] Johns, G. (2014). *Glyn Johns: Sound Man*, New York, NY: Plume/Penguin-Random House.

[20] Clemons, J. (Jul. 2, 1972). "You Can't Ignore Eagles Album," *Salina (Kan.) Journal*.

[21] *The Atlanta Constitution*. (Feb. 8, 1988). "Singer Walsh Wants Kent State Memorial," *The Atlanta Constitution*.

[22] *The Central New Jersey Home News*. (Apr. 24, 1990). "Kent State Memorial Shrouded in Controversy," *The Central New Jersey Home News*.

[23] *Wisconsin State Journal*. (Apr. 28, 1990). "Kent State Memorial to Add Victims' Names," *Wisconsin State Journal*.

[24] Valentine, P. (Feb. 5, 1972). "David Geffen: David's Talented Asylum," *Sounds*.

[25] Dr. Rock & Roll Blog, Prufer, J. (Dec. 29, 2014). Joe Walsh's Measles on the Kent State Commons Back in 1966, DrRockandroll.blogspot.com. Retrieved from http://drrockandroll.blogspot.com/2014/10/joe-walshs-measles-on-kent-state.html.

[26] *The Marshall (Texas) News Messenger*. (Mar. 21, 1971). "Shiloh Record Released."

[27] *The Marshall (Texas) News Messenger*. (Jun. 16, 1971). "Group to Perform on National TV."

[28] Duncan, Z. (Oct. 20, 1979). "Blue Steel Plotting Fun Rock Revolution," *The Indianapolis News*.

[29] Oermann, R. (Sep. 28, 1983). "'New Kid in Town' Is Jim Ed Norman," *The Tennessean*.

[30] McCollum, B. (Feb. 19, 2016). "Glenn Frey Remembered in Sign Ceremony in Royal Oak," *Detroit Free Press*.

[31] Seger, B. (1978). Album Credits/Liner Notes: *Stranger in Town*.

[32] Marsh, D. (May 15, 1980). "Bob Seger's 'Wind' Is Mostly Hot Air," *Rolling Stone*.

[33] Hurst, J. (Feb. 26, 1984). "When These Two Country Writers Finally Met, Something Funny Started," *Chicago Tribune*.

[34] Nicks, S. (1981). Album Credits/Liner Notes: *Bella Donna*.

[35] Taylor, J. (1976). Album Credits/Liner Notes: *Sweet Baby James*.

[36] Holloway, D. (Mar. 10, 1973). "The Eagles: Takin' It Easy," *New Musical Express*.

[37] Walker, J. (Jun. 1, 1973). "Tom Waits: Thursday Afternoon, Sober as a Judge," *Music World*.

[38] Rensin, D. (Jan. 1, 1974). "Jackson Browne: Such a Clever Innocence," *Crawdaddy*.

[39] Crowe, C. (May 18, 1975). "America Starts to Rediscover Itself," *Los Angeles Times*.

[40] Soeder, J. (Mar. 18, 2009). "With Eagles Ready to Land at the Q, Don Henley Sounds Off on the Band's New Album, Musicians' Rights and Misinterpreted Lyrics," *The Cleveland Plain Dealer*.

[41] Charlesworth, C. (Dec. 11, 1976). "Eagles: Where Eagles Dare," *Melody Maker*.

[42] Poet, J. (Jun. 7, 1974). "Sarah Kernochan: *House of Pain*; Tom Waits: *Closing Time*; Eagles: *On the Border*," *Berkeley Barb*.

[43] Burgess, S. (Jan. 1, 1977). "Echoes: An Interview with Gene Clark," *Dark Star*.

[44] Charone, B. (Jan. 8, 1977). "The Eagles: Life in the Fast Lane," *Sounds*.

[45] Silverton, P. (May 14, 1977). "Frankie Miller: Be Good to Yourself," *Sounds*.

[46] Gans, D. (Jan. 1, 1980). "The Eagles' Don Felder: A Short Run to the Top," *Axe Magazine*.

[47] Thomas, M. (1981). Album Credits/Liner Notes: *Alive Alone*.

[48] Zimmer, D. (Nov. 7, 1980). "Randy Meisner: Ex-Eagle Flies High Solo," *BAM*.

[49] Meisner, R. (1980). Album Credits/Liner Notes: *One More Song*.

[50] Seger, B. (1969). Album Credits/Liner Notes: *Ramblin' Gamblin' Man*.

[51] Seger, B. (1980). Album Credits/Liner Notes: *Against the Wind*.

[52] Seger, B. (1982). Album Credits/Liner Notes: *The Distance*.

[53] Seger, B. (1986). Album Credits/Liner Notes: *Like a Rock*.

[54] Seger, B. (1991). Album Credits/Liner Notes: *The Fire Inside*.

[55] Ronstadt, L. (1972). Album Credits/Liner Notes: *Linda Ronstadt*.

[56] Ronstadt, L. (1973). Album Credits/Liner Notes: *Don't Cry Now*.

[57] Ronstadt, L. (1974). Album Credits/Liner Notes: *Heart Like a Wheel*.

[58] Ronstadt, L. (1976). Album Credits/Liner Notes: *Hasten Down the Wind*.

[59] Ronstadt, L. (1977). Album Credits/Liner Notes: *Simple Dreams*.

[60] Ronstadt, L. (1998). Album Credits/Liner Notes: *We Ran*.

[61] Smyth, P. (1992). Album Credits/Liner Notes: *Patty Smyth*.

[62] Nicks, S. (1983). Album Credits/Liner Notes: *The Wild Heart*.

[63] Nicks, S. (1994). Album Credits/Liner Notes: *Street Angel*.

[64] Nelson, R. (1971). Album Credits/Liner Notes: *Rudy the Fifth*.

[65] Nelson, R. (1970). Album Credits/Liner Notes: *In Concert at the Troubadour, 1969*.

[66] Rensin, D. (Jul. 1, 1974). "The Eagles Have Stopped Takin' It Easy," *Crawdaddy*.

[67] Charone, B. (Jan. 1, 1975). "The Eagles," *Hit Parader*.

[68] Rensin, D. (Jan. 2, 1975). "Tom Rush's Circle: Joni, James & Cows," *Rolling Stone*.

[69] Rensin, D. (Mar. 13, 1975). "Dan Fogelberg: Home Free at Last," *Rolling Stone*.

[70] Fogelberg, D. (1974). Album Credits/Liner Notes: *Souvenirs*.

[71] Fogelberg, D. (1977). Album Credits/Liner Notes: *Nether Lands*.

[72] Fogelberg, D. (1981). Album Credits/Liner Notes: *The Innocent Age*.

[73] Fogelberg, D. (1984). Album Credits/Liner Notes: *Windows and Walls*.

[74] Fogelberg, D. (1990). Album Credits/Liner Notes: *The Wild Places*.

[75] Scoppa, B. (Jun. 1, 1975). "The Eagles: *One of These Nights*," *Phonograph Record*.

[76] Rosen, S. (Dec. 1, 1975). "Fishing with the Eagles for the Universal Trout," *Circus Raves*.

[77] Charone, B. (Mar. 27, 1976). "The Eagles: Desperados in Blue Jeans and Sneakers," *Sounds*.

[78] Gilbert, J. (Oct. 1, 1972). "Flying Burrito Brothers: After the Burritos," *Let It Rock*.

[79] Gilbert, J. (Mar. 10, 1973). "Eagles Make it Easy," *Sounds*.

[80] Tobler, J. (May 1, 1973). "Jac Holzman: Then and Now," *ZigZag*.

[81] Charlesworth, C. (Apr. 12, 1975). "The Eagles: Eagle Eyed," *Melody Maker*.

[82] Uhelszki, J. (Jun. 1, 1975). "Joe Walsh: Lonely in the Spotlight," *Creem*.

[83] Nolan, T. (Jun. 1, 1975). "The Eagles: California Dreamin'," *Phonograph Record*.

[84] Case, B. (Jul. 26, 1975). "Billy Cobham: When This Man Plays Drums, He Thinks of a Box Trying to Roll," *New Musical Express*.

[85] Gambaccini, P. (Jul. 31, 1975). "Elton & Company Seduce Wembley," *Rolling Stone*.

[86] Gambaccini, P. (Aug. 28, 1975). "Eagles Fly High with Disco 'Nights,'" *Rolling Stone*.

[87] Goldstein, P. (1993). *The Rolling Stone Interviews*, pp. 333-341, New York, NY: Back Bay Books/Little, Brown & Co.

[88] Crowe, C. (Sep. 25, 1975). "Eagles: Chips Off the Old Buffalo," *Rolling Stone*.

[89] Rosen, S. (Sep. 27, 1975). "Eagles: The Earthpeople's Band," *Sounds*.

[90] Partridge, R. (Nov. 1, 1975). "Tanya Tucker: Country Girl," *Melody Maker*.

[91] Woffinden, B. (Jan. 10, 1976). "A Cat Stevens Spiritual Tours Vacation," *New Musical Express*.

[92] Brown, M. (Jan. 24, 1976). "The Soulful Return of Gene Clark," *Sounds*.

[93] Brown, M. (Feb. 21, 1976). "You Don't Buck the Rules on the Bus: Buck Owens," *Street Life*.

[94] Charone, B. (Feb. 28, 1976). "*Eagles: Their Greatest Hits 1971-1975* (Asylum)," *Sounds*.

[95] Uhelszki, J. (Mar. 1, 1976). "Lynyrd Skynyrd: Fifths and Fists for the Common Man," *Creem*.

[96] Charone, B. (Mar. 6, 1976). "Bill Wyman: Lone Stone," *Sounds*.

[97] Bell, M. (May 8, 1976). "Steely Dan: *The Royal Scam*," *New Musical Express*.

[98] Charlesworth, C. (May 15, 1976). "Boz Scaggs: Scaggs in Silk," *Melody Maker*.

[99] Deller, F. (Jun. 5, 1976). "Tom Waits: Would You Say This Man Was Attempting to Convey an Impression of Sordid Bohemianism?" *New Musical Express*.

[100] Brown, M. (Jun. 12, 1976). "Tom Waits: Warm Beer, Cold Women," *Sounds*.

[101] Connolly, K. (Jul. 1, 2013). "Richard Thompson," *BOMB*.

[102] Charone, B. (Sep. 4, 1976). "Linda Ronstadt: *Hand Sewn*[sic] *Home Grown*," *Sounds*.

[103] Bangs, L. (Oct. 1, 1976). "How the Eagles Cleaned Up the Wild West," *Music Gig*.

[104] Goldman, V. (Oct. 30, 1976). "Fleetwood Mac: John and Christine and Stevie and Lindsay and Mick...," *Sounds*.

[105] Cohen, M. (Nov. 1, 1976). "Jackson Browne, Winning," *Phonograph Record*.

[106] Farren, M. (Nov. 13, 1976). "Nashville," *New Musical Express*.

[107] Charone, B. (Nov. 20, 1976). "Linda Ronstadt: Hey, Mister That's Me Up on the Jukebox," *Sounds*.

[108] Kent, N. (Dec. 18, 1976). "The Eagles: *Hotel California* (Asylum)," *New Musical Express*.

[109] Hancock, D. (Feb. 5, 1977). "Eagles Get the Bird," *National RockStar*.

[110] Demorest, S. (Mar. 17, 1977). "The Eagles: *Hotel California* (Asylum)," *Circus*.

[111] Whitall, S. (May 1, 1977). "Rock Stars Talk Back," *Creem*.

[112] Shapiro, S. (May 14, 1977). "Bob Seger: Rock 'n' Roll's Mr. Nice Guy," *Sounds*.

[113] Cromelin, R. (Jun. 1, 1977). "Steely Dan: Excerpts from a Teenage Opera," *Phonograph Record*.

[114] Makowski, P. (Jun. 25, 1977). "There'll Always Be a Rainbow as Long as Ritchie's Here," *Sounds*.

[115] Morthland, J. (Jul. 1, 1977). "Bob Seger Conquers the World (And About Time!),"

[116] Snowden, D. (Jul. 12, 1977). "Little Feat: The Rock and Roll Doctors," *Rock Around the World*.

[117] Bell, M. (Jan. 14, 1978). "Boz Scaggs: Portrait of the Image as a Reality," *New Musical Express*.

[118] Swenson, J. (Oct. 5, 1978). "REO Speedwagon Makes Its Own Way," *Rolling Stone*.

[119] Robins, W. (Dec. 10, 1978). "Steely Dan's Greatest-Hits & Quips," *Los Angeles Times*.

[120] Leviton, M. (Mar. 2, 1979). "McGuinn Clark and Hillman: Flight from the Past," *BAM*.

[121] Bell, M. (May 19, 1979). "J. Geils Band: Return of the Hard-Drivin' Man," *New Musical Express*.

[122] Williams, M. (Sep. 29, 1979). "The Eagles: *The Long Run* (Asylum),"

[123] Kent, N. (Sep. 29, 1979). "The Eagles: *The Long Run* (Asylum)," *New Musical Express*.

[124] Aronowitz, A. (Nov. 14, 1979). "Fleetwood Mac's *Tusk* and the Eagles' *The Long Run*," *Washington Post*.

[125] Rambali, P. (Dec. 8, 1979). "Standing Up for the Small Man,"

[126] Zimmer, D. (Feb. 1, 1980). "Graham Nash: The Winds of Change," *BAM*.

[127] Leviton, M. (Mar. 7, 1980). "More Hot Burritos: The Flying Burrito Brothers," *BAM*.

[128] Robertson, S. (Mar. 15, 1980). "Warren Zevon: Bad Luck Streak in Dancing School (Asylum) And Wanted Dead or Alive (Pickwick)," *Sounds*.

[129] Bell, M. (Mar. 15, 1980). "Call Tom Petty the New Springsteen and He'll Cut You!" *New Musical Express*.

[130] Cooper, M. (Mar. 22, 1980). "The Eagles: Oakland Coliseum," *Record Mirror*.

[131] Marsh, D. (Jun. 1, 1980). "Father-Figure Knows Best: Rock Managers from Elvis to Elvis," *Trouser Press*.

[132] Tobler, J. (Jan. 1, 1982). "Bill Szymczyk," *The Record Producers*.

[133] Tobler, J. (Jan. 1, 1982). "Glyn Johns," *The Record Producers*.

[134] Rensin, D. (Jul. 1, 1982). "20 Questions: Stevie Nicks," *Playboy*.

[135] Tobler, J. (1983). *The Guitar Greats - The 1982 BBC Interviews*, Buckinghamshire, UK: Northdown Publishing Ltd.

[136] Zimmer, D. (Mar. 1, 1983). "Danny Kortchmar: The Stand-up Rocker," *Record*.

[137] Holdship, B. (May 1, 1983). "Bob Seger: Big Victories," *Creem*.

[138] Cook, R. (Feb. 23, 1985). "Don Henley," *New Musical Express*.

[139] Tannenbaum, R. (Oct. 1, 1985). "Pino Palladino Doesn't Fret," *Musician*.

[140] Scoppa, B. (Jan. 1, 1986). "Don Henley in Conversation," *Record*.

[141] Simmons, S. (Oct. 1, 1986). "I Confronted Metallica on Their Own Terms!" *Creem*.

[142] Sweeting, A. (Oct. 1, 1987). "The Jesus & Mary Chain: Ah, Showbusiness..," *Q*.

[143] Rowland, M. (Dec. 1, 1988). "If Guns N' Roses Are Outlawed, Only Outlaws Will Have Guns N' Roses," *Musician*.

[144] Zimmer, D. (Dec. 2, 1988). "The Desert Rose Band: Chris Hillman's Hot Burrito #3," *BAM*.

[145] Walker, C. (Jan. 1, 1990). "Guy Clark: Cold Dog Soup, Steve Young: Primal Young, Conway Savage: Nothing Broken, Bap Kennedy: Lonely Street," *HQ*.

[146] Maconie, S. (Feb. 2, 1991). "Motorhead: Don't Lemmy Be Misunderstood," *New Musical Express*.

[147] Tannenbaum, R. (Apr. 16, 1992). "Country's New Gold Rush," *Rolling Stone*.

[148] Bradley, L. (Jul. 2, 1992). "Glenn Frey: Life After the Eagles," *Independent*.

[149] DeCurtis, A. (Apr. 1, 1993). "Garth Brooks: Ropin' The Wind," *Rolling Stone*.

[150] Simmons, S. (Jan. 1, 1994). "Sheryl Crow," *Rolling Stone*.

[151] Eggar, R. (Jan. 23, 1994). "Garth Brooks," *The Sunday Times*.

[152] DiMartino, D. (Aug. 1, 1994). "The Eagles: Irvine Meadows Amphitheatre, California," *MOJO*.

[153] Hoskyns, B. (Sep. 1, 1994). "Neil Young: A Conversation with Elliot Roberts," *MOJO*.

[154] Wheeler, S.P. (Sep. 1, 1994). "Bob Seger: Turning the Page," *Music Connection*.

[155] DeYoung, B. (Jan. 6, 1995). "Willie Nelson: Funny How Time Slips Away," *Goldmine*.

[156] Selvin, J. (Mar. 19, 1995). "Ronstadt Proves She Can Go Home Again," *San Francisco Chronicle*.

[157] Weizmann, D. (Apr. 7, 1995). "Techno Queen of Melrose Place: Traci Lords," *Los Angeles Reader*.

[158] Roeser, S. (Aug. 18, 1995). "Warren Zevon: Left Jabs and Roundhouse Rights," *Goldmine*.

[159] Hutton, J. (Jan. 1, 1996). "L.A. Confidential: Life in the Fast Lane with Redd Kross's Jeffrey & Steven McDonald," *Bucketful of Brains*.

[160] Hibbert, T. (Aug. 1, 1996). "'We're the F***in' Eagles. Kiss My Ass!'," *Q*.

[161] Associated Press (Mar. 21, 1980). "'Desperate Trucker' Frees Hostage for a Song," *Fort Myers News-Press*.

[162] Hoskyns, B. (Dec. 1, 1996). "Ed Sanders and the Fugs," *MOJO*.

[163] Zolo, P. (Jan. 1, 1997). "Portrait - The Music of Dan Fogelberg from 1972-1997," *Columbia Legacy*.

[164] Black, J. (Jan. 1, 1997). "The Troubadour Club: A History," *Troubadour*.

[165] Simmons, S. (Jul. 1, 1997). "Crazy Horse: Ralph, Billy, Poncho.. And Neil," *MOJO*.

[166] DiMartino, D. (Sep. 1, 1997). "Fleetwood Mac: The Way We Were," *MOJO*.

[167] Kruger, D. (Jun. 17, 1998). "The Linda Ronstadt Interview," *DebbieKruger.com*.

[168] Hoskyns, B. (Jul. 1, 1998). "Gram Parsons: The Good Ol' Boy," *MOJO*.

[169] Himmelsbach, E. (Jul. 12, 1998). "Brian Wilson: The Last Brother," *Los Angeles Times*.

[170] O'Hagan, S. (Sep. 12, 1998). "Gram Parsons: Another Country," *Guardian*.

[171] Kruger, D. (Oct. 9, 1998). "J D Souther," *Goldmine*.

[172] Lynskey, D. (Nov. 1, 1998). "Pras: Playa for Today," *Face*.

[173] Hoskyns, B. (Apr. 1, 1999). "What's He Building in There? An Interview with Tom Waits," *MOJO*.

[174] George-Warren, H. (Jul. 1, 1999). "The Long Way Around: Gram Parsons," *No Depression*.

[175] Cameron, K. (Sep. 11, 1999). "Leftfield: \"We Waited. That's What We Did.\"," *New Musical Express*.

[176] Himmelsbach, E. (Mar. 3, 2000). "Sons of the Pioneers: Beachwood Sparks," *LA Weekly*.

[177] George-Warren, H. (Jul. 15, 2000). "Southern Gallery: Tom Petty," *Oxford American*.

[178] Hardy, P. (2001). *The Faber Companion to 20th Century Popular Music: The Eagles*, London, UK: Faber & Faber.

[179] Hoskyns, B. (Jan. 1, 2001). "Hotel Roberto," *Rock's Backpages*.

[180] Hoskyns, B. (Jan. 26, 2001). "Almost Infamous," *Rock's Backpages*.

[181] Bennettt, M. (Aug. 19, 1972). "A Fine Singing Band, But Elusive," *The Brandon (Manitoba, Canada) Sun*.

[182] Weller, D. (May 24, 1973). "Eagles Soar Into Diversity," *Honolulu Star-Bulletin*.

[183] Hilburn, R. (Apr. 14, 1974). "The Eagles: Hatched in a Barroom," *Los Angeles Times*.

[184] Garfield, K. (Jun. 2, 1974). "Eagles Waiting to Fly Higher," *The (Nashville) Tennessean*.

[185] McDonough, J. (Jul. 29, 1973). "Eagles with a Tale of Young Man in the West," *San Francisco Examiner*.

[186] Isenberg, B. (Jun. 27, 1976). "Putting Stars in Their Places," *Los Angeles Times*.

[187] Arar, Y. (Dec. 24, 1980). "Randy Meisner: A Former Eagle Wings it Alone," *Washington (Pa.) Observer-Reporter*.

[188] Martin, G. (Jan. 1, 2003). "Rings Around Cardiff: Super Furry Animals," *Daily Mirror*.

[189] Mack, J. (1982). Album Credits/Liner Notes: *Jack Mack and the Heart Attack: Cardiac Party*.

[190] Campbell, M. (Aug. 2, 1988). "Little River Band is Back and Has Shorrock Singing," *Fon Du Lac Commonwealth Reporter*.

[191] Campbell, M. (Aug. 25, 1988). "Little River Band Hopes Eagle Combination Flies," *Richmond (Ind.) Palladium-Item*.

[192] *Waterloo (Iowa) Courier*. (Jul. 24, 1988). "Little River Band Back with Shorrock."

[193] Footman, T. (Nov. 1, 2003). "Gathering Moss: The Fossilisation of *Rolling Stone*," *Rock's Backpages*.

[194] Sutcliffe, P. (Dec. 1, 2003). "Fleetwood Mac: Take it to the Limit," *MOJO*.

[195] Willman, C. (Oct. 11, 2018). "Lindsey Buckingham's Fleetwood Mac Attack: 21 Things We Learned from His Lawsuit," *Variety*.

[196] Wood, M. (Jul. 17, 2017). "Why I Felt Betrayed by Fleetwood Mac at Classic West," *Los Angeles Times*.

[197] Wood, M. (Jul. 16, 2017). "The Eagles Fly Again at the Classic West," *Los Angeles Times*.

[198] Gans, D. (Sep. 1, 1982). "Fleetwood Mac: Where's Stevie?" *The Record*.

[199] Reckard, E.S. (Sep. 5, 1989). "Azoff Quits As Chairman of MCA's Music Unit," *Washington Post*.

[200] Grein, P. (May 7, 1983). "Azoff Looking Beyond Records," *Billboard*.

[201] *Billboard*. (Jan. 25, 2018). "No. 4: Irving Azoff | Power 100," *Billboard*.

[202] *Billboard*. (Jun. 17, 1972). "Eagles - Asylum SD 5054 (Atlantic)," *Billboard*.

[203] *Billboard*. (Jul. 1, 1972). "Hot Chart Action," *Billboard*.

[204] Freedland, N. (Jul. 8, 1972). "Two Neophyte Labels Compare Early Notes," *Billboard*.

[205] *Billboard*. (Jul. 22, 1972). "Young Bloods Lend Zest to Management, Agency Fields," *Billboard*.

[206] *Billboard*. (Jul. 22, 1972). "Being Involved with the Music is the Key to Running a Successful Night Club," *Billboard*.

[207] Greene, A. (Feb. 7, 2013). "Flashback: All the Eagles Unite for Rock and Roll Hall of Fame Induction," *Rolling Stone*.

[208] *K-SHE-95 - Real Rock Radio*. (Jun. 6, 2016). "Don Henley Reveals the Inspiration to 'Witchy Woman'."

[209] TheUncool.com, Crowe, C. (Aug. 1, 2003). Eagles: Very Best Of - Conversations with Don Henley and Glenn Frey, Retrieved from http://www.theuncool.com/journalism/the-very-best-of-the-eagles/.

[210] Ragland, J. (Aug. 24, 2000). "Channel Island Now is Public Property," *Los Angeles Times*.

[211] Eagles. (2003). Album Credits/Liner Notes: *The Very Best Of*.

[212] Kuntzman, G. (Jan. 19, 2016). "Glenn Frey's Death is Sad, But the Eagles Were a Horrific Band," *New York Daily News*.

[213] Christgau, R. (Jun. 1, 1972). "Trying to Understand the Eagles," *Newsday*.

[214] Klosterman, C. (2013). *I Wear the Black Hat: Grappling with Villains (Real and Imagined)*, New York, NY: Scribner.

[215] Deusner, S. (Aug. 9, 2013). "Quit Defending the Eagles! They're Simply Terrible," *Salon*.

[216] Willman, C. (Jan. 20, 2016). "Why Are the Eagles So Hated? An Explainer on the Immensely Popular Yet Divisive Rock Band," *Billboard*.

[217] Fanelli, D. (Sep. 21, 2017). "Don Felder Talks Eagles Gear, 'Hotel California' And His Slide Guitar Influences," *Guitar World*.

[218] Felder, D. (2008). *Heaven and Hell: My Life In The Eagles (1974-2001)*, Hoboken, NJ: John Wiley & Sons.

[220] MLive.com, Liberty, J. (Sep. 7, 2014). Kalamazoo DJ to meet the Eagles almost 4 decades after helping band get No. 1 hit, Retrieved from https://www.mlive.com/entertainment/kalamazoo/index.ssf/2014/09/longtime_kalamazoo_dj_to_meet.html.

[221] Localspins.com, Craker, L. (Sep. 9, 2014). The Eagles' energetic encore tops nostalgic night (Review, photo gallery), Retrieved from https://localspins.com/eagles-energetic-encore-tops/.

[222] Interview, Bacher, D. (Oct. 8, 2012). Joe Walsh's Long Run, Retrieved from https://www.interviewmagazine.com/music/joe-walsh-analog-man.

[223] Clary, M. (May 4, 1975). "The Return of Joe Walsh," *Akron (Ohio) Beacon Journal*.

[224] Taylor, C. (Oct. 24, 2010). "Emma's Fountain Lives Long After Rock 'n' Roll Tragedy," *Boulder (Colo.) Daily Camera*.

[225] Bienstock, R. (May 19, 2016). "Joe Walsh: My Life in 15 Songs," *Rolling Stone*.

[226] Kiefer, P. (Nov. 1, 2018). "Irving Azoff, Hollywood a-Listers Team to Save Legendary Deli Nate 'n Al," *The Hollywood Reporter*.

[227] Aswad, J. (Jul. 10, 2018). "Mega-Manager Irving Azoff Grows Business with Diverse Portfolio," *Variety*.

[228] Carson, C. (Aug. 13, 1977). "Friends Together for 'Progressions'," *Binghamton (N.Y.) Press and Sun-Bulletin*.

[229] GainesvilleRockHistory.com, Laughton, T. (Aug. 1, 2016). Tom Laughton - The Maudy Quintet, Retrieved from http://www.gainesvillerockhistory.com/MaundyQuintet.htm.

[230] George-Warren, H. (Jul. 15, 2000). "Southern Gallery: Tom Petty," *Oxford American*.

[231] Einarson, J. (2001). *Desperados: The Roots of Country Rock*, New York, NY: Cooper Square Press.

[232] Gullbuy Music Review (Mar. 25, 2003). Hearts and Flow-

ers, Gullbuy Music Review. Retrieved from http://gullbuy.com/buy/2003/3_25/heartsflo.php.

[233] Lewis, R. (Jul. 17, 2015). "Disneyland at 60: Five Great Musical Moments at the Magic Kingdom," *Los Angeles Times*.

[234] Broeske, P. (Feb. 12, 1989). "A 'Wiseguy' Who's Really a Regular Guy : TV's Ken Wahl, A Star Who Shuns the Star Label, Relishes His Real-Life Role As an 'Anti-Celebrity'," *Los Angeles Times*.

[235] Oermann, R.K. (Sep. 15, 1985). "Fabulous McGuire Sisters Revive Sweet Trio Harmony," *The (Nashville) Tennessean*.

[236] Lewis, R. (Jan. 19, 2016). "Linda Ronstadt, Whose Backing Band Was the Hub for the Eagles, Remembers Glenn Frey," *Los Angeles Times*.

[237] The Madison Square Garden Company. (Oct. 8, 2018). "Azoff Music Management Reaches Agreement to Acquire the Madison Square Garden Company's 50 Percent Interest," The Madison Square Garden Company.

[238] Green, S. (Sep. 11, 2013). "Irving Azoff Teams Up Again with James Dolan at the Madison Square Garden," *Jewish Business News*.

[239] Aswad, J. (Oct. 8, 2018). "Azoff Management to Buy Out MSG's Interest in Azoff-MSG Entertainment for $125 Million," *Variety*.

[240] Begley, S. (Mar. 7, 2016). "Eagles Co-Founder's Wife Lana Ray Meisner Dies in Accidental Shooting," *Time*.

[241] Walker, T. (Mar. 7, 2016). "Eagles Founder Randy Meisner's Wife Lana Rae Meisner Dies at Couple's Home After Accidental Gunshot to the Head," *Independent*.

[242] Smith, E. (Jan. 1, 2013). "Live Nation Chairman Azoff Resigns," *Wall Street Journal*.

[243] Live Nation Entertainment. (Dec. 31, 2012). "Irving Azoff Resigns As Live Nation Entertainment Chairman and Front Line CEO," Live Nation Entertainment.

[244] Ellis, R. (Nov. 10, 2018). "California Wildfire Burns Film Set Used in HBO's 'Westworld,' Other TV Shows and Movies," *CNN*.

[245] Cacciola, S. (Mar. 24, 2014). "The Man in the Middle," *New York Times*.

[246] Smith, E. (Feb. 21, 2009). "Can He Save Rock 'n' Roll?" *Wall Street Journal*.

[247] Hoskyns, B. (2006). *Hotel California*, Hoboken, NJ: John Wiley & Sons.

[248] Reid, G. (Feb. 25, 2006). "Stevie Nicks," *New Zealand Herald*.

[249] Sutcliffe, P. (Jan. 1, 2006). "David Gilmour: And This is Me..," *MOJO*.

[250] Cameron, K. (Apr. 1, 2007). "The Stooges: Return to the Fun House," *MOJO*.

[251] Brown, M. (Sep. 8, 2007). "Stevie Nicks: A Survivor's Story," *Telegraph Magazine*.

[252] Simmons, S. (May 1, 2008). "The Q Interview: Stevie Nicks," *Q*.

[253] Snow, M. (Oct. 1, 2009). "Tom Petty," *MOJO*.

[254] Fogerty, J. (2009). Album Credits/Liner Notes: *The Blue Ridge Rangers Ride Again*.

[255] Hoskyns, B. (Mar. 1, 2013). "Heartaches and Hangovers: Gram Parsons' GP," *MOJO*.

[256] Butcher, S. (Feb. 1, 2018). "Boyd Elder is the Most Famous Artist You've Never Heard Of," *Texas Monthly*.

[257] Fauerso, N. (Oct. 8, 2018). "Boyd Elder Dies at 74," *Glassfire*.

[258] Bloch, M. (Sep. 27, 1978). "The West is Won!" *The Palm Beach (Fla.) Post*.

[259] Kruger, D. (Jun. 1, 2013). "The Eagles: Birds of Pray," *Rhythms*.

[260] Sutcliffe, P. (Jun. 1, 2013). "The Eagles: History of the Eagles: The Story of an American Band," *MOJO*.

[261] Martin, G. (Nov. 17, 2014). "Charles Manson and the Death of the Californian Dream," *Sabotage Times*.

[262] Peeples, S.K. (Mar. 1, 1978). "Boyd Elder: Encounters of the Southwestern Kind," *Rocky Mountain Musical Express*.

[263] Hoskyns, B. (Jan. 28, 2016). "Glenn Frey, 1948-2016," *Billboard*.

[264] *San Diego Reader*. (May 10, 2007). "Scottsville Squirrel Barkers," *San Diego Reader*

[265] Patterson, J. (Aug. 16, 1992). "\Common Thread\" Raising Money for Walden Woods," *Indiana (Pa.) Gazette*.

[266] Spevak, J. (Jun. 6, 1993). "Ex-Eagles in Concert: Frey Glided, Walsh Soared," *Rochester (N.Y.) Democrat and Chronicle*.

[267] Graff, G. (Jun. 7, 1993). "2 Old Birds Still Fly," *Detroit Free Press*.

[268] Knight-Ridder News Service. (Jul. 24, 1993). "Musician Segues Into Own TV Series," Knight-Ridder News Service.

[269] Ciliberti, D.F. (Aug. 27, 1993). "\"Glenn Frey Live\" Laces with 1970s Eagles Hits," *Morristown (N.J.) Daily Record*.

[270] Bobbin, J. (Oct. 23, 1993). "Former Eagle Glenn Frey Moves to TV," *Tribune Media Service*.

[271] Goldstein, P. (Sep. 29, 1985). "Frey Continues to Spread His Wings," *Los Angeles Times*.

[272] Vare, E.A. (Dec. 15, 1985). "Musician Frey Enters Filmland," *Hattiesburg (Miss.) American*.

[273] Shriver Jr., J. (May 20, 1990). "New Record Companies Scour the Globe in Hopes of Swinging on a Star," *Los Angeles Times*.

[274] Scapelliti, C. (May 20, 2017). "Did Jethro Tull Inspire the Eagles' \"Hotel California?\"," *Guitar Player*.

[275] Aspden, P. (Apr. 3, 2017). "Why Hotel California Marked a Watershed for Rock," *Financial Times*.

[276] Asgar, R. (Jun. 25, 2014). "Theft by Led Zeppelin and Apple? No, Just Innovation," *Forbes*.

[277] *Billboard*. (Jun. 11, 2001). "Eagles Drop Suit Against Eagle Group," *Billboard*

[278] Reckard, E.S. (Sep. 5, 1989). "Azoff Quits As Chairman of MCA's Music Unit," Associated Press.

[279] *Los Angeles Times*. (Sep. 6, 1989). "Azoff Resigns As Head of MCA Music Unit to Form Own Firm."

[280] Grow, K. (Nov. 15, 2014). "Joe Walsh on His 'Sonic Highways' Appearance: 'I'm an Honorary Foo Fighter'," *Rolling Stone*.

[281] Baltin, S. (May 14, 2014). "Joe Walsh Records with Foo Fighters, Talks Eagles & Blues Album," *Billboard*.

[282] *Chapel Hill (N.C.) Daily Tar Heel*. (Jun. 1, 1978). "Randy Meisner: Randy Meisner," Chapel Hill (N.C.) Daily Tar Heel

[283] Meisner, R. (1978). Album Credits/Liner Notes: *Randy Meisner*.

[284] Meisner, R. (1982). Album Credits/Liner Notes: *Randy Meisner: Randy Meisner*.

[285] Williams, J. (Feb. 22, 1980). "Souther - Co-Founder of California Rock," *The Gaffney (S.C.) Ledger*.

[286] Kishbaugh, J. (Nov. 14, 1980). "Meisner Learns from His Early Mistakes," *Wilkes-Barre (Pa.) Citizens' Voice*.

[287] Arar, Y. (Nov. 27, 1980). "Ex-Eagle's Solo Flight Seems to Be Soaring After Flying the Coop," *Fort Meyers (Fla.) News-Press*.

[288] Kowalski, J. (Aug. 26, 1984). "\"The Allnighter\" By Frey Has \"Flashes\"," *Fon Du Lac (Wis.) Commonwealth Reporter*.

[289] Ferguson, R. (Dec. 22, 1984). "Alone, Timothy B.'s a Crowd," *Mattoon (Ill.) Journal Gazette*.

[290] Hilburn, R. (May 23, 1982). "The Eagles - The Long Run is Over," *Los Angeles Times*.

[291] Jones, P. (Jul. 12, 1975). "British Boxoffice Receipts Sizzling," *Billboard*.

[292] Recording Industry Association of America. (Jul. 12, 1975). *RIAA Gold Record Winners*.

[293] Recording Industry Association of America. (Aug. 2, 1975). *Eagles: One of These Nights*.

[294] Hilburn, R. (Dec. 13, 1975). "One of Eagles Leaves the Nest," *Los Angeles Times*.

[295] Palmer, R. (Mar. 26, 1981). "Rock Tycoon's Musical Domain Keeps Him Busy and Successful," *New York Times*.

[296] Bream, J. (Feb. 21, 1995). "The Egos Have Landed," *Minneapolis Star Tribune*.

[297] Reynolds, L. (Aug. 11, 1982). "Secret Messages in Music?," *Mount Carmel (Ill.) Daily Republican-Register*.

[298] U.S. House of Representatives. (May 12, 1982). *H.R.6363 - Phonograph Record Backward Masking Labeling Act of 1982*,

[299] Recording Industry Association of America, *Eagles: Lyin' Eyes, Asylum*, (Nov. 8, 1975).

[300] Snopes.com. (Apr. 24, 2014). "The Eagles song "Hotel California" is about Satanism," Snopes.com. Retrieved from https://www.snopes.com/fact-check/hotel-california/.

[301] Selvin, J. (Nov. 26, 1995). "Q&A with Don Henley," *San Francisco Examiner*.

[302] Richey, R. (Feb. 5, 1984). "Catering to Satan," *Muncie (Ind.) Star Press*.

[303] Marsh, D. (Jul. 3, 1975). "'One of These Nights' Lacks Sense of Unity - Eagles Have Done Better," *Rolling Stone*.

[304] Greene, A. (Jul. 16, 2015). "Flashback: The Eagles Play 'Take it to the Limit' In 1977," *Rolling Stone*.

[305] Gallagher, B. (Jun. 9, 2017). "Final Cars 3 Trailer Pushes Lightning McQueen to the Limit," Movieweb. Retrieved from https://movieweb.com/cars-3-trailer-final/.

[306] Sullivan, P. (Oct. 25, 1973). "Gram Parsons: The Mysterious Death – And Aftermath," *Rolling Stone*.

[307] *Los Angeles Times*. (Sep. 20, 1973). "Gram Parsons Dies; Country, Rock Musician," *Los Angeles Times*

[308] *New York Times*. (Nov. 7, 1973). "2 Plead in Theft and Burning of Coffin with Rock Singer," *New York Times*.

[309] *Billboard*. (Feb. 12, 2001). "Fired Eagles Guitarist Felder Sues Henley, Frey."

[310] NPR, Kennedy, M. (Jan. 19, 2018). Eagles v. Hotel California: After Lawsuit, Band Reaches A Settlement, NPR. Retrieved from https://www.npr.org/sections/thetwo-way/2018/01/19/579145980/eagles-v-hotel-california-after-lawsuit-band-reaches-a-settlement.

[311] Stempel, J. (Jan. 16, 2018). "Widow of Eagles Guitarist Frey Sues NYC Hospital for Wrongful Death," *Reuters*.

[312] Itzkoff, D. (Feb. 12, 2013). "The Long, Long Run: Glenn Frey and Don Henley Reflect on 'History of the Eagles,'" *New York Times*.

[313] Edgers, G. (Nov. 28, 2016). "Don Henley Says the Eagles Are Done. It Was Always Glenn Frey's Band.," *Washington Post*.

[314] Scoppa, B. (Mar. 9, 2013). "Don Felder Gives 'History of the Eagles' A Mixed Review," *The Hollywood Reporter*.

[315] Collins, J. (Jun. 1, 2017). "Welcome to the Hotel California (Trademark)," *Forbes*.

[316] *Variety*. (Jan. 10, 2018). "Joe Walsh Signs with Sony/ATV Music Publishing," *Variety*.

[317] Treleven, E. (Apr. 17, 2015). "Don Henley and Duluth Trading Settle Lawsuit, Apology Issued," *Wisconsin State Journal*.

[318] Michaels, S. (Jun. 4, 2014). "The Eagles' Don Henley Accuses Frank Ocean and Okkervil River of Song Theft," *Guardian*.

[319] Amplify, Brooks, D. (Oct. 3, 2016). Irving Azoff says the "Pirates" at YouTube are "Really Evil," Amplify. Retrieved from http://www.ampthemag.com/the-real/irving-azoff-says-pirates-youtube-really-evil/.

[320] Associated Press. (Oct. 15, 2000). "Henley Sued by Longtime Fan," Associated Press.

[321] Brown, H. (Oct. 10, 2016). "Bad Vibrations: Where Did it All Go Wrong for the Beach Boys?" *The Telegraph*.

[322] Halperin, S. (Sep. 17, 2018). "Paul McCartney, Don Henley, Katy Perry, More Pen Letter to SiriusXm: 'We Will Boycott,'" *Variety*.

[323] *New York Daily News*. (Nov. 20, 2017). "Glenn Frey's Son Deacon Joins Eagles As the Band Eyes a New Tour," *New York Daily News*

[324] Tunis, W. (Apr. 5, 2018). "Don Henley on the Eagles Carrying on: \"We Wanted Everybody to Be All In.\"," *Lexington (Ky.) Herald-Leader*.

[325] K-SHE-95 - Real Rock Radio (Aug. 7, 2018). "Pre-Eagles Glenn Frey & J.D. Souther album set for reissue," K-SHE-95. Retrieved from https://www.kshe95.com/real-rock-news/pre-eagles-glenn-frey-j-d-souther-album-set-for-reissue/.

[326] Waddell, R. (Oct. 12, 2007). "The Billboard Q&A: The Eagles' Glenn Frey," *Billboard*.

[327] Edgers, G. (Jan. 18, 2016). "Glenn Frey, 'the One Who Started it All' With the Eagles," *Washington Post*.

[328] Graff, G. (Oct. 11, 2018). "Deacon Frey Flies Like an Eagle in His Father's Old Band," *The Oakland Press*.

[329] Atkinson, K. (Sep. 26, 2018). "Eagles Announce 'Legacy' CD & LP Box Sets," *Billboard*.

[330] *Eau Claire (Wis.) Leader-Telegram*. (Mar. 24, 1994). "Hell Hath Frozen Over for the Eagles."

[331] Billboard (Mar. 16, 1985). "Chart History: Glenn Frey," Billboard. Retrieved from https://www.billboard.com/music/glenn-frey/chart-history.

[332] Berry, W. (Mar. 22, 1980). "Everything's Coming Up Megabucks for Frey," Associated Press.

[333] Hartford 102.9 The Whale, Picozzi, M. (Nov. 6, 2018). "And he had a part in the show too!", Hartford 102.9. Retrieved from http://www.1029thewhale.com/2018/11/06/and-he-had-a-part-in-the-show-too/.

[334] MovieCityNews, Dretzka, G. (Apr. 23, 2014). "Down and Dangerous," MovieCityNews. Retrieved from http://moviecitynews.com/author/gary-dretzka./page/13/.

[335] Broadway World (Jan. 14, 2019). "Eagles Songwriter Jack

Tempchin To Be Inducted Into The Songwriters Hall of Fame," Broadway World. Retrieved from https://www.broadwayworld.com/bwwmusic/article/Eagles-Songwriter-Jack-Tempchin-To-Be-Inducted-Into-The-Songwriters-Hall-of-Fame-20190114.

[336] Kawashima, D. (Jun. 28, 2017). "Interview with Jack Tempchin, Singer/Songwriter and Hit Songwriter for the Eagles (\"Peaceful Easy Feeling,\" \"Already Gone\") And Glenn Frey," Songwriter Universe.

[337] Graff, G. (Jun. 29, 1992). "Ex-Eagle Flies Solo," Detroit Free Press.

[338] Hilburn, R. (Jun. 5, 1994). "Hotel California: Back in Business," The Age (Melbourne, Victoria, Australia).

[339] Skiba, K. (Dec. 6, 2016). "Staples, Eagles Get Kennedy Center Honors," Chicago Tribune.

[340] Graff, G. (Jan. 18, 2016). "How Glenn Frey & Don Henley Became the Eagles, As Told by Linda Ronstadt," Billboard.

[341] Epting, C. (Jun. 4, 2013). "Ten Places the Eagles Took Flight," Rock Cellar Magazine.

[342] Edgers, G. (Dec. 4, 2016). "Eagles: Hell Has Really Frozen Over," Washington Post.

[343] Young, C.M. (Nov. 29, 1979). "The Eagles: Hell is for Heroes," Rolling Stone.

[344] McConnell, M. (Jan. 19, 2016). "Glenn Frey's Musical Sojourn Started at His Royal Oak High School with an $18 Gig," The Oakland Press.

[345] Johnson, G. (Jan. 1, 2009). MRRL Hall of Fame: Glenn Frey, Michigan Rock and Roll Hall of Fame. Retrieved from https://www.michiganrockandrolllegends.com/mrrl-hall-of-fame/105-glenn-frey.

[346] Hilburn, R. (Aug. 12, 1972). "Souther Album Rewarding," The Honolulu Advertiser.

[347] James, J. (Aug. 21, 1966). "Animals in Action - One Teenager's View," Santa Rosa (Ca.) Press Democrat.

[348] James, J. (Feb. 12, 1967). "Spotlight - The New Breed," Santa Rosa (Ca.) Press Democrat.

[349] Steele, G. (Apr. 21, 1967). "Washington High School - Benefit for Adopted Son," The Argus (Fremont, Ca.).

[350] Santa Rosa (Ca.) Press Democrat. (Dec. 16, 1968). "Glad!", Santa Rosa (Ca.) Press Democrat

[351] San Francisco Examiner. (Apr. 27, 1986). "The New Breed: Want Ad Reader," San Francisco Examiner

[352] Schmit, T.B. (2009). Album Credits/Liner Notes: Expando.

[353] Schmit, T.B. (2001). Album Credits/Liner Notes: Feed the Fire.

[354] Schmit, T.B. (1990). Album Credits/Liner Notes: Tell Me the Truth.

[355] Schmit, T.B. (1987). Album Credits/Liner Notes: Timothy B.

[356] Schmit, T.B. (1984). Album Credits/Liner Notes: Playin' It Cool.

[357] Schmit, T.B. (2016). Album Credits/Liner Notes: Leap of Faith.

[358] Dayton Daily News. (Sep. 24, 1972). "Ex-Gangster Joe Walsh Man of Many Talents," Dayton Daily News.

[359] Walsh, J. (1973). Album Credits/Liner Notes: The Smoker You Drink, the Player You Get.

[360] Williams, R. (Sep. 1, 1973). "Joe Walsh: The Smoker You Drink, The Player You Get," Melody Maker.

[361] Charlesworth, C. (Sep. 29, 1973). "Joe Walsh: Barnstorming the USA," Melody Maker.

[362] Rosen, S. (Nov. 1, 1974). "R.E.O. Speedwagon: The Band That Flies Together," Circus Raves.

[363] Crowe, C. (Feb. 1, 1975). "Joe Walsh Tends His Garden," Rolling Stone.

[364] Larkin, C. (2011). The Encyclopedia of Popular Music, London, UK: Omnibus Press.

[365] Heath, C. (Sep. 15, 2019). "Creating While Clean," GQ.

[366] James Gang. (1969). Album Credits/Liner Notes: Yer' Album.

[367] World United Music. (Sep. 24, 2015). "Legends of Rock: Joe Walsh," World United Music.

[368] Goldstein, P. (Jul. 15, 1990). "Atlantic Bites Back with Free-Speech Album," Los Angeles Times.

[369] St. Louis Post-Dispatch. (Nov. 25, 1980). "People: Don Henley," St. Louis Post-Dispatch.

[370] Lansing State Journal. (Jan. 15, 1981). "Rights Waived," Lansing State Journal.

[371] Loder, K. (Jan. 16, 1981). "Stiffs Have Rough Time on Tour," The Greensville (S.C.) News.

[372] Dayton Daily News. (Jan. 29, 1981). "Henley Asks for Drug Diversion Help," Dayton Daily News.

[373] Chicago Tribune. (Feb. 26, 1981). "Eagles Rock Star Fined in Teen-Girl Drug Case," Chicago Tribune

[374] DemocraticUnderground.com. (Nov. 21, 2017). "Don Henley, On This Day 1980," DemocraticUnderground.com.

[375] James Gang. (1970). Album Credits/Liner Notes: James Gang Rides Again.

[376] Olszewski, M. (2003). Radio Daze: Stories from the Front in Cleveland's FM Air Wars, Kent, OH: The Kent State University Press.

[377] Recording Industry Association of America. (Oct. 26, 1971)., James Gang: James Gang Rides Again.

[378] Recording Industry Association of America. (Jun. 26, 1972). James Gang: Live in Concert.

[379] Recording Industry Association of America. (Jul. 12, 1972). James Gang: Thirds.

[380] Recording Industry Association of America. (Nov. 2, 1973). Joe Walsh: The Smoker You Drink, The Player You Get.

[381] Recording Industry Association of America. (Jan. 14, 1975). Joe Walsh: So What.

[382] Recording Industry Association of America. (Aug. 7, 1978). Joe Walsh: But Seriously Folks.

[383] Recording Industry Association of America. (Dec. 8, 1982). Glenn Frey: No Fun Aloud.

[384] Recording Industry Association of America. (Aug. 6, 1985). Glenn Frey: The Allnighter.

[385] Recording Industry Association of America. (May 31, 1978). Joe Walsh: But Seriously Folks.

[386] Associated Press. (Jul. 12, 1985). "In Contrast to Songs, Glenn Frey Has a Lot Going Right for Him," Minneapolis Star Tribune.

[387] Cedrone, L. (May 25, 1971). "Very Different Western," Baltimore Evening Sun.

[388] Bishop, P. (Sep. 5, 1985). "Joe Walsh Keeps it Lean and Gritty," The Pittsburgh Press.

[389] Heldenfels, R.D. (Aug. 22, 2001). "Drew Carey: Sitcom

Aiming for More Laughs This Season," *Akron Beacon Journal*.

[390] Associated Press. (Aug. 25, 1998). *Rocker Joe Walsh Joins Drew Carey's Band*, Associated Press.

[391] Righi, L. (Aug. 10, 2007). "Joe Walsh Will Do More Than Fly Like an Eagle," *The Morning Call (Allentown, Pa.)*.

[392] McCollum, B. (Jan. 19, 2016). "Glenn Frey Details Detroit Days in Free Press Interview," *Detroit Free Press*.

[393] Gilbert, M. (Nov. 20, 2012). "'American Masters' Profiles Mogul David Geffen," *Boston Globe*.

[394] The Star Press (Muncie, Ind.). (Jul. 6, 1985). "Why Has Rock Star Don Henley Taken on the Plight of the American Farmer As His Champion Cause?," *The Star Press (Muncie, Ind.)*.

[395] IMDB.com. (May 9, 2000). *Just Shoot Me! (TV Series) -- A&E Biography: Nina Van Horn (Parody)*, IMDB.com.

[396] U.S. Senate. (Jan. 30, 2033). "Media Ownership: Hearing Before the Committee on Commerce, Science and Transportation, United States Senate, One-Hundred Eighth Congress, First Session, Jan. 30, 2003; Testimony of Don Henley," U.S. Senate.

[397] *Scribd*. (Apr. 30, 2016). "Don Henley's Runaway Tours Appearance.," *Scribd*.

[398] Barton, D. (Jul. 15, 1990). "Henley Crusades to Alert Fans to Environmental Decay," *The San Bernardino County Sun*.

[399] Connelly, C. (Apr. 24, 1985). "The Former Eagle Has Landed," *Arizona Republic*.

[400] Hilburn, R. (Aug. 8, 1982). "Henley Rises After the Fall of 1980," *Los Angeles Times*.

[401] The Drive 97.1 FM (Jan. 16, 2019). "Don Henley," The Drive 97.1 FM. Retrieved from https://live.wdrv.com/listen/artist/b2c2d4fe-8c1e-44ec-8be6-ff500e105a90.

[402] Unterberger, A. (Jul. 30, 2017). "Eagles Are Their Own Special Guests at Day One of Classic East Festival," *Billboard*.

[403] Hall, R. (May 1, 2017). "Timothy B. Schmit of the Eagles: An Intimate Chat," BestClassicBands.com. Retrieved from https://bestclassicbands.com/timothy-b-schmit-interview-5-17-17/.

[404] Willman, C. (Jul. 17, 2017). "Concert Review: 'Yesterday's Gone,' But the Music Lives on for Fleetwood Mac, Journey, Classic West Crowd," *Variety*.

[405] Grammy Awards. (Mar. 14, 2015). *16th Annual Grammy Awards (1973)*, Grammy Awards.

[406] Grammy Awards. (Feb. 28, 1976). *18th Annual Grammy Awards*, Grammy Awards.

[407] Rock and Roll Hall of Fame. (Jan. 12, 1998). *Eagles - 1998*, Rock and Roll Hall of Fame.

[408] Grammy Awards. (Feb. 23, 1978). *20th Annual Grammy Awards*, Grammy Awards.

[409] Hilburn, R. (Jan. 12, 1998). "The Long Run," *Los Angeles Times*.

[410] Hinckley, D. (Jun. 15, 2000). "Songwriters Take Measures," *New York Daily News*.

[411] Songwriters Hall of Fame. (Jun. 15, 2000). *Glenn Frey: Eagles Co-Founder and Lead Vocalist*, Songwriters Hall of Fame.

[412] Songwriters Hall of Fame. (Jun. 15, 2000). *Don Henley: Eagles Lead Vocalist, Lyricist, Producer*, Songwriters Hall of Fame.

[413] Pareles, J. (Jun. 17, 2000). "Humming the Way Into the Hall of Fame," *New York Times*.

[414] Francischine, T. (Feb. 21, 2017). "Don Felder to Be Inducted Into Florida Artists Hall of Fame," *The Gainesville (Fla.) Sun*.

[415] Talbot, C. (Feb. 23, 2013). "Tyler, Perry Lead 2013 Class for

Songwriters Hall of Fame," *The Jackson (Tenn.) Sun*.

[416] Songwriters Hall of Fame. (Jun. 1, 2007). *Jackson Browne*, Songwriters Hall of Fame

[417] Art of the Song Coffeehouse. (Jan. 1, 2012). "Glenn Frey Interview: A Tribute," Art of the Song Coffeehouse.

[418] Ferrara, L. (Nov. 15, 2012). "Eagles' Glenn Frey Teaches Songwriting; Talks Tour," *The Washington Times*.

[419] Fricke, D. (Sep. 21, 2015). "Cass County," *Rolling Stone*.

[420] *Cashbox*. (Jun. 21, 1986). "If Anybody Had a Heart," *Cashbox*.

[421] Newman, M. (Jan. 9, 2012). "Bob Seger Moves New Fans with Classic Songs," *Daily Press (Newport News, Va.)*.

[422] Bream, J. (Mar. 13, 2004). "A Devoted Dad, Seger Still Finds Time to Write and Sing," *Minneapolis Star Tribune*.

[423] The Windsor Star (Windsor, Ontario, Canada). (Dec. 20, 2016). "Glenn Frey, 67," *The Windsor Star (Windsor, Ontario, Canada)*

[424] Campbell, M. (Jan. 12, 1984). "Don Felder Enjoys Creating the Music," *Lancaster (Ohio) Eagle-Gazette*.

[425] Maza, M. (Feb. 7, 1984). "Fractured Friendships," *Arizona Republic*.

[426] Tampa Tribune. (Aug. 17, 1984). "Lou Ann Barton - Old Enough," *Tampa Tribune*.

[427] Washington Post. (Mar. 5, 1982). "Lou Ann Barton's 'Old Enough'," *Washington Post*.

[428] Associated Press. (Feb. 7, 1985). "Henley Wants to Show Down Isn't Out," Associated Press.

[429] Facebook. (Jan. 19, 2016). "Don Henley, *He Was Like a Brother to Me*," Facebook.

[430] Powers, B. (Jan. 14, 2019). "The Late Glenn Frey's Wife Continues Negligence Case Against Doctor," Radio.com 98.7 KLUV.

[431] Lynch, J. (Jan. 19, 2016). "Eagles Manager Says Glenn Frey's Death Caused Partly by Medications," *Billboard*.

[432] Seemayer, Z. (Jan. 18, 2016). "Glenn Frey Dies at 67: Travis Tritt, Niall Horan, Sheryl Crow and Other Celebs Share Touching Tributes," *ETOnline.com*.

[433] Aswad, J. (Oct. 13, 2017). "Bob Seger Dedicates New Album, 'I Knew You When,' To the Eagles' Glenn Frey," *Variety*.

[434] Lockett, D. (Jan. 18, 2017). "Bob Seger Wrote a Tribute Song to His Old Friend Glenn Frey for the First Anniversary of Frey's Death," *Vulture*.

[435] Edgers, G. (Nov. 4, 2015). "Eagles Founder Glenn Frey Facing Surgery; Band to Put Off Kennedy Center Honor," *Washington Post*.

[436] Whitaker, S. (Jan. 23, 2016). "Bob Seger Recounts Glenn Frey's Last Days," *Taste of Country*.

[437] Graff, G. (Jan. 18, 2016). "Bob Seger Remembers Glenn Frey As \"Brilliant,\" \"Titanic\" Talent," *The Oakland Press*.

[438] McCollum, B. (Apr. 20, 1997). "Unity is the Theme for the Detroit Music Awards," *Detroit Free Press*.

[439] Graff, G. (Dec. 5, 2016). "Bob Seger Performs for Glenn Frey, Eagles at Kennedy Center Honors," *The Oakland Press*.

[440] Appleford, S. (Jan. 10, 1993). "Learning from a Pro: Glenn Frey Takes Slight Detour from His Post-Eagles Career to Teach the Craft of Songwriting at UCLA Extension," *Los Angeles Times*.

[441] Felder, D. (1981). Album Credits/Liner Notes: *Heavy Metal soundtrack: Heavy Metal (Takin' A Ride)*.

[442] Mettler, M. (Apr. 4, 2014). "Q&A: Don Felder on the Soundtrack of Summer and the Secret to the Eagles' Greatest Hits," *Fox News Live.*

[443] Teverbaugh, K. (Aug. 16, 1981). "'Heavy Metal' Album Sounds Good by Itself," *Muncie (Ind.) Star Press.*

[444] Latrobe (Pa.) Bulletin. (Sep. 18, 1991). "Nicks Explains Song on Album," *Latrobe (Pa.) Bulletin.*

[445] Salem (Ore.) Statesman Journal. (Jul. 6, 1992). "Buffett-Speak: Changes in Attitudes," *Salem (Ore.) Statesman Journal.*

[446] Graff, G. (Jul. 21, 1994). "Buffett Embraces Florida," *Daily Record (Morristown, N.J.).*

[447] Island Jay Islander Blog. (Feb. 22, 2014). "What is a Parrothead?," *Island Jay Islander Blog.*

[448] Palmer, R. (Aug. 7, 1982). "Former Eagles' Solo LP Debut Distinctive," *The Indianapolis Star.*

[449] Henley, D. (1982). Album Credits/Liner Notes: *I Can't Stand Still.*

[450] Hilburn, R. (May 30, 1982). "Henley, Frey Discuss the Eagles, The Breakup," *Los Angeles Times.*

[451] McNally, J. (Jun. 25, 1982). "Eagle Glenn Frey Cuts Loose with Raw Rhythm and Blues," *The Petaluma (Ca.) Argus-Courier.*

[452] Frey, G. (1982). Album Credits/Liner Notes: *No Fun Aloud.*

[453] Van Matre, L. (Oct. 15, 1982). "Eagles' Breakup Was No Near-Miss," *Tallahassee Democrat.*

[454] Beebe, G. (Nov. 30, 1984). "Henley Builds Perfect Beast," *Santa Cruz (Ca.) Sentinel.*

[455] Hilburn, R. (Jan. 20, 1985). "Don Henley More at Home Out of the Eagles' Nest," *Los Angeles Times.*

[456] Campbell, M. (Feb. 5, 1985). "Ex-Eagle Don Henley Proves He's Not Finished with Rock 'n Roll," *The Paducah (Ky.) Sun.*

[457] Rosenberg, H. (Sep. 1, 1982). "Vengeful Song Turns Rock Musician Into Television Critic," *Los Angeles Times.*

[458] Teverbaugh, K. (Sep. 5, 1982). "Can't Stand Still: Multi-Talented Don Henley is One High-Flying Ex-Eagle," *The Star Press (Muncie, Ind.).*

[459] Tucker, K. (Sep. 15, 1982). "3 Eagles Make Solo Flights," *Austin American-Statesman.*

[460] Condon, S. (Jan. 21, 2016). "Frey Had Strong Ties to Aspen 'Partytown'," *The Aspen Times.*

[461] Oksenhorn, S. (Sep. 3, 2010). "The Long Run is Not Over for Eagles' Frey," *The Aspen Times.*

[462] San Francisco Weekly. (Apr. 29, 1998). "Fake it to the Limit," *San Francisco Weekly.*

[463] Sharp, K. (Nov. 10, 2016). "Catching Up with Eagles and Poco Co-Founder Randy Meisner (Interview)," *Rock Cellar Magazine.*

[464] Bowden, J. (Jun. 11, 2017). Randy Meisner Remembers Fist Fight With Glenn Frey & Other Eagles Regrets, RockHistoryMusic.com. Retrieved from https://www.youtube.com/watch?v=ZEUElqyN5CM.

[465] Dillon, N. (Jan. 19, 2016). "Eagles Bassist Randy Meisner Sad He and the Late Glenn Frey Can't 'Take it to the Limit' One More Time," *New York Daily News.*

[466] Sheff, D. (Jan. 12, 1981). "Bassist-Composer Randy Meisner Courageously Bailed Out of the Eagles So That He Could Rock His Own Boat," *People.*

[467] Young, C. (Aug. 9, 1977). "2 Eagles Get Into Altercation," *Mansfield (Oh.) News-Journal.*

[468] Newman, M. (Jun. 19, 2015). "Don Henley Talks Solo Album: 'I Do Not Want to Spend the Rest of My Life Being a Jukebox'," *Billboard.*

[469] Mansfield, B. (Sep. 23, 2015). "Don Henley: Music 'Keeps Me from Going Nuts'," *USA Today.*

[470] Gilbert, C. (Sep. 30, 2015). "Don Henley: The CmT.Com Interview," CMT.com.

[471] The Marshall (Texas) News Messenger. (Oct. 29, 1963). "The Four Speeds Perform at the Corral Club," *The Marshall (Texas) News Messenger.*

[472] Graff, G. (Jan. 18, 2016). "Glenn Frey, The Lone Arranger, Spark Plug, Man with the Plan: An Appreciation of the Eagles Leader," *Billboard.*

[473] Journal and Courier (Lafayette, Ind.). (Jun. 29, 1963). "The Dillards - \"Back Porch Bluegrass\"," *Journal and Courier (Lafayette, Ind.).*

[474] Van Matre, L. (Mar. 20, 1985). "Ex-Members of Eagles Talking Again, But Reunion Not Near," *The Des Moines Register.*

[475] Knopper, S. (Jan. 20, 2016). "How the Eagles' 'Greatest Hits' Invented a New Kind of Blockbuster," *Rolling Stone.*

[476] Salem (Ore.) Statesman Journal. (Dec. 9, 1999). "The Eagles Claim Record Title," *Salem (Ore.) Statesman Journal*

[477] Horgan, R. (Jan. 20, 2016). "A Desperado Absconded with Journalist's Eagles Softball Souvenir," *AdWeek.*

[478] Greene, A. (May 11, 2017). "Rolling Stone at 50: When the Editors Took on the Eagles in Softball," *Rolling Stone.*

[479] Crowe, C. (Jan. 21, 2016). "Remembering Glenn Frey: Cameron Crowe on Eagles' Teen King," *Rolling Stone.*

[480] Crowe, C. (Aug. 17, 2015). "Cameron Crowe Looks Back on His 1975 Eagles Cover Story," *Rolling Stone.*

[481] Crowe, C. (Jul. 15, 1978). "They Call Him Big Shorty," *Rolling Stone.*

[482] Uncut. (Feb. 14, 2014). "Glyn Johns – Album by Album," *Uncut*

[483] Anderson, T. (Mar. 1, 1998). "Montana Artist Sculpts a Tribute to Musical Eagles," *Great Falls (Montana) Tribune.*

[484] Sweitzer, P. (Sep. 12, 1999). "Rain Doesn't Dampen Winslow Corner Dedication," *Arizona Daily Sun (Flagstaff, Arizona).*

[485] The Republic (Columbus, Indiana). (Jan. 25, 2000). "Fans 'Take it Easy' At Winslow Corner," *The Republic (Columbus, Indiana).*

[486] Nebraska Music Hall of Fame Foundation. (Jan.1, 2000). *Biography: Randy Meisner.*

[487] Hurst, J. (Sep. 21, 1980). "Johnny Lee Cons His Way to Country Stardom," *Chicago Tribune.*

[488] Los Angeles Times. (Oct. 5, 1980). "Irv Azoff's Front Line Management is Taking Over the Management Chores for Chicago," *Los Angeles Times*

[489] Palmer, R. (Mar. 18, 1981). "The Pop Life: How a Rock Tycoon Made it to the Top," *New York Times.*

[490] Rockwell, J. (May 21, 1978). "When the Soundtrack Makes the Film," *New York Times.*

[491] Maslin, J. (Sep. 3, 1982). "'Ridgemont High'," *New York Times.*

[492] New York Times. (Apr. 27, 1983). "MCA Hires Irving Azoff," *New York Times.*

[493] Fabrikant, G. (Oct. 20, 1985). "A Movie Giant's Unfinished Script," *New York Times.*

[494] Holden, S. (Mar. 1, 1987). "\"Starlight Express\" Rolls to Market with a Rock Beat," *New York Times*.

[495] Fabrikant, G. (Sep. 6, 1989). "MCA Music Group Names New Chairman," *New York Times*.

[496] Fabrikant, G. (Oct. 31, 1989). "Ex-Head of MCA Unit Talks to Time Warner," *New York Times*.

[497] Fabrikant, G. (Oct. 22, 1990). "New Products Help to Bolster Music Sales," *New York Times*.

[498] Lev, M. (Jan. 5, 1992). "Can All Those Upstart Record Labels Survive?" *New York Times*.

[499] Goodman, F. (May 10, 1992). "Vanity Labels: Good Business or an Ego Boost?" *New York Times*.

[500] Holden, S. (Apr. 22, 1994). "Review/Film; Young, Black and Confused in the Complicated 1970's," *New York Times*.

[501] Smith, T.W. (Apr. 28, 1997). "Foreman Looking for Who's Next," *New York Times*.

[502] Strauss, N. (Apr. 29, 1998). "The Pop Life; Mike Tyson Faces the Music," *New York Times*.

[503] Meier, B. (May 24, 1998). "Big Money, Big Fallout for Tyson; The Ex-Champion Blames the Promoter for Financial Problems," *New York Times*.

[504] Maslin, J. (Dec. 11, 1998). "Dad's a Snowman. (Is Mom Santa?)," *New York Times*.

[505] Hirschorn, M. (Mar. 26, 2000). "Up from the Mailroom," *New York Times*.

[506] Gelt, J. (Oct. 4, 2017). "David Geffen Pledges $150 Million for New LACMA Building," *Los Angeles Times*.

[507] James, M. (Feb. 7, 2018). "Billionaire Patrick Soon-Shiong Reaches Deal to Buy L.A. Times and San Diego Union-Tribune," *Los Angeles Times*.

[508] Biography.com. (Apr. 2, 2014). "David Geffen," Biography.com. Retrieved from https://www.biography.com/people/david-geffen-9542656.

[509] Sisario, B. (Feb. 11, 2016). "A Word with: Irving Azoff, A Hard-Charging Artists' Manager," *New York Times*.

[510] Holson, L. (Jan. 10, 2002). "Importance of Being Important, With Music," *New York Times*.

[511] Strauss, N. (Aug. 18, 2002). "The Lost Boys: How a Pop Sensation Came Undone," *New York Times*.

[512] Leeds, J. (Jan. 6, 2005). "Talent Managing Business to Reunite Industry Figures," *New York Times*.

[513] Leeds, J. (Nov. 8, 2007). "A Trade Publication Alters a Rule, Lifting an Eagles Album to No. 1," *New York Times*.

[514] Levine, R. (Jun. 9, 2008). "For Some Music, It Has to Be Wal-Mart and Nowhere Else," *New York Times*.

[515] New York Times. (Oct. 23, 2008). "Ticketmaster to Buy Front Line, Report Says," *New York Times*.

[516] *New York Times*. (Nov. 12, 2008). "Ticketmaster Reduces Fees for Eagles Tickets," *New York Times*.

[517] *New York Times*. (Feb. 5, 2009). "Springsteen: This Merger Isn't Born to Run," *New York Times*.

[518] Sorkin, A.R. (Feb. 8, 2009). "Merger Expected of Ticketmaster and Live Nation," *New York Times*.

[519] New York Times. (Feb. 11, 2009). "Live Nation and Ticketmaster Defend Merger," *New York Times*.

[520] Bloomberg. (Feb. 25, 2010). "Eagles Put the Squeeze on Scalpers," *Bloomberg*.

[521] Chmielewski, D.C. (Jan. 26, 2010). "Ticketmaster-Live Nation Merger Gets Us Approval," *Los Angeles Times*.

[522] Segal, D. (Apr. 24, 2010). "Calling Almost Everyone's Tune," *New York Times*.

[523] Sisario, B. (Sep. 4, 2013). "Irving Azoff Starts New Entertainment Business," *New York Times*.

[524] Iannazzone, A. (Mar. 19, 2014). "Jackson Returns to 'Glory Days'," *Hartford Courant*.

[525] Cacciola, S. (Mar. 18, 2014). "Full-Court Press Wooed Jackson to Knicks," *New York Times*.

[526] Sisario, B. (Oct. 29, 2014). "New Venture Seeks Higher Royalties for Songwriters," *New York Times*.

[527] Ross, P. (Jan. 9, 1977). "Dark Songs by California's Eagles," *New York Times*.

[528] MTV.com. (Sep. 13, 1985). "1985 MTV Video Music Awards," MTV.com.

[529] *Los Angeles Times*. (Dec. 17, 1968). "Comic Larry Hankin Opens at Troubadour."

[530] Gorrell, J. (Jan. 17, 1964). "Linda Ronstadt Signs Contract," *Arizona Daily Star*.

[531] Pavillard, D. (Nov. 25, 1966). "2 Tusconians Leave Home and Become Stone Poneys," *Tuscon Daily Citizen*.

[532] Los Angeles Times. (Feb. 12, 1967). "Latest Group to Emerge in the Lucrative Folk Field," *Los Angeles Times*.

[533] Boston Globe. (May 7, 1967). "Revere Raiders Rock," *Boston Globe*.

[534] Ronstadt, L. (2013). *Linda Ronstadt: Simple Dreams*, New York, NY: Simon & Schuster.

[535] Hartford Courant. (Feb. 21, 1997). "Frey Reunited with Don Johnson on Nash Bridges," *Hartford Courant*.

[536] Penrose, N. (Sep. 14, 2016). "Fred Armisen & Bill Hader Explain How 'Documentary Now!' Cast Irving Azoff & His Son in Eagles Spoof," *Billboard*.

[537] Callahan, M. (Sep. 28, 2000). "Full Moon Records," Both Sides Now Publications. Retrieved from https://www.bsnpubs.com/elektra/fullmoon.html.

[538] Oliver, M. (Feb. 15, 1999). "Doug Weston, Troubadour Founder, Dies," *Los Angeles Times*.

[539] Los Angeles Times. (Apr. 17, 1951). "Arnold Antiques," *Los Angeles Times*.

[540] PBS: American Masters. (Nov. 1, 2012). "Timeline: Year by Year, How David Geffen Invented Himself," *American Masters*.

[541] Coolidge, R. (1972). Album Credits/Liner Notes: *The Lady's Not for Sale*.

[542] Souther, J.D. (1972). Album Credits/Liner Notes: *John David Souther*.

[543] Betts, S.L. (Mar. 15, 2016). "Flashback: The Byrds Flip the Opry Script," *Rolling Stone*.

[544] Fong-Torres, B. (Sep. 22, 1991). "Gram Parsons: The Father of Country Rock," *San Francisco Chronicle*.

[545] Rocky Mount (N.C.) Telegram. (May 5, 1974). "Sunday Highlights," *Rocky Mount (N.C.) Telegram*.

[546] Beck, M. (Sep. 17, 1973). "TV Rock Producer," *The Orlando Sentinel*.

[547] Everett, T. (Nov. 29, 1975). "Tom Waits: Not So Much a Poet, More a Purveyor of Improvisational Travelogue," *New Musical Express*.

[548] Jarvis, E. (Jun. 24, 1977). "Eagles Soar to Success," *Pensacola News Journal*.

[549] Kilday, G. (Aug. 22, 1977). "Rock Goes to the Movies in 'FM'," *Los Angeles Times*.

[550] Ivans, M. (Aug. 17, 1977). "Elvis Presley Dies; Rock Singer Was 42; Heart Failure is Cited by Coroner—Acclaim Followed Early Scorn," *New York Times*.

[551] Selway, J. (Sep. 26, 2015). "Don Henley: My Voice Won't Last Much Longer. But I'm Lucky to Have Had an Amazing Career," *The Daily Express*.

[552] Fricke, D. (Nov. 21, 2017). "Don Henley Talks 'Hotel California' Reissue, Eagles' Future," *Rolling Stone*.

[553] Lewis, R. (Oct. 15, 2017). "Hotel California Gets a 40th Anniversary Release," *Los Angeles Times*.

[554] Azoff, I. (May 9, 2016). "Dear YouTube: An Open Letter from Irving Azoff," *Recode*.

[555] Twitter. (Jul. 25, 2013). "#EaglesonSpotify," Twitter.

[556] Gartner, E. (Nov. 12, 2014). "Irving Azoff Threatens to Yank 20,000 Songs from YouTube," *The Hollywood Reporter*.

[557] Shaw, L. (Nov. 18, 2014). "Irving Azoff Demands YouTube Remove Pharrell, The Eagles," *Bloomberg*.

[558] Owsinski, B. (Sep. 9, 2013). "Irving Azoff Reinvents the Major Record Label," *Forbes*.

[559] Knopper, S. (Dec. 12, 2016). "Irving Azoff, Top Radio Group Sue Each Other Over Songwriter Rates," *Rolling Stone*.

[560] Billboard. (Oct. 13, 2018). "'A Conscious Uncoupling': What's Next After the MSG-Azoff Split?" *Billboard*.

[561] SomethingElseReviews.com. (Nov. 3, 2014). For Don Henley, a Beatles star remains his primary influence: 'I loved what he stood for, what he believed in', SomethingElseReviews.com. Retrieved from http://somethingelsereviews.com/2014/11/03/don-henley-john-lennon/.

[562] Baltin, S. (Dec. 28, 2018). "Why John Lennon Remains the Ultimate Rock Star," *Forbes*.

[563] Fricke, D. (Dec. 27, 2001). "'Imagine': The Anthem of 2001," *Rolling Stone*.

[564] Newman, M. (Jun. 11, 2012). "Before the Fast Lane," *New Jersey Monthly*.

[565] Briggs, A. (Feb. 11, 1966). "Impresario for Big Beat Generation," *Los Angeles Times*.

[566] Hilburn, R. (Aug. 2, 1970). "Atmosphere, Talent Key to Club's Success," *Los Angeles Times*.

[567] Cromelin, R. (Mar. 4, 1979). "Whiz Kid Returns to Active Duty," *Los Angeles Times*.

[568] Hilburn, R. (Mar. 25, 1972). "Jackson Browne: Acclaim at Last," *Los Angeles Times*.

[569] Hilburn, R. (Sep. 2, 1972). "David Geffen: From Mailroom Boy to Head of Record Company," *Los Angeles Times*.

[570] Chicago Daily News. (Aug. 1, 1974). "American Dream Molded in Vinyl," *Chicago Daily News*.

[571] Bate, M. (Aug. 23, 1974). "Paul Does it His Way," *The Ottawa Journal* (Ottawa, Ontario, Canada).

[572] Young, C.M. (Jun. 5, 1977). "Eagles File Suit Against Warner," *Rolling Stone*.

[573] Schruers, F. (May 19, 1978). "*Rolling Stone* Notes," *Poughkeepsie Journal*

[574] Allen, J. (Feb. 25, 1981). "What Makes David Geffen," *New York Daily News*.

[575] Klinger, J. (Feb. 22, 1980). "JD Souther Feels Like a Singer for the First Time with Top 10 Disc," *Fort Lauderdale News*.

[576] Campbell, M. (Dec. 31, 1976). "Eagles Become an American Band," *Tampa Tribune*.

[577] Nordyke, K. (Feb. 15, 2016). "Grammys: Eagles' Glenn Frey Honored with \"Take it Easy\" Performance," *The Hollywood Reporter*.

[578] Webster, A. (Dec. 18, 2008). "The Eagles Land in Guitar Hero: World Tour," *ARS Technica*.

[579] Nisbet, C. (Jan. 27, 2016). "Machine Head's Flynn on His Love of the Eagles," *Louder*.

[580] Lefsetz, B. (Jan. 18, 2016). "Op Ed: Glenn Frey – Bob Lefsetz," *Encore*.

[581] Carson, C. (Sep. 25, 1976). "Kings Like Eagles," *Press and Sun-Bulletin (Binghampton, N.Y.)*.

[582] Holden, S. (Dec. 7, 1978). "Jack Tempchin Lacks That Peaceful Easy L.A. Feeling," *Rolling Stone*.

[583] Frolick, J. (Feb. 12, 1979). "Jules, Polar Bears Melt Skepticism with New LP," *Austin American-Statesman*.

[584] MacIntosh, D. (Dec. 8, 2011). "Songwriter Interviews: J.D. Souther," *SongFacts.com*.

[585] Ledbetter, L. (Dec. 9, 1980). "John Lennon of Beatles is Killed; Suspect Held in Shooting at Dakota," *New York Times*.

[586] *Cashbox*. (May 13, 1972). "Eagles Ink Asylum Deal,.

[587] *Cashbox*. (May 27, 1972). "Ronstadt Signs with Asylum."

[588] Everett, T. (Jun. 10, 1972). "Insights & Sounds," *Cashbox*.

[589] *Cashbox*. (Nov. 25, 1972). "Warner Comm. Buys Asylum; Geffen 7 Yr Deal."

[590] *Cashbox*. (May 5, 1973). "Desperado - Eagles - Asylum SD 5068."

[591] *Cashbox*. (Jun. 2, 1973). "The Promotional Stage."

[592] *Cashbox*. (Aug. 18, 1973). "Flying High."

[593] *Cashbox*. (Aug. 25, 1973). "Geffen Chairs Elektra-Asylum."

[594] *Cashbox*. (Apr. 6, 1974). "On the Border - Eagles - Asylum 7e-1004."

[595] *Cashbox*. (Apr. 6, 1974). "High Flying Jam."

[596] Kelly, D. (Jun. 7, 1974). "200,000 Struggle Through the Jam," *The San Bernardino County Sun*.

[597] *Cashbox*. (Apr. 20, 1974). "Irv Azoff Sets Mgmt."

[598] *Cashbox*. (May 4, 1974). "Eagles (Asylum 11036) - Already Gone."

[599] *Cashbox*. (Jun. 22, 1974). "Souther Hillman & Furay Asylum LP As Tour is Set."

[600] *Cashbox*. (Jul. 6, 1974). "The Eagles Have Reportedly Embarked on a Venture."

[601] *Cashbox*. (Jul. 27, 1974). "Epic Prod. Deal W/ Full Moon Co."

[602] *Cashbox*. (Aug. 24, 1974). "Eagles (Asylum 45202) - James Dean."

[603] *Cashbox*. (Aug. 24, 1974). "Eagles Re-Sign with Asylum."

[604] *Cashbox*. (Sep. 14, 1974). "Eagles Cancel European Tour."

[605] Dougherty, P. (Jun. 19, 1981). "Music Channel on Cable TV," *New York Times*.

[606] *Cashbox*. (Sep. 14, 1974). "New Atl Acts," *Cashbox*.

[607] *Cashbox*. (Sep. 21, 1974). "NALF Benefit Scores $105,000."

[608] *Cashbox*. (Sep. 21, 1974). "Ladies Love Outlaws - Tom Rush - Columbia KC-330054."

[609] *Cashbox*. (Nov. 16, 1974). "Eagles (Asylum 45218) - The Best of My Love."

[610] *Cashbox*. (Dec. 7, 1974). "Kellman to Front Line; Brings Riperton In."

[611] Cashbox. (Jan. 11, 1975). "Points West, East Coastings," *Cashbox*.

[612] Cashbox. Breschard, J. (Jan. 11, 1975). "Talent on Stage: Eagles, Dan Fogelberg," *Cashbox*.

[613] Cashbox. (Nov. 22, 1975). "Front Line Files Countersuit in Walsh Battle," *Cashbox*.

[614] Cashbox. (Mar. 22, 1975). "Don Kirshner's Rock Concert," *Cashbox*.

[615] O'Keefe, D. (1975). Album Credits/Liner Notes: *So Long Harry Truman*.

[616] Cashbox. (Apr. 26, 1975). "Eagles, Fogelberg Top U.S. Package," *Cashbox*.

[617] Cashbox. (May 31, 1975). "Eagles (Asylum E-45257) One of These Nights," *Cashbox*.

[618] Cashbox. (Jun. 7, 1975). "4th Eagles LP to Receive Special Attention from EA," *Cashbox*.

[619] Cashbox. (Jun. 21, 1975). "One of These Nights - Eagles - Asylum 7e-1039," *Cashbox*.

[620] Cashbox. (Aug. 2, 1975). "Breaks from Bob in NY," *Cashbox*.

[621] Cashbox. (Aug. 16, 1975). "Epic Pacts Azoff's Full Moon Records," *Cashbox*.

[622] Cashbox. (Aug. 23, 1975). "Columbia, Epic Dominate First Annual Rock Music Awards Show," *Cashbox*.

[623] Cashbox. (Aug. 30, 1975). "Eagles Go Platinum 2nd Time This Year," *Cashbox*.

[624] Cashbox. (Sep. 6, 1975). "Station Breaks," Cashbox.

[625] Cashbox. (Sep. 13, 1975). "Picks of the Week: Lyin' Eyes," *Cashbox*.

[626] Cashbox. (Oct. 11, 1975). "Points West," *Cashbox*.

[627] Cashbox. (Nov. 8, 1975). "Joni Mitchell, Jackson Browne Re-Sign with Asylum Records."

[628] Comanor, J. (1976). Album Credits/Liner Notes: *A Rumor In His Own Time*.

[629] Cashbox. (Dec. 13, 1975). "For the Record," *Cashbox*.

[630] Cashbox. (Dec. 20, 1975). "Points West," *Cashbox*.

[631] Cashbox. (Dec. 20, 1975). "Picks of the Week," *Cashbox*.

[632] Cashbox. (Jan. 10, 1976). "Million Midnight," *Cashbox*.

[633] *Cashbox*. (Jan. 17, 1976). "Post-Christmas Release Falloff Hurts Retailers."

[634] Cohen, G. (Jan. 17, 1976). "Rock Shows Debut on Cable TV," *Cashbox*.

[635] Cashbox. (Jan. 24, 1976). "Ian, Eagles Receive Most 1976 Grammy Nominations," *Cashbox*.

[636] Cashbox. (Jan. 24, 1976). "Arista Pacts with Azoff's Morning Sky," *Cashbox*.

[637] Cashbox. (Feb. 14, 1976). "Eagles 'Greatest' Keys E/A/N LPS," *Cashbox*.

[638] Cashbox. (Mar. 6, 1976). "Eagles Greatest Hits First RIAA Platinum," *Cashbox*.

[639] Cashbox. (Mar. 6, 1976). "Go East, Young Man," *Cashbox*.

[640] Cashbox. (Mar. 20, 1976). "Scaggs Signs with Azoff's Front Line," *Cashbox*.

[641] Cashbox. (Apr. 10, 1976). "Eagles' Hits Remain in #1 Spot by Wide Margin, But Perhaps Not for Long," *Cashbox*.

[642] Carmicle, J.B. (May 1, 1976.) "The Artists: Music and Lyrics," *Cashbox*.

[643] Cashbox. (May 22, 1976). "For the Record," *Cashbox*.

[644] Cashbox. (Jun. 26, 1976). "Leber-Krebs," *Cashbox*.

[645] DiMauro, P. (Aug. 7, 1976). "For the Record," *Cashbox*.

[646] Cashbox. (Aug. 28, 1976). "Turntable Go-Round," *Cashbox*.

[647] Cashbox. (Sep. 11, 1976). "Hooked on Lunacy," *Cashbox*.

[648] Cashbox. (Oct. 2, 1976). "For the Record," *Cashbox*.

[649] Cashbox. (Oct. 16, 1976). "Funky Kings (Arista As 0209) Slow Dancing," *Cashbox*.

[650] Doheny, N. (1976). Album Credits/Liner Notes: *Hard Candy*.

[651] Cashbox. (Oct. 30, 1976). "Eagles Play Sold Out Forum, 3 New Songs," *Cashbox*.

[652] Cashbox. (Oct. 30, 1976). "Eagles Celebrate," *Cashbox*.

[653] Carmicle, J.B. (Nov. 27, 1976). "RKO's Abrupt Eagles' Airing Forces E/A Into Rush Release," *Cashbox*.

[654] Cashbox. (Dec. 12, 1976). "Hotel California – Eagles," *Cashbox*.

[655] Cashbox. (Dec. 12, 1976). "Eagles (Asylum 45373) New Kid in Town," *Cashbox*.

[656] Cashbox. (Dec. 25, 1976). "Eagles Earn Platinum," *Cashbox*.

[657] Cashbox. (Mar. 5, 1977). "Modell's Advertises Eagles Album for $2," *Cashbox*.

[658] Cashbox. (Mar. 12, 1977). "Eagles (Asylum 45386) (Dist. Elektra) Hotel California," *Cashbox*.

[659] Cashbox. (Mar. 12, 1977). "Eagles 2x Platinum," *Cashbox*.

[660] Cashbox. (Apr. 2, 1977). "East Coastings," *Cashbox*.

[661] Terry, K. (Apr. 9, 1977). "Eagles at the Garden," *Cashbox*.

[662] Cashbox. (May 14, 1977). "Eagles (Elektra/Asylum 45386) Life in the Fast Lane."

[663] Weber, J. (May 21, 1977). "The Eagles Sue David Geffen, WB Music, In Publ. Dispute," *Cashbox*.

[664] Cashbox. (May 21, 1977). "East Coastings, Points West," *Cashbox*.

[665] DiMauro, P. (May 28, 1977). "\"Beatlemania\" Points to Broadway Despite Possible Legal Problems," *Cashbox*.

[666] Cashbox. (Jun. 11, 1977). "East Coastings, Points West," *Cashbox*.

[667] Cashbox. (Jul. 2, 1977). "East Coastings, Points West," *Cashbox*.

[668] Cashbox. (Jul. 2, 1977). "Country Roundup," *Cashbox*.

[669] Cashbox. (Jul. 30, 1977). "East Coastings, Points West: Eyes of Texas on Eagles," *Cashbox*.

[670] Cashbox. (Aug. 27, 1977). "East Coastings, Points West: Jeans On," *Cashbox*.

[671] Cashbox. (Sep. 24, 1977). "The Bernie Leadon/Michael Georgiades Band (Elektra/Asylum 45433)," *Cashbox*.

[672] *Cashbox*. (Oct. 1, 1977). "Soft-Rock Stations Providing Early Exposure for New Acts," *Cashbox*.

[673] Fulton, D. (Oct. 8, 1977). "Talent on Stage: Linda Ronstadt/Leadon-Michael Georgiades Band," *Cashbox*.

[674] Cashbox. (Oct. 15, 1977). "East Coastings, Points West: As the Eagle Flies," *Cashbox*.

[675] Cashbox. (Oct. 22, 1977). "East Coastings, Points West: Life in the Solo Lane," *Cashbox*.

[676] Cashbox. (Oct. 22, 1977). "East Coastings, Points West: Who Were Those Guys?", *Cashbox*.

[677] Lewis, R. (Nov. 12, 1977). "Punk Rock in England: There's More to it Than Meets the Ear, Strangler's Mgr. Says," *Cashbox*.

[678] Cashbox. (Nov. 19, 1977). "East Coasting, Points West: International Gold," *Cashbox*.

[679] Cashbox. (Nov. 26, 1977). "Glenda Griffith," *Cashbox*.

[680] Hilburn, R. (Jan. 22, 1977). "Beyond the Gold and Platinum," *Los Angeles Times*.

[681] Kilday, G. (Aug. 22, 1977). "Rock Goes the the Movies in \"FM\"," *Los Angeles Times*.

[682] Young, C.M. (Sep. 11, 1977). "Jaggers Still Together, Despite Constant Rumors," *Rolling Stone*.

[683] Cashbox. (Dec. 31, 1977). "East Coastings, Points West: Life in the Film Lane," *Cashbox*.

[684] Associated Press. (Dec. 4, 1977). "Singer Linda Ronstadt Joins List of Movie Stars," Associated Press.

[685] Kleiner, D. (Mar. 30, 1978). "'FM'. A Movie About DJS Trying to Maintain Dignity," *Chambersburg (Pa.) Public Opinion*.

[686] Fort Lauderdale News. (Mar. 3, 1978). "Stones Put Touches on Their New Album," Fort Lauderdale News

[687] The Daily Utah Chronicle. (May 3, 1978). "What Price Integrity?", *The Daily Utah Chronicle*

[688] Knoedelseder Jr., W.K. (Apr. 16, 1978). "A Rock/Film Honeymoon in Splitsville: The Makers of 'FM' Aren't Speaking to Each Other," *Los Angeles Times*.

[689] Baltake, J. (Aug. 13, 1978). "Film Feud: Culture vs. Hard Cash," *Chicago Tribune*.

[690] Kilday, G. (Nov. 8, 1978). "Film Clips: The Western Spurred On," *Los Angeles Times*.

[691] Serril, T. (May 10, 1978). "'FM' Called a Pleasant Surprise," *The Central New Jersey Home News*.

[692] McGuinn, R. (1991). Album Credits/Liner Notes: *Back from Rio*.

[693] *Record World*. (Sep. 11, 1971). "Asylum to Atlantic."

[694] Lawrence, T. (Jul. 31, 1971). "New Asylum Label Readies First Product," *Record World*.

[695] Record World. (Oct. 7, 1971). "Geffen-Roberts to WB," *Record World*.

[696] Record World. (Dec. 11, 1971). "Production Pacts Big Atlantic Factor," *Record World*.

[697] Ross, R. (Aug. 7, 1971). "Burritos, Lomas Crowd Pleasers," *Record World*.

[698] Ovens, D. (Jul. 1, 1972). "Billboard Pick Singles: Hot Chart Action," *Billboard*.

[699] Billboard. (Aug. 4, 1973). "Geffen & Roberts Splitting Asylum Reins; Build Staff," *Billboard*.

[700] Billboard. (Aug. 11, 1973). "Inside Track," *Billboard*.

[701] Billboard. (Nov. 17, 1973). "DJ Assn Issues Drug-Abuse Spots," *Billboard*.

[702] Rogers, K. (1982). Album Credits/Liner Notes: *Love Will Turn You Around*.

[703] Cashbox. (Apr. 24, 1982). "East Coasting, Points West," *Cashbox*.

[704] Cashbox. (Jun. 12, 1982). "Airplay: Station to Station," *Cashbox*.

[705] Cashbox. (Jun. 19, 1982). "No Fun Aloud - Glenn Frey," *Cashbox*.

[706] Cashbox. (Aug. 14, 1982). "Ravyns (Full Moon/Asylum) Raised on Radio," *Cashbox*.

[707] Cashbox. (Aug. 21, 1982). "Glenn Frey, The One You Love," *Cashbox*.

[708] Cashbox. (Aug. 21, 1982). "Don Henley, Johnny Can't Read," *Cashbox*.

[709] Cashbox. (Aug. 28, 1982). "Don Henley, I Can't Stand Still," *Cashbox*.

[710] Albert, M. (Aug. 13, 1982). "Merchandising: Top 200 Albums," *Cashbox*.

[711] Cashbox. (Jan. 5, 1980). "Eagles Come Home for Christmas," *Cashbox*.

[712] Cashbox. (Jan. 19, 1980). "International Dateline," *Cashbox*.

[713] Cashbox. (Jan. 25, 1980). "East Coastings: The Music of Business," *Cashbox*.

[714] Zevon, W. (1980). Album Credits/Liner Notes: *Bad Luck Streak in Dancing School*.

[715] Cashbox. (Jan. 26, 1980). "Air Play: Network News," *Cashbox*.

[716] Cashbox. (Feb. 9, 1980). "Artist Development is Being Redefined by Record Labels," *Cashbox*.

[717] Cashbox. (Feb. 16, 1980). "Solters Appointed VP, Front Line Management Co.," *Cashbox*.

[718] Cashbox. (Feb. 16, 1980). "Eagles, I Can't Tell You Why," *Cashbox*.

[719] Cashbox. (Feb. 23, 1980). "The Long Run for Real," *Cashbox*.

[720] Cashbox. (Mar. 8, 1980). "East Coastings," *Cashbox*.

[721] Cashbox. (Mar. 8, 1980). "Station to Station," *Cashbox*.

[722] Cashbox. (Mar. 29, 1980). "East Coastings, Points West," *Cashbox*.

[723] Cross, C. (1979). Album Credits/Liner Notes: *Christopher Cross*.

[724] Cashbox. (May 3, 1980). "Urban Cowboy, Soundtrack," *Cashbox*.

[725] Cashbox. (Jun. 21, 1980). "Points West," *Cashbox*.

[726] Hilburn, J.D. (Feb. 15, 2015). "Desperado," Setlist.fm. Retrieved from https://www.setlist.fm/setlist/eagles/1974/fant-ewing-coliseum-monroe-la-23ca54db.html.

[727] Morse, S. (Apr. 26, 1990). "A Night of Rock Nirvana at the Centrum," *Boston Globe*.

[728] Tampa Tribune. (Jan. 29, 2014). "All-Stars Honor Beatles," *Tampa Tribune*.

[729] Bauder, D. (Mar. 16, 2010). "Genesis, ABBA Inducted into Rock Hall of Fame," Associated Press.

[730] Weisman, J. (Jul. 10, 1972). "Pine Knob Cancels Rock Concerts," *Detroit Free Press*.

[731] Lewis, R. (Jan. 23, 2016). "Linda Ronstadt Remembers Glenn Frey," *Los Angeles Times*.

[732] Calgary Herald. (Jul. 31, 1990). "Singer Switches Tracks: J.D. Souther Makes His Name in Film," *Calgary Herald*.

[733] Rodgers, L. (Mar. 15, 2009). "J.D. Takes Souther-ly Route Back to the Stage," *Arizona Republic*.

[734] Lipton, L. (Sep. 29, 1990). "Troubadour JD Souther Found Acting an Offer He Couldn't Refuse," *Los Angeles Times*.

[735] Rodman, S. (Nov. 11, 2008). "He Feels Like a New Kid Again," *Boston Globe*.

[736] Lewis, R. (Sep. 27, 2008). "The Ballad of a Classic Guitar Shop," *Los Angeles Times*.

[737] BestClassicBands.com, Brown, M. (Nov. 21, 2017). "'Hotel California' Producer on the Making of the LP," BestClassicBands.com. Retrieved from https://bestclassicbands.com/bill-szymczyk-interview-11-21-17/.

[738] Sexton, P. (Jun. 21, 2018). "Beach Boys Triumph at Elton John's Wembley Extravaganza," UDiscovermusic.com.

[739] Einarson, J. (2008). *Hot Burritos: The True Story of the Flying Burrito Brothers*, p. 147, London, UK: Jawbone Press.

[740] Tom, L. (Jan. 21, 2010). "None Other: Gene Clark & the Rise of Country Rock," PopCulturePress.com. Retrieved from http://popculturepress.blogspot.com/.

[741] Creamer, J. (Oct. 9, 1987). "The Nitty Gritty Dirt Band: After 21 Years, Band Hopes American Sound Defies Classification," *The Montgomery (Ala.) Advertiser*.

[742] Parlin, G. (Aug. 1, 1987). "Nitty Gritty Dirt Band: Still Together," *La Crosse (Wis.) Tribune*.

[743] Meehan, J. (Sep. 21, 1977). "Music Notes," *The Newspaper (Park City, Utah)*.

[744] Creighton, J. (May 3, 1987). "New Nitty Gritty Dirt Band Dazzles Fans at Westport," *St. Louis Post-Dispatch*.

[745] Brodeur, N. (Dec. 9, 2016). "Rocker Joe Walsh Gets MOPOP Founders Award, Joined by Ringo Starr, Dave Grohl in Seattle," *Seattle Times*.

[746] Irving, C. (May 15, 1976). "High-Riding Carter Turns to Party Rifts," *San Francisco Examiner*.

[747] Butkiewicz, J. (Jan. 31, 1986). "From Many Bands They Came to Form the Group Black Tie," *The Times Leader (Wilkes-Barre, Pa.)*.

[748] Devault, R. (Feb. 8, 1986). "Black Tie: Pedigreed Rock," *The Atlanta Constitution*.

[749] Surkamp, D. (Feb. 6, 1986). "Black Tie is a Star-Studded Act," *St. Louis Post-Dispatch*.

[750] Fleming, M. (May 25, 2007). "The Scottsville Squirrel Barkers - From Blue Guitar to Country Rock," *Northern Georgia Bluegrass Chronicles*.

[751] Wiser, C. (Nov. 15, 2003). "Songwriter Interviews: Mike Campbell," Songfacts.com.

[752] Devenish, C. (Mar. 19, 2002). "Henley Fires Back at RIAA," *Rolling Stone*.

[753] Andrews, T.M. (Aug. 20, 2018). "The Eagles Once Again Have the All-Time Best-Selling Album in the U.S., Upstaging Michael Jackson," *Washington Post*.

[754] Detroit Free Press. (Aug. 11, 1981). "'Heavy Metal' Can't Find Right Track," *Detroit Free Press*.

[755] Associated Press. (Dec. 19, 1983). "Guitarist Says Creating is Best Part of Music," Associated Press.

[756] Graff, G. (Jan. 5, 1984). "Taking Flight—Don Felder's Solo Career Soars After Eagles Call it Quits," *Austin American-Statesman*.

[757] Yearwood, T. (1992). Album Credits/Liner Notes: *Hearts in Armor*.

[758] Duffey, M. (Apr. 22, 1978). "Stones' Tour to Begin in June," *Rolling Stone*.

[759] Cashbox. (Feb. 14, 1970). "Film Role Set for Ensemble," *Cashbox*.

[760] Cashbox. (Feb. 21, 1970). "Hollywood: Meanwhile, Back at the Ranch," *Cashbox*.

[761] Cashbox. (May 9, 1970). "Producer Profile: Bill Szymczyk," *Cashbox*.

[762] Cashbox. (Jul. 18, 1970). "ABC/Dunhill Gives Ray and James Big Push," *Cashbox*.

[763] Cashbox. (Jul. 18, 1970). "James Gang Rides Again - James Gang," *Cashbox*.

[764] Cashbox. (Jul. 18, 1970). "James Gang - Funk #49," *Cashbox*.

[765] Cashbox. (Oct. 31, 1970). "James Gang Ends European Tour," *Cashbox*.

[766] Billboard. (Dec. 19, 1970). "How WNCR-FM Became a Showcase 'by Accident'," *Billboard*.

[767] Record World. (Jul. 25, 1970). "James Gang Rides Again," *Record World*.

[768] Record World. (Jul. 25, 1970). "James Gang - Funk #49," *Record World*.

[769] Sigman, M. (Aug. 15, 1970). "Kooper Joins James Gang for Record World Visit," *Record World*.

[770] Record World. (Nov. 28, 1970). "James Gang Takes Over," *Record World*.

[771] Cashbox. (Sep. 14, 1974). "The Kids & Me - Billy Preston," *Cashbox*.

[772] Starr, R. (1983). Album Credits/Liner Notes: *Old Wave*.

[773] Horowitz, J. (Jul. 17, 1980). "Nights of Sounds and Music," *Minneapolis Star Tribune*.

[775] Carrack, P. (2009). Album Credits/Liner Notes: *I Know That Name*.

[776] Patterson, J. (Nov. 30, 1993). "'Thread' Exudes Legacy of Eagles," Associated Press.

[777] Marsh, D. (Feb. 4, 2015). "The Grammys in 1976: Was the Captain & Tennille Really Better Than Jefferson Starship?" *The Guardian*.

[778] Billboard. (Feb. 15, 2016). "Eagles Get Presented Grammy for \"Hotel California\" That They Didn't Accept in 1977," *Billboard*.

[779] Oppel, P. (Apr. 19, 1980). "Where Eagles Dare," *Los Angeles Times*.

[780] Johnson, G. (Oct. 15, 2018). "Rick Nelson: Rockabilly Ricky, The Pop Years & The Crash," Michigan Rock and Roll Legends. Retrieved from https://www.michiganrockandrolllegends.com/dr-js-blog/278-rick-nelson-pt-1-rockabilly-ricky.

[781] Homer, S. (2012). *Rick Nelson, Rock 'n' Roll Pioneer*, Jefferson, NC: McFarland & Company, Inc.

[782] Tiegel, E. (Jan. 4, 1981). "'Aces' Unlucky for Producers," *Billboard*.

[783] Abbott, J. (Sep. 10, 1989). "Paul Shaffer, Coast to Coast," *The Orlando Sentinel*.

[784] Arizona Republic. (Dec. 14, 1990). "'Blues' A Big Hit for 'Simpsons'," *Arizona Republic*.

[785] The Honolulu Advertiser. (Oct. 3, 1990). "The Jam is on Tonight," *The Honolulu Advertiser*.

[786] Antczak, J. (Jan. 8, 1991). "Starr Intent on Getting Beyond Beatle Days; Releases New CD," *Fon Du Lac Commonwealth Reporter*.

[787] The Newark (Ohio) Advocate. (Apr. 13, 1993). "Ringo is Going Home," *The Newark (Ohio) Advocate*.

[788] Gunderson, E. (Feb. 9, 1994). "Whitney and Baby Stole the Show," *The Honolulu Advertiser*.

[789] CMT.com. (Jun. 22, 2012). "Joe Walsh and Friends Meet at CMT Crossroads," CMT.com.

[790] Goodman, F. (1998). *The Mansion on the Hill*, New York, NY: Vintage Books.

[791] Eng, S. (1996). *Jimmy Buffett: The Man from Margaritaville Revealed*, New York, NY: St. Martin's Griffin.

[792] Firefall. (1977). Album Credits/Liner Notes: *Luna Sea*.

[793] Henley, D. (1995). Album Credits/Liner Notes: *Actual*

Miles: Don Henley's Greatest Hits.

[794] Roberts, R. (1972). Album Credits/Liner Notes: Windmills.

[795] Roberts, R. (1973). Album Credits/Liner Notes: She Is a Song.

[796] Browne, J. (1973). Album Credits/Liner Notes: For Everyman.

[797] Browne, J. (1974). Album Credits/Liner Notes: Late for the Sky.

[798] Newman, R. (1974). Album Credits/Liner Notes: Good Old Boys.

[799] Walsh, J. (1974). Album Credits/Liner Notes: So What.

[800] The Souther–Hillman–Furay Band. (1974). Album Credits/Liner Notes: The Souther–Hillman–Furay Band.

[801] Browne, J. (1976). Album Credits/Liner Notes: The Pretender.

[802] Souther, J.D. (1974). Album Credits/Liner Notes: You're Only Lonely.

[803] Souther, J.D. (1976). Album Credits/Liner Notes: Black Rose.

[804] Barton, L. (1982). Album Credits/Liner Notes: Old Enough.

[805] Souther, J.D. (1984). Album Credits/Liner Notes: Home by Dawn.

[806] Zevon, W. (1976). Album Credits/Liner Notes: Warren Zevon.

[807] Zevon, W. (1982). Album Credits/Liner Notes: The Envoy.

[808] Zevon, W. (1987). Album Credits/Liner Notes: Sentimental Hygiene.

[809] Zevon, W. (2003). Album Credits/Liner Notes: The Wind.

[810] Zevon, W. (2006). Album Credits/Liner Notes: Reconsider Me: The Love Songs.

[811] Boylan, T. (Dec. 1, 1978). "The L-PS (Terence Boylan - Don't Hang Up Those Dancin' Shoes)," The (Saskatchewan) Leader-Post.

[812] Newman, R. (1977). Album Credits/Liner Notes: Little Criminals.

[813] Newman, R. (1983). Album Credits/Liner Notes: Trouble in Paradise.

[814] Newman, R. (1995). Album Credits/Liner Notes: Randy Newman's Faust.

[815] The Stone Poneys. (1967). Album Credits/Liner Notes: Evergreen, Vol. 2.

[816] Ronstadt, L. (1999). Album Credits/Liner Notes: Western Wall: The Tucson Sessions.

[817] Ronstadt, L. (2014). Album Credits/Liner Notes: Duets.

[818] Fogelberg, D. (1978). Album Credits/Liner Notes: Twin Sons of Different Mothers.

[819] Walsh, J. (1976). Album Credits/Liner Notes: You Can't Argue with a Sick Mind.

[820] Walsh, J. (1978). Album Credits/Liner Notes: But Seriously, Folks...

[821] Walsh, J. (1981). Album Credits/Liner Notes: There Goes the Neighborhood.

[822] Walsh, J. (1983). Album Credits/Liner Notes: You Bought It – You Name It.

[823] Walsh, J. (1985). Album Credits/Liner Notes: The Confessor.

[824] Bonoff, K. (1977). Album Credits/Liner Notes: Karla Bonoff.

[825] Bonoff, K. (1979). Album Credits/Liner Notes: Restless Nights.

[826] Bonoff, K. (1982). Album Credits/Liner Notes: Wild Heart of the Young.

[827] Cross, C. (1983). Album Credits/Liner Notes: Another Page.

[828] Goffin, L. (1979). Album Credits/Liner Notes: Kid Blue.

[829] Boylan, T. (1980). Album Credits/Liner Notes: Suzy.

[830] John, E. (1980). Album Credits/Liner Notes: 21 at 33.

[831] Manchester, M. (1980). Album Credits/Liner Notes: For the Working Girl.

[832] Burnett, B. (Feb. 1, 1981). "On Music: Blue Steel," Jackson (Miss.) Clarion-Ledger.

[833] Nicks, S. (1998). Album Credits/Liner Notes: Enchanted.

[834] Various Artists. (1982). Album Credits/Liner Notes: Fast Times at Ridgemont High - Soundtrack.

[835] Mitchell, J. (1977). Album Credits/Liner Notes: Don Juan's Reckless Daughter.

[836] Mitchell, J. (1985). Album Credits/Liner Notes: Dog Eat Dog.

[837] Mitchell, J. (1988). Album Credits/Liner Notes: Chalk Mark in a Rain Storm.

[838] Taylor, J. (1985). Album Credits/Liner Notes: That's Why I'm Here.

[839] Walsh, J. (1992). Album Credits/Liner Notes: Songs for a Dying Planet.

[840] Aerosmith. (1993). Album Credits/Liner Notes: Get a Grip.

[841] Browne, J. (1993). Album Credits/Liner Notes: I'm Alive.

[842] John, E. (1993). Album Credits/Liner Notes: Duets.

[843] Webb, J. (1993). Album Credits/Liner Notes: Suspending Disbelief.

[844] Storyville. (1993). Album Credits/Liner Notes: Bluest Eyes.

[845] Donohue, D. (1992). Album Credits/Liner Notes: Dane Donohue.

[846] Lawrence, K. (Jan. 11, 2002). "Musicians Battling Record Labels Over Copyright for Songs," Owensboro (Ky.) Messenger-Inquirer.

[847] Carla Olson & The Textones. (1984). Album Credits/Liner Notes: Midnight Mission.

[848] Carla Olson & The Textones. (1995). Album Credits/Liner Notes: Wave of the Hand: The Best of Carla Olson.

[849] Blue, D. (1973). Album Credits/Liner Notes: Nice Baby and the Angel.

[850] Blue, D. (1975). Album Credits/Liner Notes: Com'n Back for More.

[851] Prine, J. (1975). Album Credits/Liner Notes: Common Sense.

[852] Fool's Gold. (1976). Album Credits/Liner Notes: Fool's Gold.

[853] Simon, C. (1976). Album Credits/Liner Notes: Another Passenger.

[854] Scaggs, B. (1980). Album Credits/Liner Notes: Hits!.

[855] Scaggs, B. (1988). Album Credits/Liner Notes: Other Roads.

[856] Buffett, J. (1985). Album Credits/Liner Notes: Last Mango in Paris.

[857] Buffett, J. (1988). Album Credits/Liner Notes: Hot Water.

[858] Buffett, J. (1989). Album Credits/Liner Notes: Off to See the Lizard.

[859] Little River Band. (1994). Album Credits/Liner Notes: Reminiscing: The Twentieth Anniversary Collection.

[860] Tempchin, J. (1978). Album Credits/Liner Notes: Jack

Tempchin.

[861] Nelson, R. (1963). Album Credits/Liner Notes: *A Long Vacation*.

[862] Gayden, M. (1976). Album Credits/Liner Notes: *Hymn To The Seeker*.

[863] Welch, B. (1990). Album Credits/Liner Notes: *Man Overboard*.

[864] Souther-Hillman-Furay Band. (1975). Album Credits/Liner Notes: *Trouble in Paradise*.

[865] Furay, R. (2006). Album Credits/Liner Notes: *Heartbeat of Love*.

[866] Stills, S. (1984). Album Credits/Liner Notes: *Right By You*.

[867] Manassas. (1973). Album Credits/Liner Notes: *Down the Road*.

[868] Crosby, Stills & Nash. (1982). Album Credits/Liner Notes: *Daylight Again*.

[869] Furay, R. (1979). Album Credits/Liner Notes: *I Still Have Dreams*.

[870] Marx, R. (1987). Album Credits/Liner Notes: *Richard Marx*.

[871] Marx, R. (1994). Album Credits/Liner Notes: *Paid Vacation*.

[872] Compton & Batteau. (1970). Album Credits/Liner Notes: *In California*.

[873] Dillard, D. (1970). Album Credits/Liner Notes: *The Banjo Album*.

[874] Nitty Gritty Dirt Band. (1968). Album Credits/Liner Notes: *Rare Junk*.

[875] Brooks, D. (1969). Album Credits/Liner Notes: *Denny Brooks*.

[876] Clifford, B. (1969). Album Credits/Liner Notes: *See Your Way Clear*.

[877] Hedge & Donna Capers. (1970). Album Credits/Liner Notes: *Special Circumstances*.

[878] Sings, O. (1970). Album Credits/Liner Notes: *Odetta Sings*.

[879] Giguere, R. (1971). Album Credits/Liner Notes: *Hexagram 16*.

[880] Gibson, B. (1971). Album Credits/Liner Notes: *Bob Gibson*.

[881] Taylor, K. (1971). Album Credits/Liner Notes: *Sister Kate*.

[882] Siebel, P. (1971). Album Credits/Liner Notes: *Jack-Knife Gypsy*.

[883] Barry McGuire & The Doctor. (1971). Album Credits/Liner Notes: *Barry McGuire & The Doctor*.

[884] Lind, B. (1971). Album Credits/Liner Notes: *Since There Were Circles*.

[885] Parrish, M. (1972). Album Credits/Liner Notes: *It's A Cinch To Give Legs To Old Hard-Boiled Eggs*.

[886] Parsons, G. (1974). Album Credits/Liner Notes: *Grievous Angel*.

[887] David Bromberg Band. (1975). Album Credits/Liner Notes: *Midnight On The Water*.

[888] Fairweather-Low, A. (1975). Album Credits/Liner Notes: *La Booga Rooga*.

[889] Harris, E. (1976). Album Credits/Liner Notes: *Elite Hotel*.

[890] Harris, E. (1975). Album Credits/Liner Notes: *Pieces Of The Sky*.

[891] Fairweather-Low, A. (1976). Album Credits/Liner Notes: *Be Bop 'N' Holla*.

[892] Toto. (1986). Album Credits/Liner Notes: *Fahrenheit*.

[893] Hillman, C. (1976). Album Credits/Liner Notes: *Slippin' Away*.

[894] Reddy, H. (1977). Album Credits/Liner Notes: *Ear Candy*.

[895] McCorison, D. (1977). Album Credits/Liner Notes: *Dan McCorison*.

[896] Various Artists. (1978). Album Credits/Liner Notes: *White Mansions - A Tale from The American Civil War 1861-1865*.

[897] Woodstock Mountains Revue. (1978). Album Credits/Liner Notes: *Pretty Lucky*.

[898] Nuttycombe, C. (1978). Album Credits/Liner Notes: *It's Just a Lifetime*.

[899] Various Artists. (1980). Album Credits/Liner Notes: *The Legend Of Jesse James*.

[900] Various Artists. (1981). Album Credits/Liner Notes: *God Loves Country Music*.

[901] Coltrane, C. (1981). Album Credits/Liner Notes: *Silk & Steel*.

[902] Hillman, C. (1983). Album Credits/Liner Notes: *Morning Sky*.

[903] Harry Browning and Laury Boone. (1983). Album Credits/Liner Notes: *Sweet Harmony*.

[904] Down Home Praise. (1983). Album Credits/Liner Notes: *Down Home Praise*.

[905] Denver, J. (1984). Album Credits/Liner Notes: *John Denver's Greatest Hits, Volume 3*.

[906] Francisco, D. (1984). Album Credits/Liner Notes: *Holiness*.

[907] Hillman, C. (1984). Album Credits/Liner Notes: *Desert Rose*.

[908] Clark, G. (1986). Album Credits/Liner Notes: *Roadmaster*.

[909] Watson, H. (1987). Album Credits/Liner Notes: *Blue Slipper*.

[910] Durham, B. (1987). Album Credits/Liner Notes: *Where I Grew Up*.

[911] Watson, H. (1987). Album Credits/Liner Notes: *Helen Watson*.

[912] Hiatt, J. (1988). Album Credits/Liner Notes: *Slow Turning*.

[913] Alabama. (1988). Album Credits/Liner Notes: *Southern Star*.

[914] Neuwirth, B. (1988). Album Credits/Liner Notes: *Back To The Front*.

[915] Nitty Gritty Dirt Band. (1989). Album Credits/Liner Notes: *Will The Circle Be Unbroken (Volume Two)*.

[916] Watson, H. (1989). Album Credits/Liner Notes: *The Weather Inside*.

[917] Green on Red. (1989). Album Credits/Liner Notes: *This Time Around*.

[918] Griffith, N. (1989). Album Credits/Liner Notes: *Storms*.

[919] Berg, M. (1990). Album Credits/Liner Notes: *Lying to the Moon*.

[920] Rogers, K. (1990). Album Credits/Liner Notes: *Love Is Strange*.

[921] Foster & Lloyd. (1990). Album Credits/Liner Notes: *Version of the Truth*.

[922] Bashung. (1991). Album Credits/Liner Notes: *Osez Joséphine*.

[923] Tritt, T. (1991). Album Credits/Liner Notes: *It's All About to Change*.

[924] Astor, T. (1991). Album Credits/Liner Notes: *Voll Aus Dem Leben*.

[925] Malloy, M. (1992). Album Credits/Liner Notes: *Nobody Wins in This War*.

[926] Alabama. (1992). Album Credits/Liner Notes: *American Pride*.

[927] Restless Heart. (1992). Album Credits/Liner Notes: *Big Iron Horses*.

[928] Rivière, V. (1992). Album Credits/Liner Notes: *Mojave*.

[929] Shocked, M. (1992). Album Credits/Liner Notes: *Arkansas Traveler*.

[930] Reeves, R. (1992). Album Credits/Liner Notes: *The More I Learn*.

[931] Reeves, R. (1993). Album Credits/Liner Notes: *What Comes Naturally*.

[932] Bashung. (1993). Album Credits/Liner Notes: *J'écume*.

[933] Crosby, D. (1993). Album Credits/Liner Notes: *Thousand Roads*.

[934] Berg, M. (1994). Album Credits/Liner Notes: *The Speed of Grace*.

[935] Malloy, M. (1994). Album Credits/Liner Notes: *Ceilings and Walls*.

[936] The Amazing Rhythm Aces. (1996). Album Credits/Liner Notes: *Ride Again - Volume 1*.

[937] Woodruff, B. (1994). Album Credits/Liner Notes: *Dreams & Saturday Nights*.

[938] Neuwirth, B. (1996). Album Credits/Liner Notes: *Look Up*.

[939] Groovegrass. (1998). Album Credits/Liner Notes: *GrooveGrass 101*.

[940] McCaslin, M. (1999). Album Credits/Liner Notes: *Rain: The Lost Album*.

[941] Hart, T.L. (1999). Album Credits/Liner Notes: *Tara Lyn Hart*.

[942] Harris, E. (2001). Album Credits/Liner Notes: *Anthology (The Warner / Reprise Years)*.

[943] The Jayhawks. (2003). Album Credits/Liner Notes: *Rainy Day Music*.

[944] Harris, E. (2003). Album Credits/Liner Notes: *Stumble Into Grace*.

[945] Eagles. (2003). Album Credits/Liner Notes: *The Very Best of the Eagles*.

[946] Cowan, J. (2014). Album Credits/Liner Notes: *Sixty*.

[947] Crow, S. (2002). Album Credits/Liner Notes: *C'mon C'mon*.

[948] Cash, J. (2002). Album Credits/Liner Notes: *American IV: The Man Comes Around*.

[949] Barris, S. (2016). Album Credits/Liner Notes: *The Road in Me*.

[950] Dana, V. (1970). Album Credits/Liner Notes: *If I Never Knew Your Name*.

[951] Eve. (1970). Album Credits/Liner Notes: *You Go Your Way*.

[952] Browne, J. (1977). Album Credits/Liner Notes: *Running on Empty*.

[953] Larson, N. (1978). Album Credits/Liner Notes: *Nicolette Larson*.

[954] Carl, M. (1983). Album Credits/Liner Notes: *The Lonely Guy soundtrack*.

[955] Lee, J. (1984). Album Credits/Liner Notes: *'Til The Bars Burn Down*.

[956] Farren, C. (1985). Album Credits/Liner Notes: *Girls Just Want to Have Fun soundtrack*.

[957] Tempchin, J. (1994). Album Credits/Liner Notes: *After the Rain*.

[958] King, B. (2005). Album Credits/Liner Notes: *B.B. King & Friends - 80*.

[959] Souther, J.D. (2007). Album Credits/Liner Notes: *Border Town - The Very Best Of J.D. Souther*.

[960] Salisbury, S. (2000). Album Credits/Liner Notes: *Falling to Pieces*.

[961] Mallory, L. (2002). Album Credits/Liner Notes: *That's The Way It's Gonna Be*.

[962] Salisbury, S. (2005). Album Credits/Liner Notes: *Sandy*.

[963] Dinner, M. (1974). Album Credits/Liner Notes: *The Great Pretender*.

[964] Pure Prairie League. (1975). Album Credits/Liner Notes: *Two Lane Highway*.

[965] Angelle. (1977). Album Credits/Liner Notes: *Angelle*.

[966] Gibb, A. (1978). Album Credits/Liner Notes: *Shadow Dancing*.

[967] Bee Gees. (1981). Album Credits/Liner Notes: *Paradise*.

[968] Vitale, J. (1981). Album Credits/Liner Notes: *Plantation Harbor*.

[969] Bee Gees. (1981). Album Credits/Liner Notes: *Living Eyes*.

[970] Shorrock, G. (1982). Album Credits/Liner Notes: *Villain of the Peace*.

[971] Felder, D. (1983). Album Credits/Liner Notes: *Airborne*.

[972] Ann, R. (1983). Album Credits/Liner Notes: *Hello It's Me*.

[973] Streisand, B. (1984). Album Credits/Liner Notes: *Emotion*.

[974] Ross, D. (1985). Album Credits/Liner Notes: *Eaten Alive*.

[975] Bon Jovi, J. (1992). Album Credits/Liner Notes: *A Very Special Christmas 2*.

[976] Zander, R. (1993). Album Credits/Liner Notes: *Robin Zander*.

[977] Nelson. (1995). Album Credits/Liner Notes: *Because They Can*.

[978] Henely, D. (2000). Album Credits/Liner Notes: *Inside Job*.

[979] Zevon, W. (2002). Album Credits/Liner Notes: *Genius: The Best of Warren Zevon*.

[980] Bishop, S. (1984). Album Credits/Liner Notes: *Sleeping with Girls*.

[981] Styx. (2015). Album Credits/Liner Notes: *Live at The Orleans Arena Las Vegas*.

[982] king, B. (1970). Album Credits/Liner Notes: *Indianola Mississippi Seeds*.

[983] Haskell, J. (1971). Album Credits/Liner Notes: *California '99*.

[984] Witherspoon, J. (1971). Album Credits/Liner Notes: *Handbags and Gladrags*.

[985] King, B. (1972). Album Credits/Liner Notes: *L.A. Midnight*.

[986] America. (1973). Album Credits/Liner Notes: *Hat Trick*.

[987] The Fabulous Rhinestones. (1973). Album Credits/Liner Notes: *Freewheelin'*.

[988] REO Speedwagon. (1973). Album Credits/Liner Notes: *Ridin' The Storm Out*.

[989] Stanley, M. (1973). Album Credits/Liner Notes: *Michael Stanley*.

[990] Derringer, R. (1973). Album Credits/Liner Notes: *All American Boy*.

[991] King, B. (1973). Album Credits/Liner Notes: *The Best of B.B. King*.

[992] Vitale, J. (1975). Album Credits/Liner Notes: *Roller Coaster Weekend*.

[993] Manzarek, R. (1975). Album Credits/Liner Notes: *The Whole Thing Started with Rock & Roll Now It's Out Of Control*.

[994] Moon, K. (1975). Album Credits/Liner Notes: *Two Sides of the Moon*.

[995] Ferguson, J. (1976). Album Credits/Liner Notes: *All Alone in The End Zone*.

[996] Kooper, A. (1976). Album Credits/Liner Notes: *Act Like Nothing's Wrong*.

[997] Stewart, R. (1976). Album Credits/Liner Notes: *A Night on the Town*.

[998] Talton, Stewart & Sandlin. (1976). Album Credits/Liner Notes: *Happy to Be Alive*.

[999] Wyman, B. (1976). Album Credits/Liner Notes: *Stand Alone*.

[1000] Ferguson, J. (1977). Album Credits/Liner Notes: *Thunder Island*.

[1001] Emerson, Lake & Palmer. (1977). Album Credits/Liner Notes: *Works (Volume 1)*.

[1002] Gibb, A. (1977). Album Credits/Liner Notes: *Flowing Rivers*.

[1003] Ferguson, J. (1978). Album Credits/Liner Notes: *Real Life Ain't This Way*.

[1004] The Beach Boys. (1980). Album Credits/Liner Notes: *Keepin' The Summer Alive*.

[1005] Entwistle, J. (1981). Album Credits/Liner Notes: *Too Late The Hero*.

[1006] Richie, L. (1982). Album Credits/Liner Notes: *Lionel Richie*.

[1007] Henley, D. (1982). Album Credits/Liner Notes: *I Can't Stand Still*.

[1008] Ferguson, J. (1981). Album Credits/Liner Notes: *White Noise*.

[1009] Quarterflash. (1982). Album Credits/Liner Notes: *Take Another Picture*.

[1010] Ross, D. (1983). Album Credits/Liner Notes: *Ross*.

[1011] The Party Boys. (1985). Album Credits/Liner Notes: *You Need Professional Help*.

[1012] McDonald, M. (1985). Album Credits/Liner Notes: *No Lookin' Back*.

[1013] Winwood, S. (1986). Album Credits/Liner Notes: *Back in the High Life*.

[1014] Dolby's Cube. (1986). Album Credits/Liner Notes: *Howard the Duck soundtrack*.

[1015] Jimmy Davis & Junction. (1987). Album Credits/Liner Notes: *Kick the Wall*.

[1016] The Oak Ridge Boys. (1987). Album Credits/Liner Notes: *Where the Fast Lane Ends*.

[1017] Bar-Kays. (1989). Album Credits/Liner Notes: *Animal*.

[1018] Staff, R. (1990). Album Credits/Liner Notes: *Live from the Pacific Amphitheatre*.

[1019] Starr, R. (1989). Album Credits/Liner Notes: *Starr Struck: Best of Ringo Starr, Vol. 2*.

[1020] Wilson Phillips. (1990). Album Credits/Liner Notes: *Wilson Phillips*.

[1021] Herbs. (1990). Album Credits/Liner Notes: *Homegrown*.

[1022] Gibb, A. (1991). Album Credits/Liner Notes: *Andy Gibb*.

[1023] King, A. (1991). Album Credits/Liner Notes: *Red House*.

[1024] Summer, H.L. (1991). Album Credits/Liner Notes: *Way Past Midnight*.

[1025] Kaye, T.J. (1992). Album Credits/Liner Notes: *Not Alone*.

[1026] Emmanuel, T. (1993). Album Credits/Liner Notes: *The Journey*.

[1027] Billy Bacon and the Forbidden Pigs. (1995). Album Credits/Liner Notes: *The Other White Meat*.

[1028] Starr, R. (1998). Album Credits/Liner Notes: *Ringo Starr - VH1 Storytellers*.

[1029] Nelson, W. (2004). Album Credits/Liner Notes: *Outlaws and Angels*.

[1030] May 4 Task Force. (2005). Album Credits/Liner Notes: *The Kent State May 4 CD Project*.

[1031] Chesney, K. (2007). Album Credits/Liner Notes: *Just Who I Am: Poets & Pirates*.

[1032] Various Artists. (2007). Album Credits/Liner Notes: *Dear Mr. Fantasy*.

[1033] JD & The Straight Shot. (2008). Album Credits/Liner Notes: *Right on Time*.

[1034] Voormann, K. (2010). Album Credits/Liner Notes: *A Sideman's Journey*.

[1035] Starr, R. (2010). Album Credits/Liner Notes: *Y Not*.

[1036] McCartney, P. (2012). Album Credits/Liner Notes: *iTunes Live From Capitol Studios*.

[1037] Starr, R. (2012). Album Credits/Liner Notes: *Ringo 2012*.

[1038] Brooks, K. (2012). Album Credits/Liner Notes: *New To This Town*.

[1039] The Colorodas. (2013). Album Credits/Liner Notes: *Big Empty*.

[1040] Campbell, M. (Feb. 3, 1977). "Record Industry Goes Platinum," *Cashbox*.

[1041] Moore, L. (Aug. 16, 1979). "Clamping Down on Gold Records," *San Francisco Examiner*.

[1042] Peck, A. (Mar. 13, 1977). "Diamond Records Suggested When Gold, Platinum Too Easy," *Chicago Daily News*.

[1043] Kot, G. (Nov. 3, 2013). "Eminem Rekindles the Bad Old Days," *Baltimore Sun*.

[1044] The Stanley Clark Band. (2014). Album Credits/Liner Notes: *Up*.

[1045] Foo Fighters. (2014). Album Credits/Liner Notes: *Sonic Highways*.

[1046] Hollywood Vampires. (2015). Album Credits/Liner Notes: *Hollywood Vampires*.

[1047] Starr, R. (2015). Album Credits/Liner Notes: *Postcards From Paradise*.

[1048] Mayall, J. (2017). Album Credits/Liner Notes: *Talk About That*.

[1049] Bolton, M. (2017). Album Credits/Liner Notes: *Songs of Cinema*.

[1050] Mahal, T. (2017). Album Credits/Liner Notes: *TajMo*.

[1051] Starr, R. (2017). Album Credits/Liner Notes: *Give More Love*.

[1052] Redwing. (1972). Album Credits/Liner Notes: *What This Country Needs*.

[1053] Neuwirth, B. (1974). Album Credits/Liner Notes: *Bob Neuwirth*.

[1054] Steely Dan. (1974). Album Credits/Liner Notes: *Pretzel Logic*.

[1055] Quarterflash. (1981). Album Credits/Liner Notes: *Quarterflash*.

[1056] Prism. (1983). Album Credits/Liner Notes: *Beat Street*.

[1057] Little America. (1987). Album Credits/Liner Notes: *Little America*.

[1058] The Jeff Healey Band. (1988). Album Credits/Liner Notes: *See the Light*.

[1059] Toto. (1990). Album Credits/Liner Notes: *Past to Present 1977-1990*.

[1060] Jordan, M. (1990). Album Credits/Liner Notes: *Cow*.

[1061] Buffett, J. (1992). Album Credits/Liner Notes: *Boats, Beaches, Bars & Ballads*.

[1062] Boel, H. (1992). Album Credits/Liner Notes: *My Kindred Spirit*.

[1063] Open Skyz. (1993). Album Credits/Liner Notes: *Open Skyz*.

[1064] Gaitsch, B. (2006). Album Credits/Liner Notes: *A Lyre in A Windstorm*.

[1065] Henley, D. (1997). Album Credits/Liner Notes: *The Bridge School Concerts, Vol. One*.

[1066] Gaitsch, B. (2003). Album Credits/Liner Notes: *Aphasia*.

[1067] Fogelberg, D. (2000). Album Credits/Liner Notes: *Something Old, New, Borrowed, and Some Blues*.

[1068] Toto. (1983). Album Credits/Liner Notes: *IV*.

[1069] The Beach Boys. (1996). Album Credits/Liner Notes: *Stars and Stripes*.

[1070] Pack, D. (2005). Album Credits/Liner Notes: *The Secret of Movin' On*.

[1071] The Blind Boys of Alabama. (2009). Album Credits/Liner Notes: *Duets*.

[1072] Jordan, M. (2010). Album Credits/Liner Notes: *Crucifix in Dreamland*.

[1073] Colvin, S. (2015). Album Credits/Liner Notes: *Uncovered*.

[1074] Wynonna & The Big Noise. (2016). Album Credits/Liner Notes: *Wynonna & The Big Noise*.

[1075] Carrack, P. (2017). Album Credits/Liner Notes: *The Singles Collection*.

[1076] Harrison, G. (1992). Album Credits/Liner Notes: *George's Last Concert - The Royal Albert Hall*.

[1077] Kenny Wayne Shepherd Band. (2014). Album Credits/Liner Notes: *Goin' Home*.

[1078] Miller, F. (2016). Album Credits/Liner Notes: *Double Take*.

[1079] Rundgren, T. (2017). Album Credits/Liner Notes: *White Knight*.

[1080] David Bromberg Band. (1976). Album Credits/Liner Notes: *How Late'll Ya Play 'Til*.

[1081] Johns, E. (2015). Album Credits/Liner Notes: *Silver Liner*.

[1082] Bromberg, D. (1977). Album Credits/Liner Notes: *Out of the Blues: The Best of David Bromberg*.

[1083] Tiny Town. (1998). Album Credits/Liner Notes: *Tiny Town*.

[1084] Carnes, K. (2003). Album Credits/Liner Notes: *The Best of Kim Carnes*.

[1085] Newton, J. (2010). Album Credits/Liner Notes: *Duets: Friends & Memories*.

[1086] Marx, R. (1984). Album Credits/Liner Notes: *The Way She Loves Me*.

[1087] Nelson, R. (1972). Album Credits/Liner Notes: *Garden Party*.

[1088] Electric Range. (1996). Album Credits/Liner Notes: *Electric Range*.

[1089] Springsteen, B. (2003). Album Credits/Liner Notes: *Atlantic City (import)*.

[1090] Rogers, K. (2006). Album Credits/Liner Notes: *Water & Bridges*.

[1091] Travis, R. (2011). Album Credits/Liner Notes: *Anniversary Celebration*.

[1092] Paisley, B. (2011). Album Credits/Liner Notes: *This Is Country Music*.

[1093] Blind Pilot. (2014). Album Credits/Liner Notes: *Looking Into You—A Tribute to Jackson Browne*.

[1094] Gill, V. (2018). Album Credits/Liner Notes: *Restoration: Reimagining the Songs of Elton John and Bernie Taupin*.

[1095] Bottle Company. (1968). Album Credits/Liner Notes: *Lives for No One*.

[1096] Jack Mack and The Heart Attack. (1982). Album Credits/Liner Notes: *True Lovin' Woman*.

[1097] The Daily Oklahoman. (Dec. 23, 1984). "Van Halen Grabs Most Heavy Metal: Platinum," *The Daily Oklahoman*

[1098] Richmond, D. (Dec. 21, 1984). "Spinoffs: Making Platinum," *St. Louis Post-Dispatch*.

[1099] Gamboa, G. (Mar. 15, 1999). "Rock Hall Ceremonies Keep Everyone Guessing," *The Akron Beacon Journal*.

[1100] Horn, J. (May 28, 1994). "Eagles Reunion Plagued by Legal Questions," Associated Press.

[1101] The Signal (Santa Clarita, Calif.). (Dec. 19, 2001). "Eagle Degree," *The Signal (Santa Clarita, Calif.)*

[1102] Billboard. (Oct. 9, 2018). "Joe Walsh Tells His Recovery Story at Facing Addiction/NCADD Gala," *Billboard*.

[1103] Hoad, J. (Dec. 11, 2018). "Ringo Starr Blackout Drunk," RecoveryBootCamp.com.

[1104] Selvin, J. (Dec. 18, 2006). "The Worst Christmas Song Ever? Father Guido Sarducci Takes a Shot, To the Tune of '99 Bottles of Beer on the Wall.'," *San Francisco Chronicle*.

[1105] Thornton, B.B. (2003). Album Credits/Liner Notes: *The Edge of the World*.

[1106] last.fm. (Jan. 28, 2008). "Lacewing (The Measles)," *last.fm*.

[1107] Nebraska Music Hall of Fame Foundation. (Jan. 1, 2001). "Biography: The Drivin' Dynamics," *Nebraska Music Hall of Fame Foundation*.

[1109] Wiseman, R. (1982). *Jackson Browne: The Story of a Hold Out*, Garden City, NY: Doubleday Books.

[1110] Rodman, S. (Sep. 7, 2014). "Back to the Woods," *Boston Globe*.

[1111] Henry Diltz, H. (May 1, 2007). "The Eagles," *The Uncut*.

[1112] Campbell, M. (Dec. 29, 1976). "Eagles: The 'Song Band' Soars Still Higher," Associated Press.

[1113] Helt, J. (Apr. 24, 2015). "Interview with Former Eagles Guitarist Don Felder," MusicRecallMagazine.com.

[1114] Rochester (N.Y.) Democrat and Chronicle. (Dec. 8, 1973). "Dylan Forms Co," *Rochester (N.Y.) Democrat and Chronicle*.

[1115] Hilburn, R. (Sep. 1, 1973). "Showcase Goal of the New Roxy," *Los Angeles Times*.

[1116] Arizona Republic. (May 8, 1985). "Stick: A Review," *Arizona Republic*.

[1117] WCSX 94.7 - Detroit's Classic Rock. (Jan. 18, 2019).

"WCSX Classic Cuts: Smuggler's Blues," WCSX.94.7.

[1118] O'Neill, S. (1983). Album Credits/Liner Notes: *Foreign Affairs*.

[1119] Glynn, M. (May 7, 1983). "Azoff Named as MCA Disc Group Head, Corporate VP," *Cashbox*.

[1120] Cashbox. (Jan. 8, 1983). "Singles Out of the Box: Don Henley, \"I Can't Stand Still\," *Cashbox*.

[1121] Philips, C. (Apr. 29, 1993). "EMI Offer Intensifies Henley Feud with Geffen," *Los Angeles Times*.

[1122] Philips, C. (Sep. 1, 1993). "Henley Ups the Ante in Geffen Fight," *Los Angeles Times*.

[1123] Wickham, P.J. (Jan. 23, 1988). "Sun Rhythm Section Brings Back the Memphis Sound," *Cashbox*.

[1124] Goldstein, P. (May 8, 1983). "The Azoff Wars: High-Decibel Pop," *Los Angeles Times*.

[1125] Shefchik, R. (Apr. 4, 1985). "Soundtrack LPS Stage a Strong Comeback with Aid of MTV Stars," *Muncie Evening Press*.

[1126] Cashbox. (Feb. 23, 1985). "East Coastings," *Cashbox*.

[1127] Heaton, M. (Jul. 7, 2013). "David Spero, Artist-Manager, Talks About What Went on Behind the Scenes with the Eagles," Cleveland.com.

[1128] The Times (Shreveport, La.). (Mar. 28, 1948). "KWKH Inaugurates New Radio-Stage Show," *The Times (Shreveport, La.)*

[1129] Wilson, E. (Feb. 15, 1956). "Rock & Roll Set Adores Elvis Presley," *The Tennessean*.

[1130] Bonfiglio, J. (Dec. 29, 2016). "Don Felder Content with Life Outside the Fast Lane," *The Herald-Palladium (St. Joseph, Mich.)*.

[1131] Chula Vista Star News. (Sep. 12, 1963). "Hootenanny is Set for Saturday Night," *Chula Vista Star News*.

[1132] Goldsmith, T. (Feb. 24, 1987). "Musician Gets Down to the 'Nitty Gritty'," *The Tennessean*.

[1133] Associated Press. (Jul. 22, 1978). "Folks Are Different Now That He's Famous," *Associated Press*.

[1134] Associated Press. (Jun. 16, 1994). "Meisner, Leadon Omitted from Eagles Reunion Tour," *Associated Press*.

[1135] The Journal Times (Racine, Wisc.). (Nov. 28, 1994). "Former Eagles Bassist Forms New Band," *The Journal Times (Racine, Wisc.)*.

[1136] Frey, G. (April 21, 2012). "Glenn Frey Pays Homage to the Beach Boys," (Film/Video), YouTube.

[1137] George-Warren, H. (2005). *The Rolling Stone Encyclopedia of Rock & Roll*, London, UK: Simon & Schuster.

[1138] Uber Rock, Taylor, M. (Jul. 8, 2012). Glenn Frey - Interview Exclusive, Retrieved from https://www.uberrock.co.uk/interviews/58-july-interviews/5430-glenn-frey-interview-exclusive.html.

[1139] Poco. (1984). Album Credits/Liner Notes: *Inamorata*.

[1140] Floegel, R. (Jan. 1, 2011). "Sacramento Rock & Radio Museum: The New Breed," Sacramento Rock & Radio Museum. Retrieved from http://www.sacrockmuseum.org/the-new-breed.html.

[1141] Discogs Blog, Cannon, S. (Oct. 7, 2018). "Bob Seger's Rarest Records," Retrieved from https://blog.discogs.com/en/bob-seger-rarest-records/.

[1142] Devault, R. (Dec. 20, 1986). "Bob Seger Rolls Like a Rocker One Last Time," *The Atlanta Constitution*.

[1143] Rich Jr., C. (Aug. 14, 2004). "Randy Meisner," CharlieRichJr.com.

[1144] Corcoran, M. (Sep. 17, 1994). "Don Henley Pleased with Eagles' Reunion Tour," *Dallas Morning News*.

[1145] Abeles, N. (Jul. 23, 2014). "In the Beginning: The Four Speeds," *Texarkana Gazette*.

[1146] Christensen, T. (Feb. 10, 2007). "A Duet That Began Long Ago," *Dallas Morning News*.

[1147] Texarkana Gazette. (Jul. 23, 2014). "Band Shows Off Instruments, Outfits in Photo," *Texarkana Gazette*.

[1148] Browne, D. (Oct. 18, 2015). "Songwriter J.D. Souther Stumbles Into His Role in 'Nashville'," *Rolling Stone*.

[1149] Greene, A. (Aug. 28, 2012). "The Dude Survives: Jeff Bridges on the Enduring \"Big Lebowski\"," *Rolling Stone*.

[1150] Bell, M. (Mar. 27, 2015). "Musician Jessie Bridges Making Her Own Way and Her Own Name Outside of Her Famous Acting Family," *Calgary Herald*.

[1151] Leahy, A. (Dec. 17, 2014). "Flashback: See Feuding Eagles 'Take it Easy' With Travis Tritt," *Rolling Stone*.

[1152] Ellwood, A. (2013). "History of the Eagles: The Story of an American Band," (Film/Video), Jigsaw Productions.

[1153] Klinger, J. (Feb. 23, 1980). "Souther Making Name on His Own," *Colorado Springs Gazette Telegraph*.

[1154] Murray, T. (Mar. 10, 2012). "Rebels with a Musical Cause," *Edmonton Journal (Edmonton, Alberta, Canada)*.

[1155] Pensacola News Journal. (May 18, 2000). "The Eagles Sue Hotel California Grill," *Pensacola News Journal*.

[1156] Sharp, K. (Mar. 8, 2014). "Rock Hall-Bound Linda Ronstadt Reflects on Her Life, Legacy and Music," *Goldmine*.

[1157] Einarson, J. (2005). *Mr. Tambourine Man: The Life and Legacy of the Byrds' Gene Clark*, New York, NY: Backbeat Books.

[1158] Unterberger, R. (2002). *All Music Guide to Rock*, New York, NY: Backbeat Books.

[1159] Los Angeles Times. (May 2, 1963). "Hootenanny Included in La Mirada Festival," *Los Angeles Times*.

[1160] Palladium-Item (Wayne, Ind.). (Jul. 26, 1949). "2 Air Force Pilots Killed in Plane Crash," *Palladium-Item (Wayne, Ind.)*

[1161] The Daily Oklahoman. (Feb. 15, 1959). "Danny Cuts a New Disc at City Recording Studio."

[1162] Plasketes, G. (Jun. 6, 2016). *Warren Zevon: Desperado of Los Angeles*, Lanham, MD: Rowman & Littlefield.

[1163] Martin, S. (2007). *Born Standing Up: A Comic's Life*, New York, NY: Scribner.

[1164] Public Broadcasting System. (Nov. 1, 2012). "Timeline: Year by Year, How David Geffen Invented Himself," Public Broadcasting System.

[1165] Criscione, L. (Sep. 10, 1966). "Buffalo Springfield: Buffalo Herding Clancy," *KRLA Beat*.

[1166] Gormley, M. (May 19, 1967). "The Buffalo Springfield; For What They're Worth," *The Ottawa Journal (Ottawa, Ontario, Canada)*.

[1167] Star-Gazette (Elmira, N.Y.). (May 27, 1967). "What Does \"Buffalo Springfield\" Mean?," *Star-Gazette (Elmira, N.Y.)*.

[1168] Express and News (San Antonio, Tex.). (Aug. 13, 1966). "Pop Group on TV," *Express and News (San Antonio, Tex.)*

[1169] Kening, D. (Jan. 30, 1990). "Poco and the Pastor," *Chicago Tribune*.

[1170] Campbell, M. (Sep. 8, 1990). "\"Straight and Narrow\" Detours Poco Tour," *Associated Press*.

[1171] Browning, N.L. (Dec. 17, 1966). "A Golden Name Change," *Detroit Free Press*.

[1172] The News Journal (Wilmington, Delaware). (May 15, 1998). "What's Cool: Benefit Concert for Tiger Woods Foundation," *The News Journal*.

[1173] Los Angeles Times. (Jun. 17, 1998). "Tiger Jam I," *Los Angeles Times*.

[1174] Eder, B. (Jan. 1, 2010). "Valarie Mountain," AllMusic. Retrieved from https://www.allmusic.com/artist/valerie-mountain-mn0002312701/biography.

[1175] Cashbox (Mar. 18, 2019). "The Eagles Return to Touring." Cashbox, Retrieved from https://cashboxmagazine.com.

[1176] Kart, L. (Apr. 25, 1982). "Record World's Demise a Bad Note for Consumers," *Chicago Tribune*.

[1177] Messenger, B. (Apr. 24, 1979). "Record World Keys Hits," *Jackson (Miss.) Clarion-Ledger*.

[1178] Kazenoff, I. (Mar. 1, 1998). "Trivia Sign Language," *Ad Age*.

[1179] Traube, L. (May 25, 1946). "The Billboard Presents.," *Billboard*.

[1180] Tayler, P. (Sep. 12, 2009). "Forty Years After Woodstock, A Gentler Generation Gap," *Pew Research Center, Social & Demographic Trends*.

[1181] Lufkin, L. (Mar. 22, 1981). "An Ex-Eagle's Flight from the Nest," *San Francisco Examiner*.

[1182] Voger, M. (Nov. 9, 2007). "Loco for Poco," *Asbury Park Press (N.J.)*.

[1183] Record World. (Mar. 18, 1967). "R&B Beat: The Poor: She's Got the Time," *Record World*.

[1184] Record World. (Mar. 11, 1967). "The Poor: She's Got the Time (She's Got the Changes)," *Record World*.

[1185] Cashbox. (Feb. 11, 1967). "Green Stone Inks 5," *Cashbox*.

[1186] Einarson, J. (2001). *Desperados: The Roots of Country Rock*, p. 72. New York, NY: Cooper Square Press.

[1187] Cashbox. (Aug. 5, 1967). "'Intimate' Disko in Ny; Called 'Salvation'," *Cashbox*.

[1188] Cashbox. (Aug. 12, 1967). "Smash Rushes Track of \"Hells Angels on Wheels\"," *Cashbox*.

[1189] Cashbox. (Feb. 4, 1967). "Capitol Markets New Album, Tape Product," *Cashbox*.

[1190] Fong-Torres, B. (2011). *Eagles: Taking It to the Limit*, p. 65, Philadelphia, PA: Running Press Book Publishers.

[1191] Connelly, C. (Aug. 1, 1991). "The Second Life of Don Henley," *GQ*.

[1192] Wenner, J. (Nov. 9, 1967). "Letter from the Editor," *Rolling Stone*.

[1193] Cohen, R. (Dec. 1, 2017). "The Rise and Fall of *Rolling Stone*," *The Atlantic*.

[1194] Hagan, J. (2017). *Sticky Fingers: The Life and Times of Jann Wenner and Rolling Stone Magazine*, New York, NY: Vintage Books.

[1195] Rock Cellar Magazine. (Apr. 1, 2014). "Linda Ronstadt: Long, Long Time Simple Dreams," *Rock Cellar Magazine*.

[1196] Finkle, D. (Mar. 2, 1968). "It's Where the Girls Are with 'Happening' Groups," *Cashbox*.

[1197] Brown, J. (Sep. 1, 2014). "The Architect of 70'S AOR: Bill Szymczyk on Recording Joe Walsh, B.B. King, & The Eagles," *TapeOp*.

[1198] Smith, B. (Jun. 25, 2004). "A Mood That Flows," *The Gainesville (Fla.) Sun*.

[1199] Crowe, C. (Apr. 26, 1973). "Poor Poco: They Were 'the Next Big Thing' Four Years Ago," *Rolling Stone*.

[1200] Warburton, N. (Oct. 1, 2009). "Down in LA – The Brewer and Shipley Interview," The Strange Brew Blog. Retrieved from: https://thestrangebrew.co.uk/interviews/down-in-la-the-brewer-and-shipley-interview-part-1/

[1201] Music Archive (Apr. 19, 2012). The Poor (1966-1968), Retrieved from http://musicofsixties.blogspot.com/2012/04/the-poor-poor-1966-1968.html.

[1202] Randy Meisner Concert Dates (Mar. 12, 2018). Chronology, Retrieved from http://www.angelfire.com/rock3/deliverin/MEISNER/randyconcerts.htm.

[1203] Hinson, M. (Jan. 19, 2016). "A Beer Run for Glenn Frey: A Local Remembrance," *Tallahassee Democrat*.

[1204] Weschler, T. (2010). *Travelin' Man: On the Road and Behind the Scenes with Bob Seger*, Detroit, MI: Wayne State University Press.

[1205] Graff, G. (Oct. 31, 2017). "Bob Seger: The Legend of the Ramblin' Gamblin' Man," *Louder*.

[1206] Graff, G. (Jan. 18, 2016). "Bob Seger on Glenn Frey: 'He Had a Drive, An Imagination & A Talent That Was Just Titanic'," *Billboard*.

[1207] Crowe, C. (May 23, 1974). "A Child's Garden of Jackson Browne," *Rolling Stone*.

[1208] Goldstein, R. (Feb. 16, 1967). "Los Angeles: The Vanishing Underground," *Village Voice (Los Angeles, CA)*.

[1209] Johnson, P. (Nov. 13, 1966). "Youths on Strip Pelt Buses, Police," *Los Angeles Times*.

[1210] Associated Press. (Nov. 13, 1966). "Tenn-Agers Riot on Sunset Strip, Set Bus on Fire," *Associated Press*.

[1211] Einarson, J. (1997). *For What It's Worth: The Story of Buffalo Springfield*, New York, NY: Cooper Square Press.

[1212] Cashbox. (Jan. 7, 1967). "Pick of the Week: Buffalo Springfield, \"For What It's Worth\"," *Cashbox*.

[1213] Greenfield, R. (2011). *The Last Sultan: The Life and Times of Ahmet Ertegun*, New York, NY: Simon & Schuster.

[1214] Sims, J. (Aug. 17, 1972). "The Eagles Take it Easy & Soar," *Rolling Stone*.

[1215] Sharp, K. (Mar. 13, 2019). "Bob Seger Recalls Opening for KISS in the 1970s and the Stories Behind His Most Celebrated Songs (The Interview)," *Rock Cellar Magazine*.

[1216] Long Beach (Calif.) Independent. (Jan. 23, 1970). "Far-Out Group for Nearby Concert," *Long Beach (Calif.) Independent*.

[1217] Bowen, J. (1997). *Rough Mix*, New York, NY: Simon & Schuster.

[1218] Millar, B. (Jan. 1, 1972). "Buddy Knox," Pye Records.

[1219] Rumble, J. (Apr. 12, 2014). "Producer Playback: An Interview with Jimmy Bowen," Country Music Hall of Fame.

[1220] Schone, M. (Oct. 24, 1993). "In Nashville, The Eagles' Pedestal Perch," *Washington Post*.

[1221] Thodoris, ⊠. (Apr. 11, 2012). "Interview: Bernie Leadon," *Hit Channel*.

[1222] Cashbox. (Jun. 17, 1967). "Now is the Time for Hearts and Flowers," *Cashbox*.

[1223] Hearts and Flowers. (2003). Album Credits/Liner Notes: *The Complete Hearts and Flowers Collection*.

[1224] Seger, B. (Jan. 14, 2019). Glenn Frey fondly remembered by Bob Seger, *In the Studio with Redbeard*.

[1225] Scapelliti, C. (Jan. 21, 2016). "Glenn Frey: 13 Of His Greatest Recorded Moments," *Guitar Player*.

[1226] Browne, D. (Jan. 28, 2016). "Glenn Frey: An Oral History," *Rolling Stone*.

[1227] Aydlette, L. (Oct. 19, 2013). "Joan and Alex's Sisterhood of Song," *The Palm Beach (Fla.) Post*.

[1228] Holiday Fitness Center. (Jul. 3, 1989). "Holiday Fitness Center Ad Campaign: Glenn Frey - Hard Rock, Rock Hard," Holiday Fitness Center.

[1229] Catlan, R. (Feb. 16, 1989). "Madonna, Glenn Frey Sell Out to Corporate Concerns," *Hartford Courant*.

[1230] Baltin, S. (Oct. 20, 2018). "Jackson Browne Helps McCabe's Guitar Shop Turn 60 In Transcendent Night," *Forbes*.

[1231] Everett, T. (Jan. 30, 1982). "McCabe's Hippie Spirit Celebrates Anniversary," *Los Angeles Herald Examiner*.

[1232] The San Bernardino County Sun. (Jun. 8, 1971). "'Date Nites' Conclude Saturday," *The San Bernardino County Sun*.

[1233] Ward, J. (Mar. 1, 2005). "The Honey Ltd. Story: Loud Harmonic Transcendence," *Perfect Sound Forever magazine*.

[1234] Hoby, H. (Jul. 27, 2013). "Honey LTD: 'After 45 Years, We're Finally Going to Get Copies of Our Own Record'," *The Guardian*.

[1235] Cashbox. (Mar. 9, 1968). "Newcomer Picks: Honey Ltd," *Cashbox*.

[1236] Forgo, R. (Apr. 5, 2019). Interview with Alexandra Sliwin Collins, *Time Passages*.

[1237] Cashbox. (Nov. 9, 1968). "Dillard & Clark: Out on the Side," *Cashbox*.

[1238] *Record World*. (Aug. 24, 1968). "A&M Signs Dillard & Clark," *Record World*.

[1239] Bickhart, J. (Feb. 15, 1969). "The Fantastic Expedition of Dillard & Clark," *Rolling Stone*.

[1240] Cashbox. (Mar. 23, 1968). "Glad: Say What You Mean [Egg, Bml-Floegel]," *Cashbox*.

[1241] Cashbox. (Jul. 20, 1968). "Glad: A New Tomorrow," *Cashbox*.

[1242] Cashbox. (Dec. 7, 1968). "Glad: Johnny Silver's Ride," *Cashbox*.

[1243] Glad. (1968). Album Credits/Liner Notes: *Feeling Glad*.

[1244] Feenstra, P. (Sep. 1, 2012). "Interview: Don Felder," GetReadyRock.com. Retrieved from http://www.getreadytorock.com/rock_stars/don_felder.htm.

[1245] DonFelder.com. (Jan. 25, 2019). "Don Felder to Release New Album | American Rock 'N' Roll Out April 5," DonFelder.com.

[1246] Bennington, R. (Jun. 22, 2013). "JD Souther, American Songwriter," *The Interrobang*.

[1247] Geffen Records. (Aug. 6, 2016). "Longbranch/Pennywhistle - The Legendary 1969 Collaboration of Late Eagles Co-Founder Glenn Frey and Acclaimed Songwriter JD Souther to Be Released on CD and Vinyl on September 28 Via Geffen/Ume," Geffen Records.

[1248] Stewart, A. (May 19, 2016). "JD Souther Has Written Everything, For Everyone," *Chicago Tribune*.

[1249] Orloff, K. (Aug. 15, 1970). "Now Sound of the Troubadour," *Chicago Sun-Times*.

[1250] Perkins, T. (Aug. 30, 2013). "J.D. Souther Returns to Touring with a Little 'Nashville' On the Side," *St. Louis Post-Dispatch*.

[1251] Haber, J. (Mar. 20, 1968). "Honey Ltd. -- Just for the Record," *Los Angeles Times*.

[1252] Boston Globe. (Feb. 20, 1969). "The Byrds, Flying Burrito Brothers Share Bill at Boston Tea Party," *Boston Globe*.

[1253] San Francisco Examiner. (Nov. 1, 1969). "Flying Burrito Brothers Add Rhythm Guitarist Bernie Leadon," *San Francisco Examiner*.

[1254] Wahlquist, G. (Sep. 6, 1970). "Flying with the Burrito Brothers," *The Sydney Morning Herald*.

[1255] Record World. (Oct. 11, 1969). "James Gang: Yer' Album," *Record World*.

[1256] Rock of Ages Interviews. (Mar. 9, 2010). "Bernie Leadon," Rock of Ages Interviews.

[1257] The Remingtons. (1993). Album Credits/Liner Notes: *Aim for the Heart*.

[1258] Leo, J. (1983). Album Credits/Liner Notes: *Rockin' on the 6th*.

[1259] Nitty Gritty Dirt Band. (1988). Album Credits/Liner Notes: *Workin' Band*.

[1260] Miller, J. (Nov. 7, 2017). "Interview: John McEuen," The ArtsCenter (Carrboro, NC). Retrieved from https://artscenter-live.org/2017/11/07/interview-john-mceuen/.

[1261] Trussell, R. (Aug. 6, 1987). "The Revamped Dirt Band is Alive and Kicking Up Dust," *Chicago Tribune*.

[1262] Dean, V. (Sep. 27, 2016). "John McEuen on Making His New Album 'Made in Brooklyn': Interview," *Sarasota Herald-Tribune*.

[1263] Beaudoin, J. (Nov. 9, 2016). "All Acoustic Instruments and Kitchen Utensils: Nitty Gritty Dirt Band History with Jeff Hanna," *Pop Matters*.

[1264] Goldmine. (Mar. 27, 2009). "Backstage Pass: Chris Darrow – A Brilliant Disguise," *Goldmine*.

[1265] Jourard, M. (2016). *Music Everywhere: The Rock and Roll Roots of a Southern Town*, Gainesville, FL: University Press of Florida.

[1266] Campbell, R. (Nov. 19, 2008). "Poco Picked Up the Pieces and Found Magic in the Music," *Chron*.

[1267] Hilburn, R. (Dec. 18, 1969). "Poco Highlights Its Albums," *Los Angeles Times*.

[1268] The Atlanta Journal-Constitution. (Oct. 15, 1977). "Quick Cuts from the Rock Scene," *The Atlanta Journal-Constitution*.

[1269] Furay, R. (2006). *Pickin' Up the Pieces: The Heart and Soul of Country Rock Pioneer Richie Furay*, Colorado Springs, CO: Waterbook Press.

[1270] Rudis, A. (Jun. 14, 1969). "Buffalo Springfield Transformed," *Chicago Sun-Times*.

[1271] Los Angeles Times. (Jan. 2, 1965). "McCabe's Guitar Shops," *Los Angeles Times*.

[1272] The Californian (Salinas, Calif.). (Dec. 8, 2008). "Rock Club Co-Founder Elmer Valentine Dies," *The Californian (Salinas, Calif.)*.

[1273] Tuck, M. (Dec. 17, 1966). "Chaos on the Sunset Strip: Teens Demonstrate for Dance Rights," *KRLA Beat*.

[1274] (Apr. 14, 2019). "Whiskey a Go Go: History," WhiskeyaGoGo.com. Retrieved from https://whiskyagogo.com/calendar/history/.

[1275] Daley, D. (May 1, 2005). "Greg Ladanyi: Jackson Browne, Don Henley & The SoCal Sound," *Sound on Sound*.

[1276] McCabe's Guitar Shop. (Apr. 13, 2019). "Beware: History Happens," McCabe's Guitar Shop.

[1277] Riskin, B. (Aug. 7, 2013). "McCabe's Guitar Shop: Bob Riskin," National Association of Music Merchants.

[1278] Simmons, M. (Sep. 24, 2008). "A Half-Century of McCabe's Guitar Shop," *LA Weekly*.

[1279] Lewis, R. (Sep. 27, 2008). "The Ballad of a Classic Guitar Shop," *Los Angeles Times*.

[1280] Basler, B. (Nov. 5, 1969). "Musical Merger is a Convincing Paradox," *The Indianapolis News*.

[1281] Houghton, M. (Sep. 1, 1973). "A Guide to Contemporary Country Groups," *Let It Rock*.

[1282] Dillard & Clark. (1969). Album Credits/Liner Notes: *Through the Morning, Through the Night*.

[1283] Allen, J. (Mar. 29, 1981). "With New Label Bearing His Name, Record Biz Wiz Has Done it Again," *New York Daily News*.

[1284] Hoskyns, B. (Oct. 16, 2005). "Lady of the Canyon," *The Guardian*.

[1285] Miller, S. (Dec. 3, 2004). "Artie Mogull, 77; A&R Man Signed Legendary Acts," *New York Sun*.

[1286] Hilburn, R. (Sep. 2, 1972). "A Rise from Mailroom to Record Asylum," *Los Angeles Times*.

[1287] Lacey, S. (2012). "American Masters: Inventing David Geffen," (Film/Video), Public Broadcasting System.

[1288] Hoskyns, B. (Nov. 18, 2005). "Sex, Drugs and the Billion-Dollar Rise of David Geffen," *The Independent*.

[1289] Henke, J. (Jul. 29, 1977). "Dan Fogelberg Has Everything His Own Way," *Rolling Stone*.

[1291] Associated Press. (Mar. 16, 1976). "Boz Scaggs: Columbia Records Ordered Nothing But the Finest," Associated Press.

[1292] Bego, M. (2005). *Joni Mitchell*, Lanham, MD: Taylor Trade Publishing.

[1293] Kubernik, H. (2009). *Canyon of Dreams: The Magic and the Music of Laurel Canyon*, New York, NY: Sterling Publishing.

[1294] Knipperberg, J. (Aug. 2, 1970). "King of Spanish Rock on New Disc," *The Cincinnati Enquirer*.

[1295] Patterson, R. (May 10, 2018). "Glenn Frey Collaborator Jack Tempchin Talks Songs," BestClassicBands.com.

[1296] Lass, D. (Aug. 2, 1970). "Record Previews: Flow (CTL)," *Asbury Park Press (N.J.)*.

[1297] Record World. (Aug. 2, 1981). "Shell Shocked (Joe Walsh Promo)," *Record World*.

[1298] Graham, S. (May 9, 1981). "Elektra/Asylum Calls Out the Tanks to Push Joe Walsh's New Album," *Record World*.

[1299] *Record World*. (Aug. 15, 1981). "Joe Walsh is the Man for the Job," *Record World*.

[1300] Rolling Stone. (Jul. 9, 1981). "Eagles Won't Fly This Year," *Rolling Stone*.

[1301] Good, D. (Jan. 20, 2012). "Joe Walsh: Saving the World, One Monk at a Time," *San Diego Reader*.

[1302] Valentine, P. (Oct. 17, 1970). "The James Gang," *Sounds*.

[1303] *Guitar Player*. (May 1, 1972). "Pete Townshend," *Guitar Player*.

[1304] *Guitar Player*. (May 1, 1982). "Pete Townshend," *Guitar Player*.

[1305] Rosen, S. (Apr. 1, 1980). "Townshend Talking," *Sound International*.

[1306] Scoppa, B. (Apr. 10, 1975). "Joe Walsh - Forms and Textures of Rock Today," *Rolling Stone*.

[1307] Hilburn, R. (Dec. 1, 1973). "Joe Walsh Will Wait and See," *Los Angeles Times*.

[1308] Amendola, B. (Oct. 1, 2015). "Features: Joe Vitale," *Modern Drummer*.

[1309] Konczak, H. (Oct. 18, 2016). "Joe Vitale - Drummer for Joe Walsh," (Film/Video), Henry J. Productions, YouTube.

[1310] Kurtz, W. (Oct. 24, 2017). "The Days of Joe Walsh's 'Barnstorm'," *Goldmine*.

[1311] Cashbox. (Feb. 28, 1970). "Creed Taylor Forms CTI Label, Operation Sets Indie Status," *Cashbox*.

[1312] Cashbox. (May 16, 1970). "CTI Flows On," *Cashbox*.

[1313] Cashbox. (May 30, 1970). "Insight & Sounds: Flow," *Cashbox*.

[1314] Record World. (May 16, 1970). "Album Reviews: Flow (CTI 1003)," *Record World*.

[1315] Record World. (Jun. 6, 1970). "Success Comes in No Easy Flow," *Record World*.

[1316] Billboard. (Apr. 18, 1970). "Flow-CTI CTI 1003 (S)," *Billboard*.

[1317] Craft, D. (Jul. 27, 2006). "Return to the '70s," *The Pantograph (Bloomington, Illinois)*.

[1318] Howie, M. (Feb. 6, 2015). "Whatever Happened to: Irving Azoff," *The News-Gazette (Champaign, Illinois)*.

[1319] Frazier, T. (Dec. 1, 2004). "The Shades of Blue," 60sGarageBands.com. Retrieved from http://home.unet.nl/kesteloo/shadesofblue.html.

[1320] The Indianapolis Star. (Sep. 11, 1971). "Sherwood Sets Black Sabbath," *The Indianapolis Star*.

[1321] Fey, B. (2012). *Backstage Past (Barry Fey)*, Los Angeles, CA: Lone Wolf Press.

[1322] Record World. (Apr. 20, 1974). "Azoff Forms Front Line," *Record World*.

[1323] Harutunian, G. (Jul. 17, 2015). "Chasing Ghosts at Lake Geneva's Majestic Hills Theater," *The Beacon (Williams Bay, Wisconsin)*.

[1324] K-SHE-95 - Real Rock Radio (May 15, 2015). "Pete Townshend, Eddie Vedder, Joe Walsh, Rick Nielsen, and Joan Jett rock Chicago cancer benefit," K-SHE-95. Retrieved from https://www.kshe95.com/real-rock-news/pete-townshend-eddie-vedder-joe-walsh-rick-nielsen-and-joan-jett-rock-chicago-cancer-benefit/.

[1325] Setlist.fm. (Aug. 3, 2016). "Jethro Tull Setlist at Majestic Hills Theater, Lake Geneva, WI, USA," Setlistfm.com. Retrieved from https://www.setlist.fm/setlist/jethro-tull/1970/majestic-hills-theater-lake-geneva-wi-3c7996b.html.

[1326] di Perna, A. (Jun. 5, 2012). "Joe Walsh Discusses His Career, Gear and New Album, 'Analog Man'," *Guitar World*.

[1327] Meyers, D. (Mar. 2, 2016). "The Glorious and Weird History of the Talk Box," Ocean 104.7.

[1328] Billboard. (Sep. 9, 2016). "Irving Azoff Remembers Early N.W.A Manager Jerry Heller, His Former Boss," *Billboard*.

[1329] Dannen, F. (1990). *Hit Men*, New York, NY: Straight Arrow Publishers (Random House).

[1330] Billboard. (Jan. 27, 2012). "Billboard Reveals 2012 Power 11," *Billboard*.

[1331] *Record World*. (May 14, 1966). "Dot Appoints Minor, Vescevo," *Record World*.

[1332] Henke, J. (Mar. 19, 1981). "REO Speedwagon's Big Breakout," *Rolling Stone*.

[1333] BestClassicBands.com. (Sep. 15, 2015). "REO Speedwagon's A&R Exec Talks About Gary Richrath," *BestClassicBands*.

com.

[1334] Amabile Angermiller, M. (Mar. 24, 2017). "Journey's True Believer: Manager John Baruck on How Synchs and Touring Helped the Band Reach the Rock Hall," *Billboard*.

[1335] Sheff, D. (Mar. 23, 1981). "Now It's Cheat to the Beat, As REO Speedwagon Finally Arrives with 'Hi Infidelity'," *People*.

[1336] Downs, D. (May 2, 2019). "REO Speedwagon - Biography," *Amoeba Music*.

[1337] MusicianGuide.com. (Aug. 20, 2008). "REO Speedwagon Biography," MusicianGuide.com.

[1338] Forsythe, N. (Oct. 7, 2016). "The Red Lion Inn: 50 Years of a Campustown Rock Icon," SmilePolitely.com.

[1339] Nooger, D. (May 9, 1981). "Manager Profile: John Baruck Reaches the Top After 11 Years Guiding REO," *Cashbox*.

[1340] Rettgen, G. (Apr. 4, 1968). "Fun and Night Life," *The Capital Times (Madison, Wisc.)*.

[1341] Megan, G. (Mar. 15, 2018). "Jay B. Ross 1942-2018: Attorney Fought for the Rights of Musicians," *Chicago Tribune*.

[1342] Sullivan, M. (Jun. 8, 1985). "They're Playing Our Song: Remembering the Guild, One-Eyed Jacks, REO," *The Pantograph (Bloomington, Illinois)*.

[1343] The Metro St. Louis Live Music Historical Society (Oct. 16, 2018). "Irving Azoff/Bob Nutt/Blytham Ltd., Metro St. Louis Live Music Historical Society. Retrieved from https://web.archive.org/web/20181016204650/http://www.stlmusicyesterdays.com/Irving%20Azoff.htm.

[1344] Dey, J. (Nov. 18, 2018). "Jim Dey | 'I Was Comforted by the Fact That Bob Was So Involved in the Church'," *The News-Gazette (Champaign, Illinois)*.

[1345] Vitale, J. (2008). *Joe Vitale: Backstage Pass*, Ashland, OH: Hit Records LLC.

[1346] Hatch, D. (Jun. 3, 2010). "Cue Card: This 1970 'Incident' Full of Memories," *Peoria Journal-Star*.

[1347] Luciano, P. (Jun. 3, 2010). "Luciano: Remembering the Kickapoo Creek Rock Festival, 40 Years Later," *Peoria Journal-Star*.

[1348] The Pantograph (Bloomington, Illinois). (Jun. 30, 1970). "Bought LSD, Marijuana at Festival – Policeman."

[1349] Gorner, P. (May 28, 1970). "Rock Festival Forbidden, But...," *Chicago Tribune*.

[1350] Kickapoo Creek Film, National Public Radio, (May 29, 2017).

[1351] Roland, T. (Oct. 14, 1998). "Biography Takes Eagles Story 'to the Limit'," *The Tennessean*.

[1352] Hunter, A. (Aug. 21, 2014). "Indiana Beach Music Scene, Part 2," *The Weekly View (Indianapolis, Indiana)*.

[1353] McGrady, P. (2017). *Dan Fogelberg: Story in Song*, Seattle, WA: Amazon Digital Services LLC.

[1354] Lema, J. (Feb. 15, 2014). "Revisiting the Rec," *The State-Journal Register (Springfield, Illinois)*.

[1355] McLane, B. (Jan. 1, 1997). "The One-Eyed Jacks," BenMcLane.com. Retrieved from https://www.benmclane.com/OneEyed.htm.

[1356] IllinoisAlumni.org, Peterson, D. (Sep. 17, 2012). "The School of Rock," IllinoisAlumni.org. Retrieved from https://illinoisalumni.org/2012/09/17/the-school-of-rock/.

[1357] Clarke, S. (Jan. 1, 1975). "A Certain Western Charisma," *Melody Maker*.

[1358] Record World. (Mar. 1, 1975). "Azoff Countersuit," *Record World*.

[1359] Sekuler, E. (Apr. 5, 1975). "Irv Azoff: Manning the Front Line," *Record World*.

[1360] Lake, D. (Oct. 2, 2017). "New Eagles Track Featured on Dan Fogelberg Tribute Album," 94.7 WLS - Chicago.

[1361] Record World. (May 10, 1975). "Walsh Heads for Wembley," *Record World*.

[1362] Record World. (Aug. 2, 1975). "Flying High," *Record World*.

[1363] Edmonds, B. (Dec. 20, 1975). "The Coast: Broken Wing," *Record World*.

[1364] Kruger, D. (Oct. 2, 1997). "J.D. Souther Interview," *DebbieKruger.com*.

[1365] Facebook, Vitale, J. (Aug. 4, 2018). Joe Vitale/Joe Walsh Post, Retrieved from https://www.facebook.com/joe.vitale.395/posts/2113783515354681?__xts__[0]=68.ARAemvEB-dex1tr

[1366] Cashbox. (Aug. 15, 1970). "Shiloh (Amos 140)," *Cashbox*.

[1367] Owens, T. (Dec. 26, 1976). "From East Texas to the Eagles: Henley Returns for 'Identity Fix'," *Longview (Texas) News-Journal*.

[1368] Soundtrack. (2002). Album Credits/Liner Notes: Disney's *The Country Bears*.

[1369] Dunkerley, B. (Aug. 21, 2014). "Kenny Rogers on Working with Dolly, Dottie and Mall Cops," *Rolling Stone*.

[1370] Cavuto, N. (Apr. 18, 2012). "Kenny Rogers Remembers Dick Clark," *Fox News Live*.

[1371] MacKensie, B.S. (Dec. 9, 2015). "Joe Walsh's Power Trio Apotheosis," *Medium*.

[1372] Kutner, R. (Aug. 16, 2006). "James Gang: Interview with Joe Walsh," *The Aquarian*.

[1373] Daley, D. (Nov. 1, 2004). "Bill Szymczyk: Producer," *Sound on Sound*.

[1374] Los Angeles College of Music. (Aug. 11, 2017). "LACM's Let's Talk Music Presents: Joe Walsh," (Film/Video).

[1375] Wilson, B. (2016). *I Am Brian Wilson*, New York, NY: Da Capo Press.

[1376] Hilburn, R. (Jun. 1, 1971). "Burritos Switch to a Gentle Sound," *Los Angeles Times*.

[1377] Hugg, J. (Aug. 23, 1973). "Eagles Set for Special on TV," *Vidette-Messenger of Porter County (Valparaiso, Ind.)*.

[1378] Gannett News Service. (Feb. 13, 1990). "Henley, His Music Makes Hometown Sing," *St. Cloud (Minn.) Times*.

[1379] Hartmann, J. (Aug. 24, 2009). "Hartmann's Law - If It's Not Good Live Dump It," Holodigm Music. Retrieved from http://theholodigm.blogspot.com/2009/08/hartmanns-law-if-its-not-good-live-dump.html.

[1380] Fleysher, E. (Oct. 11, 1971). "A Hip Rick Nelson Has Changed His Image," *New York Daily News*.

[1381] MaltShopCruise.com. (Jul. 17, 2014). "Featured Artists: Matthew and Gunnar Nelson," MaltShopCruise.com.

[1382] Roberts, M. (Jan. 11, 1995). "Taken Past the Limit," *Westword*.

[1383] Edwards-Rinkle, C. (Jun. 22, 1986). "Distance Doesn't Diminish Pride for Hughlene Henley," *The Marshall (Texas) News Messenger*.

[1384] Cashbox. (Sep. 11, 1971). "Geffen's Asylum Co. Teamed with Atlantic Label Family," *Cashbox*.

[1385] Billboard. (Sep. 11, 1971). "Full Talent Line-Up for Atl, Geffen Label," *Billboard*.

[1386] Rook, J.H. (Sep. 4, 2014). "WLS Bound," JohnRook.com.

[1387] Bashe, P. (1992). *Teenage Idol, Travelin' Man: The Complete Biography of Ricky Nelson*, New York, NY: Hyperion.

[1388] Cole, J. (May 22, 2019). Interview: Jim Cole, *Time Passages*.

[1389] Faber, G. (May 22, 2019). Interview: George Faber, *Time Passages*.

[1390] Price, D.E. (Oct. 27, 2016). "Jack Tempchin on New Album, Glenn Frey Tribute and Eagles Classics," *Rolling Stone*.

[1391] Zollo, P. (Mar. 4, 2016). "Jack Tempchin, Who Wrote \"Peaceful Easy Feeling,\" Looks Back on His Partnership with Glenn Frey," *American Songwriter*.

[1392] Wenzel, J. (Oct. 11, 2015). "Don Henley Dishes on Colorado Past, New Album, State of Country Music," *Denver Post*.

[1393] Sebastian, M. (Jan. 19, 2016). "Glenn Frey and the Eagles: A Storied Part of Boulder's Music History," *The Daily Camera (Boulder, Colo.)*.

[1394] Brown, G. (2004). *Colorado Rocks! A Half-Century of Music in Colorado*, Boulder, CO: Pruett Publishing Company.

[1395] Engel, J. (Aug. 1, 1994). "Jackson Browne: Going Home," (Film/Video), Mojo Productions.

[1396] Gratzer, A. (May 26, 2019). Interview: Alan Gratzer, *Time Passages*.

[1397] Welch, C. (Oct. 1, 1971). "Judee Sill: Judee Sill (Asylum)," *Melody Maker*.

[1398] Welch, C. (Mar. 25, 1972). "Judee Sill: Lunch and Judee," *Melody Maker*.

[1399] *Cashbox*. (Oct. 9, 1971). "Linda Ronstatdt: I Fall to Pieces (Capitol 3210)," *Cashbox*.

[1400] Edmonds, B. (Apr. 1, 1972). "Linda Ronstadt: Linda Ronstadt," *Creem*.

[1401] Record World. (Aug. 19, 1972). "Album Picks: John David Souther," *Record World*.

[1402] Carney, J. (Nov. 19, 2013). "Henry Diltz: The TVD Interview," *The Vinyl District*.

[1403] James, G. (May 14, 2016). "Interview with Rock Photographer Henry Diltz," ClassicBands.com.

[1404] Jackson, L. (2005). *The Eagles: Flying High*, London, UK: Piatkus.

[1405] Figment News (May 8, 2013). :Embrace Collaboration: A Conversation with Gary Burden," Figment News. Retrieved from http://figment.cc/2013/05/08/embrace-collaboration-a-conversation-with-gary-burden/.

[1406] Segal, D. (Apr. 24, 2010). "Calling Almost Everyone's Tune," *New York Times*.

[1407] Kurutz, S. (Aug. 22, 2019). "Bill Szymczyk," *AllMusic*.

[1408] Walsh, J. (Oct. 31, 2014). "Glyn Johns Interview: My 50 Years of Producing Rock Classics," *The Independent*.

[1409] Morrison, J. (Oct. 22, 2018). "Country-Rock Icon JD Souther Comes to Attucks," *Veer*.

[1410] *MPR*. (Nov. 28, 2016). "The Song 'Reed Petite' Boosted Motown," *MPR*.

[1411] Brown, M. (Jan. 23, 2016). "Berry Gordy: The Man Who Built Motown," *The Telegraph*.

[1412] Graham, A. (Jan. 18, 2016). "Eagles' Glenn Frey a 'Soul Guy in a Country Rock Band'," *The Detroit News*.

[1413] McEuen, J. (Apr. 1, 2018). "John McEuen: The Life I've Picked: A Banjo Player's Nitty Gritty Journey," Chicago Review Press.

[1414] Young, R. (Apr. 11, 2017). "Timothy B. Schmit On Going Solo, The Eagles And His Life In Music," WBUR 90.9 FM.

[1415] Larsen, P. (Jan. 4, 2017). "Eagles' Bassist Timothy B. Schmit is Back on His Own," *Orange County Register*.

[1416] DeMasi, V. (Nov. 15, 2017). "Timothy B. Schmit Returns to His Roots on 'Leap of Faith'," *Guitar Player*.

[1417] Parks, J. (May 11, 2012). "The Eagles' Timothy B. Schmit Talks About the Long Run, His Solo Career and Life as an Eagle," *Legendary Rock Interviews*.

[1418] (Jun. 1, 2009). "Don Henley: Off the Record," *Off the Record with Joe Benson*.

[1419] Harry, B. (Oct. 1, 2000). "The Ultimate Beatles Encyclopedia," MJF Books.

[1420] Cromelin, R. (Sep. 1, 1973). "Jackson Browne: In Concert at McCabe's," *Phonograph Record*.

[1421] Worrell, B. (Nov. 23, 2015). "The Gear of the Eagles Guitarists," *Reverb*.

[1422] Rickenbacker International Corp. (Jan. 24, 2006). "The Earliest Days of the Electric Guitar," Rickenbacker International Corp. Retrieved from http://www.rickenbacker.com/history_early.asp.

[1423] Burrows, T. (2013). *1001 Guitars to Dream of Playing Before You Die*, London, UK: Universe Publishing.

[1424] Wagner, D. (Apr. 26, 1970). "James Gang - Yer' Album," *Green Bay (Wis.) Press-Gazette*.

[1425] Knippenberg, J. (Oct. 12, 1969). "Cultists Like James Gang," *Cincinnati Enquirer*.

[1426] Johnson, J. (Jun. 7, 1969). "'Who' Creates an Ambitious 75-Minute 'Pop, Rock Opera'," *Atlanta Journal-Constitution*.

[1427] Goodman, J. (Jul. 4, 1948). "Capsule Disc Will Prove Boon to Lazy," *Salt Lake Tribune*.

[1428] Tucker, G. (Mar. 17, 1949). "Disk Gets Us in an Old Groove Once More," *Salem Statesman-Journal*.

[1429] St. Louis Post-Dispatch. (Feb. 15, 1949). "Rainbow Music," *St. Louis Post-Dispatch*.

[1430] Tampa Bay Times. (Sep. 14, 1958). "Stereo on Singles," *Tampa Bay Times*.

[1431] McCash, D. (Jun. 21, 2018). "The Eagles Walked to New Orleans Wednesday and Won Our Hearts," *New Orleans Times-Picayune*.

[1432] Sublette, N. (2009). *The Year Before the Flood: A Story of New Orleans*, Chicago, IL: Chicago Review Press.

[1433] Puschmann, K. (Mar. 16, 2017). "The Eagles' Don Henley Reveals the Secret to Writing a Classic Song," *New Zealand Herald*.

[1434] Martin, T. (Jul. 10, 1987). "'Dirty' Song Coming to Town," *The Gaffney (S.C.) Ledger*.

[1435] Gillette, C. (). *The Sound of the City: The Rise of Rock and Roll*, New York, NY: Da Capo Press.

[1436] Soulwalking.co.uk (Jun. 13, 2013). "Billy Ward and the Dominoes," Soulwalking.co.uk. Retrieved from http://www.soulwalking.co.uk/Billy%20Ward%20&%20Dominoes.html.

[1437] Van Matre, L. (Aug. 9, 1989). "Lone Eagle," *Chicago Tribune*.

[1438] Rock and Roll Hall of Fame (Jan. 1, 1986). "Alan Freed: The Boundary Smashing, Trend-Setting Evangelist of Rock and Roll," Rock and Roll Hall of Fame. Retrieved from https://www.

rockhall.com/inductees/alan-freed.

[1439] Sheerin, J. (Mar. 21, 2012). "How the World's First Rock Concert Ended in Chaos," BBC News.

[1440] Sun Records (Oct. 17, 2017). "Elvis Presley," Sun Records. Retrieved from https://www.sunrecords.com/artists/elvis-presley.

[1441] Rock and Roll Hall of Fame (Nov. 6, 2019). "Elvis Presley," Rock and Roll Hall of Fame. Retrieved from https://www.rockhall.com/inductees/elvis-presley.

[1442] Young, C.M. (May 29, 2008). "Eagles: Peaceful, Uneasy Feeling," Rolling Stone.

[1443] Reading Between the Grooves, Owston, J. (Oct. 26, 2013). "Asylum Records: James Dean," Reading Between the Grooves. Retrieved from http://zeegrooves.blogspot.com/2013/10/asylum-records-james-dean.html.

[1444] Vozick-Levinson, S. (Mar. 7, 2009). "The Eagles Get Censored. Wait, What?" Entertainment Weekly.

[1445] Iorio, P. (Dec. 6, 2017). "Don Henley's 'Goddamn' Problem," Huffington Post.

[1446] National Coalition Against Censorship (Nov. 28, 2014). "Music Censorship in America; A Brief History," NCOC.

[1447] Garside, S. (Feb. 15, 1977). "Robb Strandlund Promising," Paterson (N.J.) News.

[1448] Applefeld Olson, C. (Jun. 4, 2019). "2019 ShoF Inductee Jack Tempchin Tells the Tale Behind 'Peaceful Easy Feeling'," Billboard.

[1449] Calgary Herald. (Jul. 25, 1969). "Steve Young: Rock Salt and Nails," Calgary Herald.

[1450] Moriarty, E. (Mar. 18, 1978). "Steve Young: Worth the Wait," Johnson City (Tenn.) Press.

[1451] McNally, J. (Dec. 19, 1980). "'Eagles Live' Is a Passable Album of Some of the Band's Best Songs," The Petaluma (Calif.) Argus-Courier.

[1452] Betts, S. (Mar. 18, 2016). "'Seven Bridges Road' Singer Steve Young Dead at 73," Rolling Stone.

[1453] Freeland, D. (Sep. 23, 2019). "Behind the Song: The Eagles \"Seven Bridges Road\"," American Songwriter.

[1454] Elber, L. (May 1, 2002). "'American Bandstand' Celebrates in Style," Associated Press.

[1455] Scranton (Pa.) Times-Tribune. (Aug. 3, 1957). "'American Bandstand' Makes Debut Aug. 5," Scranton (Pa.) Times-Tribune.

[1456] Philadelphia Inquirer. (Jan. 21, 1964). "Taping of 'Bandstand' Goes West in Wake of Clark's Departure," Philadelphia Inquirer.

[1457] Sacduto, A. (1974). Mick Jagger: Everybody's Lucifer, London, UK: Berkley Medallion.

[1458] Cedrone Jr., L.R. (Jun. 17, 1964). "Hair Gets Longer and Longer," Baltimore Evening Sun.

[1459] Gilmore, E. (Jun. 1, 1964). "Recovered from the Beatles? Rolling Stones Arrive Tuesday," Associated Press.

[1460] Route Blog. (Jan. 11, 2019). "The Story Behind the Music: Seven Bridges Road," Route Blog. Retrieved from https://routepublishing.wordpress.com/2019/01/11/the-story-behind-the-music-seven-bridges-road/.

[1461] Kazek, K. (Nov. 8, 2018). "Alabama is Home to the Real 'Seven Bridges Road'," The Birmingham (Ala.) News.

[1462] Redwing Online. (Feb. 24, 2003). "Redwing? Glad? New Breed? Sorting it all out: A brief history," Redwing Online. Retrieved from http://www.desktop21.com/redwing/.

[1463] Basler, B. (Nov. 5, 1969). "Musical Merger is a Convincing Paradox," The Indianapolis News.

[1464] Roberts, R. (2015). Lame Brain: My Journey Back to Real Life, Longmont, CO: Mount James Publishing.

[1465] Segal, D. (Apr. 24, 2010). "Calling Almost Everyone's Tune," New York Times.

[1466] Gibson.com (Jun. 8, 2012). "Joe Walsh Says Duane Allman Taught Him Slide Guitar," Gibson.com. Retrieved from http://es.gibson.com/News-Lifestyle/News/en-us/joe-walsh-says-duane-allman-0608-2012.aspx.

[1467] Aledort, A. (Nov. 20, 2018). "Slidedog: The Slide Guitar Mastery of Duane Allman," Guitar World.

[1468] Poe, R. (2006). Skydog: The Duane Allman Story, New York, NY: Backbeat Books.

[1469] Hits Daily Double, (Jan. 8, 2019). "A Taste of Rainmakers: Irving Azoff." Retrieved from https://hitsdailydouble.com/news&id=314719&title=a-taste-of-rainmakers:-irving-azoff

[1470] Greenhaw, W. (2001). My Heart Is in the Earth: True Stories of Alabama & Mexico, Montgomery, AL: River City Publishing.

[1471] Malone, J. (Oct. 11, 1996). Interview, Mike Nesmith, The Janice Malone Show.

[1472] Matthews, I. (1993). Album Credits/Liner Notes: The Soul of Many Places: The Elektra Years, 1972-1974.

[1473] Davis, C. (2013). Clive Davis: The Soundtrack of My Life, New York, NY: Simon & Schuster.

[1474] Kreps, D. (Mar. 5, 2009). "Eagles at Center of Goddamn \"Fast Lane\" Censorship Battle," Rolling Stone.

[1475] Hamilton, A. (Nov. 5, 2015). "Celebrating Seniors - JD Souther Turns 70," 50+ World. Retrieved from https://50plusworld.com/celebrating-seniors-jd-souther-turns-70/.

[1476] Scoppa, B. (Jun. 22, 1972). "The Flying Burrito Brothers: Last of the Red Hot Burritos," Rolling Stone.

[1477] (Sep. 1, 2019). "Glenn Frey," EquipBoard.com. Retrieved from https://equipboard.com/pros/glenn-frey.

[1478] Waits, T. (1973). Album Credits/Liner Notes: Ol' '55.

[1479] Curtis, B. (Mar. 15, 2017). "The Outsider," The Ringer. Retrieved from https://www.theringer.com/2017/3/15/16037818/pat-o-brien-cbs-sports-access-hollywood-sobriety-voice-mails-3265e474ce7b.

[1480] Italie, L. (Oct. 9, 2018). "Eagles' Joe Walsh Tells His Addiction Story at Gala Evening," Associated Press.

[1481] Rensin, D. (Mar. 15, 1975). "Dan Fogelberg: Home Free at Last," Rolling Stone.

[1482] Hoskyns, B. (Dec. 5, 2004). David Geffen, Rock's Backpages Audio.

[1483] Charone, B. (Jun. 12, 1976). "JD Souther: Black Rose (Asylum)," Sounds.

[1484] Murray, C.S. (May 26, 1973). "The Eagles: Desperado (Asylum)," New Musical Express.

[1485] Lewis, R. (Mar. 6, 2020). "Joe Smith, 'Well Loved Executive'," Los Angeles Times.

[1486] Forgo, R. (Dec. 15, 2019). Interview with Robb Strandlund, Time Passages.

[1487] Brannigan, P. (Jul. 1, 2012). "Heavy Load," Classic Rock Magazine.

[1488] Bosso, J. (Jun. 24, 2012). "Interview: The Eagles' Glenn Frey on His Album After Hours Track-By-Track," Music Radar.

[1489] Foster, S. (May 16, 2012). "Glenn Frey: After Hours," *Pop Matters*.

[1490] PennyBlack, Clarkson, J. (Apr. 7, 2012). "Interview: Glenn Frey," PennyBlack. Retrieved from http://www.pennyblackmusic.co.uk/MagSitePages/Article/6560/Glenn-Frey.

[1491] Beaudin, J. (Apr. 16, 2020). Henry Diltz Looks Back At The Eagles Desperado Shoot, Rock History Music. *RockMusicHistory.com*.

[1492] The Annenberg Space for Photography. (Jul. 27, 2012). Who Shot Rock & Roll: The Film - Henry Diltz.

[1493] Betts, S.L. (Mar. 5, 2015). "Henry Diltz: The Stories Behind Iconic Photos of Dolly, Garth and More," *Rolling Stone*. Retrieved from https://www.rollingstone.com/music/music-lists/henry-diltz-the-stories-behind-iconic-photos-of-dolly-garth-and-more-11112/.

[1494] Williamson, N. (Aug. 1, 2002). "Take it to the Limit," *Uncut*.

[1495] Vaughan, A. (2010). *The Eagles: An American Band*, New York, NY: Sterling.

[1496] Stern, H. (Jan. 1, 2015). Don Henley Live on the Howard Stern Show (2015) , *Howard Stern Show*.

[1497] Billboard. (Oct. 27, 1973). "The Hot 100 Week of October 27, 1973," Billboard. Retrieved from https://www.billboard.com/charts/hot-100/1973-10-27.

[1498] *Don Kirshner's Rock Concert*. (Nov. 26, 1975). "Joe Walsh - Don Kirshner's Rock Concert," (Film/Video).

[1499] Caddo Lake Institute (Jan. 1, 2002). "Caddo Lake & 'The Institute'," Caddo Lake Institute. Retrieved from https://data.lca.gov/clidata/cliinfo.htm.

[1500] Stern, H. (Jun. 1, 2012). Howard Stern Interview with Joe Walsh, *The Howard Stern Show*.

[1501] Tobler, J. (Apr. 1, 1977). The Eagles (1977) Interview by John Tobler, BBC.

[1502] Roberts, R. (1972). Album Credits/Liner Notes: *Windmills/She is a Song (Gott Discs Re-Issue with liner notes)*.

[1503] Furay, Roberts, R. (2006). *Pickin' Up the Pieces*, pp. 153-156, Colorado Springs, CO: Water Brook Press.

[1504] Fuentes, J. (2008). *Legend: The Story of Poco*, pp. 73-84, Stockton, CA: Groundhog Press.

[1505] Diltz, H. (May 7, 2020). "Henry Diltz Fav Album Covers, CSN, Eagles, James Taylor," RockMusicHistory.com (Film/Video).

[1506] Costas, B. (Jun. 10, 1992). Glenn Frey Interview with Bob Costas, NBC.

[1507] Fong-Torres, B. (1998). *Hickory Wind: The Life and Times of Gram Parsons (Revised and Expanded)*, pp. 193, New York, NY: St. Martin's Griffin.

[1508] Esposito, J. (Jan. 1, 1972). "Poco: A Good Feelin' To Know," *Rock*.

[1509] Scoppa, B. (Dec. 21, 1972). "Poco: A Good Feelin' To Know," *Rolling Stone*.

[1510] Gilbert, J. (Dec. 22, 1973). "Poco's Rebirth," *Sounds*.

[1511] Gold, M. (Apr. 1, 1973). "Poco: A Good Feeling to Know," *Let it Rock*.

[1512] de Walley, C. (Apr. 23, 1977). "Poco : Indian Summer (ABC)," *Sounds*.

[1513] Beaudin, J. (Jan. 1, 2000). "Randy Meisner Remembers Fist Fight With Glenn Frey & Other Eagles Regrets," Rock History Music.

[1514] Unknown, U. (Jan. 1, 2015). "Eagles' Randy Meisner -- Take It Easy. I'm Doing Just Fine," *TMZ*.

[1515] Gilbert, J. (Oct. 4, 1975). "Poco: Keep on Trying," *Sounds*.

[1516] Wosahla, S. (Aug. 21, 1975). "The First Annual Rock Award Show: A Start Into Getting Into Real Music," *Allentown (N.J.) Messenger-Press*.

[1517] Tarkiff, J. (Nov. 3, 1979). "Live! This Week," *Philadelphia Daily News*.

[1518] Beaudin, J. (Dec. 1, 2019). "Bernie Leadon On What Led To Don Felder Joining The Eagles," *Rock History Music*.

[1519] Deville, C. (Jun. 12, 2020). "Bob Dylan Talks COVID-19, George Floyd, His Favorite Eagles Songs in Rare Interview," *Stereogum*.

[1520] Brinkley, D. (Jun. 12, 2020). "Bob Dylan Has a Lot on His Mind," *New York Times*.

[1521] Dylan, B. (2020). Album Credits/Liner Notes: *Murder Most Foul*.

[1522] Radio Report. (Dec. 11, 1972). "Top of the Hour: The First Communicator Network Board of Directors," *Radio Report*.

[1523] *VH1* (May 20, 1994). "The Eagles Family Tree - VH1 Special," VH1 (Film/Video).

[1524] Bego, M. (2005). *Jackson Browne: His Life and Music*, p. 71, New York, NY: Kensington Publishing Corp.

[1525] Middlecamp, D. (May 14, 2016). "Don Henley's upcoming visit spurs memories of SLO County's desperados," *The Tribune*. Retrieved from https://www.sanluisobispo.com/news/local/news-columns-blogs/photos-from-the-vault/article77634742.html.

[1526] Deriso, N. (Jul. 6, 2020). "Why Guitarist Steuart Smith is Still Not a Member of Eagles," UltimateClassicRock.com.

[1527] Hill, D. (Jan. 1, 2018). "Joe Walsh - The Smoker You Drink/ But Seriously Folks," *In the Studio with Redbeard*.

[1528] Addams, D.R. (2002). *Rock 'n' Roll and the Cleveland Connection*, p. 308, Kent, OH: Kent State University Press.

[1529] Maher, Jr., P. (2011). *Tom Waits on Tom Waits: Interviews and Encounters*, Chicago, IL: Chicago Review Press.

[1530] Hoskyns, B. (2009). *Lowside of the Road: A Life of Tom Waits*, p. 120, New York, NY: Broadway Books.

[1531] Charone, B. (Jan. 1, 1975). "The Eagles," *Hit Parader*.

[1532] Tom Waits Library (Jan. 1, 1996). "The Heritage Coffeehouse," Tom Waits Library. Retrieved from http://tomwaitslibrary.info/topography/heritage/.

[1533] Anderson, K. (Nov. 19, 2015). "The New York Dolls' Sylvain Sylvain on the Band's Groundbreaking Style and His Clothing Line," *Vogue*.

[1534] Lester, P. (May 11, 2016). "Glyn Johns: My Top 6 Productions," *Classic Rock*.

[1535] Beaudin, J. (Oct. 25, 2019). "How Eagles Producer Glyn Johns Tried to Create a Balance of Power in the Band," (Film/Video).

[1536] Griffin, S. (1985). *Gram Parsons: A Music Biography*, pp. 83-97, and more, Pasadena, CA: Sierra Books.

[1537] Hennig, G. (Apr. 29, 2004). "Gram Parsons: Fallen Angel," BBC Music Entertainment (Film/Video).

[1538] Rabin, N. (Jun. 28, 2012). "Where to Start with the Father of \"Cosmic American Music,\" Gram Parsons," *AV Club*.

[1539] Shapiro, M. (1995). *The Story of the Eagles; The Long Run*, pp. 1-165, New York, England: Omnibus Press.

[1540] Lester, P. (May 11, 2016). "Glyn Johns: My Top 6 Productions," *Classic Rock*.

[1541] The Roxy Theatre. (Jan. 1, 2020). "The Roxy Theatre: History," The Roxy Theatre. Retrieved from https://www.theroxy.com/venue-info/history.

[1542] Epting, C. (Mar. 21, 2020). "The Roxy: A Legacy of Music and NIghtlife," West Hollywood. Retrieved from https://www.visitwesthollywood.com.

[1543] Atkinson, R. (Aug. 5, 1973). "To Settle a Debate, Mention Joe Walsh," *The Record*.

[1544] AllMusic (Jan. 1, 2020). "The Smoker You Drink, the Player You Get," Retrieved from https://www.allmusic.com/album/the-smoker-you-drink-the-player-you-get-mw0000651568.

[1545] *Rolling Stone*. (Jul. 1, 2016). Eagles: The Ultimate Guide. "The 40 Greatest Songs: The Eagles Finest Moments from Car Radio Classics to the Deep Cuts."

[1546] AllMusic (Jan. 1, 2000). Jim Ed Norman (bio and credits), Retrieved from https://www.allmusic.com/artist/jim-ed-norman-mn0000340972/biography.

[1547] Watts, C. (Feb. 24, 2016). "Don Henley, Lee Brice, More Honor Jim Ed Norman," *The Tennessean*.

[1548] Record World. (Dec. 20, 1975). "Walsh to Tour with the Eagles," *Record World*.

[1549] Record World. (Nov. 16, 1974). "Eagles-Asylum, Best of My Love," *Record World*.

[1550] Record World. (Jan. 15, 1977). "The Retail Report," *Record World*.

[1551] Fleming, K. (Sep. 21, 1974). "The Coast," *Record World*.

[1552] Beer, L. (Jan. 15, 1977). "Eagles, 'Car Wash' Top Album, Singles Charts," *Record World*.

[1553] Record World. (Mar. 12, 1977). "Powerhouse Picks," *Record World*.

[1554] *Record World*. (Feb. 12, 1977). "The FM Airplay Report," *Record World*.

[1555] Beer, L. (Mar. 26, 1977). "AbBa Breaks Through with #1 Single; Fleetwood Mac Tops LPS," *Record World*.

[1556] Beer, L. (Apr. 16, 1977). "Eagles, David Soul Top LP, Singles Charts," *Record World*.

[1557] Beer, L. (Apr. 23, 1977). "The Eagles Top Both Pop Charts with 'Hotel California'," *Record World*.

[1558] Taylor, B. (Dec. 31, 1977). "Superstars Dominate Charts in '77; Soundtracks Yield Big Singles Hits," *Record World*.

[1559] *Record World*. (Jan. 10, 1976). "Winning Welcome," *Record World*.

[1560] Record World. (Jan. 24, 1976). "Arista, Morning Sky Pact," *Record World*.

[1561] Record World. (Mar. 15, 1975). "'the Mythical Group'," *Record World*.

[1562] *Record World*. (Mar. 1, 1975). "Azoff Countersuit," *Record World*.

[1563] Record World. (Mar. 6, 1976). "Movin' With Minnie," *Record World*.

[1564] *Record World*. (Nov. 29, 1975). "Too Crowded for Irving?," *Record World*.

[1565] Record World. (May 27, 1978). "Eagles Conquer Stone," *Record World*.

[1566] LaFong, C. (Nov. 21, 1970). "Notes from the Underground," *Record World*.

[1567] Lawrence, T. (Jul. 31, 1971). "New Asylum Label Readies First Product," *Record World*.

[1568] *Record World*. (Oct. 9, 1971). "Judee Sill, \"Judee Sill\"," *Record World*.

[1569] Record World. (Oct. 9, 1971). "Strong Response for New Atlantic LPS," *Record World*.

[1570] Record World. (Dec. 11, 1971). "Production Pacts Big Atlantic Factor," *Record World*.

[1571] McReight, R. (Mar. 4, 1972). "U.K. Picks of the Week for U.S.," *Record World*.

[1572] Hutchinson, L. (Aug. 13, 2013). "Remembering Dan Fogelberg," Performing Songwriter. Retrieved from https://performingsongwriter.com/dan-fogelberg-interview-songs/.

[1573] Charlesworth, C. (Apr. 12, 1975). "Joe Walsh: Slowhand Cowboy," *Melody Maker*.

[1574] Cartwright, G. (Jan. 11, 2008). "Dan Fogelberg: American Singer-Songwriter Whose Albums Sold Millions," *The Guardian*.

[1575] Dan Fogelberg (Jan. 1, 2000). FAQs, Retrieved from https://www.danfogelberg.com/faqs.

[1576] Fogelberg, D. (1974). Album Credits/Liner Notes: *Souvenirs*.

[1577] Kielty, M. (Oct. 1, 2017). "Eagles Contribute New Cover Song to Dan Fogelberg Tribute Album," Ultimate Classic Rock.

[1578] Lifton, D. (Nov. 2, 2020). "Why Tom Petty Let Don Henley Record "The Boys of Summer," Ultimate Classic Rock. Retrieved from https://ultimateclassicrock.com/don-henley-boys-of-summer-tom-petty/.

[1579] Scoppa, B. (Apr. 24, 1975). "Joe Walsh: So What," *Rolling Stone*.

[1580] Unterberger, R. (2002). *All Music Guide to Rock*, pp. 1204-1205, New York, NY: Backbeat Books.

[1581] King, T. (2000). *The Operator*, p. 186, New York, NY: Broadway Books.

[1582] King, T. (2000). *The Operator*, pp. 53, 173, 187-189, New York, NY: Broadway Books.

[1583] Crowe, C. (May 18, 1975). "America Starts to Rediscover Itself," *Los Angeles Times*.

[1584] Limnios, M. (May 8, 2015). "John Hartmann: Holodigm Music," Blues.GR. Retrieved from http://blues.gr/profiles/blogs/veteran-agent-manager-and-record-executive-john-hartmann-talks.

[1585] Markowitz, A. (Dec. 7, 2012). "A Music Documentary Brings Jerry Garcia Back from the Dead," MusicFilmWeb. Retrieved from http://www.musicfilmweb.com/2012/12/jerry-garcia-malcolm-leo-john-hartmann-music-documentary/.

[1586] Lavinthal, D. (Dec. 18, 2014). "Irving: The HITS Interview, Part 1," HITS Daily Double. Retrieved from https://hitsdailydouble.com/news&id=272086.

[1587] Poague, G. (Sep. 4, 1999). "Moral Ambiguity? Try the Eagles," *Clarksville (Tenn.) Leaf-Chronicle*.

[1588] Viglione, J. (Jan. 1, 2018). "Music from Free Creek: The Long Lost Super Session Album," AllMusic. Retrieved from https://www.allmusic.com/album/music-from-free-creek-the-long-lost-super-session-album-mw0000995315.

[1589] Timerow, I.C. (Jan. 1, 2001). "The Free Creek Sessions: Interview with Moogie," *Heavy Metal Mayhem*.

[1590] Record World. (Mar. 8, 1975). "The Singles Chart: Turn to Stone, Joe Walsh, ABC-Dunhill," *Record World*.

[1591] Record World. (Apr. 22, 1972). "Yes + Atlantic = Gold," *Record World*.

[1592] Record World. (May 5, 1972). "Ahern Asylum Nat. Promo Director," *Record World*.

[1593] Himes, G. (Sep. 30, 1985). "Guitarist 4-Time Winner at D.C. Awards," *Baltimore Sun*.

[1594] Snider, E. (Oct. 11, 1986). "BoDeans: Simple Head-On Rock," *St. Petersburg Times*.

[1595] Gleason, H. (Jan. 14, 1988). "Rosanne Cash Changes the Rules for Women," *Los Angeles Times*.

[1596] Crowe, C. (Aug. 17, 2015). "Cameron Crowe Looks Back on His 1975 Eagles Cover Story," *Rolling Stone*.

[1597] Brown, K. (Jun. 16, 1972). "Music in Mid-America," *Kansas City Star*.

[1598] Mann, B. (Jul. 20, 1972). "Eagles Soar Through Pierrefonds Arena," *The Gazette (Montreal, Quebec, Canada)*.

[1599] Baltimore Sun. (Jun. 25, 1972). "Week's Top 40," *Baltimore Sun*.

[1600] "Redbeard" Hill, D. (Apr. 16, 2017). "Interview with Gary Brooker, Procol Harum," Raised on Radio Archives.

[1601] Forrest, R. (Aug. 19, 2020). "Interview with Jon Anderson (Yes)," The Eagle - KKGL, Boise, Idaho.

[1602] Charone, B. (Mar. 27, 1976). "The Eagles: Desperados in Blue Jeans and Sneakers," *Sounds*.

[1603] Browne, D. (Jul. 1, 2016). "Henley Looks Back," *Rolling Stone Special: Eagles the Ultimate Guide*.

[1604] HITS Daily Double. (Jan. 1, 2008). "The Long Run: An Irving Azoff Timeline," HITS Daily Double. Retrieved from https://hitsdailydouble.com/news&id=280194&title+THE-LONG-RUN:-AN-IRVING-AZOFF-TIMELINE&redirect=mobile.

[1605] Smith, W.M. (Jul. 27, 2012). "Lou Ann Barton: The Blues Queen is Working Her Butt Off," *Houston Press*.

[1606] Browning, B. (Mar. 5, 1982). "Lou Ann Barton's 'Old Enough'," *Washington Post*.

[1607] Young, C. (Jun. 5, 1977). "If Eagles Win Suit They Will Get Millions," *Rolling Stone*.

[1608] Knobler, P. (Jul. 1, 1975). "Souther, Hillman & Furay... and Geffen," *Crawdaddy*.

[1609] Discogs (Jan. 1, 2000). "Joe Walsh - So What," Discogs. Retrieved from https://www.discogs.com/Joe-Walsh-So-What/release/1673395.

[1610] AllMusic Guide (Jan. 1, 2000). "Joe Walsh - So What," AllMusic Guide. Retrieved from https://www.allmusic.com/album/so-what-mw0000094627.

[1611] *Rolling Stone*, Bienstock, R. (May 19, 2016). "Joe Walsh: My Life in 15 Songs," *Rolling Stone*. Retrieved from https://www.rollingstone.com/music/music-lists/joe-walsh-my-life-in-15-songs-66390/.

[1612] Eder, B. (Jan. 1, 2020). "Dan Fogelberg Artist Biography," Danfogelberg.com. Retrieved from https://www.danfogelberg.com/bruce-eder.

[1613] Beaudin, J. (Jul. 26, 2019). "How "I Wish You Peace" Created a Divide In The Eagles - "One of These Nights" Stories," YouTube. Retrieved from https://www.youtube.com/watch?v=-jQZ5QCXRy_A.

[1614] Podolsky, J. (May 18, 1992). "A Daughter's Lament," *People*.

[1615] Davis, P. (1992). *The Way I See It*, pp. 198-213, New York, NY: G.P. Putnam's Aons.

[1616] Crowe, C. (Nov. 4, 1972). "Movin' Up with the Eagles," *The San Diego Door*.

[1617] Connelly, C. (Mar. 20, 1982). "Patti Davis Victim of Don Henley's 'Vendetta'," *Colorado Springs Gazette Telegraph*.

[1618] The Uncool (Nov. 11, 2011). "Cameron Crowe Biography," The Uncool. Retrieved from https://www.theuncool.com/bio/.

[1619] Mitchell, K.M. (Aug. 4, 2017). "Richard Fernandez: Tour Manager for Faces, Eagles and Tom Petty," ParnelliAwards.com. Retrieved from http://digitaleditiononline.com/publication/?i=347279&article_id=2613024&view=articleBrowser.

[1620] ParnelliAwards.com. (Dec. 16, 2018). "Richard Fernandez: Partnelli Awards Lifetime Achievement Award 2016," ParnelliAwards.com. Retrieved from https://parnelliawards.com/videos/parnelli-lifetime-achievement-award-videos/.

[1621] Forgo, R. (Jan. 6, 2021). Interview with Danny O'Keefe, *Time Passages*.

[1622] Poco, n. (1975). Album Credits/Liner Notes: *Head Over Heels*.

[1623] Greene, A. (Aug. 27, 2020). "Drummer Joe Vitale on His 50-Year Saga with CSNY, Joe Walsh, The Eagles, And John Lennon," *Rolling Stone*.

[1624] Bertram, C. (Apr. 5, 2019). "Inside John Lennon's 'Lost Weekend' Period," biography.com.

[1625] DeCurtis, A. (Sep. 20, 1990). "The Eagles," *Rolling Stone*.

[1626] Smith, J. (1988). *Off the Record: An Oral History of Popular Music*, pp. 350-354, New York, NY: Warner Books.

[1627] Kelton, J. (Dec. 28, 1984). "Songwriter Taking the Future 'Day by Day'," *Washington Post*.

[1628] Pollock, B. (Sep. 28, 1980). "Danny O'Keefe After the Big One," *The (N.Y.) Herald Statesman*.

[1629] Pond, S. (Apr. 27, 1975). "So Long Harry Truman," *Los Angeles Times*.

[1630] Santasuosso, E. (Apr. 20, 1975). "Truman Songs May Create a New Folk Hero," *Boston Globe*.

[1631] Zimmerman, L. (Oct. 24, 2020). "Danny O'Keefe: From Good Time Charlie to Tales of the Nez Perce, He Furthers His Musical Mission," *American Songwriter*.

[1632] Fools Gold, N.N. (1976). Album Credits/Liner Notes: *Fools Gold*.

[1633] AllMusic, Chrispell, J. (Jan. 1, 1976). Fools Gold, Retrieved from https://www.allmusic.com/album/fools-gold-mw0000670563.

[1634] Songwriters Hall of Fame (Jan. 1, 2011). Tom Kelly: 1980s powerhouse duo with Billy Steinberg, Retrieved from https://www.songhall.org/profile/tom_kelly.

[1635] Felder, D. (2008). *Heaven and Hell: My Life In The Eagles (1974-2001)*, p. 183, Hoboken, NJ: John Wiley & Sons.

[1636] Sexton, P. (Jun. 21, 2020). "California Stealin': Beach Boys Win Elton John's Wembley Extravaganza," udiscovermusic.com.

[1637] Beaudin, J. (Jun. 21, 2017). "Kenny Passarelli on Famous Elton John Summer of '75 Wembley Show," RockHistoryMusic.com (Film/Video).

[1638] setlist.fm. (Jun. 1, 2014). Eagles Setlist at Wembley Stadium, London, England. setlist.fm. Retrieved from https://www.setlist.fm/setlist/eagles/1975/wembley-stadium-london-england-2bc0c48a.html.

[1639] Concert Archives (Jan. 1, 2000). Elton John/The Beach Boys/Eagles/Joe Walsh/Rufus featuring Chaka Khan/Stackridge - Jun 21, 1975 - Wembley Stadium - London, UK, Retrieved from https://www.concertarchives.org/concerts/elton-john-the-beach-boys-eagles-joe-walsh-rufus-featuring-chaka-khan-stackridge.

[1640] Yetnikoff, W. (Oct. 11, 1975). "CBS, Epic and Custom Labels.," *Record World.*

[1641] Record World. (Sep. 8, 1979). "Record World Album Picks: Blue Steel, No More Lonely Nights," *Record World.*

[1642] Cashbox. (Sep. 15, 1979). "Mca Distributing Holds Meet," *Cashbox.*

[1643] *Record World.* (Sep. 15, 1979). "Blue Steel, No Ballads Promo," *Record World.*

[1644] Felder, D. (2008). *Heaven and Hell: My Life In The Eagles (1974-2001)*, pp. 212-216, Hoboken, NJ: John Wiley & Sons.

[1645] Eliot, M. (2005). *To the Limit: The Untold Story of the Eagles*, pp. 194-195, Cambridge, MA: Da Capo Press.

[1646] Thompson, G. (May 21, 2014). "The Eagles on Desperado: \"We Were Quite Taken with the Idea of Being Outlaws...\"," *Uncut.*

[1647] Lifton, D. (Aug. 30, 2020). "How 'Outlaw Man' Helped Shape the Eagles' 'Desperado'," UltimateClassicRock.com.

[1648] Hunter, J.M. (1951). *The Album of Gunfighters*, pp. 26-28, Bandera, TX: Hunter & Rose, Publishers.

[1649] *Don Kirshner's Rock Concert* (Jul. 19, 1974). "Don Kirshner's Rock Concert—1974," Viacom Productions (Film/Video).

[1650] Cetner, M. (Feb. 9, 1980). "Points West: Bullet Bob Returns," *Cashbox.*

[1651] Felder, D. (2008). *Heaven and Hell: My Life In The Eagles (1974-2001)*, pp. 169-175, Hoboken, NJ: John Wiley & Sons.

[1652] Eliot, M. (2005). *To the Limit: The Untold Story of the Eagles*, pp. 147-153, Cambridge, MA: Da Capo Press.

[1653] Musicholics. (Jan. 21, 2021). "Songsplaining: Decoding the Eagles' Signature Song, Hotel California," *Musicholics.*

[1654] Country Daily. (Mar. 5, 2021). "If Everything Comes to an End, Where Will Our Last Resort Be?", *Country Daily.*

[1655] Gilmore, M. (Dec. 10, 1987). "Don Henley," *Rolling Stone's 20th Anniversary Issue #512.*

[1656] *Record World.* (Aug. 21, 1976). "The Country Singles Chart, Buck Owens, #38," *Record World.*

[1657] Vitale, J. (2008). *Joe Vitale: Backstage Pass*, pp. 132-133, Ashland, OH: Hit Records LLC.

[1658] Chambers, C. (Feb. 21, 2018). Interview -- Joe Vitale (Classic Rock Drummer, Musician, Singer-songwriter), The College Crowd Digs Me Blog.

[1659] Greene, A. (Aug. 27, 2020). "Drummer Joe Vitale on His 50-Year Saga with CSNY, Joe Walsh, The Eagles, And John Lennon," *Rolling Stone.*

[1660] Brinkley, D. (Jun. 12, 2020). "Bob Dylan Has a Lot on His Mind," *New York Times.*

[1661] Eliot, M. (2005). *To the Limit: The Untold Story of the Eagles*, p. 149, Cambridge, MA: Da Capo Press.

[1662] Felder, D. (2008). *Heaven and Hell: My Life In The Eagles (1974-2001)*, p. 175, Hoboken, NJ: John Wiley & Sons.

[1663] Felder, D. (2008). *Heaven and Hell: My Life In The Eagles (1974-2001)*, p. 174, Hoboken, NJ: John Wiley & Sons.

[1664] Record World. (Apr. 24, 1976). "Record World Hits of the Week: John David Souther, \"Black Rose\"," *Record World.*

[1665] Felder, D. (2008). *Heaven and Hell: My Life In The Eagles (1974-2001)*, pp. 187-188, Hoboken, NJ: John Wiley & Sons.

[1666] Eliot, M. (2005). *To the Limit: The Untold Story of the Eagles*, pp. 162-163, Cambridge, MA: Da Capo Press.

[1667] Browning, B. (Jan. 29, 1982). "L.P. Graffiti," *Washington Post.*

[1668] AllMusic. (Jan. 1, 2000). "Planet Waves," AllMusic. Retrieved from https://www.allmusic.com/album/planet-waves-mw0000195528.

[1669] AllMusic. (Jan. 1, 2000). "Before the Flood," AllMusic. Retrieved from https://www.allmusic.com/album/before-the-flood-mw0000650102.

[1670] Bream, J. (Jun. 9, 2002). "This Eagle is Finally Flying Solo," *Minneapolis Star Tribune.*

[1671] Carr, T. (Jan. 6, 1977). "Concert Brings Bernie Leadon Home," *Minneapolis Star Tribune.*

[1672] Hoskyns, B. (2006). *Hotel California*, p. 196, Hoboken, NJ: John Wiley & Sons.

[1673] Guitars and Things Blog. (Nov. 29, 2015). "The Gear of the Eagles' Guitarists," Guitars and Things Blog.

[1674] Drozdowski, T. (Jan. 9, 2016). "The Eagles' Glenn Frey: 1948–2016," *Premiere Guitar.*

[1675] Ariza, M.Á. (Dec. 25, 2018). "In the Style of Glenn Frey," *Guitars Exchange.*

[1676] The Sound. (Apr. 18, 2019). "Don Felder on How He Ended Up with Iconic Double-Neck 'Hotel California' Guitar," *The Sound.*

[1677] Vinnicombe , C. (Aug. 19, 2010). "Gibson's Don Felder Signature 'Hotel California' EdS-1275 Double Neck," *MusicRadar.*

[1678] Fanelli, D. (Aug. 22, 2012). "Interview: Don Felder Discusses His Signature \"Hotel California\" EdS-1275 And 1959 Les Paul Gibson Guitars," *Guitar World.*

[1679] Worrell, B. (Nov. 23, 2015). "The Gear of the Eagles' Guitarists," *Reverb.*

[1680] Meeker, W. (Aug. 1, 2012). "Joe Walsh: Life's Still Good," *Vintage Guitar Magazine.*

[1681] Ariza, M.A. (Dec. 23, 2018). "In the Style of Joe Walsh," *Guitars Exchange.*

[1682] Guitars and Things Blog. (Nov. 29, 2015). "Bernie Leadon: Guitars and Amps," Guitars and Things Blog.

[1683] Eliot, M. (2005). *To the Limit: The Untold Story of the Eagles*, p. 83, 118Cambridge, MA: Da Capo Press.

[1684] McLane, B. (Jan. 1, 1998). "John Boylan - Producer," McLane & Wong Entertainment Law.

[1685] Forgo, R. (Apr. 20, 2021). Interview with Richard Fernandez, *Time Passages.*

[1686] Ultimate Classic Rock. Deriso, N. (Jun. 10, 2020). "How Randy Meisner's 'Take it to the Limit' Fractured the Eagles," Ultimate Classic Rock. Retrieved from https://ultimateclassicrock.com/eagles-take-it-to-the-limit/.

[1687] Tune Groover. (Sep. 19, 2013). "Former Gainesville Musician David Mason Remembered," Tune Groover. Retrieved from http://tunegroover.com/former-gainesville-musician-david-mason-remembered/.

[1688] AllMusic (Jan. 1, 2000). Various Entries, AllMusic. Retrieved from https://www.allmusic.com.

[1690] Forgo, R. (Apr. 20, 2021). Interview with Richard Fernandez, *Time Passages.*

[1691] Martino, A. (Sep. 22, 2014). "Behind the Bartender: Michael Gotovac of Dan Tana's," *Los Angeles Magazine.*

[1692] Eliot, M. (2005). *To the Limit: The Untold Story of the Eagles*, pp. 157-158, Cambridge, MA: Da Capo Press.

[1693] Felder, D. (2008). *Heaven and Hell: My Life In The Eagles (1974-2001)*, p. 144, Hoboken, NJ: John Wiley & Sons.

[1694] Hartmann, J. (Oct. 5, 2009). *Inventing David Geffen*, PBS.

[1695] Miles, (1981). *John Lennon In His Own Words*, pp. 125-126, New York, New York: Quick Fox.

[1696] Eliot, M. (1998). *To The Limit--The Untold Story of The Eagles*, p. 202, Boston, MA: Little, Brown and Company.

[1697] Felder, D. (2008). *Heaven and Hell: My Life In The Eagles (1974-2001)*, p. 38, Hoboken, NJ: John Wiley & Sons.

[1698] Something Else Reviews. (Nov. 3, 2014). "For Don Henley, a Beatles Star Remains His Primary Influence: 'I Loved What He Stood For'," Something Else Reviews. Retrieved from https://somethingelsereviews.com/2014/11/03/don-henley-john-lennon/.

[1699] http://beatlesnumber9.com (???). Stars Remember John Lennon And His Murder , Retrieved from http://beatlesnumber9.com/remember.html.

[1700] Goldman, A. (1988). *The Lives of John Lennon*, p. 684, New York, NY: William Morrow and Company.

[1701] Wosahla, S. (Dec. 6, 2015). "\"John Lennon's Been Shot\"": The Marshall Tucker Band's Ghosts of Christmas Past," *No Depression.*

[1702] Vaughan, A. (2015). *The Eagles FAQ*, pp. 4-5, Milwaukee, WI: Backbeat Books.

[1703] Felder, D. (2008). *Heaven and Hell: My Life In The Eagles (1974-2001)*, p. 215Hoboken, NJ: John Wiley and Sons.

[1704] Rate Your Music. (Jan. 1, 2000). "L.A. Reggae," Rate Your Music. Retrieved from https://rateyourmusic.com/release/album/johnny-rivers/l_a-reggae/.

[1705] Discogs. (Jan. 1, 2000). "Blue Suede Shoes," Discogs. Retrieved from https://www.discogs.com/Johnny-Rivers-Blue-Suede-Shoes/release/1844003.

[1706] Norman's Rare Guitars Podcast. (Dec. 3, 2019). Michael Georgiades and James Santiago.

[1707] Varga, G. (Aug. 19, 2017). "Jack Tempchin Revisits His Musical Partnership with the Eagles' Glenn Frey on Heartfelt New CD," *San Diego Union-Tribune.*

[1708] Perkel, C. (Sep. 17, 2019). "Clive Davis: The Soundtrack of Our Lives," Hotwells Productions (Film/Video).

[1709] King, T. (Feb. 25, 2000). "The Operator: Book Explains David Geffen," *The Wall Street Journal.*

[1710] Best Classic Bands. "Label Exec Reflects on Signing John Lennon to Solo Deal," Retrieved from https://bestclassicbands.com/eddie-rosenblatt-john-lennon-6-26-16/

[1711] Kirkeby, M. (Sep. 1, 1980). "Geffen Signs Lennons, Elton John," *Associated Press.*

[1712] Kawashima, D. (Jun. 28, 2017). "Interview with Jack Tempchin, Singer/Songwriter and Hit Songwriter for the Eagles (\"Peaceful Easy Feeling,\" \"Already Gone\") And Glenn Frey," *Songwriter Universe.*

[1713] Varga, G. (Nov. 10, 2012). "Jack Tempchin's 'Peaceful Easy Feeling' At 40," *San Diego Union Tribune.*

[1714] The Eagles (). "History of the Eagles: The Story of an American Band," (Film/Video),

[1715] imdb.com (Apr. 20, 2013). "Eagles: Live at the Capital Centre," imdb.com. (Mar. 1977) Retrieved from https://www.imdb.com/title/tt11585296/.

[1716] Felder, D. (2009). *Heaven and Hell: My Life In The Eagles (1974-2001)*, pp. 181-182, Hoboken, NJ: Wiley; 1st edition (Apr. 1, 2009).

[1717] Fernandez, R. (Apr. 20, 2021). Interview With Richard Fernandez, Rik Forgo.

[1718] Hilburn, R. (Jul. 29, 1980). "The Eagles Return to the Civic," *Los Angeles Times.*

[1719] Felder, D. (2009). *Heaven and Hell: My Life In The Eagles (1974-2001)*, pp. 106-120, Hoboken, NJ: Wiley; 1st edition (Apr. 1, 2009).

[1720] Gans, D. (Jan. 1, 1980). "The Eagles' Don Felder: A Short Run to the Top," *Axe Magazine.*

[1721] Poco, n. (1976). Album Credits/Liner Notes: *Poco Live.*

[1722] Johns, G. (2014). *Glyn Johns: Sound Man*, pp. 201-201, New York, NY: Plume/Penguin-Random House.

[1723] Forgo, R. (Jun. 8, 2021). Interview with Jim Higgs, former WKMI Program Director, *Time Passages.*

[1724] The Flying Burrito Brothers, n. (1970). Album Credits/Liner Notes: *Farther Along: The Best of the Flying Burrito Brothers.*

[1725] Parsons/The Flying Burrito Brothers, G. (1976). Album Credits/Liner Notes: *Sleepless Nights.*

[1726] Johns, G. (2014). *Glyn Johns: Sound Man*, pp. 200-201New York, NY: Plume/Penguin-Random House.

[1727] The Acoustic Storm. (Nov. 22, 2014). "The Acoustic Storm Interviews: J.D. Souther." Retrieved from https://www.acousticstorm.com/artists/interview/96

[1728] Eliot, M. (1998). *To The Limit--The Untold Story of the Eagles*, pp. 102, 112-113, Boston, MA: Little, Brown and Company.

[1729] Eliot, M. (1998). *To The Limit--The Untold Story of the Eagles*, pp. 112-113, Boston, MA: Little, Brown and Company.

[1730] Forgo, R. (Jun. 9, 2021). Interview with Rip Pelley, *Time Passages.*

[1731] Browne, D. (Jun. 10, 2016). "Eagles' Complete Discography: Don Henley Looks Back," *Rolling Stone.*

[1732] Frey, G. (Mar. 31, 2014). "Glenn Frey Honors Linda Ronstadt at the 2014 Hall of Fame Induction Ceremony," Rock and Roll Hall of Fame. (Film/Video).

[1733] Eagles. (Oct. 23, 2003). Album Credits/Liner Notes: *Very Best of the Eagles.*

[1734] Holden, S. (Nov. 8, 1973). "Don't Cry Now: Review," *Rolling Stone.*

[1735] Billboard. (Jan. 12, 1974). "Chart History: Linda Ronstadt," *Billboard.*

[1736] Felder, D. (2008). *Heaven and Hell: My Life In The Eagles (1974-2001)*, pp. 214-215, Hoboken, NJ: John Wiley & Sons.

[1737] Eliot, M. (2008). *To The Limit: The Untold Story of the Eagles*, pp. 190-194, Boston, MA: Little, Brown and Company.

[1738] Greene, A. (Feb. 7, 2013). "Flashback: All the Eagles Unite for Rock and Roll Hall of Fame Induction," *Rolling Stone.*

[1739] *Billboard.* (Mar. 13, 1976). "The Hot 100: Week of March 13, 1976," *Billboard.*

[1740] Greene, A. (Jul. 16, 2015). "Flashback: The Eagles Play 'Take it to the Limit' In 1977," *Rolling Stone.*

[1741] Browne, D. (Sep. 22, 2019). "The 40 Greatest Eagles Songs," *Rolling Stone.*

[1742] Sharp, K. (Oct. 10, 2016). "Catching Up with Eagles and Poco Co-Founder Randy Meisner," *Rock Cellar Magazine*.

[1743] Gill, A. (Jul. 21, 2017). "Don Henley: \"I Know All the Drummer Jokes!\"," *Uncut*.

[1744] Frey, G. (Jun. 11, 1992). "Glenn Frey Interview: Later with Bob Costas," (Film/Video).

[1745] Glass, N. (Mar. 10, 2021). "American Journal TV Show: Interview with Randy Meisner." Retrieved from https://randy-meisnerheartsonfire.com/wp-content/uploads/2021/08/American-Journal.mp4

[1746] *Artisan News* (Feb. 10, 2016). "Timothy B Schmit on Joining the Eagles," (Film/Video).

[1747] Ferguson, J. (May 24, 2012). "Timothy B. Schmit Went from Envying the Eagles to Becoming One," *LancasterOnline*.com

[1748] Marten, N. (Jan. 8, 2021). "Timothy B. Schmit: 'I didn't peak in my 20s or 30s, like a lot of songwriters do. I'm starting to get it now, which keeps me feeling hopeful'," Guitar World. Retrieved from https://www.guitarworld.com/features/timothy-b-schmit-i-didnt-peak-in-my-20s-or-30s-like-a-lot-of-songwriters-do-im-starting-to-get-it-now-which-keeps-me-feeling-hopeful.

[1749] Meisner, R. (1978). Album Credits/Liner Notes: *Randy Meisner*.

[1750] Scheuers, F. (Nov. 26, 1978). "Stevie, Wife Skating Wonders," *Fort Worth Star-Telegram*.

[1751] Randall, R. (Jan. 1, 1994). Randy Meisner, KKYV.

[1752] Lloyd, J. (Jun. 8, 1980). "New Lead Singer, New Lease on Life," *Philadelphia Inquirer*.

[1753] Delaplane, G. (Jun. 24, 1997). "Vince Gill Skips the Fanfare and Delivers Just Good Music," *Asheville Citizen-Times*.

[1754] Edwards, J. (Oct. 25, 1990). "Vince Gill Resurrects Career with a Weeper," *Park City Daily News*.

[1755] Lloyd, J. (Jun. 6, 1980). "Pure Prairie League Hits the Right Formula," *Ft. Worth Star Telegram*.

[1756] Davis, S. (Oct. 24, 1993). "Hearts Won't Lie About Vince Gill Family, Friends Shed Light on Star's Roots," *Daily Oklahoman*.

[1757] Billboard. (May 17, 1980). "Billboard's Top Singles Picks," *Billboard*.

[1758] Italie, L. (Oct. 9, 2018). "Eagles' Joe Walsh Tells His Addiction Story at Gala Evening," *Associated Press*.

[1759-60] Harward, R. (Sep. 1, 2002). "Joe Walsh Talks Satan, Foxyboxing, Presidents, Wedgies, Wee-Wee and, Oh Yeah--The Eagles," *Salt Lake City Weekly*.

[1761] Billboard. (May 17, 1980). "Billboard's Top Single Picks," *Billboard*.

[1762] Setlist.fm. (Jul. 31, 2020). "'All Night Long' By Joe Walsh: Statistics," *Setlist.fm*.

[1763] Hutchinson, M. (Jul. 3, 2009). "Interview: Joe Walsh of the Eagles," *Lancashire Telegraph*.

[1764] *Rolling Stone*. (Aug. 26, 2012). "The Eagles and Charles M. Young: Behind the Cover Story."

[1765] Kurtz, P. (Jan. 1, 2000). "Indian Summer," AllMusic. Retrieved from https://www.allmusic.com/album/indian-summer-mw0000205832.

[1766] HIllburn, R. (May 9, 1978)." Of Sticks and Stones and Eagles And..," *Los Angeles Times*.

[1767] WOGB-FM (Sep. 19, 2017). "AOTM: The Day the Eagles Kicked Rolling Stone's Ass," WOGB-FM. Retrieved from https://www.wogb.fm/2017/09/19/aotm-the-day-the-eagles-kicked-rolling-stones-ass/.

[1768] Young, C.M. (Dec. 22, 201). "Eagles vs. *Rolling Stone* Baseball Game," (Film/Video), Retrieved from https://www.youtube.com/watch?v=Pm04HNXXPl8

[1769] Grobaty, T. (Jul. 31, 2018). "38 years ago, the Eagles crashed in 'Long Night in Wrong Beach'," The HiLo. Retrieved from https://lbpost.com/hi-lo/eagles-crashed-long-night-wrong-beach.

[1770] Grobaty, T. (Jun. 30, 2009). "Glenn Frey: Remembering the Eagles' split and the 'Long Night in Wrong Beach'," Press-Telegram. Retrieved from https://www.presstelegram.com/2016/01/18/glenn-frey-remembering-the-eagles-split-and-the-long-night-in-wrong-beach/.

[1771] Greene, A. (Jul. 21, 2020). "Flashback: The Eagles Play 'All Night Long' At Final Show Before 1980 Split," *Rolling Stone*.

[1772] Files, J. (Jul. 31, 2015). "The Night Eagles Imploded," Ultimate Classic Rock. Retrieved from https://ultimateclassicrock.com/the-eagles-break-up/.

[1773] Lange, A. (Jun. 27, 2013). "The Artie Lange Show - Don Felder," *The Artie Lange Show*.

[1774] Setlist.fm. (Jan. 1, 2000). "7/31/80 - Eagles Setlist at Long Beach Arena, Long Beach, CA, USA," Setlist.fm. Retrieved from https://www.setlist.fm/setlist/eagles/1980/long-beach-arena-long-beach-ca-bdb2526.html.

[1775] Campbell, M. (Dec. 19, 1976). "Eagles Fly High on Song," Associated Press.

[1776] Browne, D. (Jun. 10, 2016). "Eagles' Complete Discography: Don Henley Looks Back," *Rolling Stone*.

[1777] Songfacts.com (Dec. 20, 2020). "Rose of Cimarron By Poco," Songfacts.com. Retrieved from https://www.songfacts.com/facts/poco/rose-of-cimarron.

[1778] Stoller, G. (Oct. 24, 2020). "Poco's Rusty Young Puts a Cherry on Top of a Brilliant Career," No Depression. Retrieved from https://www.nodepression.com/pocos-rusty-young-puts-a-cherry-on-top-of-a-brilliant-career/.

[1779] Auerbach, B. (Feb. 8, 2018). "World Premiere Exclusive -- New Track from Poco," *Forbes*. Retrieved from https://www.forbes.com/sites/bradauerbach/2018/02/08/world-premiere-exclusive-new-track-from-poco/?sh=4aff3c073514#287484143514.

[1780] Wosahla, S. (Nov. 29, 2018). "Still Poco After All These Years," Americana Highways. Retrieved from https://americanahighways.org/2018/11/29/show-review-still-poco-after-all-these-years/.

[1781] Musicians Hall of Fame & Museum (Jan. 15, 2020). "The Story of How \"Hotel California\" By the Eagles Was Written & Recorded - Don Felder," (Film/Video). Retrieved from https://www.youtube.com/watch?v=qDeoCZw_LE0.

[1782] Hilburn, R. (Feb. 22, 1980). "Eagles' 'Long Run' Success Leads to More Encores," *Los Angeles Times*.

[1783] Eliot, M. (1998). *To The Limit--The Untold Story of The Eagles*, pp. 182-185, Boston, MA: Little, Brown and Company.

[1784] Felder, D. (2009). *Heaven and Hell: My Life In The Eagles (1974-2001)*, pp. 198-206, Hoboken, NJ: Wiley; 1st edition (Apr. 1, 2009).

[1785] Sharpe, K. (Nov. 10, 2006). "Catching Up with Eagles and

Poco Co-Founder Randy Meisner," *Rock Cellar Magazine.*

[1786] Corcoran, M. (May 11, 2016). "Keeper of the Flame: Artist Boyd Elder, Beacon of West Texas Art," *Texas Highways.*

[1787] Elder, B. (Oct. 11, 2018). "Remembering The Late Boyd Elder," *West Texas Talk - Interviews from West Texas Public Radio.*

[1788] Marino, T. (Mar. 7, 2019). "'One of These Nights' Eagles Would Score a Number One Album," *Pure Music Manufacturing.*

[1789] Bale Creek Allen Gallery (Jan. 1, 2000). Boyd Elder, Retrieved from http://balecreekallengallery.com/boyd-elder-bio.

[1790] Corcoran, M. (Feb. 10, 2018). "Respect Boyd Elder, Valentine, Texas' Greatest Hit," *Lonestar Music Magazine.*

[1791] Peeples, S.K. (Oct. 31, 2021). "Artlaw Boyd Elder's 'Chingadero Show,' 4-2-72," StephenKPeeples.com.

[1792] Felder, D. (2009). *Heaven and Hell: My Life In The Eagles (1974-2001)*, pp. 192-193, Hoboken, NJ: Wiley; 1st edition (Apr. 1, 2009).

[1793] Hilburn, R. (Nov. 25, 1978). "Eagles Soar for Holidays," *Los Angeles Times.*

[1794] DeRiso, N. (Dec. 21, 2020). "How 'Please Come Home for Christmas' Emerged from Eagles' Time Out," UltimateClassicRock.com.

[1795] Rhino. (Feb. 17, 2021). "In Memoriam: Eagles Artist Boyd Elder." Retrieved from https://www.rhino.com/article/in-memoriam-eagles-artist-boyd-elder.

[1796] RIAA (Aug. 20, 2018). "RIAA Awards the Eagles with the #1 And #3 Top-certified Albums of All Time," RIAA. Retrieved from https://www.riaa.com/riaa-awards-eagles-1-3-top-certified-albums-time/.

[1797] Hill, D. (Jul. 4, 2020). "Echoes in the Studio - Voices of Fallen Rockers," In the Studio with Redbeard.

[1798] White, T. (May 1, 1980). "The Fire This Time," *Rolling Stone.*

[1799] Local 10 News-South Florida. (Dec. 3, 2015). "Familiar Eagles Christmas Song Recorded in Miami."

[1800] Sampson, J. (Dec. 16, 1978). "Record World International: Germany," *Record World.*

[1801] Gambaccini, P. (Aug. 28, 1975). "Eagles Fly High with Disco 'Nights'," *Rolling Stone.*

[1802] Felder, D. (2009). *Heaven and Hell: My Life In The Eagles (1974-2001)*, pp. 132-133, Hoboken, NJ: Wiley; 1st edition (Apr. 1, 2009).

[1803] Eliot, M. (1998). *To The Limit--The Untold Story of The Eagles*, pp. 91-98, Boston, MA: Little, Brown and Company.

[1804] King, T. (2000). *The Operator*, pp. 184-199, New York, NY: Broadway Books.

[1805] Singular, S. (1997). *The Rise and Rise of David Geffen*, pp. 46-49, Secaucus, NJ: Birch Lane Press.

[1806] PBS. (Oct. 5, 2009). *Inventing David Geffen: Elliot Roberts*, PBS.

[1807] Geffen, D. (). *Inventing David Geffen* (Film/Video),

[1808] Williams, R. (Sep. 1, 1973). "Joe Walsh: The Smoker You Drink, The Player You Get," *Melody Maker.*

[1809] Vitale, J. (2008). *Joe Vitale: Backstage Pass*, pp. 83-84, Ashland, OH: Hit Records LLC.

[1810] Goggin, D. (Mar. 8, 2019). "Bill Szymczyk and Joe Walsh: "Hotel California," *The Record Plant Diaries Project*. Retrieved from https://www.recordplantdiaries.com/2019/03/08/bill-szymczyk-and-joe-walsh-hotel-california/.

[1811] Johns, G. (2014). *Glyn Johns: Sound Man*, pp. 200-202,

New York, NY: Plume/Penguin-Randon House.

[1812] Bashe, P. (1992). *Teenage Idol, Travelin' Man: The Complete Biography of Ricky Nelson*, pp. 162-167, New York, NY: Hyperion.

[1813] Monrovia (CA) Daily News-Post. (Sep. 8, 1973). "Rick Nelson's 'Easy to Be Free'," *Monrovia (CA) Daily News-Post.*

[1814] Wood, P. (Jun. 25, 2019). "Final Encore at the Red Lion Inn," *Champaign News-Gazette.*

[1815] Zollo, P. (Aug. 13, 2020). "Behind the Song: America, \"Horse with No Name\"," *American Songwriter.*

[1816] Hilburn, R. (Mar. 3, 1973). "Grammy Choices Ignore Progressive Elements," *Los Angeles Times.*

[1817] Warne, J. (2020). *America, The Band*, pp. 98-99, Lanham, MD: Rowman & Littlefield.

[1818] Associated Press. (Mar. 4, 1973). "At Grammy Awards, God is 'She' And Roberta Wins," Associated Press.

[1819] Goodman, F. (1998). *The Mansion on the Hill*, p. 238, New York, NY: Vintage Books.

[1820] Hermann, D. (Mar. 23, 1980). "A Conversation with the Eagles," DIR Broadcasting Corp.

[1821] Ronstadt, L. (1972). Album Credits/Liner Notes: *Linda Ronstadt.*

[1822] Ronstadt, L. (1972). Album Credits/Liner Notes: *Heart Like a Wheel.*

[1823] Ronstadt, L. (1972). Album Credits/Liner Notes: *Don't Cry Now.*

[1824] Clark, T. (Sep. 17, 2020). "The 50 Best Selling Albums of All-Time," *Business Insider.*

[1825] CNN.com. (Dec. 8, 1999). "Eagles Hits Album Named Best-Selling of Century," CNN.com.

[1826] Felder, D. (2009). *Heaven and Hell: My Life In The Eagles (1974-2001)*, pp. 118-120, Hoboken, NJ: Wiley; 1st edition (Apr. 1, 2009).

[1827] Roberts, M. (Aug. 6, 2008). "Q&A with Former Eagles Guitarist Don Felder," *Westword.*

[1828] (May 13, 2018). "Joe Walsh – The Smoker You Drink/But Seriously, Folks..." *In the Studio.*

[1829] Stern, H. (Jun. 4, 2012). "What's the Greatest Song Joe Walsh Ever Wrote?", *The Howard Stern Show.*

[1830] Cohen, H. (Jun. 2, 1995). "Fogelberg Reunites with Weisberg," *The Oklahoman.*

[1831] Hirschhorn, J. (Jun. 26, 2003). "Dan Fogelberg's Lengthy Career Finally Takes Him 'Full Circle'," Scripps.

[1832] Hirschhorn, J. (Jun. 26, 2003). "Dan Fogelberg's Lengthy Career Finally Takes Him 'Full Circle'," Scripps Howard Foundation Wire.

[1833] Rock Around the World. (Jun. 19, 1977). "To the Netherlands - And Beyond," *Rock Around the World.*

[1834] Various Artists, n. (2017). Album Credits/Liner Notes: *A Tribute to Dan Fogelberg.*

[1835] Eliot, M. (2005). *To the Limit: The Untold Story of the Eagles*, p. 113, Cambridge, MA: Da Capo Press.

[1836] Eng, S. (1996). *Jimmy Buffett: The Man from Margaritaville Revealed*, p. 183, New York, NY: St. Martin's Griffin.

[1837] Felder, D. (2008). *Heaven and Hell: My Life In The Eagles (1974-2001)*, p. 123, Hoboken, NJ: John Wiley & Sons.

[1838] 102.9 WMGK.com. (Feb. 9, 2018). "Jimmy Buffett's Connection to the Eagles," 102.9 WMGK.com.

[1839] Blistein, J. (Jan. 21, 2016). "Jimmy Buffett on Glenn Frey:

'a True Friend and Inspiration'," *Rolling Stone*.

[1840] Browne, D. (Jun. 10, 2016). "Eagles' Complete Discography: Don Henley Looks Back," *Rolling Stone*.

[1841] The Uncool, Crowe, C. (Aug. 1, 2003). "Eagles: Very Best of (Conversations With Don Henley and Glenn Frey)," *The Uncool*. Retrieved from https://www.theuncool.com/journalism/the-very-best-of-the-eagles/.

[1842] Bosso, J. (Nov. 15, 2011). "Interview: Timothy B. Schmit on playing with The Eagles, solo touring," Music Radar. Retrieved from https://www.musicradar.com/news/guitars/interview-timothy-b-schmit-on-playing-with-the-eagles-solo-touring-513119.

[1843] Hall, R. (May 1, 2017). "Timothy B. Schmit of the Eagles: An Intimate Chat," Best Classic Bands. Retrieved from https://bestclassicbands.com/timothy-b-schmit-interview-5-17-17/.

[1844] MacIntosh, D. (Nov. 10, 2011). "Timothy B. Schmit of the Eagles," *Songfacts*.

[1845] Lester, P. (Feb. 23, 2017). Timothy B Schmit: "I knew what my place was in the Eagles. I had to fit in.", Louder. Retrieved from https://www.loudersound.com/features/timothy-b-schmit-i-knew-what-my-place-was-in-the-eagles-i-had-to-fit-in.

[1846] Morse, S. (Nov. 10, 1980). "Bob Seger: Keeping a Low Profile," *Boston Globe*.

[1847] Smyntek, J. (Jul. 30, 1980). "New Seger Album Due Out This Fall," *Detroit Free Press*.

[1848] Shuster, F. (Jan. 20, 1996). "Bob Seger Hitting the Road for the First Time in Nine Years," *New York Times News Service*.

[1849] McAuliffe, K. (Apr. 13, 1980). "Bob's Journey Lands Him Against the Heart of Rock," *Detroit Free Press*.

[1850] Considine, J. (Jul. 19, 1996). "At Age 51, Bob Seger's Long Career is Still Like a Rock," *The Baltimore Sun*.

[1851] Jourard, M. (2016). *Music Everywhere: The Rock and Roll Roots of a Southern Town*, pp. 177-178, Gainesville, FL: University Press of Florida.

[1852] Charone, B. (Apr. 1, 1977). "The Eagles: One of These Nightmares," *Crawdaddy*.

[1853] Whitall, S. (Aug. 24, 1991). "Bob Seger's Long Way Home," *The Detroit News*.

[1854] McCollum, B. (Jan. 24, 2016). "Glenn Frey Remembers Detroit Days," *Detroit Free Press*.

[1855] Hilburn, R. (May 11, 1980). "Bob Seger: Moving Against the Wind," *Los Angeles Times*.

[1856] proz.com (Feb. 1, 2007). "chingandero," proz.com. Retrieved from https://www.proz.com/kudoz/spanish-to-english/poetry-literature/1749674-chingandero.html.

[1857] MacIntosh, D. (Dec. 8, 2011). "J.D. Souther: Interview," *Songfacts*.

[1858] Browne, D. (Sep. 22, 2019). "The 40 Greatest Eagles Songs," *Rolling Stone*.

[1859] Eagles, N. (2003). Album Credits/Liner Notes: *Eagles: Very Best Of*.

[1860] Graff, G. (Jan. 18, 2016). "Bob Seger on Glenn Frey: 'He Had a Drive, An Imagination & A Talent That Was Just Titanic'," *Billboard*.

[1861] McCollum, B. (Jan. 18, 2016). "Bob Seger on Friend Glenn Frey: 'He Was My Cheerleader'," *Detroit Free Press*.

[1862] Kushins, C.M. (2019). *Warren Zevon: Nothing's Bad Luck*, pp. 142-143, New York, NY: Da Capo Press.

[1863] Sullivan, J. (Apr. 10, 1980). "Warren Zevon: How L.A.'s 'Excitable Boy' Won the Battle with the Bottle," *Boston Globe*.

[1864] DeRogatis, J. (Sep. 9, 2003). "Edgy, Satirical Rocker Dies After Yearlong Cancer Battle," *jimdero.com*.

[1865] Bessman, J. (Jan. 20, 2016). "Glenn Frey: An Appreciation," *jimbessman.com*.

[1866] CBS. (Dec. 8, 1999). "Album of Century? The Eagles," CBS.

[1867] Knopper, S. (Jan. 20, 2016). "How the Eagles' 'Greatest Hits' Invented a New Kind of Blockbuster," *Rolling Stone*.

[1868] McLelland, J. (Jan. 17, 1978). "Randy Newman Redux:," *Washington Post*.

[1869] Hoskyns, B. (2006). *Hotel California*, p. 254, Hoboken, NJ: Joihn Wiley & Sons.

[1870] *Time*. (Aug. 18, 1975). "Music: Desert Singers," *Time*.

[1871] Cashbox. (May 4, 1974). "Eagles Head to UK As Headliners," *Cashbox*.

[1872] Crowe, C. (Jun. 15, 1978). "They Call Him Big Shorty," *Rolling Stone*.

[1873] Martoccio, A. (Dec. 3, 2020). "'RS Interview: Special Edition' With Joe Walsh," *Rolling Stone*.

[1874] Redmond, R. (Sep. 1, 2020). "Giving it All That You Got, Even to 10 People," *RichRedmond.com*.

[1875] Bosso, J. (Jan. 6, 2015). "Production Legend Bill Szymczyk on 12 Career-Defining Records," *Music Radar*.

[1876] Wardlaw, M. (Jun. 26, 2012). "Joe Walsh Says the Eagles Were Lucky to Break-Up Before Their Relationships Were Irreparably Damaged," Ultimate Classic Rock.

[1877] Basso, J. (Nov. 5, 2011). "Interview: Timothy B. Schmit on Playing with the Eagles, Solo Touring," *MusicRadar*.

[1878] Crowe, C. (Aug. 1, 2003). "Conversations with Don Henley and Glenn Frey," *The Uncool*.

[1879] Deriso, N. (Feb. 6, 2016). "The Day the Eagles Fired Don Felder," UltimateClassicRock.com.

[1880] Associated Press, (Feb. 13, 2013). "'History of the Eagles' Documents Their Break Up, And Make Up," *Oregon Live*.

[1881] Morse, S. (Oct. 10, 1979). "Eagles' Return is Gratifying," *Boston Globe*.

[1882] United Press International. (Oct. 11, 1979). "Eagles' Joe Walsh Presidential Hopeful," United Press International.

[1883] Makowski, P. (Nov. 20, 2017). "Interview: Joe Walsh on Rock 'N' Roll Excess and Running for President," Louder.

[1884] Jahn, M. (Nov. 26, 1972). "Fillmore of the Air," *Baltimore Sun*.

[1885] Browne, D. (Jun. 10, 2016). "Eagles' Complete Discography: Don Henley Looks Back," *Rolling Stone*.

[1886] Eagles, N. (2003). Album Credits/Liner Notes: *The Very Best Of*.

[1887] Greene, A. (Aug. 27, 2020). "Drummer Joe Vitale on His 50-Year Saga with CSNY, Joe Walsh, The Eagles, And John Lennon," *Rolling Stone*.

[1888] The Tribune-Chronicle. (Sep. 14, 2015). "Walsh-Vitale Continues on Tour," *The Tribune-Chronicle*.

[1889] Lisko, B. (Sep. 9, 2020). "Catching Up with Legendary Drummer Joe Vitale," *Canton Repository*.

[1890] Gans, D. (Jun. 14, 1981). "Interview with Joe Walsh," BAM.

[1891] Felder, D. (Oct. 4, 2018). How Don Felder Missed Out on Eagles' 'Victim of Love', *Ultimate Classic Rock Nights*.

[1892] MacIntosh, D. (Feb. 4, 2014). "Don Felder: Songfacts Interview," *Songfacts*.

[1893] AllMusic. (Jan. 1, 2000). "Randy Meisner, One More Song," AllMusic. Retrieved from https://www.allmusic.com/album/one-more-song-mw0000264230.

[1894] AllMusic. (Jan. 1, 2000). "Eric Kaz," AllMusic. Retrieved from https://www.allmusic.com/artist/eric-kaz-mn0000189565/songs.

[1895] Meisner, R. (1980). Album Credits/Liner Notes: One More Song.

[1896] Zimmer, D. (Nov. 7, 1980). "Randy Meisner: Ex-Eagle Flies High Solo," BAM.

[1897] Wikipedia. (Jan. 1, 2000). "Kim Carnes," Wikipedia. Retrieved from https://en.wikipedia.org/wiki/Kim_Carnes.

[1898] Hartman, K. (2017). Goodnight, L.A.: The Rise and Fall of Classic Rock, p. 142, New York, United States: Hachette Books.

[1899] Gallagher, M. (Nov. 19, 2014). "Interview with Don Felder," Sweetwater Guitars and Gear.

[1900] Bishop, A. (Oct. 7, 2015). "Don Henley Extended Interview," Studio 10 Extra.

[1901] Kennedy Center (Dec. 30, 2013). "Don Henley She's Got a Way—Billy Joel Kennedy Center Honors," (Film/Video).

[1902] Ganick, E. (Sep. 22, 1985). "Interview with Don Henley at Farm Aid, 1985," Entertainment Tonight (Film/Video).

[1903] Billboard. (Sep. 6, 1975). "Billboard Top LPS & Tape."

[1904] Edmunds, B. (Apr. 19, 1975). "The Coast," Record World.

[1905] Felder, D. (2008). Heaven and Hell: My Life In The Eagles (1974-2001), pp. 198-203,Hoboken, NJ: John Wiley and Sons.

[1906] Mettler, M. (Apr. 4, 2014). "Q&A: Don Felder on the Soundtrack of Summer and the Secret to the Eagles' Greatest Hits," Fox News.

[1907] Morse, S. (Oct. 10, 1979). "Eagles' Return is Satisfying," The Boston Globe.

[1908] Songfacts.com (Mar. 2, 2021). "The Long Run by Eagles." Retrieved from https://www.songfacts.com/facts/eagles/the-long-run.

[1909] Bienstock, R. (May 19, 2016). "Joe Walsh: My Life in 15 Songs," Rolling Stone.

[1910] MacIntosh, D. (Dec. 8, 2011). "J.D. Souther: Interview," Songfacts.

[1911] MacIntosh, D. (Feb. 4, 2013). Don Felder: Interview, Songfacts.

[1912] Eagles, N. (2003). Album Credits/Liner Notes: The Very Best Of.

[1913] Hilburn, R. (Nov. 25, 1978). "Eagles Soar for Holidays," Los Angeles Times.

[1914] Young, C. (Nov. 12, 1976). "Rolling Stone Notes," Los Angeles Times.

[1915] CBS Sunday Morning. (Dec. 8, 2016). "What Does \"Hotel California\" Really Mean? (And Other Questions for Don Henley)," CBS Sunday Morning.

[1916] Boucher, G. (Nov. 15, 2017). "Long, Hard Road Leads Eagles to 'Eden'," Los Angeles Times.

[1917] Boucher, G. (Nov. 15, 2017). "Long, Hard Road Leads Eagles to 'Eden'," Los Angeles Times.

[1918] Browne, D. (Jun. 10, 2016). "Eagles' Complete Discography: Don Henley Looks Back," Rolling Stone.

[1919] Perrone, P. (Jan. 19, 2016). "Glenn Frey: Singer and Songwriter Who Co-Founded the Eagles, The Biggest-Selling American Rock Band of All Time," The Independent.

[1920] Browne, D. (Sep. 22, 2019). "The 40 Greatest Eagles Songs," Rolling Stone.

[1921] Hoskyns, B. (Nov. 18, 2005). "Sex, Drugs and the Billion-Dollar Rise of David Geffen," The Independent.

[1922] Greene, A. (Jul. 30, 2017). "The Last Word: Joe Walsh on the Future of the Eagles, Trump and Turning 70," Rolling Stone.

[1923] Varga, G. (May 4, 2016). "Joe Walsh Talks Music, Politics & Artistic Seniority," San Diego Union-Tribune.

[1924] Makowsk, P. (Nov. 20, 2017). "Interview: Joe Walsh on Rock'N'Roll Excess and Running for President," Loudersound.

[1925] Crowe, C. (Sep. 1, 1975). "The Eagles: Chips Off the Old Buffalo," Rolling Stone.

[1926] Widon, L. (Nov. 10, 2015). "7 Questions for Singer-Songwriter Jackson Browne," On Milwaukee.

[1927] Campion, J. (2018). Accidentally Like a Martyr: The Tortured Art of Warren Zevon, p. 129, London, UK: Backbeat.

[1928] Hoskyns, B. (1996). Waiting for the Sun: A Rock 'n' Roll History of Los Angeles, p. 281, Milwaukee, USA: Backbeat Books.

[1929] Rolling Stone. (Sep. 19, 2003). "Browne Remembers Zevon."

[1930] Forgo, R. (Sep. 22, 2021). Interview with Tom Leadon, Time Passages.

[1931] Guitar World. (Jul. 18, 2013). "Greatest Guitar Solos of All Time," Guitar World.

[1932] Lindquist, D. (May 18, 2016). "In Post-Eagles Life, Don Felder Enjoys the Long Run," Indianapolis Star.

[1933] Foley, M. (Jul. 23, 2021). "Music Journeys Reprise: Don Felder," WCBE.

[1934] Jennings, N. (Nov. 9, 2018). "The Eagles' Joe Walsh Talks Concert for Vets, Music Career, And 25 Years of Sobriety," KIRO.

[1935] Bosso, J. (Aug. 12, 2012). "Interview: Don Felder on the Eagles' Classic Song, Hotel California," MusicRadar.

[1936] Hall, R. (Aug. 26, 2016). "10 Classic Solos Played on a Les Paul," Gibson.com.

[1937] Fox, D. (Jul. 21, 2014). "Voices Down the Corridor: Don Felder Welcomes Chat About 'Hotel California,' Summer Tour, Solo Record," Daily Herald.

[1938] KSHE. (Apr. 18, 2019). "Don Felder on how he ended up with iconic double-neck 'Hotel California' guitar," KSHE.

[1939] Geller, A. (Mar. 21, 1980). "Tune Ends the Siege of a Tearful Trucker," United Press International.

[1940] Gentile, D. (Mar. 21, 1980). "Hostage Situation Ends on a Happy Note," New York Daily News.

[1941] Tucker, R. (Mar. 19, 2020). "40 Years Ago, A NYC Gunman Had One Request: 'Desperado'," New York Post.

[1942] Hyman, D. (Sep. 8, 2015). "Meet the Men Behind the Distinctive Soundtrack of 'the Warriors'," Village Voice.

[1943] Bienstock, R. (May 19, 2016). "Joe Walsh: My Life in 15 Songs," Rolling Stone.

[1944] People. (Mar. 12, 1979). "A Street-Gang Movie Called the Warriors Triggers a Puzzling, Tragic Wave of Audience Violence and Death," People.

[1945] Gundy, S. (Jan. 1, 1983). The Guitar Greats - The 1982 BBC Interviews, Buckinghamshire, UK: Northdown Publishing Ltd.

[1946] Browne, D. (Sep. 22, 2019). "The 40 Greatest Eagles Songs," Rolling Stone.

[1947] Young, C. (Nov. 29, 1979). "The Eagles: Hell is for Heroes," Rolling Stone.

[1948] Redbeard, (Dec. 4, 2016). "Eagles' Hotel California: Don Henley, Joe Walsh, the Late Glenn Frey," *In the Studio with Redbeard*.

[1949] Suto, J. (May 11, 2014). "A Conversation with Don Felder," *Rock Show Critique*.

[1950] history.com. (Apr. 5, 2010). "Manifest Destiny," history.com.

[1951] Grein, P. (Mar. 11, 1978). "A Day in the Life of Pierre Cossette," *Billboard*.

[1952] Runtagh, J. (Dec. 8, 2016). "The Eagles' 'Hotel California': 10 Things You Didn't Know," *Rolling Stone*.

[1953] Scapelliti, C. (Jan. 11, 2019). "Did the Eagles Get the \"Hotel California\" Chords from Jethro Tull?" *Guitar World*.

[1954] Epstein, D. (Apr. 1, 2016). "20 Insane Music Pranks and Hoaxes," *Rolling Stone*.

[1955] Heath, C. (Jan. 15, 2019). "Creating While Clean," *GQ*.

[1956] Holson, L. (Jan. 10, 2002). "Importance of Being Important, With Music," *New York Times*.

[1957] Segal, D. (Apr. 24, 2010). "Calling Almost Everyone's Tune," *New York Times*.

[1958] Heaton, M. (Jul. 7, 2013). "David Spero, Artist-Manager, Talks About What Went on Behind the Scenes with the Eagles," *Cleveland Plain Dealer*.

[1959] Hedegaard, E. (Aug. 24, 2006). "Joe Walsh, One of Rock's Most Underrated Guitarists, Is Ready to Hit the Road with His Original Band," *Rolling Stone*.

[1960] Bells, K. (Oct. 3, 1986). "Joe Walsh Comes Back to His KsU Roots," *Daily Kent Stater*.

[1961] Kutner, R. (Aug. 16, 2006). "James Gang: Interview with Joe Walsh," *The Aquarian*.

[1962] O'Brien, C. (Sep. 27, 2016). "That Time Joe Walsh & John Belushi Trashed a Penthouse," Conan O'Brien Show, (Film/Video).

[1963] Dodge, J. (Jan. 19, 2016). "Remembering Glenn Frey, And the Night Belushi and Walsh Trashed a Chicago Hotel Room," CBS Chicago.

[1964] Bienstock, R. (Jun. 19, 2016). "Joe Walsh: My Life in 15 Songs," *Rolling Stone*.

[1965] Bienstock, R. (May 19, 2016). "Joe Walsh: My Life in 15 Songs," *Rolling Stone*.

[1966] Record World. (Jul. 12, 1975). "Don Kirshner Announces Rock Music Awards Panel," *Record World*.

[1967] Felder, D. (2009). *Heaven and Hell: My Life In The Eagles (1974-2001)*, p. 201, Nashville, TN: Turner.

[1968] Browne, D. (Sep. 22, 2019). "The 40 Greatest Eagles Songs," *Rolling Stone*.

[1969] Record Collector. (Apr. 5, 2008). "The Eagles Heaven & Hell," *Record Collector*.

[1970] Felder, D. (2009). *Heaven and Hell: My Life In The Eagles (1974-2001)*, p. 201, Nashville, TN: Turner Publishing Company.

[1971] Browne, D. (Sep. 22, 2018). "The 40 Greatest Eagles Songs," *Rolling Stone*.

[1972] Mettle, M. (Apr. 4, 2014). "Don Felder on the Soundtrack of Summer and Secret to the Eagles' Greatest Hits," *Fox News*.

[1973] DeRiso, N. (Dec. 15, 2020). "How Eagles' 'Seven Bridges Road' Ended a Winding Path in Top 40," Ultimate Classic Rock.

[1974] DeRiso, N. (Dec. 15, 2020). "How Eagles' 'Seven Bridges Road' Ended a Winding Path in Top 40," Ultimate Classic Rock.

[1975] Crowe, C. (Aug. 1, 2003). "Eagles: Very Best of Conversations With Don Henley and Glenn Frey," The Uncool. Retrieved from https://www.theuncool.com/journalism/the-very-best-of-the-eagles/.

[1976] Felder, D. (2008). *Heaven and Hell: My Life In The Eagles (1974-2001)*, p. 124, 181, 215, Hoboken, NJ: John Wiley and Sons.

[1977] Cashbox. (Oct. 30, 1976). "Talent on Stage: Eagles Play Sold Out Forum 3 New," *Cashbox*.

[1978] McCullaugh, J. (Sep. 4, 1976). "Studio Track, Pp. 30," *Billboard*.

[1979] Billboard. (Oct. 2, 1976). "Inside Track, Pp. 118," *Billboard*.

[1980] *Arizona Republic*. (Oct. 5, 1976). "Liner Notes," *Arizona Republic*.

[1981] Long, J.S. (Oct. 18, 1976). "McKale Crowd Sedate as the Eagles Soar," *Arizona Daily Star*.

[1982] Goffin, L. (Apr. 3, 2020). "Episode 3: J.D. Souther," Song Chronicles Podcast with Louise Goffin. Retrieved from https://www.songchroniclespodcast.com/e/ep-3-jd-souther/.

[1983] Souther, J. (1976). Album Credits/Liner Notes: *Black Rose*.

[1984] Kawashima, D. (Jul. 31, 2017). "Interview with JD Souther, Renowned Singer-Songwriter and Co-Writer of Hits for the Eagles, James Taylor, Linda Ronstadt and Don Henley," *Songwriter Universe Magazine*.

[1985] Kawashima, D. (Jul. 31, 2017). "Interview with JD Souther, Renowned Singer-Songwriter and Co-Writer of Hits for the Eagles, James Taylor, Linda Ronstadt and Don Henley," *Songwriter Universe Magazine*.

[1986] Felder, D. (2009). *Heaven and Hell: My Life In The Eagles (1974-2001)*, pp. 180-181, Hoboken, NJ: Wiley; 1st edition (Apr. 1, 2009).

[1987] Pinnock, T. (Oct. 30, 2015). "Black Sabbath: \"The Eagles Were Recording Next Door, But We Were Too Loud for Them\"," *Uncut*.

[1988] Eliot, M. (2005). *To the Limit: The Untold Story of the Eagles*, pp. 146-153, Cambridge, MA: Da Capo Press.

[1989] Felder, D. (2008). *Heaven and Hell: My Life In The Eagles (1974-2001)*, pp. 174-176, Hoboken, NJ: John Wiley & Sons.

[1990] Young, C. (Jun. 3, 1977). "Eagles Ex-Manager, Ex-Publisher Sued," *Rolling Stone*.

[1991] King, T. (2000). *The Operator*, pp. 280-281, New York, NY: Broadway Books.

[1992] Eliot, M. (2005). *To the Limit: The Untold Story of the Eagles*, pp. 180-181, Cambridge, MA: Da Capo Press.

[1993] *Record World*. (May 21, 1977). "Eagles Sue Geffen, Three Publishing Cos," *Record World*.

[1994] Weber, J. (May 21, 1977). "The Eagles Sue David Geffen, WB Music, In Publ. Dispute," *Cashbox*.

[1995] Browne, D. (Jun. 10, 2016). "Eagles' Complete Discography: Don Henley Looks Back," *Rolling Stone*.

[1996] Springsteen, B. (Sep. 8, 1978). "Sherry Darling—Bruce Springsteen (9-08-1978), The Agora, Cleveland, Ohio," (Film/Video). Retrieved from https://www.youtube.com/watch?v=T-jvKYIjxW1E.

[1997] Pentreath, R. (May 11, 2021). "Why Are There Only 12 Notes in Western Music?" Classic FM.

[1998] Eder, B. (Jan. 1, 2000). "Jethro Tull - Stand Up," AllMusic. Retrieved from https://www.allmusic.com/album/stand-up-mw0000190387.

[1999] Greene, A. (Aug. 27, 2020). "Drummer Joe Vitale on His 50-Year Saga," *Rolling Stone*.

[2000] Felder, D. (2008). *Heaven and Hell: My Life In The Eagles (1974-2001)*, p. 157, Hoboken, NJ: John Wiley & Sons.

[2001] Young, C. (Nov. 15, 1976). "Random Notes," *Rolling Stone*.

[2002] Kozak, R. (Dec. 13, 1980). "Leber-Krebs: We're a Series of Boutiques," *Billboard*.

[2003] Billboard. (Feb. 15, 2016). "Eagles Get Presented Grammy for 'Hotel California' That They Didn't Accept in 1977," *Billboard*.

[2004] Walsh, J. (1976). Album Credits/Liner Notes: *You Can't Argue With a Sick Mind*.

[2005] Chrispell, J. (Jan. 1, 2000). "You Can't Argue With a Sick Mind - Joe Walsh," AllMusic. Retrieved from https://www.allmusic.com/album/you-cant-argue-with-a-sick-mind-mw0000666259.

[2006] Sexton, P. (Aug. 10, 2021). "'You Can't Argue with a Sick Mind': Joe Walsh Rocks Out in San Francisco," uDiscoverMusic.

[2007] Forgo, R. (Jul. 26, 2021). Interview with Rip Pelley, *Time Passages*.

[2008] Buckley, D. (2007). *Elton: The Biography*, pp. l-3168, 3158, 3581, 3583 and 3737, London, United Kingdom: Calton Publishing Group.

[2009] John, E. (2019). *Me*, p. 125, 181, 290, 382, New York, NY: St. Martin's Publishing Group.

[2010] Wheeler, S.P. (Aug. 1, 1989). "Bernie Taupin: Elton's Write Hand Man," *Music Connection*.

[2011] Sandall, R. (Jul. 1, 1992). "Bernie Taupin: Him Indoors," *Q*.

[2012] Tannenbaum, R. (May 23, 2019). "When Elton John Became a Rock Star: The Untold Story of the Troubadour Concert," *Los Angeles Times*.

[2013] Billboard, (Jan. 1, 2000). "Life's Been Good - Joe Walsh," *Billboard*. Retrieved from https://www.billboard.com/music/joe-walsh/chart-history/HSI/song/344304.

[2014] YouTube (May 10, 2012). "Joe Walsh - Life's Been Good (Live Spoken Word Version) at the Troubadour," Joe Walsh YouTube, (Film/Video). Retrieved from https://www.youtube.com/watch?v=NIzyTk1fuf0.

[2015] Rosenthal, E.J. (2001). *His Song: The Musical Journey of Elton John*, p. 180, New York, NY: Watson-Guptill Publications.

[2016] Grammys.com (Oct. 8, 2021). "39th Annual Grammy Awards (1996)," Grammy.com. Retrieved from https://www.grammy.com/grammys/awards/39th-annual-grammy-awards-1996.

[2017] Grammys.com (Oct. 8, 2021). 22nd Annual Grammy Awards, Retrieved from https://www.grammy.com/grammys/awards/22nd-annual-grammy-awards-1979.

[2018] Forgo, R. (Aug. 8, 2021). "Eagles Cover Sea Cruise," *Time Passages*.

[2019] Wosahla, S. (Jul. 31, 2018). "The Eagles Then and Now & The Ghosts of Americana," *Americana Highways*.

[2020] AllMusic.com. (Sep. 20, 2019). "Artist Biography: Huey Smith." Retrieved from https://www.allmusic.com/artist/huey-piano-smith-mn0000830028/biography.

[2021] setlist.fm (Apr. 6, 2013). "Eagles'Texxas Jam, June 21, 1980," setlist.fm. Retrieved from https://www.setlist.fm/setlist/eagles/1980/cotton-bowl-dallas-tx-73dfae65.html.

[2022] Lingeman, J. (May 7, 1975). "Success!" *The McHenry Plain-dealer*.

[2023] Ames, C. (May 16, 1975). "McHenry Students Win a Free Eagles Concert," *The Daily Sentinel*.

[2024] Billboard. (Oct. 18, 1980). "Billboard's Top Album Picks," *Billboard*.

[2025] Vintage Rock TV Archive (Jan. 1, 2000). "Vintage Rock TV Archive: The Midnight Special," Retrieved from https://sites.google.com/site/vintagerocktv/usa/midnight-special.

[2026] Billboard. (Jan. 1, 2000). "Hearts on Fire - Randy Meisner," *Billboard*. Retrieved from https://www.billboard.com/music/randy-meisner/chart-history/hot-100/song/334803.

[2027] Billboard (Jan. 1, 2000). "Don't Fall In Love With A Dreamer," *Billboard*. Retrieved from https://www.billboard.com/music/kenny-rogers/chart-history/HSI/song/578523.

[2028] Billboard. (Jan. 1, 2020). "Deep Inside my Heart," *Billboard*. Retrieved from https://www.billboard.com/music/randy-meisner/chart-history/hot-100/song/574140.

[2029] AllMusic. (Jan. 1, 2000). "Gideon," AllMusic. Retrieved from https://www.allmusic.com/album/gideon-mw0000625946.

[2030] Bego, M. (2005). *Joni Mitchell*, p. 135, Lanham, MD: Taylor Trade.

[2031] Holden, S. (Jan. 15, 1976). "Review: The Hissing of Summer Lawns," *Rolling Stone*.

[2032] Browning, B. (Jan. 29, 1982). "L.P. Graffiti," *Washington Post*.

[2033] Eagles, N. (2003). Album Credits/Liner Notes: *The Very Best of the Eagles*.

[2034] RIAA (Apr. 14, 2018). "Gold & Platinum Turns 60," RIAA.com. retrieved from https://www.riaa.com/goldandplatinum60/.

[2035] Bilstein, J. (Jan. 21, 2016). "Jimmy Buffett on Glenn Frey: 'a True Friend and Inspiration'" *Rolling Stone*.

[2036] Charlesworth, C. (Sep. 1, 1973). "Joe Walsh: Barnstorming the USA," *Melody Maker*.

[2037] *Rolling Stone*. (1983). *Rolling Stone Record Guide*, p. 158, New York, NY: Random House.

[2038] Bossi, J. (Aug. 2, 2012). "Interview: Don Felder on the Eagles' Classic Song, Hotel California," *MusicRadar*.

[2039] Shirecore, I. (Aug. 1, 1994). "Douglas Adams: The First and Last Tapes.," *Darkermatters.com*.

[2040] Cartlidge, A. (Oct. 31, 2014). "John Cleese: Interview," *Varsity*.

[2041] Duka, J. (Oct. 3, 1982). "The Ego and the Art of David Geffen," *New York Times*.

[2042] Shewey, D. (Jul. 21, 1985). "On the Go with David Geffen," *New York Times*.

[2043] Ronstadt, L. (2013). *Simple Dreams: A Musical Memoir*, p. 111, New York, NY: Simon & Schuster.

[2044] Gaunt, J. (Jun. 12, 2013). "When Politics Met Americana in 1976," *No Depression*.

[2045] Vaughan, A. (Aug. 11, 2009). *Eagles FAQ*, p. 127, New York, NY: Backbeat Books.

[2046] Ronstadt, L. (2013). *Simple Dreams: A Musical Memoir*, p. 75, New York, NY: Simon & Schuster.

[2047] Bienstock, R. (May 19, 2016). "Joe Walsh: My Life in 15 Songs," *Rolling Stone*.

[2048] Vaughan, A. (Oct. 3, 1989). Jackson Browne, *Insight*.

[2049] Duka, J. (Oct. 3, 1982). "The Ego and Art of David Geffen," *New York Times*.

[2050] Tobler, J. (Dec. 1, 1976). "Eagles," *ZigZag*.

[2051] King, G. (Dec. 8, 2016). "What does "Hotel California" really mean? (And other questions for Don Henley)," CBS News.

[2052] Mirisch, W. (2008). *I Thought We Were Making Movies*, pp. 372-373, Madison, WI: The University of Wisconsin Press.

[2053] Forgo, R. (2019). *Eagles: Before the Band*, pp. 1-163, Lake Shore, MD: *Time Passages*.

[2054] Christgau, R. (Sep. 4, 1978). "Christgau's Record Guide: Rock Albums of the '70s," *Village Voice*.

[2055] Melina, R. (Nov. 2, 2010). "Top 5 Bizarre Political Candidates," livescience.com.

[2056] Runtagh, J. (Dec. 8, 2016). "The Eagles' 'Hotel California': 10 Things You Didn't Know," *Rolling Stone*.

[2057] *Brandify*. (Mar. 17, 2011). "John Kosh Documentary Excerpt - Hotel California," (Film/Video).

[2058] TeamRock, (Nov. 13, 2016). "The Story Behind the Eagles' Hotel California Album Artwork," *Louder*.

[2059] FellNumb.com. (Dec. 30, 2009). "The Eagles 'Hotel California' Cover Location. Retrieved from http://www.feelnumb.com/2009/12/30/Eagles-Hotel-California-Cover-Location/.

[2060] Wilkins, V. (Jan. 19, 2016). "5 Things You Might Not Know About the Eagles' 'Hotel California'," *ABC News*.

[2061] The Ultimate Bootleg Experience. (Sep. 26, 2020). "The Eagles - 1976-1977 Studio Outtakes - SOUL POLE VOL. 3 (STU/FLAC)," The Ultimate Bootleg Experience. Retrieved from http://theultimatebootlegexperience7.blogspot.com/2016/03/the-eagles-1976-1977-studio-outtakes.html.

[2062] Tobler, J. (1983). *The Guitar Greats - The 1982 BBC Interviews*, Buckinghamshire, UK: Northdown Publishing Ltd.

[2063] Bienstock, R. (May 1, 2016). "Joe Walsh: My Life in 15 Songs," *Rolling Stone*.

[2064] Jigsaw Productions. (Feb. 15, 2013). "History of the Eagles," (Film/Video).

[2065] Green, T. (Jun. 19, 2012). "Interview: 10 Questions for Joe Walsh," *Artsdesk.com*. Retrieved from https://theartsdesk.com/new-music/interview-10-questions-joe-walsh.

[2066] Tobler, J. (1983). *The Guitar Greats - The 1982 BBC Interviews*, Buckinghamshire, UK: Northdown Publishing Ltd

[2067] Kooper, A. (2008). *Backstage Passes & Backstabbing Bastards: Memoirs of a Rock 'N' Roll Survivor*, p. 211, New York, NY: Backbeat Books.

[2068] Eagles, E. (2000). Album Credits/Liner Notes: *Selected Works: 1972–1999*.

[2069] Box Office Mojo. (Oct. 30, 2019). "Domestic Box Office for 1978," Box Office Mojo. Retrieved from https://www.boxofficemojo.com/year/1978/.

[2070] Crowe, C. (Jun. 15, 1978). "They Call Him Big Shorty," *Rolling Stone*.

[2071] Forgo, R. (2019). *Eagles: Before the Band*, pp. 69-71, Lake Shore, MD: Time Passage LLC.

[2072] Eliot, M. (1998). *To The Limit - The Untold Story of The Eagles*, pp. 99-109, Boston, MA: Little, Brown and Company.

[2073] Hits Daily Double. (Apr. 17, 2009). "Rumor Mill: The Long Run: An Irving Azoff Timeline," Hits Daily Double. Retrieved from https://hitsdailydouble.com/news&id=280194&title+THE-LONG-RUN:-AN-IRVING-AZOFF-TIMELINE.

[2074] *Hits Daily Double*. (Jan. 8, 2019). "Irving Azoff, Taking it to the Limit Every Time."

[2075] The Press Music Reviews. (Jul. 22, 2014). "Joe Walsh – So What (1975)," The Press Music Reviews. Retrieved from https://thepressmusicreviews.wordpress.com/2014/07/22/82-joe-walsh-so-what-1975/.

[2076] Felder, D. (2009). *Heaven and Hell: My Life in the Eagles (1974-2001)*, p. 110, 170, Hoboken, NJ: Wiley; 1st edition (Apr. 1, 2009).

[2077] Jigsaw Productions (May 31, 2020). "Laurel Canyon," (Film/Video).

[2078] Hardy, P. (2001). *The Faber Companion to 20th Century Popular Music: The Eagles*, p. 1023, London, UK: Faber & Faber.

[2079] Setlist.fm (Nov. 4, 2021). "Silver Dagger performed by Eagles," Setlist.fm. Retrieved from https://www.setlist.fm/stats/songs/eagles-6bd6bede.html?songid=4bc0835e.

[2080] Eliot, M. (1998). *To The Limit - The Untold Story of the Eagles*, p. 34, Boston, MA: Little, Brown and Company.

[2081] Uhelszki, J. (Jun. 1, 1975). "Joe Walsh: Lonely in the Spotlight," *Creem*.

[2082] Eliot, M. (1998). *To The Limit--The Untold Story of The Eagles*, pp. 100-101, Boston, MA: Little, Brown and Company.

[2083] Fuentes, J. (Jan. 1, 2000). "Randy Meisner Concert Chronology." Retrieved from https://www.angelfire.com/rock3/deliverin/MEISNER/randyconcerts.htm.

[2084] Atkinson, T. (Sep. 11, 1978). "Bob Welch, Randy Meisner on Bill," *Los Angeles Times*.

[2085] Budge, D. (Jul. 24, 1974). "Points West," *Cashbox*.

[2086] Cashbox. (Jul. 27, 1974). "Our Apologies," *Cashbox*.

[2087] Greene, A. (Jul. 29, 2015). "Readers' Poll: The 10 Best Eagles Songs," *Rolling Stone*.

[2088] The Age of Ideas (Jan. 1, 2000). "David Geffen," Retrieved from https://theageofideas.com/david-geffen/.

[2089] Westbrook, B. (Aug. 24, 1975). "New Reddy Disk Relaxing Music," *Waco (Texas) Tribune-Herald*.

[2090] Jordan, T. (Aug. 16, 1975). "Pop Records," *St. Joseph News-Press*.

[2091] Felder, D. (April 1, 2009.). *Heaven and Hell: My Life in the Eagles (1974-2001)*, pp. 170-172, Hoboken, NJ: Wiley; 1st edition.

[2092] Eliot, M. (1998). *To The Limit - The Untold Story of the Eagles*, pp. 146-148, Boston, MA: Little, Brown and Company.

[2093] Corben, B. (Jun. 1, 2011). "The Raconteurs," *Miami Pulp*.

[2094] Aydiette, L. (Dec. 5, 2016). "How Eagles Classic \"Hotel California\" Was Recorded in South Florida," *Palm Beach Post*.

[2095] Butcher, S. (Feb. 1, 2018). "Boyd Elder is the Most Famous Artist You've Never Heard Of," *Texas Monthly*.

[2096] Peeples, S.K. (Sep. 3, 2018). "Boyd Elder Skull Art Featured on Eagles' Best-Selling Album in US History," StephenKPeeples.com. Retrieved from https://stephenkpeeples.com/news-and-reviews/boyd-elder-skull-art-featured-on-eagles-best-selling-album-in-us-history/.

[2097] Beaudin, J. (Aug. 30, 2019). "Bernie Leadon on Eagles Epic 'Journey of the Sorcerer'," RockHistoryMusic.com. Retrieved from https://www.youtube.com/watch?v=jRYYF7X831s.

[2098] h2g2 The Hitchhiker's Guide to the Galaxy: Earth Edition (Apr. 25, 2008). The Music of The Hitchhiker's Guide to the Galaxy, Retrieved from https://h2g2.com/approved_entry/A32873899.

[2099] Lezard, N. (Sep. 26, 2004). "Go on Then, Call Me a Dweeb—See If I Care!", *The (London) Independent*.
[2100] Shepherd, L. (Sep. 3, 2012). "A very strange piece of music," Delightful Music. Retrieved from https://lloydshepherd-writer.wordpress.com/2012/09/03/a-very-strange-piece-of-music/.
[2101] I Like Your Old Stuff (Mar. 7, 2018). "Eagles in Space," I Like Your Old Stuff. Retrieved from https://www.ilikeyouroldstuff.com/news/eagles-in-space.
[2102] Mikkelson, D. (Apr. 24, 2014). "Hotel California: Is the Eagles song 'Hotel California' about Satanism?," Snopes.com Retrieved from https://www.snopes.com/fact-check/hotel-california/.
[2103] Kroft, S. (Nov. 20, 2007). "Eagles Album Saved Band," *60 Minutes*. (Film/Video). Retrieved from https://www.cbsnews.com/news/glenn-frey-eagles-album-saved-band/.
[2104] Edwards, R. (Dec. 1, 1980). "Iron-Poor Music Even Geritol Can't Cure," *The Daily Utah Chronicle*.
[2105] Gambaccini, P. (Jul. 31, 1975). "Elton & Company Seduce Wembley," *Rolling Stone*.
[2106] Brown, C. (Jul. 1, 1977). "Eagles Soar in Saturday," *Miami Herald*.
[2107] Betts, S.L. (Jan. 19, 2016). "Flashback: See Dolly Parton's Poignant Eagles Cover," *Rolling Stone*.
[2108] March, D. (Jul. 1, 1975). "The Eagles: One of These Nights," *Rolling Stone*.
[2109] Burden, G. (Sep. 1, 2009). "Eagles—On the Border," Gary Burden R. Twerk & Co. Retrieved from http://garyburdenforrtwerk.com/2009/09/on-the-border/.
[2110] Bonhams (May 14, 2008). "Rick Griffin: The Flying Eyeball," Bonhams. Retrieved from https://www.bonhams.com/auctions/16257/lot/87/.
[2111] Bischoff's Gallery. (Nov. 28, 2021). "Beatien Yazz, Navajo," Retrieved from https://www.bischoffsgallery.com/online-store/paintings/beatien-yazz.
[2112] Adobe Gallery - Art of the Southwestern Indian (Apr. 3, 2014). "Beatien Yazz, Navajo Nation Painter." Retrieved from https://www.adobegallery.com/artist/Beatien_Yazz_1928_Present31210631.
[2113] Davies, B. (Jan. 3, 2020). "Joe Walsh: So Far So Good," AllMusic. Retrieved from https://www.allmusic.com/album/so-far-so-good-mw0000845046.
[2114] Bausch, P. (Feb. 3, 2020). "Joe Walsh...Solo Eagles Part 3," On the Records. Retrieved from https://ontherecords.net/2018/08/joe-walsh-solo-eagles-part-3/.
[2115] Billboard. (Feb. 26, 1977). "Top 100 Singles," *Billboard*.
[2116] *Cashbox*. (Feb. 26, 1977). "Top 100 Singles," *Cashbox*.
[2117] Record World. (Feb. 26, 1977). "Record World Singles Chart," *Record World*.
[2118] Cashbox. (Apr. 23, 1977). "Top 100 Singles Chart," *Cashbox*.
[2119] *Record World*. (Apr. 23, 1977). "Record World Singles Chart," *Record World*.
[2120] *Billboard*. (May 7, 1977). "Hot 100 Singles Chart," *Billboard*.
[2121] Charone, B. (Oct. 27, 1977). "Linda Ronstadt Listens to Your Sleep," *Circus*.
[2122] Wiseman, R. (Aug. 7, 1975). "The Producers," *Crawdaddy*.
[2123] King, B. (Jul. 15, 1978). "Moody Blues' \"Octave\" Below Promise," *The Atlanta Journal-Constitution*.
[2124] Burden, G. (Nov. 5, 2014). "Under the Covers: A Magical Journey - Rock and Roll in L.A. In the 60s-70s," Triptych Pictures (Film/Video).
[2125] Eder, B. (Jul. 14, 2012). "The Eagles," AllMusic.
[2126] 45cat (Feb. 13, 2022). "The Eagles (UK), "The Desperados," 45cat. Retrieved from https://www.45cat.com/record/7n15503.
[2127] Graham, S. (Apr. 21, 1979). "The Coast," *Record World*.
[2128] Graham, S. (May 5, 1979). "The Coast," *Record World*.
[2129] Forgo, R. (Feb. 16, 2022). Interview with John Kosh, *Time Passages*.
[2130] Phillips, J. (1992). *You'll Never Eat Lunch in This Town Again*, pp. 358-363, New York, NY: Signet/Penguin.
[2131] Eliot, M. (1998). *To The Limit - The Untold Story of the Eagles*, pp. 174-177, Boston, MA: Little, Brown and Company.
[2132] Smith, J. (1988). *Off the Record: An Oral History of Popular Music*, pp. 356-357, New York, NY: Warner Books.
[2133] Porter, M. (Mar. 21, 2018). "Mirrors on the ceiling" upstairs in the Boat Room at Record Plant LA," The Record Plant Diaries Project. Retrieved from https://www.recordplantdiaries.com/2018/03/21/mirrors-on-the-ceiling-upstairs-in-the-boat-room-at-record-plant-la/.
[2134] Barackman, M. (Jun. 1, 1977). "Desperados: Poco Keeps on Tryin'," *Crawdaddy*.
[2135] Pond, S. (Jan. 11, 1981). "One More Ex-Eagle," *Los Angeles Times*.
[2136] Smith, J. (1988). *Off The Record: An Oral History of Popular Music*, pp. 347-350, 351-352, 353-354, 355-357, New York, NY: Warner Books.
[2137] Burden, G. (Sep. 1, 2009). "Eagles - One of These Nights," Gary Burden for Twerk & Co. Retrieved from http://garyburdenforrtwerk.com/2009/09/one-of-these-nights/.
[2138] Charone, B. (April 3, 1976). "Joe Walsh: You Can't Argue with a Sick Mind," *Sounds*.
[2139] Henley, D. (1991). "Don Henley Inducts the Byrds Into the Rock and Roll Hall of Fame," (Film/Video).
[2140] Honigmann, D. (Jul. 20, 2015). "The Life of a Song: 'Silver Dagger'," *The Financial Times*.
[2141] Roxon, L. (Oct. 8, 1972). "The Top of Pop - Amplifications," *New York Daily News*.
[2142] DeCurtis, A. (Oct. 15, 1992). "Don Henley & Glenn Frey; The Drugs Were Good, The Women Were Beautiful, And We Had Endless Energy," *Rolling Stone*.
[2143] Walsh, J. (1974). "Joe Walsh & Friends," (Film/Video),
[2144] Hoskyns, B. (2006). *Hotel California*, p. 249; Hoboken, NJ: John Wiley & Sons.
[2145] Eliot, M. (1998). *To The Limit: The Untold Story of The Eagles*, p. 94; Boston, MA: Little, Brown and Company.
[2146] Shapiro, M. (1995). *The Story of the Eagles; The Long Run*, pp. 102-103; New York, England: Omnibus Press.
[2147] Brown, J. (2014). Behind the Boards II, p. loc. 47; Milwaukee, WI: Hal Leonard Books.
[2148] A. Lange, (2013). The Artie Lange Show, In the Studio: Don Felder. (Film/Video).
[2149] Fawcett, A. (1978). California Rock California Sound, p. 129, Los Angeles, CA: APT Publishing AG.

PHOTO CREDITS

Every effort has been made to identify the copyright holders and obtain their permission for the use of copyrighted material. Images reproduced with permission appear below with page citation. Notification of any additions or corrections that should be incorporated in future reprints or editions of this book would be greatly appreciated.

Cover illustration: Daniel Belchí Lorente
Page 18: Ethan Russell
Page 22: Henry Diltz/Henry Diltz Photography
Page 28: Henry Diltz/Henry Diltz Photography
Page 30: Henry Diltz/Henry Diltz Photography
Page 35: Henry Diltz/Henry Diltz Photography
Page 38: Henry Diltz/Henry Diltz Photography
Page 43: Peter Sherman/Peter Sherman Photography
Page 47: Cover courtesy *Cashbox International*.
Page 54: Henry Diltz/Henry Diltz Photography
Page 58: Gary Elam/Michael Ochs Archive/Getty Images
Page 62: Henry Diltz/Henry Diltz Photography
Page 70: Jackie Greene/St. Petersburg Times via ZUMA Press
Page 76: Henry Diltz/Henry Diltz Photography
Page 77: Robert Landau
Page 78: Henry Diltz/Henry Diltz Photography
Page 79: Henry Diltz/Henry Diltz Photography
Page 80: Henry Diltz/Henry Diltz Photography
Page 86: Fotos International/Getty Images
Page 92: Peter Sherman
Page 104: Archive PL/Alamy Stock Photos
Page 111: Gijsbert Hanekroot/Alamy Stock Photo
Page 112: Michael Putland/Hulton Archive/Getty Images
Page 116: Everett Collection Inc./Alamy Stock Photo
Page 118: Henry Diltz/Henry Diltz Photography
Page 121: Henry Diltz/Henry Diltz Photography
Pages 122-123: Henry Diltz/Henry Diltz Photography
Page 126: Henry Diltz/Henry Diltz Photography
Page 130: Photo courtesy Robb Strandlund
Page 136: Henry Diltz/Henry Diltz Photography
Page 139: ABC Photo Archive/Alamy Stock Photo
Page 144: mccool/Alamy Stock Photo
Page 152: Ronald Grant Archive/Alamy Stock Photo
Page 156: ABC Photo Archive/Getty Images
Page 164: Henry Diltz/Henry Diltz Photography
Page 169: Photo courtesy Jim Higgs
Pages 176-177: Norman Seeff
Page 179: Henry Diltz/Henry Diltz Photography
Page 180: Norman Seeff
Page 182: Henry Diltz/Henry Diltz Photography
Page 192: Yvette Gilbert
Page 195: Keith Williamson
Page 199: Poster photograph, Norman Seeff
Page 199: Inset 3E button: Stephen K. Peeples
Page 202: Barry Shultz
Page 204: ZUMA Press Inc./Alamy Stock Photo

Page 208: Michael Ochs Archive/Getty Images
Page 210: Norman Seeff
Page 220: Gijsbert Hanekroot/Alamy Stock Photo
Page 228: Yvette Gilbert
Page 234: Michael Ochs Archive/Getty Images
Page 240: Henry Diltz/Henry Diltz Photography
Pages 247, 249: photos courtesy Cindy Johnson and Jeri Jenkins
Page 251: George Rose/Hulton Archive/Getty Images
Page 252: Henry Diltz/Henry Diltz Photography
Page 260: Ebet Roberts/Referns/Getty Images
Page 263: Michael Putland
Page 264: Michael Putland
Pages 268-269: David Alexander
Pages 270-271: Norman Seeff
Pages 272-273: David Alexander
Page 276: Fairfax Media Archives/Getty Images
Page 288: trekandshoot/Alamy Stock Photo
Page 290: Cavan Images/Alamy Stock Photo
Page 293: David Alexander
Page 295: David Alexander
Page 300: Henry Diltz/Henry Diltz Photography
Page 302: Gary Burden/Courtesy Burden Estate
Page 312: Rob Verhorst/Redferns/Getty Images
Page 314: Michael Putland/Hulton Archive/Getty Images
Page 328: Jimmy Wachtel
Page 330: Michael Ochs Archive/Getty Images
Page 336: Doug Griffin/Toronto Star/Getty Images
Pages 350-351: Jim Shea
Page 353: Photo courtesy Kosh
Page 354: Henry Diltz/Henry Diltz Photography
Page 358: Henry Diltz/Henry Diltz Photography
Page 364: Photo by Norman Seeff, *Rolling Stone*, ©1979 Rolling Stone LLC, All Rights Reserved, Used by Permission.
Page 366: Illustration by Greg Scott, *Rolling Stone*, ©1979 Rolling Stone LLC, All Rights Reserved, Used by Permission.
Page 372: Peter B. Sherman/Peter Sherman Photography
Page 374: Peter B. Sherman/Peter Sherman Photography
Page 384: Henry Diltz/Henry Diltz Photography
Page 393: Rik Forgo
Page 398: George Rose/Hulton Archive/Getty Images
Page 412: Aaron Rapoport
Page 414: Ebet Roberts/Redferns/Getty Images

Printed in Great Britain
by Amazon

24921381R00278